Blackstone's Statutes on
Evidence

12th edition

edited by

Phil Huxley

LLB, LLM
*Former Principal Lecturer at Nottingham Law School,
Nottingham Trent University*

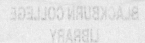

OXFORD
UNIVERSITY PRESS

OXFORD
UNIVERSITY PRESS

Great Clarendon Street, Oxford, OX2 6DP,
United Kingdom

Oxford University Press is a department of the University of Oxford.
It furthers the University's objective of excellence in research, scholarship,
and education by publishing worldwide. Oxford is a registered trade mark of
Oxford University Press in the UK and in certain other countries

This selection © Phil Huxley 2012

The moral rights of the author have been asserted

First published by Blackstone Press 1991

Ninth edition 2006
Tenth edition 2008
Eleventh edition 2010
Twelfth edition 2012

Impression: 1

British Library Cataloguing in Publication Data

Data available

ISBN 978–0–19–965630–1

Printed in Great Britain by
MPG Books Group, Bodmin and King's Lynn

Blackstone's Statutes on

Evidence

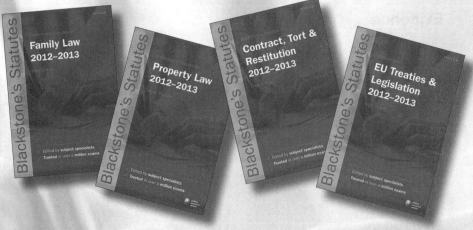

Contents

	Editor's preface	*ix*
	New to this edition	*x*

Part I	**Criminal Proceedings—Statutes**	**1**

	Criminal Procedure Act 1865	1
	Criminal Evidence Act 1898	2
	Perjury Act 1911	2
	Prevention of Crime Act 1953	3
	Homicide Act 1957	3
	Criminal Justice Act 1967	4
	Criminal Appeal Act 1968	5
	Theft Act 1968	6
	Misuse of Drugs Act 1971	8
	Rehabilitation of Offenders Act 1974	9
	Protection of Children Act 1978	16
	Magistrates' Courts Act 1980	17
	Contempt of Court Act 1981	19
	Criminal Justice Act 1982	19
	Police and Criminal Evidence Act 1984	19
	Public Order Act 1986	101
	Criminal Justice Act 1988	101
	Road Traffic Offenders Act 1988	103
	Road Traffic Act 1988	107
	Sexual Offences (Amendment) Act 1992	109
	Criminal Justice and Public Order Act 1994	110
	Criminal Evidence (Amendment) Act 1997	114
	Youth Justice and Criminal Evidence Act 1999	117
	Criminal Cases Review (Insanity) Act 1999	146
	Terrorism Act 2000	146
	Crime (International Co-operation) Act 2003	147
	Sexual Offences Act 2003	153
	Criminal Justice Act 2003	154
	Domestic Violence, Crime and Victims Act 2004	184
	Criminal Evidence (Witness Anonymity) Act 2008	186
	Coroners and Justice Act 2009	187

Part II   **Criminal Proceedings—Rules and Guidelines**   **192**

Police and Criminal Evidence Act 1984 Revised Codes of
Practice A–G   192
Appendix 7 Disclosure: Criminal Procedure and Investigations
Act 1996: Code of Practice under Part II   336
Criminal Procedure Rules 2011   343
Attorney-General's Guidelines on Disclosure of Unused
Material in Criminal Proceedings   376

Part III   **Human Rights—Act and Convention**   **384**

Human Rights Act 1998   384
Convention for the Protection of Human Rights and
Fundamental Freedoms   390

Part IV   **Civil Proceedings—Statutes and Rules**   **394**

Civil Evidence Act 1968   394
Civil Evidence Act 1972   396
Children Act 1989   396
Civil Evidence Act 1995   397
Civil Partnership Act 2004   402
Civil Procedure Rules 1998   402

Index   *443*

Alphabetical contents

A Appendix 7 Disclosure: Criminal Procedure
and Investigations Act 1996: Code of
Practice under Part II . . . 336
Attorney-General's Guidelines on
Disclosure of Unused Material in
Criminal Proceedings . . . 376

C Children Act 1989 . . . 396
Civil Evidence Act 1968 . . . 394
Civil Evidence Act 1972 . . . 396
Civil Evidence Act 1995 . . . 397
Civil Partnership Act 2004 . . . 402
Civil Procedure Rules 1998 . . . 402
Contempt of Court Act 1981 . . . 19
Convention for the Protection of
Human Rights and Fundamental
Freedoms . . . 390
Coroners and Justice Act 2009 . . . 187
Crime (International Co-operation)
Act 2003 . . . 147
Criminal Appeal Act 1968 . . . 5
Criminal Cases Review (Insanity)
Act 1999 . . . 146
Criminal Evidence Act 1898 . . . 2
Criminal Evidence (Amendment)
Act 1997 . . . 114
Criminal Evidence (Witness Anonymity)
Act 2008 . . . 186
Criminal Justice Act 1967 . . . 4
Criminal Justice Act 1982 . . . 19
Criminal Justice Act 1988 . . . 101
Criminal Justice Act 2003 . . . 154
Criminal Justice and Public Order
Act 1994 . . . 110

Criminal Procedure Act 1865 . . . 1
Criminal Procedure
Rules 2011 . . . 343

D Domestic Violence, Crime
and Victims Act 2004 . . . 184

H Homicide Act 1957 . . . 3
Human Rights Act 1998 . . . 384

M Magistrates' Courts Act 1980 . . . 17
Misuse of Drugs Act 1971 . . . 8

P Perjury Act 1911 . . . 2
Police and Criminal Evidence
Act 1984 . . . 19
Police and Criminal Evidence
Act 1984 Revised Codes of
Practice A–G . . . 192
Prevention of Crime Act 1953 . . . 3
Protection of Children Act 1978 . . . 16
Public Order Act 1986 . . . 101

R Rehabilitation of Offenders
Act 1974 . . . 9
Road Traffic Act 1988 . . . 107
Road Traffic Offenders Act 1988 . . . 103

S Sexual Offences Act 2003 . . . 153
Sexual Offences (Amendment)
Act 1992 . . . 109

T Terrorism Act 2000 . . . 146
Theft Act 1968 . . . 6

Y Youth Justice and Criminal Evidence
Act 1999 . . . 117

Chronological contents

1865 Criminal Procedure Act 1865...1
1898 Criminal Evidence Act 1898...2
1911 Perjury Act 1911...2
1950 Convention for the Protection of
      Human Rights and Fundamental
      Freedoms...390
1953 Prevention of Crime Act 1953...3
1957 Homicide Act 1957...3
1967 Criminal Justice Act 1967...4
1968 Civil Evidence Act 1968...394
      Criminal Appeal Act 1968...5
      Theft Act 1968...6
1971 Misuse of Drugs Act 1971...8
1972 Civil Evidence Act 1972...396
1974 Rehabilitation of Offenders
      Act 1974...9
1978 Protection of Children Act 1978...16
1980 Magistrates' Courts Act 1980...17
1981 Contempt of Court Act 1981...19
1982 Criminal Justice Act 1982...19
1984 Police and Criminal Evidence
      Act 1984...19
1986 Public Order Act 1986...101
1988 Criminal Justice Act 1988...101
      Road Traffic Act 1988...107
      Road Traffic Offenders Act 1988...103
1989 Children Act 1989...396
1992 Sexual Offences (Amendment)
      Act 1992...109
1994 Criminal Justice and Public Order
      Act 1994...110

1995 Civil Evidence Act 1995...397
1996 Appendix 7 Disclosure:
      Criminal Procedure and
      Investigations Act 1996: Code of
      Practice under Part II...336
1997 Criminal Evidence (Amendment)
      Act 1997...114
1998 Civil Procedure Rules 1998...402
      Human Rights Act 1998...384
1999 Criminal Cases Review (Insanity)
      Act 1999...146
      Youth Justice and Criminal Evidence
      Act 1999...117
2000 Terrorism Act 2000...146
2003 Criminal Justice Act 2003...154
      Crime (International Co-operation)
      Act 2003...147
      Sexual Offences Act 2003...153
2004 Civil Partnership Act 2004...402
      Domestic Violence, Crime and
      Victims Act 2004...184
2005 Attorney-General's Guidelines on
      Disclosure of Unused Material in
      Criminal Proceedings...376
2006 Police and Criminal Evidence Act 1984
      Revised Codes of Practice A–G...192
2008 Criminal Evidence (Witness Anonymity)
      Act 2008...186
2009 Coroners and Justice Act 2009...187
2011 Criminal Procedure Rules 2011...343

Editor's preface

There has been relatively little legislation in this area since the eleventh edition in 2010. As a result of the decision of the European Court of Human Rights in *S and Marper v United Kingdom* [2008] ECHR 1581 a large number of provisions (sections 64ZA to 64ZL) were inserted into the Police and Criminal Evidence Act 1984 by the Crime and Security Act 2010. The new provisions were designed to provide a statutory base for the retention and destruction of biometric material, including DNA samples, DNA profiles and fingerprints. The new provisions were not, however, brought into force. As a consequence of the decision in *GC and C v Commissioner of Police for the Metropolis* [2011] UKSC 21 they may never be brought into force. In *GC and C* the Supreme Court held that guidelines from the Association of Chief Police Officers regarding retention and destruction of biometric material were incompatible with Article 8 of the European Convention on Human Rights. Consequently the government introduced clauses in the Protection of Freedoms Bill 2011. On 19 March 2012 the House of Commons considered amendments to the Bill made by the Lords. The Commons disagreed with a number of those amendments and initiated a game of 'ping pong' over the changes. Once the game has ended and the Bill receives the Royal Assent, a note of the effect of the new legislation will appear on the Online Resource Centre.

This edition has benefited from the feedback of teachers of the law of Evidence in Higher Education institutions. I am grateful to them for their views though have not been able to satisfy everyone. As a result, the PACE Codes of Practice have been retained but have been moved to Part II of the book thus giving a clear run to the statutory provisions. I have also included some provisions from the Domestic Violence, Crime and Victims Act 2004.

Everyone using the book should kindly check that any particular provision is in force and has not been amended. As with any area of law, there are notable evidential legislative provisions which have been born to blush unseen. I have attempted to state the law as on St Patrick's Day 2012.

Phil Huxley

New to this edition

The twelfth edition of *Blackstone's Statutes on Evidence* has been fully revised and updated to include all relevant legislation through to April 2012.

- An extract from the Domestic Violence, Crime and Victims Act 2004
- New PACE Codes of Practice (A, B, C, D, E, F and G)
- Changes to the Criminal Procedure Rules

Part I

Criminal Proceedings—Statutes

Criminal Procedure Act 1865

(1865, c. 18)

3   How far witnesses may be discredited by the party producing

A party producing a witness shall not be allowed to impeach his credit by general evidence of bad character; but he may, in case the witness shall in the opinion of the judge prove adverse, contradict him by other evidence, or, by leave of the judge, prove that he has made at other times a statement inconsistent with his present testimony; but before such last-mentioned proof can be given the circumstances of the supposed statement, sufficient to designate the particular occasion, must be mentioned to the witness, and he must be asked whether or not he has made such statement.

4   As to proof of contradictory statements of adverse witness

If a witness, upon cross-examination as to a former statement made by him relative to the subject matter of the indictment or proceeding, and inconsistent with his present testimony, does not distinctly admit that he has made such statement, proof may be given that he did in fact make it; but before such proof can be given the circumstances of the supposed statement, sufficient to designate the particular occasion, must be mentioned to the witness, and he must be asked whether or not he has made such statement.

5   Cross-examinations as to previous statements in writing

A witness may be cross-examined as to previous statements made by him in writing, or reduced into writing, relative to the subject matter of the indictment or proceeding, without such writing being shown to him; but if it is intended to contradict such witness by the writing, his attention must, before such contradictory proof can be given, be called to those parts of the writing which are to be used for the purpose of so contradicting him: Provided always, that it shall be competent for the judge, at any time during the trial, to require the production of the writing for his inspection, and he may thereupon make such use of it for the purposes of the trial as he may think fit.

6   Proof of conviction of witness may be given

(1) If upon a witness being lawfully questioned as to whether he has been convicted he either denies or does not admit the fact, or refuses to answer, it shall be lawful for the cross examining party to prove such conviction; and a certificate containing the substance and effect only (omitting the formal part) of the indictment and conviction for such offence, purporting to be signed by the proper officer of the court where the offender was convicted having the custody of the records of the court where the offender was convicted, or by the deputy of such clerk of officer, (for which certificate a fee of (25p) and no more shall be demanded or taken), shall upon proof of the identity of the person, be sufficient evidence of the said conviction, without proof of the signature or official character of the person appearing to have signed the same.

(2) In subsection (1) 'proper officer' means—
   (a) in relation to a magistrates' court in England and Wales, the designated officer for the court; and
   (b) in relation to any other court, the clerk of the court or other officer having the custody of the records of the court, or the deputy of such clerk or other officer.

Criminal Evidence Act 1898

(1898, c. 36)

1   Competency of witnesses in criminal cases
(1) A person charged in criminal proceedings shall not be called as a witness in the proceedings except upon his own application.

(2) Subject to section 101 of the Criminal Justice Act 2003 (admissibility of evidence of defendant's bad character), a person charged in criminal proceedings who is called as a witness in the proceedings may be asked any question in cross-examination notwithstanding that it would tend to criminate him as to any offence with which he is charged in the proceedings.

(3) . . .

(4) Every person charged in criminal proceedings who is called as a witness in the proceedings shall, unless otherwise ordered by the court, give his evidence from the witness box or other place from which the other witnesses give their evidence.

2   Evidence of person charged
Where the only witness to the facts of the case called by the defence is the person charged, he shall be called as a witness immediately after the close of the evidence for the prosecution.

3   Right of reply
The fact that the person charged has been called as a witness shall not of itself confer on the prosecution the right of reply.

Perjury Act 1911

(1911, c. 6)

13   Corroboration
A person shall not be liable to be convicted of any offence against this Act, or of any offence declared by any other Act to be perjury or subornation of perjury, or to be punishable as perjury or subornation of perjury, solely upon the evidence of one witness as to the falsity of any statement alleged to be false.

14   Proof of certain proceedings on which perjury is assigned
On a prosecution—
   (a) for perjury alleged to have been committed on the trial of an indictment . . .; or
   (b) for procuring or suborning the commission of perjury on any such trial,
the fact of the former trial shall be sufficiently proved by the production of a certificate containing the substance and effect (omitting the formal parts) of the indictment and trial purporting to be signed by the clerk of the court, or other person having the custody of the records of the court where the indictment was tried, or by the deputy of that clerk or other person, without proof of the signature or official character of the clerk or person appearing to have signed the certificate.

Prevention of Crime Act 1953

(1953, c. 14)

1   Prohibition of the carrying of offensive weapons without lawful authority or reasonable excuse

(1) Any person who without lawful authority or reasonable excuse, the proof whereof shall lie on him, has with him in any public place any offensive weapon shall be guilty of an offence, and shall be liable—

    (a) on summary conviction, to imprisonment for a term not exceeding [six months] or a fine not exceeding the prescribed sum or both;

    (b) on conviction on indictment, to imprisonment for a term not exceeding [four] years or a fine . . . or both.

(2) Where any person is convicted of an offence under subsection (1) of this section the court may make an order for the forfeiture or disposal of any weapon in respect of which the offence was committed.

(3) . . .

(4) In this section 'public place' includes any highway and any other premises or place to which at the material time the public have or are permitted to have access, whether on payment or otherwise; and 'offensive weapon' means any article made or adapted for use for causing injury to the person, or intended by the person having it with him for such use by him or by some other person.

Homicide Act 1957

(1957, c. 11)

2   Persons suffering from diminished responsibility

(1) A person ("D") who kills or is a party to the killing of another is not to be convicted of murder if D was suffering from an abnormality of mental functioning which—

    (a) arose from a recognised medical condition,

    (b) substantially impaired D's ability to do one or more of the things mentioned in subsection (1A), and

    (c) provides an explanation for D's acts and omissions in doing or being a party to the killing.

(1A) Those things are—

    (a) to understand the nature of D's conduct;

    (b) to form a rational judgment;

    (c) to exercise self-control.

(1B) For the purposes of subsection (1)(c), an abnormality of mental functioning provides an explanation for D's conduct if it causes, or is a significant contributory factor in causing, D to carry out that conduct.

(2) On a charge of murder, it shall be for the defence to prove that the person charged is by virtue of this section not liable to be convicted of murder.

(3) A person who but for this section would be liable, whether as principal or as accessory, to be convicted of murder shall be liable instead to be convicted of manslaughter.

(4) The fact that one party to a killing is by virtue of this section not liable to be convicted of murder shall not affect the question whether the killing amounted to murder in the case of any other party to it.

Criminal Justice Act 1967

(1967, c. 80)

9   Proof by written statement

(1) In any criminal proceedings, a written statement by any person shall, if such of the conditions mentioned in the next following subsection as are applicable are satisfied, be admissible as evidence to the like extent as oral evidence to the like effect by that person.

(2) The said conditions are—

(a) the statement purports to be signed by the person who made it;

(b) the statement contains a declaration by the person to the effect that it is true to the best of his knowledge and belief and that he made the statement knowing that, if it were tendered in evidence, he would be liable to prosecution if he wilfully stated in it anything which he knew to be false or did not believe to be true;

(c) before the hearing at which the statement is tendered in evidence, a copy of the statement is served, by or on behalf of the party proposing to tender it, on each of the other parties to the proceedings; and

(d) none of the other parties or their solicitors, within seven days from the service of the copy of the statement, serves a notice on the party so proposing objecting to the statement being tendered in evidence under this section:

Provided that the conditions mentioned in paragraphs (c) and (d) of this subsection shall not apply if the parties agree before or during the hearing that the statement shall be so tendered.

(3) The following provisions shall also have effect in relation to any written statement tendered in evidence under this section, that is to say—

(a) if the statement is made by a person under the age of eighteen, it shall give his age;

(b) if it is made by a person who cannot read it, it shall be read to him before he signs it and shall be accompanied by a declaration by the person who so read the statement to the effect that it was so read; and

(c) if it refers to any other document as an exhibit, the copy served on any other party to the proceedings under paragraph (c) of the last foregoing subsection shall be accompanied by a copy of that document or by such information as may be necessary in order to enable the party on whom it is served to inspect that document or a copy thereof.

(3A) In the case of a statement which indicates in pursuance of subsection (3)(a) of this section that the person making it has not attained the age of 14, subsection (2)(b) of this section shall have effect as if for the words from 'made' onwards there were substituted the words 'understands the importance of telling the truth in it'.

(4) Notwithstanding that a written statement made by any person may be admissible as evidence by virtue of this section—

(a) the party by whom or on whose behalf a copy of the statement was served may call that person to give evidence; and

(b) the court may, of its own motion or on the application of any party to the proceedings, require that person to attend before the court and give evidence.

(5) An application under paragraph (b) of the last foregoing subsection to a court other than a magistrates' court may be made before the hearing and on any such application the powers of the court shall be exercisable [by a puisne judge of the High Court, a Circuit judge or Recorder sitting alone].

(6) So much of any statement as is admitted in evidence by virtue of this section shall, unless the court otherwise directs, be read aloud at the hearing and where the court so directs an account shall be given orally of so much of any statement as is not read aloud.

(7) Any document or object referred to as an exhibit and identified in a written statement tendered in evidence under this section shall be treated as if it had been produced as an exhibit and identified in court by the maker of the statement.

(8) A document required by this section to be served on any person may be served—

(a) by delivering it to him or to his solicitor; or

(b) by addressing it to him and leaving it at his usual or last known place of abode or place of business or by addressing it to his solicitor and leaving it at his office; or

(c) by sending it in a registered letter or by the recorded delivery service or by first class post addressed to him at his usual or last known place of abode or place of business or addressed to his solicitor at his office; or

(d) in the case of a body corporate, by delivering it to the secretary or clerk of the body at its registered or principal office or sending it in a registered letter or by the recorded delivery service or by first class post addressed to the secretary or clerk of that body at that office; and in paragraph (d) of this subsection references to the secretary, in relation to a limited liability partnership, are to any designated member of the limited liability partnership.

10 Proof by formal admission

(1) Subject to the provisions of this section, any fact of which oral evidence may be given in any criminal proceedings may be admitted for the purpose of those proceedings by or on behalf of the prosecutor or defendant, and the admission by any party of any such fact under this section shall as against that party be conclusive evidence in those proceedings of the fact admitted.

(2) An admission under this section—

(a) may be made before or at the proceedings;

(b) if made otherwise than in court, shall be in writing;

(c) if made in writing by an individual, shall purport to be signed by the person making it and, if so made by a body corporate, shall purport to be signed by a director or manager, or the secretary or clerk, or some other similar officer of the body corporate;

(d) if made on behalf of a defendant who is an individual, shall be made by his counsel or solicitor;

(e) if made at any stage before the trial by a defendant who is an individual, must be approved by his counsel or solicitor (whether at the time it was made or subsequently) before or at the proceedings in question.

(3) An admission under this section for the purpose of proceedings relating to any matter shall be treated as an admission for the purpose of any subsequent criminal proceedings relating to that matter (including any appeal or retrial).

(4) An admission under this section may with the leave of the court be withdrawn in the proceedings for the purpose of which it is made or any subsequent criminal proceedings relating to the same matter.

Criminal Appeal Act 1968

(1968, c. 19)

PART I APPEAL TO COURT OF APPEAL
IN CRIMINAL CASES

Appeal against conviction on indictment

1 Right of appeal

(1) [Subject to subsection (3) below] a person convicted of an offence on indictment may appeal to the Court of Appeal against his conviction.

[(2) An appeal under this section lies only—

(a) with the leave of the Court of Appeal; or

(b) if, within 28 days of the date of conviction, the judge of the court of trial grants a certificate that the case is fit for appeal.]

(3) Where a person is convicted before the Crown Court of a scheduled offence it shall not be open to him to appeal to the Court of Appeal against the conviction on the ground that the decision of the court which sent him to the Crown Court for trial as to the value involved was mistaken.

(4) In subsection (3) above 'scheduled offence' and 'the value involved' have the same meanings as they have in section 22 of the Magistrates' Courts Act 1980 (certain offences against property to be tried summarily if value of property or damage is small).]

23   Evidence

(1) For the purposes of an appeal, or on an application for leave to appeal, under this Part of this Act the Court of Appeal may, if they think it necessary or expedient in the interests of justice—

    (a) order the production of any document, exhibit or other thing connected with the proceedings, the production of which appears to them necessary for the determination of the case;

    (b) order any witness to attend for examination and be examined before the Court (whether or not he was called in the proceedings from which the appeal lies); and

    (c) receive any evidence which was not adduced in the proceedings from which the appeal lies.

(1A) The power conferred by subsection (1)(a) may be exercised so as to require the production of any document, exhibit or other thing mentioned in that subsection to—

    (a) the Court;

    (b) the appellant;

    (c) the respondent.

(2) The Court of Appeal shall, in considering whether to receive any evidence, have regard in particular to—

    (a) whether the evidence appears to the Court to be capable of belief;

    (b) whether it appears to the Court that the evidence may afford any ground for allowing the appeal;

    (c) whether the evidence would have been admissible in the proceedings from which the appeal lies on an issue which is the subject of the appeal; and

    (d) whether there is a reasonable explanation for the failure to adduce the evidence in those proceedings.

(3) Subsection (1)(c) above applies to evidence of a witness (including the appellant) who is competent but not compellable.

(4) For the purposes of an appeal, or an application for leave to appeal, under this Part of this Act, the Court of Appeal may, if they think it necessary or expedient in the interests of justice, order the examination of any witness whose attendance might be required under subsection (1)(b) above to be conducted, in manner provided by rules of court, before any judge or officer of the Court or other person appointed by the Court for the purpose, and allow the admission of any depositions so taken as evidence before the Court.

(5) A live link direction under section 22(4) does not apply to the giving of oral evidence by the appellant at any hearing unless that direction, or any subsequent direction of the court, provides expressly for the giving of such evidence through a live link.

(6) In this section, "respondent" includes a person who will be a respondent if leave to appeal is granted.

Theft Act 1968

(1968, c. 60)

22   Handling stolen goods

(1) A person handles stolen goods if (otherwise than in the course of the stealing) knowing or believing them to be stolen goods he dishonestly receives the goods, or dishonestly undertakes or

assists in their retention, removal, disposal or realisation by or for the benefit of another person, or if he arranges to do so.

(2) A person guilty of handling stolen goods shall on conviction on indictment be liable to imprisonment for a term not exceeding fourteen years.

25   Going equipped for stealing, etc.

(1) A person shall be guilty of an offence if, when not at his place of abode, he has with him any article for use in the course of or in connection with any burglary or theft.

(2) A person guilty of an offence under this section shall on conviction on indictment be liable to imprisonment for a term not exceeding three years.

(3) Where a person is charged with an offence under this section, proof that he had with him any article made or adapted for use in committing a burglary or theft shall be evidence that he had it with him for such use.

(5) For purposes of this section an offence under section 12(1) of this Act of taking a conveyance shall be treated as theft.

27   Evidence and procedure on charge of theft or handling stolen goods

(1) Any number of persons may be charged in one indictment, with reference to the same theft, with having at different times or at the same time handled all or any of the stolen goods, and the persons so charged may be tried together.

(2) On the trial of two or more persons indicted for jointly handling any stolen goods the jury may find any of the accused guilty if the jury are satisfied that he handled all or any of the stolen goods, whether or not he did so jointly with the other accused or any of them.

(3) Where a person is being proceeded against for handling stolen goods (but not for any offence other than handling stolen goods), then at any stage of the proceedings, if evidence has been given of his having or arranging to have in his possession the goods the subject of the charge, or of his undertaking or assisting in, or arranging to undertake or assist in, their retention, removal, disposal or realisation, the following evidence shall be admissible for the purpose of proving that he knew or believed the goods to be stolen goods:—

    (a) evidence that he has had in his possession, or has undertaken or assisted in the retention, removal, disposal or realisation of, stolen goods from any theft taking place not earlier than twelve months before the offence charged; and
    (b) (provided that seven days' notice in writing has been given to him of the intention to prove the conviction) evidence that he has within the five years preceding the date of the offence charged been convicted of theft or of handling stolen goods.

(4) In any proceedings for the theft of anything in the course of transmission (whether by post or otherwise), or for handling stolen goods from such a theft, a statutory declaration made by any person that he despatched or received or failed to receive any goods or postal packet, or that any goods or postal packet when despatched or received by him were in a particular state or condition, shall be admissible as evidence of the facts stated in the declaration, subject to the following conditions:—

    (a) a statutory declaration shall only be admissible where and to the extent to which oral evidence to the like effect would have been admissible in the proceedings; and
    (b) a statutory declaration shall only be admissible if at least seven days before the hearing or trial a copy of it has been given to the person charged, and he has not, at least three days before the hearing or trial or within such further time as the court may in special circumstances allow, given the prosecutor written notice requiring the attendance at the hearing or trial of the person making the declaration.

(4A) Where the proceedings mentioned in subsection (4) above are proceedings before a magistrates' court inquiring into an offence as examining justices that subsection shall have effect with the omission of the words from "subject to the following conditions" to the end of the subsection.

(5) This section is to be construed in accordance with section 24 of this Act; and in subsection (3)(b) above the reference to handling stolen goods shall include any corresponding offence committed before the commencement of this Act.

30   Spouses and civil partners

(1) This Act shall apply in relation to the parties to a marriage, and to property belonging to the wife or husband whether or not by reason of an interest derived from the marriage, as it would apply if they were not married and any such interest subsisted independently of the marriage.

(2) Subject to subsection (4) below, a person shall have the same right to bring proceedings against that person's wife or husband for any offence (whether under this Act or otherwise), as if they were not married.

(4) Proceedings shall not be instituted against a person for any offence of stealing or doing unlawful damage to property which at the time of the offence belongs to that person's wife or husband or civil partner, or for any attempt, incitement or conspiracy to commit such an offence, unless the proceedings are instituted by or with the consent of the Director of Public Prosecutions:

Provided that—

    (a) this subsection shall not apply to proceedings against a person for an offence—

        (i) if that person is charged with committing the offence jointly with the wife or husband or civil partner; or

        (ii) if by virtue of any judicial decree or order (wherever made) that person and the wife or husband are at the time of the offence under no obligation to cohabit; and

        (iii) an order (wherever made) is in force providing for the separation of that person and his or her civil partner.

(5) Notwithstanding section 6 of the Prosecution of Offences Act 1979 subsection (4) of this section shall apply—

    (a) to an arrest (if without warrant) made by the wife or husband or civil partner, and

    (b) to a warrant of arrest issued on an information laid by the wife or husband or civil partner.

31   Effect on civil proceedings and rights

(1) A person shall not be excused, by reason that to do so may incriminate that person or the spouse or civil partner of that person of an offence under this Act—

    (a) from answering any question put to that person in proceedings for the recovery or administration of any property, for the execution of any trust or for an account of any property or dealings with property; or

    (b) from complying with any order made in any such proceedings;

but no statement or admission made by a person in answering a question put or complying with an order made as aforesaid shall, in proceedings for an offence under this Act, be admissible in evidence against that person or (unless they married or became civil partners after the making of the statement of admission) against the spouse or civil partner of that person.

(2) Notwithstanding any enactment to the contrary, where property has been stolen or obtained by fraud or other wrongful means, the title to that or any other property shall not be affected by reason only of the conviction of the offender.

Misuse of Drugs Act 1971

(1971, c. 38)

5   Restriction of possession of controlled drugs

(1) Subject to any regulations under section 7 of this Act for the time being in force, it shall not be lawful for a person to have a controlled drug in his possession.

(2) Subject to section 28 of this Act and to subsection (4) below, it is an offence for a person to have a controlled drug in his possession in contravention of subsection (1) above.

(3) Subject to section 28 of this Act, it is an offence for a person to have a controlled drug in his possession, whether lawfully or not, with intent to supply it to another in contravention of section 4(1) of this Act.

(4) In any proceedings for an offence under subsection (2) above in which it is proved that the accused had a controlled drug in his possession, it shall be a defence for him to prove—

(a) that, knowing or suspecting it to be a controlled drug, he took possession of it for the purpose of preventing another from committing or continuing to commit an offence in connection with that drug and that as soon as possible after taking possession of it he took all such steps as were reasonably open to him to destroy the drug or to deliver it into the custody of a person lawfully entitled to take custody of it; or

(b) that, knowing or suspecting it to be a controlled drug, he took possession of it for the purpose of delivering it into the custody of a person lawfully entitled to take custody of it and that as soon as possible after taking possession of it he took all such steps as were reasonably open to him to deliver it into the custody of such a person.

(5) ...

(6) Nothing in subsection (4) . . . above shall prejudice any defence which it is open to a person charged with an offence under this section to raise apart from that subsection.

28 Proof of lack of knowledge etc. to be a defence in proceedings for certain offences

(1) This section applies to offences under any of the following provisions of this Act, that is to say section 4(2) and (3), section 5(2) and (3), section 6(2) and section 9.

(2) Subject to subsection (3) below, in any proceedings for an offence to which this section applies it shall be a defence for the accused to prove that he neither knew of nor suspected nor had reason to suspect the existence of some fact alleged by the prosecution which it is necessary for the prosecution to prove if he is to be convicted of the offence charged.

(3) Where in any proceedings for an offence to which this section applies it is necessary, if the accused is to be convicted of the offence charged, for the prosecution to prove that some substance or product involved in the alleged offence was the controlled drug which the prosecution alleges it to have been, and it is proved that the substance or product in question was that controlled drug, the accused—

(a) shall not be acquitted of the offence charged by reason only of proving that he neither knew nor suspected nor had reason to suspect that the substance or product in question was the particular controlled drug alleged; but

(b) shall be acquitted thereof—

(i) if he proves that he neither believed nor suspected nor had reason to suspect that the substance or product in question was a controlled drug; or

(ii) if he proves that he believed the substance or product in question to be a controlled drug, or a controlled drug of a description, such that, if it had in fact been that controlled drug or a controlled drug of that description, he would not at the material time have been committing any offence to which this section applies.

(4) Nothing in this section shall prejudice any defence which it is open to a person charged with an offence to which this section applies to raise apart from this section

Rehabilitation of Offenders Act 1974

(1974, c. 53)

4 Effect of rehabilitation

(1) Subject to sections 7 and 8 below, a person who has become a rehabilitated person for the purposes of this Act in respect of a conviction shall be treated for all purposes in law as a person who

has not committed or been charged with or prosecuted for or convicted of or sentenced for the offence or offences which were the subject of that conviction; and, notwithstanding the provisions of any other enactment or rule of law to the contrary, but subject as aforesaid—

(a) no evidence shall be admissible in any proceedings before a judicial authority exercising its jurisdiction or functions in Great Britain to prove that any such person has committed or been charged with or prosecuted for or convicted of or sentenced for any offence which was the subject of a spent conviction; and

(b) a person shall not, in any such proceedings, be asked, and, if asked, shall not be required to answer, any question relating to his past which cannot be answered without acknowledging or referring to a spent conviction or spent convictions or any circumstances ancillary thereto.

(2) Subject to the provisions of any order made under subsection (4) below, where a question seeking information with respect to a person's previous convictions, offences, conduct or circumstances is put to him or to any other person otherwise than in proceedings before a judicial authority—

(a) the question shall be treated as not relating to spent convictions or to any circumstances ancillary to spent convictions, and the answer thereto may be framed accordingly; and

(b) the person questioned shall not be subjected to any liability or otherwise prejudiced in law by reason of any failure to acknowledge or disclose a spent conviction or any circumstances ancillary to a spent conviction in his answer to the question.

(3) Subject to the provisions of any order made under subsection (4) below,—

(a) any obligation imposed on any person by any rule of law or by the provisions of any agreement or arrangement to disclose any matters to any other person shall not extend to requiring him to disclose a spent conviction or any circumstances ancillary to a spent conviction (whether the conviction is his own or another's); and

(b) a conviction which has become spent or any circumstances ancillary thereto, or any failure to disclose a spent conviction or any such circumstances, shall not be a proper ground for dismissing or excluding a person from any office, profession, occupation or employment, or for prejudicing him in any way in any occupation or employment.

(4) The Secretary of State may by order—

(a) make such provisions as seems to him appropriate for excluding or modifying the application of either or both of paragraphs (a) and (b) of subsection (2) above in relation to questions put in such circumstances as may be specified in the order;

(b) provide for such exceptions from the provisions of subsection (3) above as seem to him appropriate, in such cases or classes of case, and in relation to convictions of such a description, as may be specified in the order.

(5) For the purposes of this section and section 7 below any of the following are circumstances ancillary to a conviction, that is to say—

(a) the offence or offences which were the subject of that conviction;

(b) the conduct constituting that offence or those offences; and

(c) any process or proceedings preliminary to the conviction, any sentence imposed in respect of that conviction, any proceedings (whether by way of appeal or otherwise) for reviewing that conviction or any such sentence, and anything done in pursuance of or undergone in compliance with any such sentence.

(6) For the purposes of this section and section 7 below 'proceedings before a judicial authority' includes, in addition to proceedings before any of the ordinary courts of law, proceedings before any tribunal, body or person having power—

(a) by virtue of any enactment, law, custom or practice;

(b) under the rules governing any association, institution, profession, occupation or employment; or

(c) under any provision of an agreement providing for arbitration with respect to questions arising there under;

to determine any question affecting the rights, privileges, obligations or liabilities of any person, or to receive evidence affecting the determination of any such question.

5   Rehabilitation periods for particular sentences

(1) The sentences excluded from rehabilitation under this Act are—

    (a) a sentence of imprisonment for life;

    (b) a sentence of imprisonment, youth custody or corrective training for a term exceeding thirty months;

    (c) a sentence of preventive detention;

    (d) a sentence of detention during Her Majesty's pleasure or for life under section 90 or 91 of the Powers of Criminal Courts (Sentencing) Act 2000 . . . or a sentence of detention for a term exceeding thirty months passed under section 91 of the said Act of 2000 . . .

    (e) a sentence of custody for life;

    (f) a sentence of imprisonment for public protection under section 225 of the Criminal Justice Act 2003, a sentence of detention for public protection under section 226 of that Act or an extended sentence under section 227 or 228 of that Act . . .

and any other sentence is a sentence subject to rehabilitation under this Act.

(1A) . . .

(2) For the purposes of this Act—

    (a) the rehabilitation period applicable to a sentence specified in the first column of Table A below is the period specified in the second column of that Table in relation to that sentence, or, where the sentence was imposed on a person who was under eighteen years of age at the date of his conviction, half that period; and

    (b) the rehabilitation period applicable to a sentence specified in the first column of Table B below is the period specified in the second column of that Table in relation to that sentence;

reckoned in either case from the date of the conviction in respect of which the sentence was imposed.

Table A Rehabilitation periods subject to reduction by half for persons under 18

Sentence	Rehabilitation period
A sentence of imprisonment or youth custody or corrective training for a term exceeding six months but not exceeding thirty months.	Ten years.
A sentence of cashiering, discharge with ignominy or dismissal with disgrace from Her Majesty's service.	Ten years.
A sentence of imprisonment [or youth custody] for a term not exceeding six months.	Seven years.
A sentence of dismissal from Her Majesty's service.	Seven years.
A fine or any other sentence subject to rehabilitation under this Act, not being a sentence to which Table B below or any of subsections (3) or (8) below applies.	Five years.

Table B Rehabilitation periods for certain sentences confined to young offenders

Sentence	Rehabilitation period
A sentence of Borstal training.	Seven years.
A sentence of detention for a term exceeding six months but not exceeding thirty months passed under section 91 of the Power of Criminal Courts (Sentencing) Act 2000	Five years.
A sentence of detention for a term not exceeding six months passed under any provision mentioned in the fourth entry in this Table.	Three years.
An order for detention in a detention centre made under [section 4 of the Criminal Justice Act 1982, section 4 of the Criminal Justice Act 1961	Three years.

[

(2A) . . .

(3) The rehabilitation period applicable—

    (a) to an order discharging a person absolutely for an offence; and

    (b) . . .

shall be six months from the date of conviction.

(4) Where in respect of a conviction a person was conditionally discharged, bound over to keep the peace or be of good behaviour, the rehabilitation period applicable to the sentence shall be one year from the date of conviction or a period beginning with that date and ending when the order for conditional discharge or (as the case may be) the recognizance or bond of caution to keep the peace or be of good behaviour ceases or ceased to have effect, whichever is the longer.

(4A) Where in respect of a conviction a probation order or a community order under section 177 of the Criminal Justice Act 2003 . . . was made, the rehabilitation period applicable to the sentence shall be—

    (a) in the case of a person aged eighteen years or over at the date of his conviction, five years from the date of conviction;

    (b) in the case of a person aged under the age of eighteen years at the date of his conviction, two and a half years from the date of conviction or a period beginning with the date of conviction and ending when the order in question ceases or ceased to have effect, whichever is the longer.

(4B) Where in respect of a conviction a referral order (within the meaning of [the Powers of Criminal Courts (Sentencing) Act 2000) is made in respect of the person convicted, the rehabilitation period applicable to the sentence shall be—

    (a) if a youth offender contract takes effect under section 23 of that Act between him and a youth offender panel, the period beginning with the date of conviction and ending on the date when (in accordance with section 24 of that Act) the contract ceases to have effect;

    (b) if no such contract so takes effect, the period beginning with the date of conviction and having the same length as the period for which such a contract would (ignoring any order under paragraph 11 or 12 of Schedule 1 to that Act) have had effect had one so taken effect.

(4C) Where in respect of a conviction an order is made in respect of the person convicted under paragraph 11 or 12 of Schedule 1 to the Powers of Criminal Courts (Sentencing) Act 2000 (extension of period for which youth offender contract has effect), the rehabilitation period applicable to the sentence shall be—

    (a) if a youth offender contract takes effect under section 23 of that Act between the offender and a youth offender panel, the period beginning with the date of conviction and ending on the date when (in accordance with section 24 of that Act) the contract ceases to have effect;

(b) if no such contract so takes effect, the period beginning with the date of conviction and having the same length as the period for which, in accordance with the order, such a contract would have had effect had one so taken effect.

(5) Where in respect of a conviction any of the following sentences was imposed, that is to say—

(a) an order under section 57 of the Children and Young Persons Act 1933 . . . committing the person convicted to the care of a fit person;

(b) a supervision order under any provision of either of those Acts or of the Children and Young Persons Act 1963;

(c) . . .

(g) [*Scotland and Armed Forces*]

the rehabilitation period applicable to the sentence shall be one year from the date of conviction or a period beginning with that date and ending when the order or requirement ceases or ceased to have effect, whichever is the longer.

(6) Where in respect of a conviction any of the following orders was made, that is to say—

(a) an order under section 54 of the said Act of 1933 committing the person convicted to custody in a remand home;

(b) an approved school order under section 57 of the said Act of 1933;

(c) an attendance centre order under section 60 of the Powers of Criminal Courts (Sentencing) Act 2000; or

(d) a secure training order under section 1 of the Criminal Justice and Public Order Act 1994;

the rehabilitation period applicable to the sentence shall be a period beginning with the date of conviction and ending one year after the date on which the order ceases or ceased to have effect.

(6A) Where in respect of a conviction a detention and training order was made under section 100 of the Powers of Criminal Courts (Sentencing) Act 2000 . . . the rehabilitation period applicable to the sentence shall be—

(a) in the case of a person aged fifteen years or over at the date of his conviction, five years if the order was, and three and a half years if the order was not, for a term exceeding six months;

(b) in the case of a person aged under fifteen years at the date of his conviction, a period beginning with that date and ending one year after the date on which the order ceases to have effect.

(7) Where in respect of a conviction a hospital order under Part III of the Mental Health Act 1983 . . . was made, the rehabilitation period applicable to the sentence shall be the period of five years from the date of conviction or a period beginning with that date and ending two years after the date on which the hospital order ceases or ceased to have effect, whichever is the longer.

(8) Where in respect of a conviction an order was made imposing on the person convicted any disqualification, disability, prohibition or other penalty, the rehabilitation period applicable to the sentence shall be a period beginning with the date of conviction and ending on the date on which the disqualification, disability, prohibition or penalty (as the case may be) ceases or ceased to have effect.

(9) For the purposes of this section—

(a) . . .

(b) consecutive terms of imprisonment or of detention under section 91 of the Powers of Criminal Courts (Sentencing) Act 2000 . . . and terms which are wholly or partly concurrent (being terms of imprisonment or detention imposed in respect of offences of which a person was convicted in the same proceedings) shall be treated as a single term;

(c) no account shall be taken of any subsequent variation, made by a court in dealing with a person in respect of a suspended sentence of imprisonment, of the term originally imposed; and

(d) a sentence imposed by a court outside Great Britain shall be treated as a sentence of that one of the descriptions mentioned in this section which most nearly corresponds to the sentence imposed.

(10) References in this section to the period during which a probation order, or a supervision order under the Powers of Criminal Courts (Sentencing) Act 2000 . . . is or was in force include references to any period during which any order or requirement to which this subsection applies, being an order or requirement made or imposed directly or indirectly in substitution for the first-mentioned order or requirement, is or was in force.

This subsection applies—

    (a) to any such order or requirement as is mentioned above in this subsection;

    (b) to any order having effect under section 25(2) of the Children and Young Persons Act 1969 as if it were a training school order in Northern Ireland; and

    (c) to any supervision order made under section 72(2) of the said Act of 1968 and having effect as a supervision order under the Children and Young Persons Act (Northern Ireland) 1950.

(11) The Secretary of State may by order—

    (a) substitute different periods or terms for any of the periods or terms mentioned in subsections (1) to (8) above; and

    (b) substitute a different age for the age mentioned in subsection (2)(a) above.

6   The rehabilitation period applicable to a conviction

(1) Where only one sentence is imposed in respect of a conviction (not being a sentence excluded from rehabilitation under this Act) the rehabilitation period applicable to the conviction is, subject to the following provisions of this section, the period applicable to the sentence in accordance with section 5 above.

(2) Where more than one sentence is imposed in respect of a conviction (whether or not in the same proceedings) and none of the sentences imposed is excluded from rehabilitation under this Act, then, subject to the following provisions of this section, if the periods applicable to those sentences in accordance with section 5 above differ, the rehabilitation period applicable to the conviction shall be the longer or the longest (as the case may be) of those periods.

(3) Without prejudice to subsection (2) above, where in respect of a conviction a person was conditionally discharged or a probation order was made and after the end of the rehabilitation period applicable to the conviction in accordance with subsection (1) or (2) above he is dealt with, in consequence of a breach of conditional discharge or a breach of the order, for the offence for which the order for conditional discharge or probation order was made, then, if the rehabilitation period applicable to the conviction in accordance with subsection (2) above (taking into account any sentence imposed when he is so dealt with) ends later than the rehabilitation period previously applicable to the conviction, he shall be treated for the purposes of this Act as not having become a rehabilitated person in respect of that conviction, and the conviction shall for those purposes be treated as not having become spent, in relation to any period falling before the end of the new rehabilitation period.

(4) Subject to subsection (5) below, where during the rehabilitation period applicable to a conviction—

    (a) the person convicted is convicted of a further offence; and

    (b) no sentence excluded from rehabilitation under this Act is imposed on him in respect of the later conviction;

if the rehabilitation period applicable in accordance with this section to either of the convictions would end earlier than the period so applicable in relation to the other, the rehabilitation period which would (apart from this subsection) end the earlier shall be extended so as to end at the same time as the other rehabilitation period.

(5) Where the rehabilitation period applicable to a conviction is the rehabilitation period applicable in accordance with section 5(8) above to an order imposing on a person any disqualification, disability, prohibition or other penalty, the rehabilitation period applicable to another conviction shall not by virtue of subsection (4) above be extended by reference to that period; but if any other sentence is imposed in respect of the first-mentioned conviction for which a rehabilitation period is prescribed by any other provision of section 5 above, the rehabilitation period applicable to another conviction shall, where appropriate, be extended under subsection (4) above by reference to the

rehabilitation period applicable in accordance with that section to that sentence or, where more than one such sentence is imposed, by reference to the longer or longest of the periods so applicable to those sentences, as if the period in question were the rehabilitation period applicable to the first-mentioned conviction.

(6) For the purposes of subsection (4)(a) above there shall be disregarded—

(a) any conviction in England and Wales of a summary offence or of a scheduled offence (within the meaning of section 22 of the Magistrates' Courts Act 1980) tried summarily in pursuance of subsection (2) of that section (summary trial where value involved is small);]

(b) [*applies to Scotland only*]; and

(bb) any conviction in service disciplinary proceedings for an offence listed in Schedule 1;

(c) any conviction by or before a court outside Great Britain of an offence in respect of conduct which, if it had taken place in any part of Great Britain, would not have constituted an offence under the law in force in that part of Great Britain.

7   Limitations on rehabilitation under this Act, etc.

(1) Nothing in section 4(1) above shall affect—

(a) any right of Her Majesty, by virtue of Her Royal prerogative or otherwise, to grant a free pardon, to quash any conviction or sentence, or to commute any sentence;

(b) the enforcement by any process or proceedings of any fine or other sum adjudged to be paid by or imposed on a spent conviction;

(c) the issue of any process for the purpose of proceedings in respect of any breach of a condition or requirement applicable to a sentence imposed in respect of a spent conviction; or

(d) the operation of any enactment by virtue of which, in consequence of any conviction, a person is subject, otherwise than by way of sentence, to any disqualification, disability, prohibition or other penalty the period of which extends beyond the rehabilitation period applicable in accordance with section 6 above to the conviction.

(2) Nothing in section 4(1) above shall affect the determination of any issue, or prevent the admission or requirement of any evidence, relating to a person's previous convictions or to circumstances ancillary thereto—

(a) in any criminal proceedings before a court in Great Britain (including any appeal or reference in a criminal matter);

(b) in any service disciplinary proceedings or in any proceedings on appeal from any service disciplinary proceedings;

(bb) in any proceedings under Part 2 of the Sexual Offences Act 2003 or on an appeal from any such proceedings;

(c) [*applies to Scotland only*];

(d) in any care proceedings under section 1 of the Powers of Criminal Courts (Sentencing) Act 2000 or on appeal from any such proceedings, or in any proceedings relating to the variation or discharge of a care order or supervision order under that Act;

(e) [*applies to Scotland only*]; or

(f) in any proceedings in which he is a party or a witness, provided that, on the occasion when the issue or the admission or requirement of the evidence falls to be determined, he consents to the determination of the issue or, as the case may be, the admission or requirement of the evidence notwithstanding the provisions of section 4(1); or,

(g) . . .

(3) If at any stage in any proceedings before a judicial authority in Great Britain (not being proceedings to which, by virtue of any of paragraphs (a) to (e) of subsection (2) above or of any order for the time being in force under subsection (4) below, section 4(1) above has no application, or proceedings to which section 8 below applies) the authority is satisfied, in the light of any considerations which appear to it to be relevant (including any evidence which has been or may thereafter be put before it), that justice cannot be done in the case except by admitting or requiring evidence relating to a person's spent convictions or to circumstances ancillary thereto, that authority may admit or, as

the case may be, require the evidence in question notwithstanding the provisions of subsection (1) of section 4 above, and may determine any issue to which the evidence relates in disregard, so far as necessary, of those provisions.

(4) The Secretary of State may by order exclude the application of section 4(1) above in relation to any proceedings specified in the order (other than proceedings to which section 8 below applies) to such extent and for such purposes as may be so specified.

(5) No order made by a court with respect to any person otherwise than on a conviction shall be included in any list or statement of that person's previous convictions given or made to any court which is considering how to deal with him in respect of any offence.

Protection of Children Act 1978

(1978, c. 37)

1 Indecent photographs of children

(1) Subject to sections 1A and 1B it is an offence for a person—
- (a) to take, or permit to be taken, or to make any indecent photograph or pseudo-photograph of a child; or
- (b) to distribute or show such indecent photographs or pseudo-photographs; or
- (c) to have in his possession such indecent photographs or pseudo-photographs, with a view to their being distributed or shown by himself or others; or
- (d) to publish or cause to be published any advertisement likely to be understood as conveying that the advertiser distributes or shows such indecent photographs or pseudo-photographs, or intends to do so.

(2) For purposes of this Act, a person is to be regarded as distributing an indecent photograph or pseudo-photograph if he parts with possession of it to, or exposes or offers it for acquisition by another person.

(3) Proceedings for an offence under this Act shall not be instituted except by or with the consent of the Director of Public Prosecutions.

(4) Where a person is charged with an offence under subsection (1)(b) or (c), it shall be a defence for him to prove—
- (a) that he had a legitimate reason for distributing or showing the photographs or pseudo-photographs or (as the case may be) having them in his possession; or
- (b) that he had not himself seen the photographs or pseudo-photographs and did not know, nor had any cause to suspect, them to be indecent.

(5) References in the Children and Young Persons Act 1933 (except in sections 15 and 99) to the offences mentioned in Schedule 1 to that Act shall include an offence under subsection (1)(a) above.

1A Marriage and other relationships

(1) This section applies where, in proceedings for an offence under section 1(1)(a) of taking or making an indecent photograph of a child, or for an offence under section 1(1)(b) or (c) relating to an indecent photograph of a child, the defendant proves that the photograph was of the child aged 16 or over, and that at the time of the offence charged the child and he—
- (a) were married or civil partners of each other, or
- (b) lived together as partners in an enduring family relationship.

(2) Subsections (5) and (6) also apply where, in proceedings for an offence under section 1(1)(b) or (c) relating to an indecent photograph of a child, the defendant proves that the photograph was of the child aged 16 or over, and that at the time when he obtained it the child and he—
- (a) were married or civil partners of each other, or
- (b) lived together as partners in an enduring family relationship.

(3) This section applies whether the photograph showed the child alone or with the defendant, but not if it showed any other person.

(4) In the case of an offence under section 1(1)(a), if sufficient evidence is adduced to raise an issue as to whether the child consented to the photograph being taken or made, or as to whether the defendant reasonably believed that the child so consented, the defendant is not guilty of the offence unless it is proved that the child did not so consent and that the defendant did not reasonably believe that the child so consented.

(5) In the case of an offence under section 1(1)(b), the defendant is not guilty of the offence unless it is proved that the showing or distributing was to a person other than the child.

(6) In the case of an offence under section 1(1)(c), if sufficient evidence is adduced to raise an issue both—

(a) as to whether the child consented to the photograph being in the defendant's possession, or as to whether the defendant reasonably believed that the child so consented, and

(b) as to whether the defendant had the photograph in his possession with a view to its being distributed or shown to anyone other than the child,

the defendant is not guilty of the offence unless it is proved either that the child did not so consent and that the defendant did not reasonably believe that the child so consented, or that the defendant had the photograph in his possession with a view to its being distributed or shown to a person other than the child.

1B   Exception for criminal proceedings, investigations etc.

(1) In proceedings for an offence under section 1(1)(a) of making an indecent photograph or pseudo-photograph of a child, the defendant is not guilty of the offence if he proves that—

(a) it was necessary for him to make the photograph or pseudo-photograph for the purposes of the prevention, detection or investigation of crime, or for the purposes of criminal proceedings, in any part of the world,

(b) at the time of the offence charged he was a member of the Security Service or the Secret Intelligence Service, and it was necessary for him to make the photograph or pseudo-photograph for the exercise of any of the functions of that Service, or

(c) at the time of the offence charged he was a member of GCHQ, and it was necessary for him to make the photograph or pseudo-photograph for the exercise of any of the functions of GCHQ.

(2) In this section "GCHQ" has the same meaning as in the Intelligence Services Act 1994.

2   Evidence

(1), (2) . . .

(3) In proceedings under this Act relating to indecent photographs of children a person is to be taken as having been a child at any material time if it appears, from the evidence as a whole, that he was then under the age of 18.

Magistrates' Courts Act 1980

(1980, c. 43)

98   Evidence on oath

Subject to the provisions of any enactment or rule of law authorising the reception of unsworn evidence, evidence given before a magistrates' court shall be given on oath.

101   Onus of proving exceptions, etc.

Where the defendant to an information or complaint relies for his defence on any exception, exemption, proviso, excuse or qualification, whether or not it accompanies the description of the offence or matter of complaint in the enactment creating the offence or on which the complaint is founded, the burden of proving the exception, exemption, proviso, excuse or qualification shall be on him; and this notwithstanding that the information or complaint contains an allegation negativing the exception, exemption, proviso, excuse or qualification.

103   Evidence of persons under 14 in committal proceedings for assault, sexual offences etc.

(1) In any proceedings before a magistrates' court inquiring into an offence to which this section applies as examining justices—

(a) a child shall not be called as a witness for the prosecution; but

(b) any statement made by or taken from a child shall be admissible in evidence of any matter of which his oral testimony would be admissible,

except in a case where the application of this subsection is excluded under subsection (3) below.

(2) This section applies—

(a) to an offence which involves an assault, or injury or a threat of injury to, a person;

(b) to an offence under section 1 of the Children and Young Persons Act 1933 (cruelty to persons under 16);

(c) to an offence under the Sexual Offences Act 1956, the Indecency with Children Act 1960, the Sexual Offences Act 1967, section 54 of the Criminal Law Act 1977 or the Protection of Children Act 1978; and

(d) to an offence which consists of attempting or conspiring to commit, or of aiding, abetting, counselling, procuring or inciting the commission of, an offence falling within paragraph (a), (b) or (c) above.

(3) The application of subsection (1) above is excluded—

(a) where at or before the time when the statement is tendered in evidence the defence objects to its admission; or

(b) where the prosecution requires the attendance of the child for the purpose of establishing the identity of any person; or

(c) where the court is satisfied that it has not been possible to obtain from the child a statement that may be given in evidence under this section; or

(d) where the inquiry into the offence takes place after the court has discontinued to try it summarily and the child has given evidence in the summary trial.

(4) Section 28 above shall not apply to any statement admitted in pursuance of subsection (1) above.

(5) In this section "child" means a person under the age of 14.

104   Proof of previous convictions

Where a person is convicted of a summary offence by a magistrates' court, other than a juvenile court, and—

(a) it is proved to the satisfaction of the court, on oath or in such other manner as may be prescribed, that not less than 7 days previously a notice was served on the accused in the prescribed form and manner specifying any alleged previous conviction of the accused of a summary offence proposed to be brought to the notice of the court in the event of his conviction of the offence charged; and

(b) the accused is not present in person before the court, the court may take account of any such previous conviction so specified as if the accused had appeared and admitted it.

107   False statements in declaration proving service, etc.

If, in any solemn declaration, certificate or other writing made or given for the purpose of its being used in pursuance of rules of court as evidence of the service of any document or the handwriting or seal of any person, a person makes a statement that he knows to be false in a material particular, or recklessly makes any statement that is false in a material particular, he shall be liable on summary conviction to imprisonment for a term not exceeding 6 months or a fine not exceeding [level 3 on the standard scale] or both.

Contempt of Court Act 1981

(1981, c. 49)

10   Sources of information

No court may require a person to disclose, nor is any person guilty of contempt of court for refusing to disclose, the source of information contained in a publication for which he is responsible, unless it be established to the satisfaction of the court that disclosure is necessary in the interests of justice or national security or for the prevention of disorder or crime.

Criminal Justice Act 1982

(1982, c. 48)

Unsworn statements

72   Abolition of right of accused to make unsworn statement

    (1) Subject to subsections (2) and (3) below, in any criminal proceedings the accused shall not be entitled to make a statement without being sworn, and accordingly, if he gives evidence, he shall do so (subject to sections 55 and 56 of the Youth Justice and Criminal Evidence Act 1999) on oath and be liable to cross-examination; but this section shall not affect the right of the accused, if not represented by counsel or a solicitor, to address the court or jury otherwise than on oath on any matter on which, if he were so represented, counsel or a solicitor could address the court or jury on his behalf.

    (2) Nothing in subsection (1) above shall prevent the accused making a statement without being sworn—

      (a) if it is one which he is required by law to make personally; or

      (b) if he makes it by way of mitigation before the court passes sentence upon him.

Police and Criminal Evidence Act 1984

(1984, c. 60)

PART I   POWERS TO STOP AND SEARCH

1   Power of constable to stop and search persons, vehicles etc.

    (1) A constable may exercise any power conferred by this section—

      (a) in any place to which at the time when he proposes to exercise the power the public or any section of the public has access, on payment or otherwise, as of right or by virtue of express or implied permission; or

      (b) in any other place to which people have ready access at the time when he proposes to exercise the power but which is not a dwelling.

    (2) Subject to subsection (3) to (5) below, a constable—

      (a) may search—

         (i)   any person or vehicle;

         (ii)   anything which is in or on a vehicle, for stolen or prohibited articles or any article to which subsection (8A) below applies or any firework to which subsection (8B) below applies; and

      (b) may detain a person or vehicle for the purpose of such a search.

    (3) This section does not give a constable power to search a person or vehicle or anything in or on a vehicle unless he has reasonable grounds for suspecting that he will find stolen or prohibited articles or any article to which subsection (8A) below applies or any firework to which subsection (8B) below applies.

(4) If a person is in a garden or yard occupied with and used for the purposes of a dwelling or on other land so occupied and used, a constable may not search him in the exercise of the power conferred by this section unless the constable has reasonable grounds for believing—

(a) that he does not reside in the dwelling; and

(b) that he is not in the place in question with the express or implied permission of a person who resides in the dwelling.

(5) If a vehicle is in a garden or yard occupied with and used for the purposes of a dwelling or on other land so occupied and used, a constable may not search the vehicle or anything in or on it in the exercise of the power conferred by this section unless he has reasonable grounds for believing—

(a) that the person in charge of the vehicle does not reside in the dwelling; and

(b) that the vehicle is not in the place in question with the express or implied permission of a person who resides in the dwelling.

(6) If in the course of such a search a constable discovers an article which he has reasonable grounds for suspecting to be a stolen or prohibited article or any article to which subsection (8A) below applies or any firework to which subsection (8B) below applies, he may seize it.

(7) An article is prohibited for the purposes of this Part of this Act if it is—

(a) an offensive weapon; or

(b) an article—

(i) made or adapted for use in the course of or in connection with an offence to which this sub-paragraph applies; or

(ii) intended by the person having it with him for such use by him or by some other person.

(8) The offences to which subsection (7)(b)(i) above applies are—

(a) burglary;

(b) theft;

(c) offences under section 12 of the Theft Act 1968 (taking motor vehicle or other conveyance without authority); and

(d) fraud contrary to section 1 of the Fraud Act 2006; and

(e) offences under section 1 of the Criminal Damage Act 1971 (damaging or destroying property).

(8A) This subsection applies to any article in relation to which a person has committed, or is committing or is going to commit an offence under section 139 of the Criminal Justice Act 1988.

(8B) This subsection applies to any firework which a person possesses in contravention of a prohibition imposed by fireworks regulations.

(8C) In this section—

(a) 'firework' shall be construed in accordance with the definition of "fireworks" in section 1(1) of the Fireworks Act 2003; and

(b) 'fireworks regulations' has the same meaning as in that Act.

(9) In this Part of this Act 'offensive weapon' means any article—

(a) made or adapted for use for causing injury to persons; or

(b) intended by the person having it with him for such use by him or by some other person.

2   Provisions relating to search under section 1 and other powers

(1) A constable who detains a person or vehicle in the exercise—

(a) of the power conferred by section 1 above; or

(b) of any other power—

(i) to search a person without first arresting him; or

(ii) to search a vehicle without making an arrest,

need not conduct a search if it appears to him subsequently—

(i) that no search is required; or

(ii) that a search is impracticable.

(2) If a constable contemplates a search, other than a search of an unattended vehicle, in the exercise—

    (a) of the power conferred by section 1 above; or

    (b) of any other power, except the power conferred by section 6 below and the power conferred by section 27(2) of the Aviation Security Act 1982—

        (i) to search a person without first arresting him; or

        (ii) to search a vehicle without making an arrest,

it shall be his duty, subject to subsection (4) below, to take reasonable steps before he commences the search to bring to the attention of the appropriate person—

        (i) if the constable is not in uniform, documentary evidence that he is a constable; and

        (ii) whether he is in uniform or not, the matter specified in subsection (3) below;

and the constable shall not commence the search until he has performed that duty.

(3) The matters referred to in subsection (2)(ii) above are—

    (a) the constable's name and the name of the police station to which he is attached;

    (b) the object of the proposed search;

    (c) the constable's grounds for proposing to make it; and

    (d) the effect of section 3(7) or (8) below, as may be appropriate.

(4) A constable need not bring the effect of section 3(7) or (8) below to the attention of the appropriate person if it appears to the constable that it will not be practicable to make the record in section 3(1) below.

(5) In this section 'the appropriate person' means—

    (a) if the constable proposes to search a person, that person; and

    (b) if he proposes to search a vehicle, or anything in or on a vehicle, the person in charge of the vehicle.

(6) On completing a search of an unattended vehicle or anything in or on such a vehicle in the exercise of any such power as is mentioned in subsection (2) above a constable shall leave a notice—

    (a) stating that he has searched it;

    (b) giving the name of the police station to which he is attached;

    (c) stating that an application for compensation for any damage caused by the search may be made to that police station; and

    (d) stating the effect of section 3(8) below.

(7) The constable shall leave the notice inside the vehicle unless it is not reasonably practicable to do so without damaging the vehicle.

(8) The time for which a person or vehicle may be detained for the purposes of such a search is such time as is reasonably required to permit a search to be carried out either at the place where the person or vehicle was first detained or nearby.

(9) Neither the power conferred by section 1 above nor any other power to detain and search a person without first arresting him or to detain and search a vehicle without making an arrest is to be construed—

    (a) as authorising a constable to require a person to remove any of his clothing in public other than an outer coat, jacket or gloves; or

    (b) as authorising a constable not in uniform to stop a vehicle.

(10) This section and section 1 above apply to vessels, aircraft and hovercraft as they apply to vehicles.

3 Duty to make records concerning searches

(1) Where a constable has carried out a search in the exercise of any such power as is mentioned in section 2(1) above, other than a search—

    (a) under section 6 below; or

    (b) under section 27(2) of the Aviation Security Act 1982, a record of the search shall be made in writing unless it is not practicable to do so.

(2) If a record of a search is required to be made by subsection (1) above—

    (a) in a case where the search results in a person being arrested and taken to a police station, the constable shall secure that the record is made as part of the person's custody record;

    (b) in any other case, the constable shall make the record on the spot, or, if that is not practicable, as soon as practicable after the completion of the search.

(6) The record of a search of a person or a vehicle—

    (a) shall state—

        (i)   the object of the search;

        (ii) the grounds for making it;

        (iii) the date and time when it was made;

        (iv) the place where it was made;

        (v) except in the case of a search of an unattended vehicle, the ethnic origins of the person searched or the person in charge of the vehicle searched (as the case may be); and

    (b) shall identify the constable carrying out the search.

(6A) The requirement in subsection (6)(a)(v) above for a record to state a person's ethnic origins is a requirement to state—

    (a) the ethnic origins of the person as described by the person, and

    (b) if different, the ethnic origins of the person as perceived by the constable.

(7) If a record of a search of a person has been made under this section, the person who was searched shall be entitled to a copy of the record if he asks for one before the end of the period specified in subsection (9) below.

(8) If—

    (a) the owner of a vehicle which has been searched or the person who was in charge of the vehicle at the time when it was searched asks for a copy of the record of the search before the end of the period specified in subsection (9) below; and

    (b) a record of the search of the vehicle has been made under this section, the person who made the request shall be entitled to a copy.

(9) The period mentioned in subsections (7) and (8) above is the period of 3 months beginning with the date on which the search was made.

(10) The requirements imposed by this section with regard to records of searches of vehicles shall apply also to records of searches of vessels, aircraft and hovercraft.

4   Road checks

(1) This section shall have effect in relation to the conducting of road checks by police officers for the purpose of ascertaining whether a vehicle is carrying—

    (a) a person who has committed an offence other than a road traffic offence or a vehicle excise offence;

    (b) a person who is a witness to such an offence;

    (c) a person intending to commit such an offence; or

    (d) a person who is unlawfully at large.

(2) For the purposes of this section a road check consists of the exercise in a locality of the power conferred by section 163 of the Road Traffic Act 1988 in such a way as to stop during the period for which its exercise in that way in that locality continues all vehicles or vehicles selected by any criterion.

(3) Subject to subsection (5) below, there may only be such a road check if a police officer of the rank of superintendent or above authorises it in writing.

(4) An officer may only authorise a road check under subsection (3) above—

    (a) for the purpose specified in subsection (1)(a) above, if he has reasonable grounds—

        (i)   for believing that the offence is an indictable offence; and

        (ii) for suspecting that the person is, or is about to be, in the locality in which vehicles would be stopped if the road check were authorised;

(b) for the purpose specified in subsection (1)(b) above, if he has reasonable grounds for believing that the offence is an indictable offence;

(c) for the purpose specified in subsection (1)(c) above, if he has reasonable grounds—

    (i)   for believing that the offence would be an indictable offence; and

    (ii) for suspecting that the person is, or is about to be, in the locality in which vehicles would be stopped if the road check were authorised;

(d) for the purpose specified in subsection (1)(d) above, if he has reasonable grounds for suspecting that the person is, or is about to be, in that locality.

(5) An officer below the rank of superintendent may authorise such a road check if it appears to him that it is required as a matter of urgency for one of the purposes specified in subsection (1) above.

(6) If an authorisation is given under subsection (5) above, it shall be the duty of the officer who gives it—

(a) to make a written record of the time at which he gives it; and

(b) to cause an officer of the rank of superintendent or above to be informed that it has been given.

(7) The duties imposed by subsection (6) above shall be performed as soon as it is practicable to do so.

(8) An officer to whom a report is made under subsection (6) above may, in writing, authorise the road check to continue.

(9) If such an officer considers that the road checks should not continue, he shall record in writing—

(a) the fact that it took place; and

(b) the purpose for which it took place.

(10) An officer giving an authorisation under this section shall specify the locality in which vehicles are to be stopped.

(11) An officer giving an authorisation under this section, other than an authorisation under subsection (5) above—

(a) shall specify a period, not exceeding seven days, during which the road check may continue; and

(b) may direct that the road check—

    (i)   shall be continuous; or

    (ii) shall be conducted at specified times, during that period.

(12) If it appears to an officer of the rank of superintendent or above that a road check ought to continue beyond the period for which it has been authorised he may, from time to time, in writing specify a further period, not exceeding seven days, during which it may continue.

(13) Every written authorisation shall specify—

(a) the name of the officer giving it;

(b) the purpose of the road check; and

(c) the locality in which vehicles are to be stopped.

(14) The duties to specify the purposes of a road check imposed by subsections (9) and (13) above include duties to specify any relevant indictable offence.

(15) Where a vehicle is stopped in a road check, the person in charge of the vehicle at the time when it is stopped shall be entitled to obtain a written statement of the purpose of the road check if he applies for such a statement not later than the end of the period of twelve months from the day on which the vehicle was stopped.

(16) Nothing in this section affects the exercise by police officers of any power to stop vehicles for purposes other than those specified in subsection (1) above.

5   Reports of recorded searches and of road checks

(1) Every annual report—

(a) under section 22 of the Police Act 1996; or

(b) made by the Commissioner of Police of the Metropolis, shall contain information—
  (i) about searches recorded under section 3 above which have been carried out in the area to which the report relates during the period to which it relates; and
  (ii) about road checks authorised in that area during that period under section 4 above.

(2) The information about searches shall not include information about specific searches but shall include—
  (a) the total number of searches in each month during the period to which the report relates—
    (i) for stolen articles;
    (ii) for offensive weapons or articles to which section 1(8A) above applies; and
    (iii) for other prohibited articles;
  (b) the total number of persons arrested in each such month in consequence of searches of each of the descriptions specified in paragraph (a)(i) to (iii) above.

(3) The information about road checks shall include information—
  (a) about the reason for authorising each road check; and
  (b) about the result of each of them.

6 Statutory undertakers etc.

(1) A constable employed by statutory undertakers may stop, detain and search any vehicle before it leaves a goods area included in the premises of the statutory undertakers.

(1A) Without prejudice to any powers under subsection (1) above, a constable employed by the British Transport Police Authority may stop, detain and search any vehicle before it leaves a goods area which is included in the premises of any successor of the British Railways Board and is used wholly or mainly for the purpose of a relevant undertaking.

(2) In this section 'goods area' means any area used wholly or mainly for the storage or handling of goods and 'successor of the British Railways Board' and 'relevant undertaking' have the same meaning as in the Railways Act 1993 (Consequential Modifications) Order 1999.

7 Part I—supplementary

(1) The following enactments shall cease to have effect—
  (a) section 8 of the Vagrancy Act 1824;
  (b) section 66 of the Metropolitan Police Act 1839;
  (c) section 11 of the Canals (Offences) Act 1840;
  (d) section 19 of the Pedlars Act 1871;
  (e) section 33 of the County of Merseyside Act 1980; and
  (f) section 42 of the West Midlands County Council Act 1980.

(2) There shall also cease to have effect—
  (a) so much of any enactment contained in an Act passed before 1974, other than—
    (i) an enactment contained in a public general Act; or
    (ii) an enactment relating to statutory undertakers, as confers power on a constable to search for stolen or unlawfully obtained goods; and
  (b) so much of any enactment relating to statutory undertakers as provides that such a power shall not be exercisable after the end of a specified period.

(3) In this Part of this Act 'statutory undertakers' means persons authorised by any enactment to carry on any railway, light railway, road transport, water transport, canal, inland navigation, dock or harbour undertaking.

PART II POWERS OF ENTRY, SEARCH AND SEIZURE

Search warrants

8 Power of justice of the peace to authorise entry and search of premises

(1) If on an application made by a constable a justice of the peace is satisfied that there are reasonable grounds for believing—

(a) that an indictable offence has been committed; and

(b) that there is material on premises mentioned in subsection (1A) below which is likely to be of substantial value (whether by itself or together with other material) to the investigation of the offence; and

(c) that the material is likely to be relevant evidence; and

(d) that it does not consist of or include items subject to legal privilege, excluded material or special procedure material; and

(e) that any of the conditions specified in subsection (3) below applies in relation to each set of premises specified in the application, he may issue a warrant authorising a constable to enter and search the premises in relation to each set of premises specified in the application.

(1A) The premises referred to in subsection (1)(b) above are—

(a) one or more sets of premises specified in the application (in which case the application is for a 'specific premises warrant'); or

(b) any premises occupied or controlled by a person specified in the application, including such sets of premises as are so specified (in which case the application is for an 'all premises warrant').

(1B) If the application is for an all premises warrant, the justice of the peace must also be satisfied—

(a) that because of the particulars of the offence referred to in paragraph (a) of subsection (1) above, there are reasonable grounds for believing that it is necessary to search premises occupied or controlled by the person in question which are not specified in the application in order to find the material referred to in paragraph (b) of that subsection; and

(b) that it is not reasonably practicable to specify in the application all the premises which he occupies or controls and which might need to be searched.

(1C) The warrant may authorise entry to and search of premises on more than one occasion if, on the application, the justice of the peace is satisfied that it is necessary to authorise multiple entries in order to achieve the purpose for which he issues the warrant.

(1D) If it authorises multiple entries, the number of entries authorised may be unlimited, or limited to a maximum.

(2) A constable may seize and retain anything for which a search has been authorised under subsection (1) above.

(3) The conditions mentioned in subsection (1)(e) above are—

(a) that it is not practicable to communicate with any person entitled to grant entry to the premises;

(b) that it is practicable to communicate with a person entitled to grant entry to the premises but it is not practicable to communicate with any person entitled to grant access to the evidence;

(c) that entry to the premises will not be granted unless a warrant is produced;

(d) that the purpose of a search may be frustrated or seriously prejudiced unless a constable arriving at the premises can secure immediate entry to them.

(4) In this Act 'relevant evidence', in relation to an offence, means anything that would be admissible in evidence at a trial for the offence.

(5) The power to issue a warrant conferred by this section is in addition to any such power otherwise conferred.

(6) This section applies in relation to a relevant offence (as defined in section 28D(4) of the Immigration Act 1971) as it applies to an indictable offence.

[(7) *Execution of process of English courts in Scotland*]

9   Special provisions as to access

(1) A constable may obtain access to excluded material or special procedure material for the purposes of a criminal investigation by making an application under Schedule 1 below and in accordance with that Schedule.

(2) Any Act (including a local Act) passed before this Act under which a search of premises for the purposes of a criminal investigation could be authorised by the issue of a warrant to a constable shall cease to have effect so far as it relates to the authorisation of searches—

    (a) for items subject to legal privilege; or

    (b) for excluded material; or

    (c) for special procedure material consisting of documents or records other than documents.

[(2A) *Execution of process of English courts in Scotland and Northern Ireland*]

10   Meaning of 'items subject to legal privilege'

(1) Subject to subsection (2) below, in this Act 'items subject to legal privilege' means—

    (a) communications between a professional legal adviser and his client or any person representing his client made in connection with the giving of legal advice to the client;

    (b) communications between a professional legal adviser and his client or any person representing his client or between such an adviser or his client or any such representative and any other person made in connection with or in contemplation of legal proceedings and for the purpose of such proceedings; and

    (c) items enclosed with or referred to in such communications and made—

        (i) in connection with the giving of legal advice; or

        (ii) in connection with or in contemplation of legal proceedings and for the purposes of such proceedings,

when they are in the possession of a person who is entitled to possession of them.

(2) Items held with the intention of furthering a criminal purpose are not items subject to legal privilege.

11   Meaning of 'excluded material'

(1) Subject to the following provisions of this section, in this Act 'excluded material' means—

    (a) personal records which a person has acquired or created in the course of any trade, business, profession or other occupation or for the purposes of any paid or unpaid office and which he holds in confidence;

    (b) human tissue or tissue fluid which has been taken for the purposes of diagnosis or medical treatment and which a person holds in confidence;

    (c) journalistic material which a person holds in confidence and which consists—

        (i) of documents; or

        (ii) of records other than documents.

(2) A person holds material other than journalistic material in confidence for the purposes of this section if he holds it subject—

    (a) to an express or implied undertaking to hold it in confidence; or

    (b) to a restriction on disclosure or an obligation of secrecy contained in any enactment, including an enactment contained in an Act passed after this Act.

(3) A person holds journalistic material in confidence for the purposes of this section if—

    (a) he holds it subject to such an undertaking, restriction or obligation; and

    (b) it has been continuously held (by one or more persons) subject to such an undertaking, restriction or obligation since it was first acquired or created for the purposes of journalism.

12   Meaning of 'personal records'

In this Part of this Act 'personal records' means documentary and other records concerning an individual (whether living or dead) who can be identified from them and relating—

    (a) to his physical or mental health;

    (b) to spiritual counselling or assistance given or to be given to him; or

    (c) to counselling or assistance given or to be given to him, for the purposes of his personal welfare, by any voluntary organisation or by any individual who—

        (i)   by reason of his office or occupation has responsibilities for his personal welfare; or

        (ii) by reason of an order of a court has responsibilities for his supervision.

13   Meaning of 'journalistic material'

    (1) Subject to subsection (2) below, in this Act 'journalistic material' means material acquired or created for the purposes of journalism.

    (2) Material is only journalistic material for the purposes of this Act if it is in the possession of a person who acquired or created it for the purposes of journalism.

    (3) A person who receives material from someone who intends that the recipient shall use it for the purposes of journalism is to be taken to have acquired it for those purposes.

14   Meaning of 'special procedure material'

    (1) In this Act 'special procedure material' means—

    (a) material to which subsection (2) below applies; and

    (b) journalistic material, other than excluded material.

    (2) Subject to the following provisions of this section, this subsection applies to material, other than items subject to legal privilege and excluded material, in the possession of a person who—

    (a) acquired or created it in the course of any trade, business, profession or other occupation or for the purpose of any paid or unpaid office; and

    (b) holds it subject—

        (i)   to an express or implied undertaking to hold it in confidence; or

        (ii) to a restriction or obligation such as is mentioned in section 11(2)(b) above.

    (3) Where material is acquired—

    (a) by an employee from his employer and in the course of his employment; or

    (b) by a company from an associated company,

it is only special procedure material if it was special procedure material immediately before the acquisition.

    (4) Where material is created by an employee in the course of his employment, it is only special procedure material if it would have been special procedure material had his employer created it.

    (5) Where material is created by a company on behalf of an associated company, it is only special procedure material if it would have been special procedure material had the associated company created it.

    (6) A company is to be treated as another's associated company for the purposes of this section if it would be so treated under section 449 of the Corporation Taxes Act 2010.

15   Search warrants—safeguards

    (1) This section and section 16 below have effect in relation to the issue to constables under any enactment, including an enactment contained in an Act passed after this Act, of warrants to enter and search premises; and an entry on or search of premises under a warrant is unlawful unless it complies with this section and section 16 below.

    (2) Where a constable applies for any such warrant, it shall be his duty—

    (a) to state—

        (i)   the ground on which he makes the application;

        (ii) the enactment under which the warrant would be issued; and

(iii) if the application is for a warrant authorising entry and search on more than one occasion, the ground on which he applies for such a warrant, and whether he seeks a warrant authorising an unlimited number of entries, or (if not) the maximum number of entries desired;

(b) to specify the matters set out in subsection (2A) below; and

(c) to identify, so far as is practicable, the articles or persons to be sought.

(2A)   The matters which must be specified pursuant to subsection (2)(b) above are—

(a) if the application relates to one or more sets of premises specified in the application, each set of premises which it is desired to enter and search;

(b) if the application relates to any premises occupied or controlled by a person specified in the application—

(i)   as many sets of premises which it is desired to enter and search as it is reasonably practicable to specify;

(ii)   the person who is in occupation or control of those premises and any others which it is desired to enter and search;

(iii)   why it is necessary to search more premises than those specified under sub-paragraph (i); and

(iv)   why it is not reasonably practicable to specify all the premises which it is desired to enter and search.

(3)   An application for such a warrant shall be made ex parte and supported by an information in writing.

(4)   The constable shall answer on oath any question that the justice of the peace or judge hearing the application asks him.

(5)   A warrant shall authorise an entry on one occasion only unless it specifies that it authorises multiple entries.

(5A)   If it specifies that it authorises multiple entries, it must also specify whether the number of entries authorised is unlimited, or limited to a specified maximum.

(6)   A warrant—

(a) shall specify—

(i)   the name of the person who applies for it;

(ii)   the date on which it is issued;

(iii)   the enactment under which it is issued; and

(iv)   each set of premises to be searched, or (in the case of an all premises warrant) the person who is in occupation or control of premises to be searched, together with any premises under his occupation or control which can be specified and which are to be searched; and

(b) shall identify, so far as is practicable, the articles or persons to be sought.

(7)   Two copies shall be made of a warrant which specifies only one set of premises and does not authorise multiple entries; and as many copies as are reasonably required may be made of any other kind of warrant.

(8)   The copies shall be clearly certified as copies.

16   Execution of warrants

(1)   A warrant to enter and search premises may be executed by any constable.

(2)   Such a warrant may authorise persons to accompany any constable who is executing it.

(2A)   A person so authorised has the same powers as the constable whom he accompanies in respect of—

(a) the execution of the warrant, and

(b) the seizure of anything to which the warrant relates.

(2B)   But he may exercise those powers only in the company, and under the supervision, of a constable.

(3) Entry and search under a warrant must be within three months from the date of its issue.

(3A) If the warrant is an all premises warrant, no premises which are not specified in it may be entered or searched unless a police officer of at least the rank of inspector has in writing authorised them to be entered.

(3B) No premises may be entered or searched for the second or any subsequent time under a warrant which authorises multiple entries unless a police officer of at least the rank of inspector has in writing authorised that entry to those premises.

(4) Entry and search under a warrant must be at a reasonable hour unless it appears to the constable executing it that the purpose of a search may be frustrated on an entry at a reasonable hour.

(5) Where the occupier of premises which are to be entered and searched is present at the time when a constable seeks to execute a warrant to enter and search them, the constable—

    (a) shall identify himself to the occupier and, if not in uniform, shall produce to him documentary evidence that he is a constable;

    (b) shall produce a warrant to him; and

    (c) shall supply him with a copy of it.

(6) Where—

    (a) the occupier of such premises is not present at the time when a constable seeks to execute such a warrant; but

    (b) some other person who appears to the constable to be in charge of the premises is present,

subsection (5) above shall have effect as if any reference to the occupier were a reference to that other person.

(7) If there is no person present who appears to the constable to be in charge of the premises, he shall leave a copy of the warrant in a prominent place on the premises.

(8) A search under a warrant may only be a search to the extent required for the purpose for which the warrant was issued.

(9) A constable executing a warrant shall make an endorsement on it stating—

    (a) whether the articles or persons sought were found; and

    (b) whether any articles were seized, other than articles which were sought

and, unless the warrant is a warrant specifying one set of premises only, he shall do so separately in respect of each set of premises entered and searched, which he shall in each case state in the endorsement.

(10) A warrant shall be returned to the appropriate person mentioned in subsection (10A) below—

    (a) when it has been executed; or

    (b) in the case of a specific premises warrant which has not been executed, or an all premises warrant, or any warrant authorising multiple entries, upon the expiry of the period of three months referred to in subsection (3) above or sooner.

(10A) The appropriate person is—

    (a) if the warrant was issued by a justice of the peace, the designated officer for the local justice area in which the justice was acting when he issued the warrant;

    (b) if it was issued by a judge, the appropriate officer of the court from which he issued it.

(11) A warrant which is returned under subsection (10) above shall be retained for 12 months from its return—

    (a) by the designated officer for the local justice area, if it was returned under paragraph (i) of that subsection; and

    (b) by the appropriate officer, if it was returned under paragraph (ii).

(12) If during the period for which a warrant is to be retained the occupier of premises to which it relates asks to inspect it, he shall be allowed to do so.

Entry and search without search warrant

17   Entry for purpose of arrest etc.

(1) Subject to the following provisions of this section, and without prejudice to any other enactment, a constable may enter and search any premises for the purpose—

    (a) of executing—

        (i)   a warrant of arrest issued in connection with or arising out of criminal proceedings; or

        (ii) a warrant of commitment issued under section 76 of the Magistrates' Courts Act 1980;

    (b) of arresting a person for an indictable offence;

    (c) of arresting a person for an offence under—

        (i)   section 1 (prohibition of uniforms in connection with political objects), of the Public Order Act 1936;

        (ii) any enactment contained in sections 6 to 8 or 10 of the Criminal Law Act 1977 (offences relating to entering and remaining on property);

        (iii) section 4 of the Public Order Act 1986 (fear or provocation of violence);

        (iiia) section 4 (driving etc. when under influence of drink or drugs) or 163 (failure to stop when required to do so by constable in uniform) of the Road Traffic Act 1988;

        (iiib) section 27 of the Transport and Works Act 1992 (which relates to offences involving drink or drugs);

        (iv) section 76 of the Criminal Justice and Public Order Act 1994 (failure to comply with interim possession order);

        (v)   any of the sections 4, 5, 6(1) and (2), 7 and 8(1) and (2) of the Animal Welfare Act 2006 (offences relating to the prevention of harm to animals);

    (ca) of arresting, in pursuance of section 32(1A) of the Children and Young Persons Act 1969, any child or young person who has been remanded or committed to local authority accommodation under section 23(1) of that Act;

    (caa) of arresting a person for an offence to which section 61 of the Animal Health Act 1981 applies;

    (cb) of recapturing any person who is, or is deemed for any purpose to be, unlawfully at large while liable to be detained—

        (i)   in a prison, remand centre, young offender institution or secure training centre, or

        (ii) in pursuance of section 92 of the Powers of Criminal Courts (Sentencing) Act 2000 (dealing with children and young persons guilty of grave crimes), in any other place.

    (d) of recapturing any person whatever who is unlawfully at large and whom he is pursuing; or

    (e) of saving life or limb or preventing serious damage to property.

(2) Except for the purpose specified in paragraph (e) of subsection (1) above, the powers of entry and search conferred by this section—

    (a) are only exercisable if the constable has reasonable grounds for believing that the person whom he is seeking is on the premises; and

    (b) are limited, in relation to premises consisting of two or more separate dwellings, to powers to enter and search—

        (i)   any parts of the premises which the occupiers of any dwelling comprised in the premises use in common with the occupiers of any other such dwelling; and

        (ii) any such dwelling in which the constable has reasonable grounds for believing that the person whom he is seeking may be.

(3) The powers of entry and search conferred by this section are only exercisable for the purposes specified in subsection (1)(c)(ii) or (iv) above by a constable in uniform.

(4) The power of search conferred by this section is only a power to search to the extent that is reasonably required for the purpose for which the power of entry is exercised.

(5) Subject to subsection (6) below, all the rules of common law under which a constable has power to enter premises without a warrant are hereby abolished.

(6) Nothing in subsection (5) above affects any power of entry to deal with or prevent a breach of the peace.

18 Entry and search after arrest

(1) Subject to the following provisions of this section, a constable may enter and search any premises occupied or controlled by a person who is under arrest for an indictable offence, if he has reasonable grounds for suspecting that there is on the premises evidence, other than items subject to legal privilege, that relates—

(a) to that offence; or

(b) to some other indictable offence which is connected with or similar to that offence.

(2) A constable may seize and retain anything for which he may search under subsection (1) above.

(3) The power to search conferred by subsection (1) above is only a power to search to the extent that is reasonably required for the purpose of discovering such evidence.

(4) Subject to subsection (5) below, the powers conferred by this section may not be exercised unless an officer of the rank of inspector or above has authorised them in writing.

(5) A constable may conduct a search under subsection (1)—

(a) before the person is taken to a police station or released on bail under section 30A, and

(b) without obtaining an authorisation under subsection (4),

if the condition in subsection (5A) is satisfied.

(5A) The condition is that the presence of the person at a place (other than a police station) is necessary for the effective investigation of the offence.

(6) If a constable conducts a search by virtue of subsection (5) above, he shall inform an officer of the rank of inspector or above that he has made the search as soon as practicable after he has made it.

(7) An officer who—

(a) authorises a search; or

(b) is informed of a search under subsection (6) above,

shall make a record in writing—

(i)   of the grounds for the search; and

(ii) of the nature of the evidence that was sought.

(8) If the person who was in occupation or control of the premises at the time of the search is in police detention at the time the record is to be made, the officer shall make the record as part of his custody record.

Seizure etc.

19 General power of seizure etc.

(1) The powers conferred by subsections (2), (3) and (4) below are exercisable by a constable who is lawfully on any premises.

(2) The constable may seize anything which is on the premises if he has reasonable grounds for believing—

(a) that it has been obtained in consequence of the commission of an offence; and

(b) that it is necessary to seize it in order to prevent it being concealed, lost, damaged, altered or destroyed.

(3) The constable may seize anything which is on the premises if he has reasonable grounds for believing—

(a) that it is evidence in relation to an offence which he is investigating or any other offence; and

(b) that it is necessary to seize it in order to prevent it being concealed, lost, altered or destroyed.

(4) The constable may require any information which is stored in any electronic form and is accessible from the premises to be produced in a form in which it can be taken away and in which it is visible and legible or from which it can readily be produced in a visible and legible form if he has reasonable grounds for believing—

    (a) that—

        (i) it is evidence in relation to an offence which he is investigating or any other offence; or

        (ii) it has been obtained in consequence of the commission of an offence; and

    (b) that it is necessary to do so in order to prevent it being concealed, lost, tampered with or destroyed.

(5) The powers conferred by this section are in addition to any power otherwise conferred.

(6) No power of seizure conferred on a constable under any enactment (including an enactment contained in an Act passed after this Act) is to be taken to authorise the seizure of an item which the constable exercising the power has reasonable grounds for believing to be subject to legal privilege.

20   Extension of powers of seizure to computerised information

(1) Every power of seizure which is conferred by an enactment to which this section applies on a constable who has entered premises in the exercise of a power conferred by an enactment shall be construed as including a power to require any information stored in any electronic form and accessible from the premises to be produced in a form in which it can be taken away and in which it is visible and legible or from which it can readily be produced in a visible and legible form.

    (2) This section applies—

    (a) to any enactment contained in an Act passed before this Act;

    (b) to sections 8 and 18 above;

    (c) to paragraph 13 of Schedule 1 to this Act; and

    (d) to any enactment contained in an Act passed after this Act.

21   Access and copying

(1) A constable who seizes anything in the exercise of a power conferred by any enactment, including an enactment contained in an Act passed after this Act, shall, if so requested by a person showing himself—

    (a) to be the occupier of premises on which it was seized; or

    (b) to have had custody or control of it immediately before the seizure,

provide that person with a record of what he seized.

(2) The officer shall provide the record within a reasonable time from the making of the request for it.

(3) Subject to subsection (8) below, if a request for permission to be granted access to anything which—

    (a) has been seized by a constable; and

    (b) is retained by the police for the purpose of investigating an offence,

is made to the officer in charge of the investigation by a person who had custody or control of the thing immediately before it was so seized or by someone acting on behalf of such a person, the officer shall allow the person who made the request access to it under the supervision of a constable.

(4) Subject to subsection (8) below, if a request for a photograph or copy of any such thing is made to the officer in charge of the investigation by a person who had custody or control of the thing immediately before it was so seized, or by someone acting on behalf of such a person, the officer shall—

    (a) allow the person who made the request access to it under the supervision of a constable for the purpose of photographing or copying it; or

    (b) photograph or copy it, or cause it to be photographed or copied.

(5) A constable may also photograph or copy, or have photographed or copied, anything which he has power to seize, without a request being made under subsection (4) above.

(6) Where anything is photographed or copied under subsection (4)(b) above, the photograph or copy shall be supplied to the person who made the request.

(7) The photograph or copy shall be so supplied within a reasonable time from the making of the request.

(8) There is no duty under this section to grant access to, or to supply a photograph or copy of, anything if the officer in charge of the investigation for the purposes of which it was seized has reasonable grounds for believing that to do so would prejudice—

    (a) that investigation;

    (b) the investigation of an offence other than the offence for the purposes of investigating which the thing was seized; or

    (c) any criminal proceedings which may be brought as a result of—

        (i) the investigation of which he is in charge; or

        (ii) any such investigation as is mentioned in paragraph (b) above.

(9) The references to a constable in subsections (1), (2), (3)(a) and (5) include a person authorised under section 16(2) to accompany a constable executing a warrant.

22   Retention

(1) Subject to subsection (4) below, anything which has been seized by a constable or taken away by a constable following a requirement made by virtue of section 19 or 20 above may be retained so long as is necessary in all the circumstances.

(2) Without prejudice to the generality of subsection (1) above—

    (a) anything seized for the purposes of a criminal investigation may be retained, except as provided by subsection (4) below,—

        (i) for use as evidence at a trial for an offence; or

        (ii) for forensic examination or for investigation in connection with an offence;

        and

    (b) anything may be retained in order to establish its lawful owner, where there are reasonable grounds for believing that it has been obtained in consequence of the commission of an offence.

(3) Nothing seized on the ground that it may be used—

    (a) to cause physical injury to any person;

    (b) to damage property;

    (c) to interfere with evidence; or

    (d) to assist in escape from police detention or lawful custody,

may be retained when the person from whom it was seized is no longer in police detention or the custody of a court or is in the custody of a court but has been released on bail.

(4) Nothing may be retained for either of the purposes mentioned in subsection (2)(a) above if a photograph or copy would be sufficient for that purpose.

(5) Nothing in this section affects any power of a court to make an order under section 1 of the Police (Property) Act 1897.

(6) This section also applies to anything retained by the police under section 28H(5) of the Immigration Act 1971.

(7) The reference in subsection (1) to anything seized by a constable includes anything seized by a person authorised under section 16(2) to accompany a constable executing a warrant.

Supplementary

23   Meaning of 'premises' etc.

In this Act—

    'premises' includes any place and, in particular, includes—

        (a) any vehicle, vessel, aircraft or hovercraft;

(b) any offshore installation;

(ba) any renewable energy installation;

(c) any tent or movable structure.

'offshore installation' has the meaning given to it by section 1 of the Mineral Workings (Offshore Installations) Act 1971.

'renewable energy installation' has the same meaning as in Chapter 2 of Part 2 of the Energy Act 2004.

PART III ARREST

24 Arrest without warrant: constables

(1) A constable may arrest without a warrant—

(a) anyone who is about to commit an offence;

(b) anyone who is in the act of committing an offence;

(c) anyone whom he has reasonable grounds for suspecting to be about to commit an offence;

(d) anyone whom he has reasonable grounds for suspecting to be committing an offence.

(2) If a constable has reasonable grounds for suspecting that an offence has been committed, he may arrest without a warrant anyone whom he has reasonable grounds to suspect of being guilty of it.

(3) If an offence has been committed, a constable may arrest without a warrant—

(a) anyone who is guilty of the offence;

(b) anyone whom he has reasonable grounds for suspecting to be guilty of it.

(4) But the power of summary arrest conferred by subsection (1), (2) or (3) is exercisable only if the constable has reasonable grounds for believing that for any of the reasons mentioned in subsection (5) it is necessary to arrest the person in question.

(5) The reasons are—

(a) to enable the name of the person in question to be ascertained (in the case where the constable does not know, and cannot readily ascertain, the person's name, or has reasonable grounds for doubting whether a name given by the person as his name is his real name);

(b) correspondingly as regards the person's address;

(c) to prevent the person in question—

(i) causing physical injury to himself or any other person;

(ii) suffering physical injury;

(iii) causing loss of or damage to property;

(iv) committing an offence against public decency (subject to subsection (6)); or

(v) causing an unlawful obstruction of the highway;

(d) to protect a child or other vulnerable person from the person in question;

(e) to allow the prompt and effective investigation of the offence or of the conduct of the person in question;

(f) to prevent any prosecution for the offence from being hindered by the disappearance of the person in question.

(6) Subsection (5)(c)(iv) applies only where members of the public going about their normal business cannot reasonably be expected to avoid the person in question.

24A Arrest without warrant: other persons

(1) A person other than a constable may arrest without a warrant—

(a) anyone who is in the act of committing an indictable offence;

(b) anyone whom he has reasonable grounds for suspecting to be committing an indictable offence.

(2) Where an indictable offence has been committed, a person other than a constable may arrest without a warrant—

    (a) anyone who is guilty of the offence;

    (b) anyone whom he has reasonable grounds for suspecting to be guilty of it.

(3) But the power of summary arrest conferred by subsection (1) or (2) is exercisable only if—

    (a) the person making the arrest has reasonable grounds for believing that for any of the reasons mentioned in subsection (4) it is necessary to arrest the person in question; and

    (b) it appears to the person making the arrest that it is not reasonably practicable for a constable to make it instead.

(4) The reasons are to prevent the person in question—

    (a) causing physical injury to himself or any other person;

    (b) suffering physical injury;

    (c) causing loss of or damage to property; or

    (d) making off before a constable can assume responsibility for him.

(5) This section does not apply in relation to an offence under Part 3 or 3A of the Public Order Act 1986.

26 Repeal of statutory powers of arrest without warrant or order

(1) Subject to subsection (2) below, so much of any Act (including a local Act) passed before this Act as enables a constable—

    (a) to arrest a person for an offence without a warrant; or

    (b) to arrest a person otherwise than for an offence without a warrant or an order of a court, shall cease to have effect.

(2) Nothing in subsection (1) above affects the enactments specified in Schedule 2 to this Act.

27 Fingerprinting of certain offenders

(1) If a person—

    (a) has been convicted of a recordable offence;

    (b) has not at any time been in police detention for the offence; and

    (c) has not had his fingerprints taken—

        (i) in the course of the investigation of the offence by the police; or

        (ii) since the conviction,

any constable may at any time not later than one month after the date of the conviction require him to attend a police station in order that his fingerprints may be taken.

(1A) Where a person convicted of a recordable offence has already had his fingerprints taken as mentioned in paragraph (c) of subsection (1) above, that fact (together with any time when he has been in police detention for the offence) shall be disregarded for the purposes of that subsection if—

    (a) the fingerprints taken on the previous occasion do not constitute a complete set of his fingerprints; or

    (b) some or all of the fingerprints taken on the previous occasion are not of sufficient quality to allow satisfactory analysis, comparison or matching.

(1B) Subsections (1) and (1A) above apply—

    (a) where a person has been given a caution in respect of a recordable offence which, at the time of the caution, he has admitted, or

    (b) where a person has been warned or reprimanded under section 65 of the Crime and Disorder Act 1998 (c. 37) for a recordable offence,

as they apply where a person has been convicted of an offence, and references in this section to a conviction shall be construed accordingly.]

(2) A requirement under subsection (1) above—

    (a) shall give the person a period of at least 7 days within which he must so attend; and

    (b) may direct him to so attend at a specified time of day or between specified times of day.

(3) Any constable may arrest without warrant a person who has failed to comply with a requirement under subsection (1) above.

(4) The Secretary of State may by regulations make provision for recording in national police records convictions for such offences as are specified in the regulations.

(5) Regulations under this section shall be made by statutory instrument and shall be subject to annulment in pursuance of a resolution of either House of Parliament.

28   Information to be given on arrest

(1) Subject to subsection (5) below, where a person is arrested, otherwise than by being informed that he is under arrest, the arrest is not lawful unless the person arrested is informed that he is under arrest as soon as is practicable after his arrest.

(2) Where a person is arrested by a constable, subsection (1) above applies regardless of whether the fact of the arrest is obvious.

(3) Subject to subsection (5) below, no arrest is lawful unless the person arrested is informed of the ground for the arrest at the time of, or as soon as is practicable after, the arrest.

(4) Where a person is arrested by a constable, subsection (3) above applies regardless of whether the ground for the arrest is obvious.

(5) Nothing in this section is to be taken to require a person to be informed—

    (a) that he is under arrest; or

    (b) of the ground for the arrest,

if it was not reasonably practicable for him to be so informed by reason of his having escaped from arrest before the information could be given.

29   Voluntary attendance at police station etc.

Where for the purpose of assisting with an investigation a person attends voluntarily at a police station or at any other place where a constable is present or accompanies a constable to a police station or any such other place without having been arrested—

    (a) he shall be entitled to leave at will unless he is placed under arrest;

    (b) he shall be informed at once that he is under arrest if a decision is taken by a constable to prevent him from leaving at will.

30   Arrest elsewhere than at police station

(1) Subsection (1A) applies where a person is, at any place other than a police station—

    (a) arrested by a constable for an offence, or

    (b) taken into custody by a constable after being arrested for an offence by a person other than a constable.

(1A) The person must be taken by a constable to a police station as soon as practicable after the arrest.

(1B) Subsection (1A) has effect subject to section 30A (release on bail) and subsection (7) (release without bail).

(2) Subject to subsections (3) and (5) below, the police station to which an arrested person is taken under subsection (1A) above shall be a designated police station.

(3) A constable to whom this subsection applies may take an arrested person to any police station unless it appears to the constable that it may be necessary to keep the arrested person in police detention for more than six hours.

(4) Subsection (3) above applies—

    (a) to a constable who is working in a locality covered by a police station which is not a designated police station; and

    (b) to a constable belonging to a body of constables maintained by an authority other than a local policing body.

(5) Any constable may take an arrested person to any police station if—

    (a) either of the following conditions is satisfied—

        (i)   the constable has arrested him without the assistance of any other constable and no other constable is available to assist him;

    (ii) the constable has taken him into custody from a person other than a constable without the assistance of any other constable and no other constable is available to assist him; and

  (b) it appears to the constable that he will be unable to take the arrested person to a designated police station without the arrested person injuring himself, the constable or some other person.

(6) If the first police station to which an arrested person is taken after his arrest is not a designated police station, he shall be taken to a designated police station not more than six hours after his arrival at the first police station unless he is released previously.

(7) A person arrested by a constable at any place other than a police station must be released without bail if the condition in subsection (7A) is satisfied.

(7A) The condition is that, at any time before the person arrested reaches a police station, a constable is satisfied that there are no grounds for keeping him under arrest or releasing him on bail under section 30A.

(8) A constable who releases a person under subsection (7) above shall record the fact that he has done so.

(9) The constable shall make the record as soon as is practicable after the release.

(10) Nothing in subsection (1A) or in section 30A prevents a constable delaying taking a person to a police station or releasing him on bail if the condition in subsection (10A) is satisfied.

(10A) The condition is that the presence of the person at a place (other than a police station) is necessary in order to carry out such investigations as it is reasonable to carry out immediately.

(11) Where there is any such delay the reasons for the delay must be recorded when the person first arrives at the police station or (as the case may be) is released on bail.

(12) Nothing in subsection (1A) or section 30A above shall be taken to affect—

  (a) paragraphs 16(3) or 18(1) of Schedule 2 to the Immigration Act 1971;

  (b) section 34(1) of the Criminal Justice Act 1972; or

  (c) any provision of the Terrorism Act 2000.

(13) Nothing in subsection (10) above shall be taken to affect paragraph 18(3) of Schedule 2 to the Immigration Act 1971.

30A   Bail elsewhere than at police station

(1) A constable may release on bail a person who is arrested or taken into custody in the circumstances mentioned in section 30(1).

(2) A person may be released on bail under subsection (1) at any time before he arrives at a police station.

(3) A person released on bail under subsection (1) must be required to attend a police station.

(3A) Where a constable releases a person on bail under subsection (1)—

  (a) no recognizance for the person's surrender to custody shall be taken from the person,

  (b) no security for the person's surrender to custody shall be taken from the person or from anyone else on the person's behalf,

  (c) the person shall not be required to provide a surety or sureties for his surrender to custody, and

  (d) no requirement to reside in a bail hostel may be imposed as a condition of bail.

(3B) Subject to subsection (3A), where a constable releases a person on bail under subsection (1) the constable may impose, as conditions of the bail, such requirements as appear to the constable to be necessary—

  (a) to secure that the person surrenders to custody,

  (b) to secure that the person does not commit an offence while on bail,

  (c) to secure that the person does not interfere with witnesses or otherwise obstruct the course of justice, whether in relation to himself or any other person, or

  (d) for the person's own protection or, if the person is under the age of 17, for the person's own welfare or in the person's own interests.

(4) Where a person is released on bail under subsection (1), a requirement may be imposed on the person as a condition of bail only under the preceding provisions of this section.

(5) The police station which the person is required to attend may be any police station.

30B   Bail under section 30A: notices

(1) Where a constable grants bail to a person under section 30A, he must give that person a notice in writing before he is released.

(2) The notice must state—

(a) the offence for which he was arrested, and

(b) the ground on which he was arrested.

(3) The notice must inform him that he is required to attend a police station.

(4) It may also specify the police station which he is required to attend and the time when he is required to attend.

(4A) If the person is granted bail subject to conditions under section 30A(3B), the notice also—

(a) must specify the requirements imposed by those conditions,

(b) must explain the opportunities under sections 30CA(1) and 30CB(1) for variation of those conditions, and

(c) if it does not specify the police station at which the person is required to attend, must specify a police station at which the person may make a request under section 30CA(1)(b).

(5) If the notice does not include the information mentioned in subsection (4), the person must subsequently be given a further notice in writing which contains that information.

(6) The person may be required to attend a different police station from that specified in the notice under subsection (1) or (5) or to attend at a different time.

(7) He must be given notice in writing of any such change as is mentioned in subsection (6) but more than one such notice may be given to him.

30C   Bail under section 30A: supplemental

(1) A person who has been required to attend a police station is not required to do so if he is given notice in writing that his attendance is no longer required.

(2) If a person is required to attend a police station which is not a designated police station he must be—

(a) released, or

(b) taken to a designated police station,

not more than six hours after his arrival.

(3) Nothing in the Bail Act 1976 applies in relation to bail under section 30A.

(4) Nothing in section 30A or 30B or in this section prevents the re-arrest without a warrant of a person released on bail under section 30A if new evidence justifying a further arrest has come to light since his release.

30CA   Bail under section 30A: variation of conditions by police

(1) Where a person released on bail under section 30A(1) is on bail subject to conditions—

(a) a relevant officer at the police station at which the person is required to attend, or

(b) where no notice under section 30B specifying that police station has been given to the person, a relevant officer at the police station specified under section 30B(4A)(c),

may, at the request of the person but subject to subsection (2), vary the conditions.

(2) On any subsequent request made in respect of the same grant of bail, subsection (1) confers power to vary the conditions of the bail only if the request is based on information that, in the case of the previous request or each previous request, was not available to the relevant officer considering that previous request when he was considering it.

(3) Where conditions of bail granted to a person under section 30A(1) are varied under subsection (1)—

(a) paragraphs (a) to (d) of section 30A(3A) apply,

(b) requirements imposed by the conditions as so varied must be requirements that appear to the relevant officer varying the conditions to be necessary for any of the purposes mentioned in paragraphs (a) to (d) of section 30A(3B), and

(c) the relevant officer who varies the conditions must give the person notice in writing of the variation.

(4) Power under subsection (1) to vary conditions is, subject to subsection (3)(a) and (b), power—

(a) to vary or rescind any of the conditions, and

(b) to impose further conditions.

(5) In this section "relevant officer", in relation to a designated police station, means a custody officer but, in relation to any other police station—

(a) means a constable who is not involved in the investigation of the offence for which the person making the request under subsection (1) was under arrest when granted bail under section 30A(1), if such a constable is readily available, and

(b) if no such constable is readily available—

(i) means a constable other than the one who granted bail to the person, if such a constable is readily available, and

(ii) if no such constable is readily available, means the constable who granted bail.

30CB   Bail under section 30A: variation of conditions by court

(1) Where a person released on bail under section 30A(1) is on bail subject to conditions, a magistrates' court may, on an application by or on behalf of the person, vary the conditions if—

(a) the conditions have been varied under section 30CA(1) since being imposed under section 30A(3B),

(b) a request for variation under section 30CA(1) of the conditions has been made and refused, or

(c) a request for variation under section 30CA(1) of the conditions has been made and the period of 48 hours beginning with the day when the request was made has expired without the request having been withdrawn or the conditions having been varied in response to the request.

(2) In proceedings on an application for a variation under subsection (1), a ground may not be relied upon unless—

(a) in a case falling within subsection (1)(a), the ground was relied upon in the request in response to which the conditions were varied under section 30CA(1), or

(b) in a case falling within paragraph (b) or (c) of subsection (1), the ground was relied upon in the request mentioned in that paragraph,

but this does not prevent the court, when deciding the application, from considering different grounds arising out of a change in circumstances that has occurred since the making of the application.

(3) Where conditions of bail granted to a person under section 30A(1) are varied under subsection (1)—

(a) paragraphs (a) to (d) of section 30A(3A) apply,

(b) requirements imposed by the conditions as so varied must be requirements that appear to the court varying the conditions to be necessary for any of the purposes mentioned in paragraphs (a) to (d) of section 30A(3B), and

(c) that bail shall not lapse but shall continue subject to the conditions as so varied.

(4) Power under subsection (1) to vary conditions is, subject to subsection (3)(a) and (b), power—

(a) to vary or rescind any of the conditions, and

(b) to impose further conditions.

30D   Failure to answer to bail under section 30A

(1) A constable may arrest without a warrant a person who—

(a) has been released on bail under section 30A subject to a requirement to attend a specified police station, but

(b) fails to attend the police station at the specified time.

(2) A person arrested under subsection (1) must be taken to a police station (which may be the specified police station or any other police station) as soon as practicable after the arrest.

(2A) A person who has been released on bail under section 30A may be arrested without a warrant by a constable if the constable has reasonable grounds for suspecting that the person has broken any of the conditions of bail.

(2B) A person arrested under subsection (2A) must be taken to a police station (which may be the specified police station mentioned in subsection (1) or any other police station) as soon as practicable after the arrest.

(3) In subsection (1), 'specified' means specified in a notice under subsection (1) or (5) of section 30B or, if notice of change has been given under subsection (7) of that section, in that notice.

(4) For the purposes of—

    (a) section 30 (subject to the obligation in subsection (2)), and

    (b) section 31,

an arrest under this section is to be treated as an arrest for an offence.

31 Arrest for further offence

Where—

    (a) a person—

        (i)   has been arrested for an offence; and

        (ii) is at a police station in consequence of that arrest; and

    (b) it appears to a constable that, if he were released from that arrest, he would be liable to arrest for some other offence,

he shall be arrested for that other offence.

32 Search upon arrest

(1) A constable may search an arrested person, in any case where the person to be searched has been arrested at a place other than a police station, if the constable has reasonable grounds for believing that the arrested person may present a danger to himself or others.

(2) Subject to subsections (3) to (5) below, a constable shall also have power in any such case—

    (a) to search the arrested person for anything—

        (i)   which he might use to assist him to escape from lawful custody; or

        (ii) which might be evidence relating to an offence; and

    (b) if the offence for which he has been arrested is an indictable offence, to enter and search any premises in which he was when arrested or immediately before he was arrested for evidence relating to the offence.

(3) The power to search conferred by subsection (2) above is only a power to search to the extent that is reasonably required for the purpose of discovering any such thing or any such evidence.

(4) The powers conferred by this section to search a person are not to be construed as authorising a constable to require a person to remove any of his clothing in public other than an outer coat, jacket or gloves but they do authorise a search of a person's mouth.

(5) A constable may not search a person in the exercise of the power conferred by subsection (2)(a) above unless he has reasonable grounds for believing that the person to be searched may have concealed on him anything for which a search is permitted under that paragraph.

(6) A constable may not search premises in the exercise of the power conferred by subsection (2)(b) above unless he has reasonable grounds for believing that there is evidence for which a search is permitted under that paragraph on the premises.

(7) In so far as the power of search conferred by subsection (2)(b) above relates to premises consisting of two or more separate dwellings, it is limited to a power to search—

    (a) any dwelling in which the arrest took place or in which the person arrested was immediately before his arrest; and

    (b) any parts of the premises which the occupier of any such dwelling uses in common with the occupiers of any other dwellings comprised in the premises.

(8) A constable searching a person in the exercise of the power conferred by subsection (1) above may seize and retain anything he finds, if he has reasonable grounds for believing that the person searched might use it to cause physical injury to himself or to any other person.

(9) A constable searching a person in the exercise of the power conferred by subsection (2)(a) above may seize and retain anything he finds, other than an item subject to legal privilege, if he has reasonable grounds for believing—

(a) that he might use it to assist him to escape from lawful custody; or

(b) that it is evidence of an offence or has been obtained in consequence of the commission of an offence.

(10) Nothing in this section shall be taken to affect the power conferred by section 43 of the Terrorism Act 2000.

. . .

PART IV DETENTION

Detention—conditions and duration

34 Limitations on police detention

(1) A person arrested for an offence shall not be kept in police detention except in accordance with the provisions of this Part of this Act.

(2) Subject to subsection (3) below, if at any time a custody officer—

(a) becomes aware, in relation to any person in police detention, that the grounds for the detention of that person have ceased to apply and

(b) is not aware of any other grounds on which the continued detention of that person could be justified under the provisions of this Part of this Act,

it shall be the duty of the custody officer, subject to subsection (4) below, to order his immediate release from custody.

(3) No person in police detention shall be released except on the authority of a custody officer at the police station where his detention was authorised, or if it was authorised at more than one station, a custody officer at the station where it was last authorised.

(4) A person who appears to the custody officer to have been unlawfully at large when he was arrested is not to be released under subsection (2) above.

(5) A person whose release is ordered under subsection (2) above shall be released without bail unless it appears to the custody officer—

(a) that there is need for further investigation of any matter in connection with which he was detained at any time during the period of his detention; or

(b) that, in respect of any such matter, proceedings may be taken against him or he may be reprimanded or warned under section 65 of the Crime and Disorder Act 1998 and if it so appears he shall be released on bail.

(6) For the purposes of this Part of this Act a person arrested under section 6(5) of the Road Traffic Act 1988 or section 30(2) of the Transport and Works Act 1992 is arrested for an offence.

(7) For the purposes of this Part a person who—

(a) attends a police station to answer to bail granted under section 30A,

(b) returns to a police station to answer to bail granted under this Part, or

(c) is arrested under section 30D or 46A,

is to be treated as arrested for an offence and that offence is the offence in connection with which he was granted bail. But this subsection is subject to section 47(6) (which provides for the calculation of certain periods, where a person has been granted bail under this Part, by reference to time when the person is in police detention only).

(8) Subsection (7) does not apply in relation to a person who is granted bail subject to the duty mentioned in section 47(3)(b) and who either—

(a) attends a police station to answer to such bail, or

(b) is arrested under section 46A for failing to do so,

(provision as to the treatment of such persons for the purposes of this Part being made by section 46ZA).

35   Designated police stations

(1) The chief officer of police for each police area shall designate the police stations in his area which, subject to sections 30(3) and (5), 30A(5) and 30D(2) above, are to be the stations in that area to be used for the purpose of detaining arrested persons.

(2) A chief officer's duty under subsection (1) above is to designate police stations appearing to him to provide enough accommodation for that purpose.

(2A) The Chief Constable of the British Transport Police Force may designate police stations which (in addition to those designated under subsection (1) above) may be used for the purpose of detaining arrested persons.

(3) Without prejudice to section 12 of the Interpretation Act 1978 (continuity of duties) a chief officer—

(a) may designate a station which was not previously designated; and

(b) may direct that a designation of a station previously made shall cease to operate.

(4) In this Act 'designated police station' means a police station designated under this section.

36   Custody officers at police stations

(1) One or more custody officers shall be appointed for each designated police station.

(2) A custody officer for a police station designated under section 35(1) above shall be appointed—

(a) by the chief officer of police for the area in which the designated police station is situated; or

(b) by such other police officer as the chief officer of police for that area may direct.

(2A) A custody officer for a police station designated under section 35(2A) above shall be appointed—

(a) by the Chief Constable of the British Transport Police Force; or

(b) by such other member of that Force as that Chief Constable may direct.

(3) No officer may be appointed a custody officer unless the officer is of at least the rank of sergeant.

(4) An officer of any rank may perform the functions of a custody officer at a designated police station if a custody officer is not readily available to perform them.

(5) Subject to the following provisions of this section and to section 39(2) below, none of the functions of a custody officer in relation to a person shall be performed by an officer who at the time when the function falls to be performed is involved in the investigation of an offence for which that person is in police detention at that time.

(6) Nothing in subsection (5) above is to be taken to prevent a custody officer—

(a) performing any function assigned to custody officers—

(i)   by this Act; or

(ii)   by a code of practice issued under this Act;

(b) carrying out the duty imposed on custody officers by section 39 below;

(c) doing anything in connection with the identification of a suspect; or

(d) doing anything under sections 7 and 8 of the Road Traffic Act 1988.

(7) Where an arrested person is taken to a police station which is not a designated police station, the functions in relation to him which at a designated police station would be the functions of a custody officer shall be performed—

(a) by an officer who is not involved in the investigation of an offence for which he is in police detention, if such an officer is readily available; and

(b) if no such officer is readily available, by the officer who took him to the station or any other officer.

(7A) Subject to subsection (7B), subsection (7) applies where a person attends a police station which is not a designated station to answer to bail granted under section 30A as it applies where a person is taken to such a station.

(7B) Where subsection (7) applies because of subsection (7A), the reference in subsection (7)(b) to the officer who took him to the station is to be read as a reference to the officer who granted him bail.

(8) References to a custody officer in section 34 above or in the following provisions of this Act include references to a person other than a custody officer who is performing the functions of a custody officer by virtue of subsection (4) or (7) above.

(9) Where by virtue of subsection (7) above an officer of a force maintained by a local policing body who took an arrested person to a police station is to perform the functions of a custody officer in relation to him, the officer shall inform an officer who—

(a) is attached to a designated police station; and

(b) is of at least the rank of inspector,

that he is to do so.

(10) The duty imposed by subsection (9) above shall be performed as soon as it is practicable to perform it.

[*Note: Sections 37, 37A and 37B have effect, in relation to a person arrested following a criminal investigation by the Revenue and Customs, as if references to the Director of Public Prosecutions were references to the Director of Revenue and Customs Prosecutions. See Commissioner for Revenue and Customs Act 2005 Schedule 4 paragraph 30.*]

37   Duties of custody officer before charge

(1) Where—

(a) a person is arrested for an offence—

(i)   without a warrant; or

(ii) under a warrant not endorsed for bail,

the custody officer at each police station where he is detained after his arrest shall determine whether he has before him sufficient evidence to charge that person with the offence for which he was arrested and may detain him at the police station for such period as is necessary to enable him to do so.

(2) If the custody officer determines that he does not have such evidence before him, the person arrested shall be released either on bail or without bail, unless the custody officer has reasonable grounds for believing that his detention without being charged is necessary to secure or preserve evidence relating to an offence for which he is under arrest or to obtain such evidence by questioning him.

(3) If the custody officer has reasonable grounds for so believing, he may authorise the person arrested to be kept in police detention.

(4) Where a custody officer authorises a person who has not been charged to be kept in police detention, he shall, as soon as is practicable, make a written record of the grounds for the detention.

(5) Subject to subsection (6) below, the written record shall be made in the presence of the person arrested who shall at that time be informed by the custody officer of the grounds for his detention.

(6) Subsection (5) above shall not apply where the person arrested is, at the time when the written record is made—

(a) incapable of understanding what is said to him;

(b) violent or likely to become violent; or

(c) in urgent need of medical attention.

(7) Subject to section 41(7) below, if the custody officer determines that he has before him sufficient evidence to charge the person arrested with the offence for which he was arrested, the person arrested—

(a) shall be

(i)   released without charge and on bail, or

(ii) kept in police detention

for the purpose of enabling the Director of Public Prosecutions to make a decision under section 37B below,

    (b) shall be released without charge and on bail but not for that purpose,

    (c) shall be released without charge and without bail, or

    (d) shall be charged.

(7A) The decision as to how a person is to be dealt with under subsection (7) above shall be that of the custody officer.

(7B) Where a person is dealt with under subsection (7)(a) above, it shall be the duty of the custody officer to inform him that he is being released, or (as the case may be) detained, to enable the Director of Public Prosecutions to make a decision under section 37B below.

(8) Where—

    (a) a person is dealt with under subsection (7)(b) or (c) above; and

    (b) at the time of his release a decision whether he should be prosecuted for the offence for which he was arrested has not been taken,

it shall be the duty of the custody officer so to inform him.

(8A) Subsection (8B) applies if the offence for which the person is arrested is one in relation to which a sample could be taken under section 63B below and the custody officer—

    (a) is required in pursuance of subsection (2) above to release the person arrested and decides to release him on bail, or

    (b) decides in pursuance of subsection (7)(a) or (b) above to release the person without charge and on bail.

(8B) The detention of the person may be continued to enable a sample to be taken under section 63B, but this subsection does not permit a person to be detained for a period of more than 24 hours after the relevant time.

(9) If the person arrested is not in a fit state to be dealt with under subsection (7) above, he may be kept in police detention until he is.

(10) The duty imposed on the custody officer under subsection (1) above shall be carried out by him as soon as practicable after the person arrested arrives at the police station or, in the case of a person arrested at the police station, as soon as practicable after the arrest.

(15) In this Part of this Act—

'arrested juvenile' means a person arrested with or without a warrant who appears to be under the age of 17;

'endorsed for bail' means endorsed with a direction for bail in accordance with section 117(2) of the Magistrates' Courts Act 1980.

37A Guidance

(1) The Director of Public Prosecutions may issue guidance—

    (a) for the purpose of enabling custody officers to decide how persons should be dealt with under section 37(7) above or 37C(2) or 37CA(2) below, and

    (b) as to the information to be sent to the Director of Public Prosecutions under section 37B(1) below.

(2) The Director of Public Prosecutions may from time to time revise guidance issued under this section.

(3) Custody officers are to have regard to guidance under this section in deciding how persons should be dealt with under section 37(7) above or 37C(2) or 37CA(2) below.

(4) A report under section 9 of the Prosecution of Offences Act 1985 (report by DPP to Attorney General) must set out the provisions of any guidance issued, and any revisions to guidance made, in the year to which the report relates.

(5) The Director of Public Prosecutions must publish in such manner as he thinks fit—

    (a) any guidance issued under this section, and

    (b) any revisions made to such guidance.

(6) Guidance under this section may make different provision for different cases, circumstances or areas.

37B Consultation with the Director of Public Prosecutions

(1) Where a person is dealt with under section 37(7)(a) above, an officer involved in the investigation of the offence shall, as soon as is practicable, send to the Director of Public Prosecutions such information as may be specified in guidance under section 37A above.

(2) The Director of Public Prosecutions shall decide whether there is sufficient evidence to charge the person with an offence.

(3) If he decides that there is sufficient evidence to charge the person with an offence, he shall decide—

(a) whether or not the person should be charged and, if so, the offence with which he should be charged, and

(b) whether or not the person should be given a caution and, if so, the offence in respect of which he should be given a caution.

(4) The Director of Public Prosecutions shall give notice of his decision to an officer involved in the investigation of the offence.

(4A) Notice under subsection (4) above shall be in writing, but in the case of a person kept in police detention under section 37(7)(a) above it may be given orally in the first instance and confirmed in writing subsequently.

(5) If his decision is—

(a) that there is not sufficient evidence to charge the person with an offence, or

(b) that there is sufficient evidence to charge the person with an offence but that the person should not be charged with an offence or given a caution in respect of an offence,

a custody officer shall give the person notice in writing that he is not to be prosecuted.

(6) If the decision of the Director of Public Prosecutions is that the person should be charged with an offence, or given a caution in respect of an offence, the person shall be charged or cautioned accordingly.

(7) But if his decision is that the person should be given a caution in respect of the offence and it proves not to be possible to give the person such a caution, he shall instead be charged with the offence.

(8) For the purposes of this section, a person is to be charged with an offence either—

(a) when he is in police detention at a police station (whether because he has returned to answer bail, because he is detained under section 37(7)(a) above or for some other reason), or

(b) in accordance with section 29 of the Criminal Justice Act 2003.

(9) In this section 'caution' includes—

(a) a conditional caution within the meaning of Part 3 of the Criminal Justice Act 2003, and

(aa) a youth conditional caution within the meaning of Chapter 1 of Part 4 of the Crime and Disorder Act 1998, and

(b) a warning or reprimand under section 65 of that Act.

37C Breach of bail following release under section 37(7)(a)

(1) This section applies where—

(a) a person released on bail under section 37(7)(a) above or subsection (2)(b) below is arrested under section 46A below in respect of that bail, and

(b) at the time of his detention following that arrest at the police station mentioned in section 46A(2) below, notice under section 37B(4) above has not been given.

(2) The person arrested—

(a) shall be charged, or

(b) shall be released without charge, either on bail or without bail.

(3) The decision as to how a person is to be dealt with under subsection (2) above shall be that of a custody officer.

(4) A person released on bail under subsection (2)(b) above shall be released on bail subject to the same conditions (if any) which applied immediately before his arrest.

37CA   Breach of bail following release under section 37(7)(b)

(1) This section applies where a person released on bail under section 37(7)(b) above or subsection (2)(b) below—

    (a) is arrested under section 46A below in respect of that bail, and

    (b) is being detained following that arrest at the police station mentioned in section 46A(2) below.

(2) The person arrested—

    (a) shall be charged, or

    (b) shall be released without charge, either on bail or without bail.

(3) The decision as to how a person is to be dealt with under subsection (2) above shall be that of a custody officer.

(4) A person released on bail under subsection (2)(b) above shall be released on bail subject to the same conditions (if any) which applied immediately before his arrest.

37D   Release under section 37(7): further provision

(1) Where a person is released on bail under section 37, 37C(2)(b) or 37CA(2)(b) above, a custody officer may subsequently appoint a different time, or an additional time, at which the person is to attend at the police station to answer bail.

(2) The custody officer shall give the person notice in writing of the exercise of the power under subsection (1).

(3) The exercise of the power under subsection (1) shall not affect the conditions (if any) to which bail is subject.

(4) Where a person released on bail under section 37(7)(a) or 37C(2)(b) above returns to a police station to answer bail or is otherwise in police detention at a police station, he may be kept in police detention to enable him to be dealt with in accordance with section 37B or 37C above or to enable the power under subsection (1) above to be exercised.

(4A) Where a person released on bail under section 37(7)(b) or 37CA(2)(b) above returns to a police station to answer bail or is otherwise in police detention at a police station, he may be kept in police detention to enable him to be dealt with in accordance with section 37CA above or to enable the power under subsection (1) above to be exercised.

(5) If the person mentioned in subsection (4) or (4A) above is not in a fit state to enable him to be so dealt with as mentioned in that subsection or to enable the power under subsection (1) above to be exercised, he may be kept in police detention until he is.

(6) Where a person is kept in police detention by virtue of subsection (4), (4A) or (5) above, section 37(1) to (3) and (7) above (and section 40(8) below so far as it relates to section 37(1) to (3)) shall not apply to the offence in connection with which he was released on bail under section 37(7), 37C(2)(b) or 37CA(2)(b) above.

38   Duties of custody officer after charge

(1) Where a person arrested for an offence otherwise than under a warrant endorsed for bail is charged with an offence, the custody officer shall, subject to section 25 of the Criminal Justice and Public Order Act 1994, order his release from police detention, either on bail or without bail, unless—

    (a) if the person arrested is not an arrested juvenile—

        (i)   his name or address cannot be ascertained or the custody officer has reasonable grounds for doubting whether a name or address furnished by him as his name or address is his real name or address;

        (ii)   the custody officer has reasonable grounds for believing that the person arrested will fail to appear in court to answer to bail;

        (iii) in the case of a person arrested for an imprisonable offence, the custody officer has reasonable grounds for believing that the detention of the person arrested is necessary to prevent him from committing an offence;

(iiia) in a case where a sample may be taken from the person under section 63B below, the custody officer has reasonable grounds for believing that the detention of the person is necessary to enable the sample to be taken from him;

(iv) in the case of a person arrested for an offence which is not an imprisonable offence, the custody officer has reasonable grounds for believing that the detention of the person arrested is necessary to prevent him from causing physical injury to any other person or from causing loss of or damage to property;

(v) the custody officer has reasonable grounds for believing that the detention of the person arrested is necessary to prevent him from interfering with the administration of justice or with the investigation of offences or of a particular offence; or

(vi) the custody officer has reasonable grounds for believing that the detention of the person arrested is necessary for his own protection;

(b) if he is an arrested juvenile—

(i) any of the requirements of paragraph (a) above is satisfied (but, in the case of paragraph (a)(iiia) above, only if the arrested juvenile has attained the minimum age); or

(ii) the custody officer has reasonable grounds for believing that he ought to be detained in his own interests.

(c) the offence with which the person is charged is murder.

(2) If the release of a person arrested is not required by subsection (1) above, the custody officer may authorise him to be kept in police detention but may not authorise a person to be kept in police detention by virtue of subsection (1)(a)(iiia) after the end of the period of six hours beginning with when he was charged with the offence.

(2A) The custody officer, in taking the decisions required by subsection (1)(a) and (b) above (except (a)(i) and (vi) and (b)(ii), shall have regard to the same considerations as those which a court is required to have regard to in taking the corresponding decisions under paragraph 2 of Part I of Schedule 1 to the Bail Act 1976 disregarding paragraph 2(2) of that Part.

(3) Where a custody officer authorises a person who has been charged to be kept in police detention, he shall, as soon as practicable, make a written record of the grounds for the detention.

(4) Subject to subsection (5) below, the written record shall be made in the presence of the person charged who shall at that time be informed by the custody officer of the grounds for his detention.

(5) Subsection (4) above shall not apply where the person charged is, at the time when the written record is made—

(a) incapable of understanding what is said to him;

(b) violent or likely to become violent; or

(c) in urgent need of medical attention.

(6) Where a custody officer authorises an arrested juvenile to be kept in police detention under subsection (1) above, the custody officer shall, unless he certifies—

(a) that, by reason of such circumstances as are specified in the certificate, it is impracticable for him to do so; or

(b) in the case of an arrested juvenile who has attained the age of 12 years, that no secure accommodation is available and that keeping him in other local authority accommodation would not be adequate to protect the public from serious harm from him,

secure that the arrested juvenile is moved to local authority accommodation.

(6A) In this section, 'local authority accommodation' means accommodation provided by or on behalf of a local authority (within the meaning of the Children Act 1989);

'minimum age' means the age specified in section 63B(3)(b) below;

'secure accommodation' means accommodation provided for the purpose of restricting liberty;

'sexual offence' means an offence specified in Part 2 of Schedule 15 to the Criminal Justice Act 2003;

'violent offence' means murder or an offence specified in Part 1 of that Schedule;

and any reference, in relation to an arrested juvenile charged with a violent or sexual offence, to protecting the public from serious harm from him shall be construed as a reference to protecting members of the public from death or serious injury, whether physical or psychological, occasioned by further such offences committed by him.

(6B) Where an arrested juvenile is moved to local authority accommodation under subsection (6) above, it shall be lawful for any person acting on behalf of the authority to detain him.

(7) A certificate made under subsection (6) above in respect of an arrested juvenile shall be produced to the court before which he is first brought thereafter.

(7A) In this section 'imprisonable offence' has the same meaning as in Schedule 1 to the Bail Act 1976.

(8) In this Part of this Act 'local authority' has the same meaning as in the Children Act 1989.

39 Responsibilities in relation to persons detained
(1) Subject to subsections (2) and (4) below, it shall be the duty of the custody officer at a police station to ensure—
> (a) that all persons in police detention at that station are treated in accordance with this Act and any code of practice issued under it and relating to the treatment of persons in police detention; and
> (b) that all matters relating to such persons which are required by this Act or by such codes of practice to be recorded are recorded in the custody records relating to such persons.

(2) If this custody officer, in accordance with any code of practice issued under this Act, transfers or permits the transfer of a person in police detention—
> (a) to the custody of a police officer investigating an offence for which that person is in police detention; or
> (b) to the custody of an officer who has charge of that person outside the police station,

the custody officer shall cease in relation to that person to be subject to the duty imposed on him by subsection (1)(a) above; and it shall be the duty of the officer to whom the transfer is made to ensure that he is treated in accordance with the provisions of this Act and of any such codes of practice as are mentioned in subsection (1) above.

(3) If the person detained is subsequently returned to the custody of the custody officer, it shall be the duty of the officer investigating the offence to report to the custody officer as to the manner in which this section and the codes of practice have been complied with while that person was in his custody.

(4) If an arrested juvenile is moved to local authority accommodation under section 38(6) above, the custody officer shall cease in relation to that person to be subject to the duty imposed on him by subsection (1) above.

(6) Where—
> (a) an officer of higher rank than the custody officer gives directions relating to a person in police detention; and
> (b) the directions are at variance—
>> (i)   with any decision made or action taken by the custody officer in the performance of a duty imposed on him under this Part of this Act; or
>> (ii) with any decision or action which would but for the directions have been made or taken by him in the performance of such a duty,

the custody officer shall refer the matter at once to an officer of the rank of superintendent or above who is responsible for the police station for which the custody officer is acting as custody officer.

40 Review of police detention
(1) Reviews of the detention of each person in police detention in connection with the investigation of an offence shall be carried out periodically in accordance with the following provisions of this section—
> (a) in the case of a person who has been arrested and charged, by the custody officer; and
> (b) in the case of a person who has been arrested but not charged, by an officer of at least the rank of inspector who has not been directly involved in the investigation.

(2) The officer to whom it falls to carry out a review is referred to in this section as a 'review officer'.

(3) Subject to subsection (4) below—

  (a) the first review shall be not later than six hours after the detention was first authorised;

  (b) the second review shall be not later than nine hours after the first;

  (c) subsequent reviews shall be at intervals of not more than nine hours.

(4) A review may be postponed—

  (a) if, having regard to all the circumstances prevailing at the latest time for it specified in subsection (3) above, it is not practicable to carry out the review at that time;

  (b) without prejudice to the generality of paragraph (a) above—

    (i)   if at that time the person in detention is being questioned by a police officer and the review officer is satisfied that an interruption of the questioning for the purpose of carrying out the review would prejudice the investigation in connection with which he is being questioned; or

    (ii) if at that time no review officer is readily available.

(5) If a review is postponed under subsection (4) above it shall be carried out as soon as practicable after the latest time specified for it in subsection (3) above.

(6) If a review is carried out after postponement under subsection (4) above, the fact that it was so carried out shall not affect any requirement of this section as to the time at which any subsequent review is to be carried out.

(7) The review officer shall record the reasons for any postponement of a review in the custody record.

(8) Subject to subsection (9) below, where the person whose detention is under review has not been charged before the time of the review, section 37(1) to (6) above shall have effect in relation to him, but with the modifications specified in subsection (8A).

(8A) The modifications are—

  (a) the substitution of references to the person whose detention is under review for references to the person arrested;

  (b) the substitution of references to the review officer for references to the custody officer; and

  (c) in subsection (6), the insertion of the following paragraph after paragraph (a)—'(aa) "asleep;".'

(9) Where a person has been kept in police detention by virtue of section 37(9) or 37D(5) above, section 37(1) to (6) shall not have effect in relation to him but it shall be the duty of the review officer to determine whether he is yet in a fit state.

(10) Where the person whose detention is under review has been charged before the time of the review, section 38(1) to (6B) above shall have effect in relation to him, but with the modifications specified in subsection (10A).

(10A) The modifications are—

  (a) the substitution of a reference to the person whose detention is under review for any reference to the person arrested or to the person charged; and

  (b) in subsection (5), the insertion of the following paragraph after paragraph (a)—'(aa) "asleep;".'

(11) Where—

  (a) an officer of higher rank than the review officer gives directions relating to a person in police detention; and

  (b) the directions are at variance—

    (i)   with any decision made or action taken by the review officer in the performance of a duty imposed on him under this Part of this Act; or

    (ii) with any decision or action which would but for the directions have been made or taken by him in the performance of such a duty,

the review officer shall refer the matter at once to an officer of the rank of superintendent or above who is responsible for the police station for which the review officer is acting as review officer in connection with the detention.

(12) Before determining whether to authorise a person's continued detention the review officer shall give—

    (a) that person (unless he is asleep); or

    (b) any solicitor representing him who is available at the time of the review,

an opportunity to make representations to him about the detention.

(13) Subject to subsection (14) below, the person whose detention is under review or his solicitor may make representations under subsection (12) above either orally or in writing.

(14) The review officer may refuse to hear oral representations from the person whose detention is under review if he considers that he is unfit to make such representations by reason of his condition or behaviour.

40A   Use of telephone for review under s. 40

(1) A review under section 40(1)(b) may be carried out by means of a discussion, conducted by telephone, with one or more persons at the police station where the arrested person is held.

(2) But subsection (1) does not apply if—

    (a) the review is of a kind authorised by regulations under section 45A to be carried out using video-conferencing facilities; and

    (b) it is reasonably practicable to carry it out in accordance with those regulations.

(3) Where any review is carried out under this section by an officer who is not present at the station where the arrested person is held—

    (a) any obligation of that officer to make a record in connection with the carrying out of the review shall have effect as an obligation to cause another officer to make the record;

    (b) any requirement for the record to be made in the presence of the arrested person shall apply to the making of that record by that other officer; and

    (c) the requirements under section 40(12) and (13) above for—

        (i)   the arrested person, or

        (ii) solicitor representing him,

to be given any opportunity to make representations (whether in writing or orally to that officer shall have effect as a requirement for that person, or such a solicitor, to be given an opportunity to make representations in a manner authorised by subsection (4) below.

(4) Representations are made in a manner authorised by this subsection—

    (a) in a case where facilities exist for the immediate transmission of written representations to the officer carrying out the review, if they are made either—

        (i)   orally by telephone to that officer; or

        (ii) in writing to that officer by means of those facilities;

        and

    (b) in any other case, if they are made orally by telephone to that officer.

(5) In this section 'video-conferencing facilities' has the same meaning as in section 45A below.

41   Limits on period of detention without charge

(1) Subject to the following provisions of this section and to sections 42 and 43 below, a person shall not be kept in police detention for more than 24 hours without being charged.

(2) The time from which the period of detention of a person is to be calculated (in this Act referred to as 'the relevant time')—

    (a) in the case of a person to whom this paragraph applies, shall be—

        (i)   the time at which that person arrives at the relevant police station; or

        (ii) the time 24 hours after the time of that person's arrest,

        whichever is the earlier;

    (b) in the case of a person arrested outside England and Wales, shall be—

        (i)   the time at which that person arrives at the first police station to which he is taken in the police area in England or Wales in which the offence for which he was arrested is being investigated; or

        (ii) the time 24 hours after the time of that person's entry into England and Wales,

        whichever is the earlier;

    (c) in the case of a person who—
      (i) attends voluntarily at a police station; or
      (ii) accompanies a constable to a police station without having been arrested, and is arrested at the police station, the time of his arrest;
    (ca) in the case of a person who attends a police station to answer to bail granted under section 30A, the time when he arrives at the police station;
    (d) in any other case, except where subsection (5) below applies, shall be the time at which the person arrested arrives at the first police station to which he is taken after his arrest.

(3) Subsection (2)(a) above applies to a person if—
    (a) his arrest is sought in one police area in England and Wales;
    (b) he is arrested in another police area; and
    (c) he is not questioned in the area in which he is arrested in order to obtain evidence in relation to an offence for which he is arrested;

and in sub-paragraph (i) of that paragraph 'the relevant police station' means the first police station to which he is taken in the police area in which his arrest was sought.

(4) Subsection (2) above shall have effect in relation to a person arrested under section 31 above as if every reference in it to his arrest or his being arrested were a reference to his arrest or his being arrested for the offence for which he was originally arrested.

(5) If—
    (a) a person is in police detention in a police area in England and Wales ('the first area'); and
    (b) his arrest for an offence is sought in some other police area in England and Wales ('the second area'); and
    (c) he is taken to the second area for the purposes of investigating that offence, without being questioned in the first area in order to obtain evidence in relation to it,

the relevant time shall be—
      (i) the time 24 hours after he leaves the place where he is detained in the first area; or
      (ii) the time at which he arrives at the first police station to which he is taken in the second area,

whichever is the earlier.

(6) When a person who is in police detention at a police station is removed to hospital because he is in need of medical treatment, any time during which he is being questioned in hospital or on the way there or back by a police officer for the purpose of obtaining evidence relating to an offence shall be included in any period which falls to be calculated for the purposes of this Part of this Act, but any other time while he is in hospital or on his way there or back shall not be so included.

(7) Subject to subsection (8) below, a person who at the expiry of 24 hours after the relevant time is in police detention and has not been charged shall be released at that time either on bail or without bail.

(8) Subsection (7) above does not apply to a person whose detention for more than 24 hours after the relevant time has been authorised or is otherwise permitted in accordance with section 42 or 43 below.

(9) A person released under subsection (7) above shall not be re-arrested without a warrant for the offence for which he was previously arrested unless new evidence justifying a further arrest has come to light since his release; but this subsection does not prevent an arrest under section 46A below.

42 Authorisation of continued detention

(1) Where a police officer of the rank of superintendent or above who has not been directly involved in the investigation has reasonable grounds for believing that—
    (a) the detention of that person without charge is necessary to secure or preserve evidence relating to an offence for which he is under arrest or to obtain such evidence by questioning him;

(b) an offence for which he is under arrest is an indictable offence; and

(c) the investigation is being conducted diligently and expeditiously,

he may authorise the keeping of that person in police detention for a period expiring at or before 36 hours after the relevant time.

(2) Where an officer such as is mentioned in subsection (1) above has authorised the keeping of a person in police detention for a period expiring less than 36 hours after the relevant time, such an officer may authorise the keeping of that person in police detention for a further period expiring not more than 36 hours after that time if the conditions specified in subsection (1) above are still satisfied when he gives the authorisation.

(3) If it is proposed to transfer a person in police detention to another police area, the officer determining whether or not to authorise keeping him in detention under subsection (1) above shall have regard to the distance and the time the journey would take.

(4) No authorisation under subsection (1) above shall be given in respect of any person—

(a) more than 24 hours after the relevant time; or

(b) before the second review of his detention under section 40 above has been carried out.

(5) Where an officer authorises the keeping of a person in police detention under subsection (1) above, it shall be his duty—

(a) to inform that person of the grounds for his continued detention; and

(b) to record the grounds in that person's custody record.

(6) Before determining whether to authorise the keeping of a person in detention under subsection (1) or (2) above, an officer shall give—

(a) that person; or

(b) any solicitor representing him who is available at the time when it falls to the officer to determine whether to give the authorisation,

an opportunity to make representations to him about the detention.

(7) Subject to subsection (8) below, the person in detention or his solicitor may make representations under subsection (6) above either orally or in writing.

(8) The officer to whom it falls to determine whether to give the authorisation may refuse to hear oral representations from the person in detention if he considers that he is unfit to make such representations by reason of his condition or behaviour.

(9) Where—

(a) an officer authorises the keeping of a person in detention under subsection (1) above; and

(b) at the time of the authorisation he has not yet exercised a right conferred on him by section 56 or 58 below,

the officer—

(i)   shall inform him of that right;

(ii)   shall decide whether he should be permitted to exercise it;

(iii) shall record the decision in his custody record; and

(iv)   if the decision is to refuse to permit the exercise of the right, shall also record the grounds for the decision in that record.

(10) Where an officer has authorised the keeping of a person who has not been charged in detention under subsection (1) or (2) above, he shall be released from detention, either on bail or without bail, not later than 36 hours after the relevant time, unless—

(a) he has been charged with an offence; or

(b) his continued detention is authorised or otherwise permitted in accordance with section 43 below.

(11) A person released under subsection (10) above shall not be re-arrested without a warrant for the offence for which he was previously arrested unless new evidence justifying a further arrest has come to light since his release; but this subsection does not prevent an arrest under section 46A below.

43   Warrants of further detention

(1) Where, on an application on oath made by a constable and supported by an information, a magistrates' court is satisfied that there are reasonable grounds for believing that the further detention of the person to whom the application relates is justified, it may issue a warrant of further detention authorising the keeping of that person in police detention.

(2) A court may not hear an application for a warrant of further detention unless the person to whom the application relates—

(a) has been furnished with a copy of the information; and

(b) has been brought before the court for the hearing.

(3) The person to whom the application relates shall be entitled to be legally represented at the hearing and, if he is not so represented but wishes to be so represented—

(a) the court shall adjourn the hearing to enable him to obtain representation; and

(b) he may be kept in police detention during the adjournment.

(4) A person's further detention is only justified for the purposes of this section or section 44 below if—

(a) his detention without charge is necessary to secure or preserve evidence relating to an offence for which he is under arrest or to obtain such evidence by questioning him;

(b) an offence for which he is under arrest is an indictable offence; and

(c) the investigation is being conducted diligently and expeditiously.

(5) Subject to subsection (7) below, an application for a warrant of further detention may be made—

(a) at any time before the expiry of 36 hours after the relevant time; or

(b) in a case where—

(i)   it is not practicable for the magistrates' court to which the application will be made to sit at the expiry of 36 hours after the relevant time; but

(ii) the court will sit during the 6 hours following the end of that period, at any time before the expiry of the said 6 hours.

(6) In a case to which subsection (5)(b) above applies—

(a) the person to whom the application relates may be kept in police detention until the application is heard; and

(b) the custody officer shall make a note in that person's custody record—

(i)   of the fact that he was kept in police detention for more than 36 hours after the relevant time; and

(ii) of the reason why he was so kept.

(7) If—

(a) an application for a warrant of further detention is made after the expiry of 36 hours after the relevant time; and

(b) it appears to the magistrates' court that it would have been reasonable for the police to make it before the expiry of that period,

the court shall dismiss the application.

(8) Where on an application such as is mentioned in subsection (1) above a magistrates' court is not satisfied that there are reasonable grounds for believing that the further detention of the person to whom the application relates is justified, it shall be its duty—

(a) to refuse the application; or

(b) to adjourn the hearing of it until a time not later than 36 hours after the relevant time.

(9) The person to whom the application relates may be kept in police detention during the adjournment.

(10) A warrant of further detention shall—

(a) state the time at which it is issued;

(b) authorise the keeping in police detention of the person to whom it relates for the period stated in it.

(11) Subject to subsection (12) below, the period stated in a warrant of further detention shall be such period as the magistrates' court thinks fit, having regard to the evidence before it.

(12) The period shall not be longer than 36 hours.

(13) If it is proposed to transfer a person in police detention to a police area other than that in which he is detained when the application for a warrant of further detention is made, the court hearing the application shall have regard to the distance and the time the journey would take.

(14) Any information submitted in support of an application under this section shall state—

(a) the nature of the offence for which the person to whom the application relates has been arrested;

(b) the general nature of the evidence on which that person was arrested;

(c) what inquiries relating to the offence have been made by the police and what further inquiries are proposed by them;

(d) the reasons for believing the continued detention of that person to be necessary for the purposes of such further inquiries.

(15) Where an application under this section is refused, the person to whom the application relates shall forthwith be charged or, subject to subsection (16) below, released, either on bail or without bail.

(16) A person need not be released under subsection (15) above—

(a) before the expiry of 24 hours after the relevant time; or

(b) before the expiry of any longer period for which his continued detention is or has been authorised under section 42 above.

(17) Where an application under this section is refused, no further application shall be made under this section in respect of the person to whom the refusal relates, unless supported by evidence which has come to light since the refusal.

(18) Where a warrant of further detention is issued, the person to whom it relates shall be released from police detention, either on bail or without bail, upon or before the expiry of the warrant unless he is charged.

(19) A person released under subsection (18) above shall not be re-arrested without a warrant for the offence for which he was previously arrested unless new evidence justifying a further arrest has come to light since his release; but this subsection does not prevent an arrest under section 46A below.

44   Extension of warrants of further detention

(1) On an application made by a constable and supported by an information a magistrates' court may extend a warrant of further detention issued under section 43 above if it is satisfied that there are reasonable grounds for believing that the further detention of the person to whom the application relates is justified.

(2) Subject to subsection (3) below, the period for which a warrant of further detention may be extended shall be such period as the court thinks fit, having regard to the evidence before it.

(3) The period shall not—

(a) be longer than 36 hours; or

(b) end later than 96 hours after the relevant time.

(4) Where a warrant of further detention has been extended under subsection (1) above, or further extended under this subsection, for a period ending before 96 hours after the relevant time, on an application such as is mentioned in that subsection a magistrates' court may further extend the warrant if it is satisfied as there mentioned; and subsections (2) and (3) above apply to such further extensions as they apply to extensions under subsection (1) above.

(5) A warrant of further detention shall, if extended under this section, be endorsed with a note of the period of the extension.

(6) Subsections (2), (3) and (14) of section 43 above shall apply to an application made under this section as they apply to an application made under that section.

(7) Where an application under this section is refused, the person to whom the application relates shall forthwith be charged or, subject to subsection (8) below, released, either on bail or without bail.

(8) A person need not be released under subsection (7) above before the expiry of any period for which a warrant of further detention issued in relation to him has been extended or further extended on an earlier application made under this section.

45 Detention before charge—supplementary

(1) In sections 43 and 44 of this Act 'magistrates' court' means a court consisting of two or more justices of the peace sitting otherwise than in open court.

(2) Any reference in this Part of this Act to a period of time or a time of day is to be treated as approximate only.

45A Use of video-conferencing facilities for decisions about detention

(1) Subject to the following provisions of this section, the Secretary of State may by regulations provide that, in the case of an arrested person who is held in a police station, some or all of the functions mentioned in subsection (2) may be performed (notwithstanding anything in the preceding provisions of this Part) by an officer who—

(a) is not present in that police station; but

(b) has access to the use of video-conferencing facilities that enable him to communicate with persons in that station.

(2) Those functions are—

(a) the functions in relation to an arrested person taken to, or answering to bail at, a police station that is not a designated police station which, in the case of an arrested person taken to a station that is a designated police station, are functions of a custody officer under section 37, 38 or 40 above; and

(b) the function of carrying out a review under section 40(1)(b) above (review, by an officer of at least the rank of inspector, of the detention of person arrested but not charged).

(3) Regulations under this section shall specify the use to be made in the performance of the functions mentioned in subsection (2) above of the facilities mentioned in subsection (1) above.

(4) Regulations under this section shall not authorise the performance of any of the functions mentioned in subsection (2)(a) above by such an officer as is mentioned in subsection (1) above unless he is a custody officer for a designated police station.

(5) Where any functions mentioned in subsection (2) above are performed in a manner authorised by regulations under this section—

(a) any obligation of the officer performing those functions to make a record in connection with the performance of those functions shall have effect as an obligation to cause another officer to make the record; and

(b) any requirement for the record to be made in the presence of the arrested person shall apply to the making of that record by that other officer.

(6) Where the functions mentioned in subsection (2)(b) are performed in a manner authorised by regulations under this section, the requirements under section 40(12) and (13) above for—

(a) the arrested person, or

(b) a solicitor representing him,

to be given any opportunity to make representations (whether in writing or orally) to the person performing those functions shall have effect as a requirement for that person, or such a solicitor, to be given an opportunity to make representations in a manner authorised by subsection (7) below.

(7) Representations are made in a manner authorised by this subsection—

(a) in a case where facilities exist for the immediate transmission of written representations to the officer performing the functions, if they are made either—

(i) orally to that officer by means of the video-conferencing facilities used by him for performing those functions; or

(ii) in writing to that officer by means of the facilities available for the immediate transmission of the representations; and

(b) in any other case if they are made orally to that officer by means of the video-conferencing facilities used by him for performing the functions.

(8) Regulations under this section may make different provision for different cases and may be made so as to have effect in relation only to the police stations specified or described in the regulations.

(9) Regulations under this section shall be made by statutory instrument and shall be subject to annulment in pursuance of a resolution of either House of Parliament.

(10) Any reference in this section to video-conferencing facilities, in relation to any functions, is a reference to any facilities (whether a live television link or other facilities) by means of which the functions may be performed with the officer performing them, the person in relation to whom they are performed and any legal representative of that person all able to both see and to hear each other.

Detention—miscellaneous

46 Detention after charge

(1) Where a person—

(a) is charged with an offence; and

(b) after being charged—

(i) is kept in police detention; or

(ii) is detained by a local authority in pursuance of arrangements made under section 38(6) above,

he shall be brought before a magistrates' court in accordance with the provisions of this section.

(2) If he is to be brought before a magistrates' court in the local justice area in which the police station at which he was charged is situated, he shall be brought before such a court as soon as is practicable and in any event not later than the first sitting after he is charged with the offence.

(3) If no magistrates' court in that area is due to sit either on the day on which he is charged or on the next day, the custody officer for the police station at which he was charged shall inform the designated officer for the area that there is a person in the area to whom subsection (2) above applies.

(4) If the person charged is to be brought before a magistrates' court in a local justice area other than that in which the police station at which he was charged is situated, he shall be removed to that area as soon as is practicable and brought before such a court as soon as is practicable after his arrival in the area and in any event not later than the first sitting of a magistrates' court in that area after his arrival in the area.

(5) If no magistrates' court in that area is due to sit either on the day on which he arrives in the area or on the next day—

(a) he shall be taken to a police station in the area; and

(b) the custody officer at that station shall inform the designated officer for the area that there is a person in the area to whom subsection (4) applies.

(6) Subject to subsection (8) below, where the designated officer for a local justice area has been informed—

(a) under subsection (3) above that there is a person in the area to whom subsection (2) above applies; or

(b) under subsection (5) above that there is a person in the area to whom subsection (4) above applies,

the designated officer shall arrange for a magistrates' court to sit not later than the day next following the relevant day.

(7) In this section 'the relevant day'—

(a) in relation to a person who is to be brought before a magistrates' court in the local justice area in which the police station at which he was charged is situated, means the day on which he was charged; and

(b) in relation to a person who is to be brought before a magistrates' court in any other local justice area, means the day on which he arrives in the area.

(8) Where the day next following the relevant day is Christmas Day, Good Friday or a Sunday, the duty of the designated officer under subsection (6) above is a duty to arrange for a magistrates' court to sit not later than the first day after the relevant day which is not one of those days.

(9) Nothing in this section requires a person who is in hospital to be brought before a court if he is not well enough.

46ZA Persons granted live link bail

(1) This section applies in relation to bail granted under this Part subject to the duty mentioned in section 47(3)(b) ('live link bail').

(2) An accused person who attends a police station to answer to live link bail is not to be treated as in police detention for the purposes of this Act.

(3) Subsection (2) does not apply in relation to an accused person if—

> (b) at any time before the beginning of proceedings in relation to a live link direction under section 57C of the Crime and Disorder Act 1998 in relation to the accused person, a constable informs him that a live link will not be available for his use for the purposes of that section;
>
> or
>
> (d) the court determines for any reason not to give such a direction.

(4) If paragraph (b) or (d) of subsection (3) applies in relation to a person, he is to be treated for the purposes of this Part—

> (a) as if he had been arrested for and charged with the offence in connection with which he was granted bail, and
>
> (b) as if he had been so charged at the time when that paragraph first applied in relation to him.

(5) An accused person who is arrested under section 46A for failing to attend at a police station to answer to live link bail, and who is brought to a police station in accordance with that section, is to be treated for the purposes of this Part—

> (a) as if he had been arrested for and charged with the offence in connection with which he was granted bail, and
>
> (b) as if he had been so charged at the time when he is brought to the station.

(6) Nothing in subsection (4) or (5) affects the operation of section 47(6).

46A Power of arrest for failure to answer to police bail

(1) A constable may arrest without a warrant any person who, having been released on bail under this Part of this Act subject to a duty to attend at a police station, fails to attend at that police station at the time appointed for him to do so.

(1ZA) The reference in subsection (1) to a person who fails to attend at a police station at the time appointed for him to do so includes a reference to a person who—

> (a) attends at a police station to answer to bail granted subject to the duty mentioned in section 47(3)(b), but
>
> (b) leaves the police station at any time before the beginning of proceedings in relation to a live link direction under section 57C of the Crime and Disorder Act 1998 in relation to him.

(1ZB) The reference in subsection (1) to a person who fails to attend at a police station at the time appointed for the person to do so includes a reference to a person who—

> (a) attends at a police station to answer to bail granted subject to the duty mentioned in section 47(3)(b), but
>
> (b) refuses to be searched under section 54B.

(1A) A person who has been released on bail under section 37, 37C(2)(b) or 37CA(2)(b) above may be arrested without warrant by a constable if the constable has reasonable grounds for suspecting that the person has broken any of the conditions of bail.

(2) A person who is arrested under this section shall be taken to the police station appointed as the place at which he is to surrender to custody as soon as practicable after the arrest.

(3) For the purposes of—

> (a) section 30 above (subject to the obligation in subsection (2) above), and
>
> (b) section 31 above,

an arrest under this section shall be treated as an arrest for an offence.

47   Bail after arrest

(1)   Subject to the following provisions of this section, a release on bail of a person under this Part of this Act shall be a release on bail granted in accordance with sections 3, 3A, 5 and 5A of the Bail Act 1976 as they apply to bail granted by a constable.

(1A)   The normal powers to impose conditions of bail shall be available to him where a custody officer releases a person on bail under section 37(7)(a) above or 38(1) above (including that subsection as applied by section 40(10) above) but not in any other cases.

In this subsection, 'the normal powers to impose conditions of bail' has the meaning given in section 3(6) of the Bail Act 1976.

(1B)   No application may be made under section 5B of the Bail Act 1976 if a person is released on bail under section 37, 37C(2)(b) or 37CA(2)(b) above.

(1C)   Subsections (1D) to (1F) below apply where a person released on bail under section 37, 37C(2)(b) or 37CA(2)(b) above is on bail subject to conditions.

(1D)   The person shall not be entitled to make an application under section 43B of the Magistrates' Courts Act 1980.

(1E)   A magistrates' court may, on an application by or on behalf of the person, vary the conditions of bail; and in this subsection 'vary' has the same meaning as in the Bail Act 1976.

(1F)   Where a magistrates' court varies the conditions of bail under subsection (1E) above, that bail shall not lapse but shall continue subject to the conditions as so varied.

(2)   Nothing in the Bail Act 1976 shall prevent the re-arrest without warrant of a person released on bail subject to a duty to attend at a police station if new evidence justifying a further arrest has come to light since his release.

(3)   Subject to subsections (3A) and (4) below, in this Part of this Act references to 'bail' are references to bail subject to a duty—

  (a)   to appear before a magistrates' court at such time and such place as the custody officer may appoint;

  (b)   to attend at such police station as the custody officer may appoint at such time as he may appoint for the purposes of—

    (i)   proceedings in relation to a live link direction under section 57C of the Crime and Disorder Act 1998 (use of live link direction at preliminary hearings where accused is at police station); and

    (ii)   any preliminary hearing in relation to which such a direction is given; or

  (c)   to attend at such police station as the custody officer may appoint at such time as he may appoint for purposes other than those mentioned in paragraph (b).

(3A)   Where a custody officer grants bail to a person subject to a duty to appear before a magistrates' court, he shall appoint for the appearance—

  (a)   a date which is not later than the first sitting of the court after the person is charged with the offence; or

  (b)   where he is informed by the designated officer for the relevant local justice area that the appearance cannot be accommodated until a later date, that later date.

(4)   Where a custody officer has granted bail to a person subject to a duty to appear at a police station, the custody officer may give notice in writing to that person that his attendance at the police station is not required.

(6)   Where a person who has been granted bail under this Part and has either attended at the police station in accordance with the grant of bail or has been arrested under section 46A above is detained at a police station, any time during which he was in police detention prior to being granted bail shall be included as part of any period which falls to be calculated under this Part of this Act and any time during which he was on bail shall not be so included.

(7)   Where a person who was released on bail under this Part subject to a duty to attend at a police station is re-arrested, the provisions of this Part of this Act shall apply to him as they apply to a person arrested for the first time, but this subsection does not apply to a person who is arrested under section

46A above or has attended a police station in accordance with the grant of bail (and who accordingly is deemed by section 34(7) above to have been arrested for an offence) or to a person to whom section 46ZA(4) or (5) applies.

(8) [*Makes changes to the Magistrates' Courts Act 1980 sections 43 and 117(3)*]

47A   Early administrative hearings conducted by justices' clerk

Where a person has been charged with an offence at a police station, any requirement imposed under this Part for the person to appear or be brought before a magistrates' court shall be taken to be satisfied if the person appears or is brought before a justices' clerk in order for the clerk to conduct a hearing under section 50 of the Crime and Disorder Act 1998 (early administrative hearings).

48   Remands to police detention
[*Makes changes to the Magistrates' Court Act 1980 section 128*]

49   Police detention to count towards custodial sentence
[*Makes changes to the Criminal Justice Act 1967 section 67*]

50   Records of detention

(1) Each police force shall keep written records showing on an annual basis—
  (a) the number of persons kept in police detention for more than 24 hours and subsequently released without charge;
  (b) the number of applications for warrants of further detention and the results of the applications; and
  (c) in relation to each warrant of further detention—
    (i)   the period of further detention authorised by it;
    (ii)   the period which the person named in it spent in police detention on its authority; and
    (iii) whether he was charged or released without charge.

(2) Every annual report—
  (a) under section 22 of the Police Act 1996; or
  (b) made by the Commissioner of Police of the Metropolis,
shall contain information about the matters mentioned in subsection (1) above in respect of the period to which the report relates.

51   Savings

Nothing in this Part of this Act shall affect—
  (a) the powers conferred on immigration officers by section 4 of and Schedule 2 to the Immigration Act 1971 (administrative provisions as to control on entry etc.);
  (b) the powers conferred by or by virtue of section 41 of, or Schedule 7 to, the Terrorism Act 2000 (Power of arrest and detention);
  (d) any right of a person in police detention to apply for a writ of habeas corpus or other prerogative remedy.

PART V QUESTIONING AND TREATMENT OF PERSONS BY POLICE

53   Abolition of certain powers of constables to search persons

(1) Subject to subsection (2) below, there shall cease to have effect any Act (including a local Act) passed before this Act in so far as it authorises—
  (a) any search by a constable of a person in police detention at a police station; or
  (b) an intimate search of a person by a constable;
and any rule of common law which authorises a search such as is mentioned in paragraph (a) or (b) above is abolished.

54 Searches of detained persons

(1) The custody officer at a police station shall ascertain everything which a person has with him when he is—

    (a) brought to the station after being arrested elsewhere or after being committed to custody by an order or sentence of a court; or

    (b) arrested at the station or detained there, as a person falling within section 34(7), under section 37 above or as a person to whom section 46ZA(4) or (5) applies.

(2) The custody officer may record or cause to be recorded all or any of the things which he ascertains under subsection (1).

(2A) In the case of an arrested person, any such record may be made as part of his custody record.

(3) Subject to subsection (4) below, a custody officer may seize and retain any such thing or cause any such thing to be seized and retained.

(4) Clothes and personal effects may only be seized if the custody officer—

    (a) believes that the person from whom they are seized may use them—

        (i)   to cause physical injury to himself or any other person;

        (ii)   to damage property;

        (iii) to interfere with evidence; or

        (iv) to assist him to escape; or

    (b) has reasonable grounds for believing that they may be evidence relating to an offence.

(5) Where anything is seized, the person from whom it is seized shall be told the reason for the seizure unless he is—

    (a) violent or likely to become violent; or

    (b) incapable of understanding what is said to him.

(6) Subject to subsection (7) below, a person may be searched if the custody officer considers it necessary to enable him to carry out his duty under subsection (1) above and to the extent that the custody officer considers necessary for that purpose.

(6A) A person who is in custody at a police station or is in police detention otherwise than at a police station may at any time be searched in order to ascertain whether he has with him anything which he could use for any of the purposes specified in subsection 4(a) above.

(6B) Subject to subsection (6C) below, a constable may seize and detain, or cause to be seized and detained, anything found in such a search.

(6C) A constable may only seize clothes and personal effects in the circumstances specified in subsection (4) above.

(7) An intimate search may not be conducted under this section.

(8) A search under this section shall be carried out by a constable.

(9) The constable carrying out a search shall be of the same sex as the person searched.

54A Searches and examination to ascertain identity

(1) If an officer of at least the rank of inspector authorises it, a person who is detained in a police station may be searched or examined, or both—

    (a) for the purpose of ascertaining whether he has any mark that would tend to identify him as a person involved in the commission of an offence; or

    (b) for the purpose of facilitating the ascertainment of his identity.

(2) An officer may only give an authorisation under subsection (1) for the purpose mentioned in paragraph (a) of that subsection if—

    (a) the appropriate consent to a search or examination that would reveal whether the mark in question exists has been withheld; or

    (b) it is not practicable to obtain such consent.

(3) An officer may only give an authorisation under subsection (1) in a case in which subsection (2) does not apply if—

    (a) the person in question has refused to identify himself; or

(b) the officer has reasonable grounds for suspecting that that person is not who he claims to be.

(4) An officer may give an authorisation under subsection (1) orally or in writing but, if he gives it orally, he shall confirm it in writing as soon as is practicable.

(5) Any identifying mark found on a search or examination under this section may be photographed—

(a) with the appropriate consent; or

(b) if the appropriate consent is withheld or it is not practicable to obtain it, without it.

(6) Where a search or examination may be carried out under this section, or a photograph may be taken under this section, the only persons entitled to carry out the search or examination, or to take the photograph, are constables.

(7) A person may not under this section carry out a search or examination of a person of the opposite sex or take a photograph of any part of the body of a person of the opposite sex.

(8) An intimate search may not be carried out under this section.

(9) A photograph taken under this section—

(a) may be used by, or disclosed to, any person for any purpose related to the prevention or detection of crime, the investigation of an offence or the conduct of a prosecution; and

(b) after being so used or disclosed, may be retained but may not be used or disclosed except for a purpose so related.

(10) In subsection—

(a) the reference to crime includes a reference to any conduct which—

(i) constitutes one or more criminal offences (whether under the law of a part of the United Kingdom or of a country or territory outside the United Kingdom); or

(ii) is, or corresponds to, any conduct which, if it all took place in any one part of the United Kingdom, would constitute one or more criminal offences;

and

(b) the references to an investigation and to a prosecution include references, respectively, to any investigation outside the United Kingdom of any crime or suspected crime and to a prosecution brought in respect of any crime in a country or territory outside the United Kingdom.

(11) In this section—

(a) references to ascertaining a person's identity include references to showing that he is not a particular person; and

(b) references to taking a photograph include references to using any process by means of which a visual image may be produced, and references to photographing a person shall be construed accordingly.

(12) In this section "mark" includes features and injuries; and a mark is an identifying mark for the purposes of this section if its existence in any person's case facilitates the ascertainment of his identity or his identification as a person involved in the commission of an offence.

(13) Nothing in this section applies to a person arrested under an extradition arrest power.

54B   Searches of persons answering to live link bail

(1) A constable may search at any time—

(a) any person who is at a police station to answer to live link bail; and

(b) any article in the possession of such a person.

(2) If the constable reasonably believes a thing in the possession of the person ought to be seized on any of the grounds mentioned in subsection (3), the constable may seize and retain it or cause it to be seized and retained.

(3) The grounds are that the thing—

(a) may jeopardise the maintenance of order in the police station;

(b) may put the safety of any person in the police station at risk; or

(c) may be evidence of, or in relation to, an offence.

(4) The constable may record or cause to be recorded all or any of the things seized and retained pursuant to subsection (2).

(5) An intimate search may not be carried out under this section.

(6) The constable carrying out a search under subsection (1) must be of the same sex as the person being searched.

(7) In this section "live link bail" means bail granted under Part 4 of this Act subject to the duty mentioned in section 47(3)(b).

54C Power to retain articles seized

(1) Except as provided by subsections (2) and (3), a constable may retain a thing seized under section 54B until the time when the person from whom it was seized leaves the police station.

(2) A constable may retain a thing seized under section 54B in order to establish its lawful owner, where there are reasonable grounds for believing that it has been obtained in consequence of the commission of an offence.

(3) If a thing seized under section 54B may be evidence of, or in relation to, an offence, a constable may retain it—

(a) for use as evidence at a trial for an offence; or

(b) for forensic examination or for investigation in connection with an offence.

(4) Nothing may be retained for either of the purposes mentioned in subsection (3) if a photograph or copy would be sufficient for that purpose.

(5) Nothing in this section affects any power of a court to make an order under section 1 of the Police (Property) Act 1897.

(6) The references in this section to anything seized under section 54B include anything seized by a person to whom paragraph 27A of Schedule 4 to the Police Reform Act 2002 applies.

55 Intimate searches

(1) Subject to the following provisions of this section, if an officer of at least the rank of inspector has reasonable grounds for believing—

(a) that a person who has been arrested and is in police detention may have concealed on him anything which—

(i) he could use to cause physical injury to himself or others; and

(ii) he might so use while he is in police detention or in the custody of a court;

or

(b) that such a person—

(i) may have a Class A drug concealed on him; and

(ii) was in possession of it with the appropriate criminal intent before his arrest,

he may authorise an intimate search of that person.

(2) An officer may not authorise an intimate search of a person for anything unless he has reasonable grounds for believing that it cannot be found without his being intimately searched.

(3) An officer may give an authorisation under subsection (1) above orally or in writing but, if he gives it orally, he shall confirm it in writing as soon as is practicable.

(3A) A drug offence search shall not be carried out unless the appropriate consent has been given in writing.

(3B) Where it is proposed that a drug offence search be carried out, an appropriate officer shall inform the person who is to be subject to it—

(a) of the giving of the authorisation for it; and

(b) of the grounds for giving the authorisation.

(4) An intimate search which is only a drug offence search shall be by way of examination by a suitably qualified person.

(5) Except as provided by subsection (4) above, an intimate search shall be by way of examination by a suitably qualified person unless an officer of at least the rank of inspector considers that this is not practicable.

(6) An intimate search which is not carried out as mentioned in subsection (5) above shall be carried out by a constable.

(7) A constable may not carry out an intimate search of a person of the opposite sex.

(8) No intimate search may be carried out except—

(a) at a police station;

(b) at a hospital;

(c) at a registered medical practitioner's surgery; or

(d) at some other place used for medical purposes.

(9) An intimate search which is only a drug offence search may not be carried out at a police station.

(10) If an intimate search of a person is carried out, the custody record relating to him shall state—

(a) which parts of his body were searched; and

(b) why they were searched.

(10A) If the intimate search is a drug offence search, the custody record relating to that person shall also state—

(a) the authorisation by virtue of which the search was carried out;

(b) the grounds for giving the authorisation; and

(c) the fact that the appropriate consent was given

(11) The information required to be recorded by subsections (10) and (10A) above shall be recorded as soon as practicable after the completion of the search.

(12) The custody officer at a police station may seize and retain anything which is found on an intimate search of a person, or cause any such thing to be seized and retained—

(a) if he believes that the person from whom it is seized may use it—

(i) to cause physical injury to himself or any other person;

(ii) to damage property;

(iii) to interfere with evidence; or

(iv) to assist him to escape; or

(b) if he has reasonable grounds for believing that it may be evidence relating to an offence.

(13) Where anything is seized under this section, the person from whom it is seized shall be told the reason for the seizure unless he is—

(a) violent or likely to become violent; or

(b) incapable of understanding what is said to him.

(13A) Where the appropriate consent to a drug offence search of any person was refused without good cause, in any proceedings against that person for an offence—

(a) the court, in determining whether there is a case to answer;

(b) a judge, in deciding whether to grant an application made by the accused under paragraph 2 of Schedule 3 to the Crime and Disorder Act 1998 (applications for dismissal); and

(c) the court or jury, in determining whether that person is guilty of the offence charged,

may draw such inferences from the refusal as appear proper.

(14)–(16) [*Information to be contained in annual reports*]

(17) In this section—

'the appropriate criminal intent' means an intent to commit an offence under—

(a) section 5(3) of the Misuse of Drugs Act 1971 (possession of controlled drug with intent to supply to another); or

(b) section 68(2) of the Customs and Excise Management Act 1979 (exportation etc, with intent to evade a prohibition or restriction);

"appropriate officer" means—

(a) a constable,

(b) a person who is designated as a detention officer in pursuance of section 38 of the Police Reform Act 2002 if his designation applies paragraph 33D of Schedule 4 to that Act.

'Class A drug' has the meaning assigned to it by section 2(1)(b) of the Misuse of Drugs Act 1971;

'drug offence search' means an intimate search for a Class A drug which an officer has authorised by virtue of subsection (1)(b) above; and

'suitably qualified person' means—

(a) a registered medical practitioner; or

(b) a registered nurse.

55A X-rays and ultrasound scans

(1) If an officer of at least the rank of inspector has reasonable grounds for believing that a person who has been arrested for an offence and is in police detention—

(a) may have swallowed a Class A drug, and

(b) was in possession of it with the appropriate criminal intent before his arrest,

the officer may authorise that an x-ray is taken of the person or an ultrasound scan is carried out on the person (or both).

(2) An x-ray must not be taken of a person and an ultrasound scan must not be carried out on him unless the appropriate consent has been given in writing.

(3) If it is proposed that an x-ray is taken or an ultrasound scan is carried out, an appropriate officer must inform the person who is to be subject to it—

(a) of the giving of the authorisation for it, and

(b) of the grounds for giving the authorisation.

(4) An x-ray may be taken or an ultrasound scan carried out only by a suitably qualified person and only at—

(a) a hospital,

(b) a registered medical practitioner's surgery, or

(c) some other place used for medical purposes.

(5) The custody record of the person must also state—

(a) the authorisation by virtue of which the x-ray was taken or the ultrasound scan was carried out,

(b) the grounds for giving the authorisation, and

(c) the fact that the appropriate consent was given.

(6) The information required to be recorded by subsection (5) must be recorded as soon as practicable after the x-ray has been taken or ultrasound scan carried out (as the case may be).

(7),(8) [*Annual reports*]

(9) If the appropriate consent to an x-ray or ultrasound scan of any person is refused without good cause, in any proceedings against that person for an offence—

(a) the court, in determining whether there is a case to answer,

(b) a judge, in deciding whether to grant an application made by the accused under paragraph 2 of Schedule 3 to the Crime and Disorder Act 1998 (applications for dismissal), and

(c) the court or jury, in determining whether that person is guilty of the offence charged,

may draw such inferences from the refusal as appear proper.

(10) In this section 'the appropriate criminal intent', 'appropriate officer', 'Class A drug' and 'suitably qualified person' have the same meanings as in section 55 above.

56 Right to have someone informed when arrested

(1) Where a person has been arrested and is being held in custody in a police station or other premises, he shall be entitled, if he so requests, to have one friend or relative or other person who is known to him or who is likely to take an interest in his welfare told, as soon as is practicable except to the extent that delay is permitted by this section, that he has been arrested and is being detained there.

(2) Delay is only permitted—

(a) in the case of a person who is in police detention for an indictable offence; and

(b) if an officer of at least the rank of inspector authorises it.

(3) In any case the person in custody must be permitted to exercise the right conferred by subsection (1) above within 36 hours from the relevant time, as defined in section 41(2) above.

(4) An officer may give an authorisation under subsection (2) above orally or in writing but, if he gives it orally, he shall confirm it in writing as soon as is practicable.

(5) Subject to subsection (5A) below an officer may only authorise delay where he has reasonable grounds for believing that telling the named person of the arrest—

(a) will lead to interference with or harm to evidence connected with an indictable offence or interference with or physical injury to other persons; or

(b) will lead to the alerting of other persons suspected of having committed such an offence but not yet arrested for it; or

(c) will hinder the recovery of any property obtained as a result of such an offence.

(5A) An officer may also authorise delay where he has reasonable grounds for believing that—

(a) the person detained for the indictable offence has benefited from his criminal conduct, and

(b) the recovery of the value of the property constituting the benefit will be hindered by telling the named person of the arrest.

(5B) For the purposes of subsection (5A) above the question whether a person has benefited from his criminal conduct is to be decided in accordance with Part 2 of the Proceeds of Crime Act 2002.

(6) If a delay is authorised—

(a) the detained person shall be told the reason for it, and

(b) the reason shall be noted on his custody record.

(7) The duties imposed by subsection (6) above shall be performed as soon as is practicable.

(8) The rights conferred by this section on a person detained at a police station or other premises are exercisable whenever he is transferred from one place to another; and this section applies to each subsequent occasion on which they are exercisable as it applies to the first such occasion.

(9) There may be no further delay in permitting the exercise of the right conferred by subsection (1) above once the reason for authorising delay ceases to subsist.

(10) Nothing in this section applies to a person arrested or detained under the terrorism provisions.

57 Additional rights of children and young persons
[Amends the Children and Young Persons Act 1933 section 34(2)]

58 Access to legal advice

(1) A person arrested and held in custody in a police station or other premises shall be entitled, if he so requests, to consult a solicitor privately at any time.

(2) Subject to subsection (3) below, a request under subsection (1) above and the time at which it was made shall be recorded in the custody record.

(3) Such a request need not be recorded in the custody record of a person who makes it at a time while he is at a court after being charged with an offence.

(4) If a person makes such a request, he must be permitted to consult a solicitor as soon as is practicable except to the extent that delay is permitted by this section.

(5) In any case he must be permitted to consult a solicitor within 36 hours from the relevant time, as defined in section 41(2) above.

(6) Delay in compliance with a request is only permitted—

(a) in the case of a person who is in police detention for an indictable offence; and

(b) if an officer of at least the rank of superintendent authorises it.

(7) An officer may give an authorisation under subsection (6) above orally or in writing but, if he gives it orally, he shall confirm it in writing as soon as is practicable.

(8) Subject to subsection (8A) below an officer may only authorise delay where he has reasonable grounds for believing that the exercise of the right conferred by subsection (1) above at the time when the person detained desires to exercise it—

(a) will lead to interference with or harm to evidence connected with an indictable offence or interference with or physical injury to other persons; or

(b) will lead to the alerting of other persons suspected of having committed such an offence but not yet arrested for it; or

(c) will hinder the recovery of any property obtained as a result of such an offence.

(8A) An officer may also authorise delay where he has reasonable grounds for believing that—

(a) the person detained for the indictable offence has benefited from his criminal conduct, and

(b) the recovery of the value of the property constituting the benefit will be hindered by the exercise of the right conferred by subsection (1) above.

(8B) For the purposes of subsection (8A) above the question whether a person has benefited from his criminal conduct is to be decided in accordance with Part 2 of the Proceeds of Crime Act 2002.

(9) If delay is authorised—

(a) the detained person shall be told the reason for it; and

(b) the reason shall be noted on his custody record.

(10) The duties imposed by subsection (9) above shall be performed as soon as is practicable.

(11) There may be no further delay in permitting the exercise of the right conferred by subsection (1) above once the reason for authorising delay ceases to subsist.

(12) Nothing in this section applies to a person arrested or detained under the terrorism provisions.

60 Tape-recording of interviews

(1) It shall be the duty of the Secretary of State—

(a) to issue a code of practice in connection with the tape-recording of interviews of persons suspected of the commission of criminal offences which are held by police officers at police stations; and

(b) to make an order requiring the tape-recording of interviews of persons suspected of the commission of criminal offences, or of such descriptions of criminal offences as may be specified in the order, which are so held, in accordance with the code as it has effect for the time being.

(2) An order under subsection (1) above shall be made by statutory instrument and shall be subject to annulment in pursuance of a resolution of either House of Parliament.

60A Visual recording of interviews

(1) The Secretary of State shall have power—

(a) to issue a code of practice for the visual recording of interviews held by police officers at police stations; and

(b) to make an order requiring the visual recording of interviews so held, and requiring the visual recording to be in accordance with the code for the time being in force under this section.

(2) A requirement imposed by an order under this section may be imposed in relation to such cases or police stations in such areas, or both, as may be specified or described in the order.

(3) An order under subsection (1) above shall be made by statutory instrument and shall be subject to annulment in pursuance of a resolution of either House of Parliament.

(4) In this section—

(a) references to any interview are references to an interview of a person suspected of a criminal offence; and

(b) references to a visual recording include references to a visual recording in which an audio recording is comprised.

61 Fingerprinting

(1) Except as provided by this section no person's fingerprints may be taken without the appropriate consent.

(2) Consent to the taking of a person's fingerprints must be in writing if it is given at a time when he is at a police station.

(3) The fingerprints of a person detained at a police station may be taken without the appropriate consent if—

  (a) he is detained in consequence of his arrest for a recordable offence; and

  (b) he has not had his fingerprints taken in the course of the investigation of the offence by the police.

(3A) Where a person mentioned in paragraph (a) of subsection (3) or (4) has already had his fingerprints taken in the course of the investigation of the offence by the police, that fact shall be disregarded for the purposes of that subsection if—

  (a) the fingerprints taken on the previous occasion do not constitute a complete set of his fingerprints; or

  (b) some or all of the fingerprints taken on the previous occasion are not of sufficient quality to allow satisfactory analysis, comparison or matching (whether in the case in question or generally).

(4) The fingerprints of a person detained at a police station may be taken without the appropriate consent if—

  (a) he has been charged with a recordable offence or informed that he will be reported for such an offence; and

  (b) he has not had his fingerprints taken in the course of the investigation of the offence by the police.

(4A) The fingerprints of a person who has answered to bail at a court or police station may be taken without the appropriate consent at the court or station if—

  (a) the court, or

  (b) an officer of at least the rank of inspector,

authorises them to be taken.

(4B) A court or officer may only give an authorisation under subsection (4A) if—

  (a) the person who has answered to bail has answered to it for a person whose fingerprints were taken on a previous occasion and there are reasonable grounds for believing that he is not the same person; or

  (b) the person who has answered to bail claims to be a different person from a person whose fingerprints were taken on a previous occasion.

(5) An officer may give an authorisation under subsection (4A) above orally or in writing but, if he gives it orally, he shall confirm it in writing as soon as is practicable.

(5A) The fingerprints of a person may be taken without the appropriate consent if (before or after the coming into force of this subsection) he has been arrested for a recordable offence and released and—

  (a) in the case of a person who is on bail, he has not had his fingerprints taken in the course of the investigation of the offence by the police; or

  (b) in any case, he has had his fingerprints taken in the course of that investigation but subsection (3A)(a) or (b) above applies.

(5B) The fingerprints of a person not detained at a police station may be taken without the appropriate consent if (before or after the coming into force of this subsection) he has been charged with a recordable offence or informed that he will be reported for such an offence and—

  (a) he has not had his fingerprints taken in the course of the investigation of the offence by the police; or

  (b) he has had his fingerprints taken in the course of that investigation but subsection (3A)(a) or (b) above applies.

(6) Subject to this section, the fingerprints of a person may be taken without the appropriate consent if (before or after the coming into force of this subsection)—

(a) he has been convicted of a recordable offence,

(b) he has been given a caution in respect of a recordable offence which, at the time of the caution, he has admitted, or

(c) he has been warned or reprimanded under section 65 of the Crime and Disorder Act 1998 for a recordable offence, and

either of the conditions mentioned in subsection (6ZA) below is met.

(6ZA) The conditions referred to in subsection (6) above are—

(a) the person has not had his fingerprints taken since he was convicted, cautioned or warned or reprimanded;

(b) he has had his fingerprints taken since then but subsection (3A)(a) or (b) above applies.

(6ZB) Fingerprints may only be taken as specified in subsection (6) above with the authorisation of an officer of at least the rank of inspector.

(6ZC) An officer may only give an authorisation under subsection (6ZB) above if the officer is satisfied that taking the fingerprints is necessary to assist in the prevention or detection of crime.

(6A) A constable may take a person's fingerprints without the appropriate consent if—

(a) the constable reasonably suspects that the person is committing or attempting to commit an offence, or has committed or attempted to commit an offence; and

(b) either of the two conditions mentioned in subsection (6B) is met.

(6B) The conditions are that—

(a) the name of the person is unknown to, and cannot be readily ascertained by, the constable;

(b) the constable has reasonable grounds for doubting whether a name furnished by the person as his name is his real name.

(6C) The taking of fingerprints by virtue of subsection (6A) or (6BA) does not count for any of the purposes of this Act as taking them in the course of the investigation of an offence by the police.

(6D) Subject to this section, the fingerprints of a person may be taken without the appropriate consent if—

(a) under the law in force in a country or territory outside England and Wales the person has been convicted of an offence under that law (whether before or after the coming into force of this subsection and whether or not he has been punished for it);

(b) the act constituting the offence would constitute a qualifying offence if done in England and Wales (whether or not it constituted such an offence when the person was convicted); and

(c) either of the conditions mentioned in subsection (6E) below is met.

(6E) The conditions referred to in subsection (6D)(c) above are—

(a) the person has not had his fingerprints taken on a previous occasion under subsection (6D) above;

(b) he has had his fingerprints taken on a previous occasion under that subsection but subsection (3A)(a) or (b) above applies.

(6F) Fingerprints may only be taken as specified in subsection (6D) above with the authorisation of an officer of at least the rank of inspector.

(6G) An officer may only give an authorisation under subsection (6F) above if the officer is satisfied that taking the fingerprints is necessary to assist in the prevention or detection of crime.

(7) Where a person's fingerprints are taken without the appropriate consent by virtue of any power conferred by this section—

(a) before the fingerprints are taken, the person shall be informed of—

(i) the reason for taking the fingerprints;

(ii) the power by virtue of which they are taken; and

(iii) in a case where the authorisation of the court or an officer is required for the exercise of the power, the fact that the authorisation has been given; and

(b) those matters shall be recorded as soon as practicable after the fingerprints are taken.

(7A) If a person's fingerprints are taken at a police station or by virtue of subsection (4A), (6A) at a place other than a police station, whether with or without the appropriate consent—

(a) before the fingerprints are taken, an officer shall inform him that they may be the subject of a speculative search; and

(b) the fact that the person has been informed of this possibility shall be recorded as soon as is practicable after the fingerprints have been taken.

(8) If he is detained at a police station when the fingerprints are taken, the matters referred to in subsection (7)(a)(i) to (iii) above [and, in the case falling within subsection (7A) above, the fact referred to in paragraph (b) of that subsection] shall be recorded on his custody record.

(8B) Any power under this section to take the fingerprints of a person without the appropriate consent, if not otherwise specified to be exercisable by a constable, shall be exercisable by a constable.

(9) Nothing in this section—

(a) affects any power conferred by paragraph 18(2) of Schedule 2 to the Immigration Act 1971; or

(b) applies to a person arrested or detained under the terrorism provisions.

(10) Nothing in this section applies to a person arrested under an extradition arrest power.

61A Impressions of footwear

(1) Except as provided by this section, no impression of a person's footwear may be taken without the appropriate consent.

(2) Consent to the taking of an impression of a person's footwear must be in writing if it is given at a time when he is at a police station.

(3) Where a person is detained at a police station, an impression of his footwear may be taken without the appropriate consent if—

(a) he is detained in consequence of his arrest for a recordable offence, or has been charged with a recordable offence, or informed that he will be reported for a recordable offence; and

(b) he has not had an impression taken of his footwear in the course of the investigation of the offence by the police.

(4) Where a person mentioned in paragraph (a) of subsection (3) above has already had an impression taken of his footwear in the course of the investigation of the offence by the police, that fact shall be disregarded for the purposes of that subsection if the impression of his footwear taken previously is—

(a) incomplete; or

(b) is not of sufficient quality to allow satisfactory analysis, comparison or matching (whether in the case in question or generally).

(5) If an impression of a person's footwear is taken at a police station, whether with or without the appropriate consent—

(a) before it is taken, an officer shall inform him that it may be the subject of a speculative search; and

(b) the fact that the person has been informed of this possibility shall be recorded as soon as is practicable after the impression has been taken, and if he is detained at a police station, the record shall be made on his custody record.

(6) In a case where, by virtue of subsection (3) above, an impression of a person's footwear is taken without the appropriate consent—

(a) he shall be told the reason before it is taken; and

(b) the reason shall be recorded on his custody record as soon as is practicable after the impression is taken.

(7) The power to take an impression of the footwear of a person detained at a police station without the appropriate consent shall be exercisable by any constable.

(8) Nothing in this section applies to any person—

(a) arrested or detained under the terrorism provisions;

(b) arrested under an extradition arrest power.

62 Intimate samples

(1) Subject to section 63B below an intimate sample may be taken from a person in police detention only—

(a) if a police officer of at least the rank of inspector authorises it to be taken; and

(b) if the appropriate consent is given.

(1A) An intimate sample may be taken from a person who is not in police detention but from whom, in the course of the investigation of an offence, two or more non-intimate samples suitable for the same means of analysis have been taken which have proved insufficient—

(a) if a police officer of at least the rank of inspector authorises it to be taken; and

(b) if the appropriate consent is given.

(2) An officer may only give an authorisation under subsection (1) or (1A) above if he has reasonable grounds—

(a) for suspecting the involvement of the person from whom the sample is to be taken in a recordable offence; and

(b) for believing that the sample will tend to confirm or disprove his involvement.

(2A) An intimate sample may be taken from a person where—

(a) two or more non-intimate samples suitable for the same means of analysis have been taken from the person under section 63(3E) below (persons convicted of offences outside England and Wales etc) but have proved insufficient;

(b) a police officer of at least the rank of inspector authorises it to be taken; and

(c) the appropriate consent is given.

(2B) An officer may only give an authorisation under subsection (2A) above if the officer is satisfied that taking the sample is necessary to assist in the prevention or detection of crime.

(3) An officer may give an authorisation under subsection (1) or (1A) or (2A) above orally or in writing but, if he gives it orally, he shall confirm it in writing as soon as is practicable.

(4) The appropriate consent must be given in writing.

(5) Before an intimate sample is taken from a person, an officer shall inform him of the following—

(a) the reason for taking the sample;

(b) the fact that authorisation has been given and the provision of this section under which it has been given; and

(c) if the sample was taken at a police station, the fact that the sample may be the subject of a speculative search.

(6) The reason referred to in subsection (5)(a) above must include, except in a case where the sample is taken under subsection (2A) above, a statement of the nature of the offence in which it is suspected that the person has been involved.

(7) After an intimate sample has been taken from a person, the following shall be recorded as soon as practicable—

(a) the matters referred to in subsection (5)(a) and (b) above;

(b) if the sample was taken at a police station, the fact that the person has been informed as specified in subsection (5)(c) above; and

(c) the fact that the appropriate consent was given.

(8) If an intimate sample is taken from a person detained at a police station, the matters required to be recorded by subsection (7) above shall be recorded in his custody record.

(9) In the case of an intimate sample which is a dental impression, the sample may be taken from a person only by a registered dentist.

(9A) In the case of any other form of intimate sample, except in the case of a sample of urine, the sample may be taken from a person only by—

(a) a registered medical practitioner; or

(b) a registered health care professional.

(10) Where the appropriate consent to the taking of an intimate sample from a person was refused without good cause, in any proceedings against that person for an offence—

    (a) the court, in determining—

        (i)   whether to commit that person for trial; or

        (ii) whether there is a case to answer; and

    (aa) a judge, in deciding whether to grant an application made by the accused under—

        (i)   paragraph 2 of Schedule 3 to the Crime and Disorder Act 1998 (applications for dismissal); and

    (b) the court or jury, in determining whether that person is guilty of the offence charged,

may draw such inferences from the refusal as appear proper.

(11) Nothing in this section applies to the taking of a specimen for the purposes of any of the provisions of sections 4 to 11 of the Road Traffic Act 1988 or of sections 26 to 38 of the Transport and Works Act 1992.

(12) Nothing in this section applies to a person arrested or detained under the terrorism provisions; and subsection (1A) shall not apply where the non-intimate samples mentioned in that subsection were taken under paragraph 10 of Schedule 8 to the Terrorism Act 2000.

63 Other samples

(1) Except as provided by this section, a non-intimate sample may not be taken from a person without the appropriate consent.

(2) Consent to the taking of a non-intimate sample must be given in writing.

(2A) A non-intimate sample may be taken from a person without the appropriate consent if two conditions are satisfied.

(2B) The first is that the person is in police detention in consequence of his arrest for a recordable offence.

(2C) The second is that—

    (a) he has not had a non-intimate sample of the same type and from the same part of the body taken in the course of the investigation of the offence by the police, or

    (b) he has had such a sample taken but it proved insufficient.

(3) A non-intimate sample may be taken from a person without the appropriate consent if—

    (a) he is being held in custody by the police on the authority of a court; and

    (b) an officer of at least the rank of inspector authorises it to be taken without the appropriate consent.

(3ZA) A non-intimate sample may be taken from a person without the appropriate consent if (before or after the coming into force of this subsection) he has been arrested for a recordable offence and released and—

    (a) in the case of a person who is on bail, he has not had a non-intimate sample of the same type and from the same part of the body taken from him in the course of the investigation of the offence by the police; or

    (b) in any case, he has had a non-intimate sample taken from him in the course of that investigation but—

        (i)   it was not suitable for the same means of analysis, or

        (ii) it proved insufficient.

(3A) A non-intimate sample may be taken from a person (whether or not he is in police detention or held in custody by the police on the authority of a court) without the appropriate consent if he has been charged with a recordable offence or informed that he will be reported for such an offence and—

    (a) he has not had a non-intimate sample taken from him in the course of the investigation of the offence by the police; or

    (b) he has had a non-intimate sample taken from him in the course of that investigation but—

        (i)   it was not suitable for the same means of analysis, or

        (ii) it proved insufficient; or

(c) he has had a non-intimate sample taken from him in the course of that investigation and—
  (i)   the sample has been destroyed pursuant to section 64ZA below or any other enactment, and
  (ii) it is disputed, in relation to any proceedings relating to the offence, whether a DNA profile relevant to the proceedings is derived from the sample.

(3B) Subject to this section, a non-intimate sample may be taken from a person without the appropriate consent if (before or after the coming into force of this subsection)—
  (a) he has been convicted of a recordable offence,
  (b) he has been given a caution in respect of a recordable offence which, at the time of the caution, he has admitted, or
  (c) he has been warned or reprimanded under section 65 of the Crime and Disorder Act 1998 for a recordable offence, and
either of the conditions mentioned in subsection (3BA) below is met.

(3BA) The conditions referred to in subsection (3B) above are—
  (a) a non-intimate sample has not been taken from the person since he was convicted, cautioned or warned or reprimanded;
  (b) such a sample has been taken from him since then but—
    (i)   it was not suitable for the same means of analysis, or
    (ii) it proved insufficient.

(3BB) A non-intimate sample may only be taken as specified in subsection (3B) above with the authorisation of an officer of at least the rank of inspector.

(3BC) An officer may only give an authorisation under subsection (3BB) above if the officer is satisfied that taking the sample is necessary to assist in the prevention or detection of crime.

(3C) A non-intimate sample may also be taken from a person without the appropriate consent if he is a person to whom section 2 of the Criminal Evidence (Amendment) Act 1997 applies (persons detained following acquittal on grounds of insanity or finding of unfitness to plead).

(3D) A non-intimate sample may also be taken from a person without the appropriate consent if the person is subject to a control order.

(3E) Subject to this section, a non-intimate sample may be taken without the appropriate consent from a person if—
  (a) under the law in force in a country or territory outside England and Wales the person has been convicted of an offence under that law (whether before or after the coming into force of this subsection and whether or not he has been punished for it);
  (b) the act constituting the offence would constitute a qualifying offence if done in England and Wales (whether or not it constituted such an offence when the person was convicted); and
  (c) either of the conditions mentioned in subsection (3F) below is met.

(3F) The conditions referred to in subsection (3E)(c) above are—
  (a) the person has not had a non-intimate sample taken from him on a previous occasion under subsection (3E) above;
  (b) he has had such a sample taken from him on a previous occasion under that subsection but—
    (i)   the sample was not suitable for the same means of analysis, or
    (ii) it proved insufficient.

(3G) A non-intimate sample may only be taken as specified in subsection (3E) above with the authorisation of an officer of at least the rank of inspector.

(3H) An officer may only give an authorisation under subsection (3G) above if the officer is satisfied that taking the sample is necessary to assist in the prevention or detection of crime.

(4) An officer may only give an authorisation under subsection (3) above if he has reasonable grounds—

    (a) for suspecting the involvement of the person from whom the sample is to be taken in a recordable offence; and

    (b) for believing that the sample will tend to confirm or disprove his involvement.

(5) An officer may give an authorisation under subsection (3) above orally or in writing but, if he gives it orally, he shall confirm it in writing as soon as is practicable.

(5A) An officer shall not give an authorisation under subsection (3) above for the taking from any person of a non-intimate sample consisting of a skin impression if—

    (a) a skin impression of the same part of the body has already been taken from that person in the course of the investigation of the offence; and

    (b) the impression previously taken is not one that has proved insufficient.

(6) Where a non-intimate sample is taken from a person without the appropriate consent by virtue of any power conferred by this section—

    (a) before the sample is taken, an officer shall inform him of—

        (i) the reason for taking the sample;

        (ii) the power by virtue of which it is taken; and

        (iii) in a case where the authorisation of an officer is required for the exercise of the power, the fact that the authorisation has been given; and

    (b) those matters shall be recorded as soon as practicable after the sample is taken.

(7) The reason referred to in subsection (6)(a)(i) above must include, except in a case where the non-intimate sample is taken under subsection (3B) or (3E) above, a statement of the nature of the offence in which it is suspected that the person has been involved.

(8B) If a non-intimate sample is taken from a person at a police station, or, in a subsection (3D) case, a constable, whether with or without the appropriate consent—

    (a) before the sample is taken, an officer shall inform him that it may be the subject of a speculative search; and

    (b) the fact that the person has been informed of this possibility shall be recorded as soon as practicable after the sample has been taken.

(9) If a non-intimate sample is taken from a person detained at a police station, the matters required to be recorded by subsection (6) or (8B) above shall be recorded in his custody record.

[(9ZA) The power to take a non-intimate sample from a person without the appropriate consent shall be exercisable by any constable.]

(9A) Subsection (3B) above shall not apply to

    (a) any person convicted before 10 April 1995 unless he is a person to whom section 1 of the Criminal Evidence (Amendment) Act 1997 applies (persons imprisoned or detained by virtue of pre-existing conviction for sexual offence etc.); or

    (b) a person given a caution after 10 April 1995.

[(10) Nothing in this section applies to a person arrested or detained under the terrorism provisions.]

(11) Nothing in this section applies to a person arrested under an extradition arrest power.

63A Fingerprints and samples: supplementary provisions

(1) Where a person has been arrested on suspicion of being involved in a recordable offence or has been charged with such an offence or has been informed that he will be reported for such an offence, fingerprints, impressions of footwear or samples or the information derived from samples taken under any power conferred by this Part of this Act from the person may be checked against—

    (a) other fingerprints, impressions of footwear or samples to which the person seeking to check has access and which are held by or on behalf of any one or more relevant law-enforcement authorities or which are held in connection with or as a result of an investigation of an offence;

(b) information derived from other samples if the information is contained in records to which the person seeking to check has access and which are held as mentioned in paragraph (a) above.

(1ZA) Fingerprints taken by virtue of section 61(6A) above may be checked against other fingerprints to which the person seeking to check has access and which are held by or on behalf of any one or more relevant law-enforcement authorities or which are held in connection with or as a result of an investigation of an offence.

(1A) In subsection (1) and (1ZA) above 'relevant law-enforcement authority' means—

(a) a police force;

(b) the Serious Organised Crime Agency;

(c) a public authority (not falling within paragraphs (a) to (c)) with functions in any part of the British Islands which consist of or include the investigation of crimes or the charging of offenders;

(e) any person with functions in any country or territory outside the United Kingdom which—

(i) correspond to those of a police force; or

(ii) otherwise consist of or include the investigation of conduct contrary to the law of that country or territory, or the apprehension of persons guilty of such conduct;

(f) any person with functions under any international agreement which consist of or include the investigation of conduct which is—

(i) unlawful under the law of one or more places,

(ii) prohibited by such an agreement, or

(iii) contrary to international law,

or the apprehension of persons guilty of such conduct.

(1B) The reference in subsection (1A) above to a police force is a reference to any of the following—

(a) any police force maintained under section 2 of the Police Act 1996 (police forces in England and Wales outside London);

(b) the metropolitan police force;

(c) the City of London police force;

(d)–(o) [applies to other forces].

(1C) Where—

(a) fingerprints, impressions of footwear or samples have been taken from any person in connection with the investigation of an offence but otherwise than in circumstances to which subsection (1) above applies, and

(b) that person has given his consent in writing to the use in a speculative search of the fingerprints, of the impressions of footwear or of the samples and of information derived from them,

the fingerprints or impressions of footwear or, as the case may be, those samples and that information may be checked against any of the fingerprints, impressions of footwear, samples or information mentioned in paragraph (a) or (b) of that subsection.

(1D) A consent given for the purposes of subsection (1C) above shall not be capable of being withdrawn.

(1E) Where fingerprints or samples have been taken from any person under section 61(6) or 63(3B) above (persons convicted etc), the fingerprints or samples, or information derived from the samples, may be checked against any of the fingerprints, samples or information mentioned in subsection (1)(a) or (b) above.

(1F) Where fingerprints or samples have been taken from any person under section 61(6D), 62(2A) or 63(3E) above (offences outside England and Wales etc), the fingerprints or samples, or information derived from the samples, may be checked against any of the fingerprints, samples or information mentioned in subsection (1)(a) or (b) above.

(2) Where a sample of hair other than pubic hair is to be taken the sample may be taken either by cutting hairs or by plucking hairs with their roots so long as no more are plucked than the person taking the sample reasonably considers to be necessary for a sufficient sample.

(3) Where any power to take a sample is exercisable in relation to a person the sample may be taken in a prison or other institution to which the Prison Act 1952 applies.

(3A) Where—

(a) the power to take a non-intimate sample under section 63(3B) above is exercisable in relation to any person who is detained under Part III of the Mental Health Act 1983 in pursuance of—

(i) a hospital order or interim hospital order made following his conviction for the recordable offence in question, or

(ii) a transfer direction given at a time when he was detained in pursuance of any sentence or order imposed following that conviction, or

(b) the power to take a non-intimate sample under section 63(3C) above is exercisable in relation to any person,

the sample may be taken in the hospital in which he is detained under that Part of that Act.

Expressions used in this subsection and in the Mental Health Act 1983 have the same meaning as in that Act.

(3B) Where the power to take a non-intimate sample under section 63(3B) above is exercisable in relation to a person detained in pursuance of directions of the Secretary of State under section 92 of the Powers of Criminal Courts (Sentencing) Act 2000 the sample may be taken at the place where he is so detained.

(4) Schedule 2A (fingerprinting and samples: power to require attendance at police station) shall have effect.

63B   Testing for presence of Class A drugs

(1) A sample of urine or a non-intimate sample may be taken from a person in police detention for the purpose of ascertaining whether he has any specified Class A drug in his body if—

(a) either the arrest condition or the charge condition is met;

(b) both the age condition and the request condition are met; and

(c) the notification condition is met in relation to the arrest condition, the charge condition or the age condition (as the case may be).

(1A) The arrest condition is that the person concerned has been arrested for an offence but has not been charged with that offence and either—

(a) the offence is a trigger offence; or

(b) a police officer of at least the rank of inspector has reasonable grounds for suspecting that the misuse by that person of a specified Class A drug caused or contributed to the offence and has authorised the sample to be taken.

(2) The charge condition is either—

(a) that the person concerned has been charged with a trigger offence; or

(b) that the person concerned has been charged with an offence and a police officer of at least the rank of inspector, who has reasonable grounds for suspecting that the misuse by that person of any specified Class A drug caused or contributed to the offence, has authorised the sample to be taken.

(3) The age condition is—

(a) if the arrest condition is met, that the person concerned has attained the age of 18;

(b) if the charge condition is met, that he has attained the age of 14.

(4) The request condition is that a police officer has requested the person concerned to give the sample.

(4A) The notification condition is that—

(a) the relevant chief officer has been notified by the Secretary of State that appropriate arrangements have been made for the police area as a whole, or for the particular police station, in which the person is in police detention, and

(b) the notice has not been withdrawn.

(4B) For the purposes of subsection (4A) above, appropriate arrangements are arrangements for the taking of samples under this section from whichever of the following is specified in the notification—

(a) persons in respect of whom the arrest condition is met;

(b) persons in respect of whom the charge condition is met;

(c) persons who have not attained the age of 18.

(5) Before requesting the person concerned to give a sample, an officer must—

(a) warn him that if, when so requested, he fails without good cause to do so he may be liable to prosecution, and

(b) in a case within subsection (1A)(b) or (2)(b) above, inform him of the giving of the authorisation and of the grounds in question.

(5A) In the case of a person who has not attained the age of 17—

(a) the making of the request under subsection (4) above;

(b) the giving of the warning and (where applicable) the information under subsection (5) above; and

(c) the taking of the sample,

may not take place except in the presence of an appropriate adult.

(5B) If a sample is taken under this section from a person in respect of whom the arrest condition is met no other sample may be taken from him under this section during the same continuous period of detention but—

(a) if the charge condition is also met in respect of him at any time during that period, the sample must be treated as a sample taken by virtue of the fact that the charge condition is met;

(b) the fact that the sample is to be so treated must be recorded in the person's custody record.

(5C) Despite subsection (1)(a) above, a sample may be taken from a person under this section if—

(a) he was arrested for an offence (the first offence),

(b) the arrest condition is met but the charge condition is not met,

(c) before a sample is taken by virtue of subsection (1) above he would (but for his arrest as mentioned in paragraph (d) below) be required to be released from police detention,

(d) he continues to be in police detention by virtue of his having been arrested for an offence not falling within subsection (1A) above, and

(e) the sample is taken before the end of the period of 24 hours starting with the time when his detention by virtue of his arrest for the first offence began.

(5D) A sample must not be taken from a person under this section if he is detained in a police station unless he has been brought before the custody officer.

(6) A sample may be taken under this section only by a person prescribed by regulations made by the Secretary of State by statutory instrument.

No regulations shall be made under this subsection unless a draft has been laid before, and approved by resolution of, each House of Parliament.

(6A) The Secretary of State may by order made by statutory instrument amend—

(a) paragraph (a) of subsection (3) above, by substituting for the age for the time being specified a different age specified in the order, or different ages so specified for different police areas so specified;

(b) paragraph (b) of that subsection, by substituting for the age for the time being specified a different age specified in the order.

(6B) A statutory instrument containing an order under subsection (6A) above shall not be made unless a draft of the instrument has been laid before, and approved by a resolution of, each House of Parliament.

(7) Information obtained from a sample taken under this section may be disclosed—

(a) for the purpose of informing any decision about granting bail in criminal proceedings (within the meaning of the Bail Act 1976) to the person concerned;

(aa) for the purpose of informing any decision about the giving of a conditional caution under Part 3 of the Criminal Justice Act 2003 or a youth conditional caution under Chapter 1 of Part 4 of the Crime and Disorder Act 1998 to the person concerned;

(b) where the person concerned is in police detention or is remanded in or committed to custody by an order of a court or has been granted such bail, for the purpose of informing any decision about his supervision;

(c) where the person concerned is convicted of an offence, for the purpose of informing any decision about the appropriate sentence to be passed by a court and any decision about his supervision or release;

(ca) for the purpose of an assessment which the person concerned is required to attend by virtue of section 9(2) or 10(2) of the Drugs Act 2005;

(cb) for the purpose of proceedings against the person concerned for an offence under section 12(3) or 14(3) of that Act;

(d) for the purpose of ensuring that appropriate advice and treatment is made available to the person concerned.

(8) A person who fails without good cause to give any sample which may be taken from him under this section shall be guilty of an offence.

(10) In this section—

"appropriate adult", in relation to a person who has not attained the age of 17, means—

(a) his parent or guardian or, if he is in the care of a local authority or voluntary organisation, a person representing that authority or organisation; or

(b) a social worker of a local authority; or

(c) if no person falling within paragraph (a) or (b) is available, any responsible person aged 18 or over who is not a police officer or a person employed by the police;

"relevant chief officer" means—

(a) in relation to a police area, the chief officer of police of the police force for that police area; or

(b) in relation to a police station, the chief officer of police of the police force for the police area in which the police station is situated.

63C   Testing for presence of Class A drugs: supplementary

(1) A person guilty of an offence under section 63B above shall be liable on summary conviction to imprisonment for a term not exceeding three months, or to a fine not exceeding level 4 on the standard scale, or to both.

(2) A police officer may give an authorisation under section 63B above orally or in writing but, if he gives it orally, he shall confirm it in writing as soon as is practicable.

(3) If a sample is taken under section 63B above by virtue of an authorisation, the authorisation and the grounds for the suspicion shall be recorded as soon as is practicable after the sample is taken.

(4) If the sample is taken from a person detained at a police station, the matters required to be recorded by subsection (3) above shall be recorded in his custody record.

(5) Subsections (11) and (12) of section 62 above apply for the purposes of section 63B above as they do for the purposes of that section; and section 63B above does not prejudice the generality of sections 62 and 63 above.

(6) In section 63B above—

'Class A drug' and 'misuse' have the same meanings as in the Misuse of Drugs Act 1971;

'specified' (in relation to a Class A drug) and 'trigger offence' have the same meanings as in Part III of the Criminal Justice and Court Services Act 2000.

64 Destruction of fingerprints and samples.

(1A) Where—

   (a) fingerprints, impressions of footwear or samples are taken from a person in connection with the investigation of an offence, and

   (b) subsection (3) below does not require them to be destroyed, the fingerprints impressions of footwear or samples may be retained after they have fulfilled the purposes for which they were taken but shall not be used by any person except for purposes related to the prevention or detection of crime, the investigation of an offence, the conduct of a prosecution or the identification of a deceased person or of the person from whom a body part came.

(1B) In subsection (1A) above—

   (a) the reference to using a fingerprint or an impression of footwear includes a reference to allowing any check to be made against it under section 63A(1) or (1C) above and to disclosing it to any person;

   (b) the reference to using a sample includes a reference to allowing any check to be made under section 63A(1) or (1C) above against it or against information derived from it and to disclosing it or any such information to any person;

   (c) the reference to crime includes a reference to any conduct which–

      (i) constitutes one or more criminal offences (whether under the law of a part of the United Kingdom or of a country or territory outside the United Kingdom); or

      (ii) is, or corresponds to, any conduct which, if it all took place in any one part of the United Kingdom, would constitute one or more criminal offences; and

   (d) the references to an investigation and to a prosecution include references, respectively, to any investigation outside the United Kingdom of any crime or suspected crime and to a prosecution brought in respect of any crime in a country or territory outside the United Kingdom.

(1BA) Fingerprints taken from a person by virtue of section 61(6A) above must be destroyed as soon as they have fulfilled the purpose for which they were taken.

(3) If—

   (a) fingerprints, impressions of footwear or samples are taken from a person in connection with the investigation of an offence; and

   (b) that person is not suspected of having committed the offence, they must, except as provided in the following provisions of this section, be destroyed as soon as they have fulfilled the purpose for which they were taken.

(3AA) Samples, fingerprints and impressions of footwear are not required to be destroyed under subsection (3) above if—

   (a) they were taken for the purposes of the investigation of an offence of which a person has been convicted; and

   (b) a sample, fingerprint, (or as the case may be) an impression of footwear was also taken from the convicted person for the purposes of that investigation.

(3AB) Subject to subsection (3AC) below, where a person is entitled under subsection (1BA) or (3) above to the destruction of any fingerprint, impression of footwear or sample taken from him (or would be but for subsection (3AA) above), neither the fingerprint, nor the impression of footwear, nor the sample, nor any information derived from the sample, shall be used–

   (a) in evidence against the person who is or would be entitled to the destruction of that fingerprint, impression of footwear or sample; or

   (b) for the purposes of the investigation of any offence;

   (c) and subsection (1B) above applies for the purposes of this subsection as it applies for the purposes of subsection (1A) above.

(3AC) Where a person from whom a fingerprint, impression of footwear or sample has been taken consents in writing to its retention–

(a) that fingerprint impression of footwear or sample need not be destroyed under subsection (3) above;

(b) subsection (3AB) above shall not restrict the use that may be made of the fingerprint impression of footwear or sample or, in the case of a sample, of any information derived from it; and

(c) that consent shall be treated as comprising a consent for the purposes of section 63A(1C) above. This subsection does not apply to fingerprints taken from a person by virtue of section 61(6A) above,

and a consent given for the purpose of this subsection shall not be capable of being withdrawn.

(3AD) For the purposes of subsection (3AC) above it shall be immaterial whether the consent is given at, before or after the time when the entitlement to the destruction of the fingerprint impression of footwear or sample arises.

(4) ...

(5) If fingerprints or impressions of footwear are destroyed—

(a) any copies of the fingerprints or impressions of footwear shall also be destroyed; and

(b) any chief officer of police controlling access to computer data relating to the fingerprints or impressions of footwear shall make access to the data impossible, as soon as it is practicable to do so.

(6) A person who asks to be allowed to witness the destruction of his fingerprints or impressions of footwear or copies of them shall have a right to witness it.

(6A) If—

(a) subsection (5)(b) above falls to be complied with; and

(b) the person to whose fingerprints or impressions of footwear the data relate asks for a certificate that it has been complied with, such a certificate shall be issued to him, not later than the end of the period of three months beginning with the day on which he asks for it, by the responsible chief officer of police or a person authorised by him or on his behalf for the purposes of this section.

(6B) In this section—

"the responsible chief officer of police" means the chief officer of police in whose police area the computer data were put on to the computer.

(7) Nothing in this section—

(a) affects any power conferred by paragraph 18(2) of Schedule 2 to the Immigration Act 1971 or section 20 of the Immigration and Asylum Act 1999 (c. 33) (disclosure of police information to the Secretary of State for use for immigration purposes); or

(b) applies to a person arrested or detained under the terrorism provisions.

64ZA Destruction of samples

(1) A DNA sample to which section 64 applies must be destroyed—

(a) as soon as a DNA profile has been derived from the sample, or

(b) if sooner, before the end of the period of 6 months beginning with the date on which the sample was taken.

(2) Any other sample to which section 64 applies must be destroyed before the end of the period of 6 months beginning with the date on which it was taken.

64ZB Destruction of data given voluntarily

(1) This section applies to—

(a) fingerprints or impressions of footwear taken in connection with the investigation of an offence with the consent of the person from whom they were taken, and

(b) a DNA profile derived from a DNA sample taken in connection with the investigation of an offence with the consent of the person from whom the sample was taken.

(2) Material to which this section applies must be destroyed as soon as it has fulfilled the purpose for which it was taken or derived, unless it is—

    (a) material relating to a person who is convicted of the offence,

    (b) material relating to a person who has previously been convicted of a recordable offence, other than a person who has only one exempt conviction,

    (c) material in relation to which any of sections 64ZC to 64ZH applies, or

    (d) material which is not required to be destroyed by virtue of consent given under section 64ZL.

(3) If material to which this section applies leads to the person to whom the material relates being arrested for or charged with an offence other than the offence under investigation—

    (a) the material is not required to be destroyed by virtue of this section, and

    (b) sections 64ZD to 64ZH have effect in relation to the material as if the material was taken (or, in the case of a DNA profile, was derived from material taken) in connection with the investigation of the offence in respect of which the person is arrested or charged.

64ZC   Destruction of data relating to a person subject to a control order

(1) This section applies to material falling within subsection (2) relating to a person who—

    (a) has no previous convictions or only one exempt conviction, and

    (b) is subject to a control order.

(2) Material falls within this subsection if it is—

    (a) fingerprints taken from the person, or

    (b) a DNA profile derived from a DNA sample taken from the person.

(3) The material must be destroyed before the end of the period of 2 years beginning with the date on which the person ceases to be subject to a control order.

(4) This section ceases to have effect in relation to the material if the person is convicted—

    (a) in England and Wales or Northern Ireland of a recordable offence, or

    (b) in Scotland of an offence which is punishable by imprisonment,

before the material is required to be destroyed by virtue of this section.

(5) For the purposes of subsection (1)—

    (a) a person has no previous convictions if the person has not previously been convicted—

        (i) in England and Wales or Northern Ireland of a recordable offence, or

        (ii) in Scotland of an offence which is punishable by imprisonment, and

    (b) if the person has been previously convicted of a recordable offence in England and Wales or Northern Ireland, the conviction is exempt if it is in respect of a recordable offence other than a qualifying offence, committed when the person is aged under 18.

(6) For the purposes of that subsection—

    (a) a person is to be treated as having been convicted of an offence if—

        (i) he has been given a caution in England and Wales or Northern Ireland in respect of the offence which, at the time of the caution, he has admitted, or

        (ii) he has been warned or reprimanded under section 65 of the Crime and Disorder Act 1998 for the offence, and

    (b) if a person is convicted of more than one offence arising out of a single course of action, those convictions are to be treated as a single conviction.

(7) [*Applies to Northern Ireland*]

64ZD   Destruction of data relating to persons not convicted

(1) This section applies to material falling within subsection (2) relating to a person who—

    (a) has no previous convictions or only one exempt conviction,

    (b) is arrested for or charged with a recordable offence, and

    (c) is aged 18 or over at the time of the alleged offence.

(2) Material falls within this subsection if it is—

    (a) fingerprints or impressions of footwear taken from the person in connection with the investigation of the offence, or

    (b) a DNA profile derived from a DNA sample so taken.

(3) The material must be destroyed—

(a) in the case of fingerprints or impressions of footwear, before the end of the period of 6 years beginning with the date on which the fingerprints or impressions were taken,

(b) in the case of a DNA profile, before the end of the period of 6 years beginning with the date on which the DNA sample from which the profile was derived was taken (or, if the profile was derived from more than one DNA sample, the date on which the first of those samples was taken).

(4) But if, before the material is required to be destroyed by virtue of this section, the person is arrested for or charged with a recordable offence the material may be further retained until the end of the period of 6 years beginning with the date of the arrest or charge.

(5) This section ceases to have effect in relation to the material if the person is convicted of a recordable offence before the material is required to be destroyed by virtue of this section.

64ZE Destruction of data relating to persons under 18 not convicted: recordable offences other than qualifying offences

(1) This section applies to material falling within subsection (2) relating to a person who—

(a) has no previous convictions or only one exempt conviction,

(b) is arrested for or charged with a recordable offence other than a qualifying offence, and

(c) is aged under 18 at the time of the alleged offence.

(2) Material falls within this subsection if it is—

(a) fingerprints or impressions of footwear taken from the person in connection with the investigation of the offence, or

(b) a DNA profile derived from a DNA sample so taken.

(3) The material must be destroyed—

(a) in the case of fingerprints or impressions of footwear, before the end of the period of 3 years beginning with the date on which the fingerprints or impressions were taken,

(b) in the case of a DNA profile, before the end of the period of 3 years beginning with the date on which the DNA sample from which the profile was derived was taken (or, if the profile was derived from more than one DNA sample, the date on which the first of those samples was taken).

(4) But if, before the material is required to be destroyed by virtue of this section, the person is arrested for or charged with a recordable offence—

(a) where the person is aged 18 or over at the time of the alleged offence, the material may be further retained until the end of the period of 6 years beginning with the date of the arrest or charge,

(b) where—

(i)   the alleged offence is not a qualifying offence, and

(ii) the person is aged under 18 at the time of the alleged offence,

the material may be further retained until the end of the period of 3 years beginning with the date of the arrest or charge,

(c) where—

(i)   the alleged offence is a qualifying offence, and

(ii) the person is aged under 16 at the time of the alleged offence,

the material may be further retained until the end of the period of 3 years beginning with the date of the arrest or charge,

(d) where—

(i)   the alleged offence is a qualifying offence, and

(ii) the person is aged 16 or 17 at the time of the alleged offence,

the material may be further retained until the end of the period of 6 years beginning with the date of the arrest or charge,

(e) where—

(i)   the person is convicted of the offence,

(ii) the offence is not a qualifying offence,

          (iii) the person is aged under 18 at the time of the offence, and

          (iv) the person has no previous convictions,

the material may be further retained until the end of the period of 5 years beginning with the date of the arrest or charge.

(5) This section ceases to have effect in relation to the material if, before the material is required to be destroyed by virtue of this section, the person—

    (a) is convicted of a recordable offence and is aged 18 or over at the time of the offence,

    (b) is convicted of a qualifying offence, or

    (c) having a previous exempt conviction, is convicted of a recordable offence.

64ZF Destruction of data relating to persons under 16 not convicted: qualifying offences

(1) This section applies to material falling within subsection (2) relating to a person who—

    (a) has no previous convictions or only one exempt conviction,

    (b) is arrested for or charged with a qualifying offence, and

    (c) is aged under 16 at the time of the alleged offence.

(2) Material falls within this subsection if it is—

    (a) fingerprints or impressions of footwear taken from the person in connection with the investigation of the offence, or

    (b) a DNA profile derived from a DNA sample so taken.

(3) The material must be destroyed—

    (a) in the case of fingerprints or impressions of footwear, before the end of the period of 3 years beginning with the date on which the fingerprints or impressions were taken,

    (b) in the case of a DNA profile, before the end of the period of 3 years beginning with the date on which the DNA sample from which the profile was derived was taken (or, if the profile was derived from more than one DNA sample, the date on which the first of those samples was taken).

(4) But if, before the material is required to be destroyed by virtue of this section, the person is arrested for or charged with a recordable offence—

    (a) where the person is aged 18 or over at the time of the alleged offence, the material may be further retained until the end of the period of 6 years beginning with the date of the arrest or charge,

    (b) where—

          (i)   the alleged offence is not a qualifying offence, and

          (ii) the person is aged under 18 at the time of the alleged offence,

the material may be further retained until the end of the period of 3 years beginning with the date of the arrest or charge,

    (c) where—

          (i)   the alleged offence is a qualifying offence, and

          (ii) the person is aged under 16 at the time of the alleged offence,

the material may be further retained until the end of the period of 3 years beginning with the date of the arrest or charge,

    (d) where—

          (i)   the alleged offence is a qualifying offence, and

          (ii) the person is aged 16 or 17 at the time of the alleged offence,

the material may be further retained until the end of the period of 6 years beginning with the date of the arrest or charge,

    (e) where—

          (i)   the person is convicted of the offence,

          (ii) the offence is not a qualifying offence,

          (iii) the person is aged under 18 at the time of the offence, and

          (iv) the person has no previous convictions,

the material may be further retained until the end of the period of 5 years beginning with the date of the arrest or charge.

(5) This section ceases to have effect in relation to the material if, before the material is required to be destroyed by virtue of this section, the person—

    (a) is convicted of a recordable offence and is aged 18 or over at the time of the offence,

    (b) is convicted of a qualifying offence, or

    (c) having a previous exempt conviction, is convicted of a recordable offence.

64ZG Destruction of data relating to persons aged 16 or 17 not convicted: qualifying offences

(1) This section applies to material falling within subsection (2) relating to a person who—

    (a) has no previous convictions or only one exempt conviction,

    (b) is arrested for or charged with a qualifying offence, and

    (c) is aged 16 or 17 at the time of the alleged offence.

(2) Material falls within this subsection if it is—

    (a) fingerprints or impressions of footwear taken from the person in connection with the investigation of the offence, or

    (b) a DNA profile derived from a DNA sample so taken.

(3) The material must be destroyed—

    (a) in the case of fingerprints or impressions of footwear, before the end of the period of 6 years beginning with the date on which the fingerprints or impressions were taken,

    (b) in the case of a DNA profile, before the end of the period of 6 years beginning with the date on which the DNA sample from which the profile was derived was taken (or, if the profile was derived from more than one DNA sample, the date on which the first of those samples was taken).

(4) But if, before the material is required to be destroyed by virtue of this section, the person is arrested for or charged with a recordable offence—

    (a) where the person is aged 18 or over at the time of the alleged offence, the material may be further retained until the end of the period of 6 years beginning with the date of the arrest or charge,

    (b) where—

        (i) the alleged offence is not a qualifying offence, and

        (ii) the person is aged under 18 at the time of the alleged offence,

    the material may be further retained until the end of the period of 3 years beginning with the date of the arrest or charge,

    (c) where—

        (i) the alleged offence is a qualifying offence, and

        (ii) the person is aged 16 or 17 at the time of the alleged offence,

    the material may be further retained until the end of the period of 6 years beginning with the date of the arrest or charge,

    (d) where—

        (i) the person is convicted of the offence,

        (ii) the offence is not a qualifying offence,

        (iii) the person is aged under 18 at the time of the offence, and

        (iv) the person has no previous convictions,

    the material may be further retained until the end of the period of 5 years beginning with the date of the arrest or charge.

(5) This section ceases to have effect in relation to the material if, before the material is required to be destroyed by virtue of this section, the person—

    (a) is convicted of a recordable offence and is aged 18 or over at the time of the offence,

    (b) is convicted of a qualifying offence, or

    (c) having a previous exempt conviction, is convicted of a recordable offence.

64ZH   Destruction of data relating to persons under 18 convicted of a recordable offence other than a qualifying offence

(1) This section applies to material falling within subsection (2) relating to a person who—

    (a) has no previous convictions,

    (b) is convicted of a recordable offence other than a qualifying offence, and

    (c) is aged under 18 at the time of the offence.

(2) Material falls within this subsection if it is—

    (a) fingerprints or impressions of footwear taken from the person in connection with the investigation of the offence, or

    (b) a DNA profile derived from a DNA sample so taken.

(3) The material must be destroyed—

    (a) in the case of fingerprints or impressions of footwear, before the end of the period of 5 years beginning with the date on which the fingerprints or impressions were taken,

    (b) in the case of a DNA profile, before the end of the period of 5 years beginning with the date on which the DNA sample from which the profile was derived was taken (or, if the profile was derived from more than one DNA sample, the date on which the first of those samples was taken).

(4) But if, before the material is required to be destroyed by virtue of this section, the person is arrested for or charged with a recordable offence—

    (a) where the person is aged 18 or over at the time of the alleged offence, the material may be further retained until the end of the period of 6 years beginning with the date of the arrest or charge,

    (b) where—

        (i)   the alleged offence is not a qualifying offence, and

        (ii) the person is aged under 18 at the time of the alleged offence,

    the material may be further retained until the end of the period of 3 years beginning with the date of the arrest or charge,

    (c) where—

        (i)   the alleged offence is a qualifying offence, and

        (ii) the person is aged under 16 at the time of the alleged offence,

    the material may be further retained until the end of the period of 3 years beginning with the date of the arrest or charge,

    (d) where—

        (i)   the alleged offence is a qualifying offence, and

        (ii) the person is aged 16 or 17 at the time of the alleged offence,

    the material may be further retained until the end of the period of 6 years beginning with the date of the arrest or charge.

(5) This section ceases to have effect in relation to the material if the person is convicted of a further recordable offence before the material is required to be destroyed by virtue of this section.

64ZI   Sections 64ZB to 64ZH: supplementary provision

(1) Any reference in section 64ZB or sections 64ZD to 64ZH to a person being charged with an offence includes a reference to a person being informed that he will be reported for an offence.

(2) For the purposes of those sections—

    (a) a person has no previous convictions if the person has not previously been convicted of a recordable offence, and

    (b) if the person has been previously convicted of a recordable offence, the conviction is exempt if it is in respect of a recordable offence other than a qualifying offence, committed when the person is aged under 18.

(3) For the purposes of those sections, a person is to be treated as having been convicted of an offence if—

(a) he has been given a caution in respect of the offence which, at the time of the caution, he has admitted, or

(b) he has been warned or reprimanded under section 65 of the Crime and Disorder Act 1998 for the offence.

(4) If a person is convicted of more than one offence arising out of a single course of action, those convictions are to be treated as a single conviction for the purpose of any provision of those sections relating to an exempt, first or subsequent conviction.

(5) Subject to the completion of any speculative search that the responsible chief officer of police considers necessary or desirable, material falling within any of sections 64ZD to 64ZH must be destroyed immediately if it appears to the chief officer that—

(a) the arrest was unlawful,

(b) the taking of the fingerprints, impressions of footwear or DNA sample concerned was unlawful,

(c) the arrest was based on mistaken identity, or

(d) other circumstances relating to the arrest or the alleged offence mean that it is appropriate to destroy the material.

(6) "Responsible chief officer of police" means the chief officer of police for the police area—

(a) in which the samples, fingerprints or impressions of footwear were taken, or

(b) in the case of a DNA profile, in which the sample from which the DNA profile was derived was taken.

64ZJ Destruction of fingerprints taken under section 61(6A)

Fingerprints taken from a person by virtue of section 61(6A) (taking fingerprints for the purposes of identification) must be destroyed as soon as they have fulfilled the purpose for which they were taken.

64ZK Retention for purposes of national security

(1) Subsection (2) applies if the responsible chief officer of police determines that it is necessary for—

(a) a DNA profile to which section 64 applies, or

(b) fingerprints to which section 64 applies, other than fingerprints taken under section 61(6A), to be retained for the purposes of national security.

(2) Where this subsection applies—

(a) the material is not required to be destroyed in accordance with sections 64ZB to 64ZH, and

(b) section 64ZN(2) does not apply to the material, for as long as the determination has effect.

(3) A determination under subsection (1) has effect for a maximum of 2 years beginning with the date on which the material would otherwise be required to be destroyed, but a determination may be renewed.

(4) "Responsible chief officer of police" means the chief officer of police for the police area—

(a) in which the fingerprints were taken, or

(b) in the case of a DNA profile, in which the sample from which the DNA profile was derived was taken.

64ZL Retention with consent

(1) If a person consents in writing to the retention of fingerprints, impressions of footwear or a DNA profile to which section 64 applies, other than fingerprints taken under section 61(6A)—

(a) the material is not required to be destroyed in accordance with sections 64ZB to 64ZH, and

(b) section 64ZN(2) does not apply to the material.

(2) It is immaterial for the purposes of subsection (1) whether the consent is given at, before or after the time when the entitlement to the destruction of the material arises.

(3) Consent given under this section can be withdrawn at any time.

64ZM   Destruction of copies, and notification of destruction

(1) If fingerprints or impressions of footwear are required to be destroyed by virtue of any of sections 64ZB to 64ZJ, any copies of the fingerprints or impressions of footwear must also be destroyed.

(2) If a DNA profile is required to be destroyed by virtue of any of those sections, no copy may be kept except in a form which does not include information which identifies the person to whom the DNA profile relates.

(3) If a person makes a request to the responsible chief officer of police to be notified when anything relating to the person is destroyed under any of sections 64ZA to 64ZJ, the responsible chief officer of police or a person authorised by the chief officer or on the chief officer's behalf must within three months of the request issue the person with a certificate recording the destruction.

(4) "Responsible chief officer of police" means the chief officer of police for the police area—

  (a) in which the samples, fingerprints or impressions of footwear which have been destroyed were taken, or

  (b) in the case of a DNA profile which has been destroyed, in which the samples from which the DNA profile was derived were taken.

64ZN   Use of retained material

(1) Any material to which section 64 applies which is retained after it has fulfilled the purpose for which it was taken or derived must not be used other than—

  (a) in the interests of national security,

  (b) for the purposes of a terrorist investigation,

  (c) for purposes related to the prevention or detection of crime, the investigation of an offence or the conduct of a prosecution, or

  (d) for purposes related to the identification of a deceased person or of the person to whom the material relates.

(2) Material which is required to be destroyed by virtue of any of sections 64ZA to 64ZJ, or of section 64ZM, must not at any time after it is required to be destroyed be used—

  (a) in evidence against the person to whom the material relates, or

  (b) for the purposes of the investigation of any offence.

(3) In this section—

  (a) the reference to using material includes a reference to allowing any check to be made against it and to disclosing it to any person,

  (b) the reference to crime includes a reference to any conduct which—

    (i) constitutes one or more criminal offences (whether under the law of a part of the United Kingdom or of a country or territory outside the United Kingdom), or

    (ii) is, or corresponds to, any conduct which, if it all took place in any one part of the United Kingdom, would constitute one or more criminal offences, and

  (c) the references to an investigation and to a prosecution include references, respectively, to any investigation outside the United Kingdom of any crime or suspected crime and to a prosecution brought in respect of any crime in a country or territory outside the United Kingdom.

64A   Photographing of suspects etc.

(1) A person who is detained at a police station may be photographed—

  (a) with the appropriate consent; or

  (b) if the appropriate consent is withheld or it is not practicable to obtain it, without it.

(1A) A person falling within subsection (1B) below may, on the occasion of the relevant event referred to in subsection (1B), be photographed elsewhere than at a police station—

  (a) with the appropriate consent; or

  (b) if the appropriate consent is withheld or it is not practicable to obtain it, without it.

(1B) A person falls within this subsection if he has been—
- (a) arrested by a constable for an offence;
- (b) taken into custody by a constable after being arrested for an offence by a person other than a constable;
- (c) made subject to a requirement to wait with a community support officer under paragraph 2(3) or (3B) of Schedule 4 to the Police Reform Act 2002 ('the 2002 Act');
- (ca) given a direction by a constable under section 27 of the Violent Crime Reduction Act 2006;
- (d) given a penalty notice by a constable in uniform under Chapter 1 of Part 1 of the Criminal Justice and Police Act 2001, a penalty notice by a constable under section 444A of the Education Act 1996, or a fixed penalty notice by a constable in uniform under section 54 of the Road Traffic Offenders Act 1988;
- (e) given a notice in relation to a relevant fixed penalty offence (within the meaning of paragraph 1 of Schedule 4 to the 2002 Act) by a community support officer by virtue of a designation applying that paragraph to him;
- (f) given a notice in relation to a relevant fixed penalty offence (within the meaning of paragraph 1 of Schedule 5 to the 2002 Act) by an accredited person by virtue of accreditation specifying that that paragraph applies to him; or
- (g) given a notice in relation to a relevant fixed penalty offence (within the meaning of Schedule 5A to the 2002 Act) by an accredited inspector by virtue of accreditation specifying that paragraph 1 of Schedule 5A to the 2002 Act applies to him.

(2) A person proposing to take a photograph of any person under this section—
- (a) may, for the purpose of doing so, require the removal of any item or substance worn on or over the whole or any part of the head or face of the person to be photographed; and
- (b) if the requirement is not complied with, may remove the item or substance himself.

(3) Where a photograph may be taken under this section, the only persons entitled to take the photograph are constables.

(4) A photograph taken under this section—
- (a) may be used by, or disclosed to, any person for any purpose related to the prevention or detection of crime, the investigation of an offence or the conduct of a prosecution or to the enforcement of a sentence; and
- (b) after being so used or disclosed, may be retained but may not be used or disclosed except for a purpose so related.

(5) In subsection (4)—
- (a) the reference to crime includes a reference to any conduct which—
  - (i) constitutes one or more criminal offences (whether under the law of a part of the United Kingdom or of a country or territory outside the United Kingdom); or
  - (ii) is, or corresponds to, any conduct which, if it all took place in any one part of the United Kingdom, would constitute one or more criminal offences;

  and
- (b) the references to an investigation and to a prosecution include references, respectively, to any investigation outside the United Kingdom of any crime or suspected crime and to a prosecution brought in respect of any crime in a country or territory outside the United Kingdom; and
- (c) "sentence" includes any order made by a court in England and Wales when dealing with an offender in respect of his offence.

(6) References in this section to taking a photograph include references to using any process by means of which a visual image may be produced; and references to photographing a person shall be construed accordingly.

(6A) In this section, a 'photograph' includes a moving image, and corresponding expressions shall be construed accordingly.

(7) Nothing in this section applies to a person arrested under an extradition arrest power.

65   Part V—supplementary

(1) In this Part of this Act—

'analysis', in relation to a skin impression, includes comparison and matching;

"appropriate consent" means—

(a) in relation to a person who has attained the age of 17 years, the consent of that person;

(b) in relation to a person who has not attained that age but has attained the age of 14 years, the consent of that person and his parent or guardian; and

(c) in relation to a person who has not attained the age of 14 years, the consent of his parent or guardian;

'extradition arrest power' means any of the following—

(a) a Part 1 warrant (within the meaning given by the Extradition Act 2003) in respect of which a certificate under section 2 of that Act has been issued;

(b) section 5 of that Act;

(c) a warrant issued under section 71 of that Act;

(d) a provisional warrant (within the meaning given by that Act);

'fingerprints', in relation to any person, means a record (in any form and produced by any method) of the skin pattern and other physical characteristics or features of—

(a) any of that person's fingers; or

(b) either of his palms;

'intimate sample' means

(a) a sample of blood, semen or any other tissue fluid, urine or pubic hair;

(b) a dental impression;

(c) a swab taken from any part of a person's genitals (including pubic hair) or from a person's body orifice other than the mouth;

'intimate search' means a search which consists of the physical examination of a person's body orifices other than the mouth;

'non-intimate sample' means—

(a) a sample of hair other than pubic hair;

(b) a sample taken from a nail or from under a nail;

(c) a swab taken from any part of a person's body other than a part from which a swab taken would be an intimate sample;

(d) saliva;

(e) a skin impression;

"offence", in relation to any country or territory outside England and Wales, includes an act punishable under the law of that country or territory, however it is described;

'registered dentist' has the same meaning as in the Dentists Act 1984;

'registered health care professional' means a person (other than a medical practitioner) who is—

(a) a registered nurse; or

(b) a registered member of a health care profession which is designated for the purposes of this paragraph by an order made by the Secretary of State;

'skin impression', in relation to any person, means any record (other than a fingerprint) which is a record (in any form and produced by any method) of the skin pattern and other physical characteristics or features of the whole or any part of his foot or of any other part of his body;

'speculative search', in relation to a person's fingerprints or samples, means such a check against other fingerprints or samples or against information derived from other samples as is referred to in section 63A(1) above;

'sufficient' and 'insufficient', in relation to a sample, (subject to subsection (2) below) means sufficient or insufficient (in point of quantity or quality) for the purpose of enabling information to be produced by the means of analysis used or to be used in relation to the sample.

'the terrorism provisions' means section 41 of the Terrorism Act 2000, and any provision of Schedule 7 to that Act conferring a power of detention; and 'terrorism' has the meaning given in section 1 of that Act.

(1A) A health care profession is any profession mentioned in section 60(2) of the Health Act 1999 other than the profession of practising medicine and the profession of nursing.

(1B) An order under subsection (1) shall be made by statutory instrument and shall be subject to annulment in pursuance of a resolution of either House of Parliament.

(2) References in this Part of this Act to a sample's proving insufficient include references to where, as a consequence of—

(a) the loss, destruction or contamination of the whole or any part of the sample,

(b) any damage to the whole or a part of the sample, or

(c) the use of the whole or a part of the sample for an analysis which produced no results or which produced results some or all of which must be regarded, in the circumstances, as unreliable,

the sample has become unavailable or insufficient for the purpose of enabling information, or information of a particular description, to be obtained by means of analysis of the sample.

(3) For the purposes of this Part, a person has in particular been convicted of an offence under the law of a country or territory outside England and Wales if—

(a) a court exercising jurisdiction under the law of that country or territory has made in respect of such an offence a finding equivalent to a finding that the person is not guilty by reason of insanity; or

(b) such a court has made in respect of such an offence a finding equivalent to a finding that the person is under a disability and did the act charged against him in respect of the offence.

65A Qualifying offence

(1) In this Part, "qualifying offence" means—

(a) an offence specified in subsection (2) below, or

(b) an ancillary offence relating to such an offence.

(2) The offences referred to in subsection (1)(a) above are—

(a) murder;

(b) manslaughter;

(c) false imprisonment;

(d) kidnapping;

(e) an offence under section 4, 16, 18, 20 to 24 or 47 of the Offences Against the Person Act 1861;

(f) an offence under section 2 or 3 of the Explosive Substances Act 1883;

(g) an offence under section 1 of the Children and Young Persons Act 1933;

(h) an offence under section 4(1) of the Criminal Law Act 1967 committed in relation to murder;

(i) an offence under sections 16 to 18 of the Firearms Act 1968;

(j) an offence under section 9 or 10 of the Theft Act 1968 or an offence under section 12A of that Act involving an accident which caused a person's death;

(k) an offence under section 1 of the Criminal Damage Act 1971 required to be charged as arson;

(l) an offence under section 1 of the Protection of Children Act 1978;

(m) an offence under section 1 of the Aviation Security Act 1982;

(n) an offence under section 2 of the Child Abduction Act 1984;

(o) an offence under section 9 of the Aviation and Maritime Security Act 1990;

(p) an offence under any of sections 1 to 19, 25, 26, 30 to 41, 47 to 50, 52, 53, 57 to 59, 61 to 67, 69 and 70 of the Sexual Offences Act 2003;

(q) an offence under section 5 of the Domestic Violence, Crime and Victims Act 2004;

(r) an offence for the time being listed in section 41(1) of the Counter-Terrorism Act 2008.

(3) The Secretary of State may by order made by statutory instrument amend subsection (2) above.

(4) A statutory instrument containing an order under subsection (3) above shall not be made unless a draft of the instrument has been laid before, and approved by resolution of, each House of Parliament.

(5) In subsection (1)(b) above 'ancillary offence', in relation to an offence, means—

    (a) aiding, abetting, counselling or procuring the commission of the offence;

    (b) an offence under Part 2 of the Serious Crime Act 2007 (encouraging or assisting crime) in relation to the offence (including, in relation to times before the commencement of that Part, an offence of incitement);

    (c) attempting or conspiring to commit the offence.

PART VI CODES OF PRACTICE—GENERAL

66 Codes of practice

The Secretary of State shall issue codes of practice in connection with—

    (a) the exercise by police officers of statutory powers—

       (i)   to search a person without first arresting him;

       (ii) to search a vehicle without making an arrest; or

       (iii) to arrest a person;

    (b) the detention, treatment, questioning and identification of persons by police officers;

    (c) searches of premises by police officers; and

    (d) the seizure of property found by police officers on persons or premises.

(2) Codes shall (in particular) include provision in connection with the exercise by police officers of powers under section 63B above.

(3) [*Applies to terrorism*].

67 Codes of practice—supplementary

(1) In this section, 'code' means a code of practice under section 60, 60A or 66.

(2) The Secretary of State may at any time revise the whole or any part of a code.

(3) A code may be made, or revised, so as to—

    (a) apply only in relation to one or more specified areas,

    (b) have effect only for a specified period,

    (c) apply only in relation to specified offences or descriptions of offender.

(4) Before issuing a code, or any revision of a code, the Secretary of State must consult—

    (a)   such persons as appear to the Secretary of State to represent the views of police and crime commissioners,

    (aa) the Mayor's Office for Policing and Crime,

    (ab) the Common Council of the City of London,

    (b)   the Association of Chief Police Officers of England, Wales and Northern Ireland,

    (c)   the General Council of the Bar,

    (d)   the Law Society of England and Wales,

    (e)   the Institute of Legal Executives, and

    (f)   such other persons as he thinks fit.

(5) A code, or a revision of a code, does not come into operation until the Secretary of State by order so provides.

(6) The power conferred by subsection (5) is exercisable by statutory instrument.

(7) An order bringing a code into operation may not be made unless a draft of the order has been laid before Parliament and approved by a resolution of each House.

(7A) An order bringing a revision of a code into operation must be laid before Parliament if the order has been made without a draft having been so laid and approved by a resolution of each House.

(7B) When an order or draft of an order is laid, the code or revision of a code to which it relates must also be laid.

(7C) No order or draft of an order may be laid until the consultation required by subsection (4) has taken place.

(7D) An order bringing a code, or a revision of a code, into operation may include transitional or saving provisions.

(9) Persons other than police officers who are charged with the duty of investigating offences or charging offenders shall in the discharge of that duty have regard to any relevant provision of a code.

(9A) Persons on whom powers are conferred by—

(a) any designation under section 38 or 39 of the Police Reform Act 2002 (police powers for civilian staff), or

(b) any accreditation under section 41 of that Act (accreditation under community safety accreditation schemes),

shall have regard to any relevant provision of a code in the exercise or performance of the powers and duties conferred or imposed on them by that designation or accreditation.

(10) A failure on the part—

(a) of a police officer to comply with any provision of a code;

(b) of any person other than a police officer who is charged with the duty of investigating offences or charging offenders to have regard to any relevant provision of a code in the discharge of that duty; or

(c) of a person designated under section 38 or 39 or accredited under section 41 of the Police Reform Act 2002 to have regard to any relevant provision of a code in the exercise or performance of the powers and duties conferred or imposed on him by that designation or accreditation,

shall not of itself render him liable to any criminal or civil proceedings.

(11) In all criminal and civil proceedings any code shall be admissible in evidence; and if any provision of a code appears to the court or tribunal conducting the proceedings to be relevant to any question arising in the proceedings it shall be taken into account in determining that question.

(12) In subsection (11) 'criminal proceedings' includes service proceedings.

(13) [*Applies to service proceedings*]

PART VII DOCUMENTARY EVIDENCE IN CRIMINAL PROCEEDINGS

71 Microfilm copies

In any proceedings the contents of a document may (whether or not the document is still in existence) be proved by the production of an enlargement of a microfilm copy of that document or of the material part of it, authenticated in such manner as the court may approve. Where the proceedings concerned are proceedings before a magistrates' court inquiring into an offence as examining justices this section shall have effect with the omission of the words "authenticated in such manner as the court may approve."

72 Part VII—supplementary

(1) In this Part of this Act—

'copy' in relation to a document means anything onto which information recorded in the document has been copied, by whatever means and whether directly or indirectly, and 'statement' means any representation of fact however made; and

'proceedings' means criminal proceedings, including service proceedings

(1A) [*Defines 'service proceedings'*]

(2) Nothing in this Part of this Act shall prejudice any power of a court to exclude evidence (whether by preventing questions from being put or otherwise) at its discretion.

PART VIII EVIDENCE IN CRIMINAL PROCEEDINGS—GENERAL

Convictions and acquittals

73 Proof of convictions and acquittals

(1) Where in any proceedings the fact that a person has in the United Kingdom or any other member State been convicted or acquitted of an offence otherwise than by a Service court is admissible in evidence, it may be proved by producing a certificate of conviction or, as the case may be, of acquittal relating to that offence, and proving that the person named in the certificate as having been convicted or acquitted of the offence is the person whose conviction or acquittal of the offence is to be proved.

(2) For the purposes of this section a certificate of conviction or of acquittal—

(a) shall, as regards a conviction or acquittal on indictment, consist of a certificate, signed by the proper officer where the conviction or acquittal took place, giving the substance and effect (omitting the formal parts) of the indictment and of the conviction or acquittal; and

(b) shall, as regards a conviction or acquittal on a summary trial, consist of a copy of the conviction or of the dismissal of the information, signed by the proper officer of the court where the conviction or acquittal took place or by the proper officer of the court, if any, to which a memorandum of the conviction or acquittal was sent; and

(c) shall, as regards a conviction or acquittal by a court in a member State (other than the United Kingdom), consist of a certificate, signed by the proper officer of the court where the conviction or acquittal took place, giving details of the offence, of the conviction or acquittal, and of any sentence;

and a document purporting to be a duly signed certificate of conviction or acquittal under this section shall be taken to be such a certificate unless the contrary is proved.

(3) In subsection (2) above 'proper officer' means:

(a) in relation to a magistrates' court in England and Wales, the designated officer for the court; and

(b) in relation to any other court in the United Kingdom, the clerk of a court, his deputy and to any other person having the custody of the court record; and

(c) in relation to any court in another member State ("the EU court"), a person who would be the proper officer of the EU court if that court were in the United Kingdom.

(4) The method of proving a conviction or acquittal authorised by this section shall be in addition to and not to the exclusion of any other authorised manner of proving a conviction or acquittal.

74 Conviction as evidence of commission of offence

(1) In any proceedings the fact that a person other than the accused has been convicted of an offence by or before any court in the United Kingdom or by a Service court outside the United Kingdom shall be admissible in evidence for the purpose of proving that that person committed that offence, where evidence of his having done so is admissible, whether or not any other evidence of his having committed that offence is given.

(2) In any proceedings in which by virtue of this section a person other than the accused is proved to have been convicted of an offence by or before any court in the United Kingdom or any other member State or by a Service court outside the United Kingdom, he shall be taken to have committed that offence unless the contrary is proved.

(3) In any proceedings where evidence is admissible of that fact that the accused has committed an offence, if the accused is proved to have been convicted of the offence—

(a) by or before any court in the United Kingdom or any other member State; or

(b) by a Service court outside the United Kingdom,

he shall be taken to have committed that offence unless the contrary is proved.

(4) Nothing in this section shall prejudice—

    (a) the admissibility in evidence of any conviction which would be admissible apart from this section; or

    (b) the operation of any enactment whereby a conviction or a finding of fact in any proceedings is for the purposes of any other proceedings made conclusive evidence of any fact.

75 Provisions supplementary to section 74

(1) Where evidence that a person has been convicted of an offence is admissible by virtue of section 74 above, then without prejudice to the reception of any other admissible evidence for the purpose of identifying the facts on which the conviction was based—

    (a) the contents of any document which is admissible as evidence of the conviction; and

    (b) the contents of—

        (i) the information, complaint, indictment or chargesheet on which the person in question was convicted, or

        (ii) in the case of a conviction of an offence by a court in a member State (other than the United Kingdom), any document produced in relation to the proceedings for that offence which fulfils a purpose similar to any document or documents specified in sub-paragraph (i),

shall be admissible in evidence for that purpose.

(2) Where in any proceedings the contents of any document are admissible in evidence by virtue of subsection (1) above, a copy of that document, or of the material part of it, purporting to be certified or otherwise authenticated by or on behalf of the court or authority having custody of that document shall be admissible in evidence and shall be taken to be a true copy of that document or part unless the contrary is shown.

(3) Nothing in any of the following—

    (a) section 14 of the Powers of Criminal Courts (Sentencing) Act 2000 (under which a conviction leading to probation or discharge is to be disregarded except as mentioned in that section);

    (aa) [applies to service convictions]

    (b) [applies to Scotland and Northern Ireland only]

    (c) [applies to Scotland and Northern Ireland only]

shall affect the operation of section 74 above; . . .

(4) Nothing in section 74 above shall be construed as rendering admissible in any proceedings evidence of any conviction other than a subsisting one.

Confessions

76 Confessions

(1) In any proceedings a confession made by an accused person may be given in evidence against him in so far as it is relevant to any matter in issue in the proceedings and is not excluded by the court in pursuance of this section.

(2) If, in any proceedings where the prosecution proposes to give in evidence a confession made by an accused person, it is represented to the court that the confession was or may have been obtained—

    (a) by oppression of the person who made it; or

    (b) in consequence of anything said or done which was likely, in the circumstances existing at the time, to render unreliable any confession which might be made by him in consequence thereof,

the court shall not allow the confession to be given in evidence against him except in so far as the prosecution proves to the court beyond reasonable doubt that the confession (notwithstanding that it may be true) was not obtained as aforesaid.

(3) In any proceedings where the prosecution proposes to give in evidence a confession made by an accused person, the court may of its own motion require the prosecution, as a condition of allowing it to do so, to prove that the confession was not obtained as mentioned in subsection (2) above.

(4) The fact that a confession is wholly or partly excluded in pursuance of this section shall not affect the admissibility in evidence—

(a) of any facts discovered as a result of the confession; or

(b) where the confession is relevant as showing that the accused speaks, writes or expresses himself in a particular way, of so much of the confession as is necessary to show that he does so.

(5) Evidence that a fact to which this subsection applies was discovered as a result of a statement made by an accused person shall not be admissible unless evidence of how it was discovered is given by him or on his behalf.

(6) Subsection (5) above applies—

(a) to any fact discovered as a result of a confession which is wholly excluded in pursuance of this section; and

(b) to any fact discovered as a result of a confession which is partly so excluded, if the fact is discovered as a result of the excluded part of the confession.

(7) Nothing in Part VII of this Act shall prejudice the admissibility of a confession made by an accused person.

(8) In this section 'oppression' includes torture, inhuman or degrading treatment, and the use or threat of violence (whether or not amounting to torture).

(9) Where the proceedings mentioned in subsection (1) above are proceedings before a magistrates' court inquiring into an offence as examining justices this section shall have effect with the omission of—

(a) in subsection (1) the words "and is not excluded by the court in pursuance of this section", and

(b) subsections (2) to (6) and (8).

76A Confessions may be given in evidence for co-accused

(1) In any proceedings a confession made by an accused person may be given in evidence for another person charged in the same proceedings (a co-accused) in so far as it is relevant to any matter in issue in the proceedings and is not excluded by the court in pursuance of this section.

(2) If, in any proceedings where a co-accused proposes to give in evidence a confession made by an accused person, it is represented to the court that the confession was or may have been obtained—

(a) by oppression of the person who made it; or

(b) in consequence of anything said or done which was likely, in the circumstances existing at the time, to render unreliable any confession which might be made by him in consequence thereof,

the court shall not allow the confession to be given in evidence for the co-accused except in so far as it is proved to the court on the balance of probabilities that the confession (notwithstanding that it may be true) was not so obtained.

(3) Before allowing a confession made by an accused person to be given in evidence for a co-accused in any proceedings, the court may of its own motion require the fact that the confession was not obtained as mentioned in subsection (2) above to be proved in the proceedings on the balance of probabilities.

(4) The fact that a confession is wholly or partly excluded in pursuance of this section shall not affect the admissibility in evidence—

(a) of any facts discovered as a result of the confession; or

(b) where the confession is relevant as showing that the accused speaks, writes or expresses himself in a particular way, of so much of the confession as is necessary to show that he does so.

(5) Evidence that a fact to which this subsection applies was discovered as a result of a statement made by an accused person shall not be admissible unless evidence of how it was discovered is given by him or on his behalf.

(6) Subsection (5) above applies—

(a) to any fact discovered as a result of a confession which is wholly excluded in pursuance of this section; and

(b) to any fact discovered as a result of a confession which is partly so excluded, if the fact is discovered as a result of the excluded part of the confession.

(7) In this section 'oppression' includes torture, inhuman or degrading treatment, and the use or threat of violence (whether or not amounting to torture).

77   Confessions by mentally handicapped persons

(1) Without prejudice to the general duty of the court at a trial on indictment with a jury to direct the jury on any matter on which it appears to the court appropriate to do so, where at such a trial—

(a) the case against the accused depends wholly or substantially on a confession by him; and

(b) the court is satisfied—

(i)   that he is mentally handicapped; and

(ii)   that the confession was not made in the presence of an independent person;

the court shall warn the jury that there is special need for caution before convicting the accused in reliance on the confession, and shall explain that the need arises because of the circumstances mentioned in paragraphs (a) and (b) above.

(2) In any case where at the summary trial of a person for an offence it appears to the court that a warning under subsection (1) above would be required if the trial were on indictment with a jury, the court shall treat the case as one in which there is a special need for caution before convicting the accused on his confession.

(2A) In any case where at the trial on indictment without a jury of a person for an offence it appears to the court that a warning under subsection (1) above would be required if the trial were with a jury, the court shall treat the case as one in which there is a special need for caution before convicting the accused on his confession.

(3) In this section—

'independent person' does not include a police officer or a person employed for, or engaged on, police purposes;

'mentally handicapped', in relation to a person, means that he is in a state of arrested or incomplete development of mind which includes significant impairment of intelligence and social functioning; and

'police purposes' has the meaning assigned to it by section 101(2) of the Police Act 1996.

78   Exclusion of unfair evidence

(1) In any proceedings the court may refuse to allow evidence on which the prosecution proposes to rely to be given if it appears to the court that, having regard to all the circumstances, including the circumstances in which the evidence was obtained, the admission of the evidence would have such an adverse effect on the fairness of the proceedings that the court ought not to admit it.

(2) Nothing in this section shall prejudice any rule of law requiring a court to exclude evidence.

(3) This section shall not apply in the case of proceedings before a magistrates' court inquiring into an offences as examining justices.

79   Time for taking accused's evidence

If at the trial of any person for an offence—

(a) the defence intends to call two or more witnesses to the facts of the case; and

(b) those witnesses include the accused,

the accused shall be called before the other witness or witnesses unless the court in its discretion otherwise directs.

80   Competence and compellability of accused's spouse or civil partner

(2) In any proceedings the spouse or civil partner of a person charged in the proceedings shall, subject to subsection (4) below, be compellable to give evidence on behalf of that person.

(2A) In any proceedings spouse or civil partner of a person charged in the proceedings shall, subject to subsection (4) below, be compellable—

(a) to give evidence on behalf of any other person charged in the proceedings but only in respect of any specified offence with which that other person is charged; or

(b) to give evidence for the prosecution but only in respect of any specified offence with which any person is charged in the proceedings.

(3) In relation to the spouse or civil partner of a person charged in any proceedings, an offence is a specified offence for the purposes of subsection (2A) above if—

(a) it involves an assault on, or injury or a threat of injury to, the wife or husband or a person who was at the material time under the age of 16;

(b) it is a sexual offence alleged to have been committed in respect of a person who was at the material time under that age; or

(c) it consists of attempting or conspiring to commit, or of aiding, abetting, counselling, pro-curing or inciting the commission of, an offence falling within paragraph (a) or (b) above.

(4) No person who is charged in any proceedings shall be compellable by virtue of subsection (2) or (2A) above to give evidence in the proceedings.

(4A) References in this section to a person charged in any proceedings do not include a person who is not, or is no longer, liable to be convicted of any offence in the proceedings (whether as a result of pleading guilty or for any other reason).

(5) In any proceedings a person who has been but is no longer married to the accused shall be compellable to give evidence as if that person and the accused had never been married.

(5A) In any proceedings a person who has been but is no longer the civil partner of the accused shall be compellable to give evidence as if that person and the accused had never been civil partners.

(6) Where in any proceedings the age of any person at any time is material for the purposes of subsection (3) above, his age at the material time shall for the purposes of that provision be deemed to be or to have been that which appears to the court to be or to have been his age at that time.

(7) In subsection (3)(b) above 'sexual offence' means an offence under the Protection of Children Act 1978 or Part I of the Sexual Offences Act 2003.

(9) Section 1(d) of the Criminal Evidence Act 1898 (communications between husband and wife) and section 43(1) of the Matrimonial Causes Act 1965 (evidence as to marital intercourse) shall cease to have effect.

80A Rule where accused's spouse or civil partner not compellable

The failure of the spouse or civil partner of a person charged in any proceedings to give evidence shall not be made the subject of any comment by the prosecution.

81 Advance notice of expert evidence in crown court

(1) Criminal Procedure Rules may make provision for—

(a) requiring any party to proceedings before the Court to disclose to the other party or parties any expert evidence which he proposes to adduce in the proceedings; and

(b) prohibiting a party who fails to comply in respect of any evidence with any requirement imposed by virtue of paragraph (a) above from adducing that evidence without the leave of the court.

(2) Criminal Procedure Rules made by virtue of this section may specify the kinds of expert evidence to which they apply and may exempt facts or matters of any description specified in the rules.

PART VIII SUPPLEMENTARY

82 Part VIII—interpretation

(1) In this Part of this Act—

'confession' includes any statement wholly or partly adverse to the person who made it, whether made to a person in authority or not and whether made in words or otherwise;

'proceedings' means criminal proceedings, including service proceedings.

'Service court' means the Court Martial or the Service Civilian Court.

(1A) [Defines 'service proceedings']

(3) Nothing in this Part of this Act shall prejudice any power of a court to exclude evidence (whether by preventing questions from being put or otherwise) at its discretion.

PART X POLICE—GENERAL

107 Police officers performing duties of higher rank

(1) For the purpose of any provision of this Act or any other Act under which a power in respect of the investigation of offences or the treatment of persons in police custody is exercisable only by or with the authority of a police officer of at least the rank of superintendent, an officer of the rank of chief inspector shall be treated as holding the rank of superintendent if—

    (a) he has been authorised by an officer holding a rank above the rank of superintendent to exercise the power or, as the case may be, to give his authority for its exercise, or

    (b) he is acting during the absence of an officer holding the rank of superintendent who has authorised him, for the duration of that absence, to exercise the power, or as the case may be, to give his authority for its exercise.

(2) For the purpose of any provision of this Act or any other Act under which such a power is exercisable only by or with the authority of an officer of at least the rank of inspector, an officer of the rank of sergeant shall be treated as holding the rank of inspector if he has been authorised by an officer of at least the rank of superintendent to exercise the power or, as the case may be, to give this authority for its exercise.

111 Regulations for Police Forces and Police Cadets—Scotland

[*Applies to Scotland*]

PART XI MISCELLANEOUS AND SUPPLEMENTARY

117 Power of constable to use reasonable force

Where any provision of this Act—

    (a) confers a power on a constable; and

    (b) does not provide that the power may only be exercised with the consent of some person, other than a police officer,

the officer may use reasonable force, if necessary, in the exercise of the power.

118 General interpretation

(1) In this Act—

'designated police station' has the meaning assigned to it by section 35 above;

'document' has the same meaning as in Part I of the Civil Evidence Act 1968;

'item subject to legal privilege' has the meaning assigned to it by section 10 above;

'parent or guardian' means—

    (a) in the case of a child or young person in the care of a local authority, that authority;

'premises' has the meaning assigned to it by section 27 above;

'recordable offence' means any offence to which regulations under section 23 above apply;

'vessel' includes any ship, boat, raft or other apparatus constructed or adapted for floating on water.

(2) Subject to subsection (2A) a person is in police detention for the purposes of this Act if—

    (a) he has been taken to a police station after being arrested for an offence or after being arrested under section 41 of the Terrorism Act 2000;

    (b) he is arrested at a police station after attending voluntarily at the station or accompanying a constable to it,

and is detained there or is detained elsewhere in the charge of a constable, except that a person who is at a court after being charged is not in police detention for those purposes.

(2A) Where a person is in another's lawful custody by virtue of paragraph 22, 34(1) or 35(3) of Schedule 4 to the Police Reform Act 2002, he shall be treated as in police detention.

122 Short title

This Act may be cited as the Police and Criminal Evidence Act 1984.

SCHEDULE 2A

FINGERPRINTING AND SAMPLES: POWER TO REQUIRE ATTENDANCE AT POLICE STATION

PART 1 FINGERPRINTING

Persons arrested and released

1 (1) A constable may require a person to attend a police station for the purpose of taking his fingerprints under section 61(5A).

(2) The power under sub-paragraph (1) above may not be exercised in a case falling within section 61(5A)(b) (fingerprints taken on previous occasion insufficient etc) after the end of the period of six months beginning with the day on which the appropriate officer was informed that section 61(3A)(a) or (b) applied.

(3) In sub-paragraph (2) above "appropriate officer" means the officer investigating the offence for which the person was arrested.

Persons charged etc

2 (1) A constable may require a person to attend a police station for the purpose of taking his fingerprints under section 61(5B).

(2) The power under sub-paragraph (1) above may not be exercised after the end of the period of six months beginning with—

(a) in a case falling within section 61(5B)(a) (fingerprints not taken previously), the day on which the person was charged or informed that he would be reported, or

(b) in a case falling within section 61(5B)(b) (fingerprints taken on previous occasion insufficient etc), the day on which the appropriate officer was informed that section 61(3A)(a) or (b) applied.

(3) In sub-paragraph (2)(b) above "appropriate officer" means the officer investigating the offence for which the person was charged or informed that he would be reported.

Persons convicted etc of an offence in England and Wales

3 (1) A constable may require a person to attend a police station for the purpose of taking his fingerprints under section 61(6).

(2) Where the condition in section 61(6ZA)(a) is satisfied (fingerprints not taken previously), the power under sub-paragraph (1) above may not be exercised after the end of the period of two years beginning with—

(a) the day on which the person was convicted, cautioned or warned or reprimanded, or

(b) if later, the day on which this Schedule comes into force.

(3) Where the condition in section 61(6ZA)(b) is satisfied (fingerprints taken on previous occasion insufficient etc), the power under sub-paragraph (1) above may not be exercised after the end of the period of two years beginning with—

(a) the day on which an appropriate officer was informed that section 61(3A)(a) or (b) applied, or

(b) if later, the day on which this Schedule comes into force.

(4) In sub-paragraph (3)(a) above "appropriate officer" means an officer of the police force which investigated the offence in question.

(5) Sub-paragraphs (2) and (3) above do not apply where the offence is a qualifying offence (whether or not it was such an offence at the time of the conviction, caution or warning or reprimand).

Persons convicted etc of an offence outside England and Wales

5 A constable may require a person to attend a police station for the purpose of taking his fingerprints under section 61(6D).

Multiple attendance

6 (1) Where a person's fingerprints have been taken under section 61 on two occasions in relation to any offence, he may not under this Schedule be required to attend a police station to have his fingerprints taken under that section in relation to that offence on a subsequent occasion without the authorisation of an officer of at least the rank of inspector.

(2) Where an authorisation is given under sub-paragraph (1) above—

    (a) the fact of the authorisation, and

    (b) the reasons for giving it,

shall be recorded as soon as practicable after it has been given.

PART 2 INTIMATE SAMPLES

Persons suspected to be involved in an offence

7 A constable may require a person to attend a police station for the purpose of taking an intimate sample from him under section 62(1A) if, in the course of the investigation of an offence, two or more non-intimate samples suitable for the same means of analysis have been taken from him but have proved insufficient.

Persons convicted etc of an offence outside England and Wales

8 A constable may require a person to attend a police station for the purpose of taking a sample from him under section 62(2A) if two or more non-intimate samples suitable for the same means of analysis have been taken from him under section 63(3E) but have proved insufficient.

PART 3 NON-INTIMATE SAMPLES

Persons arrested and released

9 (1) A constable may require a person to attend a police station for the purpose of taking a non-intimate sample from him under section 63(3ZA).

(2) The power under sub-paragraph (1) above may not be exercised in a case falling within section 63(3ZA)(b) (sample taken on a previous occasion not suitable etc) after the end of the period of six months beginning with the day on which the appropriate officer was informed of the matters specified in section 63(3ZA)(b)(i) or (ii).

(3) In sub-paragraph (2) above, "appropriate officer" means the officer investigating the offence for which the person was arrested.

Persons charged etc

10 (1) A constable may require a person to attend a police station for the purpose of taking a non-intimate sample from him under section 63(3A).

(2) The power under sub-paragraph (1) above may not be exercised in a case falling within section 63(3A)(a) (sample not taken previously) after the end of the period of six months beginning with the day on which he was charged or informed that he would be reported.

(3) The power under sub-paragraph (1) above may not be exercised in a case falling within section 63(3A)(b) (sample taken on a previous occasion not suitable etc) after the end of the period of six months beginning with the day on which the appropriate officer was informed of the matters specified in section 63(3A)(b)(i) or (ii).

(4) In sub-paragraph (3) above "appropriate officer" means the officer investigating the offence for which the person was charged or informed that he would be reported.

Persons convicted etc of an offence in England and Wales

11 (1) A constable may require a person to attend a police station for the purpose of taking a non-intimate sample from him under section 63(3B).

(2) Where the condition in section 63(3BA)(a) is satisfied (sample not taken previously), the power under sub-paragraph (1) above may not be exercised after the end of the period of two years beginning with—

(a) the day on which the person was convicted, cautioned or warned or reprimanded, or

(b) if later, the day on which this Schedule comes into force.

(3) Where the condition in section 63(3BA)(b) is satisfied (sample taken on a previous occasion not suitable etc), the power under sub-paragraph (1) above may not be exercised after the end of the period of two years beginning with—

(a) the day on which an appropriate officer was informed of the matters specified in section 63(3BA)(b)(i) or (ii), or

(b) if later, the day on which this Schedule comes into force.

(4) In sub-paragraph (3)(a) above "appropriate officer" means an officer of the police force which investigated the offence in question.

(5) Sub-paragraphs (2) and (3) above do not apply where—

(a) the offence is a qualifying offence (whether or not it was such an offence at the time of the conviction, caution or warning or reprimand), or

(b) he was convicted before 10th April 1995 and is a person to whom section 1 of the Criminal Evidence (Amendment) Act 1997 applies.

Persons convicted etc of an offence outside England and Wales

13 A constable may require a person to attend a police station for the purpose of taking a non-intimate sample from him under section 63(3E).

Multiple exercise of power

14 (1) Where a non-intimate sample has been taken from a person under section 63 on two occasions in relation to any offence, he may not under this Schedule be required to attend a police station to have another such sample taken from him under that section in relation to that offence on a subsequent occasion without the authorisation of an officer of at least the rank of inspector.

(2) Where an authorisation is given under sub-paragraph (1) above—

(a) the fact of the authorisation, and

(b) the reasons for giving it,

shall be recorded as soon as practicable after it has been given.

PART 4 GENERAL AND SUPPLEMENTARY

Requirement to have power to take fingerprints or sample

15 A power conferred by this Schedule to require a person to attend a police station for the purposes of taking fingerprints or a sample under any provision of this Act may be exercised only in a case where the fingerprints or sample may be taken from the person under that provision (and, in particular, if any necessary authorisation for taking the fingerprints or sample under that provision has been obtained).

Date and time of attendance

16 (1) A requirement under this Schedule—

(a) shall give the person a period of at least seven days within which he must attend the police station; and

(b) may direct him so to attend at a specified time of day or between specified times of day.

(2) In specifying a period or time or times of day for the purposes of sub-paragraph (1) above, the constable shall consider whether the fingerprints or sample could reasonably be taken at a time when the person is for any other reason required to attend the police station.

(3) A requirement under this Schedule may specify a period shorter than seven days if—

(a) there is an urgent need for the fingerprints or sample for the purposes of the investigation of an offence; and

(b) the shorter period is authorised by an officer of at least the rank of inspector.

(4) Where an authorisation is given under sub-paragraph (3)(b) above—

    (a) the fact of the authorisation, and

    (b) the reasons for giving it,

shall be recorded as soon as practicable after it has been given.

(5) If the constable giving a requirement under this Schedule and the person to whom it is given so agree, it may be varied so as to specify any period within which, or date or time at which, the person must attend; but a variation shall not have effect unless confirmed by the constable in writing.

Enforcement

17 A constable may arrest without warrant a person who has failed to comply with a requirement under this Schedule."

(3) In that Act, in section 27 (fingerprinting of certain offenders), subsections (1) to (3) are repealed.

Public Order Act 1986

(1986, c. 64)

5 Harassment, alarm or distress

(1) A person is guilty of an offence if he—

    (a) uses threatening, abusive or insulting words or behaviour, or disorderly behaviour, or

    (b) displays any writing, sign or other visible representation which is threatening, abusive or insulting, within the hearing or sight of a person likely to be caused harassment, alarm or distress thereby.

(2) An offence under this section may be committed in a public or a private place, except that no offence is committed where the words or behaviour are used, or the writing, sign or other visible representation is displayed, by a person inside a dwelling and the other person is also inside that or another dwelling.

(3) It is a defence for the accused to prove—

    (a) that he had no reason to believe that there was any person within hearing or sight who was likely to be caused harassment, alarm or distress, or

    (b) that he was inside a dwelling and had no reason to believe that the words or behaviour used, or the writing, sign or other visible representation displayed, would be heard or seen by a person outside that or any other dwelling, or

    (c) that his conduct was reasonable.

(6) A person guilty of an offence under this section is liable on summary conviction to a fine not exceeding level 3 on the standard scale.

Criminal Justice Act 1988

(1988, c. 33)

PART III OTHER PROVISIONS ABOUT EVIDENCE IN CRIMINAL PROCEEDINGS

30 Expert reports

(1) An expert report shall be admissible as evidence in criminal proceedings, whether or not the person making it attends to give oral evidence in those proceedings.

(2) If it is proposed that the person making the report shall not give oral evidence, the report shall only be admissible with the leave of the court.

(3) For the purpose of determining whether to give leave the court shall have regard—

    (a) to the contents of the report;

    (b) to the reasons why it is proposed that the person making the report shall not give oral evidence;

    (c) to any risk, having regard in particular to whether it is likely to be possible to controvert statements in the report if the person making it does not attend to give oral evidence in the proceedings, that its admission or exclusion will result in unfairness to the accused or, if there is more than one, to any of them; and

    (d) to any other circumstances that appear to the court to be relevant.

(4) An expert report, when admitted, shall be evidence of any fact or opinion of which the person making it could have given oral evidence.

(4A) . . .

(5) In this section 'expert report' means a written report by a person dealing wholly or mainly with matters on which he is (or would if living be) qualified to give expert evidence.

31   Form of evidence and glossaries

For the purpose of helping members of juries to understand complicated issues of fact or technical terms Crown Court Rules may make provision:

    (a) as to the furnishing of evidence in any form, notwithstanding the existence of admissible material from which the evidence to be given in that form would be derived; and

    (b) as to the furnishing of glossaries for such purposes as may be specified; in any case where the court gives leave for, or requires, evidence or a glossary to be so furnished.

This section shall not apply to proceedings before a magistrates' court inquiring into an offence as examining justices.

32   Evidence through television links

(1) A person other than the accused may give evidence through a live television link in proceedings to which subsection (1A) below applies if—

    (a) the witness is outside the United Kingdom;

but evidence may not be so given without the leave of the court.

(1A) This subsection applies—

    (a) to trials on indictment, appeals to the criminal division of the Court of Appeal and hearings of references under section 9 of the Criminal Appeal Act 1995; and

    (b) to proceedings in youth courts, appeals to the Crown Court arising out of such proceedings and hearings of references under section 11 of the Criminal Appeal Act 1995 so arising'.

(3) A statement made on oath by a witness outside the United Kingdom and given in evidence through a link by virtue of this section shall be treated for the purposes of section 1 of the Perjury Act 1911 as having been made in the proceedings in which it is given in evidence.

(4) Without prejudice to the generality of any enactment conferring power to make rules to which this subsection applies, such rules may make such provision as appears to the authority making them to be necessary or expedient for the purposes of this section.

34   Abolition of requirement of corroboration for unsworn evidence of children

(2) Any requirement whereby at a trial on indictment it is obligatory for the court to give the jury a warning about convicting the accused on the uncorroborated evidence of a child is abrogated.

(3) Unsworn evidence admitted by virtue of section 56 of the Youth Justice and Criminal Evidence Act 1999 may corroborate evidence (sworn or unsworn) given by any other person.

Road Traffic Offenders Act 1988

(1988, c. 53)

11   Evidence by certificate as to driver, user or owner

(1) In any proceedings in England and Wales for an offence to which this section applies, a certificate in the prescribed form, purporting to be signed by a constable and certifying that a person specified in the certificate stated to the constable—

(a) that a particular mechanically propelled vehicle was being driven or used by, or belonged to, that person on a particular occasion, or

(b) that a particular mechanically propelled vehicle on a particular occasion was used by, or belonged to, a firm and that he was, at the time of the statement, a partner in that firm, or

(c) that a particular mechanically propelled vehicle on a particular occasion was used by, or belonged to, a corporation and that he was, at the time of the statement, a director, officer or employee of that corporation, shall be admissible as evidence for the purpose of determining by whom the vehicle was being driven or used, or to whom it belonged, as the case may be, on that occasion.

(2) Nothing in subsection (1) above makes a certificate admissible as evidence in proceedings for an offence except in a case where and to the like extent to which oral evidence to the like effect would have been admissible in those proceedings.

(3) Nothing in subsection (1) above makes a certificate admissible as evidence in proceedings for an offence—

(a) unless a copy of it has, not less than seven days before the hearing or trial, been served in the prescribed manner on the person charged with the offence, or

(b) if that person, not later than three days before the hearing or trial or within such further time as the court in special circumstances allow, serves a notice in the prescribed form and manner on the prosecutor requiring the attendance at the trial of the person who signed the certificate.

(3A) Where the proceedings mentioned in subsection (1) above are proceedings before a magistrates' court inquiring into an offence as examining justices this section shall have effect with the omission of—

(a) subsection (2), and

(b) in subsection (3), paragraph (b) and the word "or" immediately preceding it.

(4) In this section "prescribed" means prescribed by rules made by the Secretary of State by statutory instrument.

(5) Schedule 1 to this Act shows the offences to which this section applies.

12   Proof, in summary proceedings, of identity of driver of vehicle

(1) Where on the summary trial in England and Wales of an information for an offence to which this subsection applies—

(a) it is proved to the satisfaction of the court, on oath or in manner prescribed by Criminal Procedure Rules, that a requirement under section 172(2) of the Road Traffic Act 1988 to give information as to the identity of the driver of a particular vehicle on the particular occasion to which the information relates has been served on the accused by post, and

(b) a statement in writing is produced to the court purporting to be signed by the accused that the accused was the driver of that vehicle on that occasion,

the court may accept that statement as evidence that the accused was the driver of that vehicle on that occasion.

(2) Schedule 1 to this Act shows the offences to which subsection (1) above applies.

(3) Where on the summary trial in England and Wales of an information for an offence to which section 112 of the Road Traffic Regulation Act 1984 applies—

(a) it is proved to the satisfaction of the court, on oath or in manner prescribed by Criminal Procedure Rules, that a requirement under section 112(2) of the Road Traffic Regulation Act 1984 to give information as to the identity of the driver of a particular vehicle on the particular occasion to which the information relates has been served on the accused by post, and

(b) a statement in writing is produced to the court purporting to be signed by the accused that the accused was the driver of that vehicle on that occasion,

the court may accept that statement as evidence that the accused was the driver of that vehicle on that occasion.

13   Admissibility of records as evidence

(1) This section applies to a statement contained in a document purporting to be—

(a) a part of the records maintained by the Secretary of State in connection with any functions exercisable by him by virtue of Part III of the Road Traffic Act 1988 or a part of any other records maintained by the Secretary of State with respect to vehicles or of any records maintained with respect to vehicles by an approved testing authority in connection with the exercise by that authority of any functions conferred on such authority, or on that authority as such an authority, by or under any enactment or of any records maintained with respect to vehicles by an approved testing authority in connection with the exercise by that authority of any functions conferred on such authority, or on that authority as such an authority, by or under any enactment, or

(b) a copy of a document forming part of those records, or

(c) a note of any information contained in those records,

and to be authenticated by a person authorised in that behalf by the Secretary of State or (as the case may be) the approved testing authority.

(2) A statement to which this section applies shall be admissible in any proceedings as evidence . . . of any fact stated in it to the same extent as oral evidence of that fact is admissible in those proceedings.

(3) In the preceding subsections, . . .

'copy', in relation to a document, means anything onto which information recorded in the document has been copied, by whatever means and whether directly or indirectly;

'document' means anything in which information of any description is recorded; and

'statement' means any representation of fact, however made.

(3A) In any case where—

(a) a person is convicted by a magistrates' court of a summary offence under the Traffic Acts or the Road Traffic (Driver Licensing and Information Systems) Act 1989,

(b) a statement to which this section applies is produced to the court in the proceedings,

(c) the statement specifies an alleged previous conviction of the accused of an offence involving obligatory endorsement or an order made on the conviction, and

(d) the accused is not present in person before the court when the statement is produced,

the court may take account of the previous conviction or order as if the accused had appeared and admitted it.

(3B) Section 104 of the Magistrates' Courts Act 1980 (under which the previous convictions may be adduced in the absence of the accused after giving him seven days' notice of them) does not limit the effect of subsection (3A) above.

(4) In any case where—

(a) a statement to which this section applies is produced to a magistrates' court in any proceedings for an offence involving obligatory or discretionary disqualification [other than a summary offence under any of the enactments mentioned in subsection (3A) above],

(b) the statement specifies an alleged previous conviction of an accused person of any such offence or any order made on the conviction,

(c) it is proved to the satisfaction of the court, on oath or in such manner as may be prescribed by Criminal Procedure Rules, that not less than seven days before the statement is so produced a notice was served on the accused, in such form and manner as may be so prescribed, specifying the previous conviction or order and stating that it is proposed to bring it to the notice of the court in the event of or, as the case may be, in view of his conviction, and

(d) the accused is not present in person before the court when the statement is so produced,

the court may take account of the previous conviction or order as if the accused had appeared and admitted it.

(5) Nothing in the preceding provisions of this section enables evidence to be given in respect of any matter other than a matter of a description prescribed by regulations made by the Secretary of State.

(6) The power to make regulations under this section shall be exercisable by statutory instrument, which shall be subject to annulment in pursuance of a resolution of either House of Parliament.

(7) Where the proceedings mentioned in subsection (2) above are proceedings before a magistrates' court inquiring into an offence as examining justices this section shall have effect as if—

(a) in subsection (2) the words "to the same extent as oral evidence of that fact is admissible in those proceedings" were omitted;

(b) in subsection (4) the word "and" were inserted at the end of paragraph (a);

(c) in subsection (4), paragraphs (c) and (d) and the words "as if the accused had appeared and admitted it" were omitted.

16   Documentary evidence as to specimens in such proceedings

(1) Evidence of the proportion of alcohol or a drug in a specimen of breath, blood or urine may, subject to subsections (3) and (4) below and to section 15(5) and (5A) of this Act, be given by the production of a document or documents purporting to be whichever of the following is appropriate, that is to say—

(a) a statement automatically produced by the device by which the proportion of alcohol in a specimen of breath was measured and a certificate signed by a constable (which may but need not be contained in the same document as the statement) that the statement relates to a specimen provided by the accused at the date and time shown in the statement, and

(b) a certificate signed by an authorised analyst as to the proportion of alcohol or any drug found in a specimen of blood or urine identified in the certificate.

(2) Subject to subsections (3) and (4) below, evidence that a specimen of blood was taken from the accused with his consent by a medical practitioner or a registered health care professional may be given by the production of a document purporting to certify that fact and to be signed by a medical practitioner or registered health care professional.

(3) Subject to subsection (4) below—

(a) a document purporting to be such a statement or such a certificate (or both such a statement and such a certificate) as is mentioned in subsection (1)(a) above is admissible in evidence on behalf of the prosecution in pursuance of this section only if a copy of it either has been handed to the accused when the document was produced or has been served on him not later than seven days before the hearing, and

(b) any other document is so admissible only if a copy of it has been served on the accused not later than seven days before the hearing.

(4) A document purporting to be a certificate (or so much of a document as purports to be a certificate) is not so admissible if the accused, not later than three days before the hearing or within such further time as the court may in special circumstances allow, has served notice on the

prosecutor requiring the attendance at the hearing of the person by whom the document purports to be signed.

(5) [*Applies to Scotland only*]

(6) A copy of a certificate required by this section to be served on the accused or a notice required by this section to be served on the prosecutor may be served personally or sent by registered post or recorded delivery service.

(6A) Where the proceedings mentioned in section 15(1)of this Act are proceedings before a magistrates' court inquiring into an offence as examining justices this section shall have effect with the omission of subsection (4).

(7) In this section 'authorised analyst' means—

(a) any person possessing the qualifications prescribed by regulations made under section 27 of the Food Safety Act 1990 as qualifying persons for appointment as public analysts under those Acts, and

(b) any other person authorised by the Secretary of State to make analyses for the purposes of this section.

18   Evidence by certificate as to registration of driving instructors and licences to give instruction

(1) A certificate signed by the Registrar and stating that, on any date—

(a) a person's name was, or was not, in the register,

(b) the entry of a person's name was made in the register or a person's name was removed from it,

(c) a person was, or was not, the holder of a current licence under section 129 of the Road Traffic Act 1988, or

(d) a licence under that section granted to a person came into force or ceased to be in force, shall be evidence, and in Scotland sufficient evidence, of the facts stated in the certificate in pursuance of this section.

(2) A certificate so stating and purporting to be signed by the Registrar shall be deemed to be so signed unless the contrary is proved.

(3) In this section 'current licence', 'Registrar' and 'register' have the same meanings as in Part V of the Road Traffic Act 1988.

20   Speeding offences etc.: admissibility of certain evidence

(1) Evidence . . . of a fact relevant to proceedings for an offence to which this section applies may be given by the production of—

(a) a record produced by a prescribed device, and

(b) (in the same or another document) a certificate as to the circumstances in which the record was produced signed by a constable or by a person authorised by or on behalf of the chief officer of police for the police area in which the offence is alleged to have been committed;

but subject to the following provisions of this section.

(2) This section applies to—

(a) an offence under section 16 of the Road Traffic Regulation Act 1984 consisting in the contravention of a restriction on the speed of vehicles imposed under section 14 of that Act;

(b) an offence under subsection (4) of section 17 of that Act consisting in the contravention of a restriction on the speed of vehicles imposed under that section;

(c) an offence under section 88(7) of that Act (temporary minimum speed limits);

(d) an offence under section 89(1) of that Act (speeding offences generally);

(e) an offence under section 36(1) of the Road Traffic Act 1988 consisting in the failure to comply with an indication given by a light signal that vehicular traffic is not to proceed;

(f) an offence under Part I or II of the Road Traffic Regulation Act 1984 of contravening or failing to comply with an order or regulations made under either of those Parts relating to the use of an area of road which is described as a bus lane or a route for use by buses only;

(g) an offence under section 29(1) of the Vehicle Excise and Registration Act 1994 (using or keeping an unlicensed vehicle on a public road).

(3) The Secretary of State may by order amend subsection (2) above by making additions to or deletions from the list of offences for the time being set out there; and an order under this subsection may make such transitional provision as appears to him to be necessary or expedient.

(4) A record produced or measurement made by a prescribed device shall not be admissible as evidence of a fact relevant to proceedings for an offence to which this section applies unless—

(a) the device is of a type approved by the Secretary of State, and

(b) any conditions subject to which the approval was given are satisfied.

(5) Any approval given by the Secretary of State for the purposes of this section may be given subject to conditions as to the purposes for which, and the manner and other circumstances in which, any device of the type concerned is to be used.

(6) In proceedings for an offence to which this section applies, evidence (which in Scotland shall be sufficient evidence)—

(a) of a measurement made by a device, or of the circumstances in which it was made, or

(b) that a device was of a type approved for the purposes of this section, or that any conditions subject to which an approval was given were satisfied,

may be given by the production of a document which is signed as mentioned in subsection (1) above and which, as the case may be, gives particulars of the measurement or of the circumstances in which it was made, or states that the device was of such a type or that, to the best of the knowledge and belief of the person making the statement, all such conditions were satisfied.

(7) For the purposes of this section a document purporting to be a record of the kind mentioned in subsection (1) above, or to be a certificate or other document signed as mentioned in that subsection or in subsection (6) above, shall be deemed to be such a record, or to be so signed, unless the contrary is proved.

(8) Nothing in subsection (1) or (6) above makes a document admissible as evidence in proceedings for an offence unless a copy of it has, not less than seven days before the hearing or trial, been served on the person charged with the offence; and nothing in those subsections makes a document admissible as evidence of anything other than the matters shown on a record produced by a prescribed device if that person, not less than three days before the hearing or trial or within such further time as the court may in special circumstances allow, serves a notice on the prosecutor requiring attendance at the hearing or trial of the person who signed the document.

(9) In this section 'prescribed device' means device of a description specified in an order made by the Secretary of State.

(10) The powers to make orders under subsections (3) and (9) above shall be exercisable by statutory instrument, which shall be subject to annulment in pursuance of a resolution of either House of Parliament.

Road Traffic Act 1988

(1992, c. 52)

172 Duty to give information as to identity of driver etc. in certain circumstances

(1) This section applies—

(a) to any offence under the preceding provisions of this Act except—

(i) an offence under Part V, or

(ii)   an offence under section 13, 16, 51(2), 61(4), 67(9), 68(4), 96 or 120, and to an offence under section 178 of this Act,

(b)   to any offence under sections 25, 26 or 27 of the Road Traffic Offenders Act 1988,

(c)   to any offence against any other enactment relating to the use of vehicles on roads, and

(d)   to manslaughter . . . by the driver of a motor vehicle.

(2)   Where the driver of a vehicle is alleged to be guilty of an offence to which this section applies—

(a)   the person keeping the vehicle shall give such information as to the identity of the driver as he may be required to give by or on behalf of a chief officer of police, and

(b)   any other person shall if required as stated above give any information which it is in his power to give and may lead to identification of the driver.

(3)   Subject to the following provisions, a person who fails to comply with a requirement under subsection (2) above shall be guilty of an offence.

(4)   A person shall not be guilty of an offence by virtue of paragraph (a) of subsection (2) above if he shows that he did not know and could not with reasonable diligence have ascertained who the driver of the vehicle was.

(5)   Where a body corporate is guilty of an offence under this section and the offence is proved to have been committed with the consent or connivance of, or to be attributable to neglect on the part of, a director, manager, secretary or other similar officer of the body corporate, or a person who was purporting to act in any such capacity, he, as well as the body corporate, is guilty of that offence and liable to be proceeded against and punished accordingly.

(6)   Where the alleged offender is a body corporate . . . or the proceedings are brought against him by virtue of subsection (5) above or subsection (11) below, subsection (4) above shall not apply unless, in addition to the matters there mentioned, the alleged offender shows that no record was kept of the persons who drove the vehicle and that the failure to keep a record was reasonable.

(7)   A requirement under subsection (2) may be made by written notice served by post; and where it is so made—

(a)   it shall have effect as a requirement to give the information within the period of 28 days beginning with the day on which the notice is served, and

(b)   the person on whom the notice is served shall not be guilty of an offence under this section if he shows either that he gave the information as soon as reasonably practicable after the end of that period or that it has not been reasonably practicable for him to give it.

(8)   Where the person on whom a notice under subsection (7) above is to be served is a body corporate, the notice is duly served if it is served on the secretary or clerk of that body.

(9)   For the purposes of section 7 of the Interpretation Act 1978 as it applies for the purposes of this section the proper address of any person in relation to the service on him of a notice under subsection (7) above is—

(a)   in the case of the secretary or clerk of a body corporate, that of the registered or principal office of that body or (if the body corporate is the registered keeper of the vehicle concerned) the registered address, and

(b)   in any other case, his last known address at the time of service.

(10)   in this section—

'registered address', in relation to the registered keeper of a vehicle, means the address recorded in the record kept under the Vehicles Excise and Registration Act 1994 with respect to that vehicle as being that person's address, and

'registered keeper', in relation to a vehicle, means the person in whose name the vehicle is registered under that Act; and references to the driver of a vehicle include references to the rider of a cycle.

Sexual Offences (Amendment) Act 1992

(1992, c. 34)

1 Anonymity of victims of certain offences

(1) Where an allegation has been made that an offence to which this Act applies has been committed against a person, no matter relating to that person shall during that person's lifetime be included in any publication if it is likely to lead members of the public to identify that person as the person against whom the offence is alleged to have been committed.

(2) Where a person is accused of an offence to which this Act applies, no matter likely to lead members of the public to identify a person as the person against whom the offence is alleged to have been committed ('the complainant') shall during the complainant's lifetime be included in any publication.

(3) This section—

    (a) does not apply in relation to a person by virtue of subsection (1) at any time after a person has been accused of the offence, and

    (b) in its application in relation to a person by virtue of subsection (2), has effect subject to any direction given under section 3.

(3A) The matters relating to a person in relation to which the restrictions imposed by subsection (1) or (2) apply (if their inclusion in any publication is likely to have the result mentioned in that subsection) include in particular—

    (a) the person's name,

    (b) the person's address,

    (c) the identity of any school or other educational establishment attended by the person,

    (d) the identity of any place of work, and

    (e) any still or moving picture of the person.

(4) Nothing in this section prohibits the inclusion in a publication of matter consisting only of a report of criminal proceedings other than proceedings at, or intended to lead to, or on an appeal arising out of, a trial at which the accused is charged with the offence.

2 Offences to which this Act applies

(1) This Act applies to the following offences against the law of England and Wales—

    (aa) rape;

    (ab) burglary with intent to rape;

    (a) any offence under any of the provisions of the Sexual Offences Act 1956 mentioned in subsection (2);

    (b) any offence under section 128 of the Mental Health Act 1959 (intercourse with mentally handicapped person by hospital staff etc.);

    (c) any offence under section 1 of the Indecency with Children Act 1960 (indecent conduct towards young child);

    (d) any offence under section 54 of the Criminal Law Act 1977 (incitement by man of his grand-daughter, daughter or sister under the age of 16 to commit incest with him);

    (da) any offence under any of the provisions of Part 1 of the Sexual Offences Act 2003 except section 64, 65, 69 or 71;

    (e) any attempt to commit any of the offences mentioned in paragraphs (aa) to (da);

    (f) any conspiracy to commit any of those offences;

    (g) any incitement of another to commit any of those offences;

    (h) aiding, abetting, counselling or procuring the commission of any of the offences mentioned in paragraphs (aa) to (e) and (g).

(2) The provisions of the Act of 1956 are—

    (a) section 2 (procurement of a woman by threats);

(b) section 3 (procurement of a woman by false pretences);

(c) section 4 (administering drugs to obtain intercourse with a woman);

(d) section 5 (intercourse with a girl under the age of 13);

(e) section 6 (intercourse with a girl between the ages of 13 and 16);

(f) section 7 (intercourse with a mentally handicapped person);

(g) section 9 (procurement of a mentally handicapped person);

(h) section 10 (incest by a man);

(i) section 11 (incest by a woman);

(j) section 12 (buggery);

(k) section 14 (indecent assault on a woman);

(l) section 15 (indecent assault on a man);

(m) section 16 (assault with intent to commit buggery);

(n) section 17 (abduction of women by force).

Criminal Justice and Public Order Act 1994

(1994, c. 33)

Corroboration

32   Abolition of corroboration rules

(1) Any requirement whereby at a trial on indictment it is obligatory for the court to give the jury a warning about convicting the accused on the uncorroborated evidence of a person merely because that person is—

(a) an alleged accomplice of the accused, or

(b) where the offence charged is a sexual offence, the person in respect of whom it is alleged to have been committed,

is hereby abrogated.

(2) . . .

(3) Any requirement that—

(a) is applicable at the summary trial of a person for an offence, and

(b) corresponds to the requirement mentioned in subsection (1) above or that mentioned in section 34(2) of the Criminal Justice Act 1988,

is hereby abrogated.

(4) Nothing in this section applies in relation to—

(a) any trial, or

(b) any proceedings before a magistrates' court as examining justices,

which began before the commencement of this section.

33   Abolition of corroboration requirements under Sexual Offences Act 1956

(1) The following provisions of the Sexual Offences Act 1956 (which provide that a person shall not be convicted of the offence concerned on the evidence of one witness only unless the witness is corroborated) are hereby repealed—

(a) section 2(2) (procurement of woman by threats),

(b) section 3(2) (procurement of woman by false pretences),

(c) section 4(2) (administering drugs to obtain or facilitate intercourse),

(d) section 22(2) (causing prostitution of women), and

(e) section 23(2) (procuration of girl under twenty-one).

(2) Nothing in this section applies in relation to—

(a) any trial, or

(b) any proceedings before a magistrates' court as examining justices,

which began before the commencement of this section.

Inferences from accused's silence

34   Effect of accused's failure to mention facts when questioned or charged

(1) Where, in any proceedings against a person for an offence, evidence is given that the accused—

    (a) at any time before he was charged with the offence, on being questioned under caution by a constable trying to discover whether or by whom the offence had been committed, failed to mention any fact relied on in his defence in those proceedings; or

    (b) on being charged with the offence or officially informed that he might be prosecuted for it, failed to mention any such fact, being a fact which in the circumstances existing at the time the accused could reasonably have been expected to mention when so questioned, charged or informed, as the case may be, subsection (2) below applies.

(2) Where this subsection applies—

    (a) . . .

    (b) a judge, in deciding whether to grant an application made by the accused under—

        (i)   paragraph 2 of Schedule 3 to the Crime and Disorder Act 1998;

    (c) the court, in determining whether there is a case to answer; and

    (d) the court or jury, in determining whether the accused is guilty of the offence charged,

may draw such inferences from the failure as appear proper.

(2A) Where the accused was at an authorised place of detention at the time of failure, subsections (1) and (2) above do not apply if he had not been allowed an opportunity to consult a solicitor prior to being questioned, charged or informed as mentioned in subsection (1) above.

(3) Subject to any directions by the court, evidence tending to establish the failure may be given before or after evidence tending to establish the fact which the accused is alleged to have failed to mention.

(4) This section applies in relation to questioning by persons (other than constables) charged with the duty of investigating offences or charging offenders as it applies in relation to questioning by constables; and in subsection (1) above 'officially informed' means informed by a constable or any such person.

(5) This section does not—

    (a) prejudice the admissibility in evidence of the silence or other reaction of the accused in the face of anything said in his presence relating to the conduct in respect of which he is charged, in so far as evidence thereof would be admissible apart from this section; or

    (b) preclude the drawing of any inference from any such silence or other reaction of the accused which could properly be drawn apart from this section.

(6) This section does not apply in relation to a failure to mention a fact if the failure occurred before the commencement of this section.

35   Effect of accused's silence at trial

(1) At the trial of any person for an offence, subsections (2) and (3) below apply unless—

    (a) the accused's guilt is not in issue; or

    (b) it appears to the court that the physical or mental condition of the accused makes it undesirable for him to give evidence;

but subsection (2) below does not apply if, at the conclusion of the evidence for the prosecution, his legal representative informs the court that the accused will give evidence or, where he is unrepresented, the court ascertains from him that he will give evidence.

(2) Where this subsection applies, the court shall, at the conclusion of the evidence for the prosecution, satisfy itself (in the case of proceedings on indictment with a jury, in the presence of the jury) that the accused is aware that the stage has been reached at which evidence can be given for the defence and that he can, if he wishes, give evidence and that, if he chooses not to give evidence, or having been sworn, without good cause refuses to answer any question, it will be permissible for the court or jury to draw such inferences as appear proper from his failure to give evidence or his refusal, without good cause, to answer any question.

(3) Where this subsection applies, the court or jury, in determining whether the accused is guilty of the offence charged, may draw such inferences as appear proper from the failure of the accused to give evidence or his refusal, without good cause, to answer any question.

(4) This section does not render the accused compellable to give evidence on his own behalf, and he shall accordingly not be guilty of contempt of court by reason of a failure to do so.

(5) For the purposes of this section a person who, having been sworn, refuses to answer any question shall be taken to do so without good cause unless—

(a) he is entitled to refuse to answer the question by virtue of any enactment, whenever passed or made, or on the ground of privilege; or

(b) the court in the exercise of its general discretion excuses him from answering it.

(7) This section applies—

(a) in relation to proceedings on indictment for an offence, only if the person charged with the offence is arraigned on or after the commencement of this section;

(b) in relation to proceedings in a magistrates' court, only if the time when the court begins to receive evidence in the proceedings falls after the commencement of this section.

36 Effect of accused's failure or refusal to account for objects, substances or marks

(1) Where—

(a) a person is arrested by a constable, and there is—

(i)   on his person; or

(ii)   in or on his clothing or footwear; or

(iii) otherwise in his possession; or

(iv) in any place in which he is at the time of his arrest,

any object, substance or mark, or there is any mark on any such object; and

(b) that or another constable investigating the case reasonably believes that the presence of the object, substance or mark may be attributable to the participation of the person arrested in the commission of an offence specified by the constable; and

(c) the constable informs the person arrested that he so believes, and requests him to account for the presence of the object, substance or mark; and

(d) the person fails or refuses to do so,

then if, in any proceedings against the person for the offence so specified, evidence of those matters is given, subsection (2) below applies.

(2) Where this subsection applies—

(a) . . .

(b) a judge, in deciding whether to grant an application made by the accused under—

(i)   paragraph 2 of Schedule 3 to the Crime and Disorder Act 1998;

(c) the court, in determining whether there is a case to answer; and

(d) the court or jury, in determining whether the accused is guilty of the offence charged,

may draw such inferences from the failure or refusal as appear proper.

(3) Subsections (1) and (2) above apply to the condition of clothing or footwear as they apply to a substance or mark thereon.

(4) Subsections 1 and 2 above do not apply unless the accused was told in ordinary language by the constable when making the request mentioned in subsection (1)(c) above what the effect of this section would be if he failed or refused to comply with the request.

(4A) Where the accused was at an authorised place of detention at the time of the failure or refusal, subsections (1) and (2) above do not apply if he had not been allowed an opportunity to consult a solicitor prior to the request being made.

(5) This section applies in relation to officers of customs and excise as it applies in relation to constables.

(6) This section does not preclude the drawing of any inference from a failure or refusal of the accused to account for the presence of an object, substance or mark or from the condition of clothing or footwear which could properly be drawn apart from this section.

(7) This section does not apply in relation to a failure or refusal which occurred before the commencement of this section.

37 Effect of accused's failure or refusal to account for presence at a particular place

(1) Where—
(a) a person arrested by a constable was found by him at a place at or about the time the offence for which he was arrested is alleged to have been committed; and
(b) that or another constable investigating the offence reasonably believes that the presence of the person at that place and at that time may be attributable to his participation in the commission of the offence; and
(c) the constable informs the person that he so believes, and requests him to account for that presence; and
(d) the person fails or refuses to do so, then if, in any proceedings against the person for the offence, evidence of those matters is given, subsection (2) below applies.

(2) Where this subsection applies—
(a) . . .
(b) a judge, in deciding whether to grant an application made by the accused under—
(i) paragraph 2 of Schedule 3 to the Crime and Disorder Act 1998;
(c) the court, in determining whether there is a case to answer, and
(d) the court or jury, in determining whether the accused is guilty of the offence charged,
may draw such inferences from the failure or refusal as appear proper.

(3) Subsections (1) and (2) do not apply unless the accused was told in ordinary language by the constable when making the request mentioned in subsection (1)(c) above what the effect of this section would be if he failed or refused to comply with the request.

(3A) Where the accused was at an authorised place of detention at the time of the failure or refusal, subsections (1) and (2) do not apply if he had not been allowed an opportunity to consult a solicitor prior to the request being made.

(4) This section applies in relation to officers of customs and excise as it applies in relation to constables.

(5) This section does not preclude the drawing of any inference from a failure or refusal of the accused to account for his presence at a place which could properly be drawn apart from this section.

(6) This section does not apply in relation to a failure or refusal which occurred before the commencement of this section.

38 Interpretation and savings for sections 34, 35, 36 and 37

(1) In sections 34, 35, 36 and 37 of this Act—
'legal representative' means an authorised advocate or authorised litigator, as defined by section 119(1) of the Courts and Legal Services Act 1990; and
'place' includes any building or part of a building, any vehicle, vessel, aircraft or hovercraft and any other place whatsoever.

(2) In sections 34(2), 35(3), 36(2) and 37(2), references to an offence charged include references to any other offence of which the accused could lawfully be convicted on that charge.

(2A) In each of sections 34(2A), 36(4A) and 37(3A) 'authorised place of detention' means—
(a) a police station; or
(b) any other place prescribed for the purpose of that provision by the Secretary of State;
and the power to make an order under this subsection shall be exercisable by statutory instrument which shall be subject to annulment on pursuance of a resolution of either House of Parliament.

(3) A person shall not have the proceedings against him transferred to the Crown Court for trial, have a case to answer or be convicted of an offence solely on an inference drawn from such a failure or refusal as is mentioned in section 34(2), 35(3), 36(2) or 37(2).

(4) A judge shall not refuse to grant such an application as is mentioned in section 34(2)(b), 36(2)(b) and 37(2)(b) solely on an inference drawn from such a failure as is mentioned in section 34(2), 36(2) or 37(2).

(5) Nothing in sections 34, 35, 36 or 37 prejudices the operation of a provision of an enactment which provides (in whatever words) that any answer or evidence given by a person in specified circumstances shall not be admissible in evidence against him or some other person in any proceedings or class of proceedings (however described, and whether civil or criminal).
In this subsection, the reference to giving evidence is a reference to giving evidence in any manner, whether by furnishing information, making discovery, producing documents or otherwise.

(6) Nothing in sections 34, 35, 36 or 37 prejudices any power of a court, in any proceedings, to exclude evidence (whether by preventing questions being put or otherwise) at its discretion.

Criminal Evidence (Amendment) Act 1997

(1997, c. 17)

Extension of power to take non-intimate body samples without consent

1 Persons imprisoned or detained by virtue of pre-existing conviction for sexual offence etc.

(1) This section has effect for removing, in relation to persons to whom this section applies, the restriction on the operation of section 63(3B) of the Police and Criminal Evidence Act 1984 (power to take non-intimate samples without the appropriate consent from persons convicted of recordable offences)—

    (a) which is imposed by the subsection (10) inserted in section 63 by section 55(6) of the Criminal Justice and Public Order Act 1994, and

    (b) by virtue of which section 63(3B) does not apply to persons convicted before 10 April 1995.

(3) This section applies to a person who was convicted of a recordable offence before 10 April 1995 if—

    (a) that offence was one of the offences listed in Schedule 1 to this Act (which lists certain sexual, violent and other offences), and

    (b) he has at any time served or at the relevant time he is serving a sentence of imprisonment in respect of that offence.

(4) This section also applies to a person who was convicted of a recordable offence before 10 April 1995 if—

    (a) that offence was one of the offences listed in Schedule 1 to this Act, and

    (b) he has at any time been detained or at the relevant time he is detained under Part III of the Mental Health Act 1983 in pursuance of—

        (i) a hospital order or interim hospital order made following that conviction.

Expressions used in this subsection and in the Mental Health Act 1983 have the same meaning as in that Act.

(5) Where a person convicted of a recordable offence before 10 April 1995 was, following his conviction for that and any other offence or offences, sentenced to two or more terms of imprisonment (whether taking effect consecutively or concurrently), he shall be treated for the purposes of this section as serving a sentence of imprisonment in respect of that offence at any time when serving any of those terms.

(6) For the purposes of this section, references to a person serving a sentence of imprisonment include references—

(a) to his being detained in any institution to which the Prison Act 1952 applies in pursuance of any other sentence or order for detention imposed by a court in criminal proceedings, or

(b) to his being detained (otherwise than in any such institution) in pursuance of directions of the Secretary of State under section 53 of the Children and Young Persons Act 1933;

and any reference to a term of imprisonment shall be construed accordingly.

2 Persons detained following acquittal on grounds of insanity or finding of unfitness to plead

(1) This section has effect for enabling non-intimate samples to be taken from persons under section 63 of the 1984 Act without the appropriate consent where they are persons to whom this section applies.

(3) This section applies to a person if—

(a) he has at any time been detained or at the relevant time he is detained under Part III of the Mental Health Act 1983 in pursuance of an order made under—

(i) section 5(2)(a) of the Criminal Procedure (Insanity) Act 1964 or section 6 or 14 of the Criminal Appeal Act 1968 (finding of insanity or unfitness to plead), or

(ii) section 37(3) of the Mental Health Act 1983 (power of magistrates' court to make hospital order without convicting accused); and

(b) that order was made on or after the date of the passing of this Act in respect of a recordable offence.

(4) This section also applies to a person if—

(a) he has at any time been detained or at the relevant time he is detained under Part III of the Mental Health Act 1983 in pursuance of an order made under—

(i) any of the provisions mentioned in subsection (3)(a), or

(ii) section 5(1) of the Criminal Procedure (Insanity) Act 1964 as originally enacted; and

(b) that order was made before the date of the passing of this Act in respect of any offence listed in Schedule 1 to this Act.

(5) Subsection (4)(a)(i) does not apply to any order made under section 14(2) of the Criminal Appeal Act 1968 as originally enacted.

(6) For the purposes of this section an order falling within subsection (3) or (4) shall be treated as having been made in respect of an offence of a particular description—

(a) if, where the order was made following—

(i) a finding of not guilty by reason of insanity, or

(ii) a finding that the person in question was under a disability and did the act or made the omission charged against him, or

(iii) a finding for the purposes of section 37(3) of the Mental Health Act 1983 that the person in question did the act or made the omission charged against him, or

(iv) (in the case of an order made under section 5(1) of the Criminal Procedure (Insanity) Act 1964 as originally enacted) a finding that he was under a disability,

that finding was recorded in respect of an offence of that description; or

(b) if, where the order was made following the Court of Appeal forming such opinion as is mentioned in section 6(1) or 14(1) of the Criminal Appeal Act 1968, that opinion was formed on an appeal brought in respect of an offence of that description.

(7) In this section any reference to an Act 'as originally enacted' is a reference to that Act as it had effect without any of the amendments made by the Criminal Procedure (Insanity and Unfitness to Plead) Act 1991.

Supplementary

5 Interpretation

In this Act—

'the 1984 Act' means the Police and Criminal Evidence Act 1984;

'appropriate consent' has the meaning given by section 65 of the 1984 Act;

'non-intimate sample' has the meaning given by section 65 of the 1984 Act;

'recordable offence' means any offence to which regulations under section 27 of the 1984 Act (fingerprinting) apply;

'the relevant time' means, in relation to the exercise of any power to take a non-intimate sample from a person, the time when it is sought to take the sample.

SCHEDULE 1
LIST OF OFFENCES

Sexual offences and offences of indecency

1. Any offence under the Sexual Offences Act 1956, other than an offence under section 30, 31 or 33 to 36 of that Act.

2. Any offence under section 128 of the Mental Health Act 1959 (intercourse with mentally handicapped person by hospital staff etc.).

3. Any offence under section 1 of the Indecency with Children Act 1960 (indecent conduct towards young child).

4. Any offence under section 54 of the Criminal Law Act 1977 (incitement by man of his grand-daughter, daughter or sister under the age of 16 to commit incest with him).

5. Any offence under section 1 of the Protection of Children Act 1978.

Violent and other offences

6. Any of the following offences—
   (a) murder;
   (b) manslaughter;
   (c) false imprisonment; and
   (d) kidnapping.

7. Any offence under any of the following provisions of the Offences Against the Person Act 1861—
   (a) section 4 (conspiring or soliciting to commit murder);
   (b) section 16 (threats to kill);
   (c) section 18 (wounding with intent to cause grievous bodily harm);
   (d) section 20 (causing grievous bodily harm);
   (e) section 21 (attempting to choke etc. in order to commit or assist in the committing of any indictable offence);
   (f) section 22 (using chloroform etc. to commit or assist in the committing of any indictable offence);
   (g) section 23 (maliciously administering poison etc. so as to endanger life or inflict grievous bodily harm);
   (h) section 24 (maliciously administering poison etc. with intent to injure etc.); and
   (i) section 47 (assault occasioning actual bodily harm).

8. Any offence under either of the following provisions of the Explosive Substances Act 1883—
   (a) section 2 (causing explosion likely to endanger life or property); and
   (b) section 3 (attempt to cause explosion, or making or keeping explosive with intent to endanger life or property).

9. Any offence under section 1 of the Children and Young Persons Act 1933 (cruelty to person under 16).

10. Any offence under section 4(1) of the Criminal Law Act 1967 (assisting offender) committed in relation to the offence of murder.

11. Any offence under any of the following provisions of the Firearms Act 1968—
    (a) section 16 (possession of firearm with intent to injure);
    (b) section 17 (use of firearm to resist arrest); and
    (c) section 18 (carrying firearm with criminal intent).

12. Any offence under either of the following provisions of the Theft Act 1968—
    (a) section 9 (burglary); and
    (b) section 10 (aggravated burglary);
and any offence under section 12A of that Act (aggravated vehicle-taking) involving an accident which caused the death of any person.

13. Any offence under section 1 of the Criminal Damage Act 1971 (destroying or damaging property) required to be charged as arson.

14. Any offence under section 2 of the Child Abduction Act 1984 (abduction of child by person other than parent).

Conspiracy, incitement and attempts

15. Any offence under section 1 of the Criminal Law Act 1977 of conspiracy to commit any of the offences mentioned in paragraphs 1 to 14.

16. Any offence under section 1 of the Criminal Attempts Act 1981 of attempting to commit any of those offences.

17. Any offence of inciting another to commit any of those offences.

Youth Justice and Criminal Evidence Act 1999

(1999, c. 23)

PART II GIVING OF EVIDENCE OR INFORMATION FOR PURPOSES OF CRIMINAL PROCEEDINGS

Chapter I Special measures directions in case of vulnerable and intimidated witnesses

Preliminary

16 Witnesses eligible for assistance on grounds of age or incapacity

(1) For the purposes of this Chapter a witness in criminal proceedings (other than the accused) is eligible for assistance by virtue of this section—
    (a) if under the age of 18 at the time of the hearing; or
    (b) if the court considers that the quality of evidence given by the witness is likely to be diminished by reason of any circumstances falling within subsection (2).

(2) The circumstances falling within this subsection are—
    (a) that the witness—
        (i) suffers from mental disorder within the meaning of the Mental Health Act 1983, or
        (ii) otherwise has a significant impairment of intelligence and social functioning;
    (b) that the witness has a physical disability or is suffering from a physical disorder.

(3) In subsection (1)(a) 'the time of the hearing', in relation to a witness, means the time when it falls to the court to make a determination for the purposes of section 19(2) in relation to the witness.

(4) In determining whether a witness falls within subsection (1)(b) the court must consider any views expressed by the witness.

(5) In this Chapter references to the quality of a witness's evidence are to its quality in terms of completeness, coherence and accuracy; and for this purpose 'coherence' refers to a witness's ability in giving evidence to give answers which address the questions put to the witness and can be understood both individually and collectively.

17 Witnesses eligible for assistance on grounds of fear or distress about testifying

(1) For the purposes of this Chapter a witness in criminal proceedings (other than the accused) is eligible for assistance by virtue of this subsection if the court is satisfied that the quality of evidence given by the witness is likely to be diminished by reason of fear or distress on the part of the witness in connection with testifying in the proceedings.

(2) In determining whether a witness falls within subsection (1) the court must take into account, in particular—

(a) the nature and alleged circumstances of the offence to which the proceedings relate;

(b) the age of the witness;

(c) such of the following matters as appear to the court to be relevant, namely—

(i)   the social and cultural background and ethnic origins of the witness,

(ii)   the domestic and employment circumstances of the witness, and

(iii) any religious beliefs or political opinions of the witness;

(d) any behaviour towards the witness on the part of—

(i)   the accused,

(ii)   members of the family or associates of the accused, or

(iii) any other person who is likely to be an accused or a witness in the proceedings.

(3) In determining that question the court must in addition consider any views expressed by the witness.

(4) Where the complainant in respect of a sexual offence is a witness in proceedings relating to that offence (or to that offence and any other offences), the witness is eligible for assistance in relation to those proceedings by virtue of this subsection unless the witness has informed the court of the witness's wish not to be so eligible by virtue of this subsection.

18 Special measures available to eligible witnesses

(1) For the purposes of this Chapter—

(a) the provision which may be made by a special measures direction by virtue of each of sections 23 to 30 is a special measure available in relation to a witness eligible for assistance by virtue of section 16; and

(b) the provision which may be made by such a direction by virtue of each of sections 23 to 28 is a special measure available in relation to a witness eligible for assistance by virtue of section 17;

but this subsection has effect subject to subsection (2).

(2) Where (apart from this subsection) a special measure would, in accordance with subsection (1)(a) or (b), be available in relation to a witness in any proceedings, it shall not be taken by a court to be available in relation to the witness unless—

(a) the court has been notified by the Secretary of State that relevant arrangements may be made available in the area in which it appears to the court that the proceedings will take place, and

(b) the notice has not been withdrawn.

(3) In subsection (2) 'relevant arrangements' means arrangements for implementing the measure in question which cover the witness and the proceedings in question.

(4) The withdrawal of a notice under that subsection relating to a special measure shall not affect the availability of that measure in relation to a witness if a special measures direction providing for that measure to apply to the witness's evidence has been made by the court before the notice is withdrawn.

(5) The Secretary of State may by order make such amendments of this Chapter as he considers appropriate for altering the special measures which, in accordance with subsection (1)(a) or (b), are available in relation to a witness eligible for assistance by virtue of section 16 or (as the case may be) section 17, whether—

    (a) by modifying the provisions relating to any measure for the time being available in relation to such a witness,

    (b) by the addition—

        (i) (with or without modifications) of any measure which is for the time being available in relation to a witness eligible for assistance virtue of the other of those sections, or

        (ii) of any new measure, or

    (c) by the removal of any measure.

Special measures directions

19   Special measures direction relating to eligible witness

    (1) This section applies where in any criminal proceedings—

    (a) a party to the proceedings makes an application for the court to give a direction under this section in relation to a witness in the proceedings other than the accused, or

    (b) the court of its own motion raises the issue whether such a direction should be given.

    (2) Where the court determines that the witness is eligible for assistance by virtue of section 16 or 17, the court must then—

    (a) determine whether any of the special measures available in relation to the witness (or any combination of them) would, in its opinion, be likely to improve the quality of evidence given by the witness; and

    (b) if so—

        (i) determine which of those measures (or combination of them) would, in its opinion, be likely to maximise so far as practicable the quality of such evidence; and

        (ii) give a direction under this section providing for the measure or measures so determined to apply to evidence given by the witness.

    (3) In determining for the purposes of this Chapter whether any special measure or measures would or would not be likely to improve, or to maximise so far as practicable, the quality of evidence given by the witness, the court must consider all the circumstances of the case, including in particular—

    (a) any views expressed by the witness; and

    (b) whether the measure or measures might tend to inhibit such evidence being effectively tested by a party to the proceedings.

    (4) A special measures direction must specify particulars of the provision made by the direction in respect of each special measure which is to apply to the witness's evidence.

    (5) In this Chapter 'special measures direction' means a direction under this section.

    (6) Nothing in this Chapter is to be regarded as affecting any power of a court to make an order or give leave of any description (in the exercise of its inherent jurisdiction or otherwise)—

    (a) in relation to a witness who is not an eligible witness, or

    (b) in relation to an eligible witness where (as, for example, in a case where a foreign language interpreter is to be provided) the order is made or the leave is given otherwise than by reason of the fact that the witness is an eligible witness.

20   Further provisions about directions: general

    (1) Subject to subsection (2) and section 21(8), a special measures direction has binding effect from the time it is made until the proceedings for the purposes of which it is made are either—

    (a) determined (by acquittal, conviction or otherwise), or

    (b) abandoned,

in relation to the accused or (if there is more than one) in relation to each of the accused.

(2) The court may discharge or vary (or further vary) a special measures direction if it appears to the court to be in the interests of justice to do so, and may do so either—

    (a) on an application made by a party to the proceedings, if there has been a material change of circumstances since the relevant time, or

    (b) of its own motion.

(3) In subsection (2) 'the relevant time' means—

    (a) the time when the direction was given, or

    (b) if a previous application has been made under that subsection, the time when the application (or last application) was made.

(4) Nothing in section 24(2) and (3), 27(4) to (7) or 28(4) to (6) is to be regarded as affecting the power of the court to vary or discharge a special measures direction under subsection (2).

(5) The court must state in open court its reasons for—

    (a) giving or varying,

    (b) refusing an application for, or for the variation or discharge of, or

    (c) discharging,

a special measures direction and, if it is a magistrates' court, must cause them to be entered in the register of its proceedings.

(6) Criminal Procedure Rules may make provision—

    (a) for uncontested applications to be determined by the court without a hearing;

    (b) for preventing the renewal of an unsuccessful application for a special measures direction except where there has been a material change of circumstances;

    (c) for expert evidence to be given in connection with an application for, or for varying or discharging, such a direction;

    (d) for the manner in which confidential or sensitive information is to be treated in connection with such an application and in particular as to its being disclosed to, or withheld from, a party to the proceedings.

21 Special provisions relating to child witnesses

(1) For the purposes of this section—

    (a) a witness in criminal proceedings is a 'child witness' if he is an eligible witness by reason of section 16(1)(a) (whether or not he is an eligible witness by reason of any other provision of section 16 or 17); and

    (c) a 'relevant recording', in relation to a child witness, is a video recording of an interview of the witness made with a view to its admission as evidence in chief of the witness.

(2) Where the court, in making a determination for the purposes of section 19(2), determines that a witness in criminal proceedings is a child witness, the court must—

    (a) first have regard to subsections (3) to (4C) below; and

    (b) then have regard to section 19(2);

and for the purposes of section 19(2), as it then applies to the witness, any special measures required to be applied in relation to him by virtue of this section shall be treated as if they were measures determined by the court, pursuant to section 19(2)(a) and (b)(i), to be ones that (whether on their own or with any other special measures) would be likely to maximise, so far as practicable, the quality of his evidence.

(3) The primary rule in the case of a child witness is that the court must give a special measures direction in relation to the witness which complies with the following requirements—

    (a) it must provide for any relevant recording to be admitted under section 27 (video recorded evidence in chief); and

    (b) it must provide for any evidence given by the witness in the proceedings which is not given by means of a video recording (whether in chief or otherwise) to be given by means of a live link in accordance with section 24.

(4) The primary rule is subject to the following limitations—

    (a) the requirement contained in subsection (3)(a) or (b) has effect subject to the availability (within the meaning of section 18(2)) of the special measure in question in relation to the witness;

    (b) the requirement contained in subsection (2)(a) also has effect subject to section 27(2);

    (ba) if the witness informs the court of the witness's wish that the rule should not apply or should apply only in part, the rule does not apply to the extent that the court is satisfied that not complying with the rule would not diminish the quality of the witness's evidence; and

    (c) the rule does not apply to the extent that the court is satisfied that compliance with it would not be likely to maximise the quality of the witness's evidence so far as practicable (whether because the application to that evidence of one or more other special measures available in relation to the witness would have that result or for any other reason).

(4A) Where as a consequence of all or part of the primary rule being disapplied under subsection (4)(ba) a witness's evidence or any part of it would fall to be given as testimony in court, the court must give a special measures direction making such provision as is described in section 23 for the evidence or that part of it.

(4B) The requirement in subsection (4A) is subject to the following limitations—

    (a) if the witness informs the court of the witness's wish that the requirement in subsection (4A) should not apply, the requirement does not apply to the extent that the court is satisfied that not complying with it would not diminish the quality of the witness's evidence; and

    (b) the requirement does not apply to the extent that the court is satisfied that making such a provision would not be likely to maximise the quality of the witness's evidence so far as practicable (whether because the application to that evidence of one or more other special measures available in relation to the witness would have that result or for any other reason).

(4C) In making a decision under subsection (4)(ba) or (4B)(a), the court must take into account the following factors (and any others it considers relevant)—

    (a) the age and maturity of the witness;

    (b) the ability of the witness to understand the consequences of giving evidence otherwise than in accordance with the requirements in subsection (3) or (as the case may be) in accordance with the requirement in subsection (4A);

    (c) the relationship (if any) between the witness and the accused;

    (d) the witness's social and cultural background and ethnic origins;

    (e) the nature and alleged circumstances of the offence to which the proceedings relate.

(8) Where a special measures direction is given in relation to a child witness who is an eligible witness by reason only of section 16(1)(a), then—

    (a) subject to subsection (9) below, and

    (b) except where the witness has already begun to give evidence in the proceedings,

the direction shall cease to have effect at the time when the witness attains the age of 18.

(9) Where a special measures direction is given in relation to a child witness who is an eligible witness by reason only of section 16(1)(a) and—

    (a) the direction provides—

      (i) for any relevant recording to be admitted under section 27 as evidence in chief of the witness, or

      (ii) for the special measure available under section 28 to apply in relation to the witness, and

    (b) if it provides for that special measure to so apply, the witness is still under the age of 18 when the video recording is made for the purposes of section 28,

then, so far as it provides as mentioned in paragraph (a)(i) or (ii) above, the direction shall continue to have effect in accordance with section 20(1) even though the witness subsequently attains that age.

22 Extension of provisions of section 21 to certain witness over 18

(1) For the purposes of this section—

    (a) a witness in criminal proceedings (other than the accused) is a 'qualifying witness' if he—

      (i) is not an eligible witness at the time of the hearing (as defined by section 16(3)), but

      (ii) was under the age of 18 when a relevant recording was made;

    and

(c) a 'relevant recording', in relation to a witness, is a video recording of an interview of the witness made with a view to its admission as evidence in chief of the witness.

(2) Subsections (2) to (4) and (4C) of section 21, so far as relating to the giving of a direction complying with the requirement contained in section 21(3)(a), apply to a qualifying witness in respect of the relevant recording as they apply to a child witness (within the meaning of that section).

22A   Special provisions relating to sexual offences

(1) This section applies where in criminal proceedings relating to a sexual offence (or to a sexual offence and other offences) the complainant in respect of that offence is a witness in the proceedings.

(2) This section does not apply if the place of trial is a magistrates' court.

(3) This section does not apply if the complainant is an eligible witness by reason of section 16(1)(a) (whether or not the complainant is an eligible witness by reason of any other provision of section 16 or 17).

(4) If a party to the proceedings makes an application under section 19(1)(a) for a special measures direction in relation to the complainant, the party may request that the direction provide for any relevant recording to be admitted under section 27 (video recorded evidence in chief).

(5) Subsection (6) applies if—

(a) a party to the proceedings makes a request under subsection (4) with respect to the complainant, and

(b) the court determines for the purposes of section 19(2) that the complainant is eligible for assistance by virtue of section 16(1)(b) or 17.

(6) The court must—

(a) first have regard to subsections (7) to (9); and

(b) then have regard to section 19(2);

and for the purposes of section 19(2), as it then applies to the complainant, any special measure required to be applied in relation to the complainant by virtue of this section is to be treated as if it were a measure determined by the court, pursuant to section 19(2)(a) and (b)(i), to be one that (whether on its own or with any other special measures) would be likely to maximise, so far as practicable, the quality of the complainant's evidence.

(7) The court must give a special measures direction in relation to the complainant that provides for any relevant recording to be admitted under section 27.

(8) The requirement in subsection (7) has effect subject to section 27(2).

(9) The requirement in subsection (7) does not apply to the extent that the court is satisfied that compliance with it would not be likely to maximise the quality of the complainant's evidence so far as practicable (whether because the application to that evidence of one or more other special measures available in relation to the complainant would have that result or for any other reason).

(10) In this section "relevant recording", in relation to a complainant, is a video recording of an interview of the complainant made with a view to its admission as the evidence in chief of the complainant.

Special measures

23   Screening witness from accused

(1) A special measures direction may provide for the witness, while giving testimony or being sworn in court, to be prevented by means of a screen or other arrangement from seeing the accused.

(2) But the screen or other arrangement must not prevent the witness from being able to see, and to be seen by—

(a) the judge or justices (or both) and the jury (if there is one);

(b) legal representatives acting in the proceedings; and

(c) any interpreter or other person appointed (in pursuance of the direction or otherwise) to assist the witness.

(3) Where two or more legal representatives are acting for a party to the proceedings, subsection (2)(b) is to be regarded as satisfied in relation to those representatives if the witness is able to all material times to see and be seen by at least one of them.

24   Evidence by live link

(1) A special measures direction may provide for the witness to give evidence by means of a live link.

(1A) Such a direction may also provide for a specified person to accompany the witness while the witness is giving evidence by live link.

(1B) In determining who may accompany the witness, the court must have regard to the wishes of the witness.

(2) Where a direction provides for the witness to give evidence by means of a live link, the witness may not give evidence in any other way without the permission of the court.

(3) The court may give permission for the purposes of subsection (2) if it appears to the court to be in the interests of justice to do so, and may do so either—

    (a) on an application by a party to the proceedings, if there has been a material change of circumstances since the relevant time, or

    (b) of its own motion.

(4) In subsection (3) 'the relevant time' means—

    (a) the time when the direction was given, or

    (b) if a previous application has been made under that subsection, the time when the application (or last application) was made.

(8) In this Chapter 'live link' means a live television link or other arrangement whereby a witness, while absent from the courtroom or other place where the proceedings are being held, is able to see and hear a person there and to be such and heard by the persons specified in section 23(2)(a) to (c).

25   Evidence given in private

(1) A special measures direction may provide for the exclusion from the court, during the giving of the witness's evidence, of persons of any description specified in the direction.

(2) The persons who may be so excluded do not include—

    (a) the accused,

    (b) legal representatives acting in the proceedings, or

    (c) any interpreter or other person appointed (in pursuance of the direction or otherwise) to assist the witness.

(3) A special measures direction providing for representatives of news gathering or reporting organisations to be so excluded shall be expressed not to apply to one named person who—

    (a) is a representative of such an organisation, and

    (b) has been nominated for the purpose by one or more such organisations,

unless it appears to the court that no such nomination has been made.

(4) A special measures direction may only provide for the exclusion of persons under this section where—

    (a) the proceedings relate to a sexual offence; or

    (b) it appears to the court that there are reasonable grounds for believing that any person other than the accused has sought, or will seek, to intimidate the witness in connection with testifying in the proceedings.

(5) Any proceedings from which persons are excluded under this section (whether or not those persons include representatives of news gathering or reporting organisations) shall nevertheless be taken to be held in public for the purposes of any privilege or exemption from liability available in respect of fair, accurate and contemporaneous reports of legal proceedings held in public.

26   Removal of wigs and gowns

A special measures direction may provide for the wearing of wigs or gowns to be dispensed with during the giving of the witness's evidence.

27   Video recorded evidence in chief

(1) A special measures direction may provide for a video recording of an interview of the witness to be admitted as evidence in chief of the witness.

(2) A special measures direction may, however, not provide for a video recording, or a part of such a recording, to be admitted under this section if the court is of the opinion, having regard to all the circumstances of the case, that in the interests of justice the recording, or that part of it, should not be so admitted.

(3) In considering for the purposes of subsection (2) whether any part of a recording should not be admitted under this section, the court must consider whether any prejudice to the accused which might result from that part being so admitted is outweighed by the desirability of showing the whole, or substantially the whole, of the recorded interview.

(4) Where a special measures direction provides for a recording to be admitted under this section, the court may nevertheless subsequently direct that it is not to be so admitted if—

(a) it appears to the court that—
  (i) the witness will not be available for cross-examination (whether conducted in the ordinary way or in accordance with any such direction), and
  (ii) the parties to the proceedings have not agreed that there is no need for the witness to be so available; or
(b) any Criminal Procedure Rules requiring disclosure of the circumstances in which the recording was made have not been complied with to the satisfaction of the court.

(5) Where a recording is admitted under this section—

(a) the witness must be called by the party tendering it in evidence, unless—
  (i) a special measures direction provides for the witness's evidence on cross-examination to be given in any recording admissible under section 28, or
  (ii) the parties to the proceedings have agreed as mentioned in subsection (4)(a)(ii); and
(b) the witness may not without the permission of the court give evidence in chief otherwise than by means of the recording as to any matter which, in the opinion of the court, is dealt with in the witness's recorded testimony.

(6) Where in accordance with subsection (2) a special measures direction provides for part only of a recording to be admitted under this section, references in subsection (4) and (5) to the recording or to the witness's recorded testimony are references to the part of the recording or testimony which is to be so admitted.

(7) The court may give permission for the purposes of subsection (5)(b) if it appears to the court to be in the interests of justice to do so, and may do so either—

(a) on an application by a party to the proceedings, or
(b) of its own motion.

(9) The court may, in giving permission for the purposes of subsection (5)(b), direct that the evidence in question is to be given by the witness by means of a live link; and, if the court so directs, subsections (5) to (7) of section 24 shall apply in relation to that evidence as they apply in relation to evidence which is to be given in accordance with a special measures direction.

(9A) If the court directs under subsection (9) that evidence is to be given by live link, it may also make such provision in that direction as it could make under section 24(1A) in a special measures direction.

(11) Nothing in this section affects the admissibility of any video recording which would be admissible apart from this section.

28 Video recorded cross-examination or re-examination

(1) Where a special measures direction provides for a video recording to be admitted under section 27 as evidence in chief of the witness, the direction may also provide—

(a) for any cross-examination of the witness, and any re-examination, to be recorded by means of a video recording; and
(b) for such a recording to be admitted, so far as it relates to any such cross-examination or re-examination, as evidence of the witness under cross-examination or on re-examination, as the case may be.

(2) Such a recording must be made in the presence of such persons as Criminal Procedure Rules or the direction may provide and in the absence of the accused, but in circumstances in which—

(a) the judge or justices (or both) and legal representatives acting in the proceedings are able to see and hear the examination of the witness and to communicate with the persons in whose presence the recording is being made, and

(b) the accused is able to see and hear any such examination and to communicate with any legal representative acting for him.

(3) Where two or more legal representatives are acting for a party to the proceedings, subsection (2)(a) and (b) are to be regarded as satisfied in relation to those representatives if at all material times they are satisfied in relation to at least one of them.

(4) Where a special measures direction provides for a recording to be admitted under this section, the court may nevertheless subsequently direct that it is not to be so admitted if any requirement of subsection (2) or Criminal Procedure Rules or the direction has not been complied with to the satisfaction of the court.

(5) Where in pursuance of subsection (1) a recording has been made of any examination of the witness, the witness may not be subsequently cross-examined or re-examined in respect of any evidence given by the witness in the proceedings (whether in any recording admissible under section 27 or this section or otherwise than in such a recording) unless the court gives a further special measures direction making such provision as is mentioned in subsection (1)(a) and (b) in relation to any subsequent cross-examination, and re-examination, of the witness.

(6) The court may only give such a further direction if it appears to the court—

(a) that the proposed cross-examination is sought by a party to the proceedings as a result of that party having become aware, since the time when the original recording was made in pursuance of subsection (1), of a matter which that party could not with reasonable diligence have ascertained by then, or

(b) that for any other reason it is in the interests of justice to give the further direction.

(7) Nothing in this section shall be read as applying in relation to any cross-examination of the witness by the accused in person (in a case where the accused is to be able to conduct any such cross-examination).

29 Examination of witness through intermediary

(1) A special measures direction may provide for any examination of the witness (however and wherever conducted) to be conducted through an interpreter or other person approved by the court for the purposes of this section ('an intermediary').

(2) The function of an intermediary is to communicate—

(a) to the witness, questions put to the witness, and

(b) to any person asking such questions, the answers given by the witness in reply to them,

and to explain such questions or answers so far as necessary to enable them to be understood by the witness or person in question.

(3) Any examination of the witness in pursuance of subsection (1) must take place in the presence of such persons as Criminal Procedure Rules or the direction may provide, but in circumstances in which—

(a) the judge or justices (or both) and legal representatives acting in the proceedings are able to see and hear the examination of the witness and to communicate with the intermediary, and

(b) (except in the case of a video recorded examination) the jury (if there is one) are able to see and hear the examination of the witness.

(4) Where two or more legal representatives are acting for a party to the proceedings, subsection (3)(a) is to be regarded as satisfied in relation to those representatives if at all material times it is satisfied in relation to at least one of them.

(5) A person may not act as an intermediary in a particular case except after making a declaration, in such form as may be prescribed by Criminal Procedure Rules, that he will faithfully perform his function as intermediary.

(6) Subsection (1) does not apply to an interview of the witness which is recorded by means of a video recording with a view to its admission as evidence in chief of the witness; but a special measures direction may provide for such a recording to be admitted under section 27 if the interview was conducted through an intermediary and—

(a) that person complied with subsection (5) before the interview began, and

(b) the court's approval for the purposes of this action is given before the direction is given.

(7) Section 1 of the Perjury Act 1911 (perjury) shall apply in relation to a person acting as an intermediary as it applies in relation to a person lawfully sworn as an interpreter in a judicial proceeding; and for this purpose, where a person acts as an intermediary in any proceeding which is not a judicial proceeding for the purposes of that section, that proceeding shall be taken to be part of the judicial proceeding in which the witness's evidence is given.

30   Aids to communication

A special measures direction may provide for the witness, while giving evidence (whether by testimony in court or otherwise), to be provided with such device as the court considers appropriate with a view to enabling questions or answers to be communicated to or by the witness despite any disability or disorder or other impairment which the witness has or suffers from.

Supplementary

31   Status of evidence given under Chapter 1

(1) Subsections (2) to (4) apply to a statement made by a witness in criminal proceedings which, in accordance with a special measures direction, is not made by the witness in direct oral testimony in court but forms part of the witness's evidence in those proceedings.

(2) The statement shall be treated as if made by the witness in direct oral testimony in court; and accordingly—

(a) it is admissible evidence of any fact of which such testimony from the witness would be admissible;

(b) it is not capable of corroborating any other evidence given by the witness.

(3) Subsection (2) applies to a statement admitted under section 27 or 28 which is not made by the witness on oath even though it would have been required to be made on oath if made by the witness in direct oral testimony in court.

(4) In estimating the weight (if any) to be attached to the statement, the court must have regard to all the circumstances from which an inference can reasonably be drawn (as to the accuracy of the statement or otherwise).

(5) Nothing in this Chapter (apart from subsection (3)) affects the operation of any rule of law relating to evidence in criminal proceedings.

(6) Where any statement made by a person on oath in any proceeding which is not a judicial proceeding for the purposes of section 1 of the Perjury Act 1911 (perjury) is received in evidence in pursuance of a special measures direction, that proceeding shall be taken for the purposes of that section to be part of the judicial proceeding in which the statement is so received in evidence.

(7) Where in any proceeding which is not a judicial proceeding for the purposes of that Act—

(a) a person wilfully makes a false statement otherwise than on oath which is subsequently received in evidence in pursuance of a special measures direction, and

(b) the statement is made in such circumstances that had it been given on oath in any such judicial proceeding that person would have been guilty of perjury, he shall be guilty of an offence and liable to any punishment which might be imposed on conviction of an offence under section 57(2) (giving of false unsworn evidence in criminal proceedings).

(8) In this section 'statement' includes any representation of fact, whether made in words or otherwise.

32   Warning to jury

Where on a trial on indictment with a jury evidence has been given in accordance with a special measures direction, the judge must give the jury such warning (if any) as the judge considers necessary to ensure that the fact that the direction was given in relation to the witness does not prejudice the accused.

33   Interpretation etc. of Chapter 1

(1) In this Chapter—

'eligible witness' means a witness eligible for assistance by virtue of section 16 or 17;

'livelink' has the meaning given by section 24(8);

'quality', in relation to the evidence of a witness, shall be construed in accordance with section 16(5);

'special measures direction' means (in accordance with section 19(5)) a direction under section 19.

(2) In this Chapter references to the special measures available in relation to a witness shall be construed in accordance with section 18.

(3) In this Chapter references to a person being able to see or hear, or be seen or heard by, another person are to be read as not applying to the extent that either of them is unable to see or hear by reason of any impairment of eyesight or hearing.

(4) In the case of any proceedings in which there is more than one accused—

(a) any reference to the accused in sections 23 to 28 may be taken by a court, in connection with the giving of a special measures direction, as a reference to all or any of the accused, as the court may determine, and

(b) any such direction may be given on the basis of any such determination.

Chapter 1A Use of live link and intermediary for evidence of certain accused persons

33A Live link directions

(1) This section applies to any proceedings (whether in a magistrates' court or before the Crown Court) against a person for an offence.

(2) The court may, on the application of the accused, give a live link direction if it is satisfied—

(a) that the conditions in subsection (4) or, as the case may be, subsection (5) are met in relation to the accused, and

(b) that it is in the interests of justice for the accused to give evidence through a live link.

(3) A live link direction is a direction that any oral evidence to be given before the court by the accused is to be given through a live link.

(4) Where the accused is aged under 18 when the application is made, the conditions are that—

(a) his ability to participate effectively in the proceedings as a witness giving oral evidence in court is compromised by his level of intellectual ability or social functioning, and

(b) use of a live link would enable him to participate more effectively in the proceedings as a witness (whether by improving the quality of his evidence or otherwise).

(5) Where the accused has attained the age of 18 at that time, the conditions are that—

(a) he suffers from a mental disorder (within the meaning of the Mental Health Act 1983) or otherwise has a significant impairment of intelligence and social function,

(b) he is for that reason unable to participate effectively in the proceedings as a witness giving oral evidence in court, and

(c) use of a live link would enable him to participate more effectively in the proceedings as a witness (whether by improving the quality of his evidence or otherwise).

(6) While a live link direction has effect the accused may not give oral evidence before the court in the proceedings otherwise than through a live link.

(7) The court may discharge a live link direction at any time before or during any hearing to which it applies if it appears to the court to be in the interests of justice to do so (but this does not affect the power to give a further live link direction in relation to the accused).

The court may exercise this power of its own motion or on an application by a party.

(8) The court must state in open court its reasons for—

(a) giving or discharging a live link direction, or

(b) refusing an application for or for the discharge of a live link direction,

and, if it is a magistrates' court, it must cause those reasons to be entered in the register of its proceedings.

33B Section 33A: meaning of 'live link'

(1) In section 33A 'live link' means an arrangement by which the accused, while absent from the place where the proceedings are being held, is able—

(a) to see and hear a person there, and

(b) to be seen and heard by the persons mentioned in subsection (2),

and for this purpose any impairment of eyesight or hearing is to be disregarded.

(2) The persons are—

(a) the judge or justices (or both) and the jury (if there is one),

(b) where there are two or more accused in the proceedings, each of the other accused,

(c) legal representatives acting in the proceedings, and

(d) any interpreter or other person appointed by the court to assist the accused.

33BA Examination of accused through intermediary

(1) This section applies to any proceedings (whether in a magistrates' court or before the Crown Court) against a person for an offence.

(2) The court may, on the application of the accused, give a direction under subsection (3) if it is satisfied—

(a) that the condition in subsection (5) is or, as the case may be, the conditions in subsection (6) are met in relation to the accused, and

(b) that making the direction is necessary in order to ensure that the accused receives a fair trial.

(3) A direction under this subsection is a direction that provides for any examination of the accused to be conducted through an interpreter or other person approved by the court for the purposes of this section ("an intermediary").

(4) The function of an intermediary is to communicate—

(a) to the accused, questions put to the accused, and

(b) to any person asking such questions, the answers given by the accused in reply to them,

and to explain such questions or answers so far as necessary to enable them to be understood by the accused or the person in question.

(5) Where the accused is aged under 18 when the application is made the condition is that the accused's ability to participate effectively in the proceedings as a witness giving oral evidence in court is compromised by the accused's level of intellectual ability or social functioning.

(6) Where the accused has attained the age of 18 when the application is made the conditions are that—

(a) the accused suffers from a mental disorder (within the meaning of the Mental Health Act 1983) or otherwise has a significant impairment of intelligence and social function, and

(b) the accused is for that reason unable to participate effectively in the proceedings as a witness giving oral evidence in court.

(7) Any examination of the accused in pursuance of a direction under subsection (3) must take place in the presence of such persons as Criminal Procedure Rules or the direction may provide and in circumstances in which—

(a) the judge or justices (or both) and legal representatives acting in the proceedings are able to see and hear the examination of the accused and to communicate with the intermediary,

(b) the jury (if there is one) are able to see and hear the examination of the accused, and

(c) where there are two or more accused in the proceedings, each of the other accused is able to see and hear the examination of the accused.

For the purposes of this subsection any impairment of eyesight or hearing is to be disregarded.

(8) Where two or more legal representatives are acting for a party to the proceedings, subsection (7)(a) is to be regarded as satisfied in relation to those representatives if at all material times it is satisfied in relation to at least one of them.

(9) A person may not act as an intermediary in a particular case except after making a declaration, in such form as may be prescribed by Criminal Procedure Rules, that the person will faithfully perform the function of an intermediary.

(10) Section 1 of the Perjury Act 1911 (perjury) applies in relation to a person acting as an intermediary as it applies in relation to a person lawfully sworn as an interpreter in a judicial proceeding.

33BB Further provision as to directions under section 33BA(3)

(1) The court may discharge a direction given under section 33BA(3) at any time before or during the proceedings to which it applies if it appears to the court that the direction is no longer necessary in order to ensure that the accused receives a fair trial (but this does not affect the power to give a further direction under section 33BA(3) in relation to the accused).

(2) The court may vary (or further vary) a direction given under section 33BA(3) at any time before or during the proceedings to which it applies if it appears to the court that it is necessary for the direction to be varied in order to ensure that the accused receives a fair trial.

(3) The court may exercise the power in subsection (1) or (2) of its own motion or on an application by a party.

(4) The court must state in open court its reasons for—

(a) giving, varying or discharging a direction under section 33BA(3), or

(b) refusing an application for, or for the variation or discharge of, a direction under section 33BA(3),

and, if it is a magistrates' court, it must cause those reasons to be entered in the register of its proceedings.

33C Saving

Nothing in this Chapter affects—

(a) any power of a court to make an order, give directions or give leave of any description in relation to any witness (including an accused), or

(b) the operation of any rule of law relating to evidence in criminal proceedings.

Chapter II Protection of witnesses from cross-examination by accused in person

General prohibitions

34 Complainants in proceedings for sexual offences

No person charged with a sexual offence may in any criminal proceedings cross-examine in person a witness who is the complainant, either—

(a) in connection with that offence, or

(b) in connection with any other offence (or whatever nature) with which that person is charged in the proceedings.

35 Child complainants and other child witnesses

(1) No person charged with an offence to which this section applies may in any criminal proceedings cross-examine in person a protected witness, either—

(a) in connection with that offence, or

(b) in connection with any other offence (of whatever nature) with which that person is charged in the proceedings.

(2) For the purposes of subsection (1) a 'protected witness' is a witness who—

(a) either is the complainant or is alleged to have been a witness to the commission of the offence to which this section applies, and

(b) either is a child or falls to be cross-examined after giving evidence in chief (whether wholly or in part)—

(i)   by means of a video recording made (for the purposes of section 27) at a time when the witness was a child, or

(ii) in any other way at any such time.

(3) the offences to which this section applies are—

(a) any offence under—

(iva) any of sections 33 to 36 of the Sexual Offences Act 1956

(v)   the Protection of Children Act 1978; or

(vi)   Part I of the Sexual Offences Act 2003 or any relevant superseded enactment.

(b) kidnapping, false imprisonment or an offence under section 1 or 2 of the Child Abduction Act 1984;

(c) any offence under section 1 of the Children and Young Persons Act 1933;

(d) any offence (not within any of the preceding paragraphs) which involves an assault on, or injury or a threat of injury to, any person.

(3A) In subsection (3)(a)(vi) 'relevant superseded enactment' means—

(a) any of sections 1 to 32 of the Sexual Offences Act 1956;

(b) the Indecency with Children Act 1960;

(c) the Sexual Offences Act 1967;

(d) section 54 of the Criminal Law Act 1977.

(4) In this section 'child' means—

(a) where the offence falls within subsection (3)(a), a person under the age of 18; or

(b) where the offence falls within subsection (3)(b), (c) or (d), a person under the age of 14.

(5) For the purposes of this section 'witness' includes a witness who is charged with an offence in the proceedings.

Prohibition imposed by court

36 Direction prohibiting accused from cross-examining particular witness

(1) This section applies where, in a case where neither of sections 34 and 35 operates to prevent an accused in any criminal proceedings from cross-examining a witness in person—

(a) the prosecutor makes an application for the court to give a direction under this section in relation to the witness, or

(b) the court of its own motion raises the issue whether such a direction should be given.

(2) If it appears to the court—

(a) that the quality of evidence given by the witness on cross-examination—

(i)   is likely to be diminished if the cross-examination (or further cross- examination) is conducted by the accused in person, and

(ii) would be likely to be improved if a direction were given under this section, and

(b) that it would not be contrary to the interests of justice to give such a direction, the court may give a direction prohibiting the accused from cross-examining (or further cross-examining) the witness in person.

(3) In determining whether subsection (2)(a) applies in the case of a witness the court must have regard, in particular, to—

(a) any views expressed by the witness as to whether or not the witness is content to be cross-examined by the accused in person;

(b) the nature of the questions likely to be asked, having regard to the issues in the proceedings and the defence case advanced so far (if any);

   (c) any behaviour on the part of the accused at any stage of the proceedings, both generally
       and in relation to the witness;
   (d) any relationship (of whatever nature) between the witness and the accused;
   (e) whether any person (other than the accused) is or has at any time been charged in the
       proceedings with a sexual offence or an offence to which section 35 applies, and (if so)
       whether section 34 or 35 operates or would have operated to prevent that person from
       cross-examining the witness in person;
   (f) any direction under section 19 which the court has given, or proposes to give, in relation
       to the witness.
 (4) For the purposes of this section—
   (a) 'witness', in relation to an accused, does not include any other person who is charged with
       an offence in the proceedings; and
   (b) any reference to the quality of a witness's evidence shall be construed in accordance with
       section 16(5).

37 Further provisions about directions under section 36

 (1) Subject to subsection (2), a direction has binding effect from the time it is made until the witness to whom it applies is discharged.
In this section 'direction' means a direction under section 36.
 (2) The court may discharge a direction if it appears to the court to be in the interests of justice
to do so, and may do so either—
   (a) on an application made by a party to the proceedings, if there has been a material change
       of circumstances since the relevant time, or
   (b) of its own motion.
 (3) In subsection (2) 'the relevant time' means—
   (a) the time when the direction was given, or
   (b) if a previous application has been made under that subsection, the time when the applica-
       tion (or last application) was made.
 (4) The court must state in open court its reasons for—
   (a) giving, or
   (b) refusing an application for, or for the discharge of, or
   (c) discharging,
a direction and, if it is a magistrates' court, must cause them to be entered in the register of its
proceedings.
 (5) Criminal Procedure Rules may make provision—
   (a) for uncontested applications to be determined by the court without a hearing;
   (b) for preventing the renewal of an unsuccessful application for a direction except where
       there has been a material change of circumstances;
   (c) for expert evidence to be given in connection with an application for, or for discharging,
       a direction;
   (d) for the manner in which confidential or sensitive information is to be treated in connec-
       tion with such an application and in particular as to its being disclosed to, or withheld
       from, a party to the proceedings.

Cross-examination on behalf of accused

38 Defence representation for purposes of cross-examination

 (1) This section applies where an accused is prevented from cross-examining a witness in person
by virtue of section 34, 35 or 36.
 (2) Where it appears to the court that this section applies, it must—
   (a) invite the accused to arrange for a legal representative to act for him for the purpose of
       cross-examining the witness; and

(b) require the accused to notify the court, by the end of such period as it may specify, whether a legal representative is to act for him for that purpose.

(3) If by the end of the period mentioned in subsection (2)(b) either—

(a) the accused has notified the court that no legal representative is to act for him for the purpose of cross-examining the witness, or

(b) no notification has been received by the court and it appears to the court that no legal representative is to so act,

the court must consider whether it is necessary in the interests of justice for the witness to be cross-examined by a legal representative appointed to represent the interests of the accused.

(4) If the court decides that it is necessary in the interests of justice for the witness to be so cross-examined, the court must appoint a qualified legal representative (chosen by the court) to cross-examine the witness in the interests of the accused.

(5) A person so appointed shall not be responsible to the accused.

(6) Criminal Procedure Rules may make provision—

(a) as to the time when, and the manner in which, subsection (2) is to be complied with;

(b) in connection with the appointment of a legal representative under subsection (4), and in particular for securing that a person so appointed is provided with evidence or other material relating to the proceedings.

(7) Criminal Procedure Rules made in pursuance of subsection (6)(b) may make provision for the application, with such modifications as are specified in the rules, of any of the provisions of—

(a) Part I of the Criminal Procedure and Investigations Act 1996 (disclosure of material in connection with criminal proceedings), or

(b) the Sexual Offences (Protected Material) Act 1997.

(8) For the purposes of this section—

(a) any reference to cross-examination includes (in a case where a direction is given under section 36 after the accused has begun cross-examining the witness) a reference to further cross-examination; and

(b) 'qualified legal representative' means a legal representative who has a right of audience (within the meaning of the Courts and Legal Services Act 1990) in relation to the proceedings before the court.

39 Warning to jury

(1) Where on a trial on indictment with a jury an accused is prevented from cross-examining a witness in person by virtue of section 34, 35 or 36, the judge must give the jury such warning (if any) as the judge considers necessary to ensure that the accused is not prejudiced—

(a) by any inferences that might be drawn from the fact that the accused has been prevented from cross-examining the witness in person;

(b) where the witness has been cross-examined by a legal representative appointed under section 38(4), by the fact that the cross-examination was carried out by such a legal representative and not by a person acting as the accused's own legal representative.

(2) Subsection (8)(a) of section 38 applies for the purposes of this section as it applies for the purposes of section 38.

Chapter III Protection of complainants in proceedings for sexual offences

41 Restriction on evidence or questions about complainant's sexual history

(1) If at a trial a person is charged with a sexual offence, then, except with the leave of the court—

(a) no evidence may be adduced, and

(b) no question may be asked in cross-examination,

by or on behalf of any accused at the trial, about any sexual behaviour of the complainant.

(2) The court may give leave in relation to any evidence or question only on an application made by or on behalf of an accused, and may not give such leave unless it is satisfied—

(a) that subsection (3) or (5) applies, and

(b) that a refusal of leave might have the result of rendering unsafe a conclusion of the jury or (as the case may be) the court on any relevant issue in the case.

(3) This subsection applies if the evidence or question relates to a relevant issue in the case and either—

(a) that issue is not an issue of consent; or

(b) it is an issue of consent and the sexual behaviour of the complainant to which the evidence or question relates is alleged to have taken place at or about the same time as the event which is the subject matter of the charge against the accused; or

(c) it is an issue of consent and the sexual behaviour of the complainant to which the evidence or question relates is alleged to have been, in any respect, so similar—

(i) to any sexual behaviour of the complainant which (according to evidence adduced or to be adduced by or on behalf of the accused) took place as part of the event which is the subject matter of the charge against the accused, or

(ii) to any other sexual behaviour of the complainant which (according to such evidence) took place at or about the same time as the event, that the similarity cannot reasonably be explained as a coincidence.

(4) For the purposes of subsection (3) no evidence or question shall be regarded as relating to a relevant issue in the case if it appears to the court to be reasonable to assume that the purpose (or main purpose) for which it would be adduced or asked is to establish or elicit material for impugning the credibility of the complainant as a witness.

(5) This subsection applies if the evidence or question—

(a) relates to any evidence adduced by the prosecution about any sexual behaviour of the complainant; and

(b) in the opinion of the court, would go no further than is necessary to enable the evidence adduced by the prosecution to be rebutted or explained by or on behalf of the accused.

(6) For the purposes of subsections (3) and (5) the evidence or question must relate to a specific instance (or specific instances) of alleged sexual behaviour on the part of the complainant (and accordingly nothing in those subsections is capable of applying in relation to the evidence or question to the extent that it does not so relate).

(7) Where this section applies in relation to a trial by virtue of the fact that one or more of a number of persons charged in the proceedings is or are charged with a sexual offence—

(a) it shall cease to apply in relation to the trial if the prosecutor decides not to proceed with the case against that person or those persons in respect of that charge; but

(b) it shall not cease to do so in the event of that person or those persons pleading guilty to, or being convicted of, that charge.

(8) Nothing in this section authorises any evidence to be adduced or any question to be asked which cannot be adduced or asked apart from this section.

42   Interpretation and application of section 41

(1) In section 41—

(a) 'relevant issue in the case' means any issue falling to be proved by the prosecution or defence in the trial of the accused;

(b) 'issue of consent' means any issue whether the complainant in fact consented to the conduct constituting the offence with which the accused is charged (and accordingly does not include any issue as to the belief of the accused that the complainant so consented);

(c) 'sexual behaviour' means any sexual behaviour or other sexual experience, whether or not involving any accused or other person, but excluding (except in section 41(3)(c)(i) and (5)(a)) anything alleged to have taken place as part of the event which is the subject matter of the charge against the accused; and

(d) subject to any other made under subsection (2), 'sexual offence' shall be construed in accordance with section 62.

(2) The Secretary of State may by order make such provision as he considers appropriate for adding or removing, for the purposes of section 41, any offence to or from the offences which are sexual offences for the purposes of this Act by virtue of section 62.

(3) Section 41 applies in relation to the following proceedings as it applies to a trial, namely—

(c) the hearing of an application under paragraph 2(1) of Schedule 3 to the Crime and Disorder Act 1998 (application to dismiss charge by person sent for trial under section 51 or 51A of that Act),

(d) any hearing held, between conviction and sentencing, for the purpose of determining matters relevant to the court's decision as to how the accused is to be dealt with, and

(e) the hearing of an appeal,

and references (in section 41 or this section) to a person charged with an offence accordingly include a person convicted of an offence.

43 Procedure on applications under section 41

(1) An application for leave shall be heard in private and in the absence of the complainant.

In this section 'leave' means leave under section 41.

(2) Where such an application has been determined, the court must state in open court (but in the absence of the jury, if there is one)—

(a) its reasons for giving, or refusing, leave, and

(b) if it gives leave, the extent to which evidence may be adduced or questions asked in pursuance of the leave,

and, if it is a magistrates' court, must cause those matters to be entered in the register of its proceedings.

(3) Criminal Procedure Rules may make provision—

(a) requiring applications for leave to specify, in relation to each item of evidence or question to which they relate, particulars of the grounds on which it is asserted that leave should be given by virtue of subsection (3) or (5) or section 41;

(b) enabling the court to request a party to the proceedings to provide the court with information which it considers would assist it in determining an application for leave;

(c) for the manner in which confidential or sensitive information is to be treated in connection with such an application, and in particular as to its being disclosed to, or withheld from, parties to the proceedings.

Chapter IV Reporting restrictions

Reports relating to persons under 18

44 Restrictions on reporting alleged offences involving persons under 18

(1) This section applies (subject to subsection (3)) where a criminal investigation has begun in respect of—

(a) an alleged offence against the law of—

(i) England and Wales, or

(ii) . . .

(2) No matter relating to any person involved in the offence shall while he is under the age of 18 be included in any publication if it is likely to lead members of the public to identify him as a person involved in the offence.

(3) The restrictions imposed by subsection (2) cease to apply once there are proceedings in a court . . . in respect of the offence.

(4) For the purposes of subsection (2) any reference to a person involved in the offence is to—

    (a) a person by whom the offence is alleged to have been committed; or

    (b) if this paragraph applies to the publication in question by virtue of subsection (5)—

        (i) a person against or in respect of whom the offence is alleged to have been committed, or

        (ii) a person who is alleged to have been a witness to the commission of the offence;

except that paragraph (b)(i) does not include a person in relation to whom section 1 of the Sexual Offences (Amendment) Act 1992 (anonymity of victims of certain sexual offences) applies in connection with the offence.

(5) Subsection (4)(b) applies to a publication if—

    (a) where it is a relevant programme, it is transmitted, or

    (b) in the case of any other publication, it is published,

on or after such date as may be specified in an order made by the Secretary of State.

(6) The matters relating to a person in relation to which the restrictions imposed by subsection (2) apply (if their inclusion in any publication is likely to have the result mentioned in that subsection) include in particular—

    (a) his name,

    (b) his address,

    (c) the identity of an school or other educational establishment attended by him,

    (d) the identity of any place of work, and

    (e) any still or moving picture of him.

(7) Any appropriate criminal court may by order dispense, to any extent specified in the order, with the restrictions imposed by subsection (2) in relation to a person if it is satisfied that it is necessary in the interests of justice to do so.

(8) However, when deciding whether to make such an order dispensing (to any extent) with the restrictions imposed by subsection (2) in relation to a person, the court shall have regard to the welfare of that person.

(9) In subsection (7) 'appropriate criminal court' means—

    (a) in a case where this section applies by virtue of subsection (1)(a)(i) or (ii), any court . . . which has any jurisdiction in, or in relation to, any criminal proceedings (but not a service court unless the offence is alleged to have been committed by a person subject to service law);

    (b) in a case where this section applies by virtue of subsection (1)(b), any court falling within paragraph (a) or a service court.

(10) The power under subsection (7) of a magistrates' court may be exercised by a single justice.

(11) In the case of a decision of a magistrates' court . . . to make or refuse to make an order under subsection (7), the following persons, namely—

    (a) any person who was a party to the proceedings on the application for the order, and

    (b) with the leave of the Crown Court, any other person,

may, in accordance with Criminal Procedure Rules, appeal to the Crown Court against that decision or appear or be represented at the hearing of such an appeal.

(12) On such an appeal the Crown Court—

    (a) may make such order as is necessary to give effect to its determination of the appeal; and

    (b) may also make such incidental or consequential orders as appear to it to be just.

(13) In this section—

    (a) 'civil offence' means an act or omission which, if committed in England and Wales, would be an offence against the law of England and Wales;

    (b) any reference to a criminal investigation, in relation to an alleged offence, is to an investigation conducted by police officers, or other persons charged with the duty of investigation offences, with a view to it being ascertained whether a person should be charged with the offence;

    (c) . . .

45 Power to restrict reporting of criminal proceedings involving persons under 18

(1) This section applies (subject to subsection (2)) in relation to—

(a) any criminal proceedings in any court (other than a service court) . . . ; and

(b) . . .

(2) This section does not apply in relation to any proceedings to which section 49 of the Children and Young Persons Act 1933 applies.

(3) The court may direct that no matter relating to any person concerned in the proceedings shall while he is under the age of 18 be included in any publication if it is likely to lead members of the public to identify him as a person concerned in the proceedings.

(4) The court or an appellate court may by direction ('an excepting direction') dispense, to any extent specified in the excepting direction, with the restrictions imposed by a direction under subsection (3) if it is satisfied that it is necessary in the interests of justice to do so.

(5) The court or an appellate court may also by direction ('an excepting direction') dispense, to any extent specified in the excepting direction, with the restrictions imposed by a direction under subsection (3) if it is satisfied—

(a) that their effect is to impose a substantial and unreasonable restriction on the reporting of the proceedings, and

(b) that it is in the public interest to remove or relax that restriction;

but no excepting direction shall be given under this subsection by reason only of the fact that the proceedings have been determined in any way or have been abandoned.

(6) When deciding whether to make—

(a) a direction under subsection (3) in relation to a person, or

(b) an expecting direction under subsection (4) or (5) by virtue of which the restrictions imposed by a direction under subsection (3) would be dispensed with (to any extent) in relation to a person,

the court or (as the case may be) the appellate court shall have regard to the welfare of that person.

(7) For the purposes of subsection (3) any reference to a person concerned in the proceedings is to a person—

(a) against or in respect of whom the proceedings are taken, or

(b) who is a witness in the proceedings.

(8) the matters relating to a person in relation to which the restrictions imposed by a direction under subsection (3) apply (if their inclusion in any publication is likely to have the result mentioned in that subsection) include in particular—

(a) his name,

(b) his address,

(c) the identity of any school or other educational establishment attended by him,

(d) the identity of any place of work, and

(e) any still or moving picture of him.

(9) A direction under subsection (3) may be revoked by the court or an appellate court.

(10) An excepting direction—

(a) may be given at the time the direction under subsection (3) is given or subsequently; and

(b) may be varied or revoked by the court or an appellate court.

(11) In this section 'appellate court', in relation to any proceedings in a court, means a court dealing with an appeal (including an appeal by way of case stated) arising out of the proceedings or with any further appeal.

Reports relating to adult witnesses

46 Power to restrict reports about certain adult witnesses in criminal proceedings

(1) This section applies where—

(a) in any criminal proceedings in any court (other than a service court) or

(b) . . .

a party to the proceedings makes an application for the court to give a reporting direction in relation to a witness in the proceedings (other than the accused) who has attained the age of 18.

In this section 'reporting direction' has the meaning given by subsection (6).

(2) If the court determines—

    (a) that the witness is eligible for protection, and

    (b) that giving a reporting direction in relation to the witness is likely to improve—

        (i)   the quality of evidence given by the witness, or

        (ii) the level of co-operation given by the witness to any party to the proceedings in connection with that party's preparation of its case,

the court may give a reporting direction in relation to the witness.

(3) For the purposes of this section a witness is eligible for protection if the court is satisfied—

    (a) that the quality of evidence given by the witness, or

    (b) the level of co-operation given by the witness to any party to the proceedings in connection with that party's preparation of its case,

is likely to be diminished by reason of fear or distress on the part of the witness in connection with being identified by members of the public as a witness in the proceedings.

(4) In determining whether a witness is eligible for protection the court must take into account, in particular—

    (a) the nature and alleged circumstances of the offence to which the proceedings relate;

    (b) the age of the witness;

    (c) such of the following matters as appear to the court to be relevant, namely—

        (i)   the social and cultural background and ethnic origins of the witness,

        (ii) the domestic and employment circumstances of the witness, and

        (iii) any religious beliefs or political opinions of the witness;

    (d) any behaviour towards the witness on the part of—

        (i)   the accused,

        (ii) members of the family or associates of the accused, or

        (iii) any other person who is likely to be an accused or a witness in the proceedings.

(5) In determining that question the court must in addition consider any views expressed by the witness.

(6) For the purposes of this section a reporting direction in relation to a witness is a direction that no matter relating to the witness shall during the witness's lifetime be included in any publication if it is likely to lead members of the public to identify him as being a witness in the proceedings.

(7) The matters relating to a witness in relation to which the restrictions imposed by a reporting direction apply (if their inclusion in any publication is likely to have the result mentioned in subsection (6)) include in particular—

    (a) the witness's name,

    (b) the witness's address,

    (c) the identity of any educational establishment attended by the witness,

    (d) the identity of any place of work, and

    (e) any still or moving picture of the witness.

(8) In determining whether to give a reporting direction the court shall consider—

    (a) whether it would be in the interests of justice to do so, and

    (b) the public interest in avoiding the imposition of a substantial and unreasonable restriction on the reporting of the proceedings.

(9) The court or an appellate court may by direction ('an excepting direction') dispense, to any extent specified in the excepting direction, with the restrictions imposed by a reporting direction if—

    (a) it is satisfied that it is necessary in the interests of justice to do so, or

    (b) it is satisfied—

        (i)   that the effect of those restrictions is to impose a substantial and unreasonable restriction on the reporting of the proceedings, and

        (ii) that it is in the public interest to remove or relax that restriction;

but no excepting direction shall be given under paragraph (b) by reason only of the fact that the proceedings have been determined in any way or have been abandoned.

(10) A reporting direction may be revoked by the court or an appellate court.

(11) An excepting direction—

(a) may be given at the time the reporting direction is given or subsequently; and

(b) may be varied or revoked by the court or an appellate court.

(12) In this section—

(a) 'appellate court', in relation to any proceedings in a court, means a court dealing with an appeal (including an appeal by way of case stated) arising out of the proceedings or with any further appeal;

(b) references to the quality of a witness's evidence are to its quality in terms of completeness, coherence and accuracy (and for this purpose 'coherence' refers to a witness's ability in giving evidence to give answers which address the questions put to the witness and can be understood both individually and collectively);

(c) references to the preparation of the case of a party to any proceedings include, where the party is the prosecution, the carrying out of investigations into any offence at any time charged in the proceedings.

Reports relating to directions under Chapter 1, 1A or 2

47   Restrictions on reporting directions under Chapter 1A or 2.

(1) Except as provided by this section, no publication shall include a report of a matter falling within subsection (2).

(2) The matters falling within this subsection are—

(a) a direction under section 19, 33A or 36 or an order discharging, or (in the case of a direction under section 19) varying, such a direction;

(b) proceedings—

(i) on an application for such a direction or order, or

(ii) where the court acts of its own motion to determine whether to give or make any such direction or order.

(3) The court dealing with a matter falling within subsection (2) may order that subsection (1) is not to apply, or is not to apply to a specified extent, to a report of that matter.

(4) Where—

(a) there is only one accused in the relevant proceedings, and

(b) he objects to the making of an order under subsection (3),

the court shall make the order if (and only if) satisfied after hearing the representations of the accused that it is in the interests of justice to do so; and if the order is made it shall not apply to the extent that a report deals with any such objections or representations.

(5) Where—

(a) there are two or more accused in the relevant proceedings, and

(b) one or more of them object to the making of an order under subsection (3),

the court shall make the order if (and only if) satisfied after hearing the representations of each of the accused that it is in the interests of justice to do so; and if the order is made it shall not apply to the extent that a report deals with any such objections or representations.

(6) Subsection (1) does not apply to the inclusion in a publication of a report of matters after the relevant proceedings are either—

(a) determined (by acquittal, conviction or otherwise), or

(b) abandoned,

in relation to the accused or (if there is more than one) in relation to each of the accused.

(7) In this section 'the relevant proceedings' means the proceedings to which any such direction as is mentioned in subsection (2) relates or would relate.

(8) Nothing in this section affects any prohibition or restriction by virtue of any other enactment on the inclusion of matter in a publication.

Other restrictions

48 Amendments relating to other reporting restrictions

Schedule 2, which contains amendments relating to reporting restrictions under—
  (a) the Children and Young Persons Act 1933,
  (b) the Sexual Offences (Amendment) Act 1976,
  (d) the Sexual Offences (Amendment) Act 1992,
shall have effect.

Offences

49 Offences under Chapter IV

(1) This section applies if a publication—
  (a) includes any matter in contravention of section 44(2) or of a direction under section 45(3) or 46(2); or
  (b) includes a report in a contravention of section 47.
(2) Where the publication is a newspaper or periodical, any proprietor, any editor and any publisher of the newspaper or periodical is guilty of an offence.
(3) Where the publication is a relevant programme—
  (a) any body corporate . . . engaged in providing the programme service in which the programme is included, and
  (b) any person having functions in relation to the programme corresponding to those of an editor of a newspaper,
is guilty of an offence.
(4) In the case of any other publication, any person publishing it is guilty of an offence.
(5) A person guilty of an offence under this section is liable on summary conviction to a fine not exceeding level 5 on the standard scale.
(6) Proceedings for an offence under this section in respect of a publication falling within subsection (1)(b) may not be instituted—
  (a) in England and Wales otherwise than by or with the consent of the Attorney General, or

50 Defences

(1) Where a person is charged with an offence under section 49 it shall be a defence to prove that at the time of the alleged offence he was not aware, and neither suspected nor had reason to suspect, that the publication included in the matter or report in question.
(2) Where—
  (a) a person is charged with an offence under section 49, and
  (b) the offence relates to the inclusion of any matter in a publication in contravention of section 44(2),
it shall be a defence to prove that at the time of the alleged offence he was not aware, and neither suspected nor had reason to suspect, that the criminal investigation in question had begun.
(3) Where—
  (a) paragraphs (a) and (b) or subsection (2) apply, and
  (b) the contravention of section 44(2) does not relate to either—
    (i) the person by whom the offence mentioned in that provision is alleged to have been committed, or
    (ii) (where that offence is one in relation to which section 1 of the Sexual Offences (Amendment) Act 1992 applies) a person who is alleged to be a witness to the commission of the offence,
it shall be a defence to show to the satisfaction of the court that the inclusion in the publication of the matter in question was in the public interest on the ground that, to the extent that they operated to prevent that matter from being so included, the effect of the restrictions imposed by section 44(2) was to impose a substantial and unreasonable restriction on the reporting of matters connected with that offence.

(4) Subsection (5) applies where—

    (a) paragraphs (a) and (b) of subsection (2) apply, and

    (b) the contravention of section 44(2) relates to a person ('the protected person') who is neither—

        (i)   the person mentioned in subsection (3)(b)(i), nor

        (ii) a person within subsection (3)(b)(ii) who is under the age of 16.

(5) In such a case it shall be a defence, subject to subsection (6), to prove that written consent to the inclusion of the matter in question in the publication had been given—

    (a) by an appropriate person, if at the time when the consent was given the protected person was under the age of 16, or

    (b) by the protected person, if that person was aged 16 or 17 at that time,

and (where the consent was given by an appropriate person) that written notice had been previously given to that person drawing to his attention the need to consider the welfare of the protected person when deciding whether to give consent.

(6) The defence provided by subsection (5) is not available if—

    (a) (where the consent was given by an appropriate person) it is proved that written or other notice withdrawing the consent—

        (i)   was given to the appropriate recipient by any other appropriate person or by the protected person, and

        (ii) was so given in sufficient time to enable the inclusion in the publication of the matter in question to be prevented; or

    (b) subsection (8) applies.

(7) Where—

    (a) a person is charged with an offence under section 49, and

    (b) the offence relates to the inclusion of any matter in a publication in contravention of a direction under section 46(2),

it shall be a defence, unless subsection (8) applies, to prove that the person in relation to whom the direction was given had given written consent to the inclusion of that matter in the publication.

(8) Written consent is not a defence if it is proved that any person interfered—

    (a) with the peace or comfort of the person giving the consent, or

    (b) (where the consent was given by an appropriate person) with the peace or comfort of either that person or the protected person,

with intent to obtain the consent.

(9) In this section—

'an appropriate person' means (subject to subsections (10) to (12))—

    (a) . . . a person who is a parent or guardian of the protected person,

'guardian', in relation to the protected person, means any person who is not a parent of the protected person but who has parental responsibility for the protected person within the meaning of—

    (a) . . . the Children Act 1989, or

    (b) . . .

(10) Where the protected person is (within the meaning of the Children Act 1989) a child who is looked after by a local authority, 'an appropriate person' means a person who is—

    (a) a representative of that authority, or

    (b) a parent or guardian of the protected person with whom the protected person is allowed to live.

(13) However, no person by whom the offence mentioned in section 44(2) is alleged to have been committed is, by virtue of subsection (9) to (10), an appropriate person for the purposes of this section.

(14) In this section 'the appropriate recipient', in relation to a notice under subsection (6)(a), means—

    (a) the person to whom the notice giving consent was given,

    (b) (if different) the person by whom the matter in question was published, or

(c) any other person exercising, on behalf of the person mentioned in paragraph (b), any responsibility in relation to the publication of that matter;

and for this purpose 'person' includes a body of persons and a partnership.

51   Offences committed by bodies corporate

(1) If an offence under section 49 committed by a body corporate is proved—

(a) to have been committed with the consent or connivance of, or

(b) to be attributable to any neglect on the part of,

an officer, the officer as well as the body corporate is guilty of the offence and liable to be proceeded against and punished accordingly.

(2) In subsection (1) 'officer' means a director, manager, secretary or other similar officer of the body, or a person purporting to act in any such capacity.

(3) If the affairs of a body corporate are managed by its members, 'director' in subsection (2) means a member of that body.

Supplementary

52   Decisions as to public interest for purposes of Chapter IV

(1) Where for the purposes of any provision of this Chapter it falls to a court to determine whether anything is (or, as the case may be, was) in the public interest, the court must have regard, in particular, to the matters referred to in subsection (2) (so far as relevant).

(2) Those matters are—

(a) the interest in each of the following—

(i)   the open reporting of crime,

(ii)   the open reporting of matters relating to human health or safety, and

(iii) the prevention and exposure of miscarriages of justice;

(b) the welfare of any person in relation to whom the relevant restrictions imposed by or under this Chapter apply or would apply (or, as the case may be, applied); and

(c) any views expressed—

(i)   by an appropriate person on behalf of a person within paragraph (b) who is under the age of 16 ('the protected person'), or

(ii)   by a person within that paragraph who has attained that age.

(3) In subsection (2) 'an appropriate person', in relation to the protected person, has the same meaning as it has for the purposes of section 50.

Chapter V Competence of witnesses and capacity to be sworn

Competence of witnesses

53   Competence of witnesses to give evidence

(1) At every stage in criminal proceedings all persons are (whatever their age) competent to give evidence.

(2) Subsection (1) has effect subject to subsections (3) and (4).

(3) A person is not competent to give evidence in criminal proceedings if it appears to the court that he is not a person who is able to—

(a) understand questions put to him as a witness, and

(b) give answers to them which can be understood.

(4) A person charged in criminal proceedings is not competent to give evidence in the proceedings for the prosecution (whether he is the only person, or is one of two or more persons, charged in the proceedings).

(5) In subsection (4) the reference to a person charged in criminal proceedings does not include a person who is not, or is no longer, liable to be convicted of any offence in the proceedings (whether as a result of pleading guilty or for any other reason).

54   Determining competence of witnesses

(1) Any question whether a witness in criminal proceedings is competent to give evidence in the proceedings, whether raised—

    (a) by a party to the proceedings, or

    (b) by the court of its own motion,

shall be determined by the court in accordance with this section.

(2) It is for the party calling the witness to satisfy the court that, on a balance of probabilities, the witness is competent to give evidence in the proceedings.

(3) In determining the question mentioned in subsection (1) the court shall treat the witness as having the benefit of any directions under section 19 which the court has given, or proposes to give, in relation to the witness.

(4) Any proceedings held for the determination of the question shall take place in the absence of the jury (if there is one).

(5) Expert evidence may be received on the question.

(6) Any questioning of the witness (where the court considers that necessary) shall be conducted by the court in the presence of the parties.

Giving of sworn or unsworn evidence

55   Determining whether witness to be sworn

(1) Any question whether a witness in criminal proceedings may be sworn for the purpose of giving evidence on oath, whether raised—

    (a) by a party to the proceedings, or

    (b) by the court of its own motion,

shall be determined by the court in accordance with this section.

(2) The witness may not be sworn for that purpose unless—

    (a) he has attained the age of 14, and

    (b) he has a sufficient appreciation of the solemnity of the occasion and of the particular responsibility to tell the truth which is involved in taking an oath.

(3) The witness shall, if he is able to give intelligible testimony, be presumed to have a sufficient appreciation of those matters if no evidence tending to show the contrary is adduced (by any party).

(4) If any such evidence is adduced, it is for the party seeking to have the witness sworn to satisfy the court that, on a balance of probabilities, the witness has attained the age of 14 and has a sufficient appreciation of the matters mentioned in subsection (2)(b).

(5) Any proceedings held for the determination of the question mentioned in subsection (1) shall take place in the absence of the jury (if there is one).

(6) Expert evidence may be received on the question.

(7) Any questioning of the witness (where the court considers that necessary) shall be conducted by the court in the presence of the parties.

(8) For the purposes of this section a person is able to give intelligible testimony if he is able to—

    (a) understand questions put to him as a witness, and

    (b) give answers to them which can be understood.

56   Reception of unsworn evidence

(1) Subsections (2) and (3) apply to a person (of any age) who—

    (a) is competent to give evidence in criminal proceedings, but

    (b) (by virtue of section 55(2)) is not permitted to be sworn for the purpose of giving evidence on oath in such proceedings.

(2) The evidence in criminal proceedings of a person to whom this subsection applies shall be given unsworn.

(3) A deposition of unsworn evidence given by a person to whom this subsection applies may be taken for the purposes of criminal proceedings as if that evidence had been given on oath.

(4) A court in criminal proceedings shall accordingly receive in evidence any evidence given unsworn in pursuance of subsection (2) or (3).

(5) Where a person ('the witness') who is competent to give evidence in criminal proceedings gives evidence in such proceedings unsworn, no conviction, verdict or finding in those proceedings shall be taken to be unsafe for the purposes of any of sections 2(1), 13(1) and 16(1) of the Criminal Appeal Act 1968 (grounds for allowing appeals) by reason only that it appears to the Court of Appeal that the witness was a person falling within section 55(2) (and should accordingly have given his evidence on oath).

57 Penalty for giving false unsworn evidence

(1) This section applies where a person gives unsworn evidence in criminal proceedings in pursuance of section 56(2) or (3).

(2) If such a person wilfully gives false evidence in such circumstances that, had the evidence been given on oath, he would have been guilty of perjury, he shall be guilty of an offence and liable on summary conviction to—

    (a) imprisonment for a term not exceeding 6 months, or

    (b) a fine not exceeding £1,000,

or both.

(3) In relation to a person under the age of 14, subsection (2) shall have effect as if for the words following 'on summary conviction' there were substituted 'to a fine not exceeding £250'.

59 Restriction on use of answers etc. obtained under compulsion

Schedule 3, which amends enactments providing for the use of answers and statements given under compulsion so as to restrict in criminal proceedings their use in evidence against the persons giving them, shall have effect.

Chapter VII General

62 Meaning of 'sexual offence' and other references to offences

(1) In this Part 'sexual offence' means any offence under Part 1 of the Sexual Offences Act 2003 or any relevant superseded offence.

(1A) In subsection (1) 'relevant superseded offence' means—

    (a) rape or burglary with intent to rape;

    (b) an offence under any of sections 2 to 12 and 14 to 17 of the Sexual Offences Act 1956 (unlawful intercourse, indecent assault, forcible abduction etc.);

    (c) an offence under section 128 of the Mental Health Act 1959 (unlawful intercourse with person receiving treatment for mental disorder by member of hospital staff etc.);

    (d) an offence under section 1 of the Indecency with Children Act 1960 (indecent conduct towards child under 14);

    (e) an offence under section 54 of the Criminal Law Act 1977 (incitement of child under 16 to commit incest).

(2) In this part any reference (including a reference having effect by virtue of this subsection) to an offence of any description ('the substantive offence') is to be taken to include a reference to an offence which consists of attempting or conspiring to commit, or of aiding, abetting, counselling, procuring or inciting the commission of, the substantive offence.

63 General interpretation etc. of Part II

(1) In this Part (except where the context otherwise requires)—

'accused', in relation to any criminal proceedings, means any person charged with an offence to which the proceedings relate (whether or not he has been convicted);

'the complainant', in relation to any offence (or alleged offence), means a person against or in relation to whom the offence was (or is alleged to have been) committed;

'court' (except in Chapter IV or V or subsection (2)) means a magistrates' court, the Crown Court or criminal division of the Court of Appeal;

'legal representative' means a person who, for the purposes of the Legal Services Act 2007, is an authorised person in relation to an activity which constitutes the exercise of a right of audience or the conduct of litigation (within the meaning of that Act);

'picture' includes a likeness however produced;

'the prosecutor' means any person acting as prosecutor, whether an individual or body;

'publication' includes any speech, writing, relevant programme or other communication in whatever form, which is addressed to the public at large or any section of the public (and for this purpose every relevant programme shall be taken to be so addressed), but does not include an indictment or other document prepared for use in particular legal proceedings;

'relevant programme' means a programme included in a programme service, within the meaning of the Broadcasting Act 1990;

'service court' means—

. . .

'video recording' means any recording, on any medium, from which a moving image may by any means be produced, and includes the accompanying sound-track;

'witness', in relation to any criminal proceedings, means any person called, or proposed to be called, to give evidence in the proceedings.

(2) Nothing in this Part shall affect any power of a court to exclude evidence at its discretion (whether by preventing questions being put or otherwise) which is exercisable apart from this Part.

SCHEDULE 1A

RELEVANT OFFENCES FOR THE PURPOSES OF SECTION 17

Murder and manslaughter

1 Murder in a case where it is alleged that a firearm or knife was used to cause the death in question.

2 Manslaughter in a case where it is alleged that a firearm or knife was used to cause the death in question.

3 Murder or manslaughter in a case (other than a case falling within paragraph 1 or 2) where it is alleged that—

   (a) the accused was carrying a firearm or knife at any time during the commission of the offence, and

   (b) a person other than the accused knew or believed at any time during the commission of the offence that the accused was carrying a firearm or knife.

Offences against the Person Act 1861

4 An offence under section 18 of the Offences against the Person Act 1861 (wounding with intent to cause grievous bodily harm etc) in a case where it is alleged that a firearm or knife was used to cause the wound or harm in question.

5 An offence under section 20 of that Act (malicious wounding) in a case where it is alleged that a firearm or knife was used to cause the wound or inflict the harm in question.

6 An offence under section 38 of that Act (assault with intent to resist arrest) in a case where it is alleged that a firearm or knife was used to carry out the assault in question.

7 An offence under section 47 of the Offences against the Person Act 1861 (assault occasioning actual bodily harm) in a case where it is alleged that a firearm or knife was used to inflict the harm in question.

8 An offence under section 18, 20, 38 or 47 of the Offences against the Person Act 1861 in a case (other than a case falling within any of paragraphs 4 to 7) where it is alleged that—

   (a) the accused was carrying a firearm or knife at any time during the commission of the offence, and

(b) a person other than the accused knew or believed at any time during the commission of the offence that the accused was carrying a firearm or knife.

Prevention of Crime Act 1953

9 An offence under section 1 of the Prevention of Crime Act 1953 (having an offensive weapon in a public place).

Firearms Act 1968

10 An offence under section 1 of the Firearms Act 1968 (requirement of firearm certificate).

11 An offence under section 2(1) of that Act (possession etc of a shot gun without a certificate).

12 An offence under section 3 of that Act (business and other transactions with firearms and ammunition).

13 An offence under section 4 of that Act (conversion of weapons).

14 An offence under section 5(1) of that Act (weapons subject to general prohibition).

15 An offence under section 5(1A) of that Act (ammunition subject to general prohibition).

16 An offence under section 16 of that Act (possession with intent to injure).

17 An offence under section 16A of that Act (possession with intent to cause fear of violence).

18 An offence under section 17 of that Act (use of firearm to resist arrest).

19 An offence under section 18 of that Act (carrying firearm with criminal intent).

20 An offence under section 19 of that Act (carrying firearm in a public place).

21 An offence under section 20 of that Act (trespassing with firearm).

22 An offence under section 21 of that Act (possession of firearms by person previously convicted of crime).

23 An offence under section 21A of that Act (firing an air weapon beyond premises).

24 An offence under section 24A of that Act (supplying imitation firearms to minors).

Criminal Justice Act 1988

25 An offence under section 139 of the Criminal Justice Act 1988 (having article with blade or point in public place).

26 An offence under section 139A of that Act (having article with blade or point (or offensive weapon) on school premises).

Violent Crime Reduction Act 2006

27 An offence under section 28 of the Violent Crime Reduction Act 2006 (using someone to mind a weapon).

28 An offence under section 32 of that Act (sales of air weapons by way of trade or business to be face to face).

29 An offence under section 36 of that Act (manufacture, import and sale of realistic imitation firearms).

General

30 A reference in any of paragraphs 1 to 8 to an offence ("offence A") includes—
(a) a reference to an attempt to commit offence A in a case where it is alleged that it was attempted to commit offence A in the manner or circumstances described in that paragraph,
(b) a reference to a conspiracy to commit offence A in a case where it is alleged that the conspiracy was to commit offence A in the manner or circumstances described in that paragraph,
(c) a reference to an offence under Part 2 of the Serious Crime Act 2007 in relation to which offence A is the offence (or one of the offences) which the person intended or believed would be committed in a case where it is alleged that the person intended or believed offence A would be committed in the manner or circumstances described in that paragraph, and
(d) a reference to aiding, abetting, counselling or procuring the commission of offence A in a case where it is alleged that offence A was committed, or the act or omission charged in respect of offence A was done or made, in the manner or circumstances described in that paragraph.

31 A reference in any of paragraphs 9 to 29 to an offence ("offence A") includes—
  (a) a reference to an attempt to commit offence A,
  (b) a reference to a conspiracy to commit offence A,
  (c) a reference to an offence under Part 2 of the Serious Crime Act 2007 in relation to which offence A is the offence (or one of the offences) which the person intended or believed would be committed, and
  (d) a reference to aiding, abetting, counselling or procuring the commission of offence A.

Interpretation

32 In this Schedule—
"firearm" has the meaning given by section 57 of the Firearms Act 1968;
"knife" has the meaning given by section 10 of the Knives Act 1997

Criminal Cases Review (Insanity) Act 1999

(1999, c. 25)

1   Reference of former verdict of guilty but insane

(1) Where a verdict was returned . . . to the effect that a person was guilty of the act or omission charged against him but was insane at the time, the Criminal Cases Review Commission may at any time refer the verdict to the Court of Appeal if subsection (2) below applies.

(2) This subsection applies if the commission consider that there is a real possibility that the verdict would not be upheld were the reference to be made and either—
  (a) the Commission so consider because of an argument, or evidence, not raised in the proceedings which led to the verdict, or
  (b) it appears to the Commission that there are exceptional circumstances which justify the making of the reference.

(3) Section 14 of the Criminal Appeal Act 1995 (supplementary provision about the reference of a verdict) shall apply in relation to a reference under subsection (1) above as it applies in relation to references under section 9 or 10 of that Act.

2   Reference treated as appeal: England and Wales

(1) A reference under section 1(1) above of a verdict returned . . . in the case of a person shall be treated for all purposes as an appeal by the person under section 12 of the Criminal Appeal Act 1968.

(2) In their application to such a reference by virtue of subsection (1) above, sections 13 and 14 of that Act shall have effect—
  (a) as if references to the verdict of not guilty by reason of insanity were to the verdict referred under section 1(1) above, and
  (b) as if, in section 14(1)(b), for the words from the beginning to 'that he' there were substituted 'the accused was under a disability and'.

Terrorism Act 2000

(1996, c. 25)

118   Defences

(1) Subsection (2) applies where in accordance with a provision mentioned in subsection (5) it is a defence for a person charged with an offence to prove a particular matter.

(2) If the person adduces evidence which is sufficient to raise an issue with respect to the matter the court or jury shall assume that the defence is satisfied unless the prosecution proves beyond reasonable doubt that it is not.

(3) Subsection (4) applies where in accordance with a provision mentioned in subsection (5) a court—

    (a) may make an assumption in relation to a person charged with an offence unless a particular matter is proved, or

    (b) may accept a fact as sufficient evidence unless a particular matter is proved.

(4) If evidence is adduced which is sufficient to raise an issue with respect to the matter mentioned in subsection (3)(a) or (b) the court shall treat it as proved unless the prosecution disproves it beyond reasonable doubt.

(5) The provisions in respect of which subsections (2) and (4) apply are—

    (a) sections 12(4), 39(5)(a), 54, 57, 58, 77 and 103 of this Act,

120 Evidence

(1) A document which purports to be—

    (a) a notice or direction given or order made by the Secretary of State for the purposes of a provision of this Act, and

    (b) signed by him or on his behalf,

shall be received in evidence and shall, until the contrary is proved, be deemed to have been given or made by the Secretary of State.

(2) A document bearing a certificate which—

    (a) purports to be signed by or on behalf of the Secretary of State, and

    (b) states that the document is a true copy of a notice or direction given or order made by the Secretary of State for the purposes of a provision of this Act,

shall be evidence . . . of the document in legal proceedings.

(3) In subsections (1) and (2) a reference to an order does not include a reference to an order made by statutory instrument.

(4) The Documentary Evidence Act 1868 shall apply to an authorisation given in writing by the Secretary of State for the purposes of this Act as it applies to an order made by him.

Crime (International Co-operation) Act 2003

(2003, c. 32)

Chapter 2 Mutual provision of evidence

Assistance in obtaining evidence abroad

7 Requests for assistance in obtaining evidence abroad

(1) If it appears to a judicial authority in the United Kingdom on an application made by a person mentioned in subsection (3)—

    (a) that an offence has been committed or that there are reasonable grounds for suspecting that an offence has been committed, and

    (b) that proceedings in respect of the offence have been instituted or that the offence is being investigated,

the judicial authority may request assistance under this section.

(2) The assistance that may be requested under this section is assistance in obtaining outside the United Kingdom any evidence specified in the request for use in the proceedings or investigation.

(3) The application may be made—

    (a) . . . by a prosecuting authority,

    (c) where proceedings have been instituted, by the person charged in those proceedings.

(4) The judicial authorities are—

    (a) . . . any judge or justice of the peace,

(5) . . . a designated prosecuting authority may itself request assistance under this section if—

    (a) it appears to the authority that an offence has been committed or that there are reasonable grounds for suspecting that an offence has been committed, and

    (b) the authority has instituted proceedings in respect of the offence in question or it is being investigated.

'Designated' means designated by an order made by the Secretary of State.

(7) If a request for assistance under this section is made in reliance on Article 2 of the 2001 Protocol (requests for information on banking transactions) in connection with the investigation of an offence, the request must state the grounds on which the person making the request considers the evidence specified in it to be relevant for the purposes of the investigation.

8 Sending requests for assistance

(1) A request for assistance under section 7 may be sent—

    (a) to a court exercising jurisdiction in the place where the evidence is situated, or

    (b) to any authority recognised by the government of the country in question as the appropriate authority for receiving requests of that kind.

(2) Alternatively, if it is a request by a judicial authority or a designated prosecuting authority it may be sent to the Secretary of State . . . for forwarding to a court or authority mentioned in subsection (1).

(3) In cases of urgency, a request for assistance may be sent to—

    (a) the International Criminal Police Organisation, or

    (b) any body or person competent to receive it under any provisions adopted under the Treaty on European Union,

for forwarding to any court or authority mentioned in subsection (1).

9 Use of evidence obtained

(1) This section applies to evidence obtained pursuant to a request for assistance under section 7.

(2) The evidence may not without the consent of the appropriate overseas authority be used for any purpose other than that specified in the request.

(3) When the evidence is no longer required for that purpose (or for any other purpose for which such consent has been obtained), it must be returned to the appropriate overseas authority, unless that authority indicates that it need not be returned.

(6) In this section, the appropriate overseas authority means the authority recognised by the government of the country in question as the appropriate authority for receiving requests of the kind in question.

10 Domestic freezing orders

(1) If it appears to a judicial authority in the United Kingdom, on an application made by a person mentioned in subsection (4)—

    (a) that proceedings in respect of a listed offence have been instituted or such an offence is being investigated,

    (b) that there are reasonable grounds to believe that there is evidence in a participating country which satisfies the requirements of subsection (3), and

    (c) that a request has been made, or will be made, under section 7 for the evidence to be sent to the authority making the request,

the judicial authority may make a domestic freezing order in respect of the evidence.

(2) A domestic freezing order is an order for protecting evidence which is in the participating country pending its transfer to the United Kingdom.

(3) The requirements are that the evidence—

    (a) is on premises specified in the application in the participating country,

    (b) is likely to be of substantial value (whether by itself or together with other evidence) to the proceedings or investigation,

    (c) is likely to be admissible in evidence at a trial for the offence, and

    (d) does not consist of or include items subject to legal privilege.

(4) The application may be made—

    (a) in relation to England and Wales and Northern Ireland, by a constable,

(5) The judicial authorities are—

    (a) in relation to England and Wales, any judge or justice of the peace,

(6) This section does not prejudice the generality of the power to make a request for assistance under section 7.

11   Sending freezing orders

(1) A domestic freezing order made in England and Wales . . . is to be sent to the Secretary of State for forwarding to—

    (a) a court exercising jurisdiction in the place where the evidence is situated, or

    (b) any authority recognised by the government of the country in question as the appropriate authority for receiving orders of that kind.

(3) The judicial authority is to send the order to the Secretary of State . . . before the end of the period of 14 days beginning with its being made.

(4) The order must be accompanied by a certificate giving the specified information and, unless the certificate indicates when the judicial authority expects such a request to be made, by a request under section 7 for the evidence to be sent to the authority making the request.

(5) The certificate must include a translation of it into an appropriate language of the participating country (if that language is not English).

(6) The certificate must be signed by or on behalf of the judicial authority who made the order and must include a statement as to the accuracy of the information given in it.

The signature may be an electronic signature.

12   Variation or revocation of freezing orders

(1) The judicial authority that made a domestic freezing order may vary or revoke it on an application by a person mentioned below.

(2) The persons are—

    (a) the person who applied for the order,

    (b) . . . a prosecuting authority,

    (d) any other person affected by the order.

Assisting overseas authorities to obtain evidence in the UK

13   Requests for assistance from overseas authorities

(1) Where a request for assistance in obtaining evidence in a part of the United Kingdom is received by the territorial authority for that part, the authority may—

    (a) if the conditions in section 14 are met, arrange for the evidence to be obtained under section 15, or

(2) The request for assistance may be made only by—

    (a) a court exercising criminal jurisdiction, or a prosecuting authority, in a country outside the United Kingdom,

    (b) any other authority in such a country which appears to the territorial authority to have the function of making such requests for assistance,

    (c) any international authority mentioned in subsection (3).

(3) The international authorities are—

    (a) the International Criminal Police Organisation,

    (b) any other body or person competent to make a request of the kind to which this section applies under any provisions adopted under the Treaty on European Union.

14 Powers to arrange for evidence to be obtained

(1) The territorial authority may arrange for evidence to be obtained under section 15 if the request for assistance in obtaining the evidence is made in connection with—

(a) criminal proceedings or a criminal investigation, being carried on outside the United Kingdom,

(b) administrative proceedings, or an investigation into an act punishable in such proceedings, being carried on there,

(c) clemency proceedings, or proceedings on an appeal before a court against a decision in administrative proceedings, being carried on, or intended to be carried on, there.

(2) In a case within subsection (1)(a) or (b), the authority may arrange for the evidence to be so obtained only if the authority is satisfied—

(a) that an offence under the law of the country in question has been committed or that there are reasonable grounds for suspecting that such an offence has been committed, and

(b) that proceedings in respect of the offence have been instituted in that country or that an investigation into the offence is being carried on there.

An offence includes an act punishable in administrative proceedings.

(3) The territorial authority is to regard as conclusive a certificate as to the matters mentioned in subsection (2)(a) and (b) issued by any authority in the country in question which appears to him to be the appropriate authority to do so.

(4) If it appears to the territorial authority that the request for assistance relates to a fiscal offence in respect of which proceedings have not yet been instituted, the authority may not arrange for the evidence to be so obtained unless—

(a) the request is from a country which is a member of the Commonwealth or is made pursuant to a treaty to which the United Kingdom is a party, or

(b) the authority is satisfied that if the conduct constituting the offence were to occur in a part of the United Kingdom, it would constitute an offence in that part.

15 Nominating a court etc. to receive evidence

(1) Where the evidence is in England and Wales . . . the Secretary of State may by a notice nominate a court to receive any evidence to which the request relates which appears to the court to be appropriate for the purpose of giving effect to the request.

(2) But if it appears to the Secretary of State that the request relates to an offence involving serious or complex fraud, he may refer the request (or any part of it) to the Director of the Serious Fraud Office for the Director to obtain any evidence to which the request or part relates which appears to him to be appropriate for the purpose of giving effect to the request or part.

(5) Schedule 1 is to have effect in relation to proceedings before a court nominated under this section.

16 Extension of statutory search powers in England and Wales . . .

(1) Part 2 of the Police and Criminal Evidence Act 1984 (powers of entry, search and seizure) is to have effect as if references to indictable offences in section 8 of, and Schedule 1 to, that Act included any conduct which—

(a) constitutes an offence under the law of a country outside the United Kingdom, and

(b) would, if it occurred in England and Wales, constitute an indictable offence.

(2) But an application for a warrant or order by virtue of subsection (1) may be made only—

(a) in pursuance of a direction given under section 13, or

(b) if it is an application for a warrant or order under section 8 of, or Schedule 1 to, that Act by a constable for the purposes of an investigation by an international joint investigation team of which he is a member.

(5) In this section, 'international joint investigation team' has the meaning given by section 88(7) of the Police Act 1996.

17   Warrants in England and Wales . . .

(1) A justice of the peace may issue a warrant under this section if he is satisfied, on an application made by a constable, that the following conditions are met.

(2) But an application for a warrant under subsection (1) may be made only in pursuance of a direction given under section 13.

(3) The conditions are that—

(a) criminal proceedings have been instituted against a person in a country outside the United Kingdom or a person has been arrested in the course of a criminal investigation carried on there,

(b) the conduct constituting the offence which is the subject of the proceedings or investigation would, if it occurred in England and Wales . . . constitute an indictable offence, and

(c) there are reasonable grounds for suspecting that there is on premises in England and Wales . . . occupied or controlled by that person evidence relating to the offence.

(4) A warrant under this section may authorise a constable—

(a) to enter the premises in question and search the premises to the extent reasonably required for the purpose of discovering any evidence relating to the offence,

(b) to seize and retain any evidence for which he is authorised to search.

19   Seized evidence

(1) Any evidence seized by a constable under or by virtue of section 16, 17 or 18 is to be sent to the court or authority which made the request for assistance or to the territorial authority for forwarding to that court or authority.

(2) So far as may be necessary in order to comply with the request for assistance—

(a) where the evidence consists of a document, the original or a copy is to be sent, and

(b) where the evidence consists of any other article, the article itself or a description, photograph or other representation of it is to be sent.

(3) This section does not apply to evidence seized under or by virtue of section 16(2)(b) or (4)(b) or 18(2)(b).

Chapter 3 Hearing evidence through television links or by telephone

29   Hearing witnesses abroad through television links

(1) The Secretary of State may by order provide for section 32(1A) of the Criminal Justice Act 1988 . . . (proceedings in which evidence may be given through television link) to apply to any further description of criminal proceedings, or to all criminal proceedings.

(2) . . .

30   Hearing witnesses in the UK through television links

(1) This section applies where the Secretary of State receives a request, from an authority mentioned in subsection (2) ("the external authority"), for a person in the United Kingdom to give evidence through a live television link in criminal proceedings before a court in a country outside the United Kingdom.

Criminal proceedings include any proceedings on an appeal before a court against a decision in administrative proceedings.

(2) The authority referred to in subsection (1) is the authority in that country which appears to the Secretary of State to have the function of making requests of the kind to which this section applies.

(3) Unless he considers it inappropriate to do so, the Secretary of State must by notice in writing nominate a court in the United Kingdom where the witness may be heard in the proceedings in question through a live television link.

(4) Anything done by the witness in the presence of the nominated court which, if it were done in proceedings before the court, would constitute contempt of court is to be treated for that purpose as done in proceedings before the court.

(5) Any statement made on oath by a witness giving evidence in pursuance of this section is to be treated for the purposes of—

(a) section 1 of the Perjury Act 1911,

(b) ...

(c) ...

as made in proceedings before the nominated court.

(6) Part 1 of Schedule 2 (evidence given by television link) is to have effect.

(7) Subject to subsections (4) and (5) and the provisions of that Schedule, evidence given pursuant to this section is not to be treated for any purpose as evidence given in proceedings in the United Kingdom.

(8) ...

31   Hearing witnesses in the UK by telephone

(1) This section applies where the Secretary of State receives a request, from an authority mentioned in subsection (2) ('the external authority') in a participating country, for a person in the United Kingdom to give evidence by telephone in criminal proceedings before a court in that country.

Criminal proceedings include any proceedings on an appeal before a court against a decision in administrative proceedings.

(2) The authority referred to in subsection (1) is the authority in that country which appears to the Secretary of State to have the function of making requests of the kind to which this section applies.

(3) A request under subsection (1) must—

(a) specify the court in the participating country,

(b) give the name and address of the witness,

(c) state that the witness is willing to give evidence by telephone in the proceedings before that court.

(4) Unless he considers it inappropriate to do so, the Secretary of State must by notice in writing nominate a court in the United Kingdom where the witness may be heard in the proceedings in question by telephone.

(5) Anything done by the witness in the presence of the nominated court which, if it were done in proceedings before the court, would constitute contempt of court is to be treated for that purpose as done in proceedings before the court.

(6) Any statement made on oath by a witness giving evidence in pursuance of this section is to be treated for the purposes of—

(a) section 1 of the Perjury Act 1911,

(b) ...

(c) ...

as made in proceedings before the nominated court.

(7) Part 2 of Schedule 2 (evidence given by telephone link) is to have effect.

(8) Subject to subsections (5) and (6) and the provisions of that Schedule, evidence given in pursuance of this section is not to be treated for any purpose as evidence given in proceedings in the United Kingdom.

(9) ...

Sexual Offences Act 2003

(2003, c. 42)

75 Evidential presumptions about consent

(1) If in proceedings for an offence to which this section applies it is proved—

  (a) that the defendant did the relevant act,

  (b) that any of the circumstances specified in subsection (2) existed, and

  (c) that the defendant knew that those circumstances existed,

the complainant is to be taken not to have consented to the relevant act unless sufficient evidence is adduced to raise an issue as to whether he consented, and the defendant is to be taken not to have reasonably believed that the complainant consented unless sufficient evidence is adduced to raise an issue as to whether he reasonably believed it.

(2) The circumstances are that—

  (a) any person was, at the time of the relevant act or immediately before it began, using violence against the complainant or causing the complainant to fear that immediate violence would be used against him;

  (b) any person was, at the time of the relevant act or immediately before it began, causing the complainant to fear that violence was being used, or that immediate violence would be used, against another person;

  (c) the complainant was, and the defendant was not, unlawfully detained at the time of the relevant act;

  (d) the complainant was asleep or otherwise unconscious at the time of the relevant act;

  (e) because of the complainant's physical disability, the complainant would not have been able at the time of the relevant act to communicate to the defendant whether the complainant consented;

  (f) any person had administered to or caused to be taken by the complainant, without the complainant's consent, a substance which, having regard to when it was administered or taken, was capable of causing or enabling the complainant to be stupefied or overpowered at the time of the relevant act.

(3) In subsection (2)(a) and (b), the reference to the time immediately before the relevant act began is, in the case of an act which is one of a continuous series of sexual activities, a reference to the time immediately before the first sexual activity began.

76 Conclusive presumptions about consent

(1) If in proceedings for an offence to which this section applies it is proved that the defendant did the relevant act and that any of the circumstances specified in subsection (2) existed, it is to be conclusively presumed—

  (a) that the complainant did not consent to the relevant act, and

  (b) that the defendant did not believe that the complainant consented to the relevant act.

(2) The circumstances are that—

  (a) the defendant intentionally deceived the complainant as to the nature or purpose of the relevant act;

  (b) the defendant intentionally induced the complainant to consent to the relevant act by impersonating a person known personally to the complainant.

77 Sections 75 and 76: relevant acts

In relation to an offence to which sections 75 and 76 apply, references in those sections to the relevant act and to the complainant are to be read as follows—

Offence	Relevant Act
An offence under section 1 (rape).	The defendant intentionally penetrating, with his penis, the vagina, anus or mouth of another person ('the complainant').
An offence under section 2 (assault by penetration).	The defendant intentionally penetrating, with a part of his body or anything else, the vagina or anus of another person ('the complainant'), where the penetration is sexual.
An offence under section 3 (sexual assault).	The defendant intentionally touching another person ('the complainant'), where the touching is sexual.
An offence under section 4 (causing a person to engage in sexual activity without consent).	The defendant intentionally causing another person ('the complainant') to engage in an activity, where the activity is sexual.

78 'Sexual'

For the purposes of this Part (except section 71), penetration, touching or any other activity is sexual if a reasonable person would consider that—

(a) whatever its circumstances or any person's purpose in relation to it, it is because of its nature sexual, or

(b) because of its nature it may be sexual and because of its circumstances or the purpose of any person in relation to it (or both) it is sexual.

79 Part 1: general interpretation

(1) The following apply for the purposes of this Part.

(2) Penetration is a continuing act from entry to withdrawal.

(3) References to a part of the body include references to a part surgically constructed (in particular, through gender reassignment surgery).

(4) "Image" means a moving or still image and includes an image produced by any means and, where the context permits, a three-dimensional image.

(5) References to an image of a person include references to an image of an imaginary person.

(6) 'Mental disorder' has the meaning given by section 1 of the Mental Health Act 1983.

(7) References to observation (however expressed) are to observation whether direct or by looking at an image.

(8) Touching includes touching—

(a) with any part of the body,

(b) with anything else,

(c) through anything,

and in particular includes touching amounting to penetration.

(9) "Vagina" includes vulva.

(10) In relation to an animal, references to the vagina or anus include references to any similar part.

Criminal Justice Act 2003

(2003, c. 44)

PART 8 LIVE LINKS

51 Live links in criminal proceedings

(1) A witness (other than the defendant) may, if the court so directs, give evidence through a live link in the following criminal proceedings.

(2) They are—

    (a) a summary trial,

    (b) an appeal to the Crown Court arising out of such a trial,

    (c) a trial on indictment,

    (d) an appeal to the criminal division of the Court of Appeal,

    (e) the hearing of a reference under section 9 or 11 of the Criminal Appeal Act 1995,

    (f) a hearing before a magistrates' court or the Crown Court which is held after the defendant has entered a plea of guilty, and

    (g) a hearing before the Court of Appeal under section 80 of this Act.

(3) A direction may be given under this section—

    (a) on an application by a party to the proceedings, or

    (b) of the court's own motion.

(4) But a direction may not be given under this section unless—

    (a) the court is satisfied that it is in the interests of the efficient or effective administration of justice for the person concerned to give evidence in the proceedings through a live link,

    (b) it has been notified by the Secretary of State that suitable facilities for receiving evidence through a live link are available in the area in which it appears to the court that the proceedings will take place, and

    (c) that notification has not been withdrawn.

(5) The withdrawal of such a notification is not to affect a direction given under this section before that withdrawal.

(6) In deciding whether to give a direction under this section the court must consider all the circumstances of the case.

(7) Those circumstances include in particular—

    (a) the availability of the witness,

    (b) the need for the witness to attend in person,

    (c) the importance of the witness's evidence to the proceedings,

    (d) the views of the witness,

    (e) the suitability of the facilities at the place where the witness would give evidence through a live link,

    (f) whether a direction might tend to inhibit any party to the proceedings from effectively testing the witness's evidence.

(8) The court must state in open court its reasons for refusing an application for a direction under this section and, if it is a magistrates' court, must cause them to be entered in the register of its proceedings.

52 Effect of, and rescission of, direction

(1) Subsection (2) applies where the court gives a direction under section 51 for a person to give evidence through a live link in particular proceedings.

(2) The person concerned may not give evidence in those proceedings after the direction is given otherwise than through a live link (but this is subject to the following provisions of this section).

(3) The court may rescind a direction under section 51 if it appears to the court to be in the interests of justice to do so.

(4) Where it does so, the person concerned shall cease to be able to give evidence in the proceedings through a live link, but this does not prevent the court from giving a further direction under section 51 in relation to him.

(5) A direction under section 51 may be rescinded under subsection (3)—

    (a) on an application by a party to the proceedings, or

    (b) of the court's own motion.

(6) But an application may not be made under subsection (5)(a) unless there has been a material change of circumstances since the direction was given.

(7) The court must state in open court its reasons—
   (a) for rescinding a direction under section 51, or
   (b) for refusing an application to rescind such a direction,
and, if it is a magistrates' court, must cause them to be entered in the register of its proceedings.

53 Magistrates' courts permitted to sit at other locations

(1) This section applies where—
   (a) a magistrates' court is minded to give a direction under section 51 for evidence to be given through a live link in proceedings before the court, and
   (b) suitable facilities for receiving such evidence are not available at any place at which the court can (apart from subsection (2)) lawfully sit.

(2) The court may sit for the purposes of the whole or any part of the proceedings at any place at which such facilities are available and which has been authorised by a direction under section 30 of the Courts Act 2003.

(3) If the place mentioned in subsection (2) is outside the local justice area in which the justices act it shall be deemed to be in that area for the purpose of the jurisdiction of the justices acting in that area.

54 Warning to jury

(1) This section applies where, as a result of a direction under section 51, evidence has been given through a live link in proceedings before the Crown Court.

(2) The judge may give the jury (if there is one) such direction as he thinks necessary to ensure that the jury gives the same weight to the evidence as if it had been given by the witness in the courtroom or other place where the proceedings are held.

55 Rules of court

(1) Criminal Procedure Rules may make such provision as appears to the Criminal Procedure Rules Authority to be necessary or expedient for the purposes of this Part.

(2) Criminal Procedure Rules may in particular make provision—
   (a) as to the procedure to be followed in connection with applications under section 51 or 52, and
   (b) as to the arrangements or safeguards to be put in place in connection with the operation of live links.

(3) The provision which may be made by virtue of subsection (2)(a) includes provision—
   (a) for uncontested applications to be determined by the court without a hearing,
   (b) for preventing the renewal of an unsuccessful application under section 51 unless there has been a material change of circumstances,
   (c) for the manner in which confidential or sensitive information is to be treated in connection with an application under section 51 or 52 and in particular as to its being disclosed to, or withheld from, a party to the proceedings.

(4) Nothing in this section is to be taken as affecting the generality of any enactment conferring power to make Criminal Procedure Rules.

56 Interpretation of Part 8

(1) In this Part—
   'legal representative' means a person who, for the purposes of the Legal Services Act 2007, is an authorised person in relation to an activity which constitutes the exercise of a right of audience or the conduct of litigation (within the meaning of that Act),
   'local justice area' has the same meaning as in the Courts Act 2003,
   'witness', in relation to any criminal proceedings, means a person called, or proposed to be called, to give evidence in the proceedings.

(2) In this Part 'live link' means a live television link or other arrangement by which a witness, while at a place in the United Kingdom which is outside the building where the proceedings are being held, is able to see and hear a person at the place where the proceedings are being held and to be seen and heard by the following persons.

(3) They are—

(a) the defendant or defendants,

(b) the judge or justices (or both) and the jury (if there is one),

(c) legal representatives acting in the proceedings, and

(d) any interpreter or other person appointed by the court to assist the witness.

(4) The extent (if any) to which a person is unable to see or hear by reason of any impairment of eyesight or hearing is to be disregarded for the purposes of subsection (2).

(5) Nothing in this Part is to be regarded as affecting any power of a court—

(a) to make an order, give directions or give leave of any description in relation to any witness (including the defendant or defendants), or

(b) to exclude evidence at its discretion (whether by preventing questions being put or otherwise).

PART 9 PROSECUTION APPEALS

Introduction

57 Introduction

(1) In relation to a trial on indictment, the prosecution is to have the rights of appeal for which provision is made by this Part.

(2) But the prosecution is to have no right of appeal under this Part in respect of—

(a) a ruling that a jury be discharged, or

(b) a ruling from which an appeal lies to the Court of Appeal by virtue of any other enactment.

(3) An appeal under this Part is to lie to the Court of Appeal.

(4) Such an appeal may be brought only with the leave of the judge or the Court of Appeal.

General right of appeal in respect of rulings

58 General right of appeal in respect of rulings

(1) This section applies where a judge makes a ruling in relation to a trial on indictment at an applicable time and the ruling relates to one or more offences included in the indictment.

(2) The prosecution may appeal in respect of the ruling in accordance with this section.

(3) The ruling is to have no effect whilst the prosecution is able to take any steps under subsection (4).

(4) The prosecution may not appeal in respect of the ruling unless—

(a) following the making of the ruling, it—

(i) informs the court that it intends to appeal, or

(ii) requests an adjournment to consider whether to appeal, and

(b) if such an adjournment is granted, it informs the court following the adjournment that it intends to appeal.

(5) If the prosecution requests an adjournment under subsection (4)(a)(ii), the judge may grant such an adjournment.

(6) Where the ruling relates to two or more offences—

(a) any one or more of those offences may be the subject of the appeal, and

(b) if the prosecution informs the court in accordance with subsection (4) that it intends to appeal, it must at the same time inform the court of the offence or offences which are the subject of the appeal.

(7) Where—

(a) the ruling is a ruling that there is no case to answer, and

(b) the prosecution, at the same time that it informs the court in accordance with subsection (4) that it intends to appeal, nominates one or more other rulings which have been made by a judge in relation to the trial on indictment at an applicable time and which relate to the offence or offences which are the subject of the appeal,

that other ruling, or those other rulings, are also to be treated as the subject of the appeal.

(8) The prosecution may not inform the court in accordance with subsection (4) that it intends to appeal, unless, at or before that time, it informs the court that it agrees that, in respect of the offence or each offence which is the subject of the appeal, the defendant in relation to that offence should be acquitted of that offence if either of the conditions mentioned in subsection (9) is fulfilled.

(9) Those conditions are—

(a) that leave to appeal to the Court of Appeal is not obtained, and

(b) that the appeal is abandoned before it is determined by the Court of Appeal.

(10) If the prosecution informs the court in accordance with subsection (4) that it intends to appeal, the ruling mentioned in subsection (1) is to continue to have no effect in relation to the offence or offences which are the subject of the appeal whilst the appeal is pursued.

(11) If and to the extent that a ruling has no effect in accordance with this section—

(a) any consequences of the ruling are also to have no effect,

(b) the judge may not take any steps in consequence of the ruling, and

(c) if he does so, any such steps are also to have no effect.

(12) Where the prosecution has informed the court of its agreement under subsection (8) and either of the conditions mentioned in subsection (9) is fulfilled, the judge or the Court of Appeal must order that the defendant in relation to the offence or each offence concerned be acquitted of that offence.

(13) In this section 'applicable time', in relation to a trial on indictment, means any time (whether before or after the commencement of the trial) before the start of the judge's summing-up to the jury.

(14) The reference in subsection (13) to the time when the judge starts his summing-up to the jury includes the time when the judge would start his summing-up to the jury but for the making of an order under Part 7.

59 Expedited and non-expedited appeals

(1) Where the prosecution informs the court in accordance with section 58(4) that it intends to appeal, the judge must decide whether or not the appeal should be expedited.

(2) If the judge decides that the appeal should be expedited, he may order an adjournment.

(3) If the judge decides that the appeal should not be expedited, he may—

(a) order an adjournment, or

(b) discharge the jury (if one has been sworn).

(4) If he decides that the appeal should be expedited, he or the Court of Appeal may subsequently reverse that decision and, if it is reversed, the judge may act as mentioned in subsection (3)(a) or (b).

60 Continuation of proceedings for offences not affected by ruling

(1) This section applies where the prosecution informs the court in accordance with section 58(4) that it intends to appeal.

(2) Proceedings may be continued in respect of any offence which is not the subject of the appeal.

61 Determination of appeal by court of appeal

(1) On an appeal under section 58, the Court of Appeal may confirm, reverse or vary any ruling to which the appeal relates.

(2) Subsections (3) to (5) apply where the appeal relates to a single ruling.

(3) Where the Court of Appeal confirms the ruling, it must, in respect of the offence or each offence which is the subject of the appeal, order that the defendant in relation to that offence be acquitted of that offence.

(4) Where the Court of Appeal reverses or varies the ruling, it must, in respect of the offence or each offence which is the subject of the appeal, do any of the following—

(a) order that proceedings for that offence may be resumed in the Crown Court,

(b) order that a fresh trial may take place in the Crown Court for that offence,

(c) order that the defendant in relation to that offence be acquitted of that offence.

(5) But the Court of Appeal may not make an order under subsection (4)(a) or (b) in respect of an offence unless it considers that the defendant could not receive a fair trial if an order were made under subsection (4)(a) or (b).

(6) Subsections (7) and (8) apply where the appeal relates to a ruling that there is no case to answer and one or more other rulings.

(7) Where the Court of Appeal confirms the ruling that there is no case to answer, it must, in respect of the offence or each offence which is the subject of the appeal, order that the defendant in relation to that offence be acquitted of that offence.

(8) Where the Court of Appeal reverses or varies the ruling that there is no case to answer, it must in respect of the offence or each offence which is the subject of the appeal, make any of the orders mentioned in subsection (4)(a) to (c) (but subject to subsection (5)).

Right of appeal in respect of evidentiary rulings

62 Right of appeal in respect of evidentiary rulings

(1) The prosecution may, in accordance with this section and section 63, appeal in respect of—

(a) a single qualifying evidentiary ruling, or

(b) two or more qualifying evidentiary rulings.

(2) A 'qualifying evidentiary ruling' is an evidentiary ruling of a judge in relation to a trial on indictment which is made at any time (whether before or after the commencement of the trial) before the opening of the case for the defence.

(3) The prosecution may not appeal in respect of a single qualifying evidentiary ruling unless the ruling relates to one or more qualifying offences (whether or not it relates to any other offence).

(4) The prosecution may not appeal in respect of two or more qualifying evidentiary rulings unless each ruling relates to one or more qualifying offences (whether or not it relates to any other offence).

(5) If the prosecution intends to appeal under this section, it must before the opening of the case for the defence inform the court—

(a) of its intention to do so, and

(b) of the ruling or rulings to which the appeal relates.

(6) In respect of the ruling, or each ruling, to which the appeal relates—

(a) the qualifying offence, or at least one of the qualifying offences, to which the ruling relates must be the subject of the appeal, and

(b) any other offence to which the ruling relates may, but need not, be the subject of the appeal.

(7) The prosecution must, at the same time that it informs the court in accordance with subsection (5), inform the court of the offence or offences which are the subject of the appeal.

(8) For the purposes of this section, the case for the defence opens when, after the conclusion of the prosecution evidence, the earliest of the following events occurs—

(a) evidence begins to be adduced by or on behalf of a defendant,

(b) it is indicated to the court that no evidence will be adduced by or on behalf of a defendant,

(c) a defendant's case is opened, as permitted by section 2 of the Criminal Procedure Act 1865.

(9) In this section—

'evidentiary ruling' means a ruling which relates to the admissibility or exclusion of any prosecution evidence,

'qualifying offence' means an offence described in Part 1 of Schedule 4.

(10) The Secretary of State may by order amend that Part by doing any one or more of the following—

(a) adding a description of offence,

(b) removing a description of offence for the time being included,

(c) modifying a description of offence for the time being included.

(11) Nothing in this section affects the right of the prosecution to appeal in respect of an evidentiary ruling under section 58.

63   Condition that evidentiary ruling significantly weakens prosecution case

(1) Leave to appeal may not be given in relation to an appeal under section 62 unless the judge or, as the case may be, the Court of Appeal is satisfied that the relevant condition is fulfilled.

(2) In relation to an appeal in respect of a single qualifying evidentiary ruling, the relevant condition is that the ruling significantly weakens the prosecution's case in relation to the offence or offences which are the subject of the appeal.

(3) In relation to an appeal in respect of two or more qualifying evidentiary rulings, the relevant condition is that the rulings taken together significantly weaken the prosecution's case in relation to the offence or offences which are the subject of the appeal.

64   Expedited and non-expedited appeals

(1) Where the prosecution informs the court in accordance with section 62(5), the judge must decide whether or not the appeal should be expedited.

(2) If the judge decides that the appeal should be expedited, he may order an adjournment.

(3) If the judge decides that the appeal should not be expedited, he may—

(a) order an adjournment, or

(b) discharge the jury (if one has been sworn).

(4) If he decides that the appeal should be expedited, he or the Court of Appeal may subsequently reverse that decision and, if it is reversed, the judge may act as mentioned in subsection (3)(a) or (b).

65   Continuation of proceedings for offences not affected by ruling

(1) This section applies where the prosecution informs the court in accordance with section 62(5).

(2) Proceedings may be continued in respect of any offence which is not the subject of the appeal.

66   Determination of appeal by court of appeal

(1) On an appeal under section 62, the Court of Appeal may confirm, reverse or vary any ruling to which the appeal relates.

(2) In addition, the Court of Appeal must, in respect of the offence or each offence which is the subject of the appeal, do any of the following—

(a) order that proceedings for that offence be resumed in the Crown Court,

(b) order that a fresh trial may take place in the Crown Court for that offence,

(c) order that the defendant in relation to that offence be acquitted of that offence.

(3) But no order may be made under subsection (2)(c) in respect of an offence unless the prosecution has indicated that it does not intend to continue with the prosecution of that offence.

67   Reversal of rulings

The Court of Appeal may not reverse a ruling on an appeal under this Part unless it is satisfied—

   (a) that the ruling was wrong in law,
   (b) that the ruling involved an error of law or principle, or
   (c) that the ruling was a ruling that it was not reasonable for the judge to have made.

PART 10 RETRIAL FOR SERIOUS OFFENCES

Cases that may be retried

75   Cases that may be retried

   (1) This Part applies where a person has been acquitted of a qualifying offence in proceedings—
   (a) on indictment in England and Wales,
   (b) on appeal against a conviction, verdict or finding in proceedings on indictment in England and Wales, or
   (c) on appeal from a decision on such an appeal.

   (2) A person acquitted of an offence in proceedings mentioned in subsection (1) is treated for the purposes of that subsection as also acquitted of any qualifying offence of which he could have been convicted in the proceedings because of the first-mentioned offence being charged in the indictment, except an offence—
   (a) of which he has been convicted,
   (b) of which he has been found not guilty by reason of insanity, or
   (c) in respect of which, in proceedings where he has been found to be under a disability (as defined by section 4 of the Criminal Procedure (Insanity) Act 1964), a finding has been made that he did the act or made the omission charged against him.

   (3) References in subsections (1) and (2) to a qualifying offence do not include references to an offence which, at the time of the acquittal, was the subject of an order under section 77(1) or (3).

   (4) This Part also applies where a person has been acquitted, in proceedings elsewhere than in the United Kingdom, of an offence under the law of the place where the proceedings were held, if the commission of the offence as alleged would have amounted to or included the commission (in the United Kingdom or elsewhere) of a qualifying offence.

   (5) Conduct punishable under the law in force elsewhere than in the United Kingdom is an offence under that law for the purposes of subsection (4), however it is described in that law.

   (6) This Part applies whether the acquittal was before or after the passing of this Act.

   (7) References in this Part to acquittal are to acquittal in circumstances within subsection (1) or (4).

   (8) In this Part 'qualifying offence' means an offence listed in Part 1 of Schedule 5.

Application for retrial

76   Application to court of appeal

   (1) A prosecutor may apply to the Court of Appeal for an order—
   (a) quashing a person's acquittal in proceedings within section 75(1), and
   (b) ordering him to be retried for the qualifying offence.

   (2) A prosecutor may apply to the Court of Appeal, in the case of a person acquitted elsewhere than in the United Kingdom, for—
   (a) a determination whether the acquittal is a bar to the person being tried in England and Wales for the qualifying offence, and

(b) if it is, an order that the acquittal is not to be a bar.

(3) A prosecutor may make an application under subsection (1) or (2) only with the written consent of the Director of Public Prosecutions.

(4) The Director of Public Prosecutions may give his consent only if satisfied that—

(a) there is evidence as respects which the requirements of section 78 appear to be met,

(b) it is in the public interest for the application to proceed, and

(c) any trial pursuant to an order on the application would not be inconsistent with obligations of the United Kingdom under Article 31 or 34 of the Treaty on European Union relating to the principle of *ne bis in idem*.

(5) Not more than one application may be made under subsection (1) or (2) in relation to an acquittal.

77   Determination by court of appeal

(1) On an application under section 76(1), the Court of Appeal—

(a) if satisfied that the requirements of sections 78 and 79 are met, must make the order applied for;

(b) otherwise, must dismiss the application.

(2) Subsections (3) and (4) apply to an application under section 76(2).

(3) Where the Court of Appeal determines that the acquittal is a bar to the person being tried for the qualifying offence, the court—

(a) if satisfied that the requirements of sections 78 and 79 are met, must make the order applied for;

(b) otherwise, must make a declaration to the effect that the acquittal is a bar to the person being tried for the offence.

(4) Where the Court of Appeal determines that the acquittal is not a bar to the person being tried for the qualifying offence, it must make a declaration to that effect.

78   New and compelling evidence

(1) The requirements of this section are met if there is new and compelling evidence against the acquitted person in relation to the qualifying offence.

(2) Evidence is new if it was not adduced in the proceedings in which the person was acquitted (nor, if those were appeal proceedings, in earlier proceedings to which the appeal related).

(3) Evidence is compelling if—

(a) it is reliable,

(b) it is substantial, and

(c) in the context of the outstanding issues, it appears highly probative of the case against the acquitted person.

(4) The outstanding issues are the issues in dispute in the proceedings in which the person was acquitted and, if those were appeal proceedings, any other issues remaining in dispute from earlier proceedings to which the appeal related.

(5) For the purposes of this section, it is irrelevant whether any evidence would have been admissible in earlier proceedings against the acquitted person.

79   Interests of justice

(1) The requirements of this section are met if in all the circumstances it is in the interests of justice for the court to make the order under section 77.

(2) That question is to be determined having regard in particular to—

(a) whether existing circumstances make a fair trial unlikely;

(b) for the purposes of that question and otherwise, the length of time since the qualifying offence was allegedly committed;

(c) whether it is likely that the new evidence would have been adduced in the earlier proceedings against the acquitted person but for a failure by an officer or by a prosecutor to act with due diligence or expedition;

(d) whether, since those proceedings or, if later, since the commencement of this Part, any officer or prosecutor has failed to act with due diligence or expedition.

(3) In subsection (2) references to an officer or prosecutor include references to a person charged with corresponding duties under the law in force elsewhere than in England and Wales.

(4) Where the earlier prosecution was conducted by a person other than a prosecutor, subsection (2)(c) applies in relation to that person as well as in relation to a prosecutor.

80　Procedure and evidence

(1) A prosecutor who wishes to make an application under section 76(1) or (2) must give notice of the application to the Court of Appeal.

(2) Within two days beginning with the day on which any such notice is given, notice of the application must be served by the prosecutor on the person to whom the application relates, charging him with the offence to which it relates or, if he has been charged with it in accordance with section 87(4), stating that he has been so charged.

(3) Subsection (2) applies whether the person to whom the application relates is in the United Kingdom or elsewhere, but the Court of Appeal may, on application by the prosecutor, extend the time for service under that subsection if it considers it necessary to do so because of that person's absence from the United Kingdom.

(4) The Court of Appeal must consider the application at a hearing.

(5) The person to whom the application relates—

(a) is entitled to be present at the hearing, although he may be in custody, unless he is in custody elsewhere than in England and Wales or Northern Ireland, and

(b) is entitled to be represented at the hearing, whether he is present or not.

(6) For the purposes of the application, the Court of Appeal may, if it thinks it necessary or expedient in the interests of justice—

(a) order the production of any document, exhibit or other thing, the production of which appears to the court to be necessary for the determination of the application, and

(b) order any witness who would be a compellable witness in proceedings pursuant to an order or declaration made on the application to attend for examination and be examined before the court.

(7) The Court of Appeal may at one hearing consider more than one application (whether or not relating to the same person), but only if the offences concerned could be tried on the same indictment.

PART 11

Chapter 1　Evidence of bad character

Introductory

98　'Bad character'

References in this Chapter to evidence of a person's 'bad character' are to evidence of, or of a disposition towards, misconduct on his part, other than evidence which—

(a) has to do with the alleged facts of the offence with which the defendant is charged, or

(b) is evidence of misconduct in connection with the investigation or prosecution of that offence.

99　Abolition of common law rules

(1) The common law rules governing the admissibility of evidence of bad character in criminal proceedings are abolished.

(2) Subsection (1) is subject to section 118(1) in so far as it preserves the rule under which in criminal proceedings a person's reputation is admissible for the purposes of proving his bad character.

Persons other than defendants

100   Non-defendant's bad character

(1) In criminal proceedings evidence of the bad character of a person other than the defendant is admissible if and only if—

    (a) it is important explanatory evidence,

    (b) it has substantial probative value in relation to a matter which—

        (i)   is a matter in issue in the proceedings, and

        (ii)   is of substantial importance in the context of the case as a whole,

    or

    (c) all parties to the proceedings agree to the evidence being admissible.

(2) For the purposes of subsection (1)(a) evidence is important explanatory evidence if—

    (a) without it, the court or jury would find it impossible or difficult properly to understand other evidence in the case, and

    (b) its value for understanding the case as a whole is substantial.

(3) In assessing the probative value of evidence for the purposes of subsection (1)(b) the court must have regard to the following factors (and to any others it considers relevant)—

    (a) the nature and number of the events, or other things, to which the evidence relates;

    (b) when those events or things are alleged to have happened or existed;

    (c) where—

        (i)   the evidence is evidence of a person's misconduct, and

        (ii)   it is suggested that the evidence has probative value by reason of similarity between that misconduct and other alleged misconduct,

        the nature and extent of the similarities and the dissimilarities between each of the alleged instances of misconduct;

    (d) where—

        (i)   the evidence is evidence of a person's misconduct,

        (ii)   it is suggested that that person is also responsible for the misconduct charged, and

        (iii) the identity of the person responsible for the misconduct charged is disputed, the extent to which the evidence shows or tends to show that the same person was responsible each time.

(4) Except where subsection (1)(c) applies, evidence of the bad character of a person other than the defendant must not be given without leave of the court.

Defendants

101   Defendant's bad character

(1) In criminal proceedings evidence of the defendant's bad character is admissible if, but only if—

    (a) all parties to the proceedings agree to the evidence being admissible,

    (b) the evidence is adduced by the defendant himself or is given in answer to a question asked by him in cross-examination and intended to elicit it,

    (c) it is important explanatory evidence,

    (d) it is relevant to an important matter in issue between the defendant and the prosecution,

    (e) it has substantial probative value in relation to an important matter in issue between the defendant and a co-defendant,

    (f) it is evidence to correct a false impression given by the defendant, or

    (g) the defendant has made an attack on another person's character.

(2) Sections 102 to 106 contain provision supplementing subsection (1).

(3) The court must not admit evidence under subsection (1)(d) or (g) if, on an application by the defendant to exclude it, it appears to the court that the admission of the evidence would have such an adverse effect on the fairness of the proceedings that the court ought not to admit it.

(4) On an application to exclude evidence under subsection (3) the court must have regard, in particular, to the length of time between the matters to which that evidence relates and the matters which form the subject of the offence charged.

102 'Important explanatory evidence'
For the purposes of section 101(1)(c) evidence is important explanatory evidence if—
    (a) without it, the court or jury would find it impossible or difficult properly to understand other evidence in the case, and
    (b) its value for understanding the case as a whole is substantial.

103 'Matter in issue between the defendant and the prosecution'
(1) For the purposes of section 101(1)(d) the matters in issue between the defendant and the prosecution include—
    (a) the question whether the defendant has a propensity to commit offences of the kind with which he is charged, except where his having such a propensity makes it no more likely that he is guilty of the offence;
    (b) the question whether the defendant has a propensity to be untruthful, except where it is not suggested that the defendant's case is untruthful in any respect.

(2) Where subsection (1)(a) applies, a defendant's propensity to commit offences of the kind with which he is charged may (without prejudice to any other way of doing so) be established by evidence that he has been convicted of—
    (a) an offence of the same description as the one with which he is charged, or
    (b) an offence of the same category as the one with which he is charged.

(3) Subsection (2) does not apply in the case of a particular defendant if the court is satisfied, by reason of the length of time since the conviction or for any other reason, that it would be unjust for it to apply in his case.

(4) For the purposes of subsection (2)—
    (a) two offences are of the same description as each other if the statement of the offence in a written charge or indictment would, in each case, be in the same terms;
    (b) two offences are of the same category as each other if they belong to the same category of offences prescribed for the purposes of this section by an order made by the Secretary of State.

(5) A category prescribed by an order under subsection (4)(b) must consist of offences of the same type.

(6) Only prosecution evidence is admissible under section 101(1)(d).

104 'Matter in issue between the defendant and a co-defendant'
(1) Evidence which is relevant to the question whether the defendant has a propensity to be untruthful is admissible on that basis under section 101(1)(e) only if the nature or conduct of his defence is such as to undermine the co-defendant's defence.

(2) Only evidence—
    (a) which is to be (or has been) adduced by the co-defendant, or
    (b) which a witness is to be invited to give (or has given) in cross-examination by the co-defendant,
is admissible under section 101(1)(e).

105 'Evidence to correct a false impression'
(1) For the purposes of section 101(1)(f)—
    (a) the defendant gives a false impression if he is responsible for the making of an express or implied assertion which is apt to give the court or jury a false or misleading impression about the defendant;
    (b) evidence to correct such an impression is evidence which has probative value in correcting it.

(2) A defendant is treated as being responsible for the making of an assertion if—
- (a) the assertion is made by the defendant in the proceedings (whether or not in evidence given by him),
- (b) the assertion was made by the defendant—
  - (i) on being questioned under caution, before charge, about the offence with which he is charged, or
  - (ii) on being charged with the offence or officially informed that he might be prosecuted for it,

  and evidence of the assertion is given in the proceedings,
- (c) the assertion is made by a witness called by the defendant,
- (d) the assertion is made by any witness in cross-examination in response to a question asked by the defendant that is intended to elicit it, or is likely to do so, or
- (e) the assertion was made by any person out of court, and the defendant adduces evidence of it in the proceedings.

(3) A defendant who would otherwise be treated as responsible for the making of an assertion shall not be so treated if, or to the extent that, he withdraws it or disassociates himself from it.

(4) Where it appears to the court that a defendant, by means of his conduct (other than the giving of evidence) in the proceedings, is seeking to give the court or jury an impression about himself that is false or misleading, the court may if it appears just to do so treat the defendant as being responsible for the making of an assertion which is apt to give that impression.

(5) In subsection (4) 'conduct' includes appearance or dress.

(6) Evidence is admissible under section 101(1)(f) only if it goes no further than is necessary to correct the false impression.

(7) Only prosecution evidence is admissible under section 101(1)(f).

106 'Attack on another person's character'

(1) For the purposes of section 101(1)(g) a defendant makes an attack on another person's character if—
- (a) he adduces evidence attacking the other person's character,
- (b) he (or any legal representative appointed under section 38(4) of the Youth Justice and Criminal Evidence Act 1999 to cross-examine a witness in his interests) asks questions in cross-examination that are intended to elicit such evidence, or are likely to do so, or
- (c) evidence is given of an imputation about the other person made by the defendant—
  - (i) on being questioned under caution, before charge, about the offence with which he is charged, or
  - (ii) on being charged with the offence or officially informed that he might be prosecuted for it.

(2) In subsection (1) 'evidence attacking the other person's character' means evidence to the effect that the other person—
- (a) has committed an offence (whether a different offence from the one with which the defendant is charged or the same one), or
- (b) has behaved, or is disposed to behave, in a reprehensible way;

and 'imputation about the other person' means an assertion to that effect.

(3) Only prosecution evidence is admissible under section 101(1)(g).

107 Stopping the case where evidence contaminated

(1) If on a defendant's trial before a judge and jury for an offence—
- (a) evidence of his bad character has been admitted under any of paragraphs (c) to (g) of section 101(1), and
- (b) the court is satisfied at any time after the close of the case for the prosecution that—
  - (i) the evidence is contaminated, and

(ii) the contamination is such that, considering the importance of the evidence to the case against the defendant, his conviction of the offence would be unsafe,

the court must either direct the jury to acquit the defendant of the offence or, if it considers that there ought to be a retrial, discharge the jury.

(2) Where—

(a) a jury is directed under subsection (1) to acquit a defendant of an offence, and

(b) the circumstances are such that, apart from this subsection, the defendant could if acquitted of that offence be found guilty of another offence,

the defendant may not be found guilty of that other offence if the court is satisfied as mentioned in subsection (1)(b) in respect of it.

(3) If—

(a) a jury is required to determine under section 4A(2) of the Criminal Procedure (Insanity) Act 1964 whether a person charged on an indictment with an offence did the act or made the omission charged,

(b) evidence of the person's bad character has been admitted under any of paragraphs (c) to (g) of section 101(1), and

(c) the court is satisfied at any time after the close of the case for the prosecution that—

(i) the evidence is contaminated, and

(ii) the contamination is such that, considering the importance of the evidence to the case against the person, a finding that he did the act or made the omission would be unsafe,

the court must either direct the jury to acquit the defendant of the offence or, if it considers that there ought to be a rehearing, discharge the jury.

(4) This section does not prejudice any other power a court may have to direct a jury to acquit a person of an offence or to discharge a jury.

(5) For the purposes of this section a person's evidence is contaminated where—

(a) as a result of an agreement or understanding between the person and one or more others, or

(b) as a result of the person being aware of anything alleged by one or more others whose evidence may be, or has been, given in the proceedings,

the evidence is false or misleading in any respect, or is different from what it would otherwise have been.

108 Offences committed by defendant when a child

(1) Section 16(2) and (3) of the Children and Young Persons Act 1963 (offences committed by person under 14 disregarded for purposes of evidence relating to previous convictions) shall cease to have effect.

(2) In proceedings for an offence committed or alleged to have been committed by the defendant when aged 21 or over, evidence of his conviction for an offence when under the age of 14 is not admissible unless—

(a) both of the offences are triable only on indictment, and

(b) the court is satisfied that the interests of justice require the evidence to be admissible.

(3) Subsection (2) applies in addition to section 101.

General

109 Assumption of truth in assessment of relevance or probative value

(1) Subject to subsection (2), a reference in this Chapter to the relevance or probative value of evidence is a reference to its relevance or probative value on the assumption that it is true.

(2) In assessing the relevance or probative value of an item of evidence for any purpose of this Chapter, a court need not assume that the evidence is true if it appears, on the basis of any material before the court (including any evidence it decides to hear on the matter), that no court or jury could reasonably find it to be true.

110   Court's duty to give reasons for rulings

(1) Where the court makes a relevant ruling—

    (a) it must state in open court (but in the absence of the jury, if there is one) its reasons for the ruling;

    (b) if it is a magistrates' court, it must cause the ruling and the reasons for it to be entered in the register of the court's proceedings.

(2) In this section 'relevant ruling' means—

    (a) a ruling on whether an item of evidence is evidence of a person's bad character;

    (b) a ruling on whether an item of such evidence is admissible under section 100 or 101 (including a ruling on an application under section 101(3));

    (c) a ruling under section 107.

111   Rules of court

(1) Rules of court may make such provision as appears to the appropriate authority to be necessary or expedient for the purposes of this Act; and the appropriate authority is the authority entitled to make the rules.

(2) The rules may, and, where the party in question is the prosecution, must, contain provision requiring a party who—

    (a) proposes to adduce evidence of a defendant's bad character, or

    (b) proposes to cross-examine a witness with a view to eliciting such evidence,

to serve on the defendant such notice, and such particulars of or relating to the evidence, as may be prescribed.

(3) The rules may provide that the court or the defendant may, in such circumstances as may be prescribed, dispense with a requirement imposed by virtue of subsection (2).

(4) In considering the exercise of its powers with respect to costs, the court may take into account any failure by a party to comply with a requirement imposed by virtue of subsection (2) and not dispensed with by virtue of subsection (3).

(5) The rules may—

    (a) limit the application of any provision of the rules to prescribed circumstances;

    (b) subject any provision of the rules to prescribed exceptions;

    (c) make different provision for different cases or circumstances.

(6) Nothing in this section prejudices the generality of any enactment conferring power to make rules of court; and no particular provision of this section prejudices any general provision of it.

(7) In this section—

'prescribed' means prescribed by rules of court.

112   Interpretation of Chapter 1

(1) In this Chapter—

'bad character' is to be read in accordance with section 98;

'criminal proceedings' means criminal proceedings in relation to which the strict rules of evidence apply;

'defendant', in relation to criminal proceedings, means a person charged with an offence in those proceedings; and 'co-defendant', in relation to a defendant, means a person charged with an offence in the same proceedings;

'important matter' means a matter of substantial importance in the context of the case as a whole;

'misconduct' means the commission of an offence or other reprehensible behaviour;

'offence' includes a service offence;

'probative value', and 'relevant' (in relation to an item of evidence), are to be read in accordance with section 109;

'prosecution evidence' means evidence which is to be (or has been) adduced by the prosecution, or which a witness is to be invited to give (or has given) in cross-examination by the prosecution;

'service offence' has the same meaning as in the Armed Forces Act 2006;

'written charge' has the same meaning as in section 29 and also includes an information.

(2) Where a defendant is charged with two or more offences in the same criminal proceedings, this Chapter (except section 101(3)) has effect as if each offence were charged in separate proceedings; and references to the offence with which the defendant is charged are to be read accordingly.

(3) Nothing in this Chapter affects the exclusion of evidence—

    (a) under the rule in section 3 of the Criminal Procedure Act 1865 against a party impeaching the credit of his own witness by general evidence of bad character,

    (b) under section 41 of the Youth Justice and Criminal Evidence Act 1999 on grounds other than the fact that it is evidence of a person's bad character.

    (c) On grounds other than the fact that it is evidence of a person's bad character.

113　Armed Forces

[Omitted]

Chapter 2

114　Admissibility of hearsay evidence

(1) In criminal proceedings a statement not made in oral evidence in the proceedings is admissible as evidence of any matter stated if, but only if—

    (a) any provision of this Chapter or any other statutory provision makes it admissible,

    (b) any rule of law preserved by section 118 makes it admissible,

    (c) all parties to the proceedings agree to it being admissible, or

    (d) the court is satisfied that it is in the interests of justice for it to be admissible.

(2) In deciding whether a statement not made in oral evidence should be admitted under subsection (1)(d), the court must have regard to the following factors (and to any others it considers relevant)—

    (a) how much probative value the statement has (assuming it to be true) in relation to a matter in issue in the proceedings, or how valuable it is for the understanding of other evidence in the case;

    (b) what other evidence has been, or can be, given on the matter or evidence mentioned in paragraph (a);

    (c) how important the matter or evidence mentioned in paragraph (a) is in the context of the case as a whole;

    (d) the circumstances in which the statement was made;

    (e) how reliable the maker of the statement appears to be;

    (f) how reliable the evidence of the making of the statement appears to be;

    (g) whether oral evidence of the matter stated can be given and, if not, why it cannot;

    (h) the amount of difficulty involved in challenging the statement;

    (i) the extent to which that difficulty would be likely to prejudice the party facing it.

(3) Nothing in this Chapter affects the exclusion of evidence of a statement on grounds other than the fact that it is a statement not made in oral evidence in the proceedings.

115　Statements and matters stated

(1) In this Chapter references to a statement or to a matter stated are to be read as follows.

(2) A statement is any representation of fact or opinion made by a person by whatever means; and it includes a representation made in a sketch, photofit or other pictorial form.

(3) A matter stated is one to which this Chapter applies if (and only if) the purpose, or one of the purposes, of the person making the statement appears to the court to have been—

    (a) to cause another person to believe the matter, or

    (b) to cause another person to act or a machine to operate on the basis that the matter is as stated.

Principal categories of admissibility

116   Cases where a witness is unavailable

(1) In criminal proceedings a statement not made in oral evidence in the proceedings is admissible as evidence of any matter stated if—

    (a) oral evidence given in the proceedings by the person who made the statement would be admissible as evidence of that matter,

    (b) the person who made the statement (the relevant person) is identified to the court's satisfaction, and

    (c) any of the five conditions mentioned in subsection (2) is satisfied.

(2) The conditions are—

    (a) that the relevant person is dead;

    (b) that the relevant person is unfit to be a witness because of his bodily or mental condition;

    (c) that the relevant person is outside the United Kingdom and it is not reasonably practicable to secure his attendance;

    (d) that the relevant person cannot be found although such steps as it is reasonably practicable to take to find him have been taken;

    (e) that through fear the relevant person does not give (or does not continue to give) oral evidence in the proceedings, either at all or in connection with the subject matter of the statement, and the court gives leave for the statement to be given in evidence.

(3) For the purposes of subsection (2)(e) 'fear' is to be widely construed and (for example) includes fear of the death or injury of another person or of financial loss.

(4) Leave may be given under subsection (2)(e) only if the court considers that the statement ought to be admitted in the interests of justice, having regard—

    (a) to the statement's contents,

    (b) to any risk that its admission or exclusion will result in unfairness to any party to the proceedings (and in particular to how difficult it will be to challenge the statement if the relevant person does not give oral evidence),

    (c) in appropriate cases, to the fact that a direction under section 19 of the Youth Justice and Criminal Evidence Act 1999 (special measures for the giving of evidence by fearful witnesses etc) could be made in relation to the relevant person, and

    (d) to any other relevant circumstances.

(5) A condition set out in any paragraph of subsection (2) which is in fact satisfied is to be treated as not satisfied if it is shown that the circumstances described in that paragraph are caused—

    (a) by the person in support of whose case it is sought to give the statement in evidence, or

    (b) by a person acting on his behalf,

in order to prevent the relevant person giving oral evidence in the proceedings (whether at all or in connection with the subject matter of the statement).

117   Business and other documents

(1) In criminal proceedings a statement contained in a document is admissible as evidence of any matter stated if—

    (a) oral evidence given in the proceedings would be admissible as evidence of that matter,

    (b) the requirements of subsection (2) are satisfied, and

    (c) the requirements of subsection (5) are satisfied, in a case where subsection (4) requires them to be.

(2) The requirements of this subsection are satisfied if—

    (a) the document or the part containing the statement was created or received by a person in the course of a trade, business, profession or other occupation, or as the holder of a paid or unpaid office,

(b) the person who supplied the information contained in the statement (the relevant person) had or may reasonably be supposed to have had personal knowledge of the matters dealt with, and

(c) each person (if any) through whom the information was supplied from the relevant person to the person mentioned in paragraph (a) received the information in the course of a trade, business, profession or other occupation, or as the holder of a paid or unpaid office.

(3) The persons mentioned in paragraphs (a) and (b) of subsection (2) may be the same person.

(4) The additional requirements of subsection (5) must be satisfied if the statement—

(a) was prepared for the purposes of pending or contemplated criminal proceedings, or for a criminal investigation, but

(b) was not obtained pursuant to a request under section 7 of the Crime (International Co-operation) Act 2003 or an order under paragraph 6 of Schedule 13 to the Criminal Justice Act 1988 (which relate to overseas evidence).

(5) The requirements of this subsection are satisfied if—

(a) any of the five conditions mentioned in section 116(2) is satisfied (absence of relevant person etc), or

(b) the relevant person cannot reasonably be expected to have any recollection of the matters dealt with in the statement (having regard to the length of time since he supplied the information and all other circumstances).

(6) A statement is not admissible under this section if the court makes a direction to that effect under subsection (7).

(7) The court may make a direction under this subsection if satisfied that the statement's reliability as evidence for the purpose for which it is tendered is doubtful in view of—

(a) its contents,

(b) the source of the information contained in it,

(c) the way in which or the circumstances in which the information was supplied or received, or

(d) the way in which or the circumstances in which the document concerned was created or received.

118 Preservation of certain common law categories of admissibility

(1) The following rules of law are preserved.

Public information etc

1. Any rule of law under which in criminal proceedings—

(a) published works dealing with matters of a public nature (such as histories, scientific works, dictionaries and maps) are admissible as evidence of facts of a public nature stated in them,

(b) public documents (such as public registers, and returns made under public authority with respect to matters of public interest) are admissible as evidence of facts stated in them,

(c) records (such as the records of certain courts, treaties, Crown grants, pardons and commissions) are admissible as evidence of facts stated in them, or

(d) evidence relating to a person's age or date or place of birth may be given by a person without personal knowledge of the matter.

Reputation as to character

2. Any rule of law under which in criminal proceedings evidence of a person's reputation is admissible for the purpose of proving his good or bad character.

Note

The rule is preserved only so far as it allows the court to treat such evidence as proving the matter concerned.

Reputation or family tradition

3. Any rule of law under which in criminal proceedings evidence of reputation or family tradition is admissible for the purpose of proving or disproving—
- (a) pedigree or the existence of a marriage,
- (b) the existence of any public or general right, or
- (c) the identity of any person or thing.

Note

The rule is preserved only so far as it allows the court to treat such evidence as proving or disproving the matter concerned.

Res gestae

4. Any rule of law under which in criminal proceedings a statement is admissible as evidence of any matter stated if—
- (a) the statement was made by a person so emotionally overpowered by an event that the possibility of concoction or distortion can be disregarded,
- (b) the statement accompanied an act which can be properly evaluated as evidence only if considered in conjunction with the statement, or
- (c) the statement relates to a physical sensation or a mental state (such as intention or emotion).

Confessions etc

5. Any rule of law relating to the admissibility of confessions or mixed statements in criminal proceedings.

Admissions by agents etc

6. Any rule of law under which in criminal proceedings—
- (a) an admission made by an agent of a defendant is admissible against the defendant as evidence of any matter stated, or
- (b) a statement made by a person to whom a defendant refers a person for information is admissible against the defendant as evidence of any matter stated.

Common enterprise

7. Any rule of law under which in criminal proceedings a statement made by a party to a common enterprise is admissible against another party to the enterprise as evidence of any matter stated.

Expert evidence

8. Any rule of law under which in criminal proceedings an expert witness may draw on the body of expertise relevant to his field.

(2) With the exception of the rules preserved by this section, the common law rules governing the admissibility of hearsay evidence in criminal proceedings are abolished.

119   Inconsistent statements

(1) If in criminal proceedings a person gives oral evidence and—
- (a) he admits making a previous inconsistent statement, or
- (b) a previous inconsistent statement made by him is proved by virtue of section 3, 4 or 5 of the Criminal Procedure Act 1865,

the statement is admissible as evidence of any matter stated of which oral evidence by him would be admissible.

(2) If in criminal proceedings evidence of an inconsistent statement by any person is given under section 124(2)(c), the statement is admissible as evidence of any matter stated in it of which oral evidence by that person would be admissible.

120   Other previous statements of witnesses

(1) This section applies where a person (the witness) is called to give evidence in criminal proceedings.

(2) If a previous statement by the witness is admitted as evidence to rebut a suggestion that his oral evidence has been fabricated, that statement is admissible as evidence of any matter stated of which oral evidence by the witness would be admissible.

(3) A statement made by the witness in a document—

(a) which is used by him to refresh his memory while giving evidence,

(b) on which he is cross-examined, and

(c) which as a consequence is received in evidence in the proceedings,

is admissible as evidence of any matter stated of which oral evidence by him would be admissible.

(4) A previous statement by the witness is admissible as evidence of any matter stated of which oral evidence by him would be admissible, if—

(a) any of the following three conditions is satisfied, and

(b) while giving evidence the witness indicates that to the best of his belief he made the statement, and that to the best of his belief it states the truth.

(5) The first condition is that the statement identifies or describes a person, object or place.

(6) The second condition is that the statement was made by the witness when the matters stated were fresh in his memory but he does not remember them, and cannot reasonably be expected to remember them, well enough to give oral evidence of them in the proceedings.

(7) The third condition is that—

(a) the witness claims to be a person against whom an offence has been committed,

(b) the offence is one to which the proceedings relate,

(c) the statement consists of a complaint made by the witness (whether to a person in authority or not) about conduct which would, if proved, constitute the offence or part of the offence,

(e) the complaint was not made as a result of a threat or a promise, and

(f) before the statement is adduced the witness gives oral evidence in connection with its subject matter.

(8) For the purposes of subsection (7) the fact that the complaint was elicited (for example, by a leading question) is irrelevant unless a threat or a promise was involved.

Supplementary

121 Additional requirement for admissibility of multiple hearsay

(1) A hearsay statement is not admissible to prove the fact that an earlier hearsay statement was made unless—

(a) either of the statements is admissible under section 117, 119 or 120,

(b) all parties to the proceedings so agree, or

(c) the court is satisfied that the value of the evidence in question, taking into account how reliable the statements appear to be, is so high that the interests of justice require the later statement to be admissible for that purpose.

(2) In this section 'hearsay statement' means a statement, not made in oral evidence, that is relied on as evidence of a matter stated in it.

122 Documents produced as exhibits

(1) This section applies if on a trial before a judge and jury for an offence—

(a) a statement made in a document is admitted in evidence under section 119 or 120, and

(b) the document or a copy of it is produced as an exhibit.

(2) The exhibit must not accompany the jury when they retire to consider their verdict unless—

(a) the court considers it appropriate, or

(b) all the parties to the proceedings agree that it should accompany the jury.

123 Capability to make statement

(1) Nothing in section 116, 119 or 120 makes a statement admissible as evidence if it was made by a person who did not have the required capability at the time when he made the statement.

(2) Nothing in section 117 makes a statement admissible as evidence if any person who, in order for the requirements of section 117(2) to be satisfied, must at any time have supplied or received the information concerned or created or received the document or part concerned—

  (a) did not have the required capability at that time, or
  (b) cannot be identified but cannot reasonably be assumed to have had the required capability at that time.

(3) For the purposes of this section a person has the required capability if he is capable of—

  (a) understanding questions put to him about the matters stated, and
  (b) giving answers to such questions which can be understood.

(4) Where by reason of this section there is an issue as to whether a person had the required capability when he made a statement—

  (a) proceedings held for the determination of the issue must take place in the absence of the jury (if there is one);
  (b) in determining the issue the court may receive expert evidence and evidence from any person to whom the statement in question was made;
  (c) the burden of proof on the issue lies on the party seeking to adduce the statement, and the standard of proof is the balance of probabilities.

124 Credibility

(1) This section applies if in criminal proceedings—

  (a) a statement not made in oral evidence in the proceedings is admitted as evidence of a matter stated, and
  (b) the maker of the statement does not give oral evidence in connection with the subject matter of the statement.

(2) In such a case—

  (a) any evidence which (if he had given such evidence) would have been admissible as relevant to his credibility as a witness is so admissible in the proceedings;
  (b) evidence may with the court's leave be given of any matter which (if he had given such evidence) could have been put to him in cross-examination as relevant to his credibility as a witness but of which evidence could not have been adduced by the cross-examining party;
  (c) evidence tending to prove that he made (at whatever time) any other statement inconsistent with the statement admitted as evidence is admissible for the purpose of showing that he contradicted himself.

(3) If as a result of evidence admitted under this section an allegation is made against the maker of a statement, the court may permit a party to lead additional evidence of such description as the court may specify for the purposes of denying or answering the allegation.

(4) In the case of a statement in a document which is admitted as evidence under section 117 each person who, in order for the statement to be admissible, must have supplied or received the information concerned or created or received the document or part concerned is to be treated as the maker of the statement for the purposes of subsections (1) to (3) above.

125 Stopping the case where evidence is unconvincing

(1) If on a defendant's trial before a judge and jury for an offence the court is satisfied at any time after the close of the case for the prosecution that—

  (a) the case against the defendant is based wholly or partly on a statement not made in oral evidence in the proceedings, and
  (b) the evidence provided by the statement is so unconvincing that, considering its importance to the case against the defendant, his conviction of the offence would be unsafe,

the court must either direct the jury to acquit the defendant of the offence or, if it considers that there ought to be a retrial, discharge the jury.

(2) Where—

  (a) a jury is directed under subsection (1) to acquit a defendant of an offence, and

(b) the circumstances are such that, apart from this subsection, the defendant could if acquitted of that offence be found guilty of another offence,

the defendant may not be found guilty of that other offence if the court is satisfied as mentioned in subsection (1) in respect of it.

(3) If—

(a) a jury is required to determine under section 4A(2) of the Criminal Procedure (Insanity) Act 1964 whether a person charged on an indictment with an offence did the act or made the omission charged, and

(b) the court is satisfied as mentioned in subsection (1) above at any time after the close of the case for the prosecution that—

(i) the case against the defendant is based wholly or partly on a statement not made in oral evidence in the proceedings, and

(ii) the evidence provided by the statement is so unconvincing that, considering its importance to the case against the person, a finding that he did the act or made the omission would be unsafe,

the court must either direct the jury to acquit the defendant of the offence or, if it considers that there ought to be a rehearing, discharge the jury.

(4) This section does not prejudice any other power a court may have to direct a jury to acquit a person of an offence or to discharge a jury.

126 Court's general discretion to exclude evidence

(1) In criminal proceedings the court may refuse to admit a statement as evidence of a matter stated if—

(a) the statement was made otherwise than in oral evidence in the proceedings, and

(b) the court is satisfied that the case for excluding the statement, taking account of the danger that to admit it would result in undue waste of time, substantially outweighs the case for admitting it, taking account of the value of the evidence.

(2) Nothing in this Chapter prejudices—

(a) any power of a court to exclude evidence under section 78 of the Police and Criminal Evidence Act 1984 (exclusion of unfair evidence), or

(b) any other power of a court to exclude evidence at its discretion (whether by preventing questions from being put or otherwise).

Miscellaneous

127 Expert evidence: preparatory work

(1) This section applies if—

(a) a statement has been prepared for the purposes of criminal proceedings,

(b) the person who prepared the statement had or may reasonably be supposed to have had personal knowledge of the matters stated,

(c) notice is given under the appropriate rules that another person (the expert) will in evidence given in the proceedings orally or under section 9 of the Criminal Justice Act 1967 base an opinion or inference on the statement, and

(d) the notice gives the name of the person who prepared the statement and the nature of the matters stated.

(2) In evidence given in the proceedings the expert may base an opinion or inference on the statement.

(3) If evidence based on the statement is given under subsection (2) the statement is to be treated as evidence of what it states.

(4) This section does not apply if the court, on an application by a party to the proceedings, orders that it is not in the interests of justice that it should apply.

(5) The matters to be considered by the court in deciding whether to make an order under subsection (4) include—

    (a) the expense of calling as a witness the person who prepared the statement;

    (b) whether relevant evidence could be given by that person which could not be given by the expert;

    (c) whether that person can reasonably be expected to remember the matters stated well enough to give oral evidence of them.

(6) Subsections (1) to (5) apply to a statement prepared for the purposes of a criminal investigation as they apply to a statement prepared for the purposes of criminal proceedings, and in such a case references to the proceedings are to criminal proceedings arising from the investigation.

(7) The appropriate rules are Criminal Procedure Rules made by virtue of—

    (a) section 81 of the Police and Criminal Evidence Act 1984 (advance notice of expert evidence in Crown Court), or

    (b) section 20(3) of the Criminal Procedure and Investigations Act 1996 (advance notice of expert evidence in magistrates' courts).

128 Confessions

(1) . . . [Refers to section 76A Police and Criminal Evidence Act 1984.]

(2) Subject to subsection (1), nothing in this Chapter makes a confession by a defendant admissible if it would not be admissible under section 76 of the Police and Criminal Evidence Act 1984.

(3) In subsection (2) 'confession' has the meaning given by section 82 of that Act.

129 Representations other than by a person

(1) Where a representation of any fact—

    (a) is made otherwise than by a person, but

    (b) depends for its accuracy on information supplied (directly or indirectly) by a person,

the representation is not admissible in criminal proceedings as evidence of the fact unless it is proved that the information was accurate.

(2) Subsection (1) does not affect the operation of the presumption that a mechanical device has been properly set or calibrated.

General

132 Rules of court

(1) Rules of court may make such provision as appears to the appropriate authority to be necessary or expedient for the purposes of this Chapter; and the appropriate authority is the authority entitled to make the rules.

(2) The rules may make provision about the procedure to be followed and other conditions to be fulfilled by a party proposing to tender a statement in evidence under any provision of this Chapter.

(3) The rules may require a party proposing to tender the evidence to serve on each party to the proceedings such notice, and such particulars of or relating to the evidence, as may be prescribed.

(4) The rules may provide that the evidence is to be treated as admissible by agreement of the parties if—

    (a) a notice has been served in accordance with provision made under subsection (3), and

    (b) no counter-notice in the prescribed form objecting to the admission of the evidence has been served by a party.

(5) If a party proposing to tender evidence fails to comply with a prescribed requirement applicable to it—

    (a) the evidence is not admissible except with the court's leave;

    (b) where leave is given the court or jury may draw such inferences from the failure as appear proper;

    (c) the failure may be taken into account by the court in considering the exercise of its powers with respect to costs.

(6) In considering whether or how to exercise any of its powers under subsection (5) the court shall have regard to whether there is any justification for the failure to comply with the requirement.

(7) A person shall not be convicted of an offence solely on an inference drawn under subsection (5)(b).

(8) Rules under this section may—

    (a) limit the application of any provision of the rules to prescribed circumstances;

    (b) subject any provision of the rules to prescribed exceptions;

    (c) make different provision for different cases or circumstances.

(9) Nothing in this section prejudices the generality of any enactment conferring power to make rules of court; and no particular provision of this section prejudices any general provision of it.

(10) In this section—

'prescribed' means prescribed by rules of court.

133 Proof of statements in documents

Where a statement in a document is admissible as evidence in criminal proceedings, the statement may be proved by producing either—

    (a) the document, or

    (b) (whether or not the document exists) a copy of the document or of the material part of it, authenticated in whatever way the court may approve.

134 Interpretation of Chapter 2

(1) In this Chapter—

'copy', in relation to a document, means anything on to which information recorded in the document has been copied, by whatever means and whether directly or indirectly;

'criminal proceedings' means criminal proceedings in relation to which the strict rules of evidence apply;

'defendant', in relation to criminal proceedings, means a person charged with an offence in those proceedings;

'document' means anything in which information of any description is recorded;

'oral evidence' includes evidence which, by reason of any disability, disorder or other impairment, a person called as a witness gives in writing or by signs or by way of any device;

'statutory provision' means any provision contained in, or in an instrument made under, this or any other Act, including any Act passed after this Act.

(2) Section 115 (statements and matters stated) contains other general interpretative provisions.

(3) Where a defendant is charged with two or more offences in the same criminal proceedings, this Chapter has effect as if each offence were charged in separate proceedings.

Chapter 3 Miscellaneous and supplemental

137 Evidence by video recording

(1) This section applies where—

    (a) a person is called as a witness in proceedings for an offence triable only on indictment, or for a prescribed offence triable either way,

    (b) the person claims to have witnessed (whether visually or in any other way)—

        (i) events alleged by the prosecution to include conduct constituting the offence or part of the offence, or

        (ii) events closely connected with such events,

    (c) he has previously given an account of the events in question (whether in response to questions asked or otherwise),

    (d) the account was given at a time when those events were fresh in the person's memory (or would have been, assuming the truth of the claim mentioned in paragraph (b)),

(e) a video recording was made of the account,

(f) the court has made a direction that the recording should be admitted as evidence in chief of the witness, and the direction has not been rescinded, and

(g) the recording is played in the proceedings in accordance with the direction.

(2) If, or to the extent that, the witness in his oral evidence in the proceedings asserts the truth of the statements made by him in the recorded account, they shall be treated as if made by him in that evidence.

(3) A direction under subsection (1)(f)—

(a) may not be made in relation to a recorded account given by the defendant;

(b) may be made only if it appears to the court that—

(i) the witness's recollection of the events in question is likely to have been significantly better when he gave the recorded account than it will be when he gives oral evidence in the proceedings, and

(ii) it is in the interests of justice for the recording to be admitted, having regard in particular to the matters mentioned in subsection (4).

(4) Those matters are—

(a) the interval between the time of the events in question and the time when the recorded account was made;

(b) any other factors that might affect the reliability of what the witness said in that account;

(c) the quality of the recording;

(d) any views of the witness as to whether his evidence in chief should be given orally or by means of the recording.

(5) For the purposes of subsection (2) it does not matter if the statements in the recorded account were not made on oath.

(6) In this section 'prescribed' means of a description specified in an order made by the Secretary of State.

138   Video evidence: further provisions

(2) The reference in subsection (1)(f) of section 137 to the admission of a recording includes a reference to the admission of part of the recording; and references in that section and this one to the video recording or to the witness's recorded account shall, where appropriate, be read accordingly.

(3) In considering whether any part of a recording should be not admitted under section 137, the court must consider—

(a) whether admitting that part would carry a risk of prejudice to the defendant, and

(b) if so, whether the interests of justice nevertheless require it to be admitted in view of the desirability of showing the whole, or substantially the whole, of the recorded interview.

(4) A court may not make a direction under section 137(1)(f) in relation to any proceedings unless—

(a) the Secretary of State has notified the court that arrangements can be made, in the area in which it appears to the court that the proceedings will take place, for implementing directions under that section, and

(b) the notice has not been withdrawn.

(5) Nothing in section 137 affects the admissibility of any video recording which would be admissible apart from that section.

139   Use of documents to refresh memory

(1) A person giving oral evidence in criminal proceedings about any matter may, at any stage in the course of doing so, refresh his memory of it from a document made or verified by him at an earlier time if—

(a) he states in his oral evidence that the document records his recollection of the matter at that earlier time, and

(b) his recollection of the matter is likely to have been significantly better at that time than it is at the time of his oral evidence.

(2) Where—

    (a) a person giving oral evidence in criminal proceedings about any matter has previously given an oral account, of which a sound recording was made, and he states in that evidence that the account represented his recollection of the matter at that time,

    (b) his recollection of the matter is likely to have been significantly better at the time of the previous account than it is at the time of his oral evidence, and

    (c) a transcript has been made of the sound recording,

he may, at any stage in the course of giving his evidence, refresh his memory of the matter from that transcript.

140 Interpretation of Chapter 3

In this Chapter—

'criminal proceedings' means criminal proceedings in relation to which the strict rules of evidence apply;

'defendant', in relation to criminal proceedings, means a person charged with an offence in those proceedings;

'document' means anything in which information of any description is recorded, but not including any recording of sounds or moving images;

'oral evidence' includes evidence which, by reason of any disability, disorder or other impairment, a person called as a witness gives in writing or by signs or by way of any device;

'video recording' means any recording, on any medium, from which a moving image may by any means be produced, and includes the accompanying sound-track.

SCHEDULE 4

QUALIFYING OFFENCES
FOR PURPOSES OF SECTION 62

PART 1 LIST OF OFFENCES

Offences against the person

Murder

1. Murder.

Attempted murder

2. An offence under section 1 of the Criminal Attempts Act 1981 of attempting to commit murder.

Soliciting murder

3. An offence under section 4 of the Offences against the Person Act 1861.

Manslaughter

4. Manslaughter.

Corporate manslaughter

4A. An offence under section 1 of the Corporate Manslaughter and Corporate Homicide Act 2007.

Wounding or causing grievous bodily harm with intent

5. An offence under section 18 of the Offences against the Person Act 1861.

Kidnapping

6. Kidnapping.

Sexual offences

Rape

7. An offence under section 1 of the Sexual Offences Act 1956 or section 1 of the Sexual Offences Act 2003.

Attempted rape

8. An offence under section 1 of the Criminal Attempts Act 1981 of attempting to commit an offence under section 1 of the Sexual Offences Act 1956 or section 1 of the Sexual Offences Act 2003.

Intercourse with a girl under thirteen

9. An offence under section 5 of the Sexual Offences Act 1956.

Incest by a man with a girl under thirteen

10. An offence under section 10 of the Sexual Offences Act 1956 alleged to have been committed with a girl under thirteen.

Assault by penetration

11. An offence under section 2 of the Sexual Offences Act 2003.

Causing a person to engage in sexual activity without consent

12. An offence under section 4 of the Sexual Offences Act 2003 where it is alleged that the activity caused involved penetration within subsection (4)(a) to (d) of that section.

Rape of a child under thirteen

13. An offence under section 5 of the Sexual Offences Act 2003.

Attempted rape of a child under thirteen

14. An offence under section 1 of the Criminal Attempts Act 1981 of attempting to commit an offence under section 5 of the Sexual Offences Act 2003.

Assault of a child under thirteen by penetration

15. An offence under section 6 of the Sexual Offences Act 2003.

Causing a child under thirteen to engage in sexual activity

16. An offence under section 8 of the Sexual Offences Act 2003 where it is alleged that an activity involving penetration within subsection (2)(a) to (d) of that section was caused.

Sexual activity with a person with a mental disorder impeding choice

17. An offence under section 30 of the Sexual Offences Act 2003 where it is alleged that the touching involved penetration within subsection (3)(a) to (d) of that section.

Causing or inciting a person with a mental disorder impeding choice to engage in sexual activity

18. An offence under section 31 of the Sexual Offences Act 2003 where it is alleged that an activity involving penetration within subsection (3)(a) to (d) of that section was caused.

Drugs offences

Unlawful importation of Class A drug

19. An offence under section 50(2) of the Customs and Excise Management Act 1979 alleged to have been committed in respect of a Class A drug (as defined by section 2 of the Misuse of Drugs Act 1971).

Unlawful exportation of Class A drug

20. An offence under section 68(2) of the Customs and Excise Management Act 1979 alleged to have been committed in respect of a Class A drug (as defined by section 2 of the Misuse of Drugs Act 1971).

Fraudulent evasion in respect of Class A drug
21. An offence under section 170(1) or (2) of the Customs and Excise Management Act 1979 alleged to have been committed in respect of a Class A drug (as defined by section 2 of the Misuse of Drugs Act 1971).

Producing or being concerned in production of Class A drug
22. An offence under section 4(2) of the Misuse of Drugs Act 1971 alleged to have been committed in relation to a Class A drug (as defined by section 2 of that Act).

Supplying or offering to supply Class A drug
23. An offence under section 4(3) of the Misuse of Drugs Act 1971 alleged to have been committed in relation to a Class A drug (as defined by section 2 of that Act).

Theft offences

Robbery
24. An offence under section 8(1) of the Theft Act 1968 where it is alleged that, at some time during the commission of the offence, the defendant had in his possession a firearm or imitation firearm (as defined by section 57 of the Firearms Act 1968).

Criminal damage offences

Arson endangering life
25. An offence under section 1(2) of the Criminal Damage Act 1971 alleged to have been committed by destroying or damaging property by fire.

Causing explosion likely to endanger life or property
26. An offence under section 2 of the Explosive Substances Act 1883.

Intent or conspiracy to cause explosion likely to endanger life or property
27. An offence under section 3(1)(a) of the Explosive Substances Act 1883.

War crimes and terrorism

Genocide, crimes against humanity and war crimes
28. An offence under section 51 or 52 of the International Criminal Court Act 2001.

Grave breaches of the Geneva conventions
29. An offence under section 1 of the Geneva Conventions Act 1957.

Directing terrorist organisation
30. An offence under section 56 of the Terrorism Act 2000.

Hostage-taking
31. An offence under section 1 of the Taking of Hostages Act 1982.

Hijacking and other offences relating to aviation, maritime and rail security

Hijacking of aircraft
32. An offence under section 1 of the Aviation Security Act 1982.

Destroying, damaging or endangering the safety of an aircraft
33. An offence under section 2 of the Aviation Security Act 1982.

Hijacking of ships
34. An offence under section 9 of the Aviation and Maritime Security Act 1990.

Seizing or exercising control of fixed platforms
35. An offence under section 10 of the Aviation and Maritime Security Act 1990.

Destroying ships or fixed platforms or endangering their safety

    36. An offence under section 11 of the Aviation and Maritime Security Act 1990.

Hijacking of channel tunnel trains

    37. An offence under article 4 of the Channel Tunnel (Security) Order 1994 (S.I.1994/570).

Seizing or exercising control of the channel tunnel system

    38. An offence under article 5 of the Channel Tunnel (Security) Order 1994 (S.I.1994/ 570).

Conspiracy

Conspiracy

    39. An offence under section 1 of the Criminal Law Act 1977 of conspiracy to commit an offence listed in this Part of this Schedule.

PART 2   SUPPLEMENTARY

    40. A reference in Part 1 of this Schedule to an offence includes a reference to an offence of aiding, abetting, counselling or procuring the commission of the offence.

    41. A reference in Part 1 of this Schedule to an enactment includes a reference to the enactment as enacted and as amended from time to time.

SCHEDULE 5

QUALIFYING OFFENCES
FOR PURPOSES OF PART 10

PART 1   LIST OF OFFENCES FOR ENGLAND AND WALES

Offences against the person

Murder

    1. Murder.

Attempted murder

    2. An offence under section 1 of the Criminal Attempts Act 1981 of attempting to commit murder.

Soliciting murder

    3. An offence under section 4 of the Offences against the Person Act 1861.

Manslaughter

    4. Manslaughter.

Corporate manslaughter

    4A. An offence under section 1 of the Corporate Manslaughter and Corporate Homicide Act 2007.

Kidnapping

    5. Kidnapping.

Sexual offences

Rape

    6. An offence under section 1 of the Sexual Offences Act 1956 or section 1 of the Sexual Offences Act 2003.

Attempted rape

7. An offence under section 1 of the Criminal Attempts Act 1981 of attempting to commit an offence under section 1 of the Sexual Offences Act 1956 or section 1 of the Sexual Offences Act 2003.

Intercourse with a girl under thirteen

8. An offence under section 5 of the Sexual Offences Act 1956.

Incest by a man with a girl under thirteen

9. An offence under section 10 of the Sexual Offences Act 1956 alleged to have been committed with a girl under thirteen.

Assault by penetration

10. An offence under section 2 of the Sexual Offences Act 2003.

Causing a person to engage in sexual activity without consent

11. An offence under section 4 of the Sexual Offences Act 2003 where it is alleged that the activity caused involved penetration within subsection (4)(a) to (d) of that section.

Rape of a child under thirteen

12. An offence under section 5 of the Sexual Offences Act 2003.

Attempted rape of a child under thirteen

13. An offence under section 1 of the Criminal Attempts Act 1981 of attempting to commit an offence under section 5 of the Sexual Offences Act 2003.

Assault of a child under thirteen by penetration

14. An offence under section 6 of the Sexual Offences Act 2003.

Causing a child under thirteen to engage in sexual activity

15. An offence under section 8 of the Sexual Offences Act 2003 where it is alleged that an activity involving penetration within subsection (2)(a) to (d) of that section was caused.

Sexual activity with a person with a mental disorder impeding choice

16. An offence under section 30 of the Sexual Offences Act 2003 where it is alleged that the touching involved penetration within subsection (3)(a) to (d) of that section.

Causing a person with a mental disorder impeding choice to engage in sexual activity

17. An offence under section 31 of the Sexual Offences Act 2003 where it is alleged that an activity involving penetration within subsection (3)(a) to (d) of that section was caused.

Drugs offences

Unlawful importation of Class A drug

18. An offence under section 50(2) of the Customs and Excise Management Act 1979 alleged to have been committed in respect of a Class A drug (as defined by section 2 of the Misuse of Drugs Act 1971).

Unlawful exportation of Class A drug

19. An offence under section 68(2) of the Customs and Excise Management Act 1979 alleged to have been committed in respect of a Class A drug (as defined by section 2 of the Misuse of Drugs Act 1971).

Fraudulent evasion in respect of Class A drug

20. An offence under section 170(1) or (2) of the Customs and Excise Management Act 1979 alleged to have been committed in respect of a Class A drug (as defined by section 2 of the Misuse of Drugs Act 1971).

Producing or being concerned in production of Class A drug
    21. An offence under section 4(2) of the Misuse of Drugs Act 1971 alleged to have been committed in relation to a Class A drug (as defined by section 2 of that Act).

Criminal damage offences

Arson endangering life
    22. An offence under section 1(2) of the Criminal Damage Act 1971 alleged to have been committed by destroying or damaging property by fire.

Causing explosion likely to endanger life or property
    23. An offence under section 2 of the Explosive Substances Act 1883.

Intent or conspiracy to cause explosion likely to endanger life or property
    24. An offence under section 3(1)(a) of the Explosive Substances Act 1883.

War crimes and terrorism

Genocide, crimes against humanity and war crimes
    25. An offence under section 51 or 52 of the International Criminal Court Act 2001.

Grave breaches of the Geneva conventions
    26. An offence under section 1 of the Geneva Conventions Act 1957.

Directing terrorist organisation
    27. An offence under section 56 of the Terrorism Act 2000.

Hostage-taking
    28. An offence under section 1 of the Taking of Hostages Act 1982.

Conspiracy

Conspiracy
    29. An offence under section 1 of the Criminal Law Act 1977 of conspiracy to commit an offence listed in this Part of this Schedule.

Domestic Violence, Crime and Victims Act 2004

(2004, c. 28)

PART 1 DOMESTIC VIOLENCE ETC

Causing or allowing the death of a child or vulnerable adult

5   The offence
    (1) A person ("D") is guilty of an offence if—
        (a) a child or vulnerable adult ("V") dies as a result of the unlawful act of a person who—
            (i)   was a member of the same household as V, and
            (ii)   had frequent contact with him,
        (b) D was such a person at the time of that act,
        (c) at that time there was a significant risk of serious physical harm being caused to V by the unlawful act of such a person, and
        (d) either D was the person whose act caused V's death or—
            (i)   D was, or ought to have been, aware of the risk mentioned in paragraph (c),
            (ii)   D failed to take such steps as he could reasonably have been expected to take to protect V from the risk, and
            (iii) the act occurred in circumstances of the kind that D foresaw or ought to have foreseen.

(2) The prosecution does not have to prove whether it is the first alternative in subsection (1)(d) or the second (sub-paragraphs (i) to (iii)) that applies.

(3) If D was not the mother or father of V—

(a) D may not be charged with an offence under this section if he was under the age of 16 at the time of the act that caused V's death;

(b) for the purposes of subsection (1)(d)(ii) D could not have been expected to take any such step as is referred to there before attaining that age.

(4) For the purposes of this section—

(a) a person is to be regarded as a "member" of a particular household, even if he does not live in that household, if he visits it so often and for such periods of time that it is reasonable to regard him as a member of it;

(b) where V lived in different households at different times, "the same household as V" refers to the household in which V was living at the time of the act that caused V's death.

(5) For the purposes of this section an "unlawful" act is one that—

(a) constitutes an offence, or

(a) would constitute an offence but for being the act of—

(i)   a person under the age of ten, or

(ii) a person entitled to rely on a defence of insanity.

Paragraph (b) does not apply to an act of D.

(6) In this section—

"act" includes a course of conduct and also includes omission;

"child" means a person under the age of 16;

"serious" harm means harm that amounts to grievous bodily harm for the purposes of the Offences against the Person Act 1861 (c. 100);

"vulnerable adult" means a person aged 16 or over whose ability to protect himself from violence, abuse or neglect is significantly impaired through physical or mental disability or illness, through old age or otherwise.

(7) A person guilty of an offence under this section is liable on conviction on indictment to imprisonment for a term not exceeding 14 years or to a fine, or to both.

6 Evidence and procedure: England and Wales

(1) Subsections (2) to (4) apply where a person ("the defendant") is charged in the same proceedings with an offence of murder or manslaughter and with an offence under section 5 in respect of the same death ("the section 5 offence").

(2) Where by virtue of section 35(3) of the Criminal Justice and Public Order Act 1994 (c. 33) a court or jury is permitted, in relation to the section 5 offence, to draw such inferences as appear proper from the defendant's failure to give evidence or refusal to answer a question, the court or jury may also draw such inferences in determining whether he is guilty—

(a) of murder or manslaughter, or

(b) of any other offence of which he could lawfully be convicted on the charge of murder or manslaughter,

even if there would otherwise be no case for him to answer in relation to that offence.

(3) The charge of murder or manslaughter is not to be dismissed under paragraph 2 of Schedule 3 to the Crime and Disorder Act 1998 (c. 37) (unless the section 5 offence is dismissed).

(4) At the defendant's trial the question whether there is a case for the defendant to answer on the charge of murder or manslaughter is not to be considered before the close of all the evidence (or, if at some earlier time he ceases to be charged with the section 5 offence, before that earlier time).

(5) An offence under section 5 is an offence of homicide for the purposes of the following enactments—

sections 24 and 25 of the Magistrates' Courts Act 1980 (c. 43) (mode of trial of child or young person for indictable offence);

section 51A of the Crime and Disorder Act 1998 (sending cases to the Crown Court: children and young persons);

section 8 of the Powers of Criminal Courts (Sentencing) Act 2000 (c. 6) (power and duty to remit young offenders to youth courts for sentence).

Criminal Evidence (Witness Anonymity) Act 2008

(2008, c. 15)

10   Pre-commencement anonymity orders: existing proceedings

(8) In this section—

"commencement" means the day on which this Act is passed;

"pre-commencement anonymity order" means an order made before commencement that falls within section 1(2).

11   Pre-commencement anonymity orders: appeals

(1) This section applies where—

    (a) an appeal court is considering an appeal against a conviction in criminal proceedings in a case where the trial ended before commencement, and

    (b) the court from which the appeal lies ("the trial court") made a pre-commencement anonymity order in relation to a witness at the trial.

(2) The appeal court—

    (a) may not treat the conviction as unsafe solely on the ground that the trial court had no power at common law to make the order mentioned in subsection (1)(b), but

    (b) must treat the conviction as unsafe if it considers—

        (i)   that the order was not one that the trial court could have made if this Act had been in force at the material time, and

        (ii) that, as a result of the order, the defendant did not receive a fair trial.

(3) In this section—

"appeal court" means—

    (a) the Court of Appeal;

    [*applies to Northern Ireland*].

"commencement" and "pre-commencement anonymity order" have the meanings given by section 10(8).

12   Interpretation

(1) In this Act—

"court" means—

    (a) . . . a magistrates' court, the Crown Court or the criminal division of the Court of Appeal;

"criminal proceedings" means—

    (a) in relation to a court within paragraph (a) or . . . above, criminal proceedings consisting of a trial or other hearing at which evidence falls to be given;

"the defendant", in relation to any criminal proceedings, means any person charged with an offence to which the proceedings relate (whether or not convicted);

"prosecutor" means an individual or body charged with duties to conduct criminal prosecutions;

"witness", in relation to any criminal proceedings, means any person called, or proposed to be called, to give evidence at the trial or hearing in question;

"witness anonymity order" has the meaning given by section 2.

Coroners and Justice Act 2009

(2009, c. 25)

PART 2 CRIMINAL OFFENCES

Chapter 1 Murder, Infanticide and Suicide

54. Partial defence to murder: loss of control

(1) Where a person ("D") kills or is a party to the killing of another ("V"), D is not to be convicted of murder if—

(a) D's acts and omissions in doing or being a party to the killing resulted from D's loss of self-control,

(b) the loss of self-control had a qualifying trigger, and

(c) a person of D's sex and age, with a normal degree of tolerance and self-restraint and in the circumstances of D, might have reacted in the same or in a similar way to D.

(2) For the purposes of subsection (1)(a), it does not matter whether or not the loss of control was sudden.

(3) In subsection (1)(c) the reference to "the circumstances of D" is a reference to all of D's circumstances other than those whose only relevance to D's conduct is that they bear on D's general capacity for tolerance or self-restraint.

(4) Subsection (1) does not apply if, in doing or being a party to the killing, D acted in a considered desire for revenge.

(5) On a charge of murder, if sufficient evidence is adduced to raise an issue with respect to the defence under subsection (1), the jury must assume that the defence is satisfied unless the prosecution proves beyond reasonable doubt that it is not.

(6) For the purposes of subsection (5), sufficient evidence is adduced to raise an issue with respect to the defence if evidence is adduced on which, in the opinion of the trial judge, a jury, properly directed, could reasonably conclude that the defence might apply.

(7) A person who, but for this section, would be liable to be convicted of murder is liable instead to be convicted of manslaughter.

(8) The fact that one party to a killing is by virtue of this section not liable to be convicted of murder does not affect the question whether the killing amounted to murder in the case of any other party to it.

55 Meaning of "qualifying trigger"

(1) This section applies for the purposes of section 54.

(2) A loss of self-control had a qualifying trigger if subsection (3), (4) or (5) applies.

(3) This subsection applies if D's loss of self-control was attributable to D's fear of serious violence from V against D or another identified person.

(4) This subsection applies if D's loss of self-control was attributable to a thing or things done or said (or both) which—

(a) constituted circumstances of an extremely grave character, and

(b) caused D to have a justifiable sense of being seriously wronged.

(5) This subsection applies if D's loss of self-control was attributable to a combination of the matters mentioned in subsections (3) and (4).

(6) In determining whether a loss of self-control had a qualifying trigger—

(a) D's fear of serious violence is to be disregarded to the extent that it was caused by a thing which D incited to be done or said for the purpose of providing an excuse to use violence;

   (b) a sense of being seriously wronged by a thing done or said is not justifiable if D incited the
       thing to be done or said for the purpose of providing an excuse to use violence;
   (c) the fact that a thing done or said constituted sexual infidelity is to be disregarded.
(7) In this section references to "D" and "V" are to be construed in accordance with section 54.

Chapter 2 Anonymity of Witnesses

Witness anonymity orders

86 Witness anonymity orders

(1) In this Chapter a "witness anonymity order" is an order made by a court that requires such
specified measures to be taken in relation to a witness in criminal proceedings as the court considers
appropriate to ensure that the identity of the witness is not disclosed in or in connection with the
proceedings.

(2) The kinds of measures that may be required to be taken in relation to a witness include measures for securing one or more of the following—
   (a) that the witness's name and other identifying details may be—
       (i)   withheld;
       (ii) removed from materials disclosed to any party to the proceedings;
   (b) that the witness may use a pseudonym;
   (c) that the witness is not asked questions of any specified description that might lead to the
       identification of the witness;
   (d) that the witness is screened to any specified extent;
   (e) that the witness's voice is subjected to modulation to any specified extent.

(3) Subsection (2) does not affect the generality of subsection (1).

(4) Nothing in this section authorises the court to require—
   (a) the witness to be screened to such an extent that the witness cannot be seen by—
       (i)   the judge or other members of the court (if any), or
       (ii) the jury (if there is one);
   (b) the witness's voice to be modulated to such an extent that the witness's natural voice can-
       not be heard by any persons within paragraph (a)(i) or (ii).

(5) In this section "specified" means specified in the witness anonymity order concerned.

87 Applications

(1) An application for a witness anonymity order to be made in relation to a witness in criminal
proceedings may be made to the court by the prosecutor or the defendant.

(2) Where an application is made by the prosecutor, the prosecutor—
   (a) must (unless the court directs otherwise) inform the court of the identity of the witness,
       but
   (b) is not required to disclose in connection with the application—
       (i)   the identity of the witness, or
       (ii) any information that might enable the witness to be identified,
       to any other party to the proceedings or his or her legal representatives.

(3) Where an application is made by the defendant, the defendant—
   (a) must inform the court and the prosecutor of the identity of the witness, but
   (b) (if there is more than one defendant) is not required to disclose in connection with the
       application—
       (i)   the identity of the witness, or
       (ii) any information that might enable the witness to be identified,
       to any other defendant or his or her legal representatives.

(4) Accordingly, where the prosecutor or the defendant proposes to make an application
under this section in respect of a witness, any relevant material which is disclosed by or on behalf

of that party before the determination of the application may be disclosed in such a way as to prevent—

    (a) the identity of the witness, or

    (b) any information that might enable the witness to be identified,

from being disclosed except as required by subsection (2)(a) or (3)(a).

    (5) "Relevant material" means any document or other material which falls to be disclosed, or is sought to be relied on, by or on behalf of the party concerned in connection with the proceedings or proceedings preliminary to them.

    (6) The court must give every party to the proceedings the opportunity to be heard on an application under this section.

    (7) But subsection (6) does not prevent the court from hearing one or more parties in the absence of a defendant and his or her legal representatives, if it appears to the court to be appropriate to do so in the circumstances of the case.

    (8) Nothing in this section is to be taken as restricting any power to make rules of court.

88 Conditions for making order

    (1) This section applies where an application is made for a witness anonymity order to be made in relation to a witness in criminal proceedings.

    (2) The court may make such an order only if it is satisfied that Conditions A to C below are met.

    (3) Condition A is that the proposed order is necessary—

    (a) in order to protect the safety of the witness or another person or to prevent any serious damage to property, or

    (b) in order to prevent real harm to the public interest (whether affecting the carrying on of any activities in the public interest or the safety of a person involved in carrying on such activities, or otherwise).

    (4) Condition B is that, having regard to all the circumstances, the effect of the proposed order would be consistent with the defendant receiving a fair trial.

    (5) Condition C is that the importance of the witness's testimony is such that in the interests of justice the witness ought to testify and—

    (a) the witness would not testify if the proposed order were not made, or

    (b) there would be real harm to the public interest if the witness were to testify without the proposed order being made.

    (6) In determining whether the proposed order is necessary for the purpose mentioned in subsection (3)(a), the court must have regard (in particular) to any reasonable fear on the part of the witness—

    (a) that the witness or another person would suffer death or injury, or

    (b) that there would be serious damage to property,

if the witness were to be identified.

89 Relevant considerations

    (1) When deciding whether Conditions A to C in section 88 are met in the case of an application for a witness anonymity order, the court must have regard to—

    (a) the considerations mentioned in subsection (2) below, and

    (b) such other matters as the court considers relevant.

    (2) The considerations are—

    (a) the general right of a defendant in criminal proceedings to know the identity of a witness in the proceedings;

    (b) the extent to which the credibility of the witness concerned would be a relevant factor when the weight of his or her evidence comes to be assessed;

    (c) whether evidence given by the witness might be the sole or decisive evidence implicating the defendant;

(d) whether the witness's evidence could be properly tested (whether on grounds of credibility or otherwise) without his or her identity being disclosed;

(e) whether there is any reason to believe that the witness—

   (i)   has a tendency to be dishonest, or

   (ii)   has any motive to be dishonest in the circumstances of the case,

having regard (in particular) to any previous convictions of the witness and to any
relationship between the witness and the defendant or any associates of the defendant;

(f) whether it would be reasonably practicable to protect the witness by any means other than
by making a witness anonymity order specifying the measures that are under consideration by the court.

90   Warning to jury

(1) Subsection (2) applies where, on a trial on indictment with a jury, any evidence has been
given by a witness at a time when a witness anonymity order applied to the witness.

(2) The judge must give the jury such warning as the judge considers appropriate to ensure that
the fact that the order was made in relation to the witness does not prejudice the defendant.

Discharge and variation

91   Discharge or variation of order

(1) A court that has made a witness anonymity order in relation to any criminal proceedings
may in those proceedings subsequently discharge or vary (or further vary) the order if it appears to
the court to be appropriate to do so in view of the provisions of sections 88 and 89 that apply to the
making of an order.

(2) The court may do so—

(a) on an application made by a party to the proceedings if there has been a material change
of circumstances since the relevant time, or

(b) on its own initiative.

(3) The court must give every party to the proceedings the opportunity to be heard—

(a) before determining an application made to it under subsection (2);

(b) before discharging or varying the order on its own initiative.

(4) But subsection (3) does not prevent the court hearing one or more of the parties to the
proceedings in the absence of a defendant in the proceedings and his or her legal representatives, if it
appears to the court to be appropriate to do so in the circumstances of the case.

(5) "The relevant time" means—

(a) the time when the order was made, or

(b) if a previous application has been made under subsection (2), the time when the application (or the last application) was made.

92   Discharge or variation after proceedings

(1) This section applies if—

(a) a court has made a witness anonymity order in relation to a witness in criminal proceedings
("the old proceedings"), and

(b) the old proceedings have come to an end.

(2) The court that made the order may discharge or vary (or further vary) the order if it appears
to the court to be appropriate to do so in view of—

(a) the provisions of sections 88 and 89 that apply to the making of a witness anonymity
order, and

(b) such other matters as the court considers relevant.

(3) The court may do so—

(a) on an application made by a party to the old proceedings if there has been a material
change of circumstances since the relevant time, or

(b) on an application made by the witness if there has been a material change of circumstances since the relevant time.

(4) The court may not determine an application made to it under subsection (3) unless in the case of each of the parties to the old proceedings and the witness—

(a) it has given the person the opportunity to be heard, or

(b) it is satisfied that it is not reasonably practicable to communicate with the person.

(5) Subsection (4) does not prevent the court hearing one or more of the persons mentioned in that subsection in the absence of a person who was a defendant in the old proceedings and that person's legal representatives, if it appears to the court to be appropriate to do so in the circumstances of the case.

(6) "The relevant time" means—

(a) the time when the old proceedings came to an end, or

(b) if a previous application has been made under subsection (3), the time when the application (or the last application) was made.

93   Discharge or variation by appeal court

(1) This section applies if—

(a) a court has made a witness anonymity order in relation to a witness in criminal proceedings ("the trial proceedings"), and

(b) a defendant in the trial proceedings has in those proceedings—

(i)   been convicted,

(ii)   been found not guilty by reason of insanity, or

(iii) been found to be under a disability and to have done the act charged in respect of an offence.

(2) The appeal court may in proceedings on or in connection with an appeal by the defendant from the trial proceedings discharge or vary (or further vary) the order if it appears to the court to be appropriate to do so in view of—

(a) the provisions of sections 88 and 89 that apply to the making of a witness anonymity order, and

(b) such other matters as the court considers relevant.

(3) The appeal court may not discharge or vary the order unless in the case of each party to the trial proceedings—

(a) it has given the person the opportunity to be heard, or

(b) it is satisfied that it is not reasonably practicable to communicate with the person.

(4) But subsection (3) does not prevent the appeal court hearing one or more of the parties to the trial proceedings in the absence of a person who was a defendant in the trial proceedings and that person's legal representatives, if it appears to the court to be appropriate to do so in the circumstances of the case.

(5) In this section a reference to the doing of an act includes a reference to a failure to act.

(6) "Appeal court" means—

(a) the Court of Appeal,

Part II

Criminal Proceedings—Rules and Guidelines

Police and Criminal Evidence Act 1984 Revised Codes of Practice A–G

CODE OF PRACTICE FOR THE EXERCISE BY: POLICE OFFICERS OF STATUTORY POWERS OF STOP AND SEARCH POLICE OFFICERS AND POLICE STAFF OF REQUIREMENTS TO RECORD PUBLIC ENCOUNTERS (CODE A)

General

This code of practice must be readily available at all police stations for consultation by police officers, police staff, detained persons and members of the public.

The notes for guidance included are not provisions of this code, but are guidance to police officers and others about its application and interpretation. Provisions in the annexes to the code are provisions of this code.

This code governs the exercise by police officers of statutory powers to search a person or a vehicle without first making an arrest. The main stop and search powers to which this code applies are set out in Annex A, but that list should not be regarded as definitive. [See Note 1] In addition, it covers requirements on police officers and police staff to record encounters not governed by statutory powers. This code does not apply to:

(a) the powers of stop and search under;
   (i) Aviation Security Act 1982, section 27(2);
   (ii) Police and Criminal Evidence Act 1984, section 6(1) (which relates specifically to powers of constables employed by statutory undertakers on the premises of the statutory undertakers).

(b) searches carried out for the purposes of examination under Schedule 7 to the Terrorism Act 2000 and to which the Code of Practice issued under paragraph 6 of Schedule 14 to the Terrorism Act 2000 applies.

1 Principles governing stop and search

1.1 Powers to stop and search must be used fairly, responsibly, with respect for people being searched and without unlawful discrimination. The Equality Act 2010 makes it unlawful for police officers to discriminate against, harass or victimise any person on the grounds of the 'protected characteristics' of age, disability, gender reassignment, race, religion or belief, sex and sexual orientation, marriage and civil partnership, pregnancy and maternity when using their powers. When police forces are carrying out their functions they also have a duty to have regard to the need to eliminate unlawful discrimination, harassment and victimisation and to take steps to foster good relations.

1.2 The intrusion on the liberty of the person stopped or searched must be brief and detention for the purposes of a search must take place at or near the location of the stop.

1.3 If these fundamental principles are not observed the use of powers to stop and search may be drawn into question. Failure to use the powers in the proper manner reduces their effectiveness. Stop and search can play an important role in the detection and prevention of crime, and using the powers fairly makes them more effective.

1.4 The primary purpose of stop and search powers is to enable officers to allay or confirm suspicions about individuals without exercising their power of arrest. Officers may be required to justify the use or authorisation of such powers, in relation both to individual searches and the overall pattern of their activity in this regard, to their supervisory officers or in court. Any misuse of the powers is likely to be harmful to policing and lead to mistrust of the police. Officers must also be able to explain their actions to the member of the public searched. The misuse of these powers can lead to disciplinary action.

1.5 An officer must not search a person, even with his or her consent, where no power to search is applicable. Even where a person is prepared to submit to a search voluntarily, the person must not be searched unless the necessary legal power exists, and the search must be in accordance with the relevant power and the provisions of this Code. The only exception, where an officer does not require a specific power, applies to searches of persons entering sports grounds or other premises carried out with their consent given as a condition of entry.

2 Explanation of powers to stop and search

2.1 This code applies to powers of stop and search as follows:

(a) powers which require reasonable grounds for suspicion, before they may be exercised; that articles unlawfully obtained or possessed are being carried, or under Section 43 of the Terrorism Act 2000 that a person is a terrorist;

(b) authorised under section 60 of the Criminal Justice and Public Order Act 1994, based upon a reasonable belief that incidents involving serious violence may take place or that people are carrying dangerous instruments or offensive weapons within any locality in the police area or that it is expedient to use the powers to find such instruments or weapons that have been used in incidents of serious violence;

(c) authorised under section 44(1) of the Terrorism Act 2000 based upon a consideration that the exercise of the power is necessary for the prevention of acts of terrorism (see paragraph 2.18A), and

(d) powers to search a person who has not been arrested in the exercise of a power to search premises (see Code B paragraph 2.4).

Searches requiring reasonable grounds for suspicion

2.2 Reasonable grounds for suspicion depend on the circumstances in each case. There must be an objective basis for that suspicion based on facts, information, and/ or intelligence which are relevant to the likelihood of finding an article of a certain kind or, in the case of searches under section 43 of the Terrorism Act 2000, to the likelihood that the person is a terrorist. Reasonable suspicion can never be supported on the basis of personal factors. It must rely on intelligence or information about, or some specific behaviour by, the person concerned. For example, unless the police have a description of a suspect, a person's physical appearance (including any of the 'protected characteristics' set out in the Equality Act 2010 (see paragraph 1.1), or the fact that the person is known to have a previous conviction, cannot be used alone or in combination with each other, or in combination with any other factor, as the reason for searching that person. Reasonable suspicion cannot be based on generalisations or stereotypical images of certain groups or categories of people as more likely to be involved in criminal activity.

2.3 Reasonable suspicion may also exist without specific information or intelligence and on the basis of the behaviour of a person. For example, if an officer encounters someone on the street at night who is obviously trying to hide something, the officer may (depending on the other surrounding circumstances) base such suspicion on the fact that this kind of behaviour is often linked to stolen or prohibited articles being carried. Similarly, for the purposes of section 43 of the Terrorism Act 2000, suspicion that a person is a terrorist may arise from the person's behaviour at or near a location which has been identified as a potential target for terrorists.

2.4 However, reasonable suspicion should normally be linked to accurate and current intelligence or information, such as information describing an article being carried, a suspected offender, or a person who has been seen carrying a type of article known to have been stolen recently from premises in the area. Searches based on accurate and current intelligence or information are more likely to be effective. Targeting searches in a particular area at specified crime problems increases their effectiveness and minimises inconvenience to law-abiding members of the public. It also helps in justifying the use of searches both to those who are searched and to the public. This does not however prevent stop and search powers being exercised in other locations where such powers may be exercised and reasonable suspicion exists.

2.5 Searches are more likely to be effective, legitimate, and secure public confidence when reasonable suspicion is based on a range of factors. The overall use of these powers is more likely to be effective when up to date and accurate intelligence or information is communicated to officers and they are well-informed about local crime patterns.

2.6 Where there is reliable information or intelligence that members of a group or gang habitually carry knives unlawfully or weapons or controlled drugs, and wear a distinctive item of clothing or other means of identification to indicate their membership of the group or gang, that distinctive item of clothing or other means of identification may provide reasonable grounds to stop and search a person. [See Note 9]

2.7 A police officer may have reasonable grounds to suspect that a person is in innocent possession of a stolen or prohibited article or other item for which he or she is empowered to search. In that case the officer may stop and search the person even though there would be no power of arrest.

2.8 Under section 43(1) of the Terrorism Act 2000 a constable may stop and search a person whom the officer reasonably suspects to be a terrorist to discover whether the person is in possession of anything which may constitute evidence that the person is a terrorist. These searches may only be carried out by an officer of the same sex as the person searched (see Annex F). An authorisation under section 44(1) of the Terrorism Act 2000 allows vehicles to be stopped and searched by a constable in uniform who reasonably suspects that articles which could be used in connection with terrorism will be found in the vehicle or in anything in or on that vehicle. See paragraph 2.18A below.

2.9 An officer who has reasonable grounds for suspicion may detain the person concerned in order to carry out a search. Before carrying out a search the officer may ask questions about the person's behaviour or presence in circumstances which gave rise to the suspicion. As a result of questioning the detained person, the reasonable grounds for suspicion necessary to detain that person may be confirmed or, because of a satisfactory explanation, be eliminated. [See Notes 2 and 3] Questioning may also reveal reasonable grounds to suspect the possession of a different kind of unlawful article from that originally suspected. Reasonable grounds for suspicion however cannot be provided retrospectively by such questioning during a person's detention or by refusal to answer any questions put.

2.10 If, as a result of questioning before a search, or other circumstances which come to the attention of the officer, there cease to be reasonable grounds for suspecting that an article is being carried of a kind for which there is a power to stop and search, no search may take place. [See Note 3] In the absence of any other lawful power to detain, the person is free to leave at will and must be so informed.

2.11 There is no power to stop or detain a person in order to find grounds for a search. Police officers have many encounters with members of the public which do not involve detaining people against their will. If reasonable grounds for suspicion emerge during such an encounter, the officer may search the person, even though no grounds existed when the encounter began. If an officer is detaining someone for the purpose of a search, he or she should inform the person as soon as detention begins.

Searches authorised under section 60 of the Criminal Justice and Public Order Act 1994

2.12 Authority for a constable in uniform to stop and search under section 60 of the Criminal Justice and Public Order Act 1994 may be given if the authorising officer reasonably believes:

(a) that incidents involving serious violence may take place in any locality in the officer's police area, and it is expedient to use these powers to prevent their occurrence;

(b) that persons are carrying dangerous instruments or offensive weapons without good reason in any locality in the officer's police area or

(c) that an incident involving serious violence has taken place in the officer's police area, a dangerous instrument or offensive weapon used in the incident is being carried by a person in any locality in that police area, and it is expedient to use these powers to find that instrument or weapon.

2.13 An authorisation under section 60 may only be given by an officer of the rank of inspector or above and in writing, or orally if paragraph 2.12(c) applies and it is not practicable to give the authorisation in writing. The authorisation (whether written or oral) must specify the grounds on which it was given, the locality in which the powers may be exercised and the period of time for which they are in force. The period authorised shall be no longer than appears reasonably necessary to prevent, or seek to prevent incidents of serious violence, or to deal with the problem of carrying dangerous instruments or offensive weapons or to find a dangerous instrument or offensive weapon that has been used. It may not exceed 24 hours. An oral authorisation given where paragraph 2.12(c) applies must be recorded in writing as soon as practicable. [See Notes 10–13]

2.14 An inspector who gives an authorisation must, as soon as practicable, inform an officer of or above the rank of superintendent. This officer may direct that the authorisation shall be extended for a further 24 hours, if violence or the carrying of dangerous instruments or offensive weapons has occurred, or is suspected to have occurred, and the continued use of the powers is considered necessary to prevent or deal with further such activity or to find a dangerous instrument or offensive weapon used that has been used. That direction must be given in writing unless it is not practicable to do so, in which case it must be recorded in writing as soon as practicable afterwards. [See Note 12]

2.14A The selection of persons and vehicles under section 60 to be stopped and, if appropriate, searched should reflect an objective assessment of the nature of the incident or weapon in question and the individuals and vehicles thought likely to be associated with that incident or those weapons (see Notes 10 and 11). The powers must not be used to stop and search persons and vehicles for reasons unconnected with the purpose of the authorisation. When selecting persons and vehicles to be stopped in response to a specific threat or incident, officers must take care not to discriminate unlawfully against anyone on the grounds of any of the protected characteristics set out in the Equality Act 2010 (see paragraph 1.1).

2.14B The driver of a vehicle which is stopped under section 60 and any person who is searched under section 60 are entitled to a written statement to that effect if they apply within twelve months from the day the vehicle was stopped or the person was searched. This statement is a record which states that the vehicle was stopped or (as the case may be) that the person was searched under section 60 and it may form part of the search record or be supplied as a separate record.

Powers to require removal of face coverings

2.15 Section 60AA of the Criminal Justice and Public Order Act 1994 also provides a power to demand the removal of disguises. The officer exercising the power must reasonably believe that someone is wearing an item wholly or mainly for the purpose of concealing identity. There is also a power to seize such items where the officer believes that a person intends to wear them for this purpose. There is no power to stop and search for disguises. An officer may seize any such item which is discovered when exercising a power of search for something else, or which is being carried, and which the officer reasonably believes is intended to be used for concealing anyone's identity. This power can only be used if an authorisation given under section 60 or under section 60AA, is in force. [See Note 4]

2.16 Authority under section 60AA for a constable in uniform to require the removal of disguises and to seize them may be given if the authorising officer reasonably believes that activities may take place in any locality in the officer's police area that are likely to involve the commission of offences and it is expedient to use these powers to prevent or control these activities.

2.17 An authorisation under section 60AA may only be given by an officer of the rank of inspector or above, in writing, specifying the grounds on which it was given, the locality in which the powers may be exercised and the period of time for which they are in force. The period authorised shall be no longer than appears reasonably necessary to prevent, or seek to prevent the commission of offences. It may not exceed 24 hours. [See Notes 10–13]

2.18 An inspector who gives an authorisation must, as soon as practicable, inform an officer of or above the rank of superintendent. This officer may direct that the authorisation shall be extended for a further 24 hours, if crimes have been committed, or are suspected to have been committed, and the continued use of the powers is considered necessary to prevent or deal with further such activity. This direction must also be given in writing at the time or as soon as practicable afterwards. [See Note 12]

Searches authorised under section 44 of the Terrorism Act 2000

2.18A The European Court of Human Rights has ruled that the stop and search powers under sections 44 to 47 of the Terrorism Act 2000 are not compatible with the right to a private life under Article 8 of the European Convention on Human Rights. Neither the European Court ruling nor the provisions of this Code can amend these statutory provisions. However, in an oral statement made by the Home Secretary in the House of Commons on 8 July 2010, interim guidelines were announced pending a review (with a view to legislative amendment) of these provisions to ensure that police do not exercise any powers under section 44 in a way which would be incompatible with Convention rights. Under these guidelines:

(i)   Authorisations under section 44(1) should be given, and may be confirmed by the Secretary of State, only:
   • in relation to searches of vehicles and anything in or on vehicles, but not searches of drivers or passengers or anything being carried by a driver or passenger; and
   • if such searches are considered necessary for the prevention of acts of terrorism.
   Note: Section 44(3) provides that an authorising officer may give an authorisation when they consider it is 'expedient' for the prevention of acts of terrorism, but the test now to be applied is that of necessity—taking account of all of the circumstances.

(ii) A search of a vehicle or of anything in or on a vehicle under section 44(1) should only be carried out if it is reasonably suspected that articles which could be used in connection with terrorism will be found in the vehicle or in anything in or on that vehicle.
   Note: This now applies despite the provision in section 45(1)(b) which allows the power to be exercised whether or not the constable has grounds for suspecting the presence of such articles.

(iii) Authorisations to search pedestrians, drivers of vehicles and passengers in vehicles and anything carried by a driver or passenger, are not to be given under section 44(1) or (2) and if given, will not be confirmed. For these searches police must rely on the power under section 43 which requires the person who may be searched to be reasonably suspected of being a terrorist, but does not authorise the removal of headgear or footwear in public.

The provisions of paragraphs 2.1, 2.8, 2.19 to 2.26, 3.5, Annex A paragraphs 15 and 16 and Annex C paragraph 1 are amended by this Code to reflect these guidelines:

2.19 An officer of the rank of assistant chief constable (or equivalent) or above, may give authority under section 44(1) of the Terrorism Act 2000 for a constable in uniform to exercise the power to stop and search any vehicle and anything in or on any vehicle, in the whole or any part or parts of the authorising officer's police area. An authorisation may only be given if the officer considers it is necessary for the prevention of acts of terrorism.

2.20 If an authorisation is given orally at first, it must be confirmed in writing by the officer who gave it as soon as reasonably practicable.

2.21 When giving an authorisation, the officer must specify the geographical area in which the power may be used, and the time and date that the authorisation ends (up to a maximum of 28 days from the time the authorisation was given). [See Notes 12 and 13]

2.22 The officer giving an authorisation under section 44(1) must cause the Secretary of State to be informed, as soon as reasonably practicable, that such an authorisation has been given. An authorisation which is not confirmed by the Secretary of State within 48 hours of its having been given, shall have effect up until the end of that 48 hour period or the end of the period specified in the authorisation (whichever is the earlier). [See Note 14]

2.23 Following notification of the authorisation, the Secretary of State may:

   (i)   cancel the authorisation with immediate effect or with effect from such other time as he or she may direct;
   (ii) confirm it but for a shorter period than that specified in the authorisation; or
   (iii) confirm the authorisation as given.

2.24 When an authorisation under section 44(1) is given, a constable in uniform may exercise the power:

   (a) only for the purpose of stopping and searching a vehicle and anything in or on a vehicle for articles of a kind which could be used in connection with terrorism (see paragraph 2.25); and
   (b) only if there are reasonable grounds for suspecting the presence of such articles. See paragraphs 2.2 to 2.11, "Searches requiring reasonable grounds for suspicion"

2.24A When a Community Support Officer on duty and in uniform has been conferred powers under Section 44(1) of the Terrorism Act 2000 by a Chief Officer of their force, the exercise of this power must comply with the requirements of this Code of Practice, including the recording requirements.

2.25 Paragraphs 2.2 to 2.11 above ("Searches requiring reasonable grounds for suspicion") are to be applied to the stopping and searching of vehicles when an authorisation under section 44(1) is given.

2.26 The powers under sections 43 and 44(1) of the Terrorism Act 2000 allow a constable to search only for articles which could be used for terrorist purposes. However, this would not prevent a search being carried out under other powers if, in the course of exercising these powers, the officer formed reasonable grounds for suspicion.

Powers to search in the exercise of a power to search premises

2.27 The following powers to search premises also authorise the search of a person, not under arrest, who is found on the premises during the course of the search:

   (a) section 139B of the Criminal Justice Act 1988 under which a constable may enter school premises and search the premises and any person on those premises for any bladed or pointed article or offensive weapon;
   (b) under a warrant issued under section 23(3) of the Misuse of Drugs Act 1971 to search premises for drugs or documents but only if the warrant specifically authorises the search of persons found on the premises; and
   (c) under a search warrant or order issued under paragraph 1, 3 or 11 of Schedule 5 to the Terrorism Act 2000 to search premises and any person found there for material likely to be of substantial value to a terrorist investigation.

2.28 Before the power under section 139B of the Criminal Justice Act 1988 may be exercised, the constable must have reasonable grounds to believe that an offence under section 139A of the Criminal Justice Act 1988 (having a bladed or pointed article or offensive weapon on school premises) has been or is being committed. A warrant to search premises and persons found therein may be issued under section 23(3) of the Misuse of Drugs Act 1971 if there are reasonable grounds to suspect that controlled drugs or certain documents are in the possession of a person on the premises.

2.29 The powers in paragraph 2.27 do not require prior specific grounds to suspect that the person to be searched is in possession of an item for which there is an existing power to search. However, it is still necessary to ensure that the selection and treatment of those searched under these powers is based upon objective factors connected with the search of the premises, and not upon personal prejudice.

3   Conduct of searches

3.1 All stops and searches must be carried out with courtesy, consideration and respect for the person concerned. This has a significant impact on public confidence in the police. Every reasonable effort must be made to minimise the embarrassment that a person being searched may experience. [See Note 4]

3.2 The co-operation of the person to be searched must be sought in every case, even if the person initially objects to the search. A forcible search may be made only if it has been established that the person is unwilling to co-operate or resists. Reasonable force may be used as a last resort if necessary to conduct a search or to detain a person or vehicle for the purposes of a search.

3.3 The length of time for which a person or vehicle may be detained must be reasonable and kept to a minimum. Where the exercise of the power requires reasonable suspicion, the thoroughness and extent of a search must depend on what is suspected of being carried, and by whom. If the suspicion relates to a particular article which is seen to be slipped into a person's pocket, then, in the absence of other grounds for suspicion or an opportunity for the article to be moved elsewhere, the search must be confined to that pocket. In the case of a small article which can readily be concealed, such as a drug, and which might be concealed anywhere on the person, a more extensive search may be necessary. In the case of searches mentioned in paragraph 2.1(b), (c), and (d), which do not require reasonable grounds for suspicion, officers may make any reasonable search to look for items for which they are empowered to search. [See Note 5]

3.4 The search must be carried out at or near the place where the person or vehicle was first detained. [See Note 6]

3.5 There is no power to require a person to remove any clothing in public other than an outer coat, jacket or gloves, except under section 60AA of the Criminal Justice and Public Order Act 1994 (which empowers a constable to require a person to remove any item worn to conceal identity). [See Notes 4 and 6] A search in public of a person's clothing which has not been removed must be restricted to superficial examination of outer garments. This does not, however, prevent an officer from placing his or her hand inside the pockets of the outer clothing, or feeling round the inside of collars, socks and shoes if this is reasonably necessary in the circumstances to look for the object of the search or to remove and examine any item reasonably suspected to be the object of the search. For the same reasons, subject to the restrictions on the removal of headgear, a person's hair may also be searched in public (see paragraphs 3.1 and 3.3).

3.6 Where on reasonable grounds it is considered necessary to conduct a more thorough search (e.g. by requiring a person to take off a T-shirt), this must be done out of public view, for example, in a police van unless paragraph 3.7 applies, or police station if there is one nearby. [See Note 6] Any search involving the removal of more than an outer coat, jacket, gloves, headgear or footwear, or any other item concealing identity, may only be made by an officer of the same sex as the person searched and may not be made in the presence of anyone of the opposite sex unless the person being searched specifically requests it. [See Annex F and Notes 4, 7 and 8]

3.7 Searches involving exposure of intimate parts of the body must not be conducted as a routine extension of a less thorough search, simply because nothing is found in the course of the initial search. Searches involving exposure of intimate parts of the body may be carried out only at a nearby police station or other nearby location which is out of public view (but not a police vehicle). These searches must be conducted in accordance with paragraph 11 of Annex A to Code C except that an intimate search mentioned in paragraph 11(f) of Annex A to Code C may not be authorised or carried out under any stop and search powers. The other provisions of Code C do not apply to the conduct and recording of searches of persons detained at police stations in the exercise of stop and search powers. [See Note 7]

Steps to be taken prior to a search

3.8 Before any search of a detained person or attended vehicle takes place the officer must take reasonable steps, if not in uniform (see paragraph 3.9), to show their warrant card to the person to be searched or in charge of the vehicle to be searched and whether or not in uniform, to give that person the following information:

(a) that they are being detained for the purposes of a search

(b) the officer's name (except in the case of enquiries linked to the investigation of terrorism, or otherwise where the officer reasonably believes that giving his or her name might put him or her in danger, in which case a warrant or other identification number shall be given) and the name of the police station to which the officer is attached;

(c) the legal search power which is being exercised; and

(d) a clear explanation of:

   (i) the object of the search in terms of the article or articles for which there is a power to search; and

   (ii) in the case of:

- the power under section 60 of the Criminal Justice and Public Order Act 1994 (see paragraph 2.1(b)), the nature of the power, the authorisation and the fact that it has been given;
- the power under section 44 of the Terrorism Act 2000, the nature of the power, the authorisation and the fact that it has been given and the grounds for suspicion; (see *paragraph 2.1(c)* and *2.18A*).
- all other powers requiring reasonable suspicion (see *paragraph 2.1(a)*), the grounds for that suspicion.

(e) that they are entitled to a copy of the record of the search if one is made (see section 4 below) if they ask within 3 months from the date of the search and:

   (i) if they are not arrested and taken to a police station as a result of the search and it is practicable to make the record on the spot, that immediately after the search is completed they will be given, if they request, either:

- a copy of the record, or
- a receipt which explains how they can obtain a copy of the full record or access to an electronic copy of the record, or

   (ii) if they are arrested and taken to a police station as a result of the search, that the record will be made at the station as part of their custody record and they will be given, if they request, a copy of their custody record which includes a record of the search as soon as practicable whilst they are at the station. [See *Note 16*]

3.9 Stops and searches under the powers mentioned in paragraphs 2.1(b), and (c) may be undertaken only by a constable in uniform.

3.10 The person should also be given information about police powers to stop and search and the individual's rights in these circumstances.

3.11 If the person to be searched, or in charge of a vehicle to be searched, does not appear to understand what is being said, or there is any doubt about the person's ability to understand English, the officer must take reasonable steps to bring information regarding the person's rights and any relevant provisions of this Code to his or her attention. If the person is deaf or cannot understand English and is accompanied by someone, then the officer must try to establish whether that person can interpret or otherwise help the officer to give the required information.

4 Recording requirements

(a) Searches which do not result in an arrest

4.1 When an officer carries out a search in the exercise of any power to which this Code applies and the search does not result in the person searched or person in charge of the vehicle searched being arrested and taken to a police station, a record must be made of it, electronically or on paper, unless there are exceptional circumstances which make this wholly impracticable (e.g. in situations involving public disorder or when the recording officer's presence is urgently required elsewhere). If a record is to be made, the officer carrying out the search must make the record on the spot unless this is not practicable, in which case, the officer must make the record as soon as practicable after the search is completed. [See *Note 16.*]

4.2 If the record is made at the time, the person who has been searched or who is in charge of the vehicle that has been searched must be asked if they want a copy and if they do, they must be given immediately, either:

- a copy of the record, or
- a receipt which explains how they can obtain a copy of the full record or access to an electronic copy of the record

4.2A An officer is not required to provide a copy of the full record or a receipt at the time if they are called to an incident of higher priority. [See *Note 21*]

(b) Searches which result in an arrest

4.2B If a search in the exercise of any power to which this Code applies results in a person being arrested and taken to a police station, the officer carrying out the search is responsible for ensuring that a record of the search is made as part of their custody record. The custody officer must then ensure that the person is asked if they want a copy of the record and if they do, that they are given a copy as soon as practicable. [See *Note 16*].

(c) Record of search

4.3 The record of a search must always include the following information:

- (a) A note of the self defined ethnicity, and if different, the ethnicity as perceived by the officer making the search, of the person searched or of the person in charge of the vehicle searched (as the case may be); [See *Note 18*]
- (b) The date, time and place the person or vehicle was searched [See *Note 6*];
- (c) The object of the search in terms of the article or articles for which there is a power to search;
- (d) In the case of:
  - the power under section 60 of the Criminal Justice and Public Order Act 1994 (see *paragraph 2.1(b)*), the nature of the power, the authorisation and the fact that it has been given; [See *Note 17*]
  - the power under section 44 of the Terrorism Act 2000, the nature of the power, the authorisation and the fact that it has been given and the grounds for suspicion; [see *paragraphs 2.1(c)* and *2.18A and Note 17*].
  - all other powers requiring reasonable suspicion (see *paragraph 2.1(a)*), the grounds for that suspicion.
- (e) subject to paragraph 3.8(b), the identity of the officer carrying out the search. [See *Note 15*]

4.3A For the purposes of completing the search record, there is no requirement to record the name, address and date of birth of the person searched or the person in charge of a vehicle which is searched and the person is under no obligation to provide this information.

4.4 Nothing in paragraph 4.3 requires the names of police officers to be shown on the search record or any other record required to be made under this code in the case of enquiries linked to the investigation of terrorism or otherwise where an officer reasonably believes that recording names might endanger the officers. In such cases the record must show the officers' warrant or other identification number and duty station.

4.5 A record is required for each person and each vehicle searched. However, if a person is in a vehicle and both are searched, and the object and grounds of the search are the same, only one record need be completed. If more than one person in a vehicle is searched, separate records for each search of a person must be made. If only a vehicle is searched, the self-defined ethnic background of the person in charge of the vehicle must be recorded, unless the vehicle is unattended.

4.6 The record of the grounds for making a search must, briefly but informatively, explain the reason for suspecting the person concerned, by reference to the person's behaviour and/or other circumstances.

4.7 Where officers detain an individual with a view to performing a search, but the need to search is eliminated as a result of questioning the person detained, a search should not be carried out and a record is not required. [See *paragraph 2.10, Notes 3* and *22A*]

4.8 After searching an unattended vehicle, or anything in or on it, an officer must leave a notice in it (or on it, if things on it have been searched without opening it) recording the fact that it has been searched.

4.9 The notice must include the name of the police station to which the officer concerned is attached and state where a copy of the record of the search may be obtained and how (if applicable) an electronic copy may be accessed and where any application for compensation should be directed.

4.10 The vehicle must if practicable be left secure.

4.10A *Not used*

4.10B *Not used*

Recording of encounters not governed by statutory powers

4.11 *Not used.*

4.12 There is no national requirement for an officer who requests a person in a public place to account for themselves, i.e. their actions, behaviour, presence in an area or possession of anything, to make any record of the encounter or to give the person a receipt. [See *Notes 22A* and *22B*]

4.12A *Not used*

4.13 *Not used*

4.14 *Not used*

4.15 *Not used*

4.16 *Not used*

4.17 *Not used*

4.18 *Not used*

4.19 *Not used*

4.20 *Not used*

5   Monitoring and supervising the use of stop and search powers

5.1 Supervising officers must monitor the use of stop and search powers and should consider in particular whether there is any evidence that they are being exercised on the basis of stereotyped images or inappropriate generalisations. Supervising officers should satisfy themselves that the practice of officers under their supervision in stopping, searching and recording is fully in accordance with this Code. Supervisors must also examine whether the records reveal any trends or patterns which give cause for concern, and if so take appropriate action to address this.

5.2 Senior officers with area or force-wide responsibilities must also monitor the broader use of stop and search powers and, where necessary, take action at the relevant level.

5.3 Supervision and monitoring must be supported by the compilation of comprehensive statistical records of stops and searches at force, area and local level. Any apparently disproportionate use of the powers by particular officers or groups of officers or in relation to specific sections of the community should be identified and investigated.

5.4 In order to promote public confidence in the use of the powers, forces in consultation with police authorities must make arrangements for the records to be scrutinised by representatives of the community, and to explain the use of the powers at a local level. [See *Note 19*].

Notes for Guidance

Officers exercising stop and search powers

1 This code does not affect the ability of an officer to speak to or question a person in the ordinary course of the officer's duties without detaining the person or exercising any element of compulsion. It is not the purpose of the code to prohibit such encounters between the police and the community with the co-operation of the person concerned and neither does it affect the principle that all citizens have a duty to help police officers to prevent crime and discover offenders. This is a civic rather than a legal duty; but when a police officer is trying to discover whether, or by whom, an offence has been committed he or she may question any person from whom useful information might be obtained, subject to the restrictions imposed by Code C. A person's unwillingness to reply does not alter this entitlement, but in the absence of a power to arrest, or to detain in order to search, the person is free to leave at will and cannot be compelled to remain with the officer.

2 In some circumstances preparatory questioning may be unnecessary, but in general a brief conversation or exchange will be desirable not only as a means of avoiding unsuccessful searches, but to explain the grounds for the stop/search, to gain cooperation and reduce any tension there might be surrounding the stop/search.

3 Where a person is lawfully detained for the purpose of a search, but no search in the event takes place, the detention will not thereby have been rendered unlawful.

4 Many people customarily cover their heads or faces for religious reasons—for example, Muslim women, Sikh men, Sikh or Hindu women, or Rastafarian men or women. A police officer cannot order the removal of a head or face covering except where there is reason to believe that the item is being worn by the individual wholly or mainly for the purpose of disguising identity, not simply because it disguises identity. Where there may be religious sensitivities about ordering the removal of such an item, the officer should permit the item to be removed out of public view. Where practicable, the item should be removed in the presence of an officer of the same sex as the person and out of sight of anyone of the opposite sex [see Annex F].

5 A search of a person in public should be completed as soon as possible.

6 A person may be detained under a stop and search power at a place other than where the person was first detained, only if that place, be it a police station or elsewhere, is nearby. Such a place should be located within a reasonable travelling distance using whatever mode of travel (on foot or by car) is appropriate. This applies to all searches under stop and search powers, whether or not they involve the removal of clothing or exposure of intimate parts of the body (see paragraphs 3.6 and 3.7) or take place in or out of public view. It means, for example, that a search under the stop and search power in section 23 of the Misuse of Drugs Act 1971 which involves the compulsory removal of more than a person's outer coat, jacket or gloves cannot be carried out unless a place which is both nearby the place they were first detained and out of public view, is available. If a search involves exposure of intimate parts of the body and a police station is not nearby, particular care must be taken to ensure that the location is suitable in that it enables the search to be conducted in accordance with the requirements of paragraph 11 of Annex A to Code C.

7 A search in the street itself should be regarded as being in public for the purposes of paragraphs 3.6 and 3.7 above, even though it may be empty at the time a search begins. Although there is no power to require a person to do so, there is nothing to prevent an officer from asking a person voluntarily to remove more than an outer coat, jacket or gloves in public.

8 Not used

9 Other means of identification might include jewellery, insignias, tattoos or other features which are known to identify members of the particular gang or group.

Authorising officers

10 The powers under section 60 are separate from and additional to the normal stop and search powers which require reasonable grounds to suspect an individual of carrying an offensive weapon (or other article). Their overall purpose is to prevent serious violence and the widespread carrying of weapons which might lead to persons being seriously injured by disarming potential offenders or finding weapons that have been used in circumstances where other powers would not be sufficient. They should not therefore be used to replace or circumvent the normal powers for dealing with routine crime problems. A particular example might be an authorisation to prevent serious violence or the carrying of offensive weapons at a sports event by rival team supporters when the expected general appearance and age range of those likely to be responsible, alone, would not be sufficiently distinctive to support reasonable suspicion (see paragraph 2.6). The purpose of the powers under section 60AA is to prevent those involved in intimidatory or violent protests using face coverings to disguise identity.

11 Authorisations under section 60 require a reasonable belief on the part of the authorising officer. This must have an objective basis, for example: intelligence or relevant information such as a history of

antagonism and violence between particular groups; previous incidents of violence at, or connected with, particular events or locations; a significant increase in knife-point robberies in a limited area; reports that individuals are regularly carrying weapons in a particular locality; information following an incident in which weapons were used about where the weapons might be found or in the case of section 60AA previous incidents of crimes being committed while wearing face coverings to conceal identity.

12 It is for the authorising officer to determine the period of time during which the powers mentioned in paragraph 2.1(b) and (c) may be exercised. The officer should set the minimum period he or she considers necessary to deal with the risk of violence, the carrying of knives or offensive weapons, or terrorism or to find dangerous instruments or weapons that have been used. A direction to extend the period authorised under the powers mentioned in paragraph 2.1(b) may be given only once. Thereafter further use of the powers requires a new authorisation. There is no provision to extend an authorisation of the powers mentioned in paragraph 2.1(c); further use of the powers requires a new authorisation.

13 It is for the authorising officer to determine the geographical area in which the use of the powers is to be authorised. In doing so the officer may wish to take into account factors such as the nature and venue of the anticipated incident or the incident which has taken place, the number of people who may be in the immediate area of that incident, their access to surrounding areas and the anticipated or actual level of violence. The officer should not set a geographical area which is wider than that he or she believes necessary for the purpose of preventing anticipated violence, the carrying of knives or offensive weapons, acts of terrorism, finding a dangerous instrument or weapon that has been used or, in the case of section 60AA, the prevention of commission of offences. It is particularly important to ensure that constables exercising such powers are fully aware of where they may be used. If the area specified is smaller than the whole force area, the officer giving the authorisation should specify either the streets which form the boundary of the area or a divisional boundary within the force area. If the power is to be used in response to a threat or incident that straddles police force areas, an officer from each of the forces concerned will need to give an authorisation.

14 An officer who has authorised the use of powers under section 44(1) of the Terrorism Act 2000 must take immediate steps to send a copy of the authorisation to the National Joint Unit, Metropolitan Police Special Branch, who will forward it to the Secretary of State. The Secretary of State should be informed of the reasons for the authorisation. The National Joint Unit will inform the force concerned, within 48 hours of the authorisation being made, whether the Secretary of State has confirmed or cancelled or altered the authorisation. See paragraph 2.18A.

Recording

15 Where a stop and search is conducted by more than one officer the identity of all the officers engaged in the search must be recorded on the record. Nothing prevents an officer who is present but not directly involved in searching from completing the record during the course of the encounter.

16 When the search results in the person searched or in charge of a vehicle which is searched being arrested, the requirement to make the record of the search as part of the person's custody record does not apply if the person is granted "street bail" after arrest (see section 30A of PACE) to attend a police station and is not taken in custody to the police station An arrested person's entitlement to a copy of the search record which is made as part of their custody record does not affect their entitlement to a copy of their custody record or any other provisions of PACE Code C section 2 (Custody records).

17 It is important for monitoring purposes to specify whether the authority for exercising a stop and search power was given under section 60 of the Criminal Justice and Public Order Act 1994, or under section 44(1) of the Terrorism Act 2000.

18 Officers should record the self-defined ethnicity of every person stopped according to the categories used in the 2001 census question listed in Annex B. The person should be asked to select one of the five main categories representing broad ethnic groups and then a more specific cultural background from within this group. The ethnic classification should be coded for recording purposes using the coding system in Annex B. An additional "Not stated" box is available but should not be offered to respondents explicitly. Officers should be aware and explain to members of the public, especially where concerns are raised, that this information is required to obtain a true picture of stop and search activity and to help improve ethnic monitoring, tackle discriminatory practice, and promote effective use of the powers. If the person

gives what appears to the officer to be an "incorrect" answer (e.g. a person who appears to be white states that they are black), the officer should record the response that has been given and then record their own perception of the person's ethnic background by using the PNC classification system. If the "Not stated" category is used the reason for this must be recorded on the form.

19 Arrangements for public scrutiny of records should take account of the right to confidentiality of those stopped and searched. Anonymised forms and/or statistics generated from records should be the focus of the examinations by members of the public.

20 Not used

21 In situations where it is not practicable to provide a written copy of the record or immediate access to an electronic copy of the record or a receipt of the search at the time (see paragraph 4.2A above), the officer should consider giving the person details of the station which they may attend for a copy of the record. A receipt may take the form of a simple business card which includes sufficient information to locate the record should the person ask for copy, for example, the date and place of the search, a reference number or the name of the officer who carried out the search (unless paragraph 4.4 applies).

22 Not used

22A Where there are concerns which make it necessary to monitor any local disproportionality, forces have discretion to direct officers to record the self-defined ethnicity of persons they request to account for themselves in a public place or who they detain with a view to searching but do not search. Guidance should be provided locally and efforts made to minimise the bureaucracy involved. Records should be closely monitored and supervised in line with paragraphs 5.1 to 5.4 and forces can suspend or re-instate recording of these encounters as appropriate.

22B A person who is asked to account for themselves should, if they request, be given information about how they can report their dissatisfaction about how they have been treated.

Definition of Offensive Weapon

23 'Offensive weapon' is defined as any article made or adapted for use for causing injury to the person, or intended by the person having it with him for such use or by someone else. There are three categories of offensive weapons: those made for causing injury to the person; those adapted for such a purpose; and those not so made or adapted, but carried with the intention of causing injury to the person. A firearm, as defined by section 57 of the Firearms Act 1968, would fall within the definition of offensive weapon if any of the criteria above apply.

24 Not used

25 Not used

Annex A Summary of Main Stop and Search Powers

This table relates to stop and search powers only. Individual statutes below may contain other police powers of entry, search and seizure

Unlawful articles general

Power	Object of search	Extent of search	Where exercisable
1. Public Stores Act 1875, s6	HM Stores stolen or unlawfully obtained	Persons, vehicles and vessels	Anywhere where the constabulary powers are exercisable
2. Firearms Act 1968, s47	Firearms	Persons and vehicles	A public place, or anywhere in the case of reasonable suspicion of offences of carrying firearms with criminal intent or trespassing with firearms
3. Misuse of Drugs Act 1971, s23	Controlled drugs	Persons and vehicles	Anywhere
4. Customs and Excise Management Act 1979, s163	Goods: (a) on which duty has not been paid; (b) being unlawfully removed, imported or exported; (c) otherwise liable to forfeiture to HM Customs and Excise	Vehicles and vessels only	Anywhere
5. Aviation Security Act 1982, s27(1)	Stolen or unlawfully obtained goods	Airport employees and vehicles carrying airport employees or aircraft or any vehicle in a cargo area whether or not carrying an employee	Any designated airport
6. Police and Criminal Evidence Act 1984, s1	Stolen goods; articles for use in certain Theft Act offences; offensive weapons, including bladed or sharply-pointed articles (except folding pocket knives with a bladed cutting edge not exceeding 3 inches); prohibited possession of a category 4 (display grade) firework, any person under 18 in possession of an adult firework in a public place.	Persons and vehicles	Where there is public access

(cont.)

(cont.)

	Criminal Damage: Articles made, adapted or intended for use in destroying or damaging property	Persons and vehicles	Where there is public access
7.	Sporting events (Control of Alcohol etc.) Act 1985, s7	Intoxicating liquor	Persons, coaches and trains	Designated sports grounds or coaches and trains travelling to or from a designated sporting event
8.	Crossbows Act 1987, s4	Crossbows or parts of crossbows (except crossbows with a draw weight of less than 1.4 kilograms)	Persons and vehicles	Anywhere except dwellings
9.	Criminal Justice Act 1988 s139B	Offensive weapons, bladed or sharply pointed article	Persons	School premises

Evidence of game and wildlife offences

10.	Poaching Prevention Act 1862, s2	Game or poaching equipment	Persons and vehicles	A public place
11.	Deer Act 1991, s12	Evidence of offences under the Act	Persons and vehicles	Anywhere except dwellings
12.	Conservation of Seals Act 1970, s4	Seals or hunting equipment	Vehicles only	Anywhere
13.	Protection of Badgers Act 1992, s11	Evidence of offences under the Act	Persons and vehicles	Anywhere
14.	Wildlife and Countryside Act 1981, s19	Evidence of wildlife offences	Persons and vehicles	Anywhere except dwellings

Other

15.	Terrorism Act 2000, s.43(1)	*Anything which may constitute evidence that the person is a terrorist*	Persons	Anywhere
16.	Terrorism Act 2000, s.44(1)	Articles which could be used for a purpose connected with the commission, preparation or instigation of acts of terrorism	Vehicles, and anything in or on vehicles (See paragraph 2.18A)	Anywhere within the area or locality authorised under subsection (1)
17.	Not used			
18.	Paragraphs 7 and 8 of Schedule 7 to the Terrorism Act 2000	Anything relevant to determining if a person being examined falls within section 40(1)(b)	Persons, vehicles, vessels etc. (Note: These searches are subject to the Code of Practice issued under paragraph 6 or Schedule 14 to the Terrorism Act 2000)	Ports and airports
19.	Section 60 Criminal Justice and Public Order Act 1994	Offensive weapons or dangerous instruments to prevent incidents of serious violence or to deal with the carrying of such items which have been used in incidents of serious violence	Persons and vehicles	Anywhere within a locality authorised under subsection (1)

Annex B   Self-defined Ethnic Classification Categories

White	**W**
A. *White—British*	*W1*
B. *White—Irish*	*W2*
C. *Any other White background*	*W9*

Mixed	**M**
D. *White and Black Caribbean*	*M1*
E. *White and Black African*	*M2*
F. *White and Asian*	*M3*
G. *Any other Mixed Background*	*M9*

Asian/Asian—British	**A**
H. *Asian—Indian*	*A1*
I. *Asian—Pakistani*	*A2*
J. *Asian—Bangladeshi*	*A3*
K. *Any other Asian background*	*A9*

Black/Black—British	**B**
L. *Black—Caribbean*	*B1*
M. *Black African*	*B2*
N. *Any other Black background*	*B9*

Other	**O**
O. *Chinese*	*O1*
P. *Any other*	*O9*
Not Stated	**NS**

Annex C   Summary of Powers of Community Support Officers to Search and Seize

The following is a summary of the search and seizure powers that may be exercised by a community support officer (CSO) who has been designated with the relevant powers in accordance with Part 4 of the Police Reform Act 2002.

When exercising any of these powers, a CSO must have regard to any relevant provisions of this Code, including section 3 governing the conduct of searches and the steps to be taken prior to a search.

1. Power to stop and search not requiring consent

Designation	Power conferred	Object of search	Extent of search	Where exercisable
1. Police Reform Act 2002, Schedule 4, paragraph 15	Terrorism Act 2000, s44(1)(a) and (d) and 45(2); *(See paragraph 2.18A)*	Items intended to be used in connection with terrorism.	a) Vehicles or anything carried in or on the vehicle	Anywhere within area of locality authorised and in the company and under the supervision of a constable.

2. Powers to search requiring the consent of the person and seizure

A CSO may detain a person using reasonable force where necessary as set out in Part 1 of Schedule 4 to the Police Reform Act 2002. If the person has been lawfully detained, the CSO may search the person provided that person gives consent to such a search in relation to the following:

Designation	Power conferred	Object of search	Extent of search	Where exercisable
1. Police Reform Act 2002, Schedule 4, paragraph 7A	(a) Criminal Justice and Police Act 2001, s12(2)	(a) Alcohol or a container for alcohol	(a) Persons	(a) Designated public place
	(b) Confiscation of Alcohol (Young Persons) Act 1997, s1	(b) Alcohol	(b) Persons under 18 years old	(b) Public place
	(c) Children and Young Persons Act 1933, section 7(3)	(c) Tobacco or cigarette papers	(c) Persons under 16 years old found smoking	(c) Public place

3. Powers to search not requiring the consent of the person and seizure

A CSO may detain a person using reasonable force where necessary as set out in Part 1 of Schedule 4 to the Police Reform Act 2002. If the person has been lawfully detained, the CSO may search the person without the need for that person's consent in relation to the following:

Designation	Power conferred	Object of search	Extent of search	Where exercisable
Police Reform Act 2002, Schedule 4, paragraph 2A	Police and Criminal Evidence Act 1984, s.32	a) Objects that might be used to cause physical injury to the person or the CSO. b) Items that might be used to assist escape.	Persons made subject to a requirement to wait.	Any place where the requirement to wait has been made.

4. Powers to seize without consent

This power applies when drugs are found in the course of any search mentioned above.

Designation	Power conferred	Object of seizure	Where exercisable
Police Reform Act 2002, Schedule 4, paragraph 7B	Police Reform Act 2002, Schedule 4, paragraph 7B	Controlled drugs in a person's possession.	Any place where the person is in possession of the drug.

Annex D   Deleted

Annex E   Deleted

Annex F Establishing Gender of Persons for the Purpose of Searching

1. Certain provisions of this and other Codes explicitly state that searches and other procedures may only be carried out by, or in the presence of, persons of the same sex as the person subject to the search or other procedure. (See *paragraphs 2.8* and *3.6* and *Note 4 of this Code, Code C paragraph 4.1 and Annex A paragraphs 5, 6, 11 and 12 (searches, strip and intimate searches of detainees under sections 54 and 55 of PACE), Code D paragraph 5.5 and Note 5F (searches, examinations and photographing of detainees under section 54A of PACE) and 6.9 (taking samples) and Code H paragraph 4.1 and Annex A paragraphs 6, 7 and 12 (searches, strip and intimate searches under sections 54 and 55 of PACE and 43(2) of the Terrorism Act of persons arrested under section 41 of the Terrorism Act 2000).*

2. All searches should be carried out with courtesy, consideration and respect for the person concerned. Police officers should show particular sensitivity when dealing with transsexual or transvestite persons *(see Notes F1 and F2)*. The following approach is designed to minimise embarrassment and secure the co-operation of the person subject to the search.

(a) Consideration

3. At law, the gender of an individual is their gender as registered at birth unless they possess a gender recognition certificate as issued under section 9 of the Gender Recognition Act 2004, in which case the person's gender is the acquired gender.

    (a) If there is no doubt as to the sex of a person, or there is no reason to suspect that the person is not the sex that they appear to be, they should be dealt with as that sex.

    (b) A person who possesses a gender recognition certificate must be treated as their acquired gender.

    (c) If the police are not satisfied that the person possesses a gender recognition certificate and there is doubt as to a person's gender, the person should be asked what gender they consider themselves to be. If the person expresses a preference to be dealt with as a particular gender, they should be asked to sign the search record, the officer's notebook or, if applicable, their custody record, to indicate and confirm their preference. If appropriate, the person should be treated as being that gender.

    (d) If a person is unwilling to make such an election, efforts should be made to determine the predominant lifestyle of the person. For example, if they appear to live predominantly as a woman, they should be treated as such.

    (e) If there is still doubt, the person should be dealt with according to the sex that they were born.

5. Once a decision has been made about which gender an individual is to be treated as, where possible before an officer searches that person, the officer should be advised of the doubt as to the person's gender. This is important so as to maintain the dignity of the officer(s) concerned.

(b) Documentation

6. Where the gender of the detainee is established under *paragraphs 2(b)* to *(e)* above the decision should be recorded either on the search record, in the officer's notebook or, if applicable, in the person's custody record.

7. Where the person elects which gender they consider themselves to be under *paragraph 2(c)* but is not treated as their elected gender, the reason must be recorded in the search record, in the officer's notebook or, if applicable, in the person's custody record.

Note for Guidance

F1   Transsexual means a person who is proposing to undergo, is undergoing or has undergone a process (or part of a process) for the purpose of gender reassignment which is a protected characteristic under the Equality Act 2010 (see paragraph 1.1) by changing physiological or other attributes of their sex. It would apply to a woman making the transition to being a man and a man making the transition to being a woman as well as to a person who has only just started out on the process of gender reassignment and to a person who has completed the process. Both would share the characteristic of gender reassignment with each having the characteristics of one sex, but with certain characteristics of the other sex.

F2   Transvestite means a person of one gender who dresses in the clothes of a person of the opposite gender.

F3   Similar principles will apply to police officers and police staff whose duties involve carrying out, or being present at, any of the searches and other procedures mentioned in paragraph 1. Chief officers are responsible for providing corresponding operational guidance and instructions for the deployment of any transsexual officers and staff under their direction and control.

CODE OF PRACTICE FOR SEARCHES OF PREMISES BY POLICE OFFICERS AND THE SEIZURE OF PROPERTY FOUND BY POLICE OFFICERS ON PERSONS OR PREMISES (CODE B)

1   Introduction

1.1 This Code of Practice deals with police powers to:
- search premises
- seize and retain property found on premises and persons

1.1A These powers may be used to find:
- property and material relating to a crime
- wanted persons
- children who abscond from local authority accommodation where they have been remanded or committed by a court

1.2 A justice of the peace may issue a search warrant granting powers of entry, search and seizure, e.g. warrants to search for stolen property, drugs, firearms and evidence of serious offences. Police also have powers without a search warrant. The main ones provided by the Police and Criminal Evidence Act 1984 (PACE) include powers to search premises:
- to make an arrest
- after an arrest

1.3 The right to privacy and respect for personal property are key principles of the Human Rights Act 1998. Powers of entry, search and seizure should be fully and clearly justified before use because they may significantly interfere with the occupier's privacy. Officers should consider if the necessary objectives can be met by less intrusive means.

1.3A Powers to search and seize must be used fairly, responsibly, with respect for people who occupy premises being searched or are in charge of property being seized and without unlawful discrimination. The Equality Act 2010 makes it unlawful for police officers to discriminate against, harass or victimise any person on the grounds of the 'protected characteristics' of age, disability, gender reassignment, race, religion or belief, sex and sexual orientation, marriage and civil partnership, pregnancy and maternity when using their powers. When police forces are carrying out their functions they also have a duty to have regard to the need to eliminate unlawful discrimination, harassment and victimisation and to take steps to foster good relations.

1.4 In all cases, police should therefore:
- exercise their powers courteously and with respect for persons and property
- only use reasonable force when this is considered necessary and proportionate to the circumstances

1.5 If the provisions of PACE and this Code are not observed, evidence obtained from a search may be open to question.

2   General

2.1 This Code must be readily available at all police stations for consultation by:

- police officers
- police staff
- detained persons
- members of the public

2.2 The *Notes for Guidance* included are not provisions of this Code.

2.3 This Code applies to searches of premises:

(a) by police for the purposes of an investigation into an alleged offence, with the occupier's consent, other than:

- routine scene of crime searches;
- calls to a fire or burglary made by or on behalf of an occupier or searches following the activation of fire or burglar alarms or discovery of insecure premises;
- searches when *paragraph 5.4* applies;
- bomb threat calls;

(b) under powers conferred on police officers by PACE, sections 17, 18 and 32;

(c) undertaken in pursuance of search warrants issued to and executed by constables in accordance with PACE, sections 15 and 16. See *Note 2A*;

(d) subject to *paragraph 2.6*, under any other power given to police to enter premises with or without a search warrant for any purpose connected with the investigation into an alleged or suspected offence. See *Note 2B*.

For the purposes of this Code, 'premises' as defined in PACE, section 23, includes any place, vehicle, vessel, aircraft, hovercraft, tent or movable structure and any offshore installation as defined in the Mineral Workings (Offshore Installations) Act 1971, section 1. See *Note 2D*

2.4 A person who has not been arrested but is searched during a search of premises should be searched in accordance with Code A. See *Note 2C*

2.5 This Code does not apply to the exercise of a statutory power to enter premises or to inspect goods, equipment or procedures if the exercise of that power is not dependent on the existence of grounds for suspecting that an offence may have been committed and the person exercising the power has no reasonable grounds for such suspicion.

2.6 This Code does not affect any directions or requirements of a search warrant, order or other power to search and seize lawfully exercised in England or Wales that any item or evidence seized under that warrant, order or power be handed over to a police force, court, tribunal, or other authority outside England or Wales. For example, warrants and orders issued in Scotland or Northern Ireland, see *Note 2B(f)* and search warrants and powers provided for in sections 14 to 17 of the Crime (International Co-operation) Act 2003.

2.7 When this Code requires the prior authority or agreement of an officer of at least inspector or superintendent rank, that authority may be given by a sergeant or chief inspector authorised to perform the functions of the higher rank under PACE, section 107.

2.8 Written records required under this Code not made in the search record shall, unless otherwise specified, be made:

- in the recording officer's pocket book ('pocket book' includes any official report book issued to police officers) or
- on forms provided for the purpose

2.9 Nothing in this Code requires the identity of officers, or anyone accompanying them during a search of premises, to be recorded or disclosed:

(a) in the case of enquiries linked to the investigation of terrorism; or

(b) if officers reasonably believe recording or disclosing their names might put them in danger.

In these cases officers should use warrant or other identification numbers and the name of their police station. Police staff should use any identification number provided to them by the police force. See *Note 2E*

2.10 The 'officer in charge of the search' means the officer assigned specific duties and responsibilities under this Code. Whenever there is a search of premises to which this Code applies one officer must act as the officer in charge of the search. See *Note 2F*

2.11 In this Code:

   (a) 'designated person' means a person other than a police officer, designated under the Police Reform Act 2002, Part 4 who has specified powers and duties of police officers conferred or imposed on them. See *Note 2G*.

   (b) any reference to a police officer includes a designated person acting in the exercise or performance of the powers and duties conferred or imposed on them by their designation.

   (c) a person authorised to accompany police officers or designated persons in the execution of a warrant has the same powers as a constable in the execution of the warrant and the search and seizure of anything related to the warrant. These powers must be exercised in the company and under the supervision of a police officer. See *Note 3C*.

2.12 If a power conferred on a designated person:

   (a) allows reasonable force to be used when exercised by a police officer, a designated person exercising that power has the same entitlement to use force;

   (b) includes power to use force to enter any premises, that power is not exercisable by that designated person except:

      (i) in the company and under the supervision of a police officer; or

      (ii) for the purpose of:

      - saving life or limb; or
      - preventing serious damage to property.

2.13 Designated persons must have regard to any relevant provisions of the Codes of Practice.

Notes for guidance

2A PACE sections 15 and 16 apply to all search warrants issued to and executed by constables under any enactment, e.g. search warrants issued by a:

   (a) justice of the peace under the:

   - *Theft Act 1968, section 26—stolen property;*
   - *Misuse of Drugs Act 1971, section 23—controlled drugs;*
   - *PACE, section 8—evidence of an indictable offence;*
   - *Terrorism Act 2000, Schedule 5, paragraph 1;*
   - *Prevention of Terrorism Act 2005, section 7C—monitoring compliance with control order (see paragraph 10.1).*

   (b) Circuit judge under:

   - *PACE, Schedule 1;*
   - *Terrorism Act 2000, Schedule 5, paragraph 11.*

2B Examples of the other powers in paragraph 2.3(d) include:

   (a) Road Traffic Act 1988, section 6E(1) giving police power to enter premises under section 6E(1) to:

   - *require a person to provide a specimen of breath; or*
   - *arrest a person following:*
      - *~ a positive breath test;*
      - *~ failure to provide a specimen of breath;*

   (b) Transport and Works Act 1992, section 30(4) giving police powers to enter premises mirroring the powers in (a) in relation to specified persons working on transport systems to which the Act applies;

(c) *Criminal Justice Act 1988, section 139B giving police power to enter and search school premises for offensive weapons, bladed or pointed articles;*

(d) *Terrorism Act 2000, Schedule 5, paragraphs 3 and 15 empowering a superintendent in urgent cases to give written authority for police to enter and search premises for the purposes of a terrorist investigation;*

(e) *Explosives Act 1875, section 73(b) empowering a superintendent to give written authority for police to enter premises, examine and search them for explosives;*

(f) *search warrants and production orders or the equivalent issued in Scotland or Northern Ireland endorsed under the Summary Jurisdiction (Process) Act 1881 or the Petty Sessions (Ireland) Act 1851 respectively for execution in England and Wales.*

(g) *Sections 7A and 7B of the Prevention of Terrorism Act 2005, searches connected with the enforcement of control orders (see paragraph 10.1).*

2C *The Criminal Justice Act 1988, section 139B provides that a constable who has reasonable grounds to believe an offence under the Criminal Justice Act 1988, section 139A has or is being committed may enter school premises and search the premises and any persons on the premises for any bladed or pointed article or offensive weapon. Persons may be searched under a warrant issued under the Misuse of Drugs Act 1971, section 23(3) to search premises for drugs or documents only if the warrant specifically authorises the search of persons on the premises. Powers to search premises under certain terrorism provisions also authorise the search of persons on the premises, for example, under paragraphs 1, 2, 11 and 15 of Schedule 5 to the Terrorism Act 2000 and section 52 of the Anti-terrorism, Crime and Security Act 2001.*

2D *The Immigration Act 1971, Part III and Schedule 2 gives immigration officers powers to enter and search premises, seize and retain property, with and without a search warrant. These are similar to the powers available to police under search warrants issued by a justice of the peace and without a warrant under PACE, sections 17, 18, 19 and 32 except they only apply to specified offences under the Immigration Act 1971 and immigration control powers. For certain types of investigations and enquiries these powers avoid the need for the Immigration Service to rely on police officers becoming directly involved. When exercising these powers, immigration officers are required by the Immigration and Asylum Act 1999, section 145 to have regard to this Code's corresponding provisions. When immigration officers are dealing with persons or property at police stations, police officers should give appropriate assistance to help them discharge their specific duties and responsibilities.*

2E *The purpose of paragraph 2.9(b) is to protect those involved in serious organised crime investigations or arrests of particularly violent suspects when there is reliable information that those arrested or their associates may threaten or cause harm to the officers or anyone accompanying them during a search of premises. In cases of doubt, an officer of inspector rank or above should be consulted.*

2F *For the purposes of paragraph 2.10, the officer in charge of the search should normally be the most senior officer present. Some exceptions are:*

(a) *a supervising officer who attends or assists at the scene of a premises search may appoint an officer of lower rank as officer in charge of the search if that officer is:*
- *more conversant with the facts;*
- *a more appropriate officer to be in charge of the search;*

(b) *when all officers in a premises search are the same rank. The supervising officer if available must make sure one of them is appointed officer in charge of the search, otherwise the officers themselves must nominate one of their number as the officer in charge;*

(c) *a senior officer assisting in a specialist role. This officer need not be regarded as having a general supervisory role over the conduct of the search or be appointed or expected to act as the officer in charge of the search.*

Except in (c), nothing in this Note diminishes the role and responsibilities of a supervisory officer who is present at the search or knows of a search taking place.

2G *An officer of the rank of inspector or above may direct a designated investigating officer not to wear a uniform for the purposes of a specific operation.*

3 Search warrants and production orders

(a) Before making an application

3.1 When information appears to justify an application, the officer must take reasonable steps to check the information is accurate, recent and not provided maliciously or irresponsibly. An application may not be made on the basis of information from an anonymous source if corroboration has not been sought. See *Note 3A*

3.2 The officer shall ascertain as specifically as possible the nature of the articles concerned and their location.

3.3 The officer shall make reasonable enquiries to:
  (i)   establish if:
    • anything is known about the likely occupier of the premises and the nature of the premises themselves;
    • the premises have been searched previously and how recently;
  (ii) obtain any other relevant information.

3.4 An application:
  (a) to a justice of the peace for a search warrant or to a Circuit judge for a search warrant or production order under PACE, Schedule 1 must be supported by a signed written authority from an officer of inspector rank or above:
  Note: If the case is an urgent application to a justice of the peace and an inspector or above is not readily available, the next most senior officer on duty can give the written authority.
  (b) to a circuit judge under the Terrorism Act 2000, Schedule 5 for
    • a production order;
    • search warrant; or
    • an order requiring an explanation of material seized or produced under such a warrant or production order
    • must be supported by a signed written authority from an officer of superintendent rank or above.

3.5 Except in a case of urgency, if there is reason to believe a search might have an adverse effect on relations between the police and the community, the officer in charge shall consult the local police/community liaison officer:
  • before the search; or
  • in urgent cases, as soon as practicable after the search

(b) Making an application

3.6 A search warrant application must be supported in writing, specifying:
  (a) the enactment under which the application is made, see *Note 2A*;
  (b) (i) whether the warrant is to authorise entry and search of:
    • one set of premises; or
    • if the application is under PACE section 8, or Schedule 1, paragraph 12, more than one set of specified premises or all premises occupied or controlled by a specified person, and
    (ii) the premises to be searched;
  (c) the object of the search, see *Note 3B*;
  (d) the grounds for the application, including, when the purpose of the proposed search is to find evidence of an alleged offence, an indication of how the evidence relates to the investigation;
  (da) Where the application is under PACE section 8, or Schedule 1, paragraph 12 for a single warrant to enter and search:
    (i) more than one set of specified premises, the officer must specify each set of premises which it is desired to enter and search

    (ii) all premises occupied or controlled by a specified person, the officer must specify;
- as many sets of premises which it is desired to enter and search as it is reasonably practicable to specify
- the person who is in occupation or control of those premises and any others which it is desired to search
- why it is necessary to search more premises than those which can be specified
- why it is not reasonably practicable to specify all the premises which it is desired to enter and search

(db) Whether an application under PACE section 8 is for a warrant authorising entry and search on more than one occasion, and if so, the officer must state the grounds for this and whether the desired number of entries authorised is unlimited or a specified maximum.

(e)   there are no reasonable grounds to believe the material to be sought, when making application to a:

    (i) justice of the peace or a Circuit judge consists of or includes items subject to legal privilege;

    (ii) justice of the peace, consists of or includes excluded material or special procedure material;

    Note: this does not affect the additional powers of seizure in the Criminal Justice and Police Act 2001, Part 2 covered in *paragraph 7.7*, see *Note 3B;*

(f)   if applicable, a request for the warrant to authorise a person or persons to accompany the officer who executes the warrant, see *Note 3C.*

3.7 A search warrant application under PACE, Schedule 1, paragraph 12(a), shall if appropriate indicate why it is believed service of notice of an application for a production order may seriously prejudice the investigation. Applications for search warrants under the Terrorism Act 2000, Schedule 5, paragraph 11 must indicate why a production order would not be appropriate.

3.8 If a search warrant application is refused, a further application may not be made for those premises unless supported by additional grounds.

Notes for guidance

3A The identity of an informant need not be disclosed when making an application, but the officer should be prepared to answer any questions the magistrate or judge may have about:
- *the accuracy of previous information from that source*
- *any other related matters*

3B The information supporting a search warrant application should be as specific as possible, particularly in relation to the articles or persons being sought and where in the premises it is suspected they may be found. The meaning of 'items subject to legal privilege', 'excluded material' and 'special procedure material' are defined by PACE, sections 10, 11 and 14 respectively.

3C Under PACE, section 16(2), a search warrant may authorise persons other than police officers to accompany the constable who executes the warrant. This includes, e.g. any suitably qualified or skilled person or an expert in a particular field whose presence is needed to help accurately identify the material sought or to advise where certain evidence is most likely to be found and how it should be dealt with. It does not give them any right to force entry, but it gives them the right to be on the premises during the search and to search for or seize property without the occupier's permission.

4 Entry without warrant—particular powers

(a) Making an arrest etc

4.1 The conditions under which an officer may enter and search premises without a warrant are set out in PACE, section 17. It should be noted that this section does not create or confer any powers of arrest. See other powers in Note 2B(a).

(b) Search of premises where arrest takes place or the arrested person was immediately before arrest

4.2 When a person has been arrested for an indictable offence, a police officer has power under PACE, section 32 to search the premises where the person was arrested or where the person was immediately before being arrested.

(c) Search of premises occupied or controlled by the arrested person

4.3 The specific powers to search premises which are occupied or controlled by a person arrested for an indictable offence are set out in PACE, section 18. They may not be exercised, except if section 18(5) applies, unless an officer of inspector rank or above has given written authority. That authority should only be given when the authorising officer is satisfied that the premises are occupied or controlled by the arrested person and that the necessary grounds exist. If possible the authorising officer should record the authority on the Notice of Powers and Rights and, subject to *paragraph 2.9*, sign the Notice. The record of the grounds for the search and the nature of the evidence sought as required by section 18(7) of the Act should be made in:

- the custody record if there is one, otherwise
- the officer's pocket book, or
- the search record

5   Search with consent

5.1 Subject to *paragraph 5.4*, if it is proposed to search premises with the consent of a person entitled to grant entry the consent must, if practicable, be given in writing on the Notice of Powers and Rights before the search. The officer must make any necessary enquiries to be satisfied the person is in a position to give such consent. See *Notes 5A* and *5B*

5.2 Before seeking consent the officer in charge of the search shall state the purpose of the proposed search and its extent. This information must be as specific as possible, particularly regarding the articles or persons being sought and the parts of the premises to be searched. The person concerned must be clearly informed they are not obliged to consent, that any consent given can be withdrawn at any time, including before the search starts or while it is underway and anything seized may be produced in evidence. If at the time the person is not suspected of an offence, the officer shall say this when stating the purpose of the search.

5.3 An officer cannot enter and search or continue to search premises under *paragraph 5.1* if consent is given under duress or withdrawn before the search is completed.

5.4 It is unnecessary to seek consent under *paragraphs 5.1* and *5.2* if this would cause disproportionate inconvenience to the person concerned. See *Note 5C*

Notes for guidance

5A In a lodging house, hostel or similar accommodation, every reasonable effort should be made to obtain the consent of the tenant, lodger or occupier. A search should not be made solely on the basis of the landlord's consent.

5B If the intention is to search premises under the authority of a warrant or a power of entry and search without warrant, and the occupier of the premises co-operates in accordance with paragraph 6.4, there is no need to obtain written consent.

5C Paragraph 5.4 is intended to apply when it is reasonable to assume innocent occupiers would agree to, and expect, police to take the proposed action, e.g. if:

- *a suspect has fled the scene of a crime or to evade arrest and it is necessary quickly to check surrounding gardens and readily accessible places to see if the suspect is hiding*
- *police have arrested someone in the night after a pursuit and it is necessary to make a brief check of gardens along the pursuit route to see if stolen or incriminating articles have been discarded*

6 Searching premises—general considerations

(a) Time of searches

6.1 Searches made under warrant must be made within three calendar months of the date of the warrant's issue.

6.2 Searches must be made at a reasonable hour unless this might frustrate the purpose of the search.

6.3 When the extent or complexity of a search mean it is likely to take a long time, the officer in charge of the search may consider using the seize and sift powers referred to in *section 7*.

6.3A A warrant under PACE, section 8 may authorise entry to and search of premises on more than one occasion if, on the application, the justice of the peace is satisfied that it is necessary to authorise multiple entries in order to achieve the purpose for which the warrant is issued. No premises may be entered or searched on any subsequent occasions without the prior written authority of an officer of the rank of inspector who is not involved in the investigation. All other warrants authorise entry on one occasion only.

6.3B Where a warrant under PACE section 8, or Schedule 1, paragraph 12 authorises entry to and search of all premises occupied or controlled by a specified person, no premises which are not specified in the warrant may be entered and searched without the prior written authority of an officer of the rank of inspector who is not involved in the investigation.

(b) Entry other than with consent

6.4 The officer in charge of the search shall first try to communicate with the occupier, or any other person entitled to grant access to the premises, explain the authority under which entry is sought and ask the occupier to allow entry, unless:

(i) the search premises are unoccupied;

(ii) the occupier and any other person entitled to grant access are absent;

(iii) there are reasonable grounds for believing that alerting the occupier or any other person entitled to grant access would frustrate the object of the search or endanger officers or other people.

6.5 Unless *sub-paragraph 6.4(iii)* applies, if the premises are occupied the officer, subject to *paragraph 2.9*, shall, before the search begins:

(i) identify him or herself, show their warrant card (if not in uniform) and state the purpose of and grounds for the search;

(ii) identify and introduce any person accompanying the officer on the search (such persons should carry identification for production on request) and briefly describe that person's role in the process.

6.6 Reasonable and proportionate force may be used if necessary to enter premises if the officer in charge of the search is satisfied the premises are those specified in any warrant, or in exercise of the powers described in *paragraphs 4.1 to 4.3*, and if:

(i) the occupier or any other person entitled to grant access has refused entry;

(ii) it is impossible to communicate with the occupier or any other person entitled to grant access; or

(iii) any of the provisions of *paragraph 6.4* apply.

(c) Notice of Powers and Rights

6.7 If an officer conducts a search to which this Code applies the officer shall, unless it is impracticable to do so, provide the occupier with a copy of a Notice in a standard format:

(i) specifying if the search is made under warrant, with consent, or in the exercise of the powers described in *paragraphs 4.1 to 4.3*. Note: the notice format shall provide for authority or consent to be indicated, see *paragraphs 4.3* and *5.1;*

(ii) summarising the extent of the powers of search and seizure conferred by PACE and other relevant legislation as appropriate;

    (iii) explaining the rights of the occupier, and the owner of the property seized;

    (iv) explaining compensation may be payable in appropriate cases for damages caused entering and searching premises, and giving the address to send a compensation application, see *Note 6A;*

    (v) stating this Code is available at any police station.

  6.8 If the occupier is:

- present, copies of the Notice and warrant shall, if practicable, be given to them before the search begins, unless the officer in charge of the search reasonably believes this would frustrate the object of the search or endanger officers or other people
- not present, copies of the Notice and warrant shall be left in a prominent place on the premises or appropriate part of the premises and endorsed, subject to *paragraph 2.9* with the name of the officer in charge of the search, the date and time of the search

The warrant shall be endorsed to show this has been done.

(d) Conduct of searches

  6.9 Premises may be searched only to the extent necessary to achieve the purpose of the search, having regard to the size and nature of whatever is sought.

  6.9A A search may not continue under:

- a warrant's authority once all the things specified in that warrant have been found;
- any other power once the object of that search has been achieved.

  6.9B No search may continue once the officer in charge of the search is satisfied whatever is being sought is not on the premises. See *Note 6B.* This does not prevent a further search of the same premises if additional grounds come to light supporting a further application for a search warrant or exercise or further exercise of another power. For example, when, as a result of new information, it is believed articles previously not found or additional articles are on the premises.

  6.10 Searches must be conducted with due consideration for the property and privacy of the occupier and with no more disturbance than necessary. Reasonable force may be used only when necessary and proportionate because the co-operation of the occupier cannot be obtained or is insufficient for the purpose. See *Note 6C*

  6.11 A friend, neighbour or other person must be allowed to witness the search if the occupier wishes unless the officer in charge of the search has reasonable grounds for believing the presence of the person asked for would seriously hinder the investigation or endanger officers or other people. A search need not be unreasonably delayed for this purpose. A record of the action taken should be made on the premises search record including the grounds for refusing the occupier's request.

  6.12 A person is not required to be cautioned prior to being asked questions that are solely necessary for the purpose of furthering the proper and effective conduct of a search, see Code C, *paragraph 10.1(c)*. For example, questions to discover the occupier of specified premises, to find a key to open a locked drawer or cupboard or to otherwise seek co-operation during the search or to determine if a particular item is liable to be seized.

  6.12A If questioning goes beyond what is necessary for the purpose of the exemption in Code C, the exchange is likely to constitute an interview as defined by Code C, *paragraph 11.1A* and would require the associated safeguards included in Code C, *section 10.*

(e) Leaving premises

  6.13 If premises have been entered by force, before leaving the officer in charge of the search must make sure they are secure by:

- arranging for the occupier or their agent to be present
- any other appropriate means

(f) Searches under PACE Schedule 1 or the Terrorism Act 2000, Schedule 5

  6.14 An officer shall be appointed as the officer in charge of the search, see *paragraph 2.10*, in respect of any search made under a warrant issued under PACE Act 1984, Schedule 1 or the Terrorism Act 2000, Schedule 5. They are responsible for making sure the search is conducted with discretion and in a manner that causes the least possible disruption to any business or other activities carried out on the premises.

6.15 Once the officer in charge of the search is satisfied material may not be taken from the premises without their knowledge, they shall ask for the documents or other records concerned. The officer in charge of the search may also ask to see the index to files held on the premises, and the officers conducting the search may inspect any files which, according to the index, appear to contain the material sought. A more extensive search of the premises may be made only if:

- the person responsible for them refuses to:
  — produce the material sought, or
  — allow access to the index
- it appears the index is:
  — inaccurate, or
  — incomplete
  — for any other reason the officer in charge of the search has reasonable grounds for believing such a search is necessary in order to find the material sought

Notes for guidance

6A Whether compensation is appropriate depends on the circumstances in each case. Compensation for damage caused when effecting entry is unlikely to be appropriate if the search was lawful, and the force used can be shown to be reasonable, proportionate and necessary to effect entry. If the wrong premises are searched by mistake everything possible should be done at the earliest opportunity to allay any sense of grievance and there should normally be a strong presumption in favour of paying compensation.

6B It is important that, when possible, all those involved in a search are fully briefed about any powers to be exercised and the extent and limits within which it should be conducted.

6C In all cases the number of officers and other persons involved in executing the warrant should be determined by what is reasonable and necessary according to the particular circumstances.

7 Seizure and retention of property

(a) Seizure

7.1 Subject to *paragraph 7.2*, an officer who is searching any person or premises under any statutory power or with the consent of the occupier may seize anything:

    (a) covered by a warrant
    (b) the officer has reasonable grounds for believing is evidence of an offence or has been obtained in consequence of the commission of an offence but only if seizure is necessary to prevent the items being concealed, lost, disposed of, altered, damaged, destroyed or tampered with
    (c) covered by the powers in the Criminal Justice and Police Act 2001, Part 2 allowing an officer to seize property from persons or premises and retain it for sifting or examination elsewhere

See Note 7B

7.2 No item may be seized which an officer has reasonable grounds for believing to be subject to legal privilege, as defined in PACE, section 10, other than under the Criminal Justice and Police Act 2001, Part 2.

7.3 Officers must be aware of the provisions in the Criminal Justice and Police Act 2001, section 59, allowing for applications to a judicial authority for the return of property seized and the subsequent duty to secure in section 60, see *paragraph 7.12(iii)*.

7.4 An officer may decide it is not appropriate to seize property because of an explanation from the person holding it but may nevertheless have reasonable grounds for believing it was obtained in consequence of an offence by some person. In these circumstances, the officer should identify the property to the holder, inform the holder of their suspicions and explain the holder may be liable to civil or criminal proceedings if they dispose of, alter or destroy the property.

7.5 An officer may arrange to photograph, image or copy, any document or other article they have the power to seize in accordance with *paragraph 7.1*. This is subject to specific restrictions on the examination, imaging or copying of certain property seized under the Criminal Justice and Police Act 2001, Part 2. An officer must have regard to their statutory obligation to retain an original document or other article only when a photograph or copy is not sufficient.

7.6 If an officer considers information stored in any electronic form and accessible from the premises could be used in evidence, they may require the information to be produced in a form:

- which can be taken away and in which it is visible and legible; or
- from which it can readily be produced in a visible and legible form

(b) Criminal Justice and Police Act 2001: Specific procedures for seize and sift powers

7.7 The Criminal Justice and Police Act 2001, Part 2 gives officers limited powers to seize property from premises or persons so they can sift or examine it elsewhere. Officers must be careful they only exercise these powers when it is essential and they do not remove any more material than necessary. The removal of large volumes of material, much of which may not ultimately be retainable, may have serious implications for the owners, particularly when they are involved in business or activities such as journalism or the provision of medical services. Officers must carefully consider if removing copies or images of relevant material or data would be a satisfactory alternative to removing originals. When originals are taken, officers must be prepared to facilitate the provision of copies or images for the owners when reasonably practicable. See *Note 7C*

7.8 Property seized under the Criminal Justice and Police Act 2001, sections 50 or 51 must be kept securely and separately from any material seized under other powers. An examination under section 53 to determine which elements may be retained must be carried out at the earliest practicable time, having due regard to the desirability of allowing the person from whom the property was seized, or a person with an interest in the property, an opportunity of being present or represented at the examination.

7.8A All reasonable steps should be taken to accommodate an interested person's request to be present, provided the request is reasonable and subject to the need to prevent harm to, interference with, or unreasonable delay to the investigatory process. If an examination proceeds in the absence of an interested person who asked to attend or their representative, the officer who exercised the relevant seizure power must give that person a written notice of why the examination was carried out in those circumstances. If it is necessary for security reasons or to maintain confidentiality officers may exclude interested persons from decryption or other processes which facilitate the examination but do not form part of it. See *Note 7D*

7.9 It is the responsibility of the officer in charge of the investigation to make sure property is returned in accordance with sections 53 to 55. Material which there is no power to retain must be:

- separated from the rest of the seized property
- returned as soon as reasonably practicable after examination of all the seized property

7.9A Delay is only warranted if very clear and compelling reasons exist, e.g. the:

- unavailability of the person to whom the material is to be returned
- need to agree a convenient time to return a large volume of material

7.9B Legally privileged, excluded or special procedure material which cannot be retained must be returned:

- as soon as reasonably practicable
- without waiting for the whole examination

7.9C As set out in section 58, material must be returned to the person from whom it was seized, except when it is clear some other person has a better right to it. See *Note 7E*

7.10 When an officer involved in the investigation has reasonable grounds to believe a person with a relevant interest in property seized under section 50 or 51 intends to make an application under section 59 for the return of any legally privileged, special procedure or excluded material, the officer in charge of the investigation should be informed as soon as practicable and the material seized should be kept secure in accordance with section 61. See *Note 7C*

7.11 The officer in charge of the investigation is responsible for making sure property is properly secured. Securing involves making sure the property is not examined, copied, imaged or put to any other use except at the request, or with the consent, of the applicant or in accordance with the directions of the appropriate judicial authority. Any request, consent or directions must be recorded in writing and signed by both the initiator and the officer in charge of the investigation. See *Notes 7F* and *7G*

7.12 When an officer exercises a power of seizure conferred by sections 50 or 51 they shall provide the occupier of the premises or the person from whom the property is being seized with a written notice:

   (i) specifying what has been seized under the powers conferred by that section;

   (ii) specifying the grounds for those powers;

   (iii) setting out the effect of sections 59 to 61 covering the grounds for a person with a relevant interest in seized property to apply to a judicial authority for its return and the duty of officers to secure property in certain circumstances when an application is made;

   (iv) specifying the name and address of the person to whom:

      • notice of an application to the appropriate judicial authority in respect of any of the seized property must be given;

      • an application may be made to allow attendance at the initial examination of the property.

7.13 If the occupier is not present but there is someone in charge of the premises, the notice shall be given to them. If no suitable person is available, so the notice will easily be found it should either be:

      • left in a prominent place on the premises

      • attached to the exterior of the premises

(c) Retention

7.14 Subject to *paragraph 7.15*, anything seized in accordance with the above provisions may be retained only for as long as is necessary. It may be retained, among other purposes:

   (i) for use as evidence at a trial for an offence;

   (ii) to facilitate the use in any investigation or proceedings of anything to which it is inextricably linked, see *Note 7H*;

   (iii) for forensic examination or other investigation in connection with an offence;

   (iv) in order to establish its lawful owner when there are reasonable grounds for believing it has been stolen or obtained by the commission of an offence.

7.15 Property shall not be retained under *paragraph 7.14(i), (ii)* or *(iii)* if a copy or image would be sufficient.

(d) Rights of owners etc

7.16 If property is retained, the person who had custody or control of it immediately before seizure must, on request, be provided with a list or description of the property within a reasonable time.

7.17 That person or their representative must be allowed supervised access to the property to examine it or have it photographed or copied, or must be provided with a photograph or copy, in either case within a reasonable time of any request and at their own expense, unless the officer in charge of an investigation has reasonable grounds for believing this would:

   (i) prejudice the investigation of any offence or criminal proceedings; or

   (ii) lead to the commission of an offence by providing access to unlawful material such as pornography;

A record of the grounds shall be made when access is denied.

Notes for guidance

7A Any person claiming property seized by the police may apply to a magistrates' court under the Police (Property) Act 1897 for its possession and should, if appropriate, be advised of this procedure.

7B The powers of seizure conferred by PACE, sections 18(2) and 19(3) extend to the seizure of the whole premises when it is physically possible to seize and retain the premises in their totality and practical considerations make seizure desirable. For example, police may remove premises such as tents, vehicles or caravans to a police station for the purpose of preserving evidence.

7C Officers should consider reaching agreement with owners and/or other interested parties on the procedures for examining a specific set of property, rather than awaiting the judicial authority's determination. Agreement can sometimes give a quicker and more satisfactory route for all concerned and minimise costs and legal complexities.

7D What constitutes a relevant interest in specific material may depend on the nature of that material and the circumstances in which it is seized. Anyone with a reasonable claim to ownership of the material and anyone entrusted with its safe keeping by the owner should be considered.

7E Requirements to secure and return property apply equally to all copies, images or other material created because of seizure of the original property.

7F The mechanics of securing property vary according to the circumstances; "bagging up", i.e. placing material in sealed bags or containers and strict subsequent control of access is the appropriate procedure in many cases.

7G When material is seized under the powers of seizure conferred by PACE, the duty to retain it under the Code of Practice issued under the Criminal Procedure and Investigations Act 1996 is subject to the provisions on retention of seized material in PACE, section 22.

7H Paragraph 7.14 (ii) applies if inextricably linked material is seized under the Criminal Justice and Police Act 2001, sections 50 or 51. Inextricably linked material is material it is not reasonably practicable to separate from other linked material without prejudicing the use of that other material in any investigation or proceedings. For example, it may not be possible to separate items of data held on computer disk without damaging their evidential integrity. Inextricably linked material must not be examined, imaged, copied or used for any purpose other than for proving the source and/or integrity of the linked material.

8 Action after searches

8.1 If premises are searched in circumstances where this Code applies, unless the exceptions in paragraph 2.3(a) apply, on arrival at a police station the officer in charge of the search shall make or have made a record of the search, to include:

(i) the address of the searched premises;

(ii) the date, time and duration of the search;

(iii) the authority used for the search:
- if the search was made in exercise of a statutory power to search premises without warrant, the power which was used for the search:
- if the search was made under a warrant or with written consent;
  — a copy of the warrant and the written authority to apply for it, see paragraph 3.4; or
  — the written consent;
  shall be appended to the record or the record shall show the location of the copy warrant or consent.

(iv) subject to paragraph 2.9, the names of:
- the officer(s) in charge of the search;
- all other officers and authorised persons who conducted the search;

(v) the names of any people on the premises if they are known;

(vi) any grounds for refusing the occupier's request to have someone present during the search, see paragraph 6.11;

(vii) a list of any articles seized or the location of a list and, if not covered by a warrant, the grounds for their seizure;

(viii) whether force was used, and the reason;

(ix) details of any damage caused during the search, and the circumstances;

   (x)   if applicable, the reason it was not practicable;
      (a) to give the occupier a copy of the Notice of Powers and Rights, see *paragraph 6.7*;
      (b) before the search to give the occupier a copy of the Notice, see *paragraph 6.8*;
  (xi) when the occupier was not present, the place where copies of the Notice of Powers and Rights and search warrant were left on the premises, see *paragraph 6.8*.

8.2 On each occasion when premises are searched under warrant, the warrant authorising the search on that occasion shall be endorsed to show:

   (i)   if any articles specified in the warrant were found and the address where found;
  (ii) if any other articles were seized;
 (iii) the date and time it was executed and if present, the name of the occupier or if the occupier is not present the name of the person in charge of the premises;
 (iv) subject to *paragraph 2.9*, the names of the officers who executed it and any authorised persons who accompanied them;
  (v) if a copy, together with a copy of the Notice of Powers and Rights was:
- handed to the occupier; or
- endorsed as required by *paragraph 6.8*; and left on the premises and where.

8.3 Any warrant shall be returned within three calendar months of its issue or sooner on completion of the search(es) authorised by that warrant, if it was issued by a:
- justice of the peace, to the designated officer for the local justice area in which the justice was acting when issuing the warrant; or
- judge, to the appropriate officer of the court concerned,

9 Search registers

9.1 A search register will be maintained at each sub-divisional or equivalent police station. All search records required under *paragraph 8.1* shall be made, copied, or referred to in the register. See *Note 9A*

Note for guidance

9A Paragraph 9.1 also applies to search records made by immigration officers. In these cases, a search register must also be maintained at an immigration office. See also Note 2D

10 Searches under sections 7A, 7B and 7C of the Prevention of Terrorism Act 2005 in connection with control orders

10.1 This Code applies to the powers under sections 7A, 7B and 7C of the Prevention of Terrorism Act 2005 to enter and search premises subject to the modifications in the following paragraphs.

10.2 In paragraph 2.3(d), the reference to the investigation into an alleged or suspected offence include the enforcement of obligations imposed by or under a control order made under the Prevention of Terrorism Act 2005.

10.3 References to the purpose and object of the search, the nature of articles sought and what may be seized and retained include (as appropriate):
- in relation section 7A (absconding), determining whether the controlled person has absconded and if it appears so, any material or information that may assist in the pursuit and arrest of the controlled person.
- in relation to section 7B (failure to grant access to premises), determining whether any control order obligations have been contravened and if it appears so, any material or information that may assist in determining whether the controlled person is complying with the obligations imposed by the control order or in investigating any apparent contravention of those obligations.
- in relation to section 7C (monitoring compliance), determining whether the controlled person is complying with their control order obligations, and any material that may assist in that determination.
- evidence in relation to an offence under section 9 of the Prevention of Terrorism Act 2005 (offences relating to control orders).

CODE OF PRACTICE FOR THE DETENTION, TREATMENT AND QUESTIONING OF PERSONS BY POLICE OFFICERS (CODE C)

This Code applies to people in police detention after midnight on the day The Police and Criminal Evidence Act 1984 (Codes of Practice) (Revision of Codes C, G and H) Order 2012 comes into force, notwithstanding that their period of detention may have commenced before that time.

1 General

1.0 The powers and procedures in this Code must be used fairly, responsibly, with respect for the people to whom they apply and without unlawful discrimination. The Equality Act 2010 makes it unlawful for police officers to discriminate against, harass or victimise any person on the grounds of the 'protected characteristics' of age, disability, gender reassignment, race, religion or belief, sex and sexual orientation, marriage and civil partnership, pregnancy and maternity when using their powers. When police forces are carrying out their functions, they also have a duty to have regard to the need to eliminate unlawful discrimination, harassment and victimisation and to take steps to foster good relations.

1.1 All persons in custody must be dealt with expeditiously, and released as soon as the need for detention no longer applies.

1.1A A custody officer must perform the functions in this Code as soon as practicable. A custody officer will not be in breach of this Code if delay is justifiable and reasonable steps are taken to prevent unnecessary delay. The custody record shall show when a delay has occurred and the reason. See *Note 1H*

1.2 This Code of Practice must be readily available at all police stations for consultation by:
- police officers;
- police staff;
- detained persons;
- members of the public.

1.3 The provisions of this Code:
- include the *Annexes*
- do not include the *Notes for Guidance*.

1.4 If an officer has any suspicion, or is told in good faith, that a person of any age may be mentally disordered or otherwise mentally vulnerable, in the absence of clear evidence to dispel that suspicion, the person shall be treated as such for the purposes of this Code. See *Note 1G*

1.5 If anyone appears to be under 17, they shall be treated as a juvenile for the purposes of this Code in the absence of clear evidence that they are older.

1.6 If a person appears to be blind, seriously visually impaired, deaf, unable to read or speak or has difficulty orally because of a speech impediment, they shall be treated as such for the purposes of this Code in the absence of clear evidence to the contrary.

1.7 'The appropriate adult' means, in the case of a:
(a) juvenile:
    (i) the parent, guardian or, if the juvenile is in the care of a local authority or voluntary organisation, a person representing that authority or organisation;
    (ii) a social worker of a local authority;
    (iii) failing these, some other responsible adult aged 18 or over who is not a police officer or employed by the police.
(b) person who is mentally disordered or mentally vulnerable: See *Note 1D*
    (i) a relative, guardian or other person responsible for their care or custody;
    (ii) someone experienced in dealing with mentally disordered or mentally vulnerable people but who is not a police officer or employed by the police;
    (iii) failing these, some other responsible adult aged 18 or over who is not a police officer or employed by the police.

1.8 If this Code requires a person be given certain information, they do not have to be given it if at the time they are incapable of understanding what is said, are violent or may become violent or in urgent need of medical attention, but they must be given it as soon as practicable.

1.9 References to a custody officer include any police officer who for the time being, is performing the functions of a custody officer.

1.9A When this Code requires the prior authority or agreement of an officer of at least inspector or superintendent rank, that authority may be given by a sergeant or chief inspector authorised to perform the functions of the higher rank under the Police and Criminal Evidence Act 1984 (PACE), section 107.

1.10 Subject to *paragraph 1.12*, this Code applies to people in custody at police stations in England and Wales, whether or not they have been arrested, and to those removed to a police station as a place of safety under the Mental Health Act 1983, sections 135 and 136, as a last resort (see paragraph 3.16). *Section 15* applies solely to people in police detention, e.g. those brought to a police station under arrest or arrested at a police station for an offence after going there voluntarily.

1.11 No part of this Code applies to a detained person:
- (a) to whom PACE Code H applies because:
    - they are detained following arrest under section 41 of the Terrorism Act 2000 (TACT) and not charged; or
    - an authorisation has been given under section 22 of the Counter-Terrorism Act 2008 (CTACT) (post-charge questioning of terrorist suspects) to interview them.
- (b) to whom the Code of Practice issued under paragraph 6 of Schedule 14 to TACT applies because they are detained for examination under Schedule 7 to TACT. 1.12 This Code does not apply to people in custody:
    - (i) arrested on warrants issued in Scotland by officers under the Criminal Justice and Public Order Act 1994, section 136(2), or arrested or detained without warrant by officers from a police force in Scotland under section 137(2). In these cases, police powers and duties and the person's rights and entitlements whilst at a police station in England or Wales are the same as those in Scotland;
    - (ii) arrested under the Immigration and Asylum Act 1999, section 142(3) in order to have their fingerprints taken;
    - (iii) whose detention is authorised by an immigration officer under the Immigration Act 1971;
    - (iv) who are convicted or remanded prisoners held in police cells on behalf of the Prison Service under the Imprisonment (Temporary Provisions) Act 1980;
    - (v) *Not used*
    - (vi) detained for searches under stop and search powers except as required by Code A. The provisions on conditions of detention and treatment in sections 8 and 9 must be considered as the minimum standards of treatment for such detainees.

1.13 In this Code:
- (a) 'designated person' means a person other than a police officer, designated under the Police Reform Act 2002, Part 4 who has specified powers and duties of police officers conferred or imposed on them;
- (b) reference to a police officer includes a designated person acting in the exercise or performance of the powers and duties conferred or imposed on them by their designation.
- (c) where a search or other procedure to which this Code applies may only be carried out or observed by a person of the same sex as the detainee, the gender of the detainee and other parties present should be established and recorded in line with Annex L of this Code.

1.14 Designated persons are entitled to use reasonable force as follows:–
- (a) when exercising a power conferred on them which allows a police officer exercising that power to use reasonable force, a designated person has the same entitlement to use force; and
- (b) at other times when carrying out duties conferred or imposed on them that also entitle them to use reasonable force, for example:
    - when at a police station carrying out the duty to keep detainees for whom they are responsible under control and to assist any other police officer or designated person to keep any detainee under control and to prevent their escape.

- when securing, or assisting any other police officer or designated person in securing, the detention of a person at a police station.
- when escorting, or assisting any other police officer or designated person in escorting, a detainee within a police station.
- for the purpose of saving life or limb; or
- preventing serious damage to property.

1.15 Nothing in this Code prevents the custody officer, or other officer given custody of the detainee, from allowing police staff who are not designated persons to carry out individual procedures or tasks at the police station if the law allows. However, the officer remains responsible for making sure the procedures and tasks are carried out correctly in accordance with the Codes of Practice (see *Note 3F*). Any such person must be:

(a) a person employed by a police force and under the direction and control of the Chief Officer of that force; or

(b) employed by a person with whom a police force has a contract for the provision of services relating to persons arrested or otherwise in custody.

1.16 Designated persons and other police staff must have regard to any relevant provisions of the Codes of Practice.

1.17 References to pocket books include any official report book issued to police officers or other police staff.

Notes for guidance

1A Although certain sections of this Code apply specifically to people in custody at police stations, those there voluntarily to assist with an investigation should be treated with no less consideration, e.g. offered refreshments at appropriate times, and enjoy an absolute right to obtain legal advice or communicate with anyone outside the police station.

1B A person, including a parent or guardian, should not be an appropriate adult if they:
- *are:*
  — *suspected of involvement in the offence;*
  — *the victim;*
  — *a witness;*
  — *involved in the investigation.*
- *received admissions prior to attending to act as the appropriate adult.*

Note: If a juvenile's parent is estranged from the juvenile, they should not be asked to act as the appropriate adult if the juvenile expressly and specifically objects to their presence.

1C If a juvenile admits an offence to, or in the presence of, a social worker or member of a youth offending team other than during the time that person is acting as the juvenile's appropriate adult, another appropriate adult should be appointed in the interest of fairness.

1D In the case of people who are mentally disordered or otherwise mentally vulnerable, it may be more satisfactory if the appropriate adult is someone experienced or trained in their care rather than a relative lacking such qualifications. But if the detainee prefers a relative to a better qualified stranger or objects to a particular person their wishes should, if practicable, be respected.

1E A detainee should always be given an opportunity, when an appropriate adult is called to the police station, to consult privately with a solicitor in the appropriate adult's absence if they want. An appropriate adult is not subject to legal privilege.

1F A solicitor or independent custody visitor (formerly a lay visitor) present at the police station in that capacity may not be the appropriate adult.

1G 'Mentally vulnerable' applies to any detainee who, because of their mental state or capacity, may not understand the significance of what is said, of questions or of their replies. 'Mental disorder' is defined in the Mental Health Act 1983, section 1(2) as 'any disorder or disability of mind'. When the custody officer has any doubt about the mental state or capacity of a detainee, that detainee should be treated as mentally vulnerable and an appropriate adult called.

1H Paragraph 1.1A is intended to cover delays which may occur in processing detainees e.g. if:

- *a large number of suspects are brought into the station simultaneously to be placed in custody;*
- *interview rooms are all being used;*
- *there are difficulties contacting an appropriate adult, solicitor or interpreter.*

1I The custody officer must remind the appropriate adult and detainee about the right to legal advice and record any reasons for waiving it in accordance with section 6.

1J Not used

1K This Code does not affect the principle that all citizens have a duty to help police officers to prevent crime and discover offenders. This is a civic rather than a legal duty; but when police officers are trying to discover whether, or by whom, offences have been committed they are entitled to question any person from whom they think useful information can be obtained, subject to the restrictions imposed by this Code. A person's declaration that they are unwilling to reply does not alter this entitlement.

2   Custody records

2.1A When a person is brought to a police station:

- under arrest
- is arrested at the police station having attended there voluntarily or
- attends a police station to answer bail

they must be brought before the custody officer as soon as practicable after their arrival at the station or if applicable, following their arrest after attending the police station voluntarily. This applies to designated and non-designated police stations. A person is deemed to be "at a police station" for these purposes if they are within the boundary of any building or enclosed yard which forms part of that police station.

2.1 A separate custody record must be opened as soon as practicable for each person brought to a police station under arrest or arrested at the station having gone there voluntarily or attending a police station in answer to street bail. All information recorded under this Code must be recorded as soon as practicable in the custody record unless otherwise specified. Any audio or video recording made in the custody area is not part of the custody record.

2.2 If any action requires the authority of an officer of a specified rank, subject to *paragraph 2.6A*, their name and rank must be noted in the custody record.

2.3 The custody officer is responsible for the custody record's accuracy and completeness and for making sure the record or copy of the record accompanies a detainee if they are transferred to another police station. The record shall show the:

- time and reason for transfer;
- time a person is released from detention.

2.3A If a person is arrested and taken to a police station as a result of a search in the exercise of any stop and search power to which PACE Code A (Stop and search) or the 'search powers code' issued under TACT applies, the officer carrying out the search is responsible for ensuring that the record of that stop and search, is made as part of the person's custody record. The custody officer must then ensure that the person is asked if they want a copy of the search record and if they do, that they are given a copy as soon as practicable. The person's entitlement to a copy of the search record which is made as part of their custody record is in addition to, and does not affect, their entitlement to a copy of their custody record or any other provisions of section 2 (Custody records) of this Code. (See Code A *paragraph 4.2B* and the TACT search powers code *paragraph 5.3.5*).

2.4 A solicitor or appropriate adult must be permitted to inspect a detainee's custody record as soon as practicable after their arrival at the station and at any other time whilst the person is detained. Arrangements for this access must be agreed with the custody officer and may not unreasonably interfere with the custody officer's duties.

2.4A When a detainee leaves police detention or is taken before a court they, their legal representative or appropriate adult shall be given, on request, a copy of the custody record as soon as practicable. This entitlement lasts for 12 months after release.

2.5 The detainee, appropriate adult or legal representative shall be permitted to inspect the original custody record after the detainee has left police detention provided they give reasonable notice of their request. Any such inspection shall be noted in the custody record.

2.6 Subject to *paragraph 2.6A*, all entries in custody records must be timed and signed by the maker. Records entered on computer shall be timed and contain the operator's identification.

2.6A Nothing in this Code requires the identity of officers or other police staff to be recorded or disclosed:
- (a) *Not used*
- (b) if the officer or police staff reasonably believe recording or disclosing their name might put them in danger. In these cases, they shall use their warrant or other identification numbers and the name of their police station. See *Note 2A*

2.7 The fact and time of any detainee's refusal to sign a custody record, when asked in accordance with this Code, must be recorded.

Note for guidance

2A The purpose of paragraph 2.6A(b) is to protect those involved in serious organised crime investigations or arrests of particularly violent suspects when there is reliable information that those arrested or their associates may threaten or cause harm to those involved. In cases of doubt, an officer of inspector rank or above should be consulted.

3 Initial action

(a) Detained persons—normal procedure

3.1 When a person is brought to a police station under arrest or arrested at the station having gone there voluntarily, the custody officer must make sure the person is told clearly about the following continuing rights which may be exercised at any stage during the period in custody:
- (i)   the right to have someone informed of their arrest as in *section 5*;
- (ii) the right to consult privately with a solicitor and that free independent legal advice is available;
- (iii) the right to consult these Codes of Practice. See *Note 3D*

3.2 The detainee must also be given:
- a written notice setting out:
  - ~ the above three rights;
  - ~ the arrangements for obtaining legal advice;
  - ~ the right to a copy of the custody record as in *paragraph 2.4A;*
  - ~ the caution in the terms prescribed in *section 10*.
- an additional written notice briefly setting out their entitlements while in custody, see *Notes 3A* and *3B*.

Note: The detainee shall be asked to sign the custody record to acknowledge receipt of these notices. Any refusal must be recorded on the custody record.

3.3 A citizen of an independent Commonwealth country or a national of a foreign country, including the Republic of Ireland, must be informed as soon as practicable about their rights of communication with their High Commission, Embassy or Consulate. See *section 7*

3.4 The custody officer shall:
- record the offence(s) that the detainee has been arrested for and the reason(s) for the arrest on the custody record. See *paragraph 10.3 and Code G paragraphs 2.2 and 4.3.*
- note on the custody record any comment the detainee makes in relation to the arresting officer's account but shall not invite comment. If the arresting officer is not physically present when the detainee is brought to a police station, the arresting officer's account must be made available to the custody officer remotely or by a third party on the arresting officer's behalf. If the custody officer authorises a person's detention, subject to paragraph 1.8, that officer must record the grounds for detention in the detainee's presence and at

the same time, inform them of the grounds. The detainee must be informed of the grounds for their detention before they are questioned about any offence;

- note any comment the detainee makes in respect of the decision to detain them but shall not invite comment;
- not put specific questions to the detainee regarding their involvement in any offence, nor in respect of any comments they may make in response to the arresting officer's account or the decision to place them in detention. Such an exchange is likely to constitute an interview as in *paragraph 11.1A* and require the associated safeguards in *section 11*.

See *paragraph 11.13* in respect of unsolicited comments.

3.5 The custody officer or other custody staff as directed by the custody officer shall:

(a) ask the detainee, whether at this time, they:
  (i)   would like legal advice, see *paragraph 6.5*;
  (ii) want someone informed of their detention, see *section 5*;
(b) ask the detainee to sign the custody record to confirm their decisions in respect of (*a*);
(c) determine whether the detainee:
  (i)   is, or might be, in need of medical treatment or attention, see *section 9*;
  (ii) requires:
    - an appropriate adult;
    - help to check documentation;
    - an interpreter.
(d) record the decision in respect of (*c*).

Where any duties under this paragraph have been carried out by custody staff at the direction of the custody officer, the outcomes shall, as soon as practicable, be reported to the custody officer who retains overall responsibility for the detainee's care and treatment and ensuring that it complies with this Code. See *Note 3F*

3.6 When these needs are determined, the custody officer is responsible for initiating an assessment to consider whether the detainee is likely to present specific risks to custody staff or themselves. Such assessments should always include a check on the Police National Computer, to be carried out as soon as practicable, to identify any risks highlighted in relation to the detainee. Although such assessments are primarily the custody officer's responsibility, it may be necessary for them to consult and involve others, e.g. the arresting officer or an appropriate healthcare professional, see *paragraph 9.13*. Reasons for delaying the initiation or completion of the assessment must be recorded.

3.7 Chief Officers should ensure that arrangements for proper and effective risk assessments required by *paragraph 3.6* are implemented in respect of all detainees at police stations in their area.

3.8 Risk assessments must follow a structured process which clearly defines the categories of risk to be considered and the results must be incorporated in the detainee's custody record. The custody officer is responsible for making sure those responsible for the detainee's custody are appropriately briefed about the risks. If no specific risks are identified by the assessment, that should be noted in the custody record. See *Note 3E* and *paragraph 9.14*

3.8A The content of any risk assessment and any analysis of the level of risk relating to the person's detention is not required to be shown or provided to the detainee or any person acting on behalf of the detainee. But information should not be withheld from any person acting on the detainee's behalf, for example, an appropriate adult, solicitor or interpreter, if to do so might put that person at risk.

3.9 The custody officer is responsible for implementing the response to any specific risk assessment, e.g.:

- reducing opportunities for self harm;
- calling an appropriate healthcare professional;
- increasing levels of monitoring or observation;
- reducing the risk to those who come into contact with the detainee.

See *Note 3E*

3.10 Risk assessment is an ongoing process and assessments must always be subject to review if circumstances change.

3.11 If video cameras are installed in the custody area, notices shall be prominently displayed showing cameras are in use. Any request to have video cameras switched off shall be refused.

(b) Detained persons—special groups

3.12 If the detainee appears deaf or there is doubt about their hearing or speaking ability or ability to understand English, and the custody officer cannot establish effective communication, the custody officer must, as soon as practicable, call an interpreter for assistance in the action under *paragraphs 3.1–3.5*. See *section 13*

3.13 If the detainee is a juvenile, the custody officer must, if it is practicable, ascertain the identity of a person responsible for their welfare. That person:
- may be:
  - — the parent or guardian;
  - — if the juvenile is in local authority or voluntary organisation care, or is otherwise being looked after under the Children Act 1989, a person appointed by that authority or organisation to have responsibility for the juvenile's welfare;
  - — any other person who has, for the time being, assumed responsibility for the juvenile's welfare.
- must be informed as soon as practicable that the juvenile has been arrested, why they have been arrested and where they are detained. This right is in addition to the juvenile's right in *section 5* not to be held incommunicado. See *Note 3C*

3.14 If a juvenile is known to be subject to a court order under which a person or organisation is given any degree of statutory responsibility to supervise or otherwise monitor them, reasonable steps must also be taken to notify that person or organisation (the 'responsible officer'). The responsible officer will normally be a member of a Youth Offending Team, except for a curfew order which involves electronic monitoring when the contractor providing the monitoring will normally be the responsible officer.

3.15 If the detainee is a juvenile, mentally disordered or otherwise mentally vulnerable, the custody officer must, as soon as practicable:
- inform the appropriate adult, who in the case of a juvenile may or may not be a person responsible for their welfare, as in *paragraph 3.13*, of:
  - — the grounds for their detention;
  - — their whereabouts.
- ask the adult to come to the police station to see the detainee.

3.16 It is imperative that a mentally disordered or otherwise mentally vulnerable person, detained under the Mental Health Act 1983, section 136, be assessed as soon as possible. A police station should only be used as a place of safety as a last resort but if that assessment is to take place at the police station, an approved mental health professional and a registered medical practitioner shall be called to the station as soon as possible to carry it out. See *Note 9D*. The appropriate adult has no role in the assessment process and their presence is not required. Once the detainee has been assessed and suitable arrangements made for their treatment or care, they can no longer be detained under section 136. A detainee must be immediately discharged from detention under section 136 if a registered medical practitioner, having examined them, concludes they are not mentally disordered within the meaning of the Act.

3.17 If the appropriate adult is:
- already at the police station, the provisions of *paragraphs 3.1 to 3.5* must be complied with in the appropriate adult's presence;
- not at the station when these provisions are complied with, they must be complied with again in the presence of the appropriate adult when they arrive.

3.18 The detainee shall be advised that:
- the duties of the appropriate adult include giving advice and assistance;
- they can consult privately with the appropriate adult at any time.

3.19 If the detainee, or appropriate adult on the detainee's behalf, asks for a solicitor to be called to give legal advice, the provisions of *section 6* apply.

3.20 If the detainee is blind, seriously visually impaired or unable to read, the custody officer shall make sure their solicitor, relative, appropriate adult or some other person likely to take an interest in them and not involved in the investigation is available to help check any documentation. When this Code requires written consent or signing the person assisting may be asked to sign instead, if the detainee prefers. This paragraph does not require an appropriate adult to be called solely to assist in checking and signing documentation for a person who is not a juvenile, or mentally disordered or otherwise mentally vulnerable (see *paragraph 3.15*).

(c) Persons attending a police station or elsewhere voluntarily

3.21 Anybody attending a police station or other location (see *paragraph 3.22*) voluntarily to assist police with the investigation of an offence may leave at will unless arrested. See *Note 1K*. The person may only be prevented from leaving at will if their arrest on suspicion of committing the offence is necessary in accordance with Code G. See *Code G Note 2G*

If during an interview it is decided that their arrest is necessary, they must:
- be informed at once that they are under arrest and of the grounds and reasons as required by Code G, and
- be brought before the custody officer at the police station where they are arrested or, as the case may be, at the police station to which they are taken after being arrested elsewhere. The custody officer is then responsible for making sure that a custody record is opened and that they are notified of their rights in the same way as other detainees as required by this Code.

If they are not arrested but are cautioned as in *section 10*, the person who gives the caution must, at the same time, inform them they are not under arrest, they are not obliged to remain at the station or other location but if they agree to remain, they may obtain free and independent legal advice if they want. They shall also be given a copy of the notice explaining the arrangements for obtaining legal advice and told that the right to legal advice includes the right to speak with a solicitor on the telephone and be asked if they want advice. If advice is requested, the interviewer is responsible for securing its provision without delay by contacting the Defence Solicitor Call Centre and for ensuring that the provisions of this Code and Codes E and F concerning the conduct and recording of interviews of suspects are followed insofar as they can be applied to suspects who are not under arrest. See paragraph 3.2 and *Note 6B*

3.22 If the other location mentioned in paragraph 3.21 is any place or premises for which the interviewer requires the person's informed consent to remain, for example, the person's home, then the references that the person is 'not obliged to remain' and that they 'may leave at will' mean that the person may also withdraw their consent and require the officer to leave.

(d) Documentation

3.23 The grounds for a person's detention shall be recorded, in the person's presence if practicable. See *paragraph 1.8*.

3.24 Action taken under *paragraphs 3.12* to *3.20* shall be recorded.

(e) Persons answering street bail

3.25 When a person is answering street bail, the custody officer should link any documentation held in relation to arrest with the custody record. Any further action shall be recorded on the custody record in accordance with paragraphs 3.23 and 3.24 above.

Notes for guidance

3A The notice of entitlements should:
- *list the entitlements in this Code, including:*
  - *visits and contact with outside parties, including special provisions for Commonwealth citizens and foreign nationals;*
  - *reasonable standards of physical comfort;*

— *adequate food and drink;*
— *access to toilets and washing facilities, clothing, medical attention, and exercise when practicable.*
  • *mention the:*
— *provisions relating to the conduct of interviews;*
— *circumstances in which an appropriate adult should be available to assist the detainee and their statutory rights to make representation whenever the period of their detention is reviewed.*

3B In addition to notices in English, translations should be available in Welsh, the main minority ethnic languages and the principal European languages, whenever they are likely to be helpful. Audio versions of the notice should also be made available. Access 'easy read' illustrated versions should also be provided if they are available.

3C If the juvenile is in local authority or voluntary organisation care but living with their parents or other adults responsible for their welfare, although there is no legal obligation to inform them, they should normally be contacted, as well as the authority or organisation unless suspected of involvement in the offence concerned. Even if the juvenile is not living with their parents, consideration should be given to informing them.

3D The right to consult the Codes of Practice does not entitle the person concerned to delay unreasonably any necessary investigative or administrative action whilst they do so. Examples of action which need not be delayed unreasonably include:
  • *procedures requiring the provision of breath, blood or urine specimens under the Road Traffic Act 1988 or the Transport and Works Act 1992;*
  • *searching detainees at the police station;*
  • *taking fingerprints, footwear impressions or non-intimate samples without consent for evidential purposes.*

3E Home Office Circular 32/2000 and the Guidance on the Safer Detention and Handling of Persons in Police Custody Second Edition (2012) produced on behalf of the Association of Chief Police Officers provide more detailed guidance on risk assessments and identify key risk areas which should always be considered.

3F A custody officer or other officer who, in accordance with this Code, allows or directs the carrying out of any task or action relating to a detainee's care, treatment, rights and entitlements to another officer or any police staff must be satisfied that the officer or police staff concerned are suitable, trained and competent to carry out the task or action in question.

4 Detainee's property

(a) Action

4.1 The custody officer is responsible for:
  (a) ascertaining what property a detainee:
      (i) has with them when they come to the police station, whether on:
         • arrest or re-detention on answering to bail;
         • commitment to prison custody on the order or sentence of a court;
         • lodgement at the police station with a view to their production in court from prison custody;
         • transfer from detention at another station or hospital;
         • detention under the Mental Health Act 1983, section 135 or 136;
         • remand into police custody on the authority of a court.
      (ii) might have acquired for an unlawful or harmful purpose while in custody;
  (b) the safekeeping of any property taken from a detainee which remains at the police station.
The custody officer may search the detainee or authorise their being searched to the extent they consider necessary, provided a search of intimate parts of the body or involving the removal of more than outer clothing is only made as in *Annex A*. A search may only be carried out by an officer of the same sex as the detainee. See *Note 4A* and *Annex L*.

4.2 Detainees may retain clothing and personal effects at their own risk unless the custody officer considers they may use them to cause harm to themselves or others, interfere with evidence, damage property, effect an escape or they are needed as evidence. In this event the custody officer may withhold such articles as they consider necessary and must tell the detainee why.

4.3 Personal effects are those items a detainee may lawfully need, use or refer to while in detention but do not include cash and other items of value.

(b) Documentation

4.4 It is a matter for the custody officer to determine whether a record should be made of the property a detained person has with him or had taken from him on arrest. Any record made is not required to be kept as part of the custody record but the custody record should be noted as to where such a record exists. Whenever a record is made the detainee shall be allowed to check and sign the record of property as correct. Any refusal to sign shall be recorded.

4.5 If a detainee is not allowed to keep any article of clothing or personal effects, the reason must be recorded.

Notes for guidance

4A PACE, Section 54(1) and paragraph 4.1 require a detainee to be searched when it is clear the custody officer will have continuing duties in relation to that detainee or when that detainee's behaviour or offence makes an inventory appropriate. They do not require every detainee to be searched, e.g. if it is clear a person will only be detained for a short period and is not to be placed in a cell, the custody officer may decide not to search them. In such a case the custody record will be endorsed 'not searched', paragraph 4.4 will not apply, and the detainee will be invited to sign the entry. If the detainee refuses, the custody officer will be obliged to ascertain what property they have in accordance with paragraph 4.1.

4B Paragraph 4.4 does not require the custody officer to record on the custody record property in the detainee's possession on arrest if, by virtue of its nature, quantity or size, it is not practicable to remove it to the police station. 4C Paragraph 4.4 does not require items of clothing worn by the person be recorded unless withheld by the custody officer as in paragraph 4.2.

5   Right not to be held incommunicado

(a) Action

5.1 Subject to paragraph 5.7B, any person arrested and held in custody at a police station or other premises may, on request, have one person known to them or likely to take an interest in their welfare informed at public expense of their whereabouts as soon as practicable. If the person cannot be contacted the detainee may choose up to two alternatives. If they cannot be contacted, the person in charge of detention or the investigation has discretion to allow further attempts until the information has been conveyed. See *Notes 5C* and *5D*

5.2 The exercise of the above right in respect of each person nominated may be delayed only in accordance with *Annex B*.

5.3 The above right may be exercised each time a detainee is taken to another police station.

5.4 If the detainee agrees, they may at the custody officer's discretion, receive visits from friends, family or others likely to take an interest in their welfare, or in whose welfare the detainee has an interest. See *Note 5B*

5.5 If a friend, relative or person with an interest in the detainee's welfare enquires about their whereabouts, this information shall be given if the suspect agrees and *Annex B* does not apply. See *Note 5D*

5.6 The detainee shall be given writing materials, on request, and allowed to telephone one person for a reasonable time, see *Notes 5A* and *5E*. Either or both these privileges may be denied or delayed if an officer of inspector rank or above considers sending a letter or making a telephone call may result in any of the consequences in:

(a) *Annex B paragraphs 1* and *2* and the person is detained in connection with an indictable offence;

(b) *Not used*

Nothing in this paragraph permits the restriction or denial of the rights in *paragraphs 5.1* and *6.1*.

5.7 Before any letter or message is sent, or telephone call made, the detainee shall be informed that what they say in any letter, call or message (other than in a communication to a solicitor) may be read or listened to and may be given in evidence. A telephone call may be terminated if it is being abused. The costs can be at public expense at the custody officer's discretion.

5.7A Any delay or denial of the rights in this section should be proportionate and should last no longer than necessary.

5.7B In the case of a person in police custody for specific purposes and periods in accordance with a direction under the Crime (Sentences) Act 1997, Schedule 1 (productions from prison etc.), the exercise of the rights in this section shall be subject to any additional conditions specified in the direction for the purpose of regulating the detainees' contact and communication with others whilst in police custody. See *Note 5F*

(b) Documentation

5.8 A record must be kept of any:
    (a) request made under this section and the action taken;
    (b) letters, messages or telephone calls made or received or visit received;
    (c) refusal by the detainee to have information about them given to an outside enquirer. The detainee must be asked to countersign the record accordingly and any refusal recorded.

Notes for guidance

5A A person may request an interpreter to interpret a telephone call or translate a letter.

5B At the custody officer's discretion and subject to the detainee's consent, visits should be allowed when possible, subject to having sufficient personnel to supervise a visit and any possible hindrance to the investigation.

5C If the detainee does not know anyone to contact for advice or support or cannot contact a friend or relative, the custody officer should bear in mind any local voluntary bodies or other organisations who might be able to help. Paragraph 6.1 applies if legal advice is required.

5D In some circumstances it may not be appropriate to use the telephone to disclose information under paragraphs 5.1 and 5.5.

5E The telephone call at paragraph 5.6 is in addition to any communication under paragraphs 5.1 and 6.1.

5F Prison Service Order 1801 (Production of Prisoners at the Request of Police) provides detailed guidance and instructions for police officers and Governors and Directors of Prisons regarding applications for prisoners to be transferred to police custody and their safe custody and treatments which in police custody.

6   Right to legal advice

(a) Action

6.1 Unless *Annex B* applies, all detainees must be informed that they may at any time consult and communicate privately with a solicitor, whether in person, in writing or by telephone, and that free independent legal advice is available. See *paragraph 3.1, Notes 1I, 6B and 6J*

6.2 *Not used*

6.3 A poster advertising the right to legal advice must be prominently displayed in the charging area of every police station. See *Note 6H*

6.4 No police officer should, at any time, do or say anything with the intention of dissuading any person who is entitled to legal advice in accordance with this Code, whether or not they have been arrested and are detained, from obtaining legal advice. See *Note 6ZA*.

6.5 The exercise of the right of access to legal advice may be delayed only as in *Annex B*. Whenever legal advice is requested, and unless *Annex B* applies, the custody officer must act without delay to secure the provision of such advice. If the detainee has the right to speak to a solicitor in person but declines to exercise the right the officer should point out that the right includes the right to speak with a solicitor on the telephone. If the detainee continues to waive this right, or a detainee whose right to free legal advice is limited to telephone advice from the Criminal Defence Service (CDS) Direct (*see*

Note 6B) declines to exercise that right, the officer should ask them why and any reasons should be recorded on the custody record or the interview record as appropriate. Reminders of the right to legal advice must be given as in *paragraphs 3.5, 11.2, 15.4, 16.4, 2B of Annex A, 3 of Annex K* and *16.5* of this Code and Code D, *paragraphs 3.17(ii)* and *6.3*.

Once it is clear a detainee does not want to speak to a solicitor in person or by telephone they should cease to be asked their reasons. See *Note 6K*

6.5A In the case of a person who is a juvenile or is mentally disordered or otherwise mentally vulnerable, an appropriate adult should consider whether legal advice from a solicitor is required. If the person indicates that they do not want legal advice, the appropriate adult has the right to ask for a solicitor to attend if this would be in the best interests of the person. However, the person cannot be forced to see the solicitor if they are adamant that they do not wish to do so.

6.6 A detainee who wants legal advice may not be interviewed or continue to be interviewed until they have received such advice unless:

(a) *Annex B* applies, when the restriction on drawing adverse inferences from silence in *Annex C* will apply because the detainee is not allowed an opportunity to consult a solicitor; or

(b) an officer of superintendent rank or above has reasonable grounds for believing that:
  (i) the consequent delay might:
    • lead to interference with, or harm to, evidence connected with an offence;
    • lead to interference with, or physical harm to, other people;
    • lead to serious loss of, or damage to, property;
    • lead to alerting other people suspected of having committed an offence but not yet arrested for it;
    • hinder the recovery of property obtained in consequence of the commission of an offence.
       See *Note 6A*
  (ii) when a solicitor, including a duty solicitor, has been contacted and has agreed to attend, awaiting their arrival would cause unreasonable delay to the process of investigation.
  Note: In these cases the restriction on drawing adverse inferences from silence in *Annex C* will apply because the detainee is not allowed an opportunity to consult a solicitor.

(c) the solicitor the detainee has nominated or selected from a list:
  (i) cannot be contacted;
  (ii) has previously indicated they do not wish to be contacted; or
  (iii) having been contacted, has declined to attend; and
    • the detainee has been advised of the Duty Solicitor Scheme but has declined to ask for the duty solicitor;
    • in these circumstances the interview may be started or continued without further delay provided an officer of inspector rank or above has agreed to the interview proceeding.
  Note: The restriction on drawing adverse inferences from silence in *Annex C* will not apply because the detainee is allowed an opportunity to consult the duty solicitor;

(d) the detainee changes their mind about wanting legal advice or (as the case may be) about wanting a solicitor present at the interview and states that they no longer wish to speak to a solicitor. In these circumstances, the interview may be started or continued without delay provided that:
  (i) an officer of inspector rank or above:
    • speaks to the detainee to enquire about the reasons for their change of mind (see *Note 6K*), and
    • makes, or directs the making of, reasonable efforts to ascertain the solicitor's expected time of arrival and to inform the solicitor that the suspect has stated that they wish to change their mind and the reason (if given);

(ii)   the detainee's reason for their change of mind (if given) and the outcome of the action in (i) are recorded in the custody record;

(iii)   the detainee, after being informed of the outcome of the action in (i) above, confirms in writing that they want the interview to proceed without speaking or further speaking to a solicitor or (as the case may be) without a solicitor being present and do not wish to wait for a solicitor by signing an entry to this effect in the custody record;

(iv)   an officer of inspector rank or above is satisfied that it is proper for the interview to proceed in these circumstances and:

- gives authority in writing for the interview to proceed and if the authority is not recorded in the custody record, the officer must ensure that the custody record shows the date and time of authority and where it is recorded, and
- takes or directs the taking of, reasonable steps to inform the solicitor that the authority has been given and the time when the interview is expected to commence, and records or causes to be recorded, the outcome of this action in the custody record.

(v)   When the interview starts and the interviewer reminds the suspect of their right to legal advice (see *paragraph 11.2*, Code E *paragraph 4.5* and Code F *paragraph 4.5*), the interviewer shall then ensure that the following is recorded in the written interview record or the interview record made in accordance with Code E or F:

- confirmation that the detainee has changed their mind about wanting legal advice or (as the case may be) about wanting a solicitor present and the reasons for it if given;
- the fact that authority for the interview to proceed has been given and, subject to *paragraph 2.6A*, the name of the authorising officer;
- that if the solicitor arrives at the station before the interview is completed, the detainee will be so informed without delay and *a break will be taken* to allow them to speak to the solicitor if they wish, unless *paragraph 6.6(a)* applies, and
- that at any time during the interview, the detainee may again ask for legal advice and that if they do, a break will be taken to allow them to speak to the solicitor, unless *paragraph 6.6(a), (b), or (c)* applies.

Note: In these circumstances, the restriction on drawing adverse inferences from silence in *Annex C* will not apply because the detainee is allowed an opportunity to consult a solicitor if they wish.

6.7 If *paragraph 6.6(a)* applies, where the reason for authorising the delay ceases to apply, there may be no further delay in permitting the exercise of the right in the absence of a further authorisation unless *paragraph 6.6(b), (c)* or *(d)* applies. If *paragraph 6.6(b)(i)* applies, once sufficient information has been obtained to avert the risk, questioning must cease until the detainee has received legal advice unless *paragraph 6.6(a), (b)(ii), (c)* or *(d)* applies.

6.8 A detainee who has been permitted to consult a solicitor shall be entitled on request to have the solicitor present when they are interviewed unless one of the exceptions in *paragraph 6.6* applies.

6.9 The solicitor may only be required to leave the interview if their conduct is such that the interviewer is unable properly to put questions to the suspect. See *Notes 6D* and *6E*

6.10 If the interviewer considers a solicitor is acting in such a way, they will stop the interview and consult an officer not below superintendent rank, if one is readily available, and otherwise an officer not below inspector rank not connected with the investigation. After speaking to the solicitor, the officer consulted will decide if the interview should continue in the presence of that solicitor. If they decide it should not, the suspect will be given the opportunity to consult another solicitor before the interview continues and that solicitor given an opportunity to be present at the interview. *See Note 6E*

6.11 The removal of a solicitor from an interview is a serious step and, if it occurs, the officer of superintendent rank or above who took the decision will consider if the incident should be reported to the Solicitors Regulatory Authority. If the decision to remove the solicitor has been taken by an officer below superintendent rank, the facts must be reported to an officer of superintendent rank or above who will similarly consider whether a report to the Solicitors Regulatory Authority would be appropriate. When the solicitor concerned is a duty solicitor, the report should be both to the Solicitors Regulatory Authority and to the Legal Services Commission.

6.12 'Solicitor' in this Code means:

- a solicitor who holds a current practising certificate;
- an accredited or probationary representative included on the register of representatives maintained by the Legal Services Commission.

6.12A An accredited or probationary representative sent to provide advice by, and on behalf of, a solicitor shall be admitted to the police station for this purpose unless an officer of inspector rank or above considers such a visit will hinder the investigation and directs otherwise. Hindering the investigation does not include giving proper legal advice to a detainee as in *Note 6D*. Once admitted to the police station, *paragraphs 6.6 to 6.10* apply.

6.13 In exercising their discretion under *paragraph 6.12A*, the officer should take into account in particular:

- whether:
  — the identity and status of an accredited or probationary representative have been satisfactorily established;
  — they are of suitable character to provide legal advice, e.g. a person with a criminal record is unlikely to be suitable unless the conviction was for a minor offence and not recent.
- any other matters in any written letter of authorisation provided by the solicitor on whose behalf the person is attending the police station. See *Note 6F*

6.14 If the inspector refuses access to an accredited or probationary representative or a decision is taken that such a person should not be permitted to remain at an interview, the inspector must notify the solicitor on whose behalf the representative was acting and give them an opportunity to make alternative arrangements. The detainee must be informed and the custody record noted.

6.15 If a solicitor arrives at the station to see a particular person, that person must, unless *Annex B* applies, be so informed whether or not they are being interviewed and asked if they would like to see the solicitor. This applies even if the detainee has declined legal advice or, having requested it, subsequently agreed to be interviewed without receiving advice. The solicitor's attendance and the detainee's decision must be noted in the custody record.

(b) Documentation

6.16 Any request for legal advice and the action taken shall be recorded.

6.17 A record shall be made in the interview record if a detainee asks for legal advice and an interview is begun either in the absence of a solicitor or their representative, or they have been required to leave an interview.

Notes for guidance

6ZA No police officer or police staff shall indicate to any suspect, except to answer a direct question, that period for which they are liable to be detained, or if not detained, the time taken to complete the interview, might be reduced:

- *if they do not ask for legal advice or do not want a solicitor present when they are interviewed; or*
- *if they have asked for legal advice or (as the case may be) asked for a solicitor to be present when they are interviewed but change their mind and agree to be interviewed without waiting for a solicitor.*

6A In considering if paragraph 6.6(b) applies, the officer should, if practicable, ask the solicitor for an estimate of how long it will take to come to the station and relate this to the time detention is permitted, the time of day (i.e. whether the rest period under paragraph 12.2 is imminent) and the requirements of other investigations. If the solicitor is on their way or is to set off immediately, it will not normally be appropriate to begin an interview before they arrive. If it appears necessary to begin an interview before the solicitor's arrival, they should be given an indication of how long the police would be able to wait before 6.6(b) applies so there is an opportunity to make arrangements for someone else to provide legal advice.

6B A detainee has a right to free legal advice and to be represented by a solicitor. This Note for Guidance explains the arrangements which enable detainees to obtain legal advice. An outline of these arrangements is also included in the Notice of Rights and Entitlements given to detainees in accordance with paragraph 3.2. The arrangements also apply, with appropriate modifications, to persons attending a police station or other location voluntarily who are cautioned prior to being interviewed. See paragraph 3.21.

When a detainee asks for free legal advice, the Defence Solicitor Call Centre (DSCC) must be informed of the request.

Free legal advice will be limited to telephone advice provided by CDS Direct if a detainee is:

- *detained for a non-imprisonable offence;*
- *arrested on a bench warrant for failing to appear and being held for production at court (except where the solicitor has clear documentary evidence available that would result in the client being released from custody);*
- *arrested for drink driving (driving/in charge with excess alcohol, failing to provide a specimen, driving/in charge whilst unfit through drink), or*
- *detained in relation to breach of police or court bail conditions.*

unless one or more exceptions apply, in which case the DSCC should arrange for advice to be given by a solicitor at the police station, for example:

- *the police want to interview the detainee or carry out an eye-witness identification procedure;*
- *the detainee needs an appropriate adult;*
- *the detainee is unable to communicate over the telephone;*
- *the detainee alleges serious misconduct by the police;*
- *the investigation includes another offence not included in the list,*
- *the solicitor to be assigned is already at the police station.*

When free advice is not limited to telephone advice, a detainee can ask for free advice from a solicitor they know or if they do not know a solicitor or the solicitor they know cannot be contacted, from the duty solicitor.

To arrange free legal advice, the police should telephone the DSCC. The call centre will decide whether legal advice should be limited to telephone advice from CDS Direct, or whether a solicitor known to the detainee or the duty solicitor should speak to the detainee.

When a detainee wants to pay for legal advice themselves:

- *the DSCC will contact a solicitor of their choice on their behalf;*
- *they may, when free advice is only available by telephone from CDS Direct, still speak to a solicitor of their choice on the telephone for advice, but the solicitor would not be paid by legal aid and may ask the person to pay for the advice;*
- *they should be given an opportunity to consult a specific solicitor or another solicitor from that solicitor's firm. If this solicitor is not available, they may choose up to two alternatives. If these alternatives are not available, the custody officer has discretion to allow further attempts until a solicitor has been contacted and agreed to provide advice;*
- *they are entitled to a private consultation with their chosen solicitor on the telephone or the solicitor may decide to come to the police station;*
- *If their chosen solicitor cannot be contacted, the DSCC may still be called to arrange free legal advice.*

Apart from carrying out duties necessary to implement these arrangements, an officer must not advise the suspect about any particular firm of solicitors.

6B1 Not used

6B2 Not used

6C Not used

6D The solicitor's only role in the police station is to protect and advance the legal rights of their client. On occasions this may require the solicitor to give advice which has the effect of the client avoiding giving evidence which strengthens a prosecution case. The solicitor may intervene in order to seek clarification, challenge an improper question to their client or the manner in which it is put, advise their client not to reply to particular questions, or if they wish to give their client further legal advice. Paragraph 6.9 only applies if the solicitor's approach or conduct prevents or unreasonably obstructs proper questions being put to the suspect or the suspect's response being recorded. Examples of unacceptable conduct include answering questions on a suspect's behalf or providing written replies for the suspect to quote.

6E An officer who takes the decision to exclude a solicitor must be in a position to satisfy the court the decision was properly made. In order to do this they may need to witness what is happening.

6F If an officer of at least inspector rank considers a particular solicitor or firm of solicitors is persistently sending probationary representatives who are unsuited to provide legal advice, they should inform an officer of at least superintendent rank, who may wish to take the matter up with the Solicitors Regulatory Authority.

6G Subject to the constraints of Annex B, a solicitor may advise more than one client in an investigation if they wish. Any question of a conflict of interest is for the solicitor under their professional code of conduct. If, however, waiting for a solicitor to give advice to one client may lead to unreasonable delay to the interview with another, the provisions of paragraph 6.6(b) may apply.

6H In addition to a poster in English, a poster or posters containing translations into Welsh, the main minority ethnic languages and the principal European languages should be displayed wherever they are likely to be helpful and it is practicable to do so.

6I Not used

6J Whenever a detainee exercises their right to legal advice by consulting or communicating with a solicitor, they must be allowed to do so in private. This right to consult or communicate in private is fundamental. If the requirement for privacy is compromised because what is said or written by the detainee or solicitor for the purpose of giving and receiving legal advice is overheard, listened to, or read by others without the informed consent of the detainee, the right will effectively have been denied. When a detainee speaks to a solicitor on the telephone, they should be allowed to do so in private unless this is impractical because of the design and layout of the custody area or the location of telephones. However, the normal expectation should be that facilities will be available, unless they are being used, at all police stations to enable detainees to speak in private to a solicitor either face to face or over the telephone.

6K A detainee is not obliged to give reasons for declining legal advice and should not be pressed to do so.

7 Citizens of independent Commonwealth countries or foreign nationals

(a) Action

7.1 A detainee who is a citizen of an independent Commonwealth country or a national of a foreign country, including the Republic of Ireland, has the right, upon request, to communicate at any time with the appropriate High Commission, Embassy or Consulate. That detainee must be informed as soon as practicable of this right and asked if they want to have their High Commission, Embassy or Consulate told of their whereabouts and the grounds for their detention. Such a request should be acted upon as soon as practicable. See *Note 7A*.

7.2 A detainee who is is a citizen of a country with which a bilateral consular convention or agreement is in force requiring notification of arrest, must also be informed that subject to *paragraph 7.4*, notification of their arrest will be sent to the appropriate High Commission, Embassy or Consulate as soon as practicable, whether or not they request it. Details of the countries to which this requirement currently applies are available from: *http://www.fco.gov.uk/en/publications-and-documents/treaties/treaty-texts/prisoner-transfer-agreements*.

7.3 Consular officers may, if the detainee agrees, visit one of their nationals in police detention to talk to them and, if required, to arrange for legal advice. Such visits shall take place out of the hearing of a police officer.

7.4 Notwithstanding the provisions of consular conventions, if the detainee claims that they are a refugee or have applied or intend to apply for asylum, the custody officer must ensure that the United

Kingdom Borders Agency (UKBA) are informed as soon as practicable of the claim. UKBA will then determine whether compliance with relevant international obligations requires notification of arrest to be sent and will inform the custody officer as to what action police need to take.

(b) Documentation

7.5 A record shall be made:
- when a detainee is informed of their rights under this section and of any requirement in paragraph 7.2;
- of any communications with a High Commission, Embassy or Consulate, and
- of any communications with UKBA about a detainee's claim to be a refugee or to be seeking asylum and the resulting action taken by police.

Note for guidance

7A The exercise of the rights in this section may not be interfered with even though Annex B applies.

8 Conditions of detention

(a) Action

8.1 So far as it is practicable, not more than one detainee should be detained in each cell. See *Note 8C*

8.2 Cells in use must be adequately heated, cleaned and ventilated. They must be adequately lit, subject to such dimming as is compatible with safety and security to allow people detained overnight to sleep. No additional restraints shall be used within a locked cell unless absolutely necessary and then only restraint equipment, approved for use in that force by the Chief Officer, which is reasonable and necessary in the circumstances having regard to the detainee's demeanour and with a view to ensuring their safety and the safety of others. If a detainee is deaf, mentally disordered or otherwise mentally vulnerable, particular care must be taken when deciding whether to use any form of approved restraints.

8.3 Blankets, mattresses, pillows and other bedding supplied shall be of a reasonable standard and in a clean and sanitary condition. See *Note 8A*

8.4 Access to toilet and washing facilities must be provided.

8.5 If it is necessary to remove a detainee's clothes for the purposes of investigation, for hygiene, health reasons or cleaning, replacement clothing of a reasonable standard of comfort and cleanliness shall be provided. A detainee may not be interviewed unless adequate clothing has been offered.

8.6 At least two light meals and one main meal should be offered in any 24 hour period. See *Note 8B*. Drinks should be provided at meal times and upon reasonable request between meals. Whenever necessary, advice shall be sought from the appropriate healthcare professional, see *Note 9A*, on medical and dietary matters. As far as practicable, meals provided shall offer a varied diet and meet any specific dietary needs or religious beliefs the detainee may have. The detainee may, at the custody officer's discretion, have meals supplied by their family or friends at their expense. See *Note 8A*

8.7 Brief outdoor exercise shall be offered daily if practicable.

8.8 A juvenile shall not be placed in a police cell unless no other secure accommodation is available and the custody officer considers it is not practicable to supervise them if they are not placed in a cell or that a cell provides more comfortable accommodation than other secure accommodation in the station. A juvenile may not be placed in a cell with a detained adult.

(b) Documentation

8.9 A record must be kept of replacement clothing and meals offered.

8.10 If a juvenile is placed in a cell, the reason must be recorded.

8.11 The use of any restraints on a detainee whilst in a cell, the reasons for it and, if appropriate, the arrangements for enhanced supervision of the detainee whilst so restrained, shall be recorded. See *paragraph 3.9*

Notes for guidance

8A The provisions in paragraph 8.3 and 8.6 respectively are of particular importance in the case of a person likely to be detained for an extended period. In deciding whether to allow meals to be supplied by family or friends, the custody officer is entitled to take account of the risk of items being concealed in any food or package and the officer's duties and responsibilities under food handling legislation.

8B   Meals should, so far as practicable, be offered at recognised meal times, or at other times that take account of when the detainee last had a meal.

8C   Guidance on the Safer Detention and Handling of Persons in Police Custody Second Edition (2012) produced on behalf of the Association of Chief Police Officers by the provides more detailed guidance on matters concerning detainee healthcare and treatment and associated forensic issues which should be read in conjunction with sections 8 and 9 of this Code.

9   Care and treatment of detained persons

(a) General

9.1 Nothing in this section prevents the police from calling an appropriate healthcare professional to examine a detainee for the purposes of obtaining evidence relating to any offence in which the detainee is suspected of being involved. See *Notes 9A and 8C.*

9.2 If a complaint is made by, or on behalf of, a detainee about their treatment since their arrest, or it comes to notice that a detainee may have been treated improperly, a report must be made as soon as practicable to an officer of inspector rank or above not connected with the investigation. If the matter concerns a possible assault or the possibility of the unnecessary or unreasonable use of force, an appropriate healthcare professional must also be called as soon as practicable.

9.3 Detainees should be visited at least every hour. If no reasonably foreseeable risk was identified in a risk assessment, see *paragraphs 3.6–3.10*, there is no need to wake a sleeping detainee. Those suspected of being under the influence of drink or drugs or both or of having swallowed drugs, see *Note 9CA*, or whose level of consciousness causes concern must, subject to any clinical directions given by the appropriate healthcare professional, see *paragraph 9.13*:

- be visited and roused at least every half hour;
- have their condition assessed as in *Annex H;*
- and clinical treatment arranged if appropriate. See *Notes 9B, 9C* and *9H*

9.4 When arrangements are made to secure clinical attention for a detainee, the custody officer must make sure all relevant information which might assist in the treatment of the detainee's condition is made available to the responsible healthcare professional. This applies whether or not the healthcare professional asks for such information. Any officer or police staff with relevant information must inform the custody officer as soon as practicable.

(b) Clinical treatment and attention

9.5 The custody officer must make sure a detainee receives appropriate clinical attention as soon as reasonably practicable if the person:

- (a) appears to be suffering from physical illness; or
- (b) is injured; or
- (c) appears to be suffering from a mental disorder; or
- (d) appears to need clinical attention

9.5A This applies even if the detainee makes no request for clinical attention and whether or not they have already received clinical attention elsewhere. If the need for attention appears urgent, e.g. when indicated as in *Annex H*, the nearest available healthcare professional or an ambulance must be called immediately.

9.5B The custody officer must also consider the need for clinical attention as set out in Note for Guidance 9C in relation to those suffering the effects of alcohol or drugs.

9.6 *Paragraph 9.5* is not meant to prevent or delay the transfer to a hospital if necessary of a person detained under the Mental Health Act 1983, section 136. See *Note 9D*. When an assessment under that Act is to take place at a police station, see *paragraph 3.16*, the custody officer must consider whether an appropriate healthcare professional should be called to conduct an initial clinical check on the detainee. This applies particularly when there is likely to be any significant delay in the arrival of a suitably qualified medical practitioner.

9.7 If it appears to the custody officer, or they are told, that a person brought to a station under arrest may be suffering from an infectious disease or condition, the custody officer must take reasonable steps to safeguard the health of the detainee and others at the station. In deciding what action to take, advice must be sought from an appropriate healthcare professional. See *Note 9E*. The custody officer has discretion to isolate the person and their property until clinical directions have been obtained.

9.8 If a detainee requests a clinical examination, an appropriate healthcare professional must be called as soon as practicable to assess the detainee's clinical needs. If a safe and appropriate care plan cannot be provided, the appropriate healthcare professional's advice must be sought. The detainee may also be examined by a medical practitioner of their choice at their expense.

9.9 If a detainee is required to take or apply any medication in compliance with clinical directions prescribed before their detention, the custody officer must consult the appropriate healthcare professional before the use of the medication. Subject to the restrictions in *paragraph 9.10*, the custody officer is responsible for the safekeeping of any medication and for making sure the detainee is given the opportunity to take or apply prescribed or approved medication. Any such consultation and its outcome shall be noted in the custody record.

9.10 No police officer may administer or supervise the self-administration of medically prescribed controlled drugs of the types and forms listed in the Misuse of Drugs Regulations 2001, Schedule 2 or 3. A detainee may only self-administer such drugs under the personal supervision of the registered medical practitioner authorising their use or other appropriate healthcare professional. The custody officer may supervise the self-administration of, or authorise other custody staff to supervise the self-administration of, drugs listed in Schedule 4 or 5 for self-administration if the officer has consulted the appropriate healthcare professional authorising their use and both are satisfied self-administration will not expose the detainee, police officers or anyone else to the risk of harm or injury.

9.11 When appropriate healthcare professionals administer drugs or authorise the use of other medications, supervise their self-administration or consult with the custody officer about allowing self administration of drugs listed in Schedule 4 or 5, it must be within current medicines legislation and the scope of practice as determined by their relevant statutory regulatory body.

9.12 If a detainee has in their possession, or claims to need, medication relating to a heart condition, diabetes, epilepsy or a condition of comparable potential seriousness then, even though *paragraph 9.5* may not apply, the advice of the appropriate healthcare professional must be obtained.

9.13 Whenever the appropriate healthcare professional is called in accordance with this section to examine or treat a detainee, the custody officer shall ask for their opinion about:
- any risks or problems which police need to take into account when making decisions about the detainee's continued detention;
- when to carry out an interview if applicable; and
- the need for safeguards.

9.14 When clinical directions are given by the appropriate healthcare professional, whether orally or in writing, and the custody officer has any doubts or is in any way uncertain about any aspect of the directions, the custody officer shall ask for clarification. It is particularly important that directions concerning the frequency of visits are clear, precise and capable of being implemented. See *Note 9F*.

(c) Documentation

9.15 A record must be made in the custody record of:
- (a) the arrangements made for an examination by an appropriate healthcare professional under *paragraph 9.2* and of any complaint reported under that paragraph together with any relevant remarks by the custody officer;
- (b) any arrangements made in accordance with *paragraph 9.5*;
- (c) any request for a clinical examination under *paragraph 9.8* and any arrangements made in response;
- (d) the injury, ailment, condition or other reason which made it necessary to make the arrangements in (*a*) to (*c*); See *Note 9G*

    (e) any clinical directions and advice, including any further clarifications, given to police by a healthcare professional concerning the care and treatment of the detainee in connection with any of the arrangements made in (*a*) to (*c*); See *Notes E* and *9F*

    (f) if applicable, the responses received when attempting to rouse a person using the procedure in *Annex H*. See *Note 9H*

9.16 If a healthcare professional does not record their clinical findings in the custody record, the record must show where they are recorded. See *Note 9G*. However, information which is necessary to custody staff to ensure the effective ongoing care and well being of the detainee must be recorded openly in the custody record, see *paragraph 3.8* and *Annex G, paragraph 7*.

9.17 Subject to the requirements of *Section 4*, the custody record shall include:

- a record of all medication a detainee has in their possession on arrival at the police station;
- a note of any such medication they claim to need but do not have with them.

Notes for guidance

9A A 'healthcare professional' means a clinically qualified person working within the scope of practice as determined by their relevant statutory regulatory body. Whether a healthcare professional is 'appropriate' depends on the circumstances of the duties they carry out at the time.

9B Whenever possible juveniles and mentally vulnerable detainees should be visited more frequently.

9C A detainee who appears drunk or behaves abnormally may be suffering from illness, the effects of drugs or may have sustained injury, particularly a head injury which is not apparent. A detainee needing or dependent on certain drugs, including alcohol, may experience harmful effects within a short time of being deprived of their supply. In these circumstances, when there is any doubt, police should always act urgently to call an appropriate healthcare professional or an ambulance. Paragraph 9.5 does not apply to minor ailments or injuries which do not need attention. However, all such ailments or injuries must be recorded in the custody record and any doubt must be resolved in favour of calling the appropriate healthcare professional.

9CA Paragraph 9.3 would apply to a person in police custody by order of a magistrates' court under the Criminal Justice Act 1988, section 152 (as amended by the Drugs Act 2005, section 8) to facilitate the recovery of evidence after being charged with drug possession or drug trafficking and suspected of having swallowed drugs. In the case of the healthcare needs of a person who has swallowed drugs, the custody officer subject to any clinical directions, should consider the necessity for rousing every half hour. This does not negate the need for regular visiting of the suspect in the cell.

9D Whenever practicable, arrangements should be made for persons detained for assessment under the Mental Health Act 1983, section 136 to be taken to a hospital. Chapter 10 of the Mental Health Act 1983 Code of Practice (as revised) provides more detailed guidance about arranging assessments under section 136 and transferring detainees from police stations to other places of safety.

9E It is important to respect a person's right to privacy and information about their health must be kept confidential and only disclosed with their consent or in accordance with clinical advice when it is necessary to protect the detainee's health or that of others who come into contact with them.

9F The custody officer should always seek to clarify directions that the detainee requires constant observation or supervision and should ask the appropriate healthcare professional to explain precisely what action needs to be taken to implement such directions.

9G Paragraphs 9.15 and 9.16 do not require any information about the cause of any injury, ailment or condition to be recorded on the custody record if it appears capable of providing evidence of an offence.

9H The purpose of recording a person's responses when attempting to rouse them using the procedure in Annex H is to enable any change in the individual's consciousness level to be noted and clinical treatment arranged if appropriate.

10   Cautions

(a) When a caution must be given

10.1 A person whom there are grounds to suspect of an offence, see *Note 10A*, must be cautioned before any questions about an offence, or further questions if the answers provide the grounds for suspicion, are put to them if either the suspect's answers or silence, (i.e. failure or refusal to answer or answer satisfactorily) may be given in evidence to a court in a prosecution. A person need not be cautioned if questions are for other necessary purposes, e.g.:

    (a) solely to establish their identity or ownership of any vehicle;

    (b) to obtain information in accordance with any relevant statutory requirement, see *paragraph 10.9*;

    (c) in furtherance of the proper and effective conduct of a search, e.g. to determine the need to search in the exercise of powers of stop and search or to seek co-operation while carrying out a search;

    (d) to seek verification of a written record as in *paragraph 11.13*.

    (e) *Not used*

10.2 Whenever a person not under arrest is initially cautioned, or reminded they are under caution, that person must at the same time be told they are not under arrest and informed of the provisions of paragraph 3.21 which explain how they may obtain legal advice according to whether they are at a police station or elsewhere. See *Note 10C*

10.3 A person who is arrested, or further arrested, must be informed at the time if practicable, or if not, as soon as it becomes practicable thereafter, that they are under arrest and of the grounds and reasons for their arrest, see paragraph 3.4, *Note 10B* and *Code G, paragraphs 2.2 and 4.3*.

10.4 As required by *Code G, section 3*, a person who is arrested, or further arrested, must also be cautioned unless:

    (a) it is impracticable to do so by reason of their condition or behaviour at the time;

    (b) they have already been cautioned immediately prior to arrest as in *paragraph 10.1*.

(b) Terms of the cautions

10.5 The caution which must be given on:

    (a) arrest;

    (b) all other occasions before a person is charged or informed they may be prosecuted; see *section 16*,

should, unless the restriction on drawing adverse inferences from silence applies, see *Annex C*, be in the following terms:

    "You do not have to say anything. But it may harm your defence if you do not mention when questioned something which you later rely on in Court. Anything you do say may be given in evidence."

Where the use of the Welsh Language is appropriate, a constable may provide the caution directly in Welsh in the following terms:

    "Does dim rhaid i chi ddweud dim byd. Ond gall niweidio eich amddiffyniad os na fyddwch chi'n sôn, wrth gael eich holi, am rywbeth y byddwch chi'n dibynnu arno nes ymlaen yn y Llys. Gall unrhyw beth yr ydych yn ei ddweud gael ei roi fel tystiolaeth."

See *Note 10G*

10.6 *Annex C, paragraph 2* sets out the alternative terms of the caution to be used when the restriction on drawing adverse inferences from silence applies.

10.7 Minor deviations from the words of any caution given in accordance with this Code do not constitute a breach of this Code, provided the sense of the relevant caution is preserved. See *Note 10D*

10.8 After any break in questioning under caution, the person being questioned must be made aware they remain under caution. If there is any doubt the relevant caution should be given again in full when the interview resumes. See *Note 10E*

10.9 When, despite being cautioned, a person fails to co-operate or to answer particular questions which may affect their immediate treatment, the person should be informed of any relevant consequences and that those consequences are not affected by the caution. Examples are when a person's refusal to provide:

    • their name and address when charged may make them liable to detention;

    • particulars and information in accordance with a statutory requirement, e.g. under the Road Traffic Act 1988, may amount to an offence or may make the person liable to a further arrest.

(c) Special warnings under the Criminal Justice and Public Order Act 1994, sections 36 and 37

10.10 When a suspect interviewed at a police station or authorised place of detention after arrest fails or refuses to answer certain questions, or to answer satisfactorily, after due warning, see *Note 10F*, a court or jury may draw such inferences as appear proper under the Criminal Justice and Public Order Act 1994, sections 36 and 37. Such inferences may only be drawn when:

    (a) the restriction on drawing adverse inferences from silence, see *Annex C*, does not apply; and

    (b) the suspect is arrested by a constable and fails or refuses to account for any objects, marks or substances, or marks on such objects found:

- on their person;
- in or on their clothing or footwear;
- otherwise in their possession; or
- in the place they were arrested;

    (c) the arrested suspect was found by a constable at a place at or about the time the offence for which that officer has arrested them is alleged to have been committed, and the suspect fails or refuses to account for their presence there.

When the restriction on drawing adverse inferences from silence applies, the suspect may still be asked to account for any of the matters in (b) or (c) but the special warning described in *paragraph 10.11* will not apply and must not be given.

10.11 For an inference to be drawn when a suspect fails or refuses to answer a question about one of these matters or to answer it satisfactorily, the suspect must first be told in ordinary language:

    (a) what offence is being investigated;

    (b) what fact they are being asked to account for;

    (c) this fact may be due to them taking part in the commission of the offence;

    (d) a court may draw a proper inference if they fail or refuse to account for this fact;

    (e) a record is being made of the interview and it may be given in evidence if they are brought to trial.

(d) Juveniles and persons who are mentally disordered or otherwise mentally vulnerable

10.11A The information required in paragraph 10.11 must not be given to a suspect who is a juvenile or who is mentally disordered or otherwise mentally vulnerable unless the appropriate adult is present.

10.12 If a juvenile or a person who is mentally disordered or otherwise mentally vulnerable is cautioned in the absence of the appropriate adult, the caution must be repeated in the adult's presence.

(e) Documentation

10.13 A record shall be made when a caution is given under this section, either in the interviewer's pocket book or in the interview record.

Notes for guidance

10A There must be some reasonable, objective grounds for the suspicion, based on known facts or information which are relevant to the likelihood the offence has been committed and the person to be questioned committed it.

10B An arrested person must be given sufficient information to enable them to understand that they have been deprived of their liberty and the reason they have been arrested, e.g. when a person is arrested on suspicion of committing an offence they must be informed of the suspected offence's nature, when and where it was committed. The suspect must also be informed of the reason or reasons why the arrest is considered necessary. Vague or technical language should be avoided.

10C The restriction on drawing inferences from silence, see Annex C, paragraph 1, does not apply to a person who has not been detained and who therefore cannot be prevented from seeking legal advice if they want, see paragraph 3.21.

10D If it appears a person does not understand the caution, the person giving it should explain it in their own words.

10E *It may be necessary to show to the court that nothing occurred during an interview break or between interviews which influenced the suspect's recorded evidence. After a break in an interview or at the beginning of a subsequent interview, the interviewing officer should summarise the reason for the break and confirm this with the suspect.*

10F *The Criminal Justice and Public Order Act 1994, sections 36 and 37 apply only to suspects who have been arrested by a constable or an officer of Revenue and Customs officer and are given the relevant warning by the police or Revenue and Customs officer who made the arrest or who is investigating the offence. They do not apply to any interviews with suspects who have not been arrested.*

10G *Nothing in this Code requires a caution to be given or repeated when informing a person not under arrest they may be prosecuted for an offence. However, a court will not be able to draw any inferences under the Criminal Justice and Public Order Act 1994, section 34, if the person was not cautioned.*

11 Interviews—general

(a) Action

11.1A An interview is the questioning of a person regarding their involvement or suspected involvement in a criminal offence or offences which, under *paragraph 10.1*, must be carried out under caution. Whenever a person is interviewed they must be informed of the nature of the offence, or further offence. Procedures under the Road Traffic Act 1988, section 7 or the Transport and Works Act 1992, section 31 do not constitute interviewing for the purpose of this Code.

11.1 Following a decision to arrest a suspect, they must not be interviewed about the relevant offence except at a police station or other authorised place of detention, unless the consequent delay would be likely to:

    (a) lead to:
- interference with, or harm to, evidence connected with an offence;
- interference with, or physical harm to, other people; or
- serious loss of, or damage to, property;

    (b) lead to alerting other people suspected of committing an offence but not yet arrested for it; or

    (c) hinder the recovery of property obtained in consequence of the commission of an offence.

Interviewing in any of these circumstances shall cease once the relevant risk has been averted or the necessary questions have been put in order to attempt to avert that risk.

11.2 Immediately prior to the commencement or re-commencement of any interview at a police station or other authorised place of detention, the interviewer should remind the suspect of their entitlement to free legal advice and that the interview can be delayed for legal advice to be obtained, unless one of the exceptions in *paragraph 6.6* applies. It is the interviewer's responsibility to make sure all reminders are recorded in the interview record.

11.3 *Not used*

11.4 At the beginning of an interview the interviewer, after cautioning the suspect, see *section 10*, shall put to them any significant statement or silence which occurred in the presence and hearing of a police officer or other police staff before the start of the interview and which have not been put to the suspect in the course of a previous interview. See *Note 11A*. The interviewer shall ask the suspect whether they confirm or deny that earlier statement or silence and if they want to add anything.

11.4A A significant statement is one which appears capable of being used in evidence against the suspect, in particular a direct admission of guilt. A significant silence is a failure or refusal to answer a question or answer satisfactorily when under caution, which might, allowing for the restriction on drawing adverse inferences from silence, see *Annex C*, give rise to an inference under the Criminal Justice and Public Order Act 1994, Part III.

11.5 No interviewer may try to obtain answers or elicit a statement by the use of oppression. Except as in *paragraph 10.9*, no interviewer shall indicate, except to answer a direct question, what action will be taken by the police if the person being questioned answers questions, makes a statement or refuses to do either. If the person asks directly what action will be taken if they answer questions, make a statement or refuse to do either, the interviewer may inform them what action the police propose to take provided that action is itself proper and warranted.

11.6 The interview or further interview of a person about an offence with which that person has not been charged or for which they have not been informed they may be prosecuted, must cease when:

    (a) the officer in charge of the investigation is satisfied all the questions they consider relevant to obtaining accurate and reliable information about the offence have been put to the suspect, this includes allowing the suspect an opportunity to give an innocent explanation and asking questions to test if the explanation is accurate and reliable, e.g. to clear up ambiguities or clarify what the suspect said;

    (b) the officer in charge of the investigation has taken account of any other available evidence; and

    (c) the officer in charge of the investigation, or in the case of a detained suspect, the custody officer, see *paragraph 16.1*, reasonably believes there is sufficient evidence to provide a realistic prospect of conviction for that offence. See *Note 11B*

This paragraph does not prevent officers in revenue cases or acting under the confiscation provisions of the Criminal Justice Act 1988 or the Drug Trafficking Act 1994 from inviting suspects to complete a formal question and answer record after the interview is concluded.

(b) Interview records

11.7 (a) An accurate record must be made of each interview, whether or not the interview takes place at a police station.

    (b) The record must state the place of interview, the time it begins and ends, any interview breaks and, subject to *paragraph 2.6A*, the names of all those present; and must be made on the forms provided for this purpose or in the interviewer's pocket book or in accordance with the Codes of Practice E or F.

    (c) Any written record must be made and completed during the interview, unless this would not be practicable or would interfere with the conduct of the interview, and must constitute either a verbatim record of what has been said or, failing this, an account of the interview which adequately and accurately summarises it.

11.8 If a written record is not made during the interview it must be made as soon as practicable after its completion.

11.9 Written interview records must be timed and signed by the maker.

11.10 If a written record is not completed during the interview the reason must be recorded in the interview record.

11.11 Unless it is impracticable, the person interviewed shall be given the opportunity to read the interview record and to sign it as correct or to indicate how they consider it inaccurate. If the person interviewed cannot read or refuses to read the record or sign it, the senior interviewer present shall read it to them and ask whether they would like to sign it as correct or make their mark or to indicate how they consider it inaccurate. The interviewer shall certify on the interview record itself what has occurred. See *Note 11E*

11.12 If the appropriate adult or the person's solicitor is present during the interview, they should also be given an opportunity to read and sign the interview record or any written statement taken down during the interview.

11.13 A written record shall be made of any comments made by a suspect, including unsolicited comments, which are outside the context of an interview but which might be relevant to the offence. Any such record must be timed and signed by the maker. When practicable the suspect shall be given the opportunity to read that record and to sign it as correct or to indicate how they consider it inaccurate. See *Note 11E*

11.14 Any refusal by a person to sign an interview record when asked in accordance with this Code must itself be recorded.

(c) Juveniles and mentally disordered or otherwise mentally vulnerable people

11.15 A juvenile or person who is mentally disordered or otherwise mentally vulnerable must not be interviewed regarding their involvement or suspected involvement in a criminal offence or offences, or asked to provide or sign a written statement under caution or record of interview, in the absence of the appropriate adult unless *paragraphs 11.1, 11.18 to 11.20* apply. See *Note 11C*

11.16 Juveniles may only be interviewed at their place of education in exceptional circumstances and only when the principal or their nominee agrees. Every effort should be made to notify the parent(s) or other person responsible for the juvenile's welfare and the appropriate adult, if this is a different person, that the police want to interview the juvenile and reasonable time should be allowed to enable the appropriate adult to be present at the interview. If awaiting the appropriate adult would cause unreasonable delay, and unless the juvenile is suspected of an offence against the educational establishment, the principal or their nominee can act as the appropriate adult for the purposes of the interview.

11.17 If an appropriate adult is present at an interview, they shall be informed:
- they are not expected to act simply as an observer; and
- the purpose of their presence is to:
  - advise the person being interviewed;
  - observe whether the interview is being conducted properly and fairly;
  - facilitate communication with the person being interviewed.

(d) Vulnerable suspects—urgent interviews at police stations

11.18 The following persons may not be interviewed unless an officer of superintendent rank or above considers delay will lead to the consequences in *paragraph 11.1(a) to (c)*, and is satisfied the interview would not significantly harm the person's physical or mental state (see Annex G):
- (a) a juvenile or person who is mentally disordered or otherwise mentally vulnerable if at the time of the interview the appropriate adult is not present;
- (b) anyone other than in (*a*) who at the time of the interview appears unable to:
  - appreciate the significance of questions and their answers; or
  - understand what is happening because of the effects of drink, drugs or any illness, ailment or condition;
- (c) a person who has difficulty understanding English or has a hearing disability, if at the time of the interview an interpreter is not present.

11.19 These interviews may not continue once sufficient information has been obtained to avert the consequences in *paragraph 11.1(a) to (c)*.

11.20 A record shall be made of the grounds for any decision to interview a person under *paragraph 11.18*.

Notes for guidance

11A Paragraph 11.4 does not prevent the interviewer from putting significant statements and silences to a suspect again at a later stage or a further interview.

11B The Criminal Procedure and Investigations Act 1996 Code of Practice, paragraph 3.5 states 'In conducting an investigation, the investigator should pursue all reasonable lines of enquiry, whether these point towards or away from the suspect. What is reasonable will depend on the particular circumstances.' Interviewers should keep this in mind when deciding what questions to ask in an interview.

11C Although juveniles or people who are mentally disordered or otherwise mentally vulnerable are often capable of providing reliable evidence, they may, without knowing or wishing to do so, be particularly prone in certain circumstances to provide information that may be unreliable, misleading or self-incriminating. Special care should always be taken when questioning such a person, and the appropriate adult should be involved if there is any doubt about a person's age, mental state or capacity. Because of the risk of unreliable evidence it is also important to obtain corroboration of any facts admitted whenever possible.

11D Juveniles should not be arrested at their place of education unless this is unavoidable. When a juvenile is arrested at their place of education, the principal or their nominee must be informed.

11E Significant statements described in paragraph 11.4 will always be relevant to the offence and must be recorded. When a suspect agrees to read records of interviews and other comments and sign them as correct, they should be asked to endorse the record with, e.g. 'I agree that this is a correct record of what was said' and add their signature. If the suspect does not agree with the record, the interviewer should record the details of any disagreement and ask the suspect to read these details and sign them to the effect that they accurately reflect their disagreement. Any refusal to sign should be recorded.

12   Interviews in police stations

(a) Action

12.1 If a police officer wants to interview or conduct enquiries which require the presence of a detainee, the custody officer is responsible for deciding whether to deliver the detainee into the officer's custody. An investigating officer who is given custody of a detainee takes over responsibility for the detainee's care and safe custody for the purposes of this Code until they return the detainee to the custody officer when they must report the manner in which they complied with the Code whilst having custody of the detainee.

12.2 Except as below, in any period of 24 hours a detainee must be allowed a continuous period of at least 8 hours for rest, free from questioning, travel or any interruption in connection with the investigation concerned. This period should normally be at night or other appropriate time which takes account of when the detainee last slept or rested. If a detainee is arrested at a police station after going there voluntarily, the period of 24 hours runs from the time of their arrest and not the time of arrival at the police station. The period may not be interrupted or delayed, except:

    (a) when there are reasonable grounds for believing not delaying or interrupting the period would:

        (i)   involve a risk of harm to people or serious loss of, or damage to, property;

        (ii) delay unnecessarily the person's release from custody;

        (iii) otherwise prejudice the outcome of the investigation;

    (b) at the request of the detainee, their appropriate adult or legal representative;

    (c) when a delay or interruption is necessary in order to:

        (i)   comply with the legal obligations and duties arising under *section 15*;

        (ii) to take action required under *section 9* or in accordance with medical advice.

If the period is interrupted in accordance with *(a)*, a fresh period must be allowed. Interruptions under *(b)* and *(c)*, do not require a fresh period to be allowed.

12.3 Before a detainee is interviewed the custody officer, in consultation with the officer in charge of the investigation and appropriate healthcare professionals as necessary, shall assess whether the detainee is fit enough to be interviewed. This means determining and considering the risks to the detainee's physical and mental state if the interview took place and determining what safeguards are needed to allow the interview to take place. See *Annex G*. The custody officer shall not allow a detainee to be interviewed if the custody officer considers it would cause significant harm to the detainee's physical or mental state. Vulnerable suspects listed at *paragraph 11.18* shall be treated as always being at some risk during an interview and these persons may not be interviewed except in accordance with *paragraphs 11.18* to *11.20*.

12.4 As far as practicable interviews shall take place in interview rooms which are adequately heated, lit and ventilated.

12.5 A suspect whose detention without charge has been authorised under PACE, because the detention is necessary for an interview to obtain evidence of the offence for which they have been arrested, may choose not to answer questions but police do not require the suspect's consent or agreement to interview them for this purpose. If a suspect takes steps to prevent themselves being questioned or further questioned, e.g. by refusing to leave their cell to go to a suitable interview room or by trying to leave the interview room, they shall be advised their consent or agreement to interview is not required. The suspect shall be cautioned as in *section 10*, and informed if they fail or refuse to co-operate, the interview may take place in the cell and that their failure or refusal to co-operate may be given in evidence. The suspect shall then be invited to co-operate and go into the interview room.

12.6 People being questioned or making statements shall not be required to stand.

12.7 Before the interview commences each interviewer shall, subject to *paragraph 2.6A*, identify themselves and any other persons present to the interviewee.

12.8 Breaks from interviewing should be made at recognised meal times or at other times that take account of when an interviewee last had a meal. Short refreshment breaks shall be provided at approximately two hour intervals, subject to the interviewer's discretion to delay a break if there are reasonable grounds for believing it would:

  (i)   involve a:
    • risk of harm to people;
    • serious loss of, or damage to, property;
  (ii) unnecessarily delay the detainee's release;
  (iii) otherwise prejudice the outcome of the investigation.

See Note 12B

12.9 If during the interview a complaint is made by or on behalf of the interviewee concerning the provisions of any of the Codes, or it comes to the interviewer's notice that the interviewee may have been treated improperly, the interviewer should:

  (i)   record the matter in the interview record;
  (ii) inform the custody officer, who is then responsible for dealing with it as in *section 9*.

(b) Documentation

12.10 A record must be made of the:
    • time a detainee is not in the custody of the custody officer, and why
    • reason for any refusal to deliver the detainee out of that custody.

12.11 A record shall be made of:

  (a) the reasons it was not practicable to use an interview room; and
  (b) any action taken as in *paragraph 12.5*.

The record shall be made on the custody record or in the interview record for action taken whilst an interview record is being kept, with a brief reference to this effect in the custody record.

12.12 Any decision to delay a break in an interview must be recorded, with reasons, in the interview record.

12.13 All written statements made at police stations under caution shall be written on forms provided for the purpose.

12.14 All written statements made under caution shall be taken in accordance with *Annex D*. Before a person makes a written statement under caution at a police station they shall be reminded about the right to legal advice. See *Note 12A*

Notes for guidance

12A It is not normally necessary to ask for a written statement if the interview was recorded in writing and the record signed in accordance with paragraph 11.11 or audibly or visually recorded in accordance with Code E or F. Statements under caution should be taken in these circumstances only at the person's express wish. A person may however be asked if they want to make such a statement.

12B Meal breaks should normally last at least 45 minutes and shorter breaks after two hours should last at least 15 minutes. If the interviewer delays a break in accordance with paragraph 12.8 and prolongs the interview, a longer break should be provided. If there is a short interview, and another short interview is contemplated, the length of the break may be reduced if there are reasonable grounds to believe this is necessary to avoid any of the consequences in paragraph 12.8(i) to (iii).

13 Interpreters

(a) General

13.1 Chief officers are responsible for making sure appropriate arrangements are in place for provision of suitably qualified interpreters for people who:
    • are deaf;
    • do not understand English.

See *Note 13A*

(b) Foreign languages

13.2 Unless *paragraphs 11.1, 11.18* to *11.20* apply, a person must not be interviewed in the absence of a person capable of interpreting if:

(a) they have difficulty understanding English;

(b) the interviewer cannot speak the person's own language;

(c) the person wants an interpreter present.

13.3 The interviewer shall make sure the interpreter makes a note of the interview at the time in the person's language for use in the event of the interpreter being called to give evidence, and certifies its accuracy. The interviewer should allow sufficient time for the interpreter to note each question and answer after each is put, given and interpreted. The person should be allowed to read the record or have it read to them and sign it as correct or indicate the respects in which they consider it inaccurate. If the interview is audibly recorded or visually recorded, the arrangements in Code E or F apply.

13.4 In the case of a person making a statement to a police officer or other police staff other than in English:

(a) the interpreter shall record the statement in the language it is made;

(b) the person shall be invited to sign it;

(c) an official English translation shall be made in due course.

(c) Deaf people and people with speech difficulties

13.5 If a person appears to be deaf or there is doubt about their hearing or speaking ability, they must not be interviewed in the absence of an interpreter unless they agree in writing to being interviewed without one or *paragraphs 11.1, 11.18* to *11.20* apply.

13.6 An interpreter should also be called if a juvenile is interviewed and the parent or guardian present as the appropriate adult appears to be deaf or there is doubt about their hearing or speaking ability, unless they agree in writing to the interview proceeding without one or *paragraphs 11.1, 11.18* to *11.20* apply.

13.7 The interviewer shall make sure the interpreter is allowed to read the interview record and certify its accuracy in the event of the interpreter being called to give evidence. If the interview is audibly recorded or visually recorded, the arrangements in Code E or F apply.

(d) Additional rules for detained persons

13.8 All reasonable attempts should be made to make the detainee understand that interpreters will be provided at public expense.

13.9 If *paragraph 6.1* applies and the detainee cannot communicate with the solicitor because of language, hearing or speech difficulties, an interpreter must be called. The interpreter may not be a police officer or any other police staff when interpretation is needed for the purposes of obtaining legal advice. In all other cases a police officer or other police staff may only interpret if the detainee and the appropriate adult, if applicable, give their agreement in writing or if the interview is audibly recorded or visually recorded as in Code E or F.

13.10 When the custody officer cannot establish effective communication with a person charged with an offence who appears deaf or there is doubt about their ability to hear, speak or to understand English, arrangements must be made as soon as practicable for an interpreter to explain the offence and any other information given by the custody officer.

(e) Documentation

13.11 Action taken to call an interpreter under this section and any agreement to be interviewed in the absence of an interpreter must be recorded.

Note for guidance

13A Whenever possible, interpreters should be provided in accordance with national arrangements approved or prescribed by the Secretary of State.

14 Questioning—special restrictions

14.1 If a person is arrested by one police force on behalf of another and the lawful period of detention in respect of that offence has not yet commenced in accordance with PACE, section 41 no questions may be put to them about the offence while they are in transit between the forces except to clarify any voluntary statement they make.

14.2 If a person is in police detention at a hospital they may not be questioned without the agreement of a responsible doctor. See *Note 14A*

Note for guidance

14A *If questioning takes place at a hospital under paragraph 14.2, or on the way to or from a hospital, the period of questioning concerned counts towards the total period of detention permitted.*

15 Reviews and extensions of detention

(a) Persons detained under PACE

15.1 The review officer is responsible under PACE, section 40 for periodically determining if a person's detention, before or after charge, continues to be necessary. This requirement continues throughout the detention period and except as in *paragraph 15.10*, the review officer must be present at the police station holding the detainee. See *Notes 15A* and *15B*

15.2 Under PACE, section 42, an officer of superintendent rank or above who is responsible for the station holding the detainee may give authority any time after the second review to extend the maximum period the person may be detained without charge by up to 12 hours. Further detention without charge may be authorised only by a magistrates' court in accordance with PACE, sections 43 and 44. See *Notes 15C, 15D* and *15E*

15.2A An authorisation under section 42(1) of PACE extends the maximum period of detention permitted before charge for indictable offences from 24 hours to 36 hours. Detaining a juvenile or mentally vulnerable person for longer than 24 hours will be dependent on the circumstances of the case and with regard to the person's:

    (a) special vulnerability;

    (b) the legal obligation to provide an opportunity for representations to be made prior to a decision about extending detention;

    (c) the need to consult and consider the views of any appropriate adult; and

    (d) any alternatives to police custody.

15.3 Before deciding whether to authorise continued detention the officer responsible under *paragraph 15.1* or *15.2* shall give an opportunity to make representations about the detention to:

    (a) the detainee, unless in the case of a review as in *paragraph 15.1*, the detainee is asleep;

    (b) the detainee's solicitor if available at the time; and

    (c) the appropriate adult if available at the time.

See *Note 15CA*

15.3A Other people having an interest in the detainee's welfare may also make representations at the authorising officer's discretion.

15.3B Subject to *paragraph 15.10*, the representations may be made orally in person or by telephone or in writing. The authorising officer may, however, refuse to hear oral representations from the detainee if the officer considers them unfit to make representations because of their condition or behaviour. See *Note 15C*

15.3C The decision on whether the review takes place in person or by telephone or by video conferencing (see *Note 15G*) is a matter for the review officer. In determining the form the review may take, the review officer must always take full account of the needs of the person in custody. The benefits of carrying out a review in person should always be considered, based on the individual circumstances of each case with specific additional consideration if the person is:

    (a) a juvenile (and the age of the juvenile); or

    (b) suspected of being mentally vulnerable; or

(c) in need of medical attention for other than routine minor ailments; or

(d) subject to presentational or community issues around their detention.

15.4 Before conducting a review or determining whether to extend the maximum period of detention without charge, the officer responsible must make sure the detainee is reminded of their entitlement to free legal advice, see *paragraph 6.5,* unless in the case of a review the person is asleep.

15.5 If, after considering any representations, the review officer under *paragraph 15.1* decides to keep the detainee in detention or the superintendent under *paragraph 15.2* extends the maximum period for which they may be detained without charge, then any comment made by the detainee shall be recorded. If applicable, the officer shall be informed of the comment as soon as practicable. See also *paragraphs 11.4* and *11.13*

15.6 No officer shall put specific questions to the detainee:

- regarding their involvement in any offence; or
- in respect of any comments they may make:
  — when given the opportunity to make representations; or
  — in response to a decision to keep them in detention or extend the maximum period of detention.

Such an exchange could constitute an interview as in *paragraph 11.1A* and would be subject to the associated safeguards in *section 11* and, in respect of a person who has been charged, *paragraph 16.5.* See also *paragraph 11.13.*

15.7 A detainee who is asleep at a review, see *paragraph 15.1,* and whose continued detention is authorised must be informed about the decision and reason as soon as practicable after waking.

15.8 *Not used*

(b) *Review of detention by telephone and video conferencing facilities*

15.9 PACE, section 40A provides that the officer responsible under section 40 for reviewing the detention of a person who has not been charged, need not attend the police station holding the detainee and may carry out the review by telephone.

15.9A PACE, section 45A(2) provides that the officer responsible under section 40 for reviewing the detention of a person who has not been charged, need not attend the police station holding the detainee and may carry out the review by video conferencing facilities (See *Note 15G*).

15.9B A telephone review is not permitted where facilities for review by video conferencing exist and it is practicable to use them.

15.9C The review officer can decide at any stage that a telephone review or review by video conferencing should be terminated and that the review will be conducted in person. The reasons for doing so should be noted in the custody record.

See *Note 15F*

15.10 When a review is carried out by telephone or by video conferencing facilities, an officer at the station holding the detainee shall be required by the review officer to fulfil that officer's obligations under PACE section 40 and this Code by:

(a) making any record connected with the review in the detainee's custody record;

(b) if applicable, making the record in (*a*) in the presence of the detainee; and

(c) for a review by telephone, giving the detainee information about the review.

15.11 When a review is carried out by telephone or by video conferencing facilities, the requirement in *paragraph 15.3* will be satisfied:

(a) if facilities exist for the immediate transmission of written representations to the review officer, e.g. fax or email message, by allowing those who are given the opportunity to make representations, to make their representations:

(i) orally by telephone or (as the case may be) by means of the video conferencing facilities; or

(ii) in writing using the facilities for the immediate transmission of written representations; and

(b) in all other cases, by allowing those who are given the opportunity to make representations, to make their representations orally by telephone or by means of the video conferencing facilities.

(c) Documentation

15.12 It is the officer's responsibility to make sure all reminders given under *paragraph 15.4* are noted in the custody record.

15.13 The grounds for, and extent of, any delay in conducting a review shall be recorded.

15.14 When a review is carried out by telephone or video conferencing facilities, a record shall be made of:

(a) the reason the review officer did not attend the station holding the detainee;

(b) the place the review officer was;

(c) the method representations, oral or written, were made to the review officer, see *paragraph 15.11*.

15.15 Any written representations shall be retained.

15.16 A record shall be made as soon as practicable of:

(a) the outcome of each review of detention before or after charge, and if *paragraph 15.7* applies, of when the person was informed and by whom;

(b) the outcome of any determination under PACE, section 42 by a superintendent whether to extend the maximum period of detention without charge beyond 24 hours from the relevant time. If an authorisation is given, the record shall state the number of hours and minutes by which the detention period is extended or further extended.

(c) the outcome of each application under PACE, section 43, for a warrant of further detention or under section 44, for an extension or further extension of that warrant. If a warrant for further detention is granted under section 43 or extended or further extended under 44, the record shall state the detention period authorised by the warrant and the date and time it was granted or (as the case may be) the period by which the warrant is extended or further extended.

Note: Any period during which a person is released on bail does not count towards the maximum period of detention without charge allowed under PACE, sections 41 to 44.

Notes for guidance

15A *Review officer for the purposes of:*

- *PACE, sections 40, 40A and 45A means, in the case of a person arrested but not charged, an officer of at least inspector rank not directly involved in the investigation and, if a person has been arrested and charged, the custody officer.*

15B *The detention of persons in police custody not subject to the statutory review requirement in paragraph 15.1 should still be reviewed periodically as a matter of good practice. Such reviews can be carried out by an officer of the rank of sergeant or above. The purpose of such reviews is to check the particular power under which a detainee is held continues to apply, any associated conditions are complied with and to make sure appropriate action is taken to deal with any changes. This includes the detainee's prompt release when the power no longer applies, or their transfer if the power requires the detainee be taken elsewhere as soon as the necessary arrangements are made. Examples include persons:*

(a) *arrested on warrant because they failed to answer bail to appear at court;*

(b) *arrested under the Bail Act 1976, section 7(3) for breaching a condition of bail granted after charge;*

(c) *in police custody for specific purposes and periods under the Crime (Sentences) Act 1997, Schedule 1;*

(d) *convicted, or remand prisoners, held in police stations on behalf of the Prison Service under the Imprisonment (Temporary Provisions) Act 1980, section 6;*

(e) *being detained to prevent them causing a breach of the peace;*

(f) *detained at police stations on behalf of the Immigration Service;*

(g) *detained by order of a magistrates court under the Criminal Justice Act 1988, section 152 (as amended by the Drugs Act 2005, section 8) to facilitate the recovery of evidence after being charged with drug possession or drug trafficking and suspected of having swallowed drugs.*

The detention of persons remanded into police detention by order of a court under the Magistrates' Courts Act 1980, section 128 is subject to a statutory requirement to review that detention. This is to make sure the detainee is taken back to court no later than the end of the period authorised by the court or when the need for their detention by police ceases, whichever is the sooner.

15C In the case of a review of detention, but not an extension, the detainee need not be woken for the review. However, if the detainee is likely to be asleep, e.g. during a period of rest allowed as in paragraph 12.2, at the latest time a review or authorisation to extend detention may take place, the officer should, if the legal obligations and time constraints permit, bring forward the procedure to allow the detainee to make representations. A detainee not asleep during the review must be present when the grounds for their continued detention are recorded and must at the same time be informed of those grounds unless the review officer considers the person is incapable of understanding what is said, violent or likely to become violent or in urgent need of medical attention.

15CA In paragraph 15.3(b) and (c), 'available' includes being contactable in time to enable them to make representations remotely by telephone or other electronic means or in person by attending the station. Reasonable efforts should therefore be made to give the solicitor and appropriate adult sufficient notice of the time the decision is expected to be made so that they can make themselves available.

15D An application to a Magistrates' Court under PACE, sections 43 or 44 for a warrant of further detention or its extension should be made between 10am and 9pm, and if possible during normal court hours. It will not usually be practicable to arrange for a court to sit specially outside the hours of 10am to 9pm. If it appears a special sitting may be needed outside normal court hours but between 10am and 9pm, the clerk to the justices should be given notice and informed of this possibility, while the court is sitting if possible.

15E In paragraph 15.2, the officer responsible for the station holding the detainee includes a superintendent or above who, in accordance with their force operational policy or police regulations, is given that responsibility on a temporary basis whilst the appointed long-term holder is off duty or otherwise unavailable.

15F The provisions of PACE, section 40A allowing telephone reviews do not apply to reviews of detention after charge by the custody officer. When video conferencing is not required, they allow the use of a telephone to carry out a review of detention before charge. The procedure under PACE, section 42 must be done in person.

15G Video conferencing facilities means any facilities (whether a live television link or other facilities) by means of which the review can be carried out with the review officer, the detainee concerned and the detainee's solicitor all being able to both see and to hear each other. The use of video conferencing facilities for decisions about detention under section 45A of PACE is subject to regulations made by the Secretary of State being in force.

16   Charging detained persons

(a) Action

16.1 When the officer in charge of the investigation reasonably believes there is sufficient evidence to provide a realistic prospect of conviction for the offence (see *paragraph 11.6*), they shall without delay, and subject to the following qualification, inform the custody officer who will be responsible for considering whether the detainee should be charged. See *Notes 11B* and *16A*. When a person is detained in respect of more than one offence it is permissible to delay informing the custody officer until the above conditions are satisfied in respect of all the offences, but see *paragraph 11.6*. If the detainee is a juvenile, mentally disordered or otherwise mentally vulnerable, any resulting action shall be taken in the presence of the appropriate adult if they are present at the time. See *Notes 16B* and *16C*

16.1A Where guidance issued by the Director of Public Prosecutions under PACE, section 37A is in force the custody officer must comply with that Guidance in deciding how to act in dealing with the detainee. See *Notes 16AA* and *16AB*

16.1B Where in compliance with the DPP's Guidance the custody officer decides that the case should be immediately referred to the CPS to make the charging decision, consultation should take place with a Crown Prosecutor as soon as is reasonably practicable. Where the Crown Prosecutor is unable to make the charging decision on the information available at that time, the detainee may be released without charge and on bail (with conditions if necessary) under section 37(7)(a). In such circumstances, the detainee should be informed that they are being released to enable the Director of Public Prosecutions to make a decision under section 37B.

16.2 When a detainee is charged with or informed they may be prosecuted for an offence, see *Note 16B,* they shall, unless the restriction on drawing adverse inferences from silence applies, see *Annex C,* be cautioned as follows:

> 'You do not have to say anything. But it may harm your defence if you do not mention now some-thing which you later rely on in court. Anything you do say may be given in evidence.'

Where the use of the Welsh Language is appropriate, a constable may provide the caution directly in Welsh in the following terms:

> 'Does dim rhaid i chi ddweud dim byd. Ond gall niweidio eich amddiffyniad os na fyddwch chi'n sôn, yn awr, am rywbeth y byddwch chi'n dibynnu arno nes ymlaen yn y llys. Gall unrhyw beth yr ydych yn ei ddweud gael ei roi fel tystiolaeth.'

Annex C, paragraph 2 sets out the alternative terms of the caution to be used when the restriction on drawing adverse inferences from silence applies.

16.3 When a detainee is charged they shall be given a written notice showing particulars of the offence and, subject to *paragraph 2.6A,* the officer's name and the case reference number. As far as possible the particulars of the charge shall be stated in simple terms, but they shall also show the pre-cise offence in law with which the detainee is charged. The notice shall begin:

> 'You are charged with the offence(s) shown below.'

Followed by the caution. If the detainee is a juvenile, mentally disordered or otherwise mentally vulnerable, a copy of the notice should also be given to the appropriate adult.

16.4 If, after a detainee has been charged with or informed they may be prosecuted for an offence, an officer wants to tell them about any written statement or interview with another person relating to such an offence, the detainee shall either be handed a true copy of the written statement or the content of the inter-view record brought to their attention. Nothing shall be done to invite any reply or comment except to:

> (a) caution the detainee, *'You do not have to say anything, but anything you do say may be given in evidence.';*
> Where the use of the Welsh Language is appropriate, caution the detainee in the follow-ing terms:
> *'Does dim rhaid i chi ddweud dim byd, ond gall unrhyw beth yr ydych yn ei ddweud gael ei roi fel tystiolaeth.'*
> and
> (b) remind the detainee about their right to legal advice.

16.4A If the detainee:

- cannot read, the document may be read to them
- is a juvenile, mentally disordered or otherwise mentally vulnerable, the appropriate adult shall also be given a copy, or the interview record shall be brought to their attention

16.5 A detainee may not be interviewed about an offence after they have been charged with, or informed they may be prosecuted for it, unless the interview is necessary:

- to prevent or minimise harm or loss to some other person, or the public
- to clear up an ambiguity in a previous answer or statement
- in the interests of justice for the detainee to have put to them, and have an opportunity to comment on, information concerning the offence which has come to light since they were charged or informed they might be prosecuted

Before any such interview, the interviewer shall:

    (a) caution the detainee, 'You do not have to say anything, but anything you do say may be given in evidence.'

    Where the use of the Welsh Language is appropriate, the interviewer shall caution the detainee: 'Does dim rhaid i chi ddweud dim byd, ond gall unrhyw beth yr ydych yn ei ddweud gael ei roi fel tystiolaeth.'

    (b) remind the detainee about their right to legal advice.

See *Note 16B*

16.6 The provisions of *paragraphs 16.2* to *16.5* must be complied with in the appropriate adult's presence if they are already at the police station. If they are not at the police station then these provisions must be complied with again in their presence when they arrive unless the detainee has been released. See *Note 16C*

16.7 When a juvenile is charged with an offence and the custody officer authorises their continued detention after charge, the custody officer must make arrangements for the juvenile to be taken into the care of a local authority to be detained pending appearance in court *unless* the custody officer certifies in accordance with PACE, section 38(6), that:

    (a) for any juvenile; it is impracticable to do so; or,

    (b) in the case of a juvenile of at least 12 years old, no secure accommodation is available and other accommodation would not be adequate to protect the public from serious harm from that juvenile. See *Note 16D*

(b) Documentation

16.8 A record shall be made of anything a detainee says when charged.

16.9 Any questions put in an interview after charge and answers given relating to the offence shall be recorded in full during the interview on forms for that purpose and the record signed by the detainee or, if they refuse, by the interviewer and any third parties present. If the questions are audibly recorded or visually recorded the arrangements in Code E or F apply.

16.10 If arrangements for a juvenile's transfer into local authority care as in *paragraph 16.7* are not made, the custody officer must record the reasons in a certificate which must be produced before the court with the juvenile. See *Note 16D*

Notes for guidance

16A The custody officer must take into account alternatives to prosecution under the Crime and Disorder Act 1998, reprimands and warning applicable to persons under 18, and in national guidance on the cautioning of offenders, for persons aged 18 and over.

16AA When a person is arrested under the provisions of the Criminal Justice Act 2003 which allow a person to be re-tried after being acquitted of a serious offence which is a qualifying offence specified in Schedule 5 to that Act and not precluded from further prosecution by virtue of section 75(3) of that Act the detention provisions of PACE are modified and make an officer of the rank of superintendent or above who has not been directly involved in the investigation responsible for determining whether the evidence is sufficient to charge.

16AB Where Guidance issued by the Director of Public Prosecutions under section 37B is in force, a custody officer who determines in accordance with that Guidance that there is sufficient evidence to charge the detainee, may detain that person for no longer than is reasonably necessary to decide how that person is to be dealt with under PACE, section 37(7)(a) to (d), including, where appropriate, consultation with the Duty Prosecutor. The period is subject to the maximum period of detention before charge determined by PACE, sections 41 to 44. Where in accordance with the Guidance the case is referred to the CPS for decision, the custody officer should ensure that an officer involved in the investigation sends to the CPS such information as is specified in the Guidance.

16B The giving of a warning or the service of the Notice of Intended Prosecution required by the Road Traffic Offenders Act 1988, section 1 does not amount to informing a detainee they may be prosecuted for an offence and so does not preclude further questioning in relation to that offence.

16C There is no power under PACE to detain a person and delay action under paragraphs 16.2 to 16.5 solely to await the arrival of the appropriate adult. Reasonable efforts should therefore be made to give the appropriate adult sufficient notice of the time the decision (charge etc.) is to be implemented so that they can be present. If the appropriate adult is not, or cannot be, present at that time, the detainee should be released on bail to return for the decision to be implemented when the adult is present, unless the custody officer determines that the absence of the appropriate adult makes the detainee unsuitable for bail for this purpose. After charge, bail cannot be refused, or release on bail delayed, simply because an appropriate adult is not available, unless the absence of that adult provides the custody officer with the necessary grounds to authorise detention after charge under PACE, section 38.

16D *Except as in paragraph 16.7, neither a juvenile's behaviour nor the nature of the offence provides grounds for the custody officer to decide it is impracticable to arrange the juvenile's transfer to local authority care. Impracticability concerns the transport and travel requirements and the lack of secure accommodation which is provided for the purposes of restricting liberty does not make it impracticable to transfer the juvenile. The availability of secure accommodation is only a factor in relation to a juvenile aged 12 or over when other local authority accommodation would not be adequate to protect the public from serious harm from them. The obligation to transfer a juvenile to local authority accommodation applies as much to a juvenile charged during the daytime as to a juvenile to be held overnight, subject to a requirement to bring the juvenile before a court under PACE, section 46.*

17   Testing persons for the presence of specified Class A drugs

(a) Action

17.1 This section of Code C applies only in selected police stations in police areas where the provisions for drug testing under section 63B of PACE (as amended by section 5 of the Criminal Justice Act 2003 and section 7 of the Drugs Act 2005) are in force and in respect of which the Secretary of State has given a notification to the relevant chief officer of police that arrangements for the taking of samples have been made. Such a notification will cover either a police area as a whole or particular stations within a police area. The notification indicates whether the testing applies to those arrested or charged or under the age of 18 as the case may be and testing can only take place in respect of the persons so indicated in the notification. Testing cannot be carried out unless the relevant notification has been given and has not been withdrawn. See *Note 17F*

17.2 A sample of urine or a non-intimate sample may be taken from a person in police detention for the purpose of ascertaining whether they have any specified Class A drug in their body only where they have been brought before the custody officer and:

(a) either the arrest condition, see *paragraph 17.3*, or the charge condition, see *paragraph 17.4* is met;

(b) the age condition see *paragraph 17.5,* is met;

(c) the notification condition is met in relation to the arrest condition, the charge condition, or the age condition, as the case may be. (Testing on charge and/or arrest must be specifically provided for in the notification for the power to apply. In addition, the fact that testing of under 18s is authorised must be expressly provided for in the notification before the power to test such persons applies.). See *paragraph 17.1*; and

(d) a police officer has requested the person concerned to give the sample (the request condition).

17.3 The arrest condition is met where the detainee:

(a) has been arrested for a trigger offence, see *Note 17E*, but not charged with that offence; or

(b) has been arrested for any other offence but not charged with that offence and a police officer of inspector rank or above, who has reasonable grounds for suspecting that their misuse of any specified Class A drug caused or contributed to the offence, has authorised the sample to be taken.

17.4 The charge condition is met where the detainee:

(a) has been charged with a trigger offence, or

(b) has been charged with any other offence and a police officer of inspector rank or above, who has reasonable grounds for suspecting that the detainee's misuse of any specified Class A drug caused or contributed to the offence, has authorised the sample to be taken.

17.5 The age condition is met where:

    (a) in the case of a detainee who has been arrested but not charged as in *paragraph 17.3*, they are aged 18 or over;

    (b) in the case of a detainee who has been charged as in *paragraph 17.4*, they are aged 14 or over.

17.6 Before requesting a sample from the person concerned, an officer must:

    (a) inform them that the purpose of taking the sample is for drug testing under PACE. This is to ascertain whether they have a specified Class A drug present in their body;

    (b) warn them that if, when so requested, they fail without good cause to provide a sample they may be liable to prosecution;

    (c) where the taking of the sample has been authorised by an inspector or above in accordance with *paragraph 17.3(b)* or *17.4(b)* above, inform them that the authorisation has been given and the grounds for giving it;

    (d) remind them of the following rights, which may be exercised at any stage during the period in custody:

        (i) the right to have someone informed of their arrest [see section 5];

        (ii) the right to consult privately with a solicitor and that free independent legal advice is available [see section 6]; and

        (iii) the right to consult these Codes of Practice [see section 3].

17.7 In the case of a person who has not attained the age of 17—

    (a) the making of the request for a sample under *paragraph 17.2(d)* above;

    (b) the giving of the warning and the information under *paragraph 17.6* above; and

    (c) the taking of the sample,

may not take place except in the presence of an appropriate adult. See *Note 17G*

17.8 Authorisation by an officer of the rank of inspector or above within *paragraph 17.3(b)* or *17.4(b)* may be given orally or in writing but, if it is given orally, it must be confirmed in writing as soon as practicable.

17.9 If a sample is taken from a detainee who has been arrested for an offence but not charged with that offence as in *paragraph 17.3*, no further sample may be taken during the same continuous period of detention. If during that same period the charge condition is also met in respect of that detainee, the sample which has been taken shall be treated as being taken by virtue of the charge condition, see *paragraph 17.4*, being met.

17.10 A detainee from whom a sample may be taken may be detained for up to six hours from the time of charge if the custody officer reasonably believes the detention is necessary to enable a sample to be taken. Where the arrest condition is met, a detainee whom the custody officer has decided to release on bail without charge may continue to be detained, but not beyond 24 hours from the relevant time (as defined in section 41(2) of PACE), to enable a sample to be taken.

17.11 A detainee in respect of whom the arrest condition is met, but not the charge condition, see *paragraphs 17.3* and *17.4*, and whose release would be required before a sample can be taken had they not continued to be detained as a result of being arrested for a further offence which does not satisfy the arrest condition, may have a sample taken at any time within 24 hours after the arrest for the offence that satisfies the arrest condition.

(b) Documentation

17.12 The following must be recorded in the custody record:

    (a) if a sample is taken following authorisation by an officer of the rank of inspector or above, the authorisation and the grounds for suspicion;

    (b) the giving of a warning of the consequences of failure to provide a sample;

    (c) the time at which the sample was given; and

    (d) the time of charge or, where the arrest condition is being relied upon, the time of arrest and, where applicable, the fact that a sample taken after arrest but before charge is to be treated as being taken by virtue of the charge condition, where that is met in the same period of continuous detention. See *paragraph 17.9*

(c) General

17.13 A sample may only be taken by a prescribed person. See *Note 17C*

17.14 Force may not be used to take any sample for the purpose of drug testing.

17.15 The terms "Class A drug" and "misuse" have the same meanings as in the Misuse of Drugs Act 1971. "Specified" (in relation to a Class A drug) and "trigger offence" have the same meanings as in Part III of the Criminal Justice and Court Services Act 2000.

17.16 Any sample taken:

  (a) may not be used for any purpose other than to ascertain whether the person concerned has a specified Class A drug present in his body; and

  (b) can be disposed of as clinical waste unless it is to be sent for further analysis in cases where the test result is disputed at the point when the result is known, including on the basis that medication has been taken, or for quality assurance purposes.

(d) Assessment of misuse of drugs

17.17 Under the provisions of Part 3 of the Drugs Act 2005, where a detainee has tested positive for a specified Class A drug under section 63B of PACE a police officer may, at any time before the person's release from the police station, impose a requirement on the detainee to attend an initial assessment of their drug misuse by a suitably qualified person and to remain for its duration. Where such a requirement is imposed, the officer must, at the same time, impose a second requirement on the detainee to attend and remain for a follow-up assessment. The officer must inform the detainee that the second requirement will cease to have effect if, at the initial assessment they are informed that a follow-up assessment is not necessary These requirements may only be imposed on a person if:

  (a) they have reached the age of 18

  (b) notification has been given by the Secretary of State to the relevant chief officer of police that arrangements for conducting initial and follow-up assessments have been made for those from whom samples for testing have been taken at the police station where the detainee is in custody.

17.18 When imposing a requirement to attend an initial assessment and a follow-up assessment the police officer must:

  (a) inform the person of the time and place at which the initial assessment is to take place;

  (b) explain that this information will be confirmed in writing; and

  (c) warn the person that they may be liable to prosecution if they fail without good cause to attend the initial assessment and remain for it's duration and if they fail to attend the follow-up assessment and remain for its duration (if so required).

17.19 Where a police officer has imposed a requirement to attend an initial assessment and a follow-up assessment in accordance with paragraph 17.17, he must, before the person is released from detention, give the person notice in writing which:

  (a) confirms their requirement to attend and remain for the duration of the assessments; and

  (b) confirms the information and repeats the warning referred to in paragraph 17.18.

17.20 The following must be recorded in the custody record:

  (a) that the requirement to attend an initial assessment and a follow-up assessment has been imposed; and

  (b) the information, explanation, warning and notice given in accordance with paragraphs 17.17 and 17.19.

17.21 Where a notice is given in accordance with paragraph 17.19, a police officer can give the person a further notice in writing which informs the person of any change to the time or place at which the initial assessment is to take place and which repeats the warning referred to in paragraph 17.18(c).

17.22 Part 3 of the Drugs Act 2005 also requires police officers to have regard to any guidance issued by the Secretary of State in respect of the assessment provisions.

Notes for guidance

17A When warning a person who is asked to provide a urine or non-intimate sample in accordance with paragraph 17.6(b), the following form of words may be used:

"You do not have to provide a sample, but I must warn you that if you fail or refuse without good cause to do so, you will commit an offence for which you may be imprisoned, or fined, or both".

Where the Welsh language is appropriate, the following form of words may be used:

"Does dim rhaid i chi roi sampl, ond mae'n rhaid i mi eich rhybuddio y byddwch chi'n cyflawni trosedd os byddwch chi'n methu neu yn gwrthod gwneud hynny heb reswm da, ac y gellir, oherwydd hynny, eich carcharu, eich dirwyo, neu'r ddau."

17B A sample has to be sufficient and suitable. A sufficient sample is sufficient in quantity and quality to enable drug-testing analysis to take place. A suitable sample is one which by its nature, is suitable for a particular form of drug analysis.

17C A prescribed person in paragraph 17.13 is one who is prescribed in regulations made by the Secretary of State under section 63B(6) of the Police and Criminal Evidence Act 1984. [The regulations are currently contained in regulation SI 2001 No. 2645, the Police and Criminal Evidence Act 1984 (Drug Testing Persons in Police Detention) (Prescribed Persons) Regulations 2001.]

17D Samples, and the information derived from them, may not be subsequently used in the investigation of any offence or in evidence against the persons from whom they were taken.

17E Trigger offences are:

1. *Offences under the following provisions of the Theft Act 1968:*

section 1	*(theft)*
section 8	*(robbery)*
section 9	*(burglary)*
section 10	*(aggravated burglary)*
section 12	*(taking a motor vehicle or other conveyance without authority)*
section 12A	*(aggravated vehicle-taking)*
section 22	*(handling stolen goods)*
section 25	*(going equipped for stealing etc.)*

2. *Offences under the following provisions of the Misuse of Drugs Act 1971, if committed in respect of a specified Class A drug:–*

section 4	*(restriction on production and supply of controlled drugs)*
section 5(2)	*(possession of a controlled drug)*
section 5(3)	*(possession of a controlled drug with intent to supply)*

3. *Offences under the following provisions of the Fraud Act 2006:*

section 1	*(fraud)*
section 6	*(possession etc. of articles for use in frauds)*
section 7	*(making or supplying articles for use in frauds)*

   3A. *An offence under section 1(1) of the Criminal Attempts Act 1981 if committed in respect of an offence under*

   (a) *any of the following provisions of the Theft Act 1968:*

section 1	*(theft)*
section 8	*(robbery)*
section 9	*(burglary)*
section 22	*(handling stolen goods)*

   (b) *section 1 of the Fraud Act 2006 (fraud)*

4. *Offences under the following provisions of the Vagrancy Act 1824:*

section 3	*(begging)*
section 4	*(persistent begging)*

17F The power to take samples is subject to notification by the Secretary of State that appropriate arrangements for the taking of samples have been made for the police area as a whole or for the particular police station concerned for whichever of the following is specified in the notification:

(a) persons in respect of whom the arrest condition is met;

(b) persons in respect of whom the charge condition is met;

(c) persons who have not attained the age of 18.

Note: Notification is treated as having been given for the purposes of the charge condition in relation to a police area, if testing (on charge) under section 63B(2) of PACE was in force immediately before section 7 of the Drugs Act 2005 was brought into force; and for the purposes of the age condition, in relation to a police area or police station, if immediately before that day, notification that arrangements had been made for the taking of samples from persons under the age of 18 (those aged 14–17) had been given and had not been withdrawn.

17G Appropriate adult in paragraph 17.7 means the person's–

(a) parent or guardian or, if they are in the care of a local authority or voluntary organisation, a person representing that authority or organisation; or

(b) a social worker of a local authority; or

(c) if no person falling within (a) or (b) above is available, any responsible person aged 18 or over who is not a police officer or a person employed by the police.

Annex A   Intimate and Strip Searches

A   Intimate search

1. An intimate search consists of the physical examination of a person's body orifices other than the mouth. The intrusive nature of such searches means the actual and potential risks associated with intimate searches must never be underestimated.

(a) Action

2. Body orifices other than the mouth may be searched only:

(a) if authorised by an officer of inspector rank or above who has reasonable grounds for believing that the person may have concealed on themselves:

(i)   anything which they could and might use to cause physical injury to themselves or others at the station; or

(ii)   a Class A drug which they intended to supply to another or to export;

and the officer has reasonable grounds for believing that an intimate search is the only means of removing those items; and

(b) if the search is under *paragraph 2(a)(ii)* (a drug offence search), the detainee's appropriate consent has been given in writing.

2A. Before the search begins, a police officer or designated detention officer, must tell the detainee:–

(a) that the authority to carry out the search has been given;

(b) the grounds for giving the authorisation and for believing that the article cannot be removed without an intimate search.

2B. Before a detainee is asked to give appropriate consent to a search under *paragraph 2(a)(ii)* (a drug offence search) they must be warned that if they refuse without good cause their refusal may harm their case if it comes to trial, see *Note A6*. This warning may be given by a police officer or member of police staff. In the case of juveniles, mentally vulnerable or mentally disordered suspects the seeking and giving of consent must take place in the presence of the appropriate adult. A juvenile's consent is only valid if their parent's or guardian's consent is also obtained unless the juvenile is under 14, when their parent's or guardian's consent is sufficient in its own right. A detainee who is not legally represented must be reminded of their entitlement to have free legal advice, see Code C, *paragraph 6.5*, and the reminder noted in the custody record.

3. An intimate search may only be carried out by a registered medical practitioner or registered nurse, unless an officer of at least inspector rank considers this is not practicable and the search is

to take place under *paragraph 2(a)(i)*, in which case a police officer may carry out the search. See *Notes A1 to A5*

3A. Any proposal for a search under *paragraph 2(a)(i)* to be carried out by someone other than a registered medical practitioner or registered nurse must only be considered as a last resort and when the authorising officer is satisfied the risks associated with allowing the item to remain with the detainee outweigh the risks associated with removing it. See *Notes A1 to A5*

4. An intimate search under:
- *paragraph 2(a)(i)* may take place only at a hospital, surgery, other medical premises or police station
- *paragraph 2(a)(ii)* may take place only at a hospital, surgery or other medical premises and must be carried out by a registered medical practitioner or a registered nurse.

5. An intimate search at a police station of a juvenile or mentally disordered or otherwise mentally vulnerable person may take place only in the presence of an appropriate adult of the same sex (see *Annex L*), unless the detainee specifically requests a particular adult of the opposite sex who is readily available. In the case of a juvenile the search may take place in the absence of the appropriate adult only if the juvenile signifies in the presence of the appropriate adult they do not want the adult present during the search and the adult agrees. A record shall be made of the juvenile's decision and signed by the appropriate adult.

6. When an intimate search under *paragraph 2(a)(i)* is carried out by a police officer, the officer must be of the same sex as the detainee (see *Annex L*). A minimum of two people, other than the detainee, must be present during the search. Subject to *paragraph 5*, no person of the opposite sex who is not a medical practitioner or nurse shall be present, nor shall anyone whose presence is unnecessary. The search shall be conducted with proper regard to the sensitivity and vulnerability of the detainee.

(b) Documentation

7. In the case of an intimate search, the following shall be recorded as soon as practicable, in the detainee's custody record:
 (a) for searches under paragraphs 2(a)(i) and (ii);
- the authorisation to carry out the search;
- the grounds for giving the authorisation;
- the grounds for believing the article could not be removed without an intimate search;
- which parts of the detainee's body were searched;
- who carried out the search;
- who was present;
- the result.
 (b) for searches under paragraph 2(a)(ii):
- the giving of the warning required by *paragraph 2B*;
- the fact that the appropriate consent was given or (as the case may be) refused, and if refused, the reason given for the refusal (if any).

8. If an intimate search is carried out by a police officer, the reason why it was impracticable for a registered medical practitioner or registered nurse to conduct it must be recorded.

B Strip search

9. A strip search is a search involving the removal of more than outer clothing. In this Code, outer clothing includes shoes and socks.

(a) Action

10. A strip search may take place only if it is considered necessary to remove an article which a detainee would not be allowed to keep, and the officer reasonably considers the detainee might have concealed such an article. Strip searches shall not be routinely carried out if there is no reason to consider that articles are concealed.

The conduct of strip searches

11. When strip searches are conducted:

   (a) a police officer carrying out a strip search must be the same sex as the detainee (see *Annex L*);

   (b) the search shall take place in an area where the detainee cannot be seen by anyone who does not need to be present, nor by a member of the opposite sex (see *Annex L*) except an appropriate adult who has been specifically requested by the detainee;

   (c) except in cases of urgency, where there is risk of serious harm to the detainee or to others, whenever a strip search involves exposure of intimate body parts, there must be at least two people present other than the detainee, and if the search is of a juvenile or mentally disordered or otherwise mentally vulnerable person, one of the people must be the appropriate adult. Except in urgent cases as above, a search of a juvenile may take place in the absence of the appropriate adult only if the juvenile signifies in the presence of the appropriate adult that they do not want the adult to be present during the search and the adult agrees. A record shall be made of the juvenile's decision and signed by the appropriate adult. The presence of more than two people, other than an appropriate adult, shall be permitted only in the most exceptional circumstances;

   (d) the search shall be conducted with proper regard to the sensitivity and vulnerability of the detainee in these circumstances and every reasonable effort shall be made to secure the detainee's co-operation and minimise embarrassment. Detainees who are searched shall not normally be required to remove all their clothes at the same time, e.g. a person should be allowed to remove clothing above the waist and redress before removing further clothing;

   (e) if necessary to assist the search, the detainee may be required to hold their arms in the air or to stand with their legs apart and bend forward so a visual examination may be made of the genital and anal areas provided no physical contact is made with any body orifice;

   (f) if articles are found, the detainee shall be asked to hand them over. If articles are found within any body orifice other than the mouth, and the detainee refuses to hand them over, their removal would constitute an intimate search, which must be carried out as in *Part A*;

   (g) a strip search shall be conducted as quickly as possible, and the detainee allowed to dress as soon as the procedure is complete.

(b) Documentation

12. A record shall be made on the custody record of a strip search including the reason it was considered necessary, those present and any result.

Notes for guidance

A1 Before authorising any intimate search, the authorising officer must make every reasonable effort to persuade the detainee to hand the article over without a search. If the detainee agrees, a registered medical practitioner or registered nurse should whenever possible be asked to assess the risks involved and, if necessary, attend to assist the detainee.

A2 If the detainee does not agree to hand the article over without a search, the authorising officer must carefully review all the relevant factors before authorising an intimate search. In particular, the officer must consider whether the grounds for believing an article may be concealed are reasonable.

A3 If authority is given for a search under paragraph 2(a)(i), a registered medical practitioner or registered nurse shall be consulted whenever possible. The presumption should be that the search will be conducted by the registered medical practitioner or registered nurse and the authorising officer must make every reasonable effort to persuade the detainee to allow the medical practitioner or nurse to conduct the search.

A4 A constable should only be authorised to carry out a search as a last resort and when all other approaches have failed. In these circumstances, the authorising officer must be satisfied the detainee might use the article for one or more of the purposes in paragraph 2(a)(i) and the physical injury likely to be caused is sufficiently severe to justify authorising a constable to carry out the search.

A5 If an officer has any doubts whether to authorise an intimate search by a constable, the officer should seek advice from an officer of superintendent rank or above.

A6 In warning a detainee who is asked to consent to an intimate drug offence search, as in paragraph 2B, the following form of words may be used:

"You do not have to allow yourself to be searched, but I must warn you that if you refuse without good cause, your refusal may harm your case if it comes to trial."

Where the use of the Welsh Language is appropriate, the following form of words may be used:

"Nid oes rhaid i chi roi caniatâd i gael eich archwilio, ond mae'n rhaid i mi eich rhybuddio os gwrthod-wch heb reswm da, y gallai eich penderfyniad i wrthod wneud niwed i'ch achos pe bai'n dod gerbron llys."

Annex B   Delay in Notifying Arrest or Allowing Access to Legal Advice

A Persons detained under PACE

1. The exercise of the rights in *Section 5* or *Section 6*, or both, may be delayed if the person is in police detention, as in PACE, section 118(2), in connection with an indictable offence, has not yet been charged with an offence and an officer of superintendent rank or above, or inspector rank or above only for the rights in *Section 5*, has reasonable grounds for believing their exercise will:
   (i) lead to:
      - interference with, or harm to, evidence connected with an indictable offence; or
      - interference with, or physical harm to, other people; or
   (ii) lead to alerting other people suspected of having committed an indictable offence but not yet arrested for it; or
   (iii) hinder the recovery of property obtained in consequence of the commission of such an offence.

2. These rights may also be delayed if the officer has reasonable grounds to believe that:
   (i) the person detained for an indictable offence has benefited from their criminal conduct (decided in accordance with Part 2 of the Proceeds of Crime Act 2002); and
   (ii) the recovery of the value of the property constituting that benefit will be hindered by the exercise of either right.

3. Authority to delay a detainee's right to consult privately with a solicitor may be given only if the authorising officer has reasonable grounds to believe the solicitor the detainee wants to consult will, inadvertently or otherwise, pass on a message from the detainee or act in some other way which will have any of the consequences specified under *paragraphs 1 or 2*. In these circumstances the detainee must be allowed to choose another solicitor. See *Note B3*

4. If the detainee wishes to see a solicitor, access to that solicitor may not be delayed on the grounds they might advise the detainee not to answer questions or the solicitor was initially asked to attend the police station by someone else. In the latter case the detainee must be told the solicitor has come to the police station at another person's request, and must be asked to sign the custody record to signify whether they want to see the solicitor.

5. The fact the grounds for delaying notification of arrest may be satisfied does not automatically mean the grounds for delaying access to legal advice will also be satisfied.

6. These rights may be delayed only for as long as grounds exist and in no case beyond 36 hours after the relevant time as in PACE, section 41. If the grounds cease to apply within this time, the detainee must, as soon as practicable, be asked if they want to exercise either right, the custody record must be noted accordingly, and action taken in accordance with the relevant section of the Code.

7. A detained person must be permitted to consult a solicitor for a reasonable time before any court hearing.

B   Not used

C   Documentation

13. The grounds for action under this Annex shall be recorded and the detainee informed of them as soon as practicable.

14. Any reply given by a detainee under *paragraphs 6* or *11* must be recorded and the detainee asked to endorse the record in relation to whether they want to receive legal advice at this point.

D   Cautions and special warnings

15. When a suspect detained at a police station is interviewed during any period for which access to legal advice has been delayed under this Annex, the court or jury may not draw adverse inferences from their silence.

Notes for guidance

B1   Even if Annex B applies in the case of a juvenile, or a person who is mentally disordered or otherwise mentally vulnerable, action to inform the appropriate adult and the person responsible for a juvenile's welfare if that is a different person, must nevertheless be taken as in paragraph 3.13 and 3.15.

B2   In the case of Commonwealth citizens and foreign nationals, see Note 7A.

B3   A decision to delay access to a specific solicitor is likely to be a rare occurrence and only when it can be shown the suspect is capable of misleading that particular solicitor and there is more than a substantial risk that the suspect will succeed in causing information to be conveyed which will lead to one or more of the specified consequences.

Annex C   Restriction on Drawing Adverse Inferences from Silence and Terms of the Caution When the Restriction Applies

(a)   The restriction on drawing adverse inferences from silence

1. The Criminal Justice and Public Order Act 1994, sections 34, 36 and 37 as amended by the Youth Justice and Criminal Evidence Act 1999, section 58 describe the conditions under which adverse inferences may be drawn from a person's failure or refusal to say anything about their involvement in the offence when interviewed, after being charged or informed they may be prosecuted. These provisions are subject to an overriding restriction on the ability of a court or jury to draw adverse inferences from a person's silence. This restriction applies:

(a) to any detainee at a police station, see *Note 10C* who, before being interviewed, see *section 11* or being charged or informed they may be prosecuted, see *section 16*, has:

   (i)   asked for legal advice, see *section 6, paragraph 6.1*;

   (ii) not been allowed an opportunity to consult a solicitor, including the duty solicitor, as in this Code; and

   (iii) not changed their mind about wanting legal advice, see *section 6, paragraph 6.6(d)*.

   Note the condition in (ii) will:

   — apply when a detainee who has asked for legal advice is interviewed before speaking to a solicitor as in *section 6, paragraph 6.6(a)* or *(b)*;

   — not apply if the detained person declines to ask for the duty solicitor, see *section 6, paragraphs 6.6(c)* and *(d)*.

(b) to any person charged with, or informed they may be prosecuted for, an offence who:

   (i)   has had brought to their notice a written statement made by another person or the content of an interview with another person which relates to that offence, see *section 16, paragraph 16.4*;

   (ii) is interviewed about that offence, see *section 16, paragraph 16.5*; or

   (iii) makes a written statement about that offence, see *Annex D paragraphs 4* and *9*.

(b)   Terms of the caution when the restriction applies

2. When a requirement to caution arises at a time when the restriction on drawing adverse inferences from silence applies, the caution shall be:

'You do not have to say anything, but anything you do say may be given in evidence.'

Where the use of the Welsh Language is appropriate, the caution may be used directly in Welsh in the following terms:

'Does dim rhaid i chi ddweud dim byd, ond gall unrhyw beth yr ydych chi'n ei ddweud gael ei roi fel tystiolaeth.'

3. Whenever the restriction either begins to apply or ceases to apply after a caution has already been given, the person shall be re-cautioned in the appropriate terms. The changed position on drawing inferences and that the previous caution no longer applies shall also be explained to the detainee in ordinary language. See *Note C2*

Notes for guidance

C1 The restriction on drawing inferences from silence does not apply to a person who has not been detained and who therefore cannot be prevented from seeking legal advice if they want to, see paragraphs 10.2 and 3.15.

C2 The following is suggested as a framework to help explain changes in the position on drawing adverse inferences if the restriction on drawing adverse inferences from silence:

(a) begins to apply:

'The caution you were previously given no longer applies. This is because after that caution:

(i)   you asked to speak to a solicitor but have not yet been allowed an opportunity to speak to a solicitor. See paragraph 1(a); or

(ii) you have been charged with/informed you may be prosecuted. See paragraph 1(b).

'This means that from now on, adverse inferences cannot be drawn at court and your defence will not be harmed just because you choose to say nothing. Please listen carefully to the caution I am about to give you because it will apply from now on. You will see that it does not say anything about your defence being harmed.'

(b) ceases to apply before or at the time the person is charged or informed they may be prosecuted, see paragraph 1(a);

'The caution you were previously given no longer applies. This is because after that caution you have been allowed an opportunity to speak to a solicitor. Please listen carefully to the caution I am about to give you because it will apply from now on. It explains how your defence at court may be affected if you choose to say nothing.'

Annex D   Written Statements Under Caution

(a)   Written by a person under caution

1. A person shall always be invited to write down what they want to say.

2. A person who has not been charged with, or informed they may be prosecuted for, any offence to which the statement they want to write relates, shall:

(a) unless the statement is made at a time when the restriction on drawing adverse inferences from silence applies, see Annex C, be asked to write out and sign the following before writing what they want to say:

'I make this statement of my own free will. I understand that I do not have to say anything but that it may harm my defence if I do not mention when questioned something which I later rely on in court. This statement may be given in evidence.';

(b) if the statement is made at a time when the restriction on drawing adverse inferences from silence applies, be asked to write out and sign the following before writing what they want to say;

'I make this statement of my own free will. I understand that I do not have to say anything. This statement may be given in evidence.'

3. When a person, on the occasion of being charged with or informed they may be prosecuted for any offence, asks to make a statement which relates to any such offence and wants to write it they shall:

    (a) unless the restriction on drawing adverse inferences from silence, see *Annex C,* applied when they were so charged or informed they may be prosecuted, be asked to write out and sign the following before writing what they want to say:

    'I make this statement of my own free will. I understand that I do not have to say anything but that it may harm my defence if I do not mention when questioned something which I later rely on in court. This statement may be given in evidence.';

    (b) if the restriction on drawing adverse inferences from silence applied when they were so charged or informed they may be prosecuted, be asked to write out and sign the following before writing what they want to say:

    'I make this statement of my own free will. I understand that I do not have to say anything. This statement may be given in evidence.'

4. When a person, who has already been charged with or informed they may be prosecuted for any offence, asks to make a statement which relates to any such offence and wants to write it they shall be asked to write out and sign the following before writing what they want to say:

'I make this statement of my own free will. I understand that I do not have to say anything. This statement may be given in evidence.';

5. Any person writing their own statement shall be allowed to do so without any prompting except a police officer or other police staff may indicate to them which matters are material or question any ambiguity in the statement.

(b) Written by a police officer or other police staff

6. If a person says they would like someone to write the statement for them, a police officer, or other police staff shall write the statement.

7. If the person has not been charged with, or informed they may be prosecuted for, any offence to which the statement they want to make relates they shall, before starting, be asked to sign, or make their mark, to the following:

    (a) unless the statement is made at a time when the restriction on drawing adverse inferences from silence applies, see *Annex C*:

    'I, ..., wish to make a statement. I want someone to write down what I say. I understand that I do not have to say anything but that it may harm my defence if I do not mention when questioned something which I later rely on in court. This statement may be given in evidence.';

    (b) if the statement is made at a time when the restriction on drawing adverse inferences from silence applies: '

    'I, ..., wish to make a statement. I want someone to write down what I say. I understand that I do not have to say anything. This statement may be given in evidence.'

8. If, on the occasion of being charged with or informed they may be prosecuted for any offence, the person asks to make a statement which relates to any such offence they shall before starting be asked to sign, or make their mark to, the following:

    (a) unless the restriction on drawing adverse inferences from silence applied, see *Annex C,* when they were so charged or informed they may be prosecuted:

    'I, ..., wish to make a statement. I want someone to write down what I say. I understand that I do not have to say anything but that it may harm my defence if I do not mention when questioned something which I later rely on in court. This statement may be given in evidence.';

    (b) if the restriction on drawing adverse inferences from silence applied when they were so charged or informed they may be prosecuted:

    'I, ..., wish to make a statement. I want someone to write down what I say. I understand that I do not have to say anything. This statement may be given in evidence.'

9. If, having already been charged with or informed they may be prosecuted for any offence, a person asks to make a statement which relates to any such offence they shall before starting, be asked to sign, or make their mark to:

'I, ..., wish to make a statement. I want someone to write down what I say. I understand that I do not have to say anything. This statement may be given in evidence.'

10. The person writing the statement must take down the exact words spoken by the person making it and must not edit or paraphrase it. Any questions that are necessary, e.g. to make it more intelligible, and the answers given must be recorded at the same time on the statement form.

11. When the writing of a statement is finished the person making it shall be asked to read it and to make any corrections, alterations or additions they want. When they have finished reading they shall be asked to write and sign or make their mark on the following certificate at the end of the statement:

'I have read the above statement, and I have been able to correct, alter or add anything I wish. This statement is true. I have made it of my own free will.'

12. If the person making the statement cannot read, or refuses to read it, or to write the above mentioned certificate at the end of it or to sign it, the person taking the statement shall read it to them and ask them if they would like to correct, alter or add anything and to put their signature or make their mark at the end. The person taking the statement shall certify on the statement itself what has occurred.

Annex E   Summary of Provisions Relating to Mentally Disordered and Otherwise Mentally Vulnerable People

1. If an officer has any suspicion, or is told in good faith, that a person of any age may be mentally disordered or otherwise mentally vulnerable, or mentally incapable of understanding the significance of questions or their replies that person shall be treated as mentally disordered or otherwise mentally vulnerable for the purposes of this Code. See *paragraph 1.4* and *Note E4*

2. In the case of a person who is mentally disordered or otherwise mentally vulnerable, 'the appropriate adult' means:

(a) a relative, guardian or other person responsible for their care or custody;
(b) someone experienced in dealing with mentally disordered or mentally vulnerable people but who is not a police officer or employed by the police;
(c) failing these, some other responsible adult aged 18 or over who is not a police officer or employed by the police. See *paragraph 1.7(b)* and *Note 1D*

3. If the custody officer authorises the detention of a person who is mentally vulnerable or appears to be suffering from a mental disorder, the custody officer must as soon as practicable inform the appropriate adult of the grounds for detention and the person's whereabouts, and ask the adult to come to the police station to see them. If the appropriate adult:

• is already at the station when information is given as in *paragraphs 3.1* to *3.5* the information must be given in their presence;
• is not at the station when the provisions of *paragraph 3.1* to *3.5* are complied with these provisions must be complied with again in their presence once they arrive.

See *paragraphs 3.15* to *3.17*

4. If the appropriate adult, having been informed of the right to legal advice, considers legal advice should be taken, the provisions of *section 6* apply as if the mentally disordered or otherwise mentally vulnerable person had requested access to legal advice. See *paragraph 3.19* and *Note E1*.

5. The custody officer must make sure a person receives appropriate clinical attention as soon as reasonably practicable if the person appears to be suffering from a mental disorder or in urgent cases immediately call the nearest appropriate healthcare professional or an ambulance. It is not intended these provisions delay the transfer of a detainee to a place of safety under the Mental Health Act 1983,

section 136 if that is applicable. If an assessment under that Act is to take place at a police station, the custody officer must consider whether an appropriate healthcare professional should be called to conduct an initial clinical check on the detainee. See *paragraph 9.5* and *9.6*

6. It is imperative a mentally disordered or otherwise mentally vulnerable person detained under the Mental Health Act 1983, section 136 be assessed as soon as possible. A police station should only be used as a place of safety as a last resort but if that assessment is to take place at the police station, an approved social worker and registered medical practitioner shall be called to the station as soon as possible to carry it out. Once the detainee has been assessed and suitable arrangements been made for their treatment or care, they can no longer be detained under section 136. A detainee should be immediately discharged from detention if a registered medical practitioner having examined them, concludes they are not mentally disordered within the meaning of the Act. See *paragraph 3.16*

7. If a mentally disordered or otherwise mentally vulnerable person is cautioned in the absence of the appropriate adult, the caution must be repeated in the appropriate adult's presence. See *paragraph 10.12*

8. A mentally disordered or otherwise mentally vulnerable person must not be interviewed or asked to provide or sign a written statement in the absence of the appropriate adult unless the provisions of *paragraphs 11.1* or *11.18* to *11.20* apply. Questioning in these circumstances may not continue in the absence of the appropriate adult once sufficient information to avert the risk has been obtained. A record shall be made of the grounds for any decision to begin an interview in these circumstances. See *paragraphs 11.1, 11.15* and *11.18* to *11.20*

9. If the appropriate adult is present at an interview, they shall be informed they are not expected to act simply as an observer and the purposes of their presence are to:
- advise the interviewee;
- observe whether or not the interview is being conducted properly and fairly;
- facilitate communication with the interviewee. See *paragraph 11.17*

10. If the detention of a mentally disordered or otherwise mentally vulnerable person is reviewed by a review officer or a superintendent, the appropriate adult must, if available at the time, be given an opportunity to make representations to the officer about the need for continuing detention. See *paragraph 15.3*

11. If the custody officer charges a mentally disordered or otherwise mentally vulnerable person with an offence or takes such other action as is appropriate when there is sufficient evidence for a prosecution this must be carried out in the presence of the appropriate adult if they are at the police station. A copy of the written notice embodying any charge must also be given to the appropriate adult. See *paragraphs 16.1* to *16.4A*

12. An intimate or strip search of a mentally disordered or otherwise mentally vulnerable person may take place only in the presence of the appropriate adult of the same sex, unless the detainee specifically requests the presence of a particular adult of the opposite sex. A strip search may take place in the absence of an appropriate adult only in cases of urgency when there is a risk of serious harm to the detainee or others. See *Annex A, paragraphs 5* and *11(c)*

13. Particular care must be taken when deciding whether to use any form of approved restraints on a mentally disordered or otherwise mentally vulnerable person in a locked cell. See *paragraph 8.2*

Notes for guidance

E1 The purpose of the provision at paragraph 3.19 is to protect the rights of a mentally disordered or otherwise mentally vulnerable detained person who does not understand the significance of what is said to them. If the detained person wants to exercise the right to legal advice, the appropriate action should be taken and not delayed until the appropriate adult arrives. A mentally disordered or otherwise mentally vulnerable detained person should always be given an opportunity, when an appropriate adult is called to the police station, to consult privately with a solicitor in the absence of the appropriate adult if they want.

E2 Although people who are mentally disordered or otherwise mentally vulnerable are often capable of providing reliable evidence, they may, without knowing or wanting to do so, be particularly prone in certain circumstances to provide information that may be unreliable, misleading or self-incriminating. Special care should always be taken when questioning such a person, and the appropriate adult should be involved if there is any doubt about a person's mental state or capacity. Because of the risk of unreliable evidence, it is important to obtain corroboration of any facts admitted whenever possible.

E3 Because of the risks referred to in Note E2, which the presence of the appropriate adult is intended to minimise, officers of superintendent rank or above should exercise their discretion to authorise the commencement of an interview in the appropriate adult's absence only in exceptional cases, if it is necessary to avert an immediate risk of serious harm. See paragraphs 11.1, 11.18 to 11.20

E4 There is no requirement for an appropriate adult to be present if a person is detained under section 136 of the Mental Health Act 1983 for assessment.

Annex F   *Not Used*

Annex G   Fitness to be Interviewed

1. This Annex contains general guidance to help police officers and healthcare professionals assess whether a detainee might be at risk in an interview.

2. A detainee may be at risk in a interview if it is considered that:
    (a) conducting the interview could significantly harm the detainee's physical or mental state;
    (b) anything the detainee says in the interview about their involvement or suspected involvement in the offence about which they are being interviewed might be considered unreliable in subsequent court proceedings because of their physical or mental state.

3. In assessing whether the detainee should be interviewed, the following must be considered:
    (a) how the detainee's physical or mental state might affect their ability to understand the nature and purpose of the interview, to comprehend what is being asked and to appreciate the significance of any answers given and make rational decisions about whether they want to say anything;
    (b) the extent to which the detainee's replies may be affected by their physical or mental condition rather than representing a rational and accurate explanation of their involvement in the offence;
    (c) how the nature of the interview, which could include particularly probing questions, might affect the detainee.

4. It is essential healthcare professionals who are consulted consider the functional ability of the detainee rather than simply relying on a medical diagnosis, e.g. it is possible for a person with severe mental illness to be fit for interview.

5. Healthcare professionals should advise on the need for an appropriate adult to be present, whether reassessment of the person's fitness for interview may be necessary if the interview lasts beyond a specified time, and whether a further specialist opinion may be required.

6. When healthcare professionals identify risks they should be asked to quantify the risks. They should inform the custody officer:
    • whether the person's condition:
        — is likely to improve;
        — will require or be amenable to treatment; and
    • indicate how long it may take for such improvement to take effect.

7. The role of the healthcare professional is to consider the risks and advise the custody officer of the outcome of that consideration. The healthcare professional's determination and any advice or recommendations should be made in writing and form part of the custody record.

8. Once the healthcare professional has provided that information, it is a matter for the custody officer to decide whether or not to allow the interview to go ahead and if the interview is to proceed,

to determine what safeguards are needed. Nothing prevents safeguards being provided in addition to those required under the Code. An example might be to have an appropriate healthcare professional present during the interview, in addition to an appropriate adult, in order constantly to monitor the person's condition and how it is being affected by the interview.

Annex H   Detained Person: Observation List

1. If any detainee fails to meet any of the following criteria, an appropriate healthcare professional or an ambulance must be called.

2. When assessing the level of rousability, consider:

Rousability—can they be woken?
- go into the cell
- call their name
- shake gently

Response to questions—can they give appropriate answers to questions such as:
- What's your name?
- Where do you live?
- Where do you think you are?

Response to commands—can they respond appropriately to commands such as:
- Open your eyes!
- Lift one arm, now the other arm!

3. Remember to take into account the possibility or presence of other illnesses, injury, or mental condition, a person who is drowsy and smells of alcohol may also have the following:
- Diabetes
- Epilepsy
- Head injury
- Drug intoxication or overdose
- Stroke

Annex I   *Not Used*

Annex J   *Not Used*

Annex K   X-Rays and Ultrasound Scans

(a) Action

1. PACE, section 55A allows a person who has been arrested and is in police detention to have an X-ray taken of them or an ultrasound scan to be carried out on them (or both) if:

    (a) authorised by an officer of inspector rank or above who has reasonable grounds for believing that the detainee:

        (i) may have swallowed a Class A drug; and

        (ii) was in possession of that Class A drug with the intention of supplying it to another or to export; and

    (b) the detainee's appropriate consent has been given in writing.

2. Before an x-ray is taken or an ultrasound scan carried out, a police officer, designated detention officer or staff custody officer must tell the detainee:–

    (a) that the authority has been given; and

    (b) the grounds for giving the authorisation.

3. Before a detainee is asked to give appropriate consent to an x-ray or an ultrasound scan, they must be warned that if they refuse without good cause their refusal may harm their case if it comes to trial, see *Notes K1* and *K2*. This warning may be given by a police officer or member of police staff.

In the case of juveniles, mentally vulnerable or mentally disordered suspects the seeking and giving of consent must take place in the presence of the appropriate adult. A juvenile's consent is only valid if their parent's or guardian's consent is also obtained unless the juvenile is under 14, when their parent's or guardian's consent is sufficient in its own right. A detainee who is not legally represented must be reminded of their entitlement to have free legal advice, see Code C, *paragraph 6.5*, and the reminder noted in the custody record.

4. An x-ray may be taken, or an ultrasound scan may be carried out, only by a registered medical practitioner or registered nurse, and only at a hospital, surgery or other medical premises.

(b) Documentation

5. The following shall be recorded as soon as practicable in the detainee's custody record:
    (a) the authorisation to take the x-ray or carry out the ultrasound scan (or both);
    (b) the grounds for giving the authorisation;
    (c) the giving of the warning required by *paragraph 3*; and
    (d) the fact that the appropriate consent was given or (as the case may be) refused, and if refused, the reason given for the refusal (if any); and
    (e) if an x-ray is taken or an ultrasound scan carried out:
    •   where it was taken or carried out;
    •   who took it or carried it out;
    •   who was present;
    •   the result.

6 Paragraphs 1.4–1.7 of this Code apply and an appropriate adult should be present when consent is sought to any procedure under this Annex.

Notes for guidance

K1 If authority is given for an x-ray to be taken or an ultrasound scan to be carried out (or both), consideration should be given to asking a registered medical practitioner or registered nurse to explain to the detainee what is involved and to allay any concerns the detainee might have about the effect which taking an x-ray or carrying out an ultrasound scan might have on them. If appropriate consent is not given, evidence of the explanation may, if the case comes to trial, be relevant to determining whether the detainee had a good cause for refusing.

K2 In warning a detainee who is asked to consent to an X-ray being taken or an ultrasound scan being carried out (or both), as in paragraph 3, the following form of words may be used:

'You do not have to allow an x-ray of you to be taken or an ultrasound scan to be carried out on you, but I must warn you that if you refuse without good cause, your refusal may harm your case if it comes to trial.'

Where the use of the Welsh Language is appropriate, the following form of words may be provided in Welsh:

'Does dim rhaid i chi ganiatáu cymryd sgan uwchsain neu belydr-x (neu'r ddau) arnoch, ond mae'n rhaid i mi eich rhybuddio os byddwch chi'n gwrthod gwneud hynny heb reswm da, fe allai hynny niweidio eich achos pe bai'n dod gerbron llys.'

Annex L Establishing Gender of Persons for the Purpose of Searching

1. Certain provisions of this and other PACE Codes explicitly state that searches and other procedures may only be carried out by, or in the presence of, persons of the same sex as the person subject to the search or other procedure. See *Note L1*.

2. All searches and procedures must be carried out with courtesy, consideration and respect for the person concerned. Police officers should show particular sensitivity when dealing with transgender individuals (including transsexual persons) and transvestite persons (see *Notes L2, L3 and L4*).

(a) Consideration

3. In law, the gender (and accordingly the sex) of an individual is their gender as registered at birth unless they have been issued with a Gender Recognition Certificate (GRC) under the Gender Recognition Act 2004 (GRA), in which case the person's gender is their acquired gender. This means that if the acquired gender is the male gender, the person's sex becomes that of a man and, if it is the female gender, the person's sex becomes that of a woman and they must be treated as their acquired gender.

4. When establishing whether the person concerned should be treated as being male or female for the purposes of these searches and procedures, the following approach which is designed to minimise embarrassment and secure the person's co-operation should be followed:

    (a) The person must not be asked whether they have a GRC (see *paragraph 8*);

    (b) If there is no doubt as to as to whether the person concerned should be treated as being male or female, they should be dealt with as being of that sex.

    (c) If at any time (including during the search or carrying out the procedure) there is doubt as to whether the person should be treated, or continue to be treated, as being male or female:

        (i)   the person should be asked what gender they consider themselves to be. If they express a preference to be dealt with as a particular gender, they should be asked to indicate and confirm their preference by signing the custody record or, if a custody record has not been opened, the search record or the officer's notebook. Subject to (ii) below, the person should be treated according to their preference;

        (ii) if there are grounds to doubt that the preference in (i) accurately reflects the person's predominant lifestyle, for example, if they ask to be treated as woman but documents and other information make it clear that they live predominantly as a man, or vice versa, they should be treated according to what appears to be their predominant lifestyle and not their stated preference;

        (iii) If the person is unwilling to express a preference as in (i) above, efforts should be made to determine their predominant lifestyle and they should be treated as such. For example, if they appear to live predominantly as a woman, they should be treated as being female; or

        (iv) if none of the above apply, the person should be dealt with according to what reasonably appears to have been their sex as registered at birth.

5. Once a decision has been made about which gender an individual is to be treated as, each officer responsible for the search or procedure should where possible be advised before the search or procedure starts of any doubts as to the person's gender and the person informed that the doubts have been disclosed. This is important so as to maintain the dignity of the person and any officers concerned.

(b) Documentation

6. The person's gender as established under *paragraph 4(c)(i)* to *(iv)* above must be recorded in the person's custody record, or if a custody record has not been opened, on the search record or in the officer's notebook.

7. Where the person elects which gender they consider themselves to be under *paragraph 4(b)(i)* but following *4(b)(ii)* is not treated in accordance with their preference, the reason must be recorded in the search record, in the officer's notebook or, if applicable, in the person's custody record.

(c) Disclosure of information

8. Section 22 of the GRA defines any information relating to a person's application for a GRC or to a successful applicant's gender before it became their acquired gender as 'protected information'. Nothing in this Annex is to be read as authorising or permitting any police officer or any police staff who has acquired such information when acting in their official capacity to disclose that information to any other person in contravention of the GRA. Disclosure includes making a record of 'protected information' which is read by others.

Note for guidance

L1 Provisions to which paragraph 1 applies include:
- In Code C; paragraph 4.1 and Annex A paragraphs 5, 6, and 11 (searches, strip and intimate searches of detainees under sections 54 and 55 of PACE);
- In Code A; paragraphs 2.8 and 3.6 and Note 4;
- In Code D; paragraph 5.5 and Note 5F (searches, examinations and photographing of detainees under section 54A of PACE) and paragraph 6.9 (taking samples);
- In Code H; paragraph 4.1 and Annex A paragraphs 6, 7 and 12 (searches, strip and intimate searches under sections 54 and 55 of PACE of persons arrested under section 41 of the Terrorism Act 2000).

L2 While there is no agreed definition of transgender (or trans), it is generally used as an umbrella term to describe people whose gender identity (self-identification as being a woman, man, neither or both) differs from the sex they were registered as at birth. The term includes, but is not limited to, transsexual people.

L3 Transsexual means a person who is proposing to undergo, is undergoing or has undergone a process (or part of a process) for the purpose of gender reassignment which is a protected characteristic under the Equality Act 2010 (see paragraph 1.0) by changing physiological or other attributes of their sex. This includes aspects of gender such as dress and title. It would apply to a woman making the transition to being a man and a man making the transition to being a woman as well as to a person who has only just started out on the process of gender reassignment and to a person who has completed the process. Both would share the characteristic of gender reassignment with each having the characteristics of one sex, but with certain characteristics of the other sex.

L4 Transvestite means a person of one gender who dresses in the clothes of a person of the opposite gender. However, a transvestite does not live permanently in the gender opposite to their birth sex.

L5 Chief officers are responsible for providing corresponding operational guidance and instructions for the deployment of transgender officers and staff under their direction and control to duties which involve carrying out, or being present at, any of the searches and procedures described in paragraph 1. The guidance and instructions must comply with the Equality Act 2010 and should therefore complement the approach in this Annex.

CODE OF PRACTICE FOR THE IDENTIFICATION OF PERSONS BY POLICE OFFICERS (CODE D)

1 Introduction

1.1 This Code of Practice concerns the principal methods used by police to identify people in connection with the investigation of offences and the keeping of accurate and reliable criminal records. The powers and procedures in this code must be used fairly, responsibly, with respect for the people to whom they apply and without unlawful discrimination. The Equality Act 2010 makes it unlawful for police officers to discriminate against, harass or victimise any person on the grounds of the 'protected characteristics' of age, disability, gender reassignment, race, religion or belief, sex and sexual orientation, marriage and civil partnership, pregnancy and maternity when using their powers. When police forces are carrying out their functions they also have a duty to have regard to the need to eliminate unlawful discrimination, harassment and victimisation and to take steps to foster good relations.

1.2 In this code, identification by an eye-witness arises when a witness who has seen the offender committing the crime and is given an opportunity to identify a person suspected of involvement in the offence in a video identification, identification parade or similar procedure. These eye-witness identification procedures (see Part A of section 3 below) are designed to:
- test the witness' ability to identify the suspect as the person they saw on a previous occasion
- provide safeguards against mistaken identification.

While this Code concentrates on visual identification procedures, it does not preclude the police making use of aural identification procedures such as a "voice identification parade", where they judge that appropriate.

1.2A In this code, separate provisions in Part B of section 3 below apply when any person, including a police officer, is asked if they recognise anyone they see in an image as being someone they know and to test their claim that they recognise that person as someone who is known to them. Except where stated, these separate provisions are not subject to the eye-witnesses identification procedures described in paragraph 1.2.

1.3 Identification by fingerprints applies when a person's fingerprints are taken to:
- compare with fingerprints found at the scene of a crime
- check and prove convictions
- help to ascertain a person's identity.

1.3A Identification using footwear impressions applies when a person's footwear impressions are taken to compare with impressions found at the scene of a crime.

1.4 Identification by body samples and impressions includes taking samples such as blood or hair to generate a DNA profile for comparison with material obtained from the scene of a crime, or a victim.

1.5 Taking photographs of arrested people applies to recording and checking identity and locating and tracing persons who:
- are wanted for offences
- fail to answer their bail.

1.6 Another method of identification involves searching and examining detained suspects to find, e.g., marks such as tattoos or scars which may help establish their identity or whether they have been involved in committing an offence.

1.7 The provisions of the Police and Criminal Evidence Act 1984 (PACE) and this Code are designed to make sure fingerprints, samples, impressions and photographs are taken, used and retained, and identification procedures carried out, only when justified and necessary for preventing, detecting or investigating crime. If these provisions are not observed, the application of the relevant procedures in particular cases may be open to question.

2 General

2.1 This Code must be readily available at all police stations for consultation by:
- police officers and police staff
- detained persons
- members of the public

2.2 The provisions of this Code:
- include the *Annexes*
- do not include the *Notes for guidance.*

2.3 Code C, paragraph 1.4, regarding a person who may be mentally disordered or otherwise mentally vulnerable and the *Notes for guidance* applicable to those provisions apply to this Code.

2.4 Code C, paragraph 1.5, regarding a person who appears to be under the age of 17 applies to this Code.

2.5 Code C, paragraph 1.6, regarding a person who appears to be blind, seriously visually impaired, deaf, unable to read or speak or has difficulty communicating orally because of a speech impediment applies to this Code.

2.6 In this Code:
- 'appropriate adult' means the same as in Code C, paragraph 1.7
- 'solicitor' means the same as in Code C, paragraph 6.12

and the *Notes for guidance* applicable to those provisions apply to this Code.
- where a search or other procedure under this code may only be carried out or observed by a person of the same sex as the person to whom the search or procedure applies, the gender of the detainee and other persons present should be established and recorded in line with Annex F of Code A.

2.7 References to custody officers include those performing the functions of custody officer, see *paragraph 1.9* of Code C.

2.8 When a record of any action requiring the authority of an officer of a specified rank is made under this Code, subject to *paragraph 2.18,* the officer's name and rank must be recorded.

2.9 When this Code requires the prior authority or agreement of an officer of at least inspector or superintendent rank, that authority may be given by a sergeant or chief inspector who has been authorised to perform the functions of the higher rank under PACE, section 107.

2.10 Subject to *paragraph 2.18*, all records must be timed and signed by the maker.

2.11 Records must be made in the custody record, unless otherwise specified. References to 'pocket book' include any official report book issued to police officers or police staff.

2.12 If any procedure in this Code requires a person's consent, the consent of a:

- mentally disordered or otherwise mentally vulnerable person is only valid if given in the presence of the appropriate adult
- juvenile is only valid if their parent's or guardian's consent is also obtained unless the juvenile is under 14, when their parent's or guardian's consent is sufficient in its own right. If the only obstacle to an identification procedure in *section 3* is that a juvenile's parent or guardian refuses consent or reasonable efforts to obtain it have failed, the identification officer may apply the provisions of *paragraph 3.21*. See *Note 2A*

2.13 If a person is blind, seriously visually impaired or unable to read, the custody officer or identification officer shall make sure their solicitor, relative, appropriate adult or some other person likely to take an interest in them and not involved in the investigation is available to help check any documentation. When this Code requires written consent or signing, the person assisting may be asked to sign instead, if the detainee prefers. This paragraph does not require an appropriate adult to be called solely to assist in checking and signing documentation for a person who is not a juvenile, or mentally disordered or otherwise mentally vulnerable (see *Note 2B* and Code C *paragraph 3.15*).

2.14 If any procedure in this Code requires information to be given to or sought from a suspect, it must be given or sought in the appropriate adult's presence if the suspect is mentally disordered, otherwise mentally vulnerable or a juvenile. If the appropriate adult is not present when the information is first given or sought, the procedure must be repeated in the presence of the appropriate adult when they arrive. If the suspect appears deaf or there is doubt about their hearing or speaking ability or ability to understand English, and effective communication cannot be established, the information must be given or sought through an interpreter.

2.15 Any procedure in this Code involving the participation of a suspect who is mentally disordered, otherwise mentally vulnerable or a juvenile must take place in the presence of the appropriate adult. See Code C paragraph 1.4.

2.15A Any procedure in this Code involving the participation of a witness who is or appears to be mentally disordered, otherwise mentally vulnerable or a juvenile should take place in the presence of a pre-trial support person unless the witness states that they do not want a support person to be present. A support person must not be allowed to prompt any identification of a suspect by a witness. See *Note 2AB*.

2.16 References to:

- 'taking a photograph', include the use of any process to produce a single, still or moving, visual image
- 'photographing a person', should be construed accordingly
- 'photographs', 'films', 'negatives' and 'copies' include relevant visual images recorded, stored, or reproduced through any medium
- 'destruction' includes the deletion of computer data relating to such images or making access to that data impossible

2.17 Except as described, nothing in this Code affects the powers and procedures:

  (i) for requiring and taking samples of breath, blood and urine in relation to driving offences, etc, when under the influence of drink, drugs or excess alcohol under the:
  - Road Traffic Act 1988, sections 4 to 11

- Road Traffic Offenders Act 1988, sections 15 and 16
- Transport and Works Act 1992, sections 26 to 38;

(ii) under the Immigration Act 1971, Schedule 2, paragraph 18, for taking photographs and fingerprints from persons detained under that Act, Schedule 2, paragraph 16 (Administrative Controls as to Control on Entry etc.); for taking fingerprints in accordance with the Immigration and Asylum Act 1999; sections 141 and 142(3), or other methods for collecting information about a person's external physical characteristics provided for by regulations made under that Act, section 144;

(iii) under the Terrorism Act 2000, Schedule 8, for taking photographs, fingerprints, skin impressions, body samples or impressions from people:

- arrested under that Act, section 41,
- detained for the purposes of examination under that Act, Schedule 7, and to whom the Code of Practice issued under that Act, Schedule 14, paragraph 6, applies ('the terrorism provisions')

See *Note 2C*;

(iv) for taking photographs, fingerprints, skin impressions, body samples or impressions from people who have been:

- arrested on warrants issued in Scotland, by officers exercising powers under the Criminal Justice and Public Order Act 1994, section 136(2)
- arrested or detained without warrant by officers from a police force in Scotland exercising their powers of arrest or detention under the Criminal Justice and Public Order Act 1994, section 137(2), (Cross Border powers of arrest etc.).

Note: In these cases, police powers and duties and the person's rights and entitlements whilst at a police station in England and Wales are the same as if the person had been arrested in Scotland by a Scottish police officer.

2.18 Nothing in this Code requires the identity of officers or police staff to be recorded or disclosed:

(a) in the case of enquiries linked to the investigation of terrorism;

(b) if the officers or police staff reasonably believe recording or disclosing their names might put them in danger.

In these cases, they shall use warrant or other identification numbers and the name of their police station. *See Note 2D*

2.19 In this Code:

(a) 'designated person' means a person other than a police officer, designated under the Police Reform Act 2002, Part 4, who has specified powers and duties of police officers conferred or imposed on them;

(b) any reference to a police officer includes a designated person acting in the exercise or performance of the powers and duties conferred or imposed on them by their designation.

2.20 If a power conferred on a designated person:

(a) allows reasonable force to be used when exercised by a police officer, a designated person exercising that power has the same entitlement to use force;

(b) includes power to use force to enter any premises, that power is not exercisable by that designated person except:

(i) in the company, and under the supervision, of a police officer; or

(ii) for the purpose of:

- saving life or limb; or
- preventing serious damage to property.

2.21 Nothing in this Code prevents the custody officer, or other officer given custody of the detainee, from allowing police staff who are not designated persons to carry out individual procedures or tasks at the police station if the law allows. However, the officer remains responsible for making sure the procedures and tasks are carried out correctly in accordance with the Codes of Practice. Any such person must be:

(a) a person employed by a police authority maintaining a police force and under the control and direction of the Chief Officer of that force;

(b) employed by a person with whom a police authority has a contract for the provision of services relating to persons arrested or otherwise in custody. 9

2.22 Designated persons and other police staff must have regard to any relevant provisions of the Codes of Practice.

Notes for guidance

2A For the purposes of paragraph 2.12, the consent required from a parent or guardian may, for a juvenile in the care of a local authority or voluntary organisation, be given by that authority or organisation. In the case of a juvenile, nothing in paragraph 2.12 requires the parent, guardian or representative of a local authority or voluntary organisation to be present to give their consent, unless they are acting as the appropriate adult under paragraphs 2.14 or 2.15. However, it is important that a parent or guardian not present is fully informed before being asked to consent. They must be given the same information about the procedure and the juvenile's suspected involvement in the offence as the juvenile and appropriate adult. The parent or guardian must also be allowed to speak to the juvenile and the appropriate adult if they wish. Provided the consent is fully informed and is not withdrawn, it may be obtained at any time before the procedure takes place.

2AB The Youth Justice and Criminal Evidence Act 1999 guidance "Achieving Best Evidence in Criminal Proceedings" indicates that a pre-trial support person should accompany a vulnerable witness during any identification procedure unless the witness states that they do not want a support person to be present. It states that this support person should not be (or not be likely to be) a witness in the investigation.

2B People who are seriously visually impaired or unable to read may be unwilling to sign police documents. The alternative, i.e. their representative signing on their behalf, seeks to protect the interests of both police and suspects.

2C Photographs, fingerprints, samples and impressions may be taken from a person detained under the terrorism provisions to help determine whether they are, or have been, involved in terrorism, as well as when there are reasonable grounds for suspecting their involvement in a particular offence.

2D The purpose of paragraph 2.18(b) is to protect those involved in serious organised crime investigations or arrests of particularly violent suspects when there is reliable information that those arrested or their associates may threaten or cause harm to the officers. In cases of doubt, an officer of inspector rank or above should be consulted.

3 Identification and recognition of suspects

(A) Identification of a suspect by an eye-witness

3.0 This part applies when an eye-witness has seen the offender committing the crime or in any other circumstances which tend to prove or disprove the involvement of the person they saw in the crime, for example, close to the scene of the crime, immediately before or immediately after it was committed. It sets out the procedures to be used to test the ability of that eye-witness to identify a person suspected of involvement in the offence as the person they saw on the previous occasion. Except where stated, this part does not apply to the procedures described in Part B and Note 3AA.

3.1 A record shall be made of the suspect's description as first given by a potential witness. This record must:

(a) be made and kept in a form which enables details of that description to be accurately produced from it, in a visible and legible form, which can be given to the suspect or the suspect's solicitor in accordance with this Code; and

(b) unless otherwise specified, be made before the witness takes part in any identification procedures under paragraphs 3.5 to 3.10, 3.21 or 3.23.

A copy of the record shall where practicable, be given to the suspect or their solicitor before any procedures under paragraphs 3.5 to 3.10, 3.21 or 3.23 are carried out. See Note 3E

(a) Cases when the suspect's identity is not known

3.2 In cases when the suspect's identity is not known, a witness may be taken to a particular neighbourhood or place to see whether they can identify the person they saw on a previous occasion. Although the number, age, sex, race, general description and style of clothing of other people present at the location and the way in which any identification is made cannot be controlled, the principles applicable to the formal procedures under *paragraphs 3.5 to 3.10* shall be followed as far as practicable. For example:

(a) where it is practicable to do so, a record should be made of the witness' description of the suspect, as in paragraph 3.1 (a), before asking the witness to make an identification;

(b) care must be taken not to direct the witness' attention to any individual unless, taking into account all the circumstances, this cannot be avoided. However, this does not prevent a witness being asked to look carefully at the people around at the time or to look towards a group or in a particular direction, if this appears necessary to make sure that the witness does not overlook a possible suspect simply because the witness is looking in the opposite direction and also to enable the witness to make comparisons between any suspect and others who are in the area; See *Note 3F*

(c) where there is more than one witness, every effort should be made to keep them separate and witnesses should be taken to see whether they can identify a person independently;

(d) once there is sufficient information to justify the arrest of a particular individual for suspected involvement in the offence, e.g., after a witness makes a positive identification, the provisions set out from paragraph 3.4 onwards shall apply for any other witnesses in relation to that individual.;

(e) the officer or police staff accompanying the witness must record, in their pocket book, the action taken as soon as, and in as much detail, as possible. The record should include: the date, time and place of the relevant occasion the witness claims to have previously seen the suspect; where any identification was made; how it was made and the conditions at the time (e.g., the distance the witness was from the suspect, the weather and light); if the witness's attention was drawn to the suspect; the reason for this; and anything said by the witness or the suspect about the identification or the conduct of the procedure.

3.3 A witness must not be shown photographs, computerised or artist's composite likenesses or similar likenesses or pictures (including 'E-fit' images) if the identity of the suspect is known to the police and the suspect is available to take part in a video identification, an identification parade or a group identification. If the suspect's identity is not known, the showing of such images to a witness to obtain identification evidence must be done in accordance with *Annex E*.

(b) Cases when the suspect is known and available

3.4 If the suspect's identity is known to the police and they are available, the identification procedures set out in paragraphs 3.5 to 3.10 may be used. References in this section to a suspect being 'known' mean there is sufficient information known to the police to justify the arrest of a particular person for suspected involvement in the offence. A suspect being 'available' means they are immediately available or will be within a reasonably short time and willing to take an effective part in at least one of the following which it is practicable to arrange:

- video identification;
- identification parade; or
- group identification.

Video identification

3.5 A 'video identification' is when the witness is shown moving images of a known suspect, together with similar images of others who resemble the suspect. Moving images must be used unless:

- the suspect is known but not available (see paragraph 3.21 of this Code); or

- in accordance with paragraph 2A of Annex A of this Code, the identification officer does not consider that replication of a physical feature can be achieved or that it is not possible to conceal the location of the feature on the image of the suspect.

  The identification officer may then decide to make use of video identification but using **still** images.

3.6 Video identifications must be carried out in accordance with *Annex A*.

Identification parade

3.7 An 'identification parade' is when the witness sees the suspect in a line of others who resemble the suspect.

3.8 Identification parades must be carried out in accordance with *Annex B*.

Group identification

3.9 A 'group identification' is when the witness sees the suspect in an informal group of people.

3.10 Group identifications must be carried out in accordance with *Annex C*.

Arranging eye-witness identification procedures

3.11 Except for the provisions in *paragraph 3.19*, the arrangements for, and conduct of, the identification procedures in paragraphs 3.5 to 3.10 and circumstances in which an identification procedure must be held shall be the responsibility of an officer not below inspector rank who is not involved with the investigation, 'the identification officer'. Unless otherwise specified, the identification officer may allow another officer or police staff, see *paragraph 2.21*, to make arrangements for, and conduct, any of these identification procedures. In delegating these procedures, the identification officer must be able to supervise effectively and either intervene or be contacted for advice. No officer or any other person involved with the investigation of the case against the suspect, beyond the extent required by these procedures, may take any part in these procedures or act as the identification officer. This does not prevent the identification officer from consulting the officer in charge of the investigation to determine which procedure to use. When an identification procedure is required, in the interest of fairness to suspects and witnesses, it must be held as soon as practicable.

Circumstances in which an eye-witness identification procedure must be held

3.12 Whenever:

(i) an eye witness has identified a suspect or purported to have identified them prior to any identification procedure set out in paragraphs 3.5 to 3.10 having been held; or

(ii) there is a witness available who expresses an ability to identify the suspect, or where there is a reasonable chance of the witness being able to do so, and they have not been given an opportunity to identify the suspect in any of the procedures set out in paragraphs 3.5 to 3.10, and the suspect disputes being the person the witness claims to have seen, an identification procedure shall be held unless it is not practicable or it would serve no useful purpose in proving or disproving whether the suspect was involved in committing the offence, for example:

- where the suspect admits being at the scene of the crime and gives an account of what took place and the eye-witness does not see anything which contradicts that.
- when it is not disputed that the suspect is already known to the witness who claims to have recognised them when seeing them commit the crime.

3.13 An eye-witness identification procedure may also be held if the officer in charge of the investigation considers it would be useful.

Selecting an eye-witness identification procedure

3.14 If, because of paragraph 3.12, an identification procedure is to be held, the suspect shall initially be offered a video identification unless:

(a) a video identification is not practicable; or

(b) an identification parade is both practicable and more suitable than a video identification; or

(c) paragraph 3.16 applies.

The identification officer and the officer in charge of the investigation shall consult each other to determine which option is to be offered. An identification parade may not be practicable because of factors relating to the witnesses, such as their number, state of health, availability and travelling requirements. A video identification would normally be more suitable if it could be arranged and completed sooner than an identification parade. Before an option is offered the suspect must also be reminded of their entitlement to have free legal advice, see Code C, *paragraph 6.5*.

3.15 A suspect who refuses the identification procedure first offered shall be asked to state their reason for refusing and may get advice from their solicitor and/or if present, their appropriate adult. The suspect, solicitor and/or appropriate adult shall be allowed to make representations about why another procedure should be used. A record should be made of the reasons for refusal and any representations made. After considering any reasons given, and representations made, the identification officer shall, if appropriate, arrange for the suspect to be offered an alternative which the officer considers suitable and practicable. If the officer decides it is not suitable and practicable to offer an alternative identification procedure, the reasons for that decision shall be recorded.

3.16 A group identification may initially be offered if the officer in charge of the investigation considers it is more suitable than a video identification or an identification parade and the identification officer considers it practicable to arrange.

Notice to suspect

3.17 Unless *paragraph 3.20* applies, before a video identification, an identification parade or group identification is arranged, the following shall be explained to the suspect:

(i) the purposes of the video identification, identification parade or group identification;

(ii) their entitlement to free legal advice; see Code C, paragraph 6.5;

(iii) the procedures for holding it, including their right to have a solicitor or friend present;

(iv) that they do not have to consent to or co-operate in a video identification, identification parade or group identification;

(v) that if they do not consent to, and co-operate in, a video identification, identification parade or group identification, their refusal may be given in evidence in any subsequent trial and police may proceed covertly without their consent or make other arrangements to test whether a witness can identify them, see *paragraph 3.21;*

(vi) whether, for the purposes of the video identification procedure, images of them have previously been obtained, see *paragraph 3.20*, and if so, that they may co-operate in providing further, suitable images to be used instead;

(vii) if appropriate, the special arrangements for juveniles;

(viii) if appropriate, the special arrangements for mentally disordered or otherwise mentally vulnerable people;

(ix) that if they significantly alter their appearance between being offered an identification procedure and any attempt to hold an identification procedure, this may be given in evidence if the case comes to trial, and the identification officer may then consider other forms of identification, see *paragraph 3.21* and *Note 3C;*

(x) that a moving image or photograph may be taken of them when they attend for any identification procedure;

(xi) whether, before their identity became known, the witness was shown photographs a computerised or artist's composite likeness or similar likeness or image by the police, see *Note 3B;*

(xii) that if they change their appearance before an identification parade, it may not be practicable to arrange one on the day or subsequently and, because of the appearance change, the identification officer may consider alternative methods of identification, see *Note 3C;*

    (xiii)   that they or their solicitor will be provided with details of the description of the suspect as first given by any witnesses who are to attend the video identification, identification parade, group identification or confrontation, see paragraph 3.1.

3.18 This information must also be recorded in a written notice handed to the suspect. The suspect must be given a reasonable opportunity to read the notice, after which, they should be asked to sign a second copy to indicate if they are willing to co-operate with the making of a video or take part in the identification parade or group identification. The signed copy shall be retained by the identification officer.

3.19 The duties of the identification officer under *paragraphs 3.17* and *3.18* may be performed by the custody officer or other officer not involved in the investigation if:

    (a) it is proposed to release the suspect in order that an identification procedure can be arranged and carried out and an inspector is not available to act as the identification officer, see *paragraph 3.11*, before the suspect leaves the station; or

    (b) it is proposed to keep the suspect in police detention whilst the procedure is arranged and carried out and waiting for an inspector to act as the identification officer, see *paragraph 3.11,* would cause unreasonable delay to the investigation.

The officer concerned shall inform the identification officer of the action taken and give them the signed copy of the notice. See *Note 3C*

3.20 If the identification officer and officer in charge of the investigation suspect, on reasonable grounds that if the suspect was given the information and notice as in *paragraphs 3.17* and *3.18,* they would then take steps to avoid being seen by a witness in any identification procedure, the identification officer may arrange for images of the suspect suitable for use in a video identification procedure to be obtained before giving the information and notice. If suspect's images are obtained in these circumstances, the suspect may, for the purposes of a video identification procedure, co-operate in providing new images which if suitable, would be used instead, see *paragraph 3.17(vi).*

(c) Cases when the suspect is known but not available

3.21 When a known suspect is not available or has ceased to be available, see *paragraph 3.4,* the identification officer may make arrangements for a video identification (see Annex A). If necessary, the identification officer may follow the video identification procedures but using still images. Any suitable moving or still images may be used and these may be obtained covertly if necessary. Alternatively, the identification officer may make arrangements for a group identification. See *Note 3D.* These provisions may also be applied to juveniles where the consent of their parent or guardian is either refused or reasonable efforts to obtain that consent have failed. (see *paragraph 2.12).*

3.22 Any covert activity should be strictly limited to that necessary to test the ability of the witness to identify the suspect.

3.23 The identification officer may arrange for the suspect to be confronted by the witness if none of the options referred to in paragraphs 3.5 to 3.10 or 3.21 are practicable. A "confrontation" is when the suspect is directly confronted by the witness. A confrontation does not require the suspect's consent. Confrontations must be carried out in accordance with Annex D.

3.24 Requirements for information to be given to, or sought from, a suspect or for the suspect to be given an opportunity to view images before they are shown to a witness, do not apply if the suspect's lack of co-operation prevents the necessary action.

(d) Documentation

3.25 A record shall be made of the video identification, identification parade, group identification or confrontation on forms provided for the purpose.

3.26 If the identification officer considers it is not practicable to hold a video identification or identification parade requested by the suspect, the reasons shall be recorded and explained to the suspect.

3.27 A record shall be made of a person's failure or refusal to co-operate in a video identification, identification parade or group identification and, if applicable, of the grounds for obtaining images in accordance with *paragraph 3.20.*

(e) Showing films and photographs of incidents and information released to the media

3.28 Nothing in this Code inhibits showing films, photographs or other images to the public through the national or local media, or to police officers for the purposes of recognition and tracing suspects. However, when such material is shown to obtain evidence of recognition, the procedures in Part B will apply. See *Note 3AA*.

3.29 When a broadcast or publication is made, see *paragraph 3.28*, a copy of the relevant material released to the media for the purposes of recognising or tracing the suspect, shall be kept. The suspect or their solicitor shall be allowed to view such material before any eye-witness identification procedures under *paragraphs 3.5 to 3.10, 3.21 or 3.23* of Part A are carried out, provided it is practicable and would not unreasonably delay the investigation. Each eye-witness involved in the procedure shall be asked, after they have taken part, whether they have seen any film, photograph or image relating to the offence or any description of the suspect which has been broadcast or published in any national or local media or on any social networking site and if they have, they should be asked to give details of the circumstances, such as the date and place as relevant. Their replies shall be recorded. This paragraph does not affect any separate requirement under the Criminal Procedure and Investigations Act 1996 to retain material in connection with criminal investigations.

(f) Destruction and retention of photographs taken or used in eye-witness identification procedures

3.30 PACE, section 64A, see *paragraph 5.12*, provides powers to take photographs of suspects and allows these photographs to be used or disclosed only for purposes related to the prevention or detection of crime, the investigation of offences or the conduct of prosecutions by, or on behalf of, police or other law enforcement and prosecuting authorities inside and outside the United Kingdom or the enforcement of a sentence. After being so used or disclosed, they may be retained but can only be used or disclosed for the same purposes.

3.31 Subject to *paragraph 3.33,* the photographs (and all negatives and copies), of suspects not taken in accordance with the provisions in *paragraph 5.12* which are taken for the purposes of, or in connection with, the identification procedures in *paragraphs 3.5 to 3.10, 3.21 or 3.23* must be destroyed unless the suspect:

(a) is charged with, or informed they may be prosecuted for, a recordable offence;
(b) is prosecuted for a recordable offence;
(c) is cautioned for a recordable offence or given a warning or reprimand in accordance with the Crime and Disorder Act 1998 for a recordable offence; or
(d) gives informed consent, in writing, for the photograph or images to be retained for purposes described in *paragraph 3.30*.

3.32 When *paragraph 3.31* requires the destruction of any photograph, the person must be given an opportunity to witness the destruction or to have a certificate confirming the destruction if they request one within five days of being informed that the destruction is required.

3.33 Nothing in *paragraph 3.31* affects any separate requirement under the Criminal Procedure and Investigations Act 1996 to retain material in connection with criminal investigations.

(B) Evidence of recognition by showing films, photographs and other images

3.34 This Part of this section applies when, for the purposes of obtaining evidence of recognition, any person, including a police officer:

(a) views the image of an individual in a film, photograph or any other visual medium; and
(b) is asked whether they recognise that individual as someone who is known to them.
See Notes 3AA and 3G

3.35 The films, photographs and other images shall be shown on an individual basis to avoid any possibility of collusion and to provide safeguards against mistaken recognition (see *Note 3G*), the showing shall as far as possible follow the principles for video identification if the suspect is known, see *Annex A*, or identification by photographs if the suspect is not known, see *Annex E*.

3.36   record of the circumstances and conditions under which the person is given an opportunity to recognise the individual must be made and the record must include:

(a) Whether the person knew or was given information concerning the name or identity of any suspect.

(b) What the person has been told *before* the viewing about the offence, the person(s) depicted in the images or the offender and by whom.

(c) How and by whom the witness was asked to view the image or look at the individual.

(d) Whether the viewing was alone or with others and if with others, the reason for it.

(e) The arrangements under which the person viewed the film or saw the individual and by whom those arrangements were made.

(f) Whether the viewing of any images was arranged as part of a mass circulation to police and the public or for selected persons.

(g) The date time and place images were viewed or further viewed or the individual was seen.

(h) The times between which the images were viewed or the individual was seen.

(i) How the viewing of images or sighting of the individual was controlled and by whom.

(j) Whether the person was familiar with the location shown in any images or the place where they saw the individual and if so, why.

(k) Whether or not on this occasion, the person claims to recognise any image shown, or any individual seen, as being someone known to them, and if they do:

(i)   the reason

(ii)   the words of recognition

(iii) any expressions of doubt

(iv) what features of the image or the individual triggered the recognition.

3.37 The record under paragraph 3.36 may be made by:

- the person who views the image or sees the individual and makes the recognition.
- the officer or police staff in charge of showing the images to the person or in charge of the conditions under which the person sees the individual.

Notes for guidance

3AA   The eye-witness identification procedures in Part A should not be used to test whether a witness can recognise a person as someone they know and would be able to give evidence of recognition along the lines that "On (describe date, time location) I saw an image of an individual who I recognised as AB." In these cases, the procedures in Part B shall apply.

3A   Except for the provisions of Annex E, paragraph 1, a police officer who is a witness for the purposes of this part of the Code is subject to the same principles and procedures as a civilian witness.

3B   When a witness attending an identification procedure has previously been shown photographs, or been shown or provided with computerised or artist's composite likenesses, or similar likenesses or pictures, it is the officer in charge of the investigation's responsibility to make the identification officer aware of this.

3C   The purpose of paragraph 3.19 is to avoid or reduce delay in arranging identification procedures by enabling the required information and warnings, see sub-paragraphs 3.17(ix) and 3.17(xii), to be given at the earliest opportunity.

3D   Paragraph 3.21 would apply when a known suspect deliberately makes themselves 'unavailable' in order to delay or frustrate arrangements for obtaining identification evidence. It also applies when a suspect refuses or fails to take part in a video identification, an identification parade or a group identification, or refuses or fails to take part in the only practicable options from that list. It enables any suitable images of the suspect, moving or still, which are available or can be obtained, to be used in an identification procedure. Examples include images from custody and other CCTV systems and from visually recorded interview records, see Code F Note for Guidance 2D.

3E When it is proposed to show photographs to a witness in accordance with Annex E, it is the responsibility of the officer in charge of the investigation to confirm to the officer responsible for supervising and directing the showing, that the first description of the suspect given by that witness has been recorded. If this description has not been recorded, the procedure under Annex E must be postponed. See Annex E paragraph 2

3F The admissibility and value of identification evidence obtained when carrying out the procedure under paragraph 3.2 may be compromised if:

(a) before a person is identified, the witness' attention is specifically drawn to that person; or

(b) the suspect's identity becomes known before the procedure.

3G The admissibility and value of evidence of recognition obtained when carrying out the procedures in Part B may be compromised if before the person is recognised, the witness who has claimed to know them is given or is made, or becomes aware of, information about the person which was not previously known to them personally but which they have purported to rely on to support their claim that the person is in fact known to them.

4 Identification by fingerprints and footwear impressions

(A) Taking fingerprints in connection with a criminal investigation

(a) General

4.1 References to 'fingerprints' means any record, produced by any method, of the skin pattern and other physical characteristics or features of a person's:

(i)   fingers; or

(ii)   palms.

(b) Action

4.2 A person's fingerprints may be taken in connection with the investigation of an offence only with their consent or if *paragraph 4.3* applies. If the person is at a police station consent must be in writing.

4.3 PACE, section 61, provides powers to take fingerprints without consent from any person over the age of ten years:

(a)   under section 61(3), from a person detained at a police station in consequence of being arrested for a recordable offence, see *Note 4A*, if they have not had their fingerprints taken in the course of the investigation of the offence unless those previously taken fingerprints are not a complete set or some or all of those fingerprints are not of sufficient quality to allow satisfactory analysis, comparison or matching.

(b)   under section 61(4), from a person detained at a police station who has been charged with a recordable offence, see *Note 4A*, or informed they will be reported for such an offence if they have not had their fingerprints taken in the course of the investigation of the offence unless those previously taken fingerprints are not a complete set or some or all of those fingerprints are not of sufficient quality to allow satisfactory analysis, comparison or matching.

(c)   under section 61(4A), from a person who has been bailed to appear at a court or police station if the person:

(i)   has answered to bail for a person whose fingerprints were taken previously and there are reasonable grounds for believing they are not the same person; or

(ii)   who has answered to bail claims to be a different person from a person whose fingerprints were previously taken;

and in either case, the court or an officer of inspector rank or above, authorises the fingerprints to be taken at the court or police station (an inspector's authority may be given in writing or orally and confirmed in writing, as soon as practicable);

(ca) under section 61(5A) from a person who has been arrested for a recordable offence and released if the person:

(i)   is on bail and has not had their fingerprints taken in the course of the investigation of the offence, or;

(ii)   has had their fingerprints taken in the course of the investigation of the offence, but they do not constitute a complete set or some, or all, of the fingerprints are not of sufficient quality to allow satisfactory analysis, comparison or matching.

(cb) under section 61(5B) from a person not detained at a police station who has been charged with a recordable offence or informed they will be reported for such an offence if they have not had their fingerprints taken in the course of the investigation or their fingerprints have been taken in the course of the investigation of the offence, but they do not constitute a complete set or some, or all, of the fingerprints are not of sufficient quality to allow satisfactory analysis, comparison or matching.

(d)   under section 61(6), from a person who has been:

(i)   convicted of a recordable offence;

(ii)   given a caution in respect of a recordable offence which, at the time of the caution, the person admitted; or

(iii) warned or reprimanded under the Crime and Disorder Act 1998, section 65, for a recordable offence,

if, since their conviction, caution, warning or reprimand their fingerprints have not been taken or their fingerprints which have been taken since then do not constitute a complete set or some, or all, of the fingerprints are not of sufficient quality to allow satisfactory analysis, comparison or matching, and in either case, an officer of inspector rank or above, is satisfied that taking the fingerprints is necessary to assist in the prevention or detection of crime and authorises the taking;

(e)   under section 61(6A) from a person a constable reasonably suspects is committing or attempting to commit, or has committed or attempted to commit, any offence if either:

• the person's name is unknown and cannot be readily ascertained by the constable; or

• the constable has reasonable grounds for doubting whether a name given by the person is their real name.

Note: fingerprints taken under this power are not regarded as having been taken in the course of the investigation of an offence.

[See Note 4C]

(f)   under section 61(6D) from a person who has been convicted outside England and Wales of an offence which if committed in England and Wales would be a qualifying offence as defined by PACE, section 65A (see Note 4AB) if:

(i)   the person's fingerprints have not been taken previously under this power or their fingerprints have been so taken on a previous occasion but they do not constitute a complete set or some, or all, of the fingerprints are not of sufficient quality to allow satisfactory analysis, comparison or matching; and

(ii)   a police officer of inspector rank or above is satisfied that taking fingerprints is necessary to assist in the prevention or detection of crime and authorises them to be taken.

4.4 PACE, section 63A(4) and Schedule 2A provide powers to:

(a)   make a requirement (in accordance with Annex G) for a person to attend a police station to have their fingerprints taken in the exercise of certain powers in paragraph 4.3 above when that power applies at the time the fingerprints would be taken in accordance with the requirement. Those powers are:

(i)   section 61(5A)—Persons arrested for a recordable offence and released, see paragraph 4.3(ca): The requirement may not be made more than six months from the day the investigating officer was informed that the fingerprints previously taken were incomplete or below standard.

(ii) section 61(5B)—Persons charged etc. with a recordable offence, see paragraph 4.3(cb): The requirement may not be made more than six months from:
- the day the person was charged or reported if fingerprints have not been taken since then; or
- the day the investigating officer was informed that the fingerprints previously taken were incomplete or below standard.

(iii) section 61(6)—Person convicted, cautioned, warned or reprimanded for a recordable offence in England and Wales, see paragraph 4.3(d): Where the offence for which the person was convicted etc is also a qualifying offence (see *Note 4AB*), there is no time limit for the exercise of this power. Where the conviction etc. is for a recordable offence which is not a qualifying offence, the requirement may not be made more than two years from:
- the day the person was convicted, cautioned, warned or reprimanded, or the day Schedule 2A comes into force (if later), if fingerprints have not been taken since then; or
- the day an officer from the force investigating the offence was informed that the fingerprints previously taken were incomplete or below standard or the day Schedule 2A comes into force (if later).

(iv) section 61(6D)—A person who has been convicted of a qualifying offence (see *Note 4AB*) outside England and Wales, see paragraph 4.3(g): There is no time limit for making the requirement.

Note: A person who has had their fingerprints taken under any of the powers in section 61 mentioned in paragraph 4.3 on two occasions in relation to any offence may not be required under Schedule 2A to attend a police station for their fingerprints to be taken again under section 61 in relation to that offence, unless authorised by an officer of inspector rank or above. The fact of the authorisation and the reasons for giving it must be recorded as soon as practicable.

(b) arrest, without warrant, a person who fails to comply with the requirement.

4.5 A person's fingerprints may be taken, as above, electronically.

4.6 Reasonable force may be used, if necessary, to take a person's fingerprints without their consent under the powers as in *paragraphs 4.3* and *4.4*.

4.7 Before any fingerprints are taken:
(a) without consent under any power mentioned in *paragraphs 4.3* and *4.4* above, the person must be informed of:
(i) the reason their fingerprints are to be taken;
(ii) the power under which they are to be taken; and
(iii) the fact that the relevant authority has been given if any power mentioned in *paragraph 4.3(c), (d)* or *(f)* applies

(b) with or without consent at a police station or elsewhere, the person must be informed:
(i) that their fingerprints may be subject of a speculative search against other fingerprints, see *Note 4B*; and
(ii) that their fingerprints may be retained in accordance with *Annex F, Part (a)* unless they were taken under the power mentioned in paragraph 4.3(e) when they must be destroyed after they have being checked (See *Note 4C*).

(c) Documentation

4.8A A record must be made as soon as practicable after the fingerprints are taken, of:
- the matters in paragraph 4.7(a)(i) to (iii) and the fact that the person has been informed of those matters; and
- the fact that the person has been informed of the matters in paragraph 4.7(b)(i) and (ii).

The record must be made in the person's custody record if they are detained at a police station when the fingerprints are taken.

4.8 If force is used, a record shall be made of the circumstances and those present.

4.9 Not used

(B) Taking fingerprints in connection with immigration enquiries

Action

4.10 A person's fingerprints may be taken and retained for the purposes of immigration law enforcement and control in accordance with powers and procedures other than under PACE and for which the UK Border Agency (not the police) are responsible. Details of these powers and procedures which are under the Immigration Act 1971, Schedule 2 and Immigration and Asylum Act 1999, section 141, including modifications to the PACE Codes of Practice are contained in Chapter 24 of the Operational Instructions and Guidance manual which is published by the UK Border Agency (See *Note 4D*).

4.11 *Not used*

4.12 *Not used*

4.13 *Not used*

4.14 *Not used*

4.15 *Not used*

(C) Taking footwear impressions in connection with a criminal investigation

(a) Action

4.16 Impressions of a person's footwear may be taken in connection with the investigation of an offence only with their consent or if *paragraph 4.17* applies. If the person is at a police station consent must be in writing.

4.17 PACE, section 61A, provides power for a police officer to take footwear impressions without consent from any person over the age of ten years who is detained at a police station:

   (a) in consequence of being arrested for a recordable offence, see *Note 4A*; or if the detainee has been charged with a recordable offence, or informed they will be reported for such an offence; and

   (b) the detainee has not had an impression of their footwear taken in the course of the investigation of the offence unless the previously taken impression is not complete or is not of sufficient quality to allow satisfactory analysis, comparison or matching (whether in the case in question or generally).

4.18 Reasonable force may be used, if necessary, to take a footwear impression from a detainee without consent under the power in *paragraph 4.17*.

4.19 Before any footwear impression is taken with, or without, consent as above, the person must be informed:

   (a) of the reason the impression is to be taken;

   (b) that the impression may be retained and may be subject of a speculative search against other impressions, see *Note 4B*, unless destruction of the impression is required in accordance with *Annex F, Part (a)*; and

   (c) that if their footwear impressions are required to be destroyed, they may witness their destruction as provided for in *Annex F, Part (a)*.

(b) Documentation

4.20 A record must be made as soon as possible, of the reason for taking a person's footwear impressions without consent. If force is used, a record shall be made of the circumstances and those present.

4.21 A record shall be made when a person has been informed under the terms of *paragraph 4.19(b)*, of the possibility that their footwear impressions may be subject of a speculative search.

Notes for guidance

4A *References to 'recordable offences' in this Code relate to those offences for which convictions, cautions, reprimands and warnings may be recorded in national police records. See PACE, section 27(4).*

The recordable offences current at the time when this Code was prepared, are any offences which carry a sentence of imprisonment on conviction (irrespective of the period, or the age of the offender or actual sentence passed) as well as the non-imprisonable offences under the Vagrancy Act 1824 sections 3 and 4 (begging and persistent begging), the Street Offences Act 1959, section 1 (loitering or soliciting for purposes of prostitution), the Road Traffic Act 1988, section 25 (tampering with motor vehicles), the Criminal Justice and Public Order Act 1994, section 167 (touting for hire car services) and others listed in the National Police Records (Recordable Offences) Regulations 2000 as amended.

4AB A qualifying offence is one of the offences specified in PACE, section 65A. These indictable offences which concern the use or threat of violence or unlawful force against persons, sexual offences and offences against children include, for example, murder, manslaughter, false imprisonment, kidnapping and other offences such as:

- *sections 4, 16, 18, 20 to 24 or 47 of the Offences Against the Person Act 1861;*
- *sections 16 to 18 of the Firearms Act 1968;*
- *sections 9 or 10 of the Theft Act 1968 or under section 12A of that Act involving an accident which caused a person's death;*
- *section 1 of the Criminal Damage Act 1971 required to be charged as arson;*
- *section 1 of the Protection of Children Act 1978 and;*
- *sections 1 to 19, 25, 26, 30 to 41, 47 to 50, 52, 53, 57 to 59, 61 to 67, 69 and 70 of the Sexual Offences Act 2003.*

4B Fingerprints, footwear impressions or a DNA sample (and the information derived from it) taken from a person arrested on suspicion of being involved in a recordable offence, or charged with such an offence, or informed they will be reported for such an offence, may be subject of a speculative search. This means the fingerprints, footwear impressions or DNA sample may be checked against other fingerprints, footwear impressions and DNA records held by, or on behalf of, the police and other law enforcement authorities in, or outside, the UK, or held in connection with, or as a result of, an investigation of an offence inside or outside the UK. Fingerprints, footwear impressions and samples taken from a person suspected of committing a recordable offence but not arrested, charged or informed they will be reported for it, may be subject to a speculative search only if the person consents in writing. The following is an example of a basic form of words:

> *"I consent to my fingerprints, footwear impressions and DNA sample and information derived from it being retained and used only for purposes related to the prevention and detection of a crime, the investigation of an offence or the conduct of a prosecution either nationally or internationally.*
>
> *I understand that my fingerprints, footwear impressions or DNA sample may be checked against other fingerprint, footwear impressions and DNA records held by or on behalf of relevant law enforcement authorities, either nationally or internationally.*
>
> *I understand that once I have given my consent for my fingerprints, footwear impressions or DNA sample to be retained and used I cannot withdraw this consent."*

See Annex F regarding the retention and use of fingerprints and footwear impressions taken with consent for elimination purposes.

4C The power under section 61(6A) of PACE described in paragraph 4.3(e) allows fingerprints of a suspect who has not been arrested to be taken in connection with any offence (whether recordable or not) using a mobile device and then checked on the street against the database containing the national fingerprint collection. Fingerprints taken under this power cannot be retained after they have been checked. The results may make an arrest for the suspected offence based on the name condition unnecessary (See Code G paragraph 2.9(a)) and enable the offence to be disposed of without arrest, for example, by summons/charging by post, penalty notice or words of advice. If arrest for a non-recordable offence is necessary for any other reasons, this power may also be exercised at the station. Before the power is exercised, the officer should:

- *inform the person of the nature of the suspected offence and why they are suspected of committing it.*
- *give them a reasonable opportunity to establish their real name before deciding that their name is unknown and cannot be readily ascertained or that there are reasonable grounds to doubt that a name they have given is their real name.*

- *as applicable, inform the person of the reason why their name is not know and cannot be readily ascertained or of the grounds for doubting that a name they have given is their real name, including, for example, the reason why a particular document the person has produced to verify their real name, is not sufficient.*

4D *Powers to take fingerprints without consent for immigration purposes are given to police and immigration officers under the:*

(a) *Immigration Act 1971, Schedule 2, paragraph 18(2), when it is reasonably necessary for the purposes of identifying a person detained under the Immigration Act 1971, Schedule 2, paragraph 16 (Detention of person liable to examination or removal), and*

(b) *Immigration and Asylum Act 1999, section 141(7) when a person:*
  - *fails without reasonable excuse to produce, on arrival, a valid passport with a photograph or some other document satisfactorily establishing their identity and nationality;*
  - *is refused entry to the UK but is temporarily admitted if an immigration officer reasonably suspects the person might break a residence or reporting condition;*
  - *is subject to directions for removal from the UK;*
  - *has been arrested under the Immigration Act 1971, Schedule 2, paragraph 17;*
  - *has made a claim for asylum*
  - *is a dependant of any of the above.*

The Immigration and Asylum Act 1999, section 142(3), also gives police and immigration officers power to arrest without warrant, a person who fails to comply with a requirement imposed by the Secretary of State to attend a specified place for fingerprinting.

5 Examinations to establish identity and the taking of photographs

(A) Detainees at police stations

(a) Searching or examination of detainees at police stations

5.1 PACE, section 54A(1), allows a detainee at a police station to be searched or examined or both, to establish:

(a) whether they have any marks, features or injuries that would tend to identify them as a person involved in the commission of an offence and to photograph any identifying marks, see *paragraph 5.5*; or

(b) their identity, see *Note 5A*.

A person detained at a police station to be searched under a stop and search power, see Code A, is not a detainee for the purposes of these powers.

5.2 A search and/or examination to find marks under section 54A (1) (a) may be carried out without the detainee's consent, see *paragraph 2.12*, only if authorised by an officer of at least inspector rank when consent has been withheld or it is not practicable to obtain consent, see *Note 5D*.

5.3 A search or examination to establish a suspect's identity under section 54A (1) (b) may be carried out without the detainee's consent, see *paragraph 2.12*, only if authorised by an officer of at least inspector rank when the detainee has refused to identify themselves or the authorising officer has reasonable grounds for suspecting the person is not who they claim to be.

5.4 Any marks that assist in establishing the detainee's identity, or their identification as a person involved in the commission of an offence, are identifying marks. Such marks may be photographed with the detainee's consent, see *paragraph 2.12*; or without their consent if it is withheld or it is not practicable to obtain it, see Note 5D.

5.5 A detainee may only be searched, examined and photographed under section 54A, by a police officer of the same sex.

5.6 Any photographs of identifying marks, taken under section 54A, may be used or disclosed only for purposes related to the prevention or detection of crime, the investigation of offences or the conduct of prosecutions by, or on behalf of, police or other law enforcement and prosecuting authorities inside, and outside, the UK. After being so used or disclosed, the photograph may be retained but must not be used or disclosed except for these purposes, see *Note 5B*.

5.7 The powers, as in *paragraph 5.1*, do not affect any separate requirement under the Criminal Procedure and Investigations Act 1996 to retain material in connection with criminal investigations.

5.8 Authority for the search and/or examination for the purposes of *paragraphs 5.2* and *5.3* may be given orally or in writing. If given orally, the authorising officer must confirm it in writing as soon as practicable. A separate authority is required for each purpose which applies.

5.9 If it is established a person is unwilling to co-operate sufficiently to enable a search and/or examination to take place or a suitable photograph to be taken, an officer may use reasonable force to:

(a) search and/or examine a detainee without their consent; and

(b) photograph any identifying marks without their consent.

5.10 The thoroughness and extent of any search or examination carried out in accordance with the powers in section 54A must be no more than the officer considers necessary to achieve the required purpose. Any search or examination which involves the removal of more than the person's outer clothing shall be conducted in accordance with Code C, Annex A, paragraph 11.

5.11 An intimate search may not be carried out under the powers in section 54A.

(b) Photographing detainees at police stations and other persons elsewhere than at a police station

5.12 Under PACE, section 64A, an officer may photograph:

(a) any person whilst they are detained at a police station; and

(b) any person who is elsewhere than at a police station and who has been:

(i) arrested by a constable for an offence;

(ii) taken into custody by a constable after being arrested for an offence by a person other than a constable;

(iii) made subject to a requirement to wait with a community support officer under paragraph 2(3) or (3B) of Schedule 4 to the Police Reform Act 2002;

(iiia) given a direction by a constable under section 27 of the Violent Crime Reduction Act 2006.

(iv) given a penalty notice by a constable in uniform under Chapter 1 of Part 1 of the Criminal Justice and Police Act 2001, a penalty notice by a constable under section 444A of the Education Act 1996, or a fixed penalty notice by a constable in uniform under section 54 of the Road Traffic Offenders Act 1988;

(v) given a notice in relation to a relevant fixed penalty offence (within the meaning of paragraph 1 of Schedule 4 to the Police Reform Act 2002) by a community support officer by virtue of a designation applying that paragraph to him;

(vi) given a notice in relation to a relevant fixed penalty offence (within the meaning of paragraph 1 of Schedule 5 to the Police Reform Act 2002) by an accredited person by virtue of accreditation specifying that that paragraph applies to him; or

(vii) given a direction to leave and not return to a specified location for up to 48 hours by a police constable (under section 27 of the Violent Crime Reduction Act 2006).

5.12A Photographs taken under PACE, section 64A:

(a) may be taken with the person's consent, or without their consent if consent is withheld or it is not practicable to obtain their consent, see *Note 5E*; and

(b) may be used or disclosed only for purposes related to the prevention or detection of crime, the investigation of offences or the conduct of prosecutions by, or on behalf of, police or other law enforcement and prosecuting authorities inside and outside the United Kingdom or the enforcement of any sentence or order made by a court when dealing with an offence. After being so used or disclosed, they may be retained but can only be used or disclosed for the same purposes. See *Note 5B*.

5.13 The officer proposing to take a detainee's photograph may, for this purpose, require the person to remove any item or substance worn on, or over, all, or any part of, their head or face. If they do not comply with such a requirement, the officer may remove the item or substance.

5.14 If it is established the detainee is unwilling to co-operate sufficiently to enable a suitable photograph to be taken and it is not reasonably practicable to take the photograph covertly, an officer may use reasonable force, see *Note 5F*.

(a) to take their photograph without their consent; and

(b) for the purpose of taking the photograph, remove any item or substance worn on, or over, all, or any part of, the person's head or face which they have failed to remove when asked.

5.15 For the purposes of this Code, a photograph may be obtained without the person's consent by making a copy of an image of them taken at any time on a camera system installed anywhere in the police station.

(c) Information to be given

5.16 When a person is searched, examined or photographed under the provisions as in *paragraph 5.1* and *5.12*, or their photograph obtained as in *paragraph 5.15*, they must be informed of the:

(a) purpose of the search, examination or photograph;

(b) grounds on which the relevant authority, if applicable, has been given; and

(c) purposes for which the photograph may be used, disclosed or retained.

This information must be given before the search or examination commences or the photograph is taken, except if the photograph is:

(i) to be taken covertly;

(ii) obtained as in *paragraph 5.15*, in which case the person must be informed as soon as practicable after the photograph is taken or obtained.

(d) Documentation

5.17 A record must be made when a detainee is searched, examined, or a photograph of the person, or any identifying marks found on them, are taken. The record must include the:

(a) identity, subject to paragraph 2.18, of the officer carrying out the search, examination or taking the photograph;

(b) purpose of the search, examination or photograph and the outcome;

(c) detainee's consent to the search, examination or photograph, or the reason the person was searched, examined or photographed without consent;

(d) giving of any authority as in *paragraphs 5.2* and *5.3*, the grounds for giving it and the authorising officer.

5.18 If force is used when searching, examining or taking a photograph in accordance with this section, a record shall be made of the circumstances and those present.

(B) Persons at police stations not detained

5.19 When there are reasonable grounds for suspecting the involvement of a person in a criminal offence, but that person is at a police station **voluntarily** and not detained, the provisions of *paragraphs 5.1* to *5.18* should apply, subject to the modifications in the following paragraphs.

5.20 References to the 'person being detained' and to the powers mentioned in *paragraph 5.1* which apply only to detainees at police stations shall be omitted.

5.21 Force may not be used to:

(a) search and/or examine the person to:

(i)   discover whether they have any marks that would tend to identify them as a person involved in the commission of an offence; or

(ii) establish their identity, see *Note 5A*;

(b) take photographs of any identifying marks, see *paragraph 5.4*; or

(c) take a photograph of the person.

5.22 Subject to *paragraph 5.24*, the photographs of persons or of their identifying marks which are not taken in accordance with the provisions mentioned in *paragraphs 5.1* or *5.12*, must be destroyed (together with any negatives and copies) unless the person:

(a) is charged with, or informed they may be prosecuted for, a recordable offence;

(b) is prosecuted for a recordable offence;

    (c) is cautioned for a recordable offence or given a warning or reprimand in accordance with the Crime and Disorder Act 1998 for a recordable offence; or

    (d) gives informed consent, in writing, for the photograph or image to be retained as in *paragraph 5.6.*

5.23   When *paragraph 5.22* requires the destruction of any photograph, the person must be given an opportunity to witness the destruction or to have a certificate confirming the destruction provided they so request the certificate within five days of being informed the destruction is required.

5.24   Nothing in *paragraph 5.22* affects any separate requirement under the Criminal Procedure and Investigations Act 1996 to retain material in connection with criminal investigations.

Notes for guidance

5A   The conditions under which fingerprints may be taken to assist in establishing a person's identity, are described in Section 4.

5B   Examples of purposes related to the prevention or detection of crime, the investigation of offences or the conduct of prosecutions include:

    (a) checking the photograph against other photographs held in records or in connection with, or as a result of, an investigation of an offence to establish whether the person is liable to arrest for other offences;

    (b) when the person is arrested at the same time as other people, or at a time when it is likely that other people will be arrested, using the photograph to help establish who was arrested, at what time and where;

    (c) when the real identity of the person is not known and cannot be readily ascertained or there are reasonable grounds for doubting a name and other personal details given by the person, are their real name and personal details. In these circumstances, using or disclosing the photograph to help to establish or verify their real identity or determine whether they are liable to arrest for some other offence, e.g. by checking it against other photographs held in records or in connection with, or as a result of, an investigation of an offence;

    (d) when it appears any identification procedure in section 3 may need to be arranged for which the person's photograph would assist;

    (e) when the person's release without charge may be required, and if the release is:

        (i)   on bail to appear at a police station, using the photograph to help verify the person's identity when they answer their bail and if the person does not answer their bail, to assist in arresting them; or

        (ii)   without bail, using the photograph to help verify their identity or assist in locating them for the purposes of serving them with a summons to appear at court in criminal proceedings;

    (e) when the person has answered to bail at a police station and there are reasonable grounds for doubting they are the person who was previously granted bail, using the photograph to help establish or verify their identity;

    (f) when the person arrested on a warrant claims to be a different person from the person named on the warrant and a photograph would help to confirm or disprove their claim;

    (g) when the person has been charged with, reported for, or convicted of, a recordable offence and their photograph is not already on record as a result of (a) to (f) or their photograph is on record but their appearance has changed since it was taken and the person has not yet been released or brought before a court.

5C   There is no power to arrest a person convicted of a recordable offence solely to take their photograph. The power to take photographs in this section applies only where the person is in custody as a result of the exercise of another power, e.g. arrest for fingerprinting under PACE, section 27.

5D   Examples of when it would not be practicable to obtain a detainee's consent, see paragraph 2.12, to a search, examination or the taking of a photograph of an identifying mark include:

    (a) when the person is drunk or otherwise unfit to give consent;

(b) when there are reasonable grounds to suspect that if the person became aware a search or examination was to take place or an identifying mark was to be photographed, they would take steps to prevent this happening, e.g. by violently resisting, covering or concealing the mark etc and it would not otherwise be possible to carry out the search or examination or to photograph any identifying mark;

(c) in the case of a juvenile, if the parent or guardian cannot be contacted in sufficient time to allow the search or examination to be carried out or the photograph to be taken.

5E Examples of when it would not be practicable to obtain the person's consent, see paragraph 2.12, to a photograph being taken include:

(a) when the person is drunk or otherwise unfit to give consent;

(b) when there are reasonable grounds to suspect that if the person became aware a photograph, suitable to be used or disclosed for the use and disclosure described in paragraph 5.6, was to be taken, they would take steps to prevent it being taken, e.g. by violently resisting, covering or distorting their face etc, and it would not otherwise be possible to take a suitable photograph;

(c) when, in order to obtain a suitable photograph, it is necessary to take it covertly; and

(d) in the case of a juvenile, if the parent or guardian cannot be contacted in sufficient time to allow the photograph to be taken.

5F The use of reasonable force to take the photograph of a suspect elsewhere than at a police station must be carefully considered. In order to obtain a suspect's consent and co-operation to remove an item of religious headwear to take their photograph, a constable should consider whether in the circumstances of the situation the removal of the headwear and the taking of the photograph should be by an officer of the same sex as the person. It would be appropriate for these actions to be conducted out of public view.

6 Identification by body samples and impressions

(A) General

6.1 References to:

(a) an 'intimate sample' mean a dental impression or sample of blood, semen or any other tissue fluid, urine, or pubic hair, or a swab taken from any part of a person's genitals or from a person's body orifice other than the mouth;

(b) a 'non-intimate sample' means:

(i)   a sample of hair, other than pubic hair, which includes hair plucked with the root, see Note 6A;

(ii) a sample taken from a nail or from under a nail;

(iii) a swab taken from any part of a person's body other than a part from which a swab taken would be an intimate sample;

(iv) saliva;

(v)   a skin impression which means any record, other than a fingerprint, which is a record, in any form and produced by any method, of the skin pattern and other physical characteristics or features of the whole, or any part of, a person's foot or of any other part of their body.

(B) Action

(a) Intimate samples

6.2 PACE, section 62, provides that intimate samples may be taken under:

(a) section 62(1), from a person in police detention only:

(i) if a police officer of inspector rank or above has reasonable grounds to believe such an impression or sample will tend to confirm or disprove the suspect's involvement in a recordable offence, see Note 4A, and gives authorisation for a sample to be taken; and

(ii) with the suspect's written consent;

    (b) section 62(1A), from a person not in police detention but from whom two or more non-intimate samples have been taken in the course of an investigation of an offence and the samples, though suitable, have proved insufficient if:

        (i)   a police officer of inspector rank or above authorises it to be taken; and

        (ii) the person concerned gives their written consent. See *Notes 6B* and *6C*

    (c) section 62(2A), from a person convicted outside England and Wales of an offence which if committed in England and Wales would be qualifying offence as defined by PACE, section 65A (see *Note 4AB*) from whom two or more non-intimate samples taken under section 63(3E) (see paragraph 6.6(h)) have proved insufficient if:

        (i)   a police officer of inspector rank or above is satisfied that taking the sample is necessary to assist in the prevention or detection of crime and authorises it to be taken; and

        (ii) the person concerned gives their written consent.

6.2A PACE, section 63A(4) and Schedule 2A provide powers to:

    (a) make a requirement (in accordance with Annex G) for a person to attend a police station to have an intimate sample taken in the exercise of one of the following powers in paragraph 6.2 when that power applies at the time the sample is to be taken in accordance with the requirement or after the person's arrest if they fail to comply with the requirement:

        (i)   section 62(1A)—Persons from whom two or more non-intimate samples have been taken and proved to be insufficient, see paragraph 6.2(b): There is no time limit for making the requirement.

        (ii) section 62(2A)—Persons convicted outside England and Wales from whom two or more non-intimate samples taken under section 63(3E) (see paragraph 6.6(h)) have proved insufficient, see *paragraph 6.2(c)*: There is no time limit for making the requirement.

6.3 Before a suspect is asked to provide an intimate sample, they must be:

    (a) informed:

        (i)   of the reason, including the nature of the suspected offence (except if taken under *paragraph 6.2(c)* from a person convicted outside England and Wales.

        (ii) that authorisation has been given and the provisions under which given;

        (iii) that a sample taken at a police station may be subject of a speculative search;

    (b) warned that if they refuse without good cause their refusal may harm their case if it comes to trial, see *Note 6D*. If the suspect is in police detention and not legally represented, they must also be reminded of their entitlement to have free legal advice, see Code C, *paragraph 6.5*, and the reminder noted in the custody record. If *paragraph 6.2(b)* applies and the person is attending a station voluntarily, their entitlement to free legal advice as in Code C, *paragraph 3.21* shall be explained to them.

6.4 Dental impressions may only be taken by a registered dentist. Other intimate samples, except for samples of urine, may only be taken by a registered medical practitioner or registered nurse or registered paramedic.

(b) Non-intimate samples

6.5 A non-intimate sample may be taken from a detainee only with their written consent or if *paragraph 6.6* applies.

6.6 A non-intimate sample may be taken from a person without the appropriate consent in the following circumstances:

    (a) under section 63(2A) from a person who is in police detention as a consequence of being arrested for a recordable offence and who has not had a non-intimate sample of the same type and from the same part of the body taken in the course of the investigation of the offence by the police or they have had such a sample taken but it proved insufficient.

(b) Under section 63(3) from a person who is being held in custody by the police on the authority of a court if an officer of at least the rank of inspector authorises it to be taken. An authorisation may be given:

   (i) if the authorising officer has reasonable grounds for suspecting the person of involvement in a recordable offence and for believing that the sample will tend to confirm or disprove that involvement, and

   (ii) in writing or orally and confirmed in writing, as soon as practicable;

but an authorisation may not be given to take from the same part of the body a further non-intimate sample consisting of a skin impression unless the previously taken impression proved insufficient

(c) under section 63(3ZA) from a person who has been arrested for a recordable offence and released if the person:

   (i) is on bail and has not had a sample of the same type and from the same part of the body taken in the course of the investigation of the offence, or;

   (ii) has had such a sample taken in the course of the investigation of the offence, but it proved unsuitable or insufficient.

(d) under section 63(3A), from a person (whether or not in police detention or held in custody by the police on the authority of a court) who has been charged with a recordable offence or informed they will be reported for such an offence if the person:

   (i) has not had a non-intimate sample taken from them in the course of the investigation of the offence;

   (ii) has had a sample so taken, but it proved unsuitable or insufficient, see *Note 6B*; or

   (iii) has had a sample taken in the course of the investigation of the offence and the sample has been destroyed and in proceedings relating to that offence there is a dispute as to whether a DNA profile relevant to the proceedings was derived from the destroyed sample.

(e) under section 63(3B), from a person who has been:

   (i) convicted of a recordable offence;

   (ii) given a caution in respect of a recordable offence which, at the time of the caution, the person admitted; or

   (iii) warned or reprimanded under the Crime and Disorder Act 1998, section 65, for a recordable offence,

if, since their conviction, caution, warning or reprimand a non-intimate sample has not been taken from them or a sample which has been taken since then has proved to be unsuitable or insufficient and in either case, an officer of inspector rank or above, is satisfied that taking the fingerprints is necessary to assist in the prevention or detection of crime and authorises the taking;

(f) under section 63(3C) from a person to whom section 2 of the Criminal Evidence (Amendment) Act 1997 applies (persons detained following acquittal on grounds of insanity or finding of unfitness to plead).

(g) under section 63(3E) from a person who has been convicted outside England and Wales of an offence which if committed in England and Wales would be a qualifying offence as defined by PACE, section 65A (see *Note 4AB*) if:

   (i) a non-intimate sample has not been taken previously under this power or unless a sample was so taken but was unsuitable or insufficient; and

   (ii) a police officer of inspector rank or above is satisfied that taking a sample is necessary to assist in the prevention or detection of crime and authorises it to be taken.

6.6A PACE, section 63A(4) and Schedule 2A provide powers to:

(a) make a requirement (in accordance with Annex G) for a person to attend a police station to have a non-intimate sample taken in the exercise of one of the following powers in paragraph 6.6 when that power applies at the time the sample would be taken in accordance with the requirement:

    (i)   section 63(3ZA)—Persons arrested for a recordable offence and released, see paragraph 6.6(c): The requirement may not be made more than six months from the day the investigating officer was informed that the sample previously taken was unsuitable or insufficient.

    (ii) section 63(3A)—Persons charged etc. with a recordable offence, see paragraph 6.6(d): The requirement may not be made more than six months from:
- the day the person was charged or reported if a sample has not been taken since then; or
- the day the investigating officer was informed that the sample previously taken was unsuitable or insufficient.

    (iii) section 63(3B)—Person convicted, cautioned, warned or reprimanded for a recordable offence in England and Wales, see paragraph 6.6(e): Where the offence for which the person was convicted etc is also a qualifying offence (see Note 4AB), there is no time limit for the exercise of this power. Where the conviction etc was for a recordable offence that is not a qualifying offence, the requirement may not be made more than two years from:
- the day the person was convicted, cautioned, warned or reprimanded, or the day Schedule 2A comes into force (if later), if a samples has not been taken since then; or
- the day an officer from the force investigating the offence was informed that the sample previously taken was unsuitable or insufficient or the day Schedule 2A comes into force (if later).

    (iv) section 63(3E)—A person who has been convicted of qualifying offence (see Note 4AB) outside England and Wales, see paragraph 6.6(h): There is no time limit for making the requirement.

Note: A person who has had a non-intimate sample taken under any of the powers in section 63 mentioned in paragraph 6.6 on two occasions in relation to any offence may not be required under Schedule 2A to attend a police station for a sample to be taken again under section 63 in relation to that offence, unless authorised by an officer of inspector rank or above. The fact of the authorisation and the reasons for giving it must be recorded as soon as practicable.

  (b) arrest, without warrant, a person who fails to comply with the requirement.

6.7 Reasonable force may be used, if necessary, to take a non-intimate sample from a person without their consent under the powers mentioned in *paragraph 6.6*.

6.8 Before any non-intimate sample is taken:

  (a) without consent under any power mentioned in paragraphs 6.6 and 6.6A, the person must be informed of:
- (i) the reason for taking the sample;
- (ii) the power under which the sample is to be taken;
- (iii) the fact that the relevant authority has been given if any power mentioned in *paragraph 6.6(b), (e) or (h)* applies;

  (b) with or without consent at a police station or elsewhere, the person must be informed:
- (i) that their sample or information derived from it may be subject of a speculative search against other samples and information derived from them, see *Note 6E* and
- (ii) that their sample and the information derived from it may be retained in accordance with Annex F, Part (a).

  (c) Removal of clothing

6.9 When clothing needs to be removed in circumstances likely to cause embarrassment to the person, no person of the opposite sex who is not a registered medical practitioner or registered health care professional shall be present, (unless in the case of a juvenile, mentally disordered or mentally vulnerable person, that person specifically requests the presence of an appropriate adult of the opposite sex who is readily available) nor shall anyone whose presence is unnecessary. However, in the case of a juvenile, this is subject to the overriding proviso that such a removal of clothing may take place in the absence of the appropriate adult only if the juvenile signifies in their presence, that they prefer the adult's absence and they agree.

(c) Documentation

6.10 A record must be made as soon as practicable after the sample is taken of:

- The matters in paragraph 6.8(a)(i) to (iii) and the fact that the person has been informed of those matters; and
- The fact that the person has been informed of the matters in paragraph 6.8(b)(i) and (ii).

6.10A If force is used, a record shall be made of the circumstances and those present.

6.11 A record must be made of a warning given as required by *paragraph 6.3.*

6.12 *Not used*

Notes for guidance

6A When hair samples are taken for the purpose of DNA analysis (rather than for other purposes such as making a visual match), the suspect should be permitted a reasonable choice as to what part of the body the hairs are taken from. When hairs are plucked, they should be plucked individually, unless the suspect prefers otherwise and no more should be plucked than the person taking them reasonably considers necessary for a sufficient sample.

6B (a) An insufficient sample is one which is not sufficient either in quantity or quality to provide information for a particular form of analysis, such as DNA analysis. A sample may also be insufficient if enough information cannot be obtained from it by analysis because of loss, destruction, damage or contamination of the sample or as a result of an earlier, unsuccessful attempt at analysis.

(b) An unsuitable sample is one which, by its nature, is not suitable for a particular form of analysis.

6C Nothing in paragraph 6.2 prevents intimate samples being taken for elimination purposes with the consent of the person concerned but the provisions of paragraph 2.12 relating to the role of the appropriate adult, should be applied. Paragraph 6.2(b) does not, however, apply where the non-intimate samples were previously taken under the Terrorism Act 2000, Schedule 8, paragraph 10.

6D In warning a person who is asked to provide an intimate sample as in paragraph 6.3, the following form of words may be used:

'You do not have to provide this sample/allow this swab or impression to be taken, but I must warn you that if you refuse without good cause, your refusal may harm your case if it comes to trial.'

6E Fingerprints or a DNA sample and the information derived from it taken from a person arrested on suspicion of being involved in a recordable offence, or charged with such an offence, or informed they will be reported for such an offence, may be subject of a speculative search. This means they may be checked against other fingerprints and DNA records held by, or on behalf of, the police and other law enforcement authorities in or outside the UK or held in connection with, or as a result of, an investigation of an offence inside or outside the UK. Fingerprints and samples taken from any other person, e.g. a person suspected of committing a recordable offence but who has not been arrested, charged or informed they will be reported for it, may be subject to a speculative search only if the person consents in writing to their fingerprints being subject of such a search. The following is an example of a basic form of words:

"I consent to my fingerprints/DNA sample and information derived from it being retained and used only for purposes related to the prevention and detection of a crime, the investigation of an offence or the conduct of a prosecution either nationally or internationally.

I understand that this sample may be checked against other fingerprint/DNA records held by or on behalf of relevant law enforcement authorities, either nationally or internationally.

I understand that once I have given my consent for the sample to be retained and used I cannot withdraw this consent."

See Annex F regarding the retention and use of fingerprints and samples taken with consent for elimination purposes.

6F Samples of urine and non-intimate samples taken in accordance with sections 63B and 63C of PACE may not be used for identification purposes in accordance with this Code. See Code C note for guidance 17D.

Annex A Video Identification

(a) General

1. The arrangements for obtaining and ensuring the availability of a suitable set of images to be used in a video identification must be the responsibility of an identification officer, who has no direct involvement with the case.

2. The set of images must include the suspect and at least eight other people who, so far as possible, resemble the suspect in age, general appearance and position in life. Only one suspect shall appear in any set unless there are two suspects of roughly similar appearance, in which case they may be shown together with at least twelve other people.

2A If the suspect has an unusual physical feature, e.g., a facial scar, tattoo or distinctive hairstyle or hair colour which does not appear on the images of the other people that are available to be used, steps may be taken to:

(a) conceal the location of the feature on the images of the suspect and the other people; or

(b) replicate that feature on the images of the other people.

For these purposes, the feature may be concealed or replicated electronically or by any other method which it is practicable to use to ensure that the images of the suspect and other people resemble each other. The identification officer has discretion to choose whether to conceal or replicate the feature and the method to be used. If an unusual physical feature has been described by the witness, the identification officer should, if practicable, have that feature replicated. If it has not been described, concealment may be more appropriate.

2B If the identification officer decides that a feature should be concealed or replicated, the reason for the decision and whether the feature was concealed or replicated in the images shown to any witness shall be recorded.

2C If the witness requests to view an image where an unusual physical feature has been concealed or replicated without the feature being concealed or replicated, the witness may be allowed to do so.

3. The images used to conduct a video identification shall, as far as possible, show the suspect and other people in the same positions or carrying out the same sequence of movements. They shall also show the suspect and other people under identical conditions unless the identification officer reasonably believes:

(a) because of the suspect's failure or refusal to co-operate or other reasons, it is not practicable for the conditions to be identical; and

(b) any difference in the conditions would not direct a witness' attention to any individual image.

4. The reasons identical conditions are not practicable shall be recorded on forms provided for the purpose.

5. Provision must be made for each person shown to be identified by number.

6. If police officers are shown, any numerals or other identifying badges must be concealed. If a prison inmate is shown, either as a suspect or not, then either all, or none of, the people shown should be in prison clothing.

7. The suspect or their solicitor, friend, or appropriate adult must be given a reasonable opportunity to see the complete set of images before it is shown to any witness. If the suspect has a reasonable objection to the set of images or any of the participants, the suspect shall be asked to state the reasons for the objection. Steps shall, if practicable, be taken to remove the grounds for objection. If this is not practicable, the suspect and/or their representative shall be told why their objections cannot be met and the objection, the reason given for it and why it cannot be met shall be recorded on forms provided for the purpose.

8. Before the images are shown in accordance with *paragraph 7,* the suspect or their solicitor shall be provided with details of the first description of the suspect by any witnesses who are to attend the video identification. When a broadcast or publication is made, as in *paragraph 3.28,* the suspect or their solicitor must also be allowed to view any material released to the media by the police for the purpose of recognising or tracing the suspect, provided it is practicable and would not unreasonably delay the investigation.

9. The suspect's solicitor, if practicable, shall be given reasonable notification of the time and place the video identification is to be conducted so a representative may attend on behalf of the suspect. The suspect may not be present when the images are shown to the witness(es). In the absence of the suspect's solicitor, the viewing itself shall be recorded on video. No unauthorised people may be present.

(b) Conducting the video identification

10. The identification officer is responsible for making the appropriate arrangements to make sure, before they see the set of images, witnesses are not able to communicate with each other about the case, see any of the images which are to be shown, see, or be reminded of, any photograph or description of the suspect or be given any other indication as to the suspect's identity, or overhear a witness who has already seen the material. There must be no discussion with the witness about the composition of the set of images and they must not be told whether a previous witness has made any identification.

11. Only one witness may see the set of images at a time. Immediately before the images are shown, the witness shall be told that the person they saw on a specified earlier occasion may, or may not, appear in the images they are shown and that if they cannot make a positive identification, they should say so. The witness shall be advised that at any point, they may ask to see a particular part of the set of images or to have a particular image frozen for them to study. Furthermore, it should be pointed out to the witness that there is no limit on how many times they can view the whole set of images or any part of them. However, they should be asked not to make any decision as to whether the person they saw is on the set of images until they have seen the whole set at least twice.

12. Once the witness has seen the whole set of images at least twice and has indicated that they do not want to view the images, or any part of them, again, the witness shall be asked to say whether the individual they saw in person on a specified earlier occasion has been shown and, if so, to identify them by number of the image. The witness will then be shown that image to confirm the identification, see *paragraph 17.*

13. Care must be taken not to direct the witness' attention to any one individual image or give any indication of the suspect's identity. Where a witness has previously made an identification by photographs, or a computerised or artist's composite or similar likeness, the witness must not be reminded of such a photograph or composite likeness once a suspect is available for identification by other means in accordance with this Code. Nor must the witness be reminded of any description of the suspect.

14. After the procedure, each witness shall be asked whether they have seen any broadcast or published films or photographs, or any descriptions of suspects relating to the offence and their reply shall be recorded.

(c) Image security and destruction

15. Arrangements shall be made for all relevant material containing sets of images used for specific identification procedures to be kept securely and their movements accounted for. In particular, no-one involved in the investigation shall be permitted to view the material prior to it being shown to any witness.

16. As appropriate, *paragraph 3.30 or 3.31* applies to the destruction or retention of relevant sets of images.

(d) Documentation

17. A record must be made of all those participating in, or seeing, the set of images whose names are known to the police.

18. A record of the conduct of the video identification must be made on forms provided for the purpose. This shall include anything said by the witness about any identifications or the conduct of the procedure and any reasons it was not practicable to comply with any of the provisions of this Code governing the conduct of video identifications.

Annex B Identification Parades

(a) General

1. A suspect must be given a reasonable opportunity to have a solicitor or friend present, and the suspect shall be asked to indicate on a second copy of the notice whether or not they wish to do so.

2. An identification parade may take place either in a normal room or one equipped with a screen permitting witnesses to see members of the identification parade without being seen. The procedures for the composition and conduct of the identification parade are the same in both cases, subject to *paragraph 8* (except that an identification parade involving a screen may take place only when the suspect's solicitor, friend or appropriate adult is present or the identification parade is recorded on video).

3. Before the identification parade takes place, the suspect or their solicitor shall be provided with details of the first description of the suspect by any witnesses who are attending the identification parade. When a broadcast or publication is made as in *paragraph 3.28*, the suspect or their solicitor should also be allowed to view any material released to the media by the police for the purpose of recognising or tracing the suspect, provided it is practicable to do so and would not unreasonably delay the investigation.

(b) Identification parades involving prison inmates

4. If a prison inmate is required for identification, and there are no security problems about the person leaving the establishment, they may be asked to participate in an identification parade or video identification.

5. An identification parade may be held in a Prison Department establishment but shall be conducted, as far as practicable under normal identification parade rules. Members of the public shall make up the identification parade unless there are serious security, or control, objections to their admission to the establishment. In such cases, or if a group or video identification is arranged within the establishment, other inmates may participate. If an inmate is the suspect, they are not required to wear prison clothing for the identification parade unless the other people taking part are other inmates in similar clothing, or are members of the public who are prepared to wear prison clothing for the occasion.

(c) Conduct of the identification parade

6. Immediately before the identification parade, the suspect must be reminded of the procedures governing its conduct and cautioned in the terms of Code C, paragraphs 10.5 or 10.6, as appropriate.

7. All unauthorised people must be excluded from the place where the identification parade is held.

8. Once the identification parade has been formed, everything afterwards, in respect of it, shall take place in the presence and hearing of the suspect and any interpreter, solicitor, friend or appropriate adult who is present (unless the identification parade involves a screen, in which case everything said to, or by, any witness at the place where the identification parade is held, must be said in the hearing and presence of the suspect's solicitor, friend or appropriate adult or be recorded on video).

9. The identification parade shall consist of at least eight people (in addition to the suspect) who, so far as possible, resemble the suspect in age, height, general appearance and position in life. Only one suspect shall be included in an identification parade unless there are two suspects of roughly similar appearance, in which case they may be paraded together with at least twelve other people. In no circumstances shall more than two suspects be included in one identification parade and where there are separate identification parades, they shall be made up of different people.

10. If the suspect has an unusual physical feature, e.g., a facial scar, tattoo or distinctive hairstyle or hair colour which cannot be replicated on other members of the identification parade, steps may be taken to conceal the location of that feature on the suspect and the other members of the identification parade if the suspect and their solicitor, or appropriate adult, agree. For example, by use of a plaster or a hat, so that all members of the identification parade resemble each other in general appearance.

11. When all members of a similar group are possible suspects, separate identification parades shall be held for each unless there are two suspects of similar appearance when they may appear on the same identification parade with at least twelve other members of the group who are not suspects. When police officers in uniform form an identification parade any numerals or other identifying badges shall be concealed.

12. When the suspect is brought to the place where the identification parade is to be held, they shall be asked if they have any objection to the arrangements for the identification parade or to any of the other participants in it and to state the reasons for the objection. The suspect may obtain advice from their solicitor or friend, if present, before the identification parade proceeds. If the suspect has a reasonable objection to the arrangements or any of the participants, steps shall, if practicable, be taken to remove the grounds for objection. When it is not practicable to do so, the suspect shall be told why their objections cannot be met and the objection, the reason given for it and why it cannot be met, shall be recorded on forms provided for the purpose.

13. The suspect may select their own position in the line, but may not otherwise interfere with the order of the people forming the line. When there is more than one witness, the suspect must be told, after each witness has left the room, that they can, if they wish, change position in the line. Each position in the line must be clearly numbered, whether by means of a number laid on the floor in front of each identification parade member or by other means.

14. Appropriate arrangements must be made to make sure, before witnesses attend the identification parade, they are not able to:
   (i)   communicate with each other about the case or overhear a witness who has already seen the identification parade;
   (ii)   see any member of the identification parade;
   (iii) see, or be reminded of, any photograph or description of the suspect or be given any other indication as to the suspect's identity; or
   (iv)   see the suspect before or after the identification parade.

15. The person conducting a witness to an identification parade must not discuss with them the composition of the identification parade and, in particular, must not disclose whether a previous witness has made any identification.

16. Witnesses shall be brought in one at a time. Immediately before the witness inspects the identification parade, they shall be told the person they saw on a specified earlier occasion may, or may not, be present and if they cannot make a positive identification, they should say so. The witness must also be told they should not make any decision about whether the person they saw is on the identification parade until they have looked at each member at least twice.

17. When the officer or police staff (see paragraph 3.11) conducting the identification procedure is satisfied the witness has properly looked at each member of the identification parade, they shall ask the witness whether the person they saw on a specified earlier occasion is on the identification parade and, if so, to indicate the number of the person concerned, see *paragraph 28*.

18. If the witness wishes to hear any identification parade member speak, adopt any specified posture or move, they shall first be asked whether they can identify any person(s) on the identification parade on the basis of appearance only. When the request is to hear members of the identification parade speak, the witness shall be reminded that the participants in the identification parade have been chosen on the basis of physical appearance only. Members of the identification parade may then be asked to comply with the witness' request to hear them speak, see them move or adopt any specified posture.

19. If the witness requests that the person they have indicated remove anything used for the purposes of *paragraph 10* to conceal the location of an unusual physical feature, that person may be asked to remove it.

20. If the witness makes an identification after the identification parade has ended, the suspect and, if present, their solicitor, interpreter or friend shall be informed. When this occurs, consideration should be given to allowing the witness a second opportunity to identify the suspect.

21. After the procedure, each witness shall be asked whether they have seen any broadcast or published films or photographs or any descriptions of suspects relating to the offence and their reply shall be recorded.

22. When the last witness has left, the suspect shall be asked whether they wish to make any comments on the conduct of the identification parade.

(d) Documentation

23. A video recording must normally be taken of the identification parade. If that is impracticable, a colour photograph must be taken. A copy of the video recording or photograph shall be supplied, on request, to the suspect or their solicitor within a reasonable time.

24. As appropriate, *paragraph 3.30* or *3.31*, should apply to any photograph or video taken as in *paragraph 23*.

25. If any person is asked to leave an identification parade because they are interfering with its conduct, the circumstances shall be recorded.

26. A record must be made of all those present at an identification parade whose names are known to the police.

27. If prison inmates make up an identification parade, the circumstances must be recorded.

28. A record of the conduct of any identification parade must be made on forms provided for the purpose. This shall include anything said by the witness or the suspect about any identifications or the conduct of the procedure, and any reasons it was not practicable to comply with any of this Code's provisions.

Annex C Group Identification

(a) General

1. The purpose of this Annex is to make sure, as far as possible, group identifications follow the principles and procedures for identification parades so the conditions are fair to the suspect in the way they test the witness' ability to make an identification.

2. Group identifications may take place either with the suspect's consent and cooperation or covertly without their consent.

3. The location of the group identification is a matter for the identification officer, although the officer may take into account any representations made by the suspect, appropriate adult, their solicitor or friend.

4. The place where the group identification is held should be one where other people are either passing by or waiting around informally, in groups such that the suspect is able to join them and be capable of being seen by the witness at the same time as others in the group. For example people leaving an escalator, pedestrians walking through a shopping centre, passengers on railway and bus stations, waiting in queues or groups or where people are standing or sitting in groups in other public places.

5. If the group identification is to be held covertly, the choice of locations will be limited by the places where the suspect can be found and the number of other people present at that time. In these cases, suitable locations might be along regular routes travelled by the suspect, including buses or trains or public places frequented by the suspect.

6. Although the number, age, sex, race and general description and style of clothing of other people present at the location cannot be controlled by the identification officer, in selecting the location the officer must consider the general appearance and numbers of people likely to be present. In particular, the officer must reasonably expect that over the period the witness observes the group, they will be able to see, from time to time, a number of others whose appearance is broadly similar to that of the suspect.

7. A group identification need not be held if the identification officer believes, because of the unusual appearance of the suspect, none of the locations it would be practicable to use, satisfy the requirements of *paragraph 6* necessary to make the identification fair.

8. Immediately after a group identification procedure has taken place (with or without the suspect's consent), a colour photograph or video should be taken of the general scene, if practicable, to give a general impression of the scene and the number of people present. Alternatively, if it is practicable, the group identification may be video recorded.

9. If it is not practicable to take the photograph or video in accordance with *paragraph 8,* a photograph or film of the scene should be taken later at a time determined by the identification officer if the officer considers it practicable to do so.

10. An identification carried out in accordance with this Code remains a group identification even though, at the time of being seen by the witness, the suspect was on their own rather than in a group.

11. Before the group identification takes place, the suspect or their solicitor shall be provided with details of the first description of the suspect by any witnesses who are to attend the identification. When a broadcast or publication is made, as in *paragraph 3.28,* the suspect or their solicitor should also be allowed to view any material released by the police to the media for the purposes of recognising or tracing the suspect, provided that it is practicable and would not unreasonably delay the investigation.

12. After the procedure, each witness shall be asked whether they have seen any broadcast or published films or photographs or any descriptions of suspects relating to the offence and their reply recorded.

(b) Identification with the consent of the suspect

13. A suspect must be given a reasonable opportunity to have a solicitor or friend present. They shall be asked to indicate on a second copy of the notice whether or not they wish to do so.

14. The witness, the person carrying out the procedure and the suspect's solicitor, appropriate adult, friend or any interpreter for the witness, may be concealed from the sight of the individuals in the group they are observing, if the person carrying out the procedure considers this assists the conduct of the identification.

15. The person conducting a witness to a group identification must not discuss with them the forthcoming group identification and, in particular, must not disclose whether a previous witness has made any identification.

16. Anything said to, or by, the witness during the procedure about the identification should be said in the presence and hearing of those present at the procedure.

17. Appropriate arrangements must be made to make sure, before witnesses attend the group identification, they are not able to:

(i)   communicate with each other about the case or overhear a witness who has already been given an opportunity to see the suspect in the group;

(ii)   see the suspect; or

(iii)   see, or be reminded of, any photographs or description of the suspect or be given any other indication of the suspect's identity.

18. Witnesses shall be brought one at a time to the place where they are to observe the group. Immediately before the witness is asked to look at the group, the person conducting the procedure shall tell them that the person they saw may, or may not, be in the group and that if they cannot make a positive identification, they should say so. The witness shall be asked to observe the group in which the suspect is to appear. The way in which the witness should do this will depend on whether the group is moving or stationary.

Moving group

19. When the group in which the suspect is to appear is moving, e.g. leaving an escalator, the provisions of *paragraphs 20 to 24* should be followed.

20. If two or more suspects consent to a group identification, each should be the subject of separate identification procedures. These may be conducted consecutively on the same occasion.

21. The person conducting the procedure shall tell the witness to observe the group and ask them to point out any person they think they saw on the specified earlier occasion.

22. Once the witness has been informed as in *paragraph 21* the suspect should be allowed to take whatever position in the group they wish.

23. When the witness points out a person as in *paragraph 21* they shall, if practicable, be asked to take a closer look at the person to confirm the identification. If this is not practicable, or they cannot confirm the identification, they shall be asked how sure they are that the person they have indicated is the relevant person.

24. The witness should continue to observe the group for the period which the person conducting the procedure reasonably believes is necessary in the circumstances for them to be able to make comparisons between the suspect and other individuals of broadly similar appearance to the suspect as in *paragraph 6*.

Stationary groups

25. When the group in which the suspect is to appear is stationary, e.g. people waiting in a queue, the provisions of *paragraphs 26* to *29* should be followed.

26. If two or more suspects consent to a group identification, each should be subject to separate identification procedures unless they are of broadly similar appearance when they may appear in the same group. When separate group identifications are held, the groups must be made up of different people.

27. The suspect may take whatever position in the group they wish. If there is more than one witness, the suspect must be told, out of the sight and hearing of any witness, that they can, if they wish, change their position in the group.

28. The witness shall be asked to pass along, or amongst, the group and to look at each person in the group at least twice, taking as much care and time as possible according to the circumstances, before making an identification. Once the witness has done this, they shall be asked whether the person they saw on the specified earlier occasion is in the group and to indicate any such person by whatever means the person conducting the procedure considers appropriate in the circumstances. If this is not practicable, the witness shall be asked to point out any person they think they saw on the earlier occasion.

29. When the witness makes an indication as in *paragraph 28,* arrangements shall be made, if practicable, for the witness to take a closer look at the person to confirm the identification. If this is not practicable, or the witness is unable to confirm the identification, they shall be asked how sure they are that the person they have indicated is the relevant person.

All cases

30. If the suspect unreasonably delays joining the group, or having joined the group, deliberately conceals themselves from the sight of the witness, this may be treated as a refusal to co-operate in a group identification.

31. If the witness identifies a person other than the suspect, that person should be informed what has happened and asked if they are prepared to give their name and address. There is no obligation upon any member of the public to give these details. There shall be no duty to record any details of any other member of the public present in the group or at the place where the procedure is conducted.

32. When the group identification has been completed, the suspect shall be asked whether they wish to make any comments on the conduct of the procedure.

33. If the suspect has not been previously informed, they shall be told of any identifications made by the witnesses.

(c) Identification without the suspect's consent

34. Group identifications held covertly without the suspect's consent should, as far as practicable, follow the rules for conduct of group identification by consent.

35. A suspect has no right to have a solicitor, appropriate adult or friend present as the identification will take place without the knowledge of the suspect.

36. Any number of suspects may be identified at the same time.

(d) Identifications in police stations

37. Group identifications should only take place in police stations for reasons of safety, security or because it is not practicable to hold them elsewhere.

38. The group identification may take place either in a room equipped with a screen permitting witnesses to see members of the group without being seen, or anywhere else in the police station that the identification officer considers appropriate.

39. Any of the additional safeguards applicable to identification parades should be followed if the identification officer considers it is practicable to do so in the circumstances.

(e) Identifications involving prison inmates

40. A group identification involving a prison inmate may only be arranged in the prison or at a police station.

41. When a group identification takes place involving a prison inmate, whether in a prison or in a police station, the arrangements should follow those in *paragraphs 37 to 39*. If a group identification takes place within a prison, other inmates may participate. If an inmate is the suspect, they do not have to wear prison clothing for the group identification unless the other participants are wearing the same clothing.

(f) Documentation

42. When a photograph or video is taken as in *paragraph 8 or 9*, a copy of the photograph or video shall be supplied on request to the suspect or their solicitor within a reasonable time.

43. *Paragraph 3.30* or *3.31*, as appropriate, shall apply when the photograph or film taken in accordance with *paragraph 8 or 9* includes the suspect.

44. A record of the conduct of any group identification must be made on forms provided for the purpose. This shall include anything said by the witness or suspect about any identifications or the conduct of the procedure and any reasons why it was not practicable to comply with any of the provisions of this Code governing the conduct of group identifications.

Annex D Confrontation by a Witness

1. Before the confrontation takes place, the witness must be told that the person they saw may, or may not, be the person they are to confront and that if they are not that person, then the witness should say so.

2. Before the confrontation takes place the suspect or their solicitor shall be provided with details of the first description of the suspect given by any witness who is to attend. When a broadcast or publication is made, as in *paragraph 3.28*, the suspect or their solicitor should also be allowed to view any material released to the media for the purposes of recognising or tracing the suspect, provided it is practicable to do so and would not unreasonably delay the investigation.

3. Force may not be used to make the suspect's face visible to the witness.

4. Confrontation must take place in the presence of the suspect's solicitor, interpreter or friend unless this would cause unreasonable delay.

5. The suspect shall be confronted independently by each witness, who shall be asked "Is this the person?". If the witness identifies the person but is unable to confirm the identification, they shall be asked how sure they are that the person is the one they saw on the earlier occasion.

6. The confrontation should normally take place in the police station, either in a normal room or one equipped with a screen permitting a witness to see the suspect without being seen. In both cases, the procedures are the same except that a room equipped with a screen may be used only when the suspect's solicitor, friend or appropriate adult is present or the confrontation is recorded on video.

7. After the procedure, each witness shall be asked whether they have seen any broadcast or published films or photographs or any descriptions of suspects relating to the offence and their reply shall be recorded.

Annex E Showing Photographs

(a) Action

1. An officer of sergeant rank or above shall be responsible for supervising and directing the showing of photographs. The actual showing may be done by another officer or police staff, see *paragraph 3.11*.

2. The supervising officer must confirm the first description of the suspect given by the witness has been recorded before they are shown the photographs. If the supervising officer is unable to confirm the description has been recorded they shall postpone showing the photographs.

3. Only one witness shall be shown photographs at any one time. Each witness shall be given as much privacy as practicable and shall not be allowed to communicate with any other witness in the case.

4. The witness shall be shown not less than twelve photographs at a time, which shall, as far as possible, all be of a similar type.

5. When the witness is shown the photographs, they shall be told the photograph of the person they saw may, or may not, be amongst them and if they cannot make a positive identification, they should say so. The witness shall also be told they should not make a decision until they have viewed at least twelve photographs. The witness shall not be prompted or guided in any way but shall be left to make any selection without help.

6. If a witness makes a positive identification from photographs, unless the person identified is otherwise eliminated from enquiries or is not available, other witnesses shall not be shown photographs. But both they, and the witness who has made the identification, shall be asked to attend a video identification, an identification parade or group identification unless there is no dispute about the suspect's identification.

7. If the witness makes a selection but is unable to confirm the identification, the person showing the photographs shall ask them how sure they are that the photograph they have indicated is the person they saw on the specified earlier occasion.

8. When the use of a computerised or artist's composite or similar likeness has led to there being a known suspect who can be asked to participate in a video identification, appear on an identification parade or participate in a group identification, that likeness shall not be shown to other potential witnesses.

9. When a witness attending a video identification, an identification parade or group identification has previously been shown photographs or computerised or artist's composite or similar likeness (and it is the responsibility of the officer in charge of the investigation to make the identification officer aware that this is the case), the suspect and their solicitor must be informed of this fact before the identification procedure takes place.

10. None of the photographs shown shall be destroyed, whether or not an identification is made, since they may be required for production in court. The photographs shall be numbered and a separate photograph taken of the frame or part of the album from which the witness made an identification as an aid to reconstituting it.

(b) Documentation

11. Whether or not an identification is made, a record shall be kept of the showing of photographs on forms provided for the purpose. This shall include anything said by the witness about any identification or the conduct of the procedure, any reasons it was not practicable to comply with any of the provisions of this Code governing the showing of photographs and the name and rank of the supervising officer.

12. The supervising officer shall inspect and sign the record as soon as practicable.

Annex F Fingerprints, Footwear Impressions and Samples—Destruction and Speculative Searches

(a) Fingerprints, footwear impressions and samples taken in connection with a criminal investigation from a person suspected of committing the offence under investigation.

1. The retention and destruction of fingerprints, footwear impressions and samples taken in connection with a criminal investigation from a person suspected of committing the offence under investigation is subject to PACE, section 64.

(b) Fingerprints, footwear impressions and samples taken in connection with a criminal investigation from a person not suspected of committing the offence under investigation.

2. When fingerprints, footwear impressions or DNA samples are taken from a person in connection with an investigation and the person is not suspected of having committed the offence, see *Note F1*, they must be destroyed as soon as they have fulfilled the purpose for which they were taken unless:

    (a) they were taken for the purposes of an investigation of an offence for which a person has been convicted; and

    (b) fingerprints, footwear impressions or samples were also taken from the convicted person for the purposes of that investigation.

However, subject to *paragraph 2*, the fingerprints, footwear impressions and samples, and the information derived from samples, may not be used in the investigation of any offence or in evidence against the person who is, or would be, entitled to the destruction of the fingerprints, footwear impressions and samples, see *Note F2*.

3. The requirement to destroy fingerprints, footwear impressions and DNA samples, and information derived from samples, and restrictions on their retention and use in *paragraph 1* do not apply if the person gives their written consent for their fingerprints, footwear impressions or sample to be retained and used after they have fulfilled the purpose for which they were taken, see *Note F1*.

4. When a person's fingerprints, footwear impressions or sample are to be destroyed:

    (a) any copies of the fingerprints and footwear impressions must also be destroyed;

    (b) the person may witness the destruction of their fingerprints, footwear impressions or copies if they ask to do so within five days of being informed destruction is required;

    (c) access to relevant computer fingerprint data shall be made impossible as soon as it is practicable to do so and the person shall be given a certificate to this effect within three months of asking; and

    (d) neither the fingerprints, footwear impressions, the sample, or any information derived from the sample, may be used in the investigation of any offence or in evidence against the person who is, or would be, entitled to its destruction.

5. Fingerprints, footwear impressions or samples, and the information derived from samples, taken in connection with the investigation of an offence which are not required to be destroyed, may be retained after they have fulfilled the purposes for which they were taken but may be used only for purposes related to the prevention or detection of crime, the investigation of an offence or the conduct of a prosecution in, as well as outside, the UK and may also be subject to a speculative search. This includes checking them against other fingerprints, footwear impressions and DNA records held by, or on behalf of, the police and other law enforcement authorities in, as well as outside, the UK.

(b) Fingerprints taken in connection with Immigration Service enquiries

6. See *paragraph 4.10*.

Notes for guidance

F1 Fingerprints, footwear impressions and samples given voluntarily for the purposes of elimination play an important part in many police investigations. It is, therefore, important to make sure innocent volunteers are not deterred from participating and their consent to their fingerprints, footwear impressions and DNA being used for the purposes of a specific investigation is fully informed and voluntary. If the police or volunteer seek to have the fingerprints, footwear impressions or samples retained for use after the specific investigation ends, it is important the volunteer's consent to this is also fully informed and voluntary.

Examples of consent for:

- DNA/fingerprints/footwear impressions—to be used only for the purposes of a specific investigation;
- DNA/fingerprints/footwear impressions—to be used in the specific investigation and retained by the police for future use.

To minimise the risk of confusion, each consent should be physically separate and the volunteer should be asked to sign each consent.

(a) DNA:

(i)   DNA sample taken for the purposes of elimination or as part of an intelligence-led screening and to be used only for the purposes of that investigation and destroyed afterwards:

"I consent to my DNA/mouth swab being taken for forensic analysis. I understand that the sample will be destroyed at the end of the case and that my profile will only be compared to the crime stain profile from this enquiry. I have been advised that the person taking the sample may be required to give evidence and/or provide a written statement to the police in relation to the taking of it".

(ii) DNA sample to be retained on the National DNA database and used in the future:

"I consent to my DNA sample and information derived from it being retained and used only for purposes related to the prevention and detection of a crime, the investigation of an offence or the conduct of a prosecution either nationally or internationally."

"I understand that this sample may be checked against other DNA records held by, or on behalf of, relevant law enforcement authorities, either nationally or internationally".

"I understand that once I have given my consent for the sample to be retained and used I cannot withdraw this consent."

(b) Fingerprints:

(i)   Fingerprints taken for the purposes of elimination or as part of an intelligence-led screening and to be used only for the purposes of that investigation and destroyed afterwards:

"I consent to my fingerprints being taken for elimination purposes. I understand that the fingerprints will be destroyed at the end of the case and that my fingerprints will only be compared to the fingerprints from this enquiry. I have been advised that the person taking the fingerprints may be required to give evidence and/or provide a written statement to the police in relation to the taking of it."

(ii) Fingerprints to be retained for future use:

"I consent to my fingerprints being retained and used only for purposes related to the prevention and detection of a crime, the investigation of an offence or the conduct of a prosecution either nationally or internationally".

"I understand that my fingerprints may be checked against other records held by, or on behalf of, relevant law enforcement authorities, either nationally or internationally."

"I understand that once I have given my consent for my fingerprints to be retained and used I cannot withdraw this consent."

(c) Footwear impressions:

(i)   Footwear impressions taken for the purposes of elimination or as part of an intelligence-led screening and to be used only for the purposes of that investigation and destroyed afterwards:

"I consent to my footwear impressions being taken for elimination purposes. I understand that the footwear impressions will be destroyed at the end of the case and that my footwear impressions will only be compared to the footwear impressions from this enquiry. I have been advised that the person taking the footwear impressions may be

> required to give evidence and/or provide a written statement to the police in relation to the taking of it."

    (ii)   *Footwear impressions to be retained for future use:*

> "I consent to my footwear impressions being retained and used only for purposes related to the prevention and detection of a crime, the investigation of an offence or the conduct of a prosecution, either nationally or internationally".

> "I understand that my footwear impressions may be checked against other records held by, or on behalf of, relevant law enforcement authorities, either nationally or internationally."

> "I understand that once I have given my consent for my footwear impressions to be retained and used I cannot withdraw this consent."

F2 *The provisions for the retention of fingerprints, footwear impressions and samples in paragraph 1 allow for all fingerprints, footwear impressions and samples in a case to be available for any subsequent miscarriage of justice investigation.*

Annex G Requirement for a Person to Attend a Police Station for Fingerprints and Samples.

1. A requirement under Schedule 2A for a person to attend a police station to have fingerprints or samples taken:

    (a) must give the person a period of at least seven days within which to attend the police station; and

    (b) may direct them to attend at a specified time of day or between specified times of day.

2. When specifying the period and times of attendance, the officer making the requirements must consider whether the fingerprints or samples could reasonably be taken at a time when the person is required to attend the police station for any other reason. See Note G1.

3. An officer of the rank of inspector or above may authorise a period shorter than 7 days if there is an urgent need for person's fingerprints or sample for the purposes of the investigation of an offence. The fact of the authorisation and the reasons for giving it must be recorded as soon as practicable.

4. The constable making a requirement and the person to whom it applies may agree to vary it so as to specify any period within which, or date or time at which, the person is to attend. However, variation shall not have effect for the purposes of enforcement, unless it is confirmed by the constable in writing.

Notes for guidance

G1 *The specified period within which the person is to attend need not fall within the period allowed (if applicable) for making the requirement.*

G2 *To justify the arrest without warrant of a person who fails to comply with a requirement, (see paragraph 4.4(b) above), the officer making the requirement, or confirming a variation, should be prepared to explain how, when and where the requirement was made or the variation was confirmed and what steps were taken to ensure the person understood what to do and the consequences of not complying with the requirement.*

CODE OF PRACTICE ON AUDIO RECORDING INTERVIEWS WITH SUSPECTS (CODE E)

1 General

1.1 This Code of Practice must be readily available for consultation by:

- police officers
- police staff
- detained persons
- members of the public.

1.2 The *Notes for Guidance* included are not provisions of this Code.

1.3 Nothing in this Code shall detract from the requirements of Code C, the Code of Practice for the detention, treatment and questioning of persons by police officers.

1.4 This Code does not apply to those people listed in Code C, *paragraph 1.12*.

1.5 The term:
- 'appropriate adult' has the same meaning as in Code C, *paragraph 1.7*
- 'solicitor' has the same meaning as in Code C, *paragraph 6.12*.

1.5A Recording of interviews shall be carried out openly to instil confidence in its reliability as an impartial and accurate record of the interview.

1.6 In this Code:
- (aa) 'recording media' means any removable, physical audio recording medium (such as magnetic tape, optical disc or solid state memory) which can be played and copied.
- (a) 'designated person' means a person other than a police officer, designated under the Police Reform Act 2002, Part 4 who has specified powers and duties of police officers conferred or imposed on them;
- (b) any reference to a police officer includes a designated person acting in the exercise or performance of the powers and duties conferred or imposed on them by their designation.
- (c) 'secure digital network' is a computer network system which enables an original interview recording to be stored as a digital multi media file or a series of such files, on a secure file server which is accredited by the National Accreditor for Police Information Systems in the National Police Improvement Agency (NPIA) in accordance with the UK Government Protective Marking Scheme. (see section 7 of this Code).

1.7 Sections 2 to 6 of this code set out the procedures and requirements which apply to all interviews together with the provisions which apply only to interviews recorded using removable media. Section 7 sets out the provisions which apply to interviews recorded using a secure digital network and specifies the provisions in sections 2 to 6 which do not apply to secure digital network recording.

1.8 Nothing in this Code prevents the custody officer, or other officer given custody of the detainee, from allowing police staff who are not designated persons to carry out individual procedures or tasks at the police station if the law allows. However, the officer remains responsible for making sure the procedures and tasks are carried out correctly in accordance with this Code. Any such police staff must be:
- (a) a person employed by a police authority maintaining a police force and under the control and direction of the Chief Officer of that force; or
- (b) employed by a person with whom a police authority has a contract for the provision of services relating to persons arrested or otherwise in custody.

1.9 Designated persons and other police staff must have regard to any relevant provisions of the Codes of Practice.

1.10 References to pocket book include any official report book issued to police officers or police staff.

1.11 References to a custody officer include those performing the functions of a custody officer as in *paragraph 1.9* of Code C.

2 Recording and sealing master recordings

2.1 Not used.

2.2 One recording, the master recording, will be sealed in the suspect's presence. A second recording will be used as a working copy. The master recording is either of the two recordings used in a twin deck/drive machine or the only recording in a single deck/drive machine. The working copy is either the second/third recording used in a twin/triple deck/drive machine or a copy of the master recording made by a single deck/drive machine. See *Notes 2A* and *2B* [*This paragraph does not apply to interviews recorded using a secure digital network, see paragraphs 7.4 to 7.6*]

2.3 Nothing in this Code requires the identity of officers or police staff conducting interviews to be recorded or disclosed:

(a) in the case of enquiries linked to the investigation of terrorism (see *paragraph 3.2*); or

(b) if the interviewer reasonably believes recording or disclosing their name might put them in danger.

In these cases interviewers should use warrant or other identification numbers and the name of their police station. See *Note 2C*

Notes for guidance

2A *The purpose of sealing the master recording in the suspect's presence is to show the recording's integrity is preserved. If a single deck/drive machine is used the working copy of the master recording must be made in the suspect's presence and without the master recording leaving their sight. The working copy shall be used for making further copies if needed.*

2B *Not used.*

2C *The purpose of paragraph 2.3(b) is to protect those involved in serious organised crime investigations or arrests of particularly violent suspects when there is reliable information that those arrested or their associates may threaten or cause harm to those involved. In cases of doubt, an officer of inspector rank or above should be consulted.*

3   Interviews to be audio recorded

3.1 Subject to *paragraphs 3.3* and *3.4*, audio recording shall be used at police stations for any interview:

(a) with a person cautioned under Code C, *section 10* in respect of any indictable offence, including an offence triable either way, see *Note 3A*

(b) which takes place as a result of an interviewer exceptionally putting further questions to a suspect about an offence described in *paragraph 3.1(a)* after they have been charged with, or told they may be prosecuted for, that offence, see Code C, *paragraph 16.5*

(c) when an interviewer wants to tell a person, after they have been charged with, or informed they may be prosecuted for, an offence described in *paragraph 3.1(a)*, about any written statement or interview with another person, see Code C, *paragraph 16.4.*

3.2 The Terrorism Act 2000 makes separate provision for a Code of Practice for the audio recording of interviews of those arrested under Section 41 of, or Schedule 7 to, the 2000 Act. The provisions of this Code do not apply to such interviews. [See *Note 3C*].

3.3 The custody officer may authorise the interviewer not to audio record the interview when it is:

(a) not reasonably practicable because of equipment failure or the unavailability of a suitable interview room or recording equipment and the authorising officer considers, on reasonable grounds, that the interview should not be delayed; or

(b) clear from the outset there will not be a prosecution.

Note: In these cases the interview should be recorded in writing in accordance with Code C, *section 11*. In all cases the custody officer shall record the specific reasons for not audio recording. See *Note 3B*

3.4 If a person refuses to go into or remain in a suitable interview room, see Code C *paragraph 12.5*, and the custody officer considers, on reasonable grounds, that the interview should not be delayed the interview may, at the custody officer's discretion, be conducted in a cell using portable recording equipment or, if none is available, recorded in writing as in Code C, *section 11*. The reasons for this shall be recorded.

3.5 The whole of each interview shall be audio recorded, including the taking and reading back of any statement.

3.6 A sign or indicator which is visible to the suspect must show when the recording equipment is recording.

Notes for guidance

3A *Nothing in this Code is intended to preclude audio recording at police discretion of interviews at police stations with people cautioned in respect of offences not covered by paragraph 3.1, or responses made by persons after they have been charged with, or told they may be prosecuted for, an offence, provided this Code is complied with.*

3B A decision not to audio record an interview for any reason may be the subject of comment in court. The authorising officer should be prepared to justify that decision.

3C If, during the course of an interview under this Code, it becomes apparent that the interview should be conducted under one of the terrorism codes for recording of interviews the interview should only continue in accordance with the relevant code.

4   The interview

(a) General

4.1 The provisions of Code C:
  - *sections 10 and 11*, and the applicable *Notes for Guidance* apply to the conduct of interviews to which this Code applies
  - *paragraphs 11.7 to 11.14* apply only when a written record is needed.

4.2 Code C, *paragraphs 10.10, 10.11* and Annex C describe the restriction on drawing adverse inferences from a suspect's failure or refusal to say anything about their involvement in the offence when interviewed or after being charged or informed they may be prosecuted, and how it affects the terms of the caution and determines if and by whom a special warning under sections 36 and 37 of the Criminal Justice and Public Order Act 1994 can be given.

(b) Commencement of interviews

4.3 When the suspect is brought into the interview room the interviewer shall, without delay but in the suspect's sight, load the recorder with new recording media and set it to record. The recording media must be unwrapped or opened in the suspect's presence. *[This paragraph does not apply to interviews recorded using a secure digital network, see paragraphs 7.4 and 7.5].*

4.4 The interviewer should tell the suspect about the recording process and point out the sign or indicator which shows that the recording equipment is activated and recording. See *paragraph 3.6.* The interviewer shall:
  (a) say the interview is being audibly recorded
  (b) subject to *paragraph 2.3*, give their name and rank and that of any other interviewer present
  (c) ask the suspect and any other party present, e.g. a solicitor, to identify themselves
  (d) state the date, time of commencement and place of the interview
  (e) state the suspect will be given a notice about what will happen to the copies of the recording. *[This sub-paragraph does not apply to interviews recorded using a secure digital network, see paragraphs 7.4 and 7.6 to 7.7]*

See Note 4A

4.5 The interviewer shall:
  - caution the suspect, see Code C, *section 10*
  - remind the suspect of their entitlement to free legal advice, see Code C, *paragraph 11.2.*

4.6 The interviewer shall put to the suspect any significant statement or silence, see *Code C, paragraph 11.4.*

(c) Interviews with deaf persons

4.7 If the suspect is deaf or is suspected of having impaired hearing, the interviewer shall make a written note of the interview in accordance with Code C, at the same time as audio recording it in accordance with this Code. See *Notes 4B* and *4C*

(d) Objections and complaints by the suspect

4.8 If the suspect objects to the interview being audibly recorded at the outset, during the interview or during a break, the interviewer shall explain that the interview is being audibly recorded and that this Code requires the suspect's objections to be recorded on the audio recording. When any objections have been audibly recorded or the suspect has refused to have their objections recorded, the interviewer shall say they are turning off the recorder, give their reasons and turn it off. The interviewer shall then make a written record of the interview as in Code C, *section 11*. If, however, the interviewer reasonably considers they may proceed to question the suspect with the audio recording still on, the interviewer may do so. This procedure also applies in cases where the suspect has previously objected to the interview being visually recorded, see *Code F 4.8*, and the investigating officer has decided to audibly record the interview. See *Note 4D*

4.9 If in the course of an interview a complaint is made by or on behalf of the person being questioned concerning the provisions of this Code or Code C, the interviewer shall act as in Code C, *paragraph 12.9*. See *Notes 4E* and *4F*

4.10 If the suspect indicates they want to tell the interviewer about matters not directly connected with the offence and they are unwilling for these matters to be audio recorded, the suspect should be given the opportunity to tell the interviewer at the end of the formal interview.

(e) Changing recording media

4.11 When the recorder shows the recording media only has a short time left, the interviewer shall tell the suspect the recording media are coming to an end and round off that part of the interview. If the interviewer leaves the room for a second set of recording media, the suspect shall not be left unattended. The interviewer will remove the recording media from the recorder and insert the new recording media which shall be unwrapped or opened in the suspect's presence. The recorder should be set to record on the new media. To avoid confusion between the recording media, the interviewer shall mark the media with an identification number immediately after they are removed from the recorder. [*This paragraph does not apply to interviews recorded using a secure digital network as this does not use removable media, see paragraphs 1.6(c), 7.4 and 7.14 to 7.15.*]

(f) Taking a break during interview

4.12 When a break is taken, the fact that a break is to be taken, the reason for it and the time shall be recorded on the audio recording.

4.12A When the break is taken and the interview room vacated by the suspect, the recording media shall be removed from the recorder and the procedures for the conclusion of an interview followed, see *paragraph 4.18*.

4.13 When a break is a short one and both the suspect and an interviewer remain in the interview room, the recording may be stopped. There is no need to remove the recording media and when the interview recommences the recording should continue on the same recording media. The time the interview recommences shall be recorded on the audio recording.

4.14 After any break in the interview the interviewer must, before resuming the interview, remind the person being questioned that they remain under caution or, if there is any doubt, give the caution in full again. See *Note 4G*.

[*Paragraphs 4.12 to 4.14 do not apply to interviews recorded using a secure digital network, see paragraphs 7.4 and 7.8 to 7.10*]

(g) Failure of recording equipment

4.15 If there is an equipment failure which can be rectified quickly, e.g. by inserting new recording media, the interviewer shall follow the appropriate procedures as in paragraph 4.11. When the recording is resumed the interviewer shall explain what happened and record the time the interview recommences. If, however, it will not be possible to continue recording on that recorder and no replacement recorder is readily available, the interview may continue without being audibly recorded. If this happens, the interviewer shall seek the custody officer's authority as in paragraph 3.3. See *Note 4H* [*This paragraph does not apply to interviews recorded using a secure digital network, see paragraphs 7.4 and 7.11*]

(h) Removing recording media from the recorder

4.16 When recording media is removed from the recorder during the interview, they shall be retained and the procedures in *paragraph 4.18* followed. [*This paragraph does not apply to interviews recorded using a secure digital network as this does not use removable media, see 1.6(c), 7.4 and 7.14 to 7.15.*]

(i) Conclusion of interview

4.17 At the conclusion of the interview, the suspect shall be offered the opportunity to clarify anything he or she has said and asked if there is anything they want to add.

4.18 At the conclusion of the interview, including the taking and reading back of any written statement, the time shall be recorded and the recording shall be stopped. The interviewer shall seal the master recording with a master recording label and treat it as an exhibit in accordance with force standing orders. The interviewer shall sign the label and ask the suspect and any third party present during the interview to sign it. If the suspect or third party refuse to sign the label an officer of at least inspector rank, or if not available the custody officer, shall be called into the interview room and asked, subject to *paragraph 2.3*, to sign it.

4.19 The suspect shall be handed a notice which explains:

- how the audio recording will be used
- the arrangements for access to it
- that if the person is charged or informed they will be prosecuted, a copy of the audio recording will be supplied as soon as practicable or as otherwise agreed between the suspect and the police or on the order of a court.

[Paragraphs 4.17 to 4.19 do not apply to interviews recorded using a secure digital network, see paragraphs 7.4 and 7.12 to 7.13]

Notes for guidance

4A For the purpose of voice identification the interviewer should ask the suspect and any other people present to identify themselves.

4B This provision is to give a person who is deaf or has impaired hearing equivalent rights of access to the full interview record as far as this is possible using audio recording.

4C The provisions of Code C, section 13 on interpreters for deaf persons or for interviews with suspects who have difficulty understanding English continue to apply.

4D The interviewer should remember that a decision to continue recording against the wishes of the suspect may be the subject of comment in court.

4E If the custody officer is called to deal with the complaint, the recorder should, if possible, be left on until the custody officer has entered the room and spoken to the person being interviewed. Continuation or termination of the interview should be at the interviewer's discretion pending action by an inspector under Code C, paragraph 9.2.

4F If the complaint is about a matter not connected with this Code or Code C, the decision to continue is at the interviewer's discretion. When the interviewer decides to continue the interview, they shall tell the suspect the complaint will be brought to the custody officer's attention at the conclusion of the interview. When the interview is concluded the interviewer must, as soon as practicable, inform the custody officer about the existence and nature of the complaint made.

4G The interviewer should remember that it may be necessary to show to the court that nothing occurred during a break or between interviews which influenced the suspect's recorded evidence. After a break or at the beginning of a subsequent interview, the interviewer should consider summarising on the record the reason for the break and confirming this with the suspect.

4H Where the interview is being recorded and the media or the recording equipment fails the officer conducting the interview should stop the interview immediately. Where part of the interview is unaffected by the error and is still accessible on the media, that media shall be copied and sealed in the suspect's presence and the interview recommenced using new equipment/media as required. Where the content of the interview has been lost in its entirety the media should be sealed in the suspect's presence and the interview begun again. If the recording equipment cannot be fixed or no replacement is immediately available the interview should be recorded in accordance with Code C, section 11.

5   After the interview

5.1 The interviewer shall make a note in their pocket book that the interview has taken place, was audibly recorded, its time, duration and date and the master recording's identification number.

5.2 If no proceedings follow in respect of the person whose interview was recorded, the recording media must be kept securely as in *paragraph 6.1* and *Note 6A*.

[*This section (paragraphs 5.1, 5.2 and Note 5A) does not apply to interviews recorded using a secure digital network, see paragraphs 7.4 and 7.14 to 7.15*]

Note for guidance

5A *Any written record of an audibly recorded interview should be made in accordance with national guidelines approved by the Secretary of State, and with regard to the advice contained in the Manual of Guidance for the preparation, processing and submission of prosecution files.*

6   Media security

6.1 The officer in charge of each police station at which interviews with suspects are recorded shall make arrangements for master recordings to be kept securely and their movements accounted for on the same basis as material which may be used for evidential purposes, in accordance with force standing orders. See *Note 6A*

6.2 A police officer has no authority to break the seal on a master recording required for criminal trial or appeal proceedings. If it is necessary to gain access to the master recording, the police officer shall arrange for its seal to be broken in the presence of a representative of the Crown Prosecution Service. The defendant or their legal adviser should be informed and given a reasonable opportunity to be present. If the defendant or their legal representative is present they shall be invited to reseal and sign the master recording. If either refuses or neither is present this should be done by the representative of the Crown Prosecution Service. See *Notes 6B* and *6C*

6.3 If no criminal proceedings result or the criminal trial and, if applicable, appeal proceedings to which the interview relates have been concluded, the chief officer of police is responsible for establishing arrangements for breaking the seal on the master recording, if necessary.

6.4 When the master recording seal is broken, a record must be made of the procedure followed, including the date, time, place and persons present.

[*This section (paragraphs 6.1 to 6.4 and Notes 6A to 6C) does not apply to interviews recorded using a secure digital network, see paragraphs 7.4 and 7.14 to 7.15*]

Notes for guidance

6A *This section is concerned with the security of the master recording sealed at the conclusion of the interview. Care must be taken of working copies of recordings because their loss or destruction may lead to the need to access master recordings.*

6B *If the recording has been delivered to the crown court for their keeping after committal for trial the crown prosecutor will apply to the chief clerk of the crown court centre for the release of the recording for unsealing by the crown prosecutor.*

6C *Reference to the Crown Prosecution Service or to the crown prosecutor in this part of the Code should be taken to include any other body or person with a statutory responsibility for prosecution for whom the police conduct any audibly recorded interviews.*

7   Recording of Interviews by Secure Digital Network

7.1 A secure digital network does not use removable media and this section specifies the provisions which will apply when a secure digital network is used.

7.2 *Not used.*

7.3 The following requirements are solely applicable to the use of a secure digital network for the recording of interviews.

(a) *Application of sections 1 to 6 of Code E*

7.4 Sections 1 to 6 of Code E above apply except for the following paragraphs:
- Paragraph 2.2 under "Recording and sealing of master recordings"
- Paragraph 4.3 under "(b) Commencement of interviews"
- Paragraph 4.4 (e) under "(b) Commencement of interviews"

- Paragraphs 4.11–4.19 under "(e) Changing recording media", "(f) Taking a break during interview", "(g) Failure of recording equipment", "(h) Removing recording media from the recorder" and "(i) Conclusion of interview"
- Paragraphs 6.1–6.4 and Notes 6A to 6C under "Media security"

(b) Commencement of interview

7.5 When the suspect is brought into the interview room, the interviewer shall without delay and in the sight of the suspect, switch on the recording equipment and enter the information necessary to log on to the secure network and start recording.

7.6 The interviewer must then inform the suspect that the interview is being recorded using a secure digital network and that recording has commenced.

7.7 In addition to the requirements of paragraph 4.4(a–d) above, the interviewer must inform the person that:

- they will be given access to the recording of the interview in the event that they are charged or informed that they will be prosecuted but if they are not charged or informed that they will be prosecuted they will only be given access as agreed with the police or on the order of a court; and
- they will be given a written notice at the end of the interview setting out their rights to access the recording and what will happen to the recording.

(c) Taking a break during interview

7.8 When a break is taken, the fact that a break is to be taken, the reason for it and the time shall be recorded on the audio recording. The recording shall be stopped and the procedures in paragraphs 7.12 and 7.13 for the conclusion of an interview followed.

7.9 When the interview recommences the procedures in paragraphs 7.5 to 7.7 for commencing an interview shall be followed to create a new file to record the continuation of the interview. The time the interview recommences shall be recorded on the audio recording.

7.10 After any break in the interview the interviewer must, before resuming the interview, remind the person being questioned that they remain under caution or, if there is any doubt, give the caution in full again. See *Note 4G*

(d) Failure of recording equipment

7.11 If there is an equipment failure which can be rectified quickly, e.g. by commencing a new secure digital network recording, the interviewer shall follow the appropriate procedures as in *paragraphs 7.8 to 7.10*. When the recording is resumed the interviewer shall explain what happened and record the time the interview recommences. If, however, it is not possible to continue recording on the secure digital network the interview should be recorded on removable media as in *paragraph 4.3* unless the necessary equipment is not available. If this happens the interview may continue without being audibly recorded and the interviewer shall seek the custody officer's authority as in *paragraph 3.3*. See *Note 4H*.

(e) Conclusion of interview

7.12 At the conclusion of the interview, the suspect shall be offered the opportunity to clarify anything he or she has said and asked if there is anything they want to add.

7.13 At the conclusion of the interview, including the taking and reading back of any written statement:

(a) the time shall be orally recorded

(b) the suspect shall be handed a notice which explains:

- how the audio recording will be used
- the arrangements for access to it
- that if they are charged or informed that they will be prosecuted, they will be given access to the recording of the interview either electronically or by being given a copy on removable recording media, but if they are not charged or informed that they will prosecuted, they will only be given access as agreed with the police or on the order of a court.

See *Note 7A.*

    (c) the suspect must be asked to confirm that he or she has received a copy of the notice at paragraph 7.13(b) above. If the suspect fails to accept or to acknowledge receipt of the notice, the interviewer will state for the recording that a copy of the notice has been provided to the suspect and that he or she has refused to take a copy of the notice or has refused to acknowledge receipt.

    (d) the time shall be recorded and the interviewer shall notify the suspect that the recording is being saved to the secure network. The interviewer must save the recording in the presence of the suspect. The suspect should then be informed that the interview is terminated.

(f) After the interview

7.14 The interviewer shall make a note in their pocket book that the interview has taken place, was audibly recorded, its time, duration and date and the original recording's identification number.

7.15 If no proceedings follow in respect of the person whose interview was recorded, the recordings must be kept securely as in *paragraphs 7.16* and *7.17*.

See *Note 5A*

(g) Security of secure digital network interview records

7.16 Interview record files are stored in read only format on non-removable storage devices, for example, hard disk drives, to ensure their integrity. The recordings are first saved locally to a secure non-removable device before being transferred to the remote network device. If for any reason the network connection fails, the recording remains on the local device and will be transferred when the network connections are restored.

7.17 Access to interview recordings, including copying to removable media, must be strictly controlled and monitored to ensure that access is restricted to those who have been given specific permission to access for specified purposes when this is necessary. For example, police officers and CPS lawyers involved in the preparation of any prosecution case, persons interviewed if they have been charged or informed they may be prosecuted and their legal representatives.

Note for guidance

7A *The notice at paragraph 7.13 above should provide a brief explanation of the secure digital network and how access to the recording is strictly limited. The notice should also explain the access rights of the suspect, his or her legal representative, the police and the prosecutor to the recording of the interview. Space should be provided on the form to insert the date and the file reference number for the interview.*

CODE OF PRACTICE ON VISUAL RECORDING WITH SOUND OF INTERVIEWS WITH SUSPECTS (CODE F)

1 General

1.1 This code of practice must be readily available for consultation by police officers and other police staff, detained persons and members of the public.

1.2 The notes for guidance included are not provisions of this code. They form guidance to police officers and others about its application and interpretation.

1.3 Nothing in this code shall be taken as detracting in any way from the requirements of the Code of Practice for the Detention, Treatment and Questioning of Persons by Police Officers (Code C). [See *Note 1A*].

1.4 The interviews to which this Code applies are set out in paragraphs 3.1 - 3.3.

1.5 In this code, the term "appropriate adult", "solicitor" and "interview" have the same meaning as those set out in Code C. The corresponding provisions and Notes for Guidance in Code C applicable to those terms shall also apply where appropriate.

1.5A The visual recording of interviews shall be carried out openly to instil confidence in its reliability as an impartial and accurate record of the interview.

1.6 Any reference in this code to visual recording shall be taken to mean visual recording with sound and in this code:

(aa) 'recording media' means any removable, physical audio recording medium (such as magnetic tape, optical disc or solid state memory) which can be played and copied.

(a) 'designated person' means a person other than a police officer, designated under the Police Reform Act 2002, Part 4 who has specified powers and duties of police officers conferred or imposed on them;

(b) any reference to a police officer includes a designated person acting in the exercise or performance of the powers and duties conferred or imposed on them by their designation.

(c) 'secure digital network' is a computer network system which enables an original interview recording to be stored as a digital multi media file or a series of such files, on a secure file server which is accredited by the National Accreditor for Police Information Systems in the National Police Improvement Agency (NPIA) in accordance with the UK Government Protective Marking Scheme. (see section 7 of this Code).

1.7 References to "pocket book" in this Code include any official report book issued to police officers.

Note for guidance

1A As in paragraph 1.9 of Code C, references to custody officers include those carrying out the functions of a custody officer.

2   Recording and sealing of master recordings

2.1 Not used

2.2 The camera(s) shall be placed in the interview room so as to ensure coverage of as much of the room as is practicably possible whilst the interviews are taking place. [See *Note 2A*].

2.3 The certified recording medium will be of a high quality, new and previously unused. When the certified recording medium is placed in the recorder and switched on to record, the correct date and time, in hours, minutes and seconds, will be superimposed automatically, second by second, during the whole recording. [See *Note 2B*]. See section 7 regarding the use of a secure digital network to record the interview.

2.4 One copy of the certified recording medium, referred to in this code as the master copy, will be sealed before it leaves the presence of the suspect. A second copy will be used as a working copy. [See *Note 2C* and *2D*].

2.5 Nothing in this code requires the identity of an officer to be recorded or disclosed if:

(a) the interview or record relates to a person detained under the Terrorism Act 2000 (see paragraph 3.2); or

(b) otherwise where the officer reasonably believes that recording or disclosing their name might put them in danger.

2.6 In these cases, the officer will have their back to the camera and shall use their warrant or other identification number and the name of the police station to which they are attached. Such instances and the reasons for them shall be recorded in the custody record. [See *Note 2E*]

Notes for guidance

2A Interviewing officers will wish to arrange that, as far as possible, visual recording arrangements are unobtrusive. It must be clear to the suspect, however, that there is no opportunity to interfere with the recording equipment or the recording media.

2B In this context, the certified recording media should be capable of having an image of the date and time superimposed upon them as they record the interview.

2C The purpose of sealing the master copy before it leaves the presence of the suspect is to establish their confidence that the integrity of the copy is preserved.

2D The recording of the interview may be used for identification procedures in accordance with paragraph 3.21 or Annex E of Code D.

2E *The purpose of the paragraph 2.5(b) is to protect police officers and others involved in the investigation of serious organised crime or the arrest of particularly violent suspects when there is reliable information that those arrested or their associates may threaten or cause harm to the officers, their families or their personal property.*

3 Interviews to be visually recorded

3.1 Subject to paragraph 3.2 below, if an interviewing officer decides to make a visual recording these are the areas where it might be appropriate:

 (a) with a suspect in respect of an indictable offence (including an offence triable either way) [see *Notes 3A* and *3B*];

 (b) which takes place as a result of an interviewer exceptionally putting further questions to a suspect about an offence described in sub-paragraph (a) above after they have been charged with, or informed they may be prosecuted for, that offence [see *Note 3C*];

 (c) in which an interviewer wishes to bring to the notice of a person, after that person has been charged with, or informed they may be prosecuted for an offence described in sub-paragraph (a) above, any written statement made by another person, or the content of an interview with another person [see *Note 3D*]

 (d) with, or in the presence of, a deaf or deaf/blind or speech impaired person who uses sign language to communicate;

 (e) with, or in the presence of anyone who requires an "appropriate adult"; or

 (f) in any case where the suspect or their representative requests that the interview be recorded visually.

3.2 The Terrorism Act 2000 makes separate provision for a code of practice for the video recording of interviews in a police station of those detained under Schedule 7 or section 41 of the Act. The provisions of this code do not therefore apply to such interviews [see *Note 3E*].

3.3 The custody officer may authorise the interviewing officer not to record the interview visually:

 (a) where it is not reasonably practicable to do so because of failure of the equipment, or the non-availability of a suitable interview room, or recorder, and the authorising officer considers on reasonable grounds that the interview should not be delayed until the failure has been rectified or a suitable room or recorder becomes available. In such cases the custody officer may authorise the interviewing officer to audio record the interview in accordance with the guidance set out in Code E;

 (b) where it is clear from the outset that no prosecution will ensue; or

 (c) where it is not practicable to do so because at the time the person resists being taken to a suitable interview room or other location which would enable the interview to be recorded, or otherwise fails or refuses to go into such a room or location, and the authorising officer considers on reasonable grounds that the interview should not be delayed until these conditions cease to apply.

In all cases the custody officer shall make a note in the custody records of the reasons for not taking a visual record. [See *Note 3F*].

3.4 When a person who is voluntarily attending the police station is required to be cautioned in accordance with Code C prior to being interviewed, the subsequent interview shall be recorded, unless the custody officer gives authority in accordance with the provisions of paragraph 3.3 above for the interview not to be so recorded.

3.5 The whole of each interview shall be recorded visually, including the taking and reading back of any statement.

3.6 A sign or indicator which is visible to the suspect must show when the visual recording equipment is recording.

Notes for guidance

3A *Nothing in the code is intended to preclude visual recording at police discretion of interviews at police stations with people cautioned in respect of offences not covered by paragraph 3.1, or responses made by interviewees after they have been charged with, or informed they may be prosecuted for, an offence, provided that this code is complied with.*

3B Attention is drawn to the provisions set out in Code C about the matters to be considered when deciding whether a detained person is fit to be interviewed.

3C Code C sets out the circumstances in which a suspect may be questioned about an offence after being charged with it.

3D Code C sets out the procedures to be followed when a person's attention is drawn after charge, to a statement made by another person. One method of bringing the content of an interview with another person to the notice of a suspect may be to play him a recording of that interview.

3E If, during the course of an interview under this Code, it becomes apparent that the interview should be conducted under one of the terrorism codes for video recording of interviews the interview should only continue in accordance with the relevant code.

3F A decision not to record an interview visually for any reason may be the subject of comment in court. The authorising officer should therefore be prepared to justify their decision in each case.

4 The interview

(a) General

4.1 The provisions of Code C in relation to cautions and interviews and the Notes for Guidance applicable to those provisions shall apply to the conduct of interviews to which this Code applies.

4.2 Particular attention is drawn to those parts of Code C that describe the restrictions on drawing adverse inferences from a suspect's failure or refusal to say anything about their involvement in the offence when interviewed, or after being charged or informed they may be prosecuted and how those restrictions affect the terms of the caution and determine whether a special warning under Sections 36 and 37 of the Criminal Justice and Public Order Act 1994 can be given.

(b) Commencement of interviews

4.3 When the suspect is brought into the interview room the interviewer shall without delay, but in sight of the suspect, load the recording equipment and set it to record. The recording media must be unwrapped or otherwise opened in the presence of the suspect. [See *Note 4A*]

4.4 The interviewer shall then tell the suspect formally about the visual recording and point out the sign or indicator which shows that the recording equipment is activated and recording. See *paragraph 3.6*. The interviewer shall:

  (a) explain the interview is being visually recorded;
  (b) subject to paragraph 2.5, give his or her name and rank, and that of any other interviewer present;
  (c) ask the suspect and any other party present (e.g. his solicitor) to identify themselves.
  (d) state the date, time of commencement and place of the interview; and
  (e) state that the suspect will be given a notice about what will happen to the recording.

4.5 The interviewer shall then caution the suspect, which should follow that set out in Code C, and remind the suspect of their entitlement to free and independent legal advice and that they can speak to a solicitor on the telephone.

4.6 The interviewer shall then put to the suspect any significant statement or silence (i.e. failure or refusal to answer a question or to answer it satisfactorily) which occurred before the start of the interview, and shall ask the suspect whether they wish to confirm or deny that earlier statement or silence or whether they wish to add anything. The definition of a "significant" statement or silence is the same as that set out in Code C.

(c) Interviews with the deaf

4.7 If the suspect is deaf or there is doubt about their hearing ability, the provisions of Code C on interpreters for the deaf or for interviews with suspects who have difficulty in understanding English continue to apply.

(d) Objections and complaints by the suspect

4.8 If the suspect raises objections to the interview being visually recorded either at the outset or during the interview or during a break in the interview, the interviewer shall explain the fact that the interview is being visually recorded and that the provisions of this code require that the suspect's objections shall be recorded on the visual recording. When any objections have been visually recorded or the suspect has refused to have their objections recorded, the interviewer shall say that they are turning off the recording equipment, give their reasons and turn it off. If a separate audio recording is being maintained, the officer shall ask the person to record the reasons for refusing to agree to visual recording of the interview. Paragraph 4.8 of Code E will apply if the person objects to audio recording of the interview. The officer shall then make a written record of the interview. If the interviewer reasonably considers they may proceed to question the suspect with the visual recording still on, the interviewer may do so. See *Note 4G*.

4.9 If in the course of an interview a complaint is made by the person being questioned, or on their behalf, concerning the provisions of this code or of Code C, then the interviewer shall act in accordance with Code C, record it in the interview record and inform the custody officer. [See *Notes 4B* and *4C*].

4.10 If the suspect indicates that they wish to tell the interviewer about matters not directly connected with the offence of which they are suspected and that they are unwilling for these matters to be recorded, the suspect shall be given the opportunity to tell the interviewer about these matters after the conclusion of the formal interview.

(e) Changing the recording media

4.11 In instances where the recording medium is not of sufficient length to record all of the interview with the suspect, further certified recording medium will be used. When the recording equipment indicates that the recording medium has only a short time left to run, the interviewer shall advise the suspect and round off that part of the interview. If the interviewer wishes to continue the interview but does not already have further certified recording media with him, they shall obtain a set. The suspect should not be left unattended in the interview room. The interviewer will remove the recording media from the recording equipment and insert the new ones which have been unwrapped or otherwise opened in the suspect's presence. The recording equipment shall then be set to record. Care must be taken, particularly when a number of sets of recording media have been used, to ensure that there is no confusion between them. This could be achieved by marking the sets of recording media with consecutive identification numbers.

(f) Taking a break during the interview

4.12 When a break is to be taken during the course of an interview and the interview room is to be vacated by the suspect, the fact that a break is to be taken, the reason for it and the time shall be recorded. The recording equipment must be turned off and the recording media removed. The procedures for the conclusion of an interview set out in paragraph 4.19, below, should be followed.

4.13 When a break is to be a short one, and both the suspect and a police officer are to remain in the interview room, the fact that a break is to be taken, the reasons for it and the time shall be recorded on the recording media. The recording equipment may be turned off, but there is no need to remove the recording media. When the interview is recommenced the recording shall continue on the same recording media and the time at which the interview recommences shall be recorded.

4.14 When there is a break in questioning under caution, the interviewing officer must ensure that the person being questioned is aware that they remain under caution. If there is any doubt, the caution must be given again in full when the interview resumes. [See *Note 4D* and *4E*].

(g) Failure of recording equipment

4.15 If there is a failure of equipment which can be rectified quickly, the appropriate procedures set out in paragraph 4.12 shall be followed. When the recording is resumed the interviewer shall explain what has happened and record the time the interview recommences. If, however, it is not possible to continue recording on that particular recorder and no alternative equipment is readily available, the interview may continue without being recorded visually. In such circumstances, the procedures set out in paragraph 3.3 of this code for seeking the authority of the custody officer will be followed. [See *Note 4F*].

(h) Removing used recording media from recording equipment

4.16 Where used recording media are removed from the recording equipment during the course of an interview, they shall be retained and the procedures set out in paragraph 4.18 below followed.

(i) Conclusion of interview

4.17 Before the conclusion of the interview, the suspect shall be offered the opportunity to clarify anything he or she has said and asked if there is anything that they wish to add.

4.18 At the conclusion of the interview, including the taking and reading back of any written statement, the time shall be recorded and the recording equipment switched off. The master recording shall be removed from the recording equipment, sealed with a master recording label and treated as an exhibit in accordance with the force standing orders. The interviewer shall sign the label and also ask the suspect and any third party present during the interview to sign it. If the suspect or third party refuses to sign the label, an officer of at least the rank of inspector, or if one is not available, the custody officer, shall be called into the interview room and asked, subject to *paragraph 2.5*, to sign it.

4.19 The suspect shall be handed a notice which explains the use which will be made of the recording and the arrangements for access to it. The notice will also advise the suspect that a copy of the tape shall be supplied as soon as practicable if the person is charged or informed that he will be prosecuted.

Notes for guidance

4A The interviewer should attempt to estimate the likely length of the interview and ensure that an appropriate quantity of certified recording media and labels with which to seal the master copies are available in the interview room.

4B Where the custody officer is called immediately to deal with the complaint, wherever possible the recording equipment should be left to run until the custody officer has entered the interview room and spoken to the person being interviewed. Continuation or termination of the interview should be at the discretion of the interviewing officer pending action by an inspector as set out in Code C.

4C Where the complaint is about a matter not connected with this code of practice or Code C, the decision to continue with the interview is at the discretion of the interviewing officer. Where the interviewing officer decides to continue with the interview, the person being interviewed shall be told that the complaint will be brought to the attention of the custody officer at the conclusion of the interview. When the interview is concluded, the interviewing officer must, as soon as practicable, inform the custody officer of the existence and nature of the complaint made.

4D In considering whether to caution again after a break, the officer should bear in mind that he may have to satisfy a court that the person understood that he was still under caution when the interview resumed.

4E The officer should bear in mind that it may be necessary to satisfy the court that nothing occurred during a break in an interview or between interviews which influenced the suspect's recorded evidence. On the re-commencement of an interview, the officer should consider summarising on the record the reason for the break and confirming this with the suspect.

4F If any part of the recording media breaks or is otherwise damaged during the interview, it should be sealed as a master copy in the presence of the suspect and the interview resumed where it left off. The undamaged part should be copied and the original sealed as a master tape in the suspect's presence, if necessary after the interview. If equipment for copying is not readily available, both parts should be sealed in the suspect's presence and the interview begun again.

4G The interviewer should be aware that a decision to continue recording against the wishes of the suspect may be the subject of comment in court.

5 After the interview

5.1 The interviewer shall make a note in his or her pocket book of the fact that the interview has taken place and has been recorded, its time, duration and date and the identification number of the master copy of the recording media.

5.2 Where no proceedings follow in respect of the person whose interview was recorded, the recording media must nevertheless be kept securely in accordance with paragraph 6.1 and Note 6A.

Note for guidance

5A *Any written record of a recorded interview shall be made in accordance with national guidelines approved by the Secretary of State, and with regard to the advice contained in the Manual of Guidance for the preparation, processing and submission of files.*

6 Master copy security

(a) General

6.1 The officer in charge of the police station at which interviews with suspects are recorded shall make arrangements for the master copies to be kept securely and their movements accounted for on the same basis as other material which may be used for evidential purposes, in accordance with force standing orders [See *Note 6A*].

(b) Breaking master copy seal for criminal proceedings

6.2 A police officer has no authority to break the seal on a master copy which is required for criminal trial or appeal proceedings. If it is necessary to gain access to the master copy, the police officer shall arrange for its seal to be broken in the presence of a representative of the Crown Prosecution Service. The defendant or their legal adviser shall be informed and given a reasonable opportunity to be present. If the defendant or their legal representative is present they shall be invited to reseal and sign the master copy. If either refuses or neither is present, this shall be done by the representative of the Crown Prosecution Service. [See *Notes 6B* and *6C*].

(c) Breaking master copy seal: other cases

6.3 The chief officer of police is responsible for establishing arrangements for breaking the seal of the master copy where no criminal proceedings result, or the criminal proceedings, to which the interview relates, have been concluded and it becomes necessary to break the seal. These arrangements should be those which the chief officer considers are reasonably necessary to demonstrate to the person interviewed and any other party who may wish to use or refer to the interview record that the master copy has not been tampered with and that the interview record remains accurate. [See *Note 6D*]

6.4 Subject to paragraph 6.6, a representative of each party must be given a reasonable opportunity to be present when the seal is broken, the master copy copied and resealed.

6.5 If one or more of the parties is not present when the master copy seal is broken because they cannot be contacted or refuse to attend or paragraph 6.6 applies, arrangements should be made for an independent person such as a custody visitor, to be present. Alternatively, or as an additional safeguard, arrangement should be made for a film or photographs to be taken of the procedure.

6.6 Paragraph 6.5 does not require a person to be given an opportunity to be present when;
    (a) it is necessary to break the master copy seal for the proper and effective further investigation of the original offence or the investigation of some other offence; and
    (b) the officer in charge of the investigation has reasonable grounds to suspect that allowing an opportunity might prejudice any such an investigation or criminal proceedings which may be brought as a result or endanger any person. [See *Note 6E*]

(d) Documentation

6.7 When the master copy seal is broken, copied and re-sealed, a record must be made of the procedure followed, including the date time and place and persons present.

Notes for guidance

6A This section is concerned with the security of the master copy which will have been sealed at the conclusion of the interview. Care should, however, be taken of working copies since their loss or destruction may lead unnecessarily to the need to have access to master copies.

6B If the master copy has been delivered to the Crown Court for their keeping after committal for trial the Crown Prosecutor will apply to the Chief Clerk of the Crown Court Centre for its release for unsealing by the Crown Prosecutor.

6C Reference to the Crown Prosecution Service or to the Crown Prosecutor in this part of the code shall be taken to include any other body or person with a statutory responsibility for prosecution for whom the police conduct any recorded interviews.

6D The most common reasons for needing access to master copies that are not required for criminal proceedings arise from civil actions and complaints against police and civil actions between individuals arising out of allegations of crime investigated by police.

6E Paragraph 6.6 could apply, for example, when one or more of the outcomes or likely outcomes of the investigation might be; (i) the prosecution of one or more of the original suspects, (ii) the prosecution of someone previously not suspected, including someone who was originally a witness; and (iii) any original suspect being treated as a prosecution witness and when premature disclosure of any police action, particularly through contact with any parties involved, could lead to a real risk of compromising the investigation and endangering witnesses.

7   Visual recording of interviews by secure digital network

7.1   This section applies if an officer wishes to make a visual recording with sound of an interview mentioned in section 3 of this Code using a secure digital network which does not use removable media (see *paragraph 1.6(c)* above.

7.3   The provisions of sections 1 to 6 of this Code which relate or apply only to removable media will not apply to a secure digital network recording.

7.4   The statutory requirement and provisions for the audio recording of interviews using a secure digital network set out in section 7 of Code E should be applied to the visual recording with sound of interviews mentioned in section 3 of this code as if references to audio recordings of interviews include visual recordings with sound.

CODE OF PRACTICE FOR THE STATUTORY POWER OF ARREST BY POLICE OFFICERS (CODE G)

This Code applies to any arrest made by a police officer after midnight on 12 November 2012

1   Introduction

1.1   This Code of Practice deals with the statutory power of police to arrest a person who is involved, or suspected of being involved, in a criminal offence. The power of arrest must be used fairly, responsibly, with respect for people suspected of committing offences and without unlawful discrimination. The Equality Act 2010 makes it unlawful for police officers to discriminate against, harass or victimise any person on the grounds of the 'protected characteristics' of age, disability, gender reassignment, race, religion or belief, sex and sexual orientation, marriage and civil partnership, pregnancy and maternity when using their powers. When police forces are carrying out their functions they also have a duty to have regard to the need to eliminate unlawful discrimination, harassment and victimisation and to take steps to foster good relations.

1.2   The exercise of the power of arrest represents an obvious and significant interference with the Right to liberty and security under Article 5 of the European Convention on Human Rights set out in Part I of Schedule 1 to the Human Rights Act 1998.

1.3   The use of the power must be fully justified and officers exercising the power should consider if the necessary objectives can be met by other, less intrusive means. Absence of justification for exercising the power of arrest may lead to challenges should the case proceed to court. It could also lead to civil claims against police for unlawful arrest and false imprisonment. When the power of arrest is exercised it is essential that it is exercised in a non-discriminatory and proportionate manner which is compatible with the Right to liberty under Article 5. See *Note 1B*.

1.4 Section 24 of the Police and Criminal Evidence Act 1984 (as substituted by section 110 of the Serious Organised Crime and Police Act 2005) provides the statutory power for a constable to arrest without warrant for all offences. If the provisions of the Act and this Code are not observed, both the arrest and the conduct of any subsequent investigation may be open to question.

1.5 This Code of Practice must be readily available at all police stations for consultation by police officers and police staff, detained persons and members of the public.

1.6 The notes for guidance are not provisions of this code.

2. Elements of Arrest under section 24 PACE

2.1 A lawful arrest requires two elements:

A person's involvement or suspected involvement or attempted involvement in the commission of a criminal offence;

AND

Reasonable grounds for *believing* that the person's arrest is necessary.
- both elements must be satisfied, and
- it can never be necessary to arrest a person unless there are reasonable grounds to suspect them of committing an offence.

2.2 The arrested person must be informed that they have been arrested, even if this fact is obvious, and of the relevant circumstances of the arrest in relation to both the above elements. The custody officer must be informed of these matters on arrival at the police station. See *paragraphs 2.9, 3.3* and *Note 3* and *Code C paragraph 3.4*.

(a) 'Involvement in the commission of an offence'

2.3 A constable may arrest without warrant in relation to any offence (see *Notes 1* and *1A*) anyone:
- who is about to commit an offence or is in the act of committing an offence;
- whom the officer has reasonable grounds for suspecting is about to commit an offence or to be committing an offence;
- whom the officer has reasonable grounds to suspect of being guilty of an offence which he or she has reasonable grounds for suspecting has been committed;
- anyone who is guilty of an offence which has been committed or anyone whom the officer has reasonable grounds for suspecting to be guilty of that offence.

2.3A There must be some reasonable, objective grounds for the suspicion, based on known facts and information which are relevant to the likelihood the offence has been committed and the person liable to arrest committed it. See *Notes 2* and *2A*.

(b) Necessity criteria

2.4 The power of arrest is only exercisable if the constable has reasonable grounds for *believing* that it is necessary to arrest the person. The statutory criteria for what may constitute necessity are set out in paragraph 2.9 and it remains an operational decision at the discretion of the constable to decide:
- which one or more of the necessity criteria (if any) applies to the individual; and
- if any of the criteria do apply, whether to arrest, grant street bail after arrest, report for summons or for charging by post, issue a penalty notice or take any other action that is open to the officer.

2.5 In applying the criteria, the arresting officer has to be satisfied that at least one of the reasons supporting the need for arrest is satisfied.

2.6 Extending the power of arrest to all offences provides a constable with the ability to use that power to deal with any situation. However applying the necessity criteria requires the constable to examine and justify the reason or reasons why a person needs to be arrested or (as the case may be) further arrested, for an offence for the custody officer to decide whether to authorise their detention for that offence. See *Note 2C*

2.7 The criteria in paragraph 2.9 below which are set out in section 24 of PACE as substituted by section 110 of the Serious Organised Crime and Police Act 2005 are exhaustive. However, the circumstances that may satisfy those criteria remain a matter for the operational discretion of individual officers. Some examples are given to illustrate what those circumstances might be and what officers might consider when deciding whether arrest is necessary.

2.8 In considering the individual circumstances, the constable must take into account the situation of the victim, the nature of the offence, the circumstances of the suspect and the needs of the investigative process.

2.9 When it is practicable to tell a person why their arrest is necessary (as required by paragraphs 2.2, 3.3 and *Note 3*), the constable should outline the facts, information and other circumstances which provide the grounds for believing that their arrest is necessary and which the officer considers satisfy one or more of the statutory criteria in sub-paragraphs (a) to (f), namely:

    (a) to enable the name of the person in question to be ascertained (in the case where the constable does not know, and cannot readily ascertain, the person's name, or has reasonable grounds for doubting whether a name given by the person as his name is his real name): An officer might decide that a person's name cannot be readily ascertained if they fail or refuse to give it when asked, particularly after being warned that failure or refusal is likely to make their arrest necessary (see *Note 2D)*. Grounds to doubt a name given may arise if the person appears reluctant or hesitant when asked to give their name or to verify the name they have given.

    Where mobile fingerprinting is available and the suspect's name cannot be ascertained or is doubted, the officer should consider using the power under section 61(6A) of PACE (see *Code D paragraph 4.3(e)*) to take and check the fingerprints of a suspect as this may avoid the need to arrest solely to enable their name to be ascertained.

    (b) correspondingly as regards the person's address: An officer might decide that a person's address cannot be readily ascertained if they fail or refuse to give it when asked, particularly after being warned that such a failure or refusal is likely to make their arrest necessary. See *Note 2D*. Grounds to doubt an address given may arise if the person appears reluctant or hesitant when asked to give their address or is unable to provide verifiable details of the locality they claim to live in.

    When considering reporting to consider summons or charging by post as alternatives to arrest, an address would be satisfactory if the person will be at it for a sufficiently long period for it to be possible to serve them with the summons or requisition and charge; or, that some other person at that address specified by the person will accept service on their behalf. When considering issuing a penalty notice, the address should be one where the person will be in the event of enforcement action if the person does not pay the penalty or is convicted and fined after a court hearing.

    (c) to prevent the person in question:

        (i) causing physical injury to himself or any other person; This might apply where the suspect has already used or threatened violence against others and it is thought likely that they may assault others if they are not arrested. See *Note 2D*

        (ii) suffering physical injury; This might apply where the suspect's behaviour and actions are believed likely to provoke, or have provoked, others to want to assault the suspect unless the suspect is arrested for their own protection. See *Note 2D*

        (iii) causing loss or damage to property; This might apply where the suspect is a known persistent offender with a history of serial offending against property (theft and criminal damage) and it is thought likely that they may continue offending if they are not arrested.

(iv) committing an offence against public decency (only applies where members of the public going about their normal business cannot reasonably be expected to avoid the person in question);

This might apply when an offence against public decency is being committed in a place to which the public have access and is likely to be repeated in that or some other public place at a time when the public are likely to encounter the suspect. See *Note 2D*

(v) causing an unlawful obstruction of the highway;

This might apply to any offence where its commission causes an unlawful obstruction which it is believed may continue or be repeated if the person is not arrested, particularly if the person has been warned that they are causing an obstruction. See *Note 2D*

(d) to protect a child or other vulnerable person from the person in question.

This might apply when the health (physical or mental) or welfare of a child or vulnerable person is likely to be harmed or is at risk of being harmed, if the person is not arrested in cases where it is not practicable and appropriate to make alternative arrangements to prevent the suspect from having any harmful or potentially harmful contact with the child or vulnerable person.

(e) to allow the prompt and effective investigation of the offence or of the conduct of the person in question. See *Note 2E*

This may arise when it is thought likely that unless the person is arrested and then either taken in custody to the police station or granted 'street bail' to attend the station later, see *Note 2J*, further action considered necessary to properly investigate their involvement in the offence would be frustrated, unreasonably delayed or otherwise hindered and therefore be impracticable. Examples of such actions include:

(i) *interviewing the suspect* on occasions when the person's voluntary attendance is not considered to be a practicable alternative to arrest, because for example:

- it is thought unlikely that the person would attend the police station voluntarily to be interviewed.
- it is necessary to interview the suspect about the outcome of other investigative action for which their arrest is necessary, see (ii) to (v) below.
- arrest would enable the special warning to be given in accordance with Code C paragraphs 10.10 and 10.11 when the suspect is found:
  — in possession of incriminating objects, or at a place where such objects are found;
  — at or near the scene of the crime at or about the time it was committed.
- the person has made false statements and/or presented false evidence;
- it is thought likely that the person:
  — may steal or destroy evidence;
  — may collude or make contact with, co-suspects or conspirators;
  — may intimidate or threaten or make contact with, witnesses. See *Notes 2F and 2G*

(ii) when considering arrest in connection with the investigation of an *indictable offence* (see *Note 6*), there is a need:

- to enter and search without a search warrant any premises occupied or controlled by the arrested person or where the person was when arrested or immediately before arrest;
- to prevent the arrested person from having contact with others;
- to detain the arrested person for more than 24 hours before charge.

(iii) when considering arrest in connection with any *recordable offence* and it is necessary to secure or preserve evidence of that offence by taking fingerprints, footwear impressions or samples from the suspect for evidential comparison or matching with other material relating to that offence, for example, from the crime scene. See *Note 2H*

  (iv) when considering arrest in connection with any offence and it is necessary to search, examine or photograph the person to obtain evidence. See *Note 2H*

  (v) when considering arrest in connection with an offence to which the statutory Class A drug testing requirements in Code C section 17 apply, to enable testing when it is thought that drug misuse might have caused or contributed to the offence. See *Note 2I*.

(f) to prevent any prosecution for the offence from being hindered by the disappearance of the person in question.

This may arise when it is thought that:

• if the person is not arrested they are unlikely to attend court if they are prosecuted;

• the address given is not a satisfactory address for service of a summons or a written charge and requisition to appear at court because the person will not be at it for a sufficiently long period for the summons or charge and requisition to be served and no other person at that specified address will accept service on their behalf.

3   Information to be given on Arrest

(a) Cautions—when a caution must be given

3.1 Code C paragraphs 10.1 and 10.2 set out the requirement for a person whom there are grounds to suspect of an offence (see *Note 2*) to be cautioned before being questioned or further questioned about an offence.

3.2 *Not used.*

3.3 A person who is arrested, or further arrested, must be informed at the time if practicable, or if not, as soon as it becomes practicable thereafter, that they are under arrest and of the grounds and reasons for their arrest, see paragraphs 2.2 and *Note 3*.

3.4 A person who is arrested, or further arrested, must be cautioned unless:

  (a) it is impracticable to do so by reason of their condition or behaviour at the time;

  (b) they have already been cautioned immediately prior to arrest as in *paragraph 3.1*.

(b) Terms of the caution (Taken from Code C section 10)

3.5 The caution, which must be given on arrest, should be in the following terms:

"You do not have to say anything. But it may harm your defence if you do not mention when questioned something which you later rely on in Court. Anything you do say may be given in evidence."

Where the use of the Welsh Language is appropriate, a constable may provide the caution directly in Welsh in the following terms:

"Does dim rhaid i chi ddweud dim byd. Ond gall niweidio eich amddiffyniad os na fyddwch chi'n sôn, wrth gael eich holi, am rywbeth y byddwch chi'n dibynnu arno nes ymlaen yn y Llys. Gall unrhyw beth yr ydych yn ei ddweud gael ei roi fel tystiolaeth."

See *Note 5*

3.6 Minor deviations from the words of any caution given in accordance with this Code do not constitute a breach of this Code, provided the sense of the relevant caution is preserved. See *Note 6*

3.7 *Not used.*

4   Records of Arrest

(a) General

4.1 The arresting officer is required to record in his pocket book or by other methods used for recording information:

• the nature and circumstances of the offence leading to the arrest;

• the reason or reasons why arrest was necessary;

• the giving of the caution; and

• anything said by the person at the time of arrest.

4.2 Such a record should be made at the time of the arrest unless impracticable to do. If not made at that time, the record should then be completed as soon as possible thereafter.

4.3 On arrival at the police station or after being first arrested at the police station, the arrested person must be brought before the custody officer as soon as practicable and a custody record must be opened in accordance with section 2 of Code C. The information given by the arresting officer on the circumstances and reason or reasons for arrest shall be recorded as part of the custody record. Alternatively, a copy of the record made by the officer in accordance with paragraph 4.1 above shall be attached as part of the custody record. See *paragraph 2.2* and *Code C paragraphs 3.4* and *10.3*.

4.4 The custody record will serve as a record of the arrest. Copies of the custody record will be provided in accordance with paragraphs 2.4 and 2.4A of Code C and access for inspection of the original record in accordance with paragraph 2.5 of Code C.

(b) Interviews and arrests

4.5 Records of interview, significant statements or silences will be treated in the same way as set out in sections 10 and 11 of Code C and in Codes E and F (audio and visual recording of interviews).

Notes for guidance

1 For the purposes of this Code, 'offence' means any statutory or common law offence for which a person may be tried by a magistrates' court or the Crown court and punished if convicted. Statutory offences include assault, rape, criminal damage, theft, robbery, burglary, fraud, possession of controlled drugs and offences under road traffic, liquor licensing, gambling and immigration legislation and local government byelaws. Common law offences include murder, manslaughter, kidnapping, false imprisonment, perverting the course of justice and escape from lawful custody.

1A This code does not apply to powers of arrest conferred on constables under any arrest warrant, for example, a warrant issued under the Magistrates' Courts Act 1980, sections 1 or 13, or the Bail Act 1976, section 7(1), or to the powers of constables to arrest without warrant other than under section 24 of PACE for an offence. These other powers to arrest without warrant do not depend on the arrested person committing any specific offence and include:

- *PACE, section 46A, arrest of person who fails to answer police bail to attend police station or is suspected of breaching any condition of that bail for the custody officer to decide whether they should be kept in police detention which applies whether or not the person commits an offence under section 6 of the Bail Act 1976 (e.g. failing without reasonable cause to surrender to custody);*
- *Bail Act 1976, section 7(3), arrest of person bailed to attend court who is suspected of breaching, or is believed likely to breach, any condition of bail to take them to court for bail to be re-considered;*
- *Children & Young Persons Act 1969, section 32(1A) (absconding)—arrest to return the person to the place where they are required to reside;*
- *Immigration Act 1971, Schedule 2 to arrest a person liable to examination to determine their right to remain in the UK;*
- *Mental Health Act 1983, section 136 to remove person suffering from mental disorder to place of safety for assessment;*
- *Prison Act 1952, section 49, arrest to return person unlawfully at large to the prison etc. where they are liable to be detained;*
- *Road Traffic Act 1988, section 6D arrest of driver following the outcome of a preliminary roadside test requirement to enable the driver to be required to provide an evidential sample;*
- *Common law power to stop or prevent a Breach of the Peace—after arrest a person aged 18 or over may be brought before a justice of the peace court to show cause why they should not be bound over to keep the peace - not criminal proceedings.*

1B Juveniles should not be arrested at their place of education unless this is unavoidable. When a juvenile is arrested at their place of education, the principal or their nominee must be informed. (From Code C Note 11D)

2 Facts and information relevant to a person's suspected involvement in an offence should not be confined to those which tend to indicate the person has committed or attempted to commit the offence. Before making a decision to arrest, a constable should take account of any facts and information that are available, including claims of innocence made by the person, that might dispel the suspicion.

2A Particular examples of facts and information which might point to a person's innocence and may tend to dispel suspicion include those which relate to the statutory defence provided by the Criminal Law Act 1967, section 3(1) which allows the use of reasonable force in the prevention of crime or making an arrest and the common law of self-defence. This may be relevant when a person appears, or claims, to have been acting reasonably in defence of themselves or others or to prevent their property or the property of others from being stolen, destroyed or damaged, particularly if the offence alleged is based on the use of unlawful force, e.g. a criminal assault. When investigating allegations involving the use of force by school staff, the power given to all school staff under the Education and Inspections Act 2006, section 93, to use reasonable force to prevent their pupils from committing any offence, injuring persons, damaging property or prejudicing the maintenance of good order and discipline may be similarly relevant. The Association of Chief Police Officers and the Crown Prosecution Service have published joint guidance to help the public understand the meaning of reasonable force and what to expect from the police and CPS in cases which involve claims of self defence. Separate advice for school staff on their powers to use reasonable force is available from the Department for Education

2B If a constable who is dealing with an allegation of crime and considering the need to arrest becomes an investigator for the purposes of the Code of Practice under the Criminal Procedure and Investigations Act 1996, the officer should, in accordance with paragraph 3.5 of that Code, "pursue all reasonable lines of inquiry, whether these point towards or away from the suspect. What is reasonable in each case will depend on the particular circumstances."

2C For a constable to have reasonable grounds for believing it necessary to arrest, he or she is not required to be satisfied that there is no viable alternative to arrest. However, it does mean that in all cases, the officer should consider that arrest is the practical, sensible and proportionate option in all the circumstances at the time the decision is made. This applies equally to a person in police detention after being arrested for an offence who is suspected of involvement in a further offence and the necessity to arrest them for that further offence is being considered.

2D Although a warning is not expressly required, officers should if practicable, consider whether a warning which points out their offending behaviour, and explains why, if they do not stop, the resulting consequences may make their arrest necessary. Such a warning might:
- if heeded, avoid the need to arrest, or
- if it is ignored, support the need to arrest and also help prove the mental element of certain offences, for example, the person's intent or awareness, or help to rebut a defence that they were acting reasonably.

A person who is warned that they may be liable to arrest if their real name and address cannot be ascertained, should be given a reasonable opportunity to establish their real name and address before deciding that either or both are unknown and cannot be readily ascertained or that there are reasonable grounds to doubt that a name and address they have given is their real name and address. They should be told why their name is not known and cannot be readily ascertained and (as the case may be) of the grounds for doubting that a name and address they have given is their real name and address, including, for example, the reason why a particular document the person has produced to verify their real name and/or address, is not sufficient.

2E The meaning of "prompt" should be considered on a case by case basis taking account of all the circumstances. It indicates that the progress of the investigation should not be delayed to the extent that it would adversely affect the effectiveness of the investigation. The arresting officer also has discretion to release the arrested person on 'street bail' as an alternative to taking the person directly to the station. See Note 2J.

2F An officer who believes that it is necessary to interview the person suspected of committing the offence must then consider whether their arrest is necessary in order to carry out the interview. The officer is not required to interrogate the suspect to determine whether they will attend a police station voluntarily to be interviewed but they must consider whether the suspect's voluntary attendance is a practicable alternative for carrying out the interview. If it is, then arrest would not be necessary. Conversely, an officer who considers this option but is not satisfied that it is a practicable alternative, may have reasonable grounds for deciding that the arrest is necessary at the outset 'on the street'. Without such considerations, the officer would not be able to establish that arrest was necessary in order to interview.

Circumstances which suggest that a person's arrest „on the street would not be necessary to interview them might be where the officer:

- is satisfied as to their identity and address and that they will attend the police station voluntarily to be interviewed, either immediately or by arrangement at a future date and time; and
- is not aware of any other circumstances which indicate that voluntary attendance would not be a practicable alternative. See paragraph 2.9(e)(i) to (v).

When making arrangements for the person's voluntary attendance, the officer should tell the person:

- that to properly investigate their suspected involvement in the offence they must be interviewed under caution at the police station, but in the circumstances their arrest for this purpose will not be necessary if they attend the police station voluntarily to be interviewed;
- that if they attend voluntarily, they will be entitled to free legal advice before, and to have a solicitor present at, the interview;
- that the date and time of the interview will take account of their circumstances and the needs of the investigation; and
- that if they do not agree to attend voluntarily at a time which meets the needs of the investigation, or having so agreed, fail to attend, or having attended, fail to remain for the interview to be completed, their arrest will be necessary to enable them to be interviewed.

2G When the person attends the police station voluntarily for interview by arrangement as in Note 2F above, their arrest on arrival at the station prior to interview would only be justified if:

- new information coming to light after the arrangements were made indicates that from that time, voluntary attendance ceased to be a practicable alternative and the person's arrest became necessary; and
- it was not reasonably practicable for the person to be arrested before they attended the station.

If a person who attends the police station voluntarily to be interviewed decides to leave before the interview is complete, the police would at that point be entitled to consider whether their arrest was necessary to carry out the interview. The possibility that the person might decide to leave during the interview is therefore not a valid reason for arresting them before the interview has commenced. See Code C paragraph 3.21.

2H The necessity criteria do not permit arrest solely to enable the routine taking, checking (speculative searching) and retention of fingerprints, samples, footwear impressions and photographs when there are no prior grounds to believe that checking and comparing the fingerprints etc. or taking a photograph would provide relevant evidence of the person's involvement in the offence concerned or would help to ascertain or verify their real identity.

2I The necessity criteria do not permit arrest for an offence solely because it happens to be one of the statutory drug testing "trigger offences" (see Code C Note 17E) when there is no suspicion that Class A drug misuse might have caused or contributed to the offence.

2J Having determined that the necessity criteria have been met and having made the arrest, the officer can then consider the use of street bail on the basis of the effective and efficient progress of the investigation of the offence in question. It gives the officer discretion to compel the person to attend a police station at a date/time that best suits the overall needs of the particular investigation. Its use is not confined to dealing with child care issues or allowing officers to attend to more urgent operational duties and granting street bail does not retrospectively negate the need to arrest.

3 An arrested person must be given sufficient information to enable them to understand they have been deprived of their liberty and the reason they have been arrested, as soon as practicable after the arrest, e.g. when a person is arrested on suspicion of committing an offence they must be informed of the nature

of the suspected offence and when and where it was committed. The suspect must also be informed of the reason or reasons why arrest is considered necessary. Vague or technical language should be avoided. When explaining why one or more of the arrest criteria apply, it is not necessary to disclose any specific details that might undermine or otherwise adversely affect any investigative processes. An example might be the conduct of a formal interview when prior disclosure of such details might give the suspect an opportunity to fabricate an innocent explanation or to otherwise conceal lies from the interviewer.

4 Nothing in this Code requires a caution to be given or repeated when informing a person not under arrest they may be prosecuted for an offence. However, a court will not be able to draw any inferences under the Criminal Justice and Public Order Act 1994, section 34, if the person was not cautioned.

5 If it appears a person does not understand the caution, the person giving it should explain it in their own words.

6 Certain powers available as the result of an arrest—for example, entry and search of premises, detention without charge beyond 24 hours, holding a person incommunicado and delaying access to legal advice—only apply in respect of indictable offences and are subject to the specific requirements on authorisation as set out in PACE and the relevant Code of Practice.

Appendix 7 Disclosure: Criminal Procedure and Investigations Act 1996: Code of Practice under Part II

Introduction

1.1 This code of practice is issued under Part II of the Criminal Procedure and Investigations Act 1996 ('the Act'). It applies in respect of criminal investigations conducted by police officers which begin on or after the day on which this code comes into effect. Persons other than police officers who are charged with the duty of conducting an investigation as defined in the Act are to have regard to the relevant provisions of the code, and should take these into account in applying their own operating procedures.

1.2 This code does not apply to persons who are not charged with the duty of conducting an investigation as defined in the Act.

1.3 Nothing in this code applies to material intercepted in obedience to a warrant issued under section 2 of the Interception of Communications Act 1985, or to any copy of that material as defined in section 10 of that Act.

1.4 ...

Definitions

2.1 In this code:
— a *criminal investigation* is an investigation conducted by police officers with a view to it being ascertained whether a person should be charged with an offence, or whether a person charged with an offence is guilty of it. This will include:
— investigations into crimes that have been committed;
— investigations whose purpose is to ascertain whether a crime has been committed, with a view to the possible institution of criminal proceedings; and
— investigations which begin in the belief that a crime may be committed, for example when the police keep premises or individuals under observation for a period of time, with a view to the possible institution of criminal proceedings;
— charging a person with an offence includes prosecution by way of summons;
— an *investigator* is any police officer involved in the conduct of a criminal investigation. All investigators have a responsibility for carrying out the duties imposed on them under this code, including in particular recording information, and retaining records of information and other material;

— the *officer in charge of an investigation* is the police officer responsible for directing a criminal investigation. He is also responsible for ensuring that proper procedures are in place for recording information, and retaining records of information and other material, in the investigation;

— the *disclosure officer* is the person responsible for examining material retained by the police during the investigation; revealing material to the prosecutor during the investigation and any criminal proceedings resulting from it, and certifying that he has done this; and disclosing material to the accused at the request of the prosecutor;

— the *prosecutor* is the authority responsible for the conduct of criminal proceedings on behalf of the Crown. Particular duties may in practice fall to individuals acting on behalf of the prosecuting authority;

— *material* is material of any kind, including information and objects, which is obtained in the course of a criminal investigation and which may be relevant to the investigation;

— material may be *relevant to an investigation* if it appears to an investigator, or to the officer in charge of an investigation, or to the disclosure officer, that it has some bearing on any offence under investigation or any person being investigated, or on the surrounding circumstances of the case, unless it is incapable of having any impact on the case;

— *sensitive material* is material which the disclosure officer believes, after consulting the officer in charge of the investigation, it is not in the public interest to disclose;

— references to *primary prosecution disclosure* are to the duty of the prosecutor under section 3 of the Act to disclose material which is in his possession or which he has inspected in pursuance of this code, and which in his opinion might undermine the case against the accused;

— references to *secondary prosecution disclosure* are to the duty of the prosecutor under section 7 of the Act to disclose material which is in his possession or which he has inspected in pursuance of this code, and which might reasonably be expected to assist the defence disclosed by the accused in a defence statement given under the Act;

— references to the disclosure of material to a person accused of an offence include references to the disclosure of material to his legal representative;

— references to police officers and to the chief officer of police include those employed in a police force as defined in section 3(3) of the Prosecution of Offences Act 1985.

General responsibilities

3.1 The functions of the investigator, the officer in charge of an investigation and the disclosure officer are separate. Whether they are undertaken by one, two or more persons will depend on the complexity of the case and the administrative arrangements within each police force. Where they are undertaken by more than one person, close consultation between them is essential to the effective performance of the duties imposed by this code.

3.2 The chief officer of police for each police force is responsible for putting in place arrangements to ensure that in every investigation the identity of the officer in charge of an investigation and the disclosure officer is recorded.

3.3 The officer in charge of an investigation may delegate tasks to another investigator or to civilians employed by the police force, but he remains responsible for ensuring that these have been carried out and for accounting for any general policies followed in the investigation. In particular, it is an essential part of his duties to ensure that all material which may be relevant to an investigation is retained, and either made available to the disclosure officer or (in exceptional circumstances) revealed directly to the prosecutor.

3.4 In conducting an investigation, the investigator should pursue all reasonable lines of inquiry, whether these point towards or away from the suspect. What is reasonable in each case will depend on the particular circumstances.

3.5 If the officer in charge of an investigation believes that other persons may be in possession of material that may be relevant to the investigation, and if this has not been obtained under paragraph 3.4 above, he should ask the disclosure officer to inform them of the existence of the investigation and to invite them to retain the material in case they receive a request for its disclosure. The disclosure officer should inform the prosecutor that they may have such material. However, the officer in charge of an investigation is not required to make speculative enquiries of other persons: there must be some reason to believe that they may have relevant material. That reason may come from information provided to the police by the accused or from other inquiries made or from some other source.

3.6 If, during a criminal investigation, the officer in charge of an investigation or disclosure officer for any reason no longer has responsibility for the functions falling to him, either his supervisor or the police officer in charge of criminal investigations for the police force concerned must assign someone else to assume that responsibility. That person's identity must be recorded, as with those initially responsible for these functions in each investigation.

Recording of information

4.1 If material which may be relevant to the investigation consists of information which is not recorded in any form, the officer in charge of an investigation must ensure that it is recorded in a durable or retrievable form (whether in writing, on video or audio tape, or on computer disk).

4.2 Where it is not practicable to retain the initial record of information because it forms part of a larger record which is to be destroyed, its contents should be transferred as a true record to a durable and more easily-stored form before that happens.

4.3 Negative information is often relevant to an investigation. If it may be relevant it must be recorded. An example might be a number of people present in a particular place at a particular time who state that they saw nothing unusual.

4.4 Where information which may be relevant is obtained, it must be recorded at the time it is obtained or as soon as practicable after that time. This includes, for example, information obtained in house-to-house enquiries, although the requirement to record information promptly does not require an investigator to take a statement from a potential witness where it would not otherwise be taken.

Retention of material

(a)　Duty to retain material

5.1 The investigator must retain material obtained in a criminal investigation which may be relevant to the investigation. This includes not only material coming into the possession of the investigator (such as documents seized in the course of searching premises) but also material generated by him (such as interview records). Material may be photographed, or retained in the form of a copy rather than the original, if the original is perishable, or was supplied to the investigator rather than generated by him and is to be returned to its owner.

5.2 Where material has been seized in the exercise of the powers of seizure conferred by the Police and Criminal Evidence Act 1984, the duty to retain it under this code is subject to the provisions on the retention of seized material in section 22 of that Act.

5.3 If the officer in charge of an investigation becomes aware as a result of developments in the case that material previously examined but not retained (because it was not thought to be relevant) may now be relevant to the investigation, he should, wherever practicable, take steps to obtain it or ensure that it is retained for further inspection or for production in court if required.

5.4 The duty to retain material includes in particular the duty to retain material falling into the following categories, where it may be relevant to the investigation:

- crime reports (including crime report forms, relevant parts of incident report books or police officers' notebooks);
- custody records;
- records which are derived from tapes of telephone messages (for example, 999 calls) containing descriptions of an alleged offence or offender;

- final versions of witness statements (and draft versions where their content differs from the final version), including any exhibits mentioned (unless these have been returned to their owner on the understanding that they will be produced in court if required);
- interview records (written records, or audio or video tapes, of interviews with actual or potential witnesses or suspects);
- communications between the police and experts such as forensic scientists, reports of work carried out by experts, and schedules of scientific material prepared by the expert for the investigator, for the purposes of criminal proceedings;
- any material casting doubt on the reliability of a confession;
- any material casting doubt on the reliability of a witness;
- any other material which may fall within the test for primary prosecution disclosure in the Act.

5.5 The duty to retain material falling into these categories does not extend to items which are purely ancillary to such material and possess no independent significance (for example, duplicate copies of records or reports).

(b)   Length of time for which material is to be retained

5.6 All material which may be relevant to the investigation must be retained until a decision is taken whether to institute proceedings against a person for an offence.

5.7 If a criminal investigation results in proceedings being instituted, all material which may be relevant must be retained at least until the accused is acquitted or convicted or the prosecutor decides not to proceed with the case.

5.8 Where the accused is convicted after a not guilty plea, all material which may be relevant must be retained for the following minimum periods after the date of conviction:

- one year, in respect of a conviction at a summary trial;
- three years, in respect of a conviction at a trial on indictment.

5.9 If an appeal against conviction is in progress at the end of the periods specified in paragraph 5.8, all material which may be relevant must be retained until the appeal is determined.

5.10 Material need not be retained by the police for the duration of the periods specified in paragraph 5.8 in these circumstances:

- it was seized and is to be returned to its owner;
- the material is not durable and deteriorates so much that it has no evidential value;
- copies of the material are held by another criminal justice agency, and it is agreed in writing between the police and that agency that the agency will retain these for the minimum periods specified above.

Preparation of material for prosecutor

(a)   Introduction

6.1 The officer in charge of the investigation, the disclosure officer or an investigator may seek advice from the prosecutor about whether any particular item of material may be relevant to the investigation.

6.2 Material which may be relevant to an investigation, which has been retained in accordance with this code, and which the disclosure officer believes will not form part of the prosecution case, must be listed on a schedule.

6.3 Material which the disclosure officer does not believe is sensitive must be listed on a schedule of non-sensitive material. The schedule must include a statement that the disclosure officer does not believe the material is sensitive.

6.4 Any material which is believed to be sensitive must be either listed on a schedule of sensitive material or, in exceptional circumstances, revealed to the prosecutor separately.

6.5 Paragraphs 6.6 to 6.11 below apply to both sensitive and non-sensitive material. Paragraphs 6.12 to 6.14 apply to sensitive material only.

(b)   Circumstances in which a schedule is to be prepared

6.6   The disclosure officer must ensure that a schedule is prepared in the following circumstances:

— the accused is charged with an offence which is triable only on indictment;
— the accused is charged with an offence which is triable either way, and it is considered either that the case is likely to be tried on indictment or that the accused is likely to plead not guilty at a summary trial;
— the accused is charged with a summary offence, and it is considered that he is likely to plead not guilty.

6.7   In respect of either way and summary offences, a schedule may not be needed if a person has admitted the offence, or if a police officer witnessed the offence and that person has not denied it.

6.8   If it is believed that the accused is likely to plead guilty at a summary trial, it is not necessary to prepare a schedule in advance. If, contrary to this belief, the accused pleads not guilty at a summary trial, or the offence is to be tried on indictment, the disclosure officer must ensure that a schedule is prepared as soon as is reasonably practicable after that happens.

(c)   Way in which material is to be listed on schedule

6.9   The disclosure officer should ensure that each item of material is listed separately on the schedule, and is numbered consecutively. The description of each item should make clear the nature of the item and should contain sufficient detail to enable the prosecutor to decide whether he needs to inspect the material before deciding whether or not it should be disclosed.

6.10   In some enquiries it may not be practicable to list each item of material separately. For example, there may be many items of a similar or repetitive nature. These may be listed in a block and described by quantity and generic title.

6.11   Even if some material is listed in a block, the disclosure officer must ensure that any items among that material which might meet the test for primary prosecution disclosure are listed and described individually.

(d)   Treatment of sensitive material

6.12   Subject to paragraph 6.13 below, the disclosure officer must list on a sensitive schedule any material which he believes it is not in the public interest to disclose, and the reason for that belief. The schedule must include a statement that the disclosure officer believes the material is sensitive. Depending on the circumstances, examples of such material may include the following among others:

— material relating to national security;
— material received from the intelligence and security agencies;
— material relating to intelligence from foreign sources which reveals sensitive intelligence gathering methods;
— material given in confidence;
— material which relates to the use of a telephone system and which is supplied to an investigator for intelligence purposes only;
— material relating to the identity or activities of informants, or under-cover police officers, or other persons supplying information to the police who may be in danger if their identities are revealed;
— material revealing the location of any premises or other place used for police surveillance, or the identity of any person allowing a police officer to use them for surveillance;
— material revealing, either directly or indirectly, techniques and methods relied upon by a police officer in the course of a criminal investigation, for example covert surveillance techniques, or other methods of detecting crime;
— material whose disclosure might facilitate the commission of other offences or hinder the prevention and detection of crime;
— internal police communications such as management minutes;
— material upon the strength of which search warrants were obtained;
— material containing details of persons taking part in identification parades;

— material supplied to an investigator during a criminal investigation which has been generated by an official of a body concerned with the regulation or supervision of bodies corporate or of persons engaged in financial activities, or which has been generated by a person retained by such a body;

— material supplied to an investigator during a criminal investigation which relates to a child or young person and which has been generated by a local authority Social services department, an Area Child Protection Committee or other party contacted by an investigator during the investigation.

6.13 In exceptional circumstances, where an investigator considers that material is so sensitive that its revelation to the prosecutor by means of an entry on the sensitive schedule is inappropriate, the existence of the material must be revealed to the prosecutor separately. This will apply where compromising the material would be likely to lead directly to the loss of life, or directly threaten national security.

6.14 In such circumstances, the responsibility for informing the prosecutor lies with the investigator who knows the detail of the sensitive material. The investigator should act as soon as is reasonably practicable after the file containing the prosecution case is sent to the prosecutor. The investigator must also ensure that the prosecutor is able to inspect the material so that he can assess whether it needs to be brought before a court for a ruling on disclosure.

Revelation of material to prosecutor

7.1 The disclosure officer must give the schedules to the prosecutor. Wherever practicable this should be at the same time as he gives him the file containing the material for the prosecution case (or as soon as is reasonably practicable after the decision on mode of trial or the plea, in cases to which paragraph 6.8 applies).

7.2 The disclosure officer should draw the attention of the prosecutor to any material an investigator has retained (whether or not listed on a schedule) which may fall within the test for primary prosecution disclosure in the Act, and should explain why he has come to that view.

7.3 At the same time as complying with the duties in paragraphs 7.1 and 7.2, the disclosure officer must give the prosecutor a copy of any material which falls into the following categories (unless such material has already been given to the prosecutor as part of the file containing the material for the prosecution case):

— records of the first description of a suspect given to the police by a potential witness, whether or not the description differs from that of the alleged offender;

— information provided by an accused person which indicates an explanation for the offence with which he has been charged;

— any material casting doubt on the reliability of a confession;

— any material casting doubt on the reliability of a witness;

— any other material which the investigator believes may fall within the test for primary prosecution disclosure in the Act.

7.4 If the prosecutor asks to inspect material which has not already been copied to him, the disclosure officer must allow him to inspect it. If the prosecutor asks for a copy of material which has not already been copied to him, the disclosure officer must give him a copy. However, this does not apply where the disclosure officer believes, having consulted the officer in charge of the investigation, that the material is too sensitive to be copied and can only be inspected.

7.5 If material consists of information which is recorded other than in writing, whether it should be given to the prosecutor in its original form as a whole, or by way of relevant extracts recorded in the same form, or in the form of a transcript, is a matter for agreement between the disclosure officer and the prosecutor.

Subsequent action by disclosure officer

8.1 At the time a schedule of non-sensitive material is prepared, the disclosure officer may not know exactly what material will form the case against the accused, and the prosecutor may not have given advice about the likely relevance of particular items of material. Once these matters have been determined, the disclosure officer must give the prosecutor, where necessary, an amended schedule listing any additional material:

— which may be relevant to the investigation,
— which does not form part of the case against the accused,
— which is not already listed on the schedule, and
— which he believes is not sensitive,

unless he is informed in writing by the prosecutor that the prosecutor intends to disclose the material to the defence.

8.2 After a defence statement has been given, the disclosure officer must look again at the material which has been retained and must draw the attention of the prosecutor to any material which might reasonably be expected to assist the defence disclosed by the accused; and he must reveal it to him in accordance with paragraphs 7.4 and 7.5 above.

8.3 Section 9 of the Act imposes a continuing duty on the prosecutor, for the duration of criminal proceedings against the accused, to disclose material which meets the tests for disclosure (subject to public interest considerations). To enable him to do this, any new material coming to light should be treated in the same way as the earlier material.

Certification by disclosure officer

9.1 The disclosure officer must certify to the prosecutor that, to the best of his knowledge and belief, all material which has been retained and made available to him has been revealed to the prosecutor in accordance with this code. He must sign and date the certificate. It will be necessary to certify not only at the time when the schedule and accompanying material is submitted to the prosecutor, but also when material which has been retained is reconsidered after the accused has given a defence statement.

Disclosure of material to accused

10.1 If material has not already been copied to the prosecutor, and he requests its disclosure to the accused on the ground that:

— it falls within the test for primary or secondary prosecution disclosure, or
— the court has ordered its disclosure after considering an application from the accused, the disclosure officer must disclose it to the accused.

10.2 If material has been copied to the prosecutor, and it is to be disclosed, whether it is disclosed by the prosecutor or the disclosure officer is a matter for agreement between the two of them.

10.3 The disclosure officer must disclose material to the accused either by giving him a copy or by allowing him to inspect it. If the accused person asks for a copy of any material which he has been allowed to inspect, the disclosure officer must give it to him, unless in the opinion of the disclosure officer that is either not practicable (for example because the material consists of an object which cannot be copied, or because the volume of material is so great), or not desirable (for example because the material is a statement by a child witness in relation to a sexual offence).

10.4 If material which the accused has been allowed to inspect consists of information which is recorded other than in writing, whether it should be given to the accused in its original form or in the form of a transcript is a matter for the discretion of the disclosure officer. If the material is transcribed, the disclosure officer must ensure that the transcript is certified to the accused as a true record of the material which has been transcribed.

10.5 If a court concludes that it is in the public interest that an item of sensitive material must be disclosed to the accused, it will be necessary to disclose the material if the case is to proceed. This does not mean that sensitive documents must always be disclosed in their original form: for example, the court may agree that sensitive details still requiring protection should be blocked out, or that documents may be summarised, or that the prosecutor may make an admission about the substance of the material under section 10 of the Criminal Justice Act 1967.

Criminal Procedure Rules 2011

(SI 2011, No. 1709)

PART 27 WITNESS STATEMENTS

27.1. When this Part applies

This Part applies where a party wants to introduce a written statement in evidence under section 9 of the Criminal Justice Act 1967.

27.2. Content of written statement

The statement must contain—

    (a) at the beginning—

        (i)   the witness' name, and

        (ii) the witness' age, if under 18;

    (b) a declaration by the witness that—

        (i)   it is true to the best of the witness' knowledge and belief, and

        (ii) the witness knows that if it is introduced in evidence, then it would be an offence wilfully to have stated in it anything that the witness knew to be false or did not believe to be true;

    (c) if the witness cannot read the statement, a signed declaration by someone else that that person read it to the witness; and

    (d) the witness' signature.

27.3. Reference to exhibit

Where the statement refers to a document or object as an exhibit—

    (a) the statement must contain such a description of that exhibit as to identify it clearly; and

    (b) the exhibit must be labelled or marked correspondingly, and the label or mark signed by the maker of the statement.

27.4. Written statement in evidence

    (1) A party who wants to introduce in evidence a written statement must—

    (a) before the hearing at which that party wants to do so, serve a copy of the statement on—

        (i)   the court officer, and

        (ii) each other party; and

    (b) at or before that hearing, serve the statement itself on the court officer.

    (2) If that party relies on only part of the statement, that party must mark the copy in such a way as to make that clear.

    (3) A prosecutor must serve on a defendant, with the copy of the statement, a notice—

    (a) of the right within 7 days of service to object to the introduction of the statement in evidence instead of the witness giving evidence in person; and

    (b) that if the defendant does not object in time, the court—

        (i)   can nonetheless require the witness to give evidence in person, but

        (ii) may decide not to do so.

    (4) The court may exercise its power to require the witness to give evidence in person—

    (a) on application by any party; or

    (b) on its own initiative.

    (5) A party entitled to receive a copy of a statement may waive that entitlement by so informing—

    (a) the party who would have served it; and

    (b) the court.

PART 28 WITNESS SUMMONSES, WARRANTS AND ORDERS

28.1. When this Part applies
(1) This Part applies in magistrates' courts and in the Crown Court where—
    (a) a party wants the court to issue a witness summons, warrant or order under—
        (i)   section 97 of the Magistrates' Courts Act 1980,
        (ii) section 2 of the Criminal Procedure (Attendance of Witnesses) Act 1965, or
        (iii) section 7 of the Bankers' Books Evidence Act 1879;
    (b) the court considers the issue of such a summons, warrant or order on its own initiative as if a party had applied; or
    (c) one of those listed in rule 28.7 wants the court to withdraw such a summons, warrant or order.
(2) A reference to a 'witness' in this Part is a reference to a person to whom such a summons, warrant or order is directed.

28.2. Issue etc. of summons, warrant or order with or without a hearing
(1) The court may issue or withdraw a witness summons, warrant or order with or without a hearing.
(2) A hearing under this Part must be in private unless the court otherwise directs.

28.3. Application for summons, warrant or order: general rules
(1) A party who wants the court to issue a witness summons, warrant or order must apply as soon as practicable after becoming aware of the grounds for doing so.
(2) The party applying must—
    (a) identify the proposed witness;
    (b) explain—
        (i)   what evidence the proposed witness can give or produce,
        (ii) why it is likely to be material evidence, and
        (iii) why it would be in the interests of justice to issue a summons, order or warrant as appropriate.
(3) The application may be made orally unless—
    (a) rule 28.5 applies; or
    (b) the court otherwise directs.

28.4. Written application: form and service
(1) An application in writing under rule 28.3 must be in the form set out in the Practice Direction, containing the same declaration of truth as a witness statement.
(2) The party applying must serve the application—
    (a) in every case, on the court officer and as directed by the court; and
    (b) as required by rule 28.5, if that rule applies.

28.5. Application for summons to produce a document, etc.: special rules
(1) This rule applies to an application under rule 28.3 for a witness summons requiring the proposed witness—
    (a) to produce in evidence a document or thing; or
    (b) to give evidence about information apparently held in confidence,
that relates to another person.
(2) The application must be in writing in the form required by rule 28.4.
(3) The party applying must serve the application—
    (a) on the proposed witness, unless the court otherwise directs; and

(b) on one or more of the following, if the court so directs—
    (i)   a person to whom the proposed evidence relates,
    (ii) another party.

(4) The court must not issue a witness summons where this rule applies unless—
  (a) everyone served with the application has had at least 14 days in which to make representations, including representations about whether there should be a hearing of the application before the summons is issued; and
  (b) the court is satisfied that it has been able to take adequate account of the duties and rights, including rights of confidentiality, of the proposed witness and of any person to whom the proposed evidence relates.

(5) This rule does not apply to an application for an order to produce in evidence a copy of an entry in a banker's book.

28.6. Application for summons to produce a document, etc.: court's assessment of relevance and confidentiality

(1) This rule applies where a person served with an application for a witness summons requiring the proposed witness to produce in evidence a document or thing objects to its production on the ground that—
  (a) it is not likely to be material evidence; or
  (b) even if it is likely to be material evidence, the duties or rights, including rights of confidentiality, of the proposed witness or of any person to whom the document or thing relates, outweigh the reasons for issuing a summons.

(2) The court may require the proposed witness to make the document or thing available for the objection to be assessed.

(3) The court may invite—
  (a) the proposed witness or any representative of the proposed witness; or
  (b) a person to whom the document or thing relates or any representative of such a person,
to help the court assess the objection.

28.7. Application to withdraw a summons, warrant or order

(1) The court may withdraw a witness summons, warrant or order if one of the following applies for it to be withdrawn—
  (a) the party who applied for it, on the ground that it no longer is needed;
  (b) the witness, on the grounds that—
    (i)   he was not aware of any application for it, and
    (ii) he cannot give or produce evidence likely to be material evidence, or
    (iii) even if he can, his duties or rights, including rights of confidentiality, or those of any person to whom the evidence relates, outweigh the reasons for the issue of the summons, warrant or order; or
  (c) any person to whom the proposed evidence relates, on the grounds that—
    (i)   he was not aware of any application for it, and
    (ii) that evidence is not likely to be material evidence, or
    (iii) even if it is, his duties or rights, including rights of confidentiality, or those of the witness, outweigh the reasons for the issue of the summons, warrant or order.

(2) A person applying under the rule must—
  (a) apply in writing as soon as practicable after becoming aware of the grounds for doing so, explaining why he wants the summons, warrant or order to be withdrawn; and
  (b) serve the application on the court officer and as appropriate on—
    (i)   the witness,
    (ii) the party who applied for the summons, warrant or order, and

        (iii) any other person who he knows was served with the application for the summons, warrant or order.

(3) Rule 28.6 applies to an application under this rule that concerns a document or thing to be produced in evidence

28.8. Court's power to vary requirements under this Part

(1) The court may—

    (a) shorten or extend (even after it has expired) a time limit under this Part; and

    (b) where a rule or direction requires an application under this Part to be in writing, allow that application to be made orally instead.

(2) Someone who wants the court to allow an application to be made orally under paragraph (1)(b) of this rule must—

    (a) give as much notice as the urgency of his application permits to those on whom he would otherwise have served an application in writing; and

    (b) in doing so explain the reasons for the application and for wanting the court to consider it orally.

PART 29 MEASURES TO ASSIST A WITNESS OR DEFENDANT TO GIVE EVIDENCE

29.1. When this Part applies

(1) This Part applies—

    (a) where the court can give a direction (a 'special measures direction'), under section 19 of the Youth Justice and Criminal Evidence Act 1999, on an application or on its own initiative, for any of the following measures—

        (i) preventing a witness from seeing the defendant (section 23 of the 1999 Act),

        (ii) allowing a witness to give evidence by live link (section 24 of the 1999 Act),

        (iii) hearing a witness' evidence in private (section 25 of the 1999 Act),

        (iv) dispensing with the wearing of wigs and gowns (section 26 of the 1999 Act),

        (v) admitting video recorded evidence (sections 27 and 28 of the 1999 Act),

        (vi) questioning a witness through an intermediary (section 29 of the 1999 Act),

        (vii) using a device to help a witness communicate (section 30 of the 1999 Act);

    (b) where the court can vary or discharge such a direction, under section 20 of the 1999 Act;

    (c) where the court can give, vary or discharge a direction (a 'defendant's evidence direction') for a defendant to give evidence—

        (i) by live link, under section 33A of the 1999 Act, or

        (ii) through an intermediary, under sections 33BA and 33BB of the 1999 Act;

    (d) where the court can—

        (i) make a witness anonymity order, under section 86 of the Coroners and Justice Act 2009, or

        (ii) vary or discharge such an order, under section 91, 92 or 93 of the 2009 Act;

    (e) where the court can give or discharge a direction (a 'live link direction'), on an application or on its own initiative, for a witness to give evidence by live link under—

        (i) section 32 of the Criminal Justice Act 1988, or

        (ii) sections 51 and 52 of the Criminal Justice Act 2003;

    (f) where the court can exercise any other power it has to give, vary or discharge a direction for a measure to help a witness give evidence.

29.2. Meaning of 'witness'

In this Part, 'witness' means anyone (other than a defendant) for whose benefit an application, direction or order is made.

29.3. Making an application for a direction or order

A party who wants the court to exercise its power to give or make a direction or order must—

(a) apply in writing as soon as reasonably practicable, and in any event not more than—
    (i) 28 days after the defendant pleads not guilty, in a magistrates' court, or
    (ii) 14 days after the defendant pleads not guilty, in the Crown Court; and
(b) serve the application on—
    (i) the court officer, and
    (ii) each other party.

29.4. Decisions and reasons

(1) A party who wants to introduce the evidence of a witness who is the subject of an application, direction or order must—

(a) inform the witness of the court's decision as soon as reasonably practicable; and
(b) explain to the witness the arrangements that as a result will be made for him or her to give evidence.

(2) The court must announce, at a hearing in public before the witness gives evidence, the reasons for a decision—

(a) to give, make, vary or discharge a direction or order; or
(b) to refuse to do so.

29.5. Court's power to vary requirements under this Part

(1) The court may—

(a) shorten or extend (even after it has expired) a time limit under this Part; and
(b) allow an application or representations to be made in a different form to one set out in the Practice Direction, or to be made orally.

(2) A person who wants an extension of time must—

(a) apply when serving the application or representations for which it is needed; and
(b) explain the delay.

29.6. Custody of documents

Unless the court otherwise directs, the court officer may—

(a) keep a written application or representations; or
(b) arrange for the whole or any part to be kept by some other appropriate person, subject to any conditions that the court may impose.

29.7. Declaration by intermediary

(1) This rule applies where—

(a) a video recorded interview with a witness is conducted through an intermediary;
(b) the court directs the examination of a witness or defendant through an intermediary.

(2) An intermediary must make a declaration—

(a) before such an interview begins;
(b) before the examination begins (even if such an interview with the witness was conducted through the same intermediary).

(3) The declaration must be in these terms—

"I solemnly, sincerely and truly declare [or I swear by Almighty God] that I will well and faithfully communicate questions and answers and make true explanation of all matters and things as shall be required of me according to the best of my skill and understanding."

29.8. Exercise of court's powers

The court may decide whether to give, vary or discharge a special measures direction—

(a) at a hearing, in public or in private, or without a hearing;
(b) in a party's absence, if that party—
    (i) applied for the direction, variation or discharge, or
    (ii) has had at least 14 days in which to make representations.

29.9. Special measures direction for a young witness

(1) This rule applies where, under section 21 or section 22 of the Youth Justice and Criminal Evidence Act 19991, the primary rule requires the court to give a direction for a special measure to assist a child witness or a qualifying witness—

(a) on an application, if one is made; or

(b) on the court's own initiative, in any other case.

(2) A party who wants to introduce the evidence of such a witness must as soon as reasonably practicable—

(a) notify the court that the witness is eligible for assistance;

(b) provide the court with any information that the court may need to assess the witness' views, if the witness does not want the primary rule to apply; and

(c) serve any video recorded evidence on—

(i)   the court officer, and

(ii) each other party.

29.10 Content of application for a special measures direction

An applicant for a special measures direction must—

(a) explain how the witness is eligible for assistance;

(b) explain why special measures would be likely to improve the quality of the witness' evidence;

(c) propose the measure or measures that in the applicant's opinion would be likely to maximise so far as practicable the quality of that evidence;

(d) report any views that the witness has expressed about—

(i)   his or her eligibility for assistance,

(ii) the likelihood that special measures would improve the quality of his or her evidence, and

(iii) the measure or measures proposed by the applicant;

(e) in a case in which a child witness or a qualifying witness does not want the primary rule to apply, provide any information that the court may need to assess the witness' views;

(f) in a case in which the applicant proposes that the witness should give evidence by live link—

(i)   identify someone to accompany the witness while the witness gives evidence,

(ii) name that person, if possible, and

(iii) explain why that person would be an appropriate companion for the witness, including the witness' own views;

(g) in a case in which the applicant proposes the admission of video recorded evidence, identify—

(i)   the date and duration of the recording,

(ii) which part the applicant wants the court to admit as evidence, if the applicant does not want the court to admit all of it;

(h) attach any other material on which the applicant relies; and

(i) if the applicant wants a hearing, ask for one, and explain why it is needed.

29.11. Application to vary or discharge a special measures direction

(1) A party who wants the court to vary or discharge a special measures direction must—

(a) apply in writing, as soon as reasonably practicable after becoming aware of the grounds for doing so; and

(b) serve the application on—

(i)   the court officer, and

(ii) each other party.

(2) The applicant must—

    (a) explain what material circumstances have changed since the direction was given (or last varied, if applicable);

    (b) explain why the direction should be varied or discharged; and

    (c) ask for a hearing, if the applicant wants one, and explain why it is needed.

29.12. Application containing information withheld from another party

(1) This rule applies where—

    (a) an applicant serves an application for a special measures direction, or for its variation or discharge; and

    (b) the application includes information that the applicant thinks ought not be revealed to another party.

(2) The applicant must—

    (a) omit that information from the part of the application that is served on that other party;

    (b) mark the other part to show that, unless the court otherwise directs, it is only for the court; and

    (c) in that other part, explain why the applicant has withheld that information from that other party.

(3) Any hearing of an application to which this rule applies—

    (a) must be in private, unless the court otherwise directs; and

    (b) if the court so directs, may be, wholly or in part, in the absence of a party from whom information has been withheld.

(4) At any hearing of an application to which this rule applies—

    (a) the general rule is that the court will receive, in the following sequence—

        (i) representations first by the applicant and then by each other party, in all the parties' presence, and then

        (ii) further representations by the applicant, in the absence of a party from whom information has been withheld; but

    (b) the court may direct other arrangements for the hearing.

29.13. Representations in response

(1) This rule applies where a party wants to make representations about—

    (a) an application for a special measures direction;

    (b) an application for the variation or discharge of such a direction; or

    (c) a direction, variation or discharge that the court proposes on its own initiative.

(2) Such a party must—

    (a) serve the representations on—

        (i) the court officer, and

        (ii) each other party;

    (b) do so not more than 14 days after, as applicable—

        (i) service of the application, or

        (ii) notice of the direction, variation or discharge that the court proposes; and

    (c) ask for a hearing, if that party wants one, and explain why it is needed.

(3) Where representations include information that the person making them thinks ought not be revealed to another party, that person must—

    (a) omit that information from the representations served on that other party;

    (b) mark the information to show that, unless the court otherwise directs, it is only for the court; and

    (c) with that information include an explanation of why it has been withheld from that other party.

(4) Representations against a special measures direction must explain—
  (a) why the witness is not eligible for assistance; or
  (b) if the witness is eligible for assistance, why—
    (i) no special measure would be likely to improve the quality of the witness' evidence,
    (ii) the proposed measure or measures would not be likely to maximise so far as practicable the quality of the witness' evidence, or
    (iii) the proposed measure or measures might tend to inhibit the effective testing of that evidence.
  (c) in a case in which the admission of video recorded evidence is proposed, why it would not be in the interests of justice for the recording, or part of it, to be admitted as evidence.
(5) Representations against the variation or discharge of a special measures direction must explain why it should not be varied or discharged.

29.14. Exercise of court's powers
The court may decide whether to give, vary or discharge a defendant's evidence direction—
  (a) at a hearing, in public or in private, or without a hearing;
  (b) in a party's absence, if that party—
    (i) applied for the direction, variation or discharge, or
    (ii) has had at least 14 days in which to make representations.

29.15. Content of application for a defendant's evidence direction
An applicant for a defendant's evidence direction must—
  (a) explain how the proposed direction meets the conditions prescribed by the Youth Justice and Criminal Evidence Act 1999;
  (b) in a case in which the applicant proposes that the defendant give evidence by live link—
    (i) identify a person to accompany the defendant while the defendant gives evidence, and
    (ii) explain why that person is appropriate;
  (c) ask for a hearing, if the applicant wants one, and explain why it is needed.

29.16. Application to vary or discharge a defendant's evidence direction
(1) A party who wants the court to vary or discharge a defendant's evidence direction must—
  (a) apply in writing, as soon as reasonably practicable after becoming aware of the grounds for doing so; and
  (b) serve the application on—
    (i) the court officer, and
    (ii) each other party.
(2) The applicant must—
  (a) on an application to discharge a live link direction, explain why it is in the interests of justice to do so;
  (b) on an application to discharge a direction for an intermediary, explain why it is no longer necessary in order to ensure that the defendant receives a fair trial;
  (c) on an application to vary a direction for an intermediary, explain why it is necessary for the direction to be varied in order to ensure that the defendant receives a fair trial; and
  (d) ask for a hearing, if the applicant wants one, and explain why it is needed.

29.17. Representations in response
(1) This rule applies where a party wants to make representations about—
  (a) an application for a defendant's evidence direction;
  (b) an application for the variation or discharge of such a direction; or

(c) a direction, variation or discharge that the court proposes on its own initiative.

(2) Such a party must—

    (a) serve the representations on—

        (i) the court officer, and

        (ii) each other party;

    (b) do so not more than 14 days after, as applicable—

        (i) service of the application, or

        (ii) notice of the direction, variation or discharge that the court proposes; and

    (c) ask for a hearing, if that party wants one, and explain why it is needed.

(3) Representations against a direction, variation or discharge must explain why the conditions prescribed by the Youth Justice and Criminal Evidence Act 1999 are not met.

29.18. Exercise of court's powers

(1) The court may decide whether to make, vary or discharge a witness anonymity order—

    (a) at a hearing (which will be in private, unless the court otherwise directs), or without a hearing (unless any party asks for one);

    (b) in the absence of a defendant.

(2) The court must not exercise its power to make, vary or discharge a witness anonymity order, or to refuse to do so—

    (a) before or during the trial, unless each party has had an opportunity to make representations;

    (b) on an appeal by the defendant to which applies Part 63 (appeal to the Crown Court) or Part 68 (appeal to the Court of Appeal about conviction or sentence), unless in each party's case—

        (i) that party has had an opportunity to make representations, or

        (ii) the appeal court is satisfied that it is not reasonably practicable to communicate with that party;

    (c) after the trial and any such appeal are over, unless in the case of each party and the witness—

        (i) each has had an opportunity to make representations, or

        (ii) the court is satisfied that it is not reasonably practicable to communicate with that party or witness.

29.19. Content and conduct of application for a witness anonymity order

(1) An applicant for a witness anonymity order must—

    (a) include in the application nothing that might reveal the witness' identity;

    (b) describe the measures proposed by the applicant;

    (c) explain how the proposed order meets the conditions prescribed by section 88 of the Coroners and Justice Act 2009;

    (d) explain why no measures other than those proposed will suffice, such as—

        (i) an admission of the facts that would be proved by the witness,

        (ii) an order restricting public access to the trial,

        (iii) reporting restrictions, in particular under section 46 of the Youth Justice and Criminal Evidence Act 1999 or under section 39 of the Children and Young Persons Act 1933,

        (iv) a direction for a special measure under section 19 of the Youth Justice and Criminal Evidence Act 1999,

        (v) introduction of the witness' written statement as hearsay evidence, under section 116 of the Criminal Justice Act 2003, or

        (vi) arrangements for the protection of the witness;

    (e) attach to the application—

        (i) a witness statement setting out the proposed evidence, edited in such a way as not to reveal the witness' identity,

(ii) where the prosecutor is the applicant, any further prosecution evidence to be served, and any further prosecution material to be disclosed under the Criminal Procedure and Investigations Act 1996, similarly edited, and

(iii) any defence statement that has been served, or as much information as may be available to the applicant that gives particulars of the defence; and

(f) ask for a hearing, if the applicant wants one.

(2) At any hearing of the application, the applicant must—

(a) identify the witness to the court, unless at the prosecutor's request the court otherwise directs; and

(b) present to the court, unless it otherwise directs—

(i) the unedited witness statement from which the edited version has been prepared,

(ii) where the prosecutor is the applicant, the unedited version of any further prosecution evidence or material from which an edited version has been prepared, and

(iii) such further material as the applicant relies on to establish that the proposed order meets the conditions prescribed by section 88 of the 2009 Act.

(3) At any such hearing—

(a) the general rule is that the court will receive, in the following sequence—

(i) representations first by the applicant and then by each other party, in all the parties' presence, and then

(ii) information withheld from a defendant, and further representations by the applicant, in the absence of any (or any other) defendant; but

(b) the court may direct other arrangements for the hearing.

(4) Before the witness gives evidence, the applicant must identify the witness to the court—

(a) if not already done;

(b) without revealing the witness' identity to any other party or person; and

(c) unless at the prosecutor's request the court otherwise directs.

29.20. Duty of court officer to notify the Director of Public Prosecutions
The court officer must notify the Director of Public Prosecutions of an application, unless the prosecutor is, or acts on behalf of, a public authority.

29.21. Application to vary or discharge a witness anonymity order
(1) A party who wants the court to vary or discharge a witness anonymity order, or a witness who wants the court to do so when the case is over, must—

(a) apply in writing, as soon as reasonably practicable after becoming aware of the grounds for doing so; and

(b) serve the application on—

(i) the court officer, and

(ii) each other party.

(2) The applicant must—

(a) explain what material circumstances have changed since the order was made (or last varied, if applicable);

(b) explain why the order should be varied or discharged, taking account of the conditions for making an order; and

(c) ask for a hearing, if the applicant wants one.

(3) Where an application includes information that the applicant thinks might reveal the witness' identity, the applicant must—

(a) omit that information from the application that is served on a defendant;

(b) mark the information to show that it is only for the court and the prosecutor (if the prosecutor is not the applicant); and

(c) with that information include an explanation of why it has been withheld.

(4) Where a party applies to vary or discharge a witness anonymity order after the trial and any appeal are over, the party who introduced the witness' evidence must serve the application on the witness.

29.22. Representations in response

(1) This rule applies where a party or, where the case is over, a witness, wants to make representations about—

    (a) an application for a witness anonymity order;

    (b) an application for the variation or discharge of such an order; or

    (c) a variation or discharge that the court proposes on its own initiative.

(2) Such a party or witness must—

    (a) serve the representations on—

        (i)   the court officer, and

        (ii)   each other party;

    (b) do so not more than 14 days after, as applicable—

        (i)   service of the application, or

        (ii)   notice of the variation or discharge that the court proposes; and

    (c) ask for a hearing, if that party or witness wants one.

(3) Where representations include information that the person making them thinks might reveal the witness' identity, that person must—

    (a) omit that information from the representations served on a defendant;

    (b) mark the information to show that it is only for the court (and for the prosecutor, if relevant); and

    (c) with that information include an explanation of why it has been withheld.

(4) Representations against a witness anonymity order must explain why the conditions for making the order are not met.

(5) Representations against the variation or discharge of such an order must explain why it would not be appropriate to vary or discharge it, taking account of the conditions for making an order.

(6) A prosecutor's representations in response to an application by a defendant must include all information available to the prosecutor that is relevant to the conditions and considerations specified by sections 88 and 89 of the Coroners and Justice Act 2009.

29.23. Exercise of court's powers

The court may decide whether to give or discharge a live link direction—

    (a) at a hearing, in public or in private, or without a hearing;

    (b) in a party's absence, if that party—

        (i)   applied for the direction or discharge, or

        (ii)   has had at least 14 days in which to make representations.

29.24. Content of application for a live link direction

An applicant for a live link direction must—

    (a) unless the court otherwise directs, identify the place from which the witness will give evidence;

    (b) if that place is in the United Kingdom, explain why it would be in the interests of the efficient or effective administration of justice for the witness to give evidence by live link;

    (c) if the applicant wants the witness to be accompanied by another person while giving evidence—

        (i)   name that person, if possible, and

        (ii)   explain why it is appropriate for the witness to be accompanied;

        (iii) ask for a hearing, if the applicant wants one, and explain why it is needed.

29.25. Application to discharge a live link direction

(1) A party who wants the court to discharge a live link direction must—
    (a) apply in writing, as soon as reasonably practicable after becoming aware of the grounds for doing so; and
    (b) serve the application on—
        (i) the court officer, and
        (ii) each other party.

(2) The applicant must—
    (a) explain what material circumstances have changed since the direction was given;
    (b) explain why it is in the interests of justice to discharge the direction; and
    (c) ask for a hearing, if the applicant wants one, and explain why it is needed.

29.26. Representations in response

(1) This rule applies where a party wants to make representations about—
    (a) an application for a live link direction;
    (b) an application for the discharge of such a direction; or
    (c) a direction or discharge that the court proposes on its own initiative.

(2) Such a party must—
    (a) serve the representations on—
        (i) the court officer, and
        (ii) each other party;
    (b) do so not more than 14 days after, as applicable—
        (i) service of the application, or
        (ii) notice of the direction or discharge that the court proposes; and
    (c) ask for a hearing, if that party wants one, and explain why it is needed.

(3) Representations against a direction or discharge must explain, as applicable, why the conditions prescribed by the Criminal Justice Act 1988 or the Criminal Justice Act 2003 are not met.

PART 31 RESTRICTION ON CROSS-EXAMINATION BY A DEFENDANT ACTING IN PERSON

31.1. Restrictions on cross-examination of witness

(1) This rule and rules 31.2 and 31.3 apply where an accused is prevented from cross-examining a witness in person by virtue of section 34, 35 or 36 of the Youth Justice and Criminal Evidence Act 1999.

(2) The court shall explain to the accused as early in the proceedings as is reasonably practicable that he—
    (a) is prevented from cross-examining a witness in person; and
    (b) should arrange for a legal representative to act for him for the purpose of cross-examining the witness.

(3) The accused shall notify the court officer within 7 days of the court giving its explanation, or within such other period as the court may in any particular case allow, of the action, if any, he has taken.

(4) Where he has arranged for a legal representative to act for him, the notification shall include details of the name and address of the representative.

(5) The notification shall be in writing.

(6) The court officer shall notify all other parties to the proceedings of the name and address of the person, if any, appointed to act for the accused.

(7) Where the court gives its explanation under paragraph (2) to the accused either within 7 days of the day set for the commencement of any hearing at which a witness in respect of whom a prohibition under section 34, 35 or 36 of the 1999 Act applies may be cross-examined or after such

a hearing has commenced, the period of 7 days shall be reduced in accordance with any directions issued by the court.

(8) Where at the end of the period of 7 days or such other period as the court has allowed, the court has received no notification from the accused it may grant the accused an extension of time, whether on its own motion or on the application of the accused.

(9) Before granting an extension of time, the court may hold a hearing at which all parties to the proceedings may attend and be heard.

(10) Any extension of time shall be of such period as the court considers appropriate in the circumstances of the case.

(11) The decision of the court as to whether to grant the accused an extension of time shall be notified to all parties to the proceedings by the court officer.

31.2.   Appointment of legal representative by the court

(1) Where the court decides, in accordance with section 38(4) of the Youth Justice and Criminal Evidence Act 1999, to appoint a qualified legal representative, the court officer shall notify all parties to the proceedings of the name and address of the representative.

(2) An appointment made by the court under section 38(4) of the 1999 Act shall, except to such extent as the court may in any particular case determine, terminate at the conclusion of the cross-examination of the witness or witnesses in respect of whom a prohibition under section 34, 35 or 36 of the 1999 Act applies.

31.3.   Appointment arranged by the accused

(1) The accused may arrange for the qualified legal representative, appointed by the court under section 38(4) of the Youth Justice and Criminal Evidence Act 1999, to be appointed to act for him for the purpose of cross-examining any witness in respect of whom a prohibition under section 34, 35 or 36 of the 1999 Act applies.

(2) Where such an appointment is made—

    (a) both the accused and the qualified legal representative appointed shall notify the court of the appointment; and

    (b) the qualified legal representative shall, from the time of his appointment, act for the accused as though the arrangement had been made under section 38(2)(a) of the 1999 Act and shall cease to be the representative of the court under section 38(4).

(3) Where the court receives notification of the appointment either from the qualified legal representative or from the accused but not from both, the court shall investigate whether the appointment has been made, and if it concludes that the appointment has not been made, paragraph (2)(b) shall not apply.

(4) An accused may, notwithstanding an appointment by the court under section 38(4) of the 1999 Act, arrange for a legal representative to act for him for the purpose of cross-examining any witness in respect of whom a prohibition under section 34, 35 or 36 of the 1999 Act applies.

(5) Where the accused arranges for, or informs the court of his intention to arrange for, a legal representative to act for him, he shall notify the court, within such period as the court may allow, of the name and address of any person appointed to act for him.

(6) Where the court is notified within the time allowed that such an appointment has been made, any qualified legal representative appointed by the court in accordance with section 38(4) of the 1999 Act shall be discharged.

(7) The court officer shall, as soon as reasonably practicable after the court receives notification of an appointment under this rule or, where paragraph (3) applies, after the court is satisfied that the appointment has been made, notify all the parties to the proceedings—

    (a) that the appointment has been made;

    (b) where paragraph (4) applies, of the name and address of the person appointed; and

    (c) that the person appointed by the court under section 38(4) of the 1999 Act has been discharged or has ceased to act for the court.

31.4. Prohibition on cross-examination of witness

(1) An application by the prosecutor for the court to give a direction under section 36 of the Youth Justice and Criminal Evidence Act 1999 in relation to any witness must be sent to the court officer and at the same time a copy thereof must be sent by the applicant to every other party to the proceedings.

(2) In his application the prosecutor must state why, in his opinion—

(a) the evidence given by the witness is likely to be diminished if cross-examination is undertaken by the accused in person;

(b) the evidence would be improved if a direction were given under section 36(2) of the 1999 Act; and

(c) it would not be contrary to the interests of justice to give such a direction.

(3) On receipt of the application the court officer must refer it—

(a) if the trial has started, to the court of trial; or

(b) if the trial has not started when the application is received—

(i) to the judge or court designated to conduct the trial, or

(ii) if no judge or court has been designated for that purpose, to such judge or court designated for the purposes of hearing that application.

(4) Where a copy of the application is received by a party to the proceedings more than 14 days before the date set for the trial to begin, that party may make observations in writing on the application to the court officer, but any such observations must be made within 14 days of the receipt of the application and be copied to the other parties to the proceedings.

(5) A party to whom an application is sent in accordance with paragraph (1) who wishes to oppose the application must give his reasons for doing so to the court officer and the other parties to the proceedings.

(6) Those reasons must be notified—

(a) within 14 days of the date the application was served on him, if that date is more than 14 days before the date set for the trial to begin;

(b) if the trial has begun, in accordance with any directions issued by the court; or

(c) if neither paragraph (6)(a) nor (b) applies, before the date set for the trial to begin.

(7) Where the application made in accordance with paragraph (1) is made before the date set for the trial to begin and—

(a) is not contested by any party to the proceedings, the court may determine the application without a hearing;

(b) is contested by a party to the proceedings, the court must direct a hearing of the application.

(8) Where the application is made after the trial has begun—

(a) the application may be made orally; and

(b) the court may give such directions as it considers appropriate to deal with the application.

(9) Where a hearing of the application is to take place, the court officer shall notify each party to the proceedings of the time and place of the hearing.

(10) A party notified in accordance with paragraph (9) may be present at the hearing and be heard.

(11) The court officer must, as soon as possible after the determination of an application made in accordance with paragraph (1), give notice of the decision and the reasons for it to all the parties to the proceedings.

(12) A person making an oral application under paragraph (8)(a) must—

(a) give reasons why the application was not made before the trial commenced; and

(b) provide the court with the information set out in paragraph (2).

PART 33   EXPERT EVIDENCE

33.1.   Reference to expert

A reference to an 'expert' in this Part is a reference to a person who is required to give or prepare expert evidence for the purpose of criminal proceedings, including evidence required to determine fitness to plead or for the purpose of sentencing.

33.2.   Expert's duty to the court

(1) An expert must help the court to achieve the overriding objective by giving objective, un-biased opinion on matters within his expertise.

(2) This duty overrides any obligation to the person from whom he receives instructions or by whom he is paid.

(3) This duty includes an obligation to inform all parties and the court if the expert's opinion changes from that contained in a report served as evidence or given in a statement.

33.3.   Content of expert's report

(1) An expert's report must—
   - (a) give details of the expert's qualifications, relevant experience and accreditation;
   - (b) give details of any literature or other information which the expert has relied on in making the report;
   - (c) contain a statement setting out the substance of all facts given to the expert which are material to the opinions expressed in the report, or upon which those opinions are based;
   - (d) make clear which of the facts stated in the report are within the expert's own knowledge;
   - (e) say who carried out any examination, measurement, test or experiment which the expert has used for the report and—
      - (i) give the qualifications, relevant experience and accreditation of that person,
      - (ii) say whether or not the examination, measurement, test or experiment was carried out under the expert's supervision, and
      - (iii) summarise the findings on which the expert relies;
   - (f) where there is a range of opinion on the matters dealt with in the report—
      - (i) summarise the range of opinion, and
      - (ii) give reasons for his own opinion;
   - (g) if the expert is not able to give his opinion without qualification, state the qualification;
   - (h) contain a summary of the conclusions reached;
   - (i) contain a statement that the expert understands his duty to the court, and has complied and will continue to comply with that duty; and
   - (j) contain the same declaration of truth as a witness statement.

(2) Only sub-paragraphs (i) and (j) of rule 33.3(1) apply to a summary by an expert of his conclusions served in advance of that expert's report.

33.4.   Service of expert evidence

(1) A party who wants to introduce expert evidence must—
   - (a) serve it on—
      - (i) the court officer, and
      - (ii) each other party;
   - (b) serve it—
      - (i) as soon as practicable, and in any event
      - (ii) with any application in support of which that party relies on that evidence; and

(c) if another party so requires, give that party a copy of, or a reasonable opportunity to inspect—
    (i) a record of any examination, measurement, test or experiment on which the expert's findings and opinion are based, or that were carried out in the course of reaching those findings and opinion, and
    (ii) anything on which any such examination, measurement, test or experiment was carried out.

(2) A party may not introduce expert evidence if that party has not complied with this rule, unless—
    (a) every other party agrees; or
    (b) the court gives permission.

33.5. Expert to be informed of service of report

A party who serves on another party or on the court a report by an expert must, at once, inform that expert of that fact.

33.6. Pre-hearing discussion of expert evidence

(1) This rule applies where more than one party wants to introduce expert evidence.

(2) The court may direct the experts to—
    (a) discuss the expert issues in the proceedings; and
    (b) prepare a statement for the court of the matters on which they agree and disagree, giving their reasons.

(3) Except for that statement, the content of that discussion must not be referred to without the court's permission.

(4) A party may not introduce expert evidence without the court's permission if the expert has not complied with a direction under this rule.

33.7. Court's power to direct that evidence is to be given by a single joint expert

(1) Where more than one defendant wants to introduce expert evidence on an issue at trial, the court may direct that the evidence on that issue is to be given by one expert only.

(2) Where the co-defendants cannot agree who should be the expert, the court may—
    (a) select the expert from a list prepared or identified by them; or
    (b) direct that the expert be selected in another way.

33.8. Instructions to a single joint expert

(1) Where the court gives a direction under rule 33.7 for a single joint expert to be used, each of the co-defendants may give instructions to the expert.

(2) When a co-defendant gives instructions to the expert he must, at the same time, send a copy of the instructions to the other co-defendant(s).

(3) The court may give directions about—
    (a) the payment of the expert's fees and expenses; and
    (b) any examination, measurement, test or experiment which the expert wishes to carry out.

(4) The court may, before an expert is instructed, limit the amount that can be paid by way of fees and expenses to the expert.

(5) Unless the court otherwise directs, the instructing co-defendants are jointly and severally liable for the payment of the expert's fees and expenses.

33.9. Court's power to vary requirements under this Part

(1) The court may—
    (a) extend (even after it has expired) a time limit under this Part;
    (b) allow the introduction of expert evidence which omits a detail required by this Part.

(2) A party who wants an extension of time must—

    (a) apply when serving the expert evidence for which it is required; and

    (b) explain the delay.

PART 34 HEARSAY EVIDENCE

34.1. When this Part applies

This Part applies—

    (a) in a magistrates' court and in the Crown Court;

    (b) where a party wants to introduce hearsay evidence, within the meaning of section 114 of the Criminal Justice Act 2003.

34.2. Notice to introduce hearsay evidence

(1) This rule applies where a party wants to introduce hearsay evidence for admission under any of the following sections of the Criminal Justice Act 2003—

    (a) section 114(1)(d) (evidence admissible in the interests of justice);

    (b) section 116 (evidence where a witness is unavailable);

    (c) section 121 (multiple hearsay).

(2) That party must—

    (a) serve notice on—

        (i) the court officer, and

        (ii) each other party;

    (b) in the notice—

        (i) identify the evidence that is hearsay,

        (ii) set out any facts on which that party relies to make the evidence admissible,

        (iii) explain how that party will prove those facts if another party disputes them, and

        (iv) explain why the evidence is admissible; and

    (c) attach to the notice any statement or other document containing the evidence that has not already been served.

(3) A prosecutor who wants to introduce such evidence must serve the notice not more than 14 days after the defendant pleads not guilty.

(4) A defendant who wants to introduce such evidence must serve the notice as soon as reasonably practicable.

(5) A party entitled to receive a notice under this rule may waive that entitlement by so informing—

    (a) the party who would have served it; and

    (b) the court.

34.3. Opposing the introduction of hearsay evidence

(1) This rule applies where a party objects to the introduction of hearsay evidence.

(2) That party must—

    (a) apply to the court to determine the objection;

    (b) serve the application on—

        (i) the court officer, and

        (ii) each other party;

    (c) serve the application as soon as reasonably practicable, and in any event not more than 14 days after—

        (i) service of notice to introduce the evidence under rule 34.2,

        (ii) service of the evidence to which that party objects, if no notice is required by that rule, or

        (iii) the defendant pleads not guilty

        whichever of those events happens last; and

      (d) in the application, explain—
         (i)   which, if any, facts set out in a notice under rule 34.2 that party disputes,
         (ii) why the evidence is not admissible,
         (iii) any other objection to the application.
  (3) The court—
      (a) may determine an application—
         (i)   at a hearing, in public or in private, or
         (ii) without a hearing;
      (b) must not determine the application unless the party who served the notice—
         (i)   is present, or
         (ii) has had a reasonable opportunity to respond;
      (c) may adjourn the application; and
      (d) may discharge or vary a determination where it can do so under—
         (i)   section 8B of the Magistrates' Courts Act 1980 (ruling at pre-trial hearing in a magistrates' court), or
         (ii) section 9 of the Criminal Justice Act 1987, or section 31 or 40 of the Criminal Procedure and Investigations Act 1996 (ruling at preparatory or other pre-trial hearing in the Crown Court).

34.4. Unopposed hearsay evidence
  (1) This rule applies where—
      (a) a party has served notice to introduce hearsay evidence under rule 34.2; and
      (b) no other party has applied to the court to determine an objection to the introduction of the evidence.
  (2) The court will treat the evidence as if it were admissible by agreement.

34.5. Court's power to vary requirements under this Part
  (1) The court may—
      (a) shorten or extend (even after it has expired) a time limit under this Part;
      (b) allow an application or notice to be in a different form to one set out in the Practice Direction, or to be made or given orally;
      (c) dispense with the requirement for notice to introduce hearsay evidence.
  (2) A party who wants an extension of time must—
      (a) apply when serving the application or notice for which it is needed; and
      (b) explain the delay.

PART 35 EVIDENCE OF BAD CHARACTER

35.1. When this Part applies
This Part applies—
      (a) in a magistrates' court and in the Crown Court;
      (b) where a party wants to introduce evidence of bad character, within the meaning of section 98 of the Criminal Justice Act 2003.

35.2. Content of application or notice
  (1) A party who wants to introduce evidence of bad character must—
      (a) make an application under rule 35.3, where it is evidence of a non-defendant's bad character;
      (b) give notice under rule 35.4, where it is evidence of a defendant's bad character; and
  (2) An application or notice must—
      (a) set out the facts of the misconduct on which that party relies,

(b) explain how that party will prove those facts (whether by certificate of conviction, other official record, or other evidence), if another party disputes them, and

(c) explain why the evidence is admissible.

35.3.   Application to introduce evidence of a non-defendant's bad character

(1) This rule applies where a party wants to introduce evidence of the bad character of a person other than the defendant.

(2) That party must serve an application to do so on—

(a) the court officer; and

(b) each other party.

(3) The applicant must serve the application—

(a) as soon as reasonably practicable; and in any event

(b) not more than 14 days after the prosecutor discloses material on which the application is based (if the prosecutor is not the applicant).

(4) A party who objects to the introduction of the evidence must—

(a) serve notice on—

(i)   the court officer, and

(ii) each other party

not more than 14 days after service of the application; and

(b) in the notice explain, as applicable—

(i)   which, if any, facts of the misconduct set out in the application that party disputes,

(ii) what, if any, facts of the misconduct that party admits instead,

(iii) why the evidence is not admissible, and

(iv) any other objection to the application.

(5) The court—

(a) may determine an application—

(i)   at a hearing, in public or in private, or

(ii) without a hearing;

(b) must not determine the application unless each party other than the applicant—

(i)   is present, or

(ii) has had at least 14 days in which to serve a notice of objection;

(c) may adjourn the application; and

(d) may discharge or vary a determination where it can do so under—

(i)   section 8B of the Magistrates' Courts Act 1980 (ruling at pre-trial hearing in a magistrates' court), or

(ii) section 9 of the Criminal Justice Act 1987, or section 31 or 40 of the Criminal Procedure and Investigations Act 1996 (ruling at preparatory or other pre-trial hearing in the Crown Court).

35.4.   Notice to introduce evidence of a defendant's bad character

(1) This rule applies where a party wants to introduce evidence of a defendant's bad character.

(2) That party must serve notice on—

(a) the court officer; and

(b) each other party.

(3) A prosecutor who wants to introduce such evidence must serve the notice not more than—

(a) 28 days after the defendant pleads not guilty, in a magistrates' court; or

(b) 14 days after the defendant pleads not guilty, in the Crown Court.

(4) A co-defendant who wants to introduce such evidence must serve the notice—

(a) as soon as reasonably practicable; and in any event

(b) not more than 14 days after the prosecutor discloses material on which the notice is based.

(5) A party who objects to the introduction of the evidence must—
  (a) apply to the court to determine the objection;
  (b) serve the application on—
    (i) the court officer, and
    (ii) each other party
    not more than 14 days after service of the notice; and
  (c) in the application explain, as applicable—
    (i)   which, if any, facts of the misconduct set out in the notice that party disputes,
    (ii) what, if any, facts of the misconduct that party admits instead,
    (iii) why the evidence is not admissible,
    (iv) why it would be unfair to admit the evidence, and
    (v)   any other objection to the notice.
(6) The court—
  (a) may determine an application—
    (i) at a hearing, in public or in private, or
    (ii) without a hearing;
  (b) must not determine the application unless the party who served the notice—
    (i) is present, or
    (ii) has had a reasonable opportunity to respond;
  (c) may adjourn the application; and
  (d) may discharge or vary a determination where it can do so under—
    (i) section 8B of the Magistrates' Courts Act 1980 (ruling at pre-trial hearing in a magistrates' court), or
    (ii) section 9 of the Criminal Justice Act 1987, or section 31 or 40 of the Criminal Procedure and Investigations Act 1996 (ruling at preparatory or other pre-trial hearing in the Crown Court).
(7) A party entitled to receive a notice may waive that entitlement by so informing—
  (a) the party who would have served it; and
  (b) the court.

35.5. Reasons for decisions
The court must announce at a hearing in public (but in the absence of the jury, if there is one) the reasons for a decision—
  (a) to admit evidence as evidence of bad character, or to refuse to do so; or
  (b) to direct an acquittal or a retrial under section 107 of the Criminal Justice Act 2003.

35.6. Court's power to vary requirements under this Part
(1) The court may—
  (a) shorten or extend (even after it has expired) a time limit under this Part;
  (b) allow an application or notice to be in a different form to one set out in the Practice Direction, or to be made or given orally;
  (c) dispense with a requirement for notice to introduce evidence of a defendant's bad character.
(2) A party who wants an extension of time must—
  (a) apply when serving the application or notice for which it is needed; and
  (b) explain the delay.

PART 36 EVIDENCE OF A COMPLAINANT'S PREVIOUS SEXUAL BEHAVIOUR

36.1. When this Part applies
This Part applies in magistrates' courts and in the Crown Court where a defendant wants to—
  (a) introduce evidence; or
  (b) cross-examine a witness

about a complainant's sexual behaviour despite the prohibition in section 41 of the Youth Justice and Criminal Evidence Act 1999.

36.2. Application for permission to introduce evidence or cross-examine
The defendant must apply for permission to do so—
- (a) in writing; and
- (b) not more than 28 days after the prosecutor has complied or purported to comply with section 3 of the Criminal Procedure and Investigations Act 1996 (disclosure by prosecutor).

36.3. Content of application
The application must—
- (a) identify the issue to which the defendant says the complainant's sexual behaviour is relevant;
- (b) give particulars of—
  - (i) any evidence that the defendant wants to introduce, and
  - (ii) any questions that the defendant wants to ask;
- (c) identify the exception to the prohibition in section 41 of the Youth Justice and Criminal Evidence Act 1999 on which the defendant relies; and
- (d) give the name and date of birth of any witness whose evidence about the complainant's sexual behaviour the defendant wants to introduce.

36.4. Service of application
The defendant must serve the application on the court officer and all other parties.

36.5. Reply to application
A party who wants to make representations about an application under rule 36.2 must—
- (a) do so in writing not more than 14 days after receiving it; and
- (b) serve those representations on the court officer and all other parties.

36.6. Application for special measures
If the court allows an application under rule 36.2 then—
- (a) a party may apply not more than 14 days later for a special measures direction or for the variation of an existing special measures direction; and
- (b) the court may shorten the time for opposing that application.

36.7 Court's power to vary requirements under this Part
The court may shorten or extend (even after it has expired) a time limit under this Part.

PART 37 TRIAL AND SENTENCE IN A MAGISTRATES' COURT

37.1 When this Part applies
(1) This Part applies in a magistrates' court where—
- (a) the court tries a case; or
- (b) the defendant pleads guilty.

(2) Where the defendant is under 18, in this Part—
- (a) a reference to convicting the defendant includes a reference to finding the defendant guilty of an offence; and
- (b) a reference to sentence includes a reference to an order made on a finding of guilt.

37.2 General Rules
(1) Where this Part applies—
- (a) the general rule is that the hearing must be in public; but
- (b) the court may exercise any power it has to—

          (i)   impose reporting restrictions,

          (ii) withhold information from the public, or

          (iii) order a hearing in private; and

    (c) unless the court otherwise directs, only the following may attend a hearing in a youth court—

          (i)   the parties and their legal representatives,

          (ii) a defendant's parents, guardian or other supporting adult,

          (iii) a witness,

          (iv) anyone else directly concerned in the case, and

          (v) a representative of a news-gathering or reporting organisation.

(2) Unless already done, the justices' legal adviser or the court must—

    (a) read the allegation of the offence to the defendant;

    (b) explain, in terms the defendant can understand (with help, if necessary)—

          (i)   the allegation, and

          (ii) what the procedure at the hearing will be;

    (c) ask whether the defendant has been advised about the potential effect on sentence of a guilty plea;

    (d) ask whether the defendant pleads guilty or not guilty; and

    (e) take the defendant's plea.

(3) The court may adjourn the hearing—

    (a) at any stage, to the same or to another magistrates' court; or

    (b) to a youth court, where the court is not itself a youth court and the defendant is under 18.

37.3 Procedure on a plea of not guilty

(1) This rule applies—

    (a) if the defendant has—

          (i)   entered a plea of not guilty, or

          (ii) not entered a plea; or

    (b) if, in either case, it appears to the court that there may be grounds for making a hospital order without convicting the defendant.

(2) If a not guilty plea was taken on a previous occasion, the justices' legal adviser or the court must ask the defendant to confirm that plea.

(3) In the following sequence—

    (a) the prosecutor may summarise the prosecution case, identifying the relevant law and facts;

    (b) the prosecutor must introduce the evidence on which the prosecution case relies;

    (c) at the conclusion of the prosecution case, on the defendant's application or on its own initiative, the court—

          (i)   may acquit on the ground that the prosecution evidence is insufficient for any reasonable court properly to convict, but

          (ii) must not do so unless the prosecutor has had an opportunity to make representations;

    (d) the justices' legal adviser or the court must explain, in terms the defendant can understand (with help, if necessary)—

          (i)   the right to give evidence, and

          (ii) the potential effect of not doing so at all, or of refusing to answer a question while doing so;

    (e) the defendant may introduce evidence;

    (f) a party may introduce further evidence if it is then admissible (for example, because it is in rebuttal of evidence already introduced);

(g) the prosecutor may make final representations in support of the prosecution case, where—

    (i)   the defendant is represented by a legal representative, or

    (ii) whether represented or not, the defendant has introduced evidence other than his or her own; and

(h) the defendant may make final representations in support of the defence case.

(4) Where a party wants to introduce evidence or make representations after that party's opportunity to do so under paragraph (3), the court—

(a) may refuse to receive any such evidence or representations; and

(b) must not receive any such evidence or representations after it has announced its verdict.

(5) If the court—

(a) convicts the defendant; or

(b) makes a hospital order instead of doing so,

it must give sufficient reasons to explain its decision.

(6) If the court acquits the defendant, it may—

(a) give an explanation of its decision; and

(b) exercise any power it has to make—

    (i)   a civil behaviour order,

    (ii) a costs order.

37.4   Evidence of a witness in person

(1) This rule applies where a party wants to introduce evidence by calling a witness to give that evidence in person.

(2) Unless the court otherwise directs—

(a) a witness waiting to give evidence must not wait inside the courtroom, unless that witness is—

    (i)   a party, or

    (ii) an expert witness;

(b) a witness who gives evidence in the courtroom must do so from the place provided for that purpose; and

(c) a witness' address must not be announced unless it is relevant to an issue in the case.

(3) Unless other legislation otherwise provides, before giving evidence a witness must take an oath or affirm.

(4) In the following sequence—

(a) the party who calls a witness must ask questions in examination-in-chief;

(b) every other party may ask questions in cross-examination;

(c) the party who called the witness may ask questions in re-examination;

(d) at any time while giving evidence, a witness may refer to a record of that witness' recollection of events, if other legislation so permits;

(e) the party who calls a witness, in examination-in-chief may ask that witness to adopt all or part of such a record as part of that witness' evidence, but only if—

    (i)   the parties agree, and

    (ii) the court so permits;

(f) if the witness adopts any part of such a record—

    (i)   that part must be read aloud, or

    (ii) with the court's permission, its contents may be summarised aloud.

(5) The justices' legal adviser or the court may—

(a) ask a witness questions; and in particular

(b) where the defendant is not represented, ask any question necessary in the defendant's interests.

37.5   Evidence by written statement
(1) This rule applies where a party introduces in evidence the written statement of a witness.

(2) The party introducing the statement must read or summarise aloud those parts that are relevant to the issues in the case.

37.6   Evidence by admission
(1) This rule applies where—
   (a) a party introduces in evidence a fact admitted by another party; or
   (b) parties jointly admit a fact.

(2) Unless the court otherwise directs, a written record must be made of the admission.

37.7   Procedure on plea of guilty
(1) This rule applies if—
   (a) the defendant pleads guilty; and
   (b) the court is satisfied that the plea represents a clear acknowledgement of guilt.

(2) The court may convict the defendant without receiving evidence.

37.8   Written guilty plea: special rules
(1) This rule applies where—
   (a) the offence alleged—
      (i) can be tried only in a magistrates' court, and
      (ii) is not one specified under section 12(1)(a) of the Magistrates' Courts Act 1980;
   (b) the defendant is at least 16 years old;
   (c) the prosecutor has served on the defendant—
      (i) the summons or requisition,
      (ii) the material on which the prosecutor relies to set out the facts of the offence and to provide information relevant to sentence,
      (iii) a notice that the procedure set out in this rule applies, and
      (iv) a notice for the defendant's use if the defendant wants to plead guilty without attending court; and
   (d) the prosecutor has served on the court officer—
      (i) copies of those documents, and
      (ii) a certificate of service of those documents on the defendant.

(2) A defendant who wants to plead guilty without attending court must, before the hearing date specified in the summons or requisition—
   (a) serve a notice of guilty plea on the court officer; and
   (b) include with that notice any representations that the defendant wants the court to consider on that date.

(3) A defendant who wants to withdraw such a notice must notify the court officer in writing before the hearing date.

(4) The court may accept such a guilty plea on the hearing date, and if it does so must take account only of—
   (a) the material served by the prosecutor on the defendant under this rule; and
   (b) any representations by the defendant.

(5) With the defendant's agreement, the court may deal with the case in the same way as under paragraph (4) where the defendant—
   (a) is present; and
   (b) has served a notice of guilty plea under paragraph (2); or
   (c) pleads guilty there and then.

37.9   Application to withdraw a guilty plea
(1) This rule applies where the defendant wants to withdraw a guilty plea.

(2) The defendant must apply to do so—

    (a) as soon as practicable after becoming aware of the reasons for doing so; and

    (b) before sentence.

(3) Unless the court otherwise directs, the application must be in writing and the defendant must serve it on—

    (a) the court officer; and

    (b) the prosecutor.

(4) The application must—

    (a) explain why it would be unjust not to allow the defendant to withdraw the guilty plea;

    (b) identify—

        (i) any witness that the defendant wants to call, and

        (ii) any other proposed evidence; and

    (c) say whether the defendant waives legal professional privilege, giving any relevant name and date.

37.10   Procedure if the court convicts

(1) This rule applies if the court convicts the defendant.

(2) The court—

    (a) may exercise its power to require—

        (i) a statement of the defendant's financial circumstances,

        (ii) a pre-sentence report; and

    (b) may (and in some circumstances must) remit the defendant to a youth court for sentence where—

        (i) the defendant is under 18, and

        (ii) the convicting court is not itself a youth court.

(3) The prosecutor must—

    (a) summarise the prosecution case, if the sentencing court has not heard evidence;

    (b) identify any offence to be taken into consideration in sentencing;

    (c) provide information relevant to sentence; and

    (d) where it is likely to assist the court, identify any other matter relevant to sentence, including—

        (i) aggravating and mitigating factors,

        (ii) the legislation applicable, and

        (iii) any guidelines issued by the Sentencing Guidelines Council, or guideline cases.

(4) The defendant must provide information relevant to sentence, including details of financial circumstances.

(5) Where the defendant pleads guilty but wants to be sentenced on a different basis to that disclosed by the prosecution case—

    (a) the defendant must set out that basis in writing, identifying what is in dispute;

    (b) the court may invite the parties to make representations about whether the dispute is material to sentence; and

    (c) if the court decides that it is a material dispute, the court will—

        (i) invite such further representations or evidence as it may require, and

        (ii) decide the dispute.

(6) Where the court has power to order the endorsement of the defendant's driving licence, or power to order the disqualification of the defendant from holding or obtaining one—

    (a) if other legislation so permits, a defendant who wants the court not to exercise that power must introduce the evidence or information on which the defendant relies;

    (b) the prosecutor may introduce evidence; and

    (c) the parties may make representations about that evidence or information.

(7) Before the court passes sentence—
    (a) the court must—
        (i)   give the defendant an opportunity to make representations and introduce evidence relevant to sentence, and
        (ii) where the defendant is under 18, give the defendant's parents, guardian or other supporting adult, if present, such an opportunity as well; and
    (b) the justices' legal adviser or the court must elicit any further information relevant to sentence that the court may require.
(8) If the court requires more information, it may exercise its power to adjourn the hearing for not more than—
    (a) 3 weeks at a time, if the defendant will be in custody; or
    (b) 4 weeks at a time.
(9) When the court has taken into account all the evidence, information and any report available, the general rule is that the court will—
    (a) pass sentence there and then;
    (b) explain the sentence, the reasons for it, and its effect, in terms the defendant can understand (with help, if necessary); and
    (c) consider exercising any power it has to make a costs or other order.
(10) Despite the general rule—
    (a) the court must adjourn the hearing if—
        (i)   the case started with a summons or requisition, and the defendant is absent, and
        (ii) the court considers passing a custodial sentence, or
        (iii) the court considers imposing a disqualification (unless it has already adjourned the hearing to give the defendant an opportunity to attend);
    (b) the court may exercise any power it has to—
        (i)   commit the defendant to the Crown Court for sentence (and in some cases it must do so), or
        (ii) defer sentence for up to 6 months.

37.11 Procedure where a party is absent

(1) This rule—
    (a) applies where a party is absent; but
    (b) does not apply where the defendant has served a notice of guilty plea under rule 37.8 (written guilty plea: special rules).
(2) Where the prosecutor is absent, the court may—
    (a) if it has received evidence, deal with the case as if the prosecutor were present; and
    (b) in any other case—
        (i)   enquire into the reasons for the prosecutor's absence, and
        (ii) if satisfied there is no good reason, exercise its power to dismiss the allegation.
(3) Where the defendant is absent—
    (a) the general rule is that the court will proceed as if the defendant—
        (i)   were present, and
        (ii) had pleaded not guilty (unless a plea already has been taken)
        and the court must give reasons if it does not do so; but
    (b) the general rule does not apply if the defendant is under 18;
    (c) the general rule is subject to the court being satisfied that—
        (i)   any summons or requisition was served on the defendant a reasonable time before the hearing, or
        (ii) in a case in which the hearing has been adjourned, the defendant had reasonable notice of where and when it would resume;
    (d) the general rule is subject also to rule 37.10(10)(a) (restrictions on passing sentence in the defendant's absence); and

(e) the hearing must be treated as if it had not taken place at all if—
  (i) the case started with a summons or requisition,
  (ii) the defendant makes a statutory declaration of not having found out about the case until after the hearing began, and
  (iii) the defendant serves that declaration on the court officer not more than 21 days after the date of finding out about the case, unless the court extends that time limit.
(4) Where the defendant is absent, the court—
  (a) must exercise its power to issue a warrant for the defendant's arrest, if it passes a custodial sentence; and
  (b) may exercise its power to do so in any other case, if it does not apply the general rule in paragraph (3)(a) of this rule about proceeding in the defendant's absence.

37.12 Provision of documents for the court

(1) This rule applies where a party—
  (a) introduces in evidence any document; or
  (b) relies on any other document in the presentation of that party's case.
(2) Unless the court otherwise directs, that party must supply sufficient copies of such a document for—
  (a) each other party;
  (b) the court; and
  (c) the justices' legal adviser.

37.13 Place of trial

(1) Unless the court otherwise directs, the hearing must take place in a courtroom provided by the Lord Chancellor.
(2) Where the hearing takes place in Wales—
  (a) any party or witness may use the Welsh language; and
  (b) if practicable, at least one member of the court must be Welsh-speaking.

37.14 Duty of justices' legal adviser

(1) A justices' legal adviser must attend, unless the court—
  (a) includes a District Judge (Magistrates' Courts); and
  (b) otherwise directs.
(2) A justices' legal adviser must—
  (a) give the court legal advice; and
  (b) if necessary, attend the members of the court outside the courtroom to give such advice; but
  (c) inform the parties of any such advice given outside the courtroom.
(3) A justices' legal adviser must—
  (a) assist an unrepresented defendant;
  (b) assist the court by—
    (i) making a note of the substance of any oral evidence or representations, to help the court recall that information,
    (ii) if the court rules inadmissible part of a written statement introduced in evidence, marking that statement in such a way as to make that clear,
    (iii) ensuring that an adequate record is kept of the court's decisions and the reasons for them, and
    (iv) making any announcement, other than of the verdict or sentence.
(4) Where the defendant has served a notice of guilty plea to which rule 37.8 (written guilty plea: special rules) applies, a justices' legal adviser must read aloud to the court—
  (a) the material on which the prosecutor relies to set out the facts of the offence and to provide information relevant to sentence (or summarise any written statement included in that material, if the court so directs); and
  (b) any written representations by the defendant.

37.15   Duty of court officer

The court officer must—

(a) serve on each party notice of where and when an adjourned hearing will resume, unless—

    (i)   the party was present when that was arranged, or

    (ii) the defendant has served a notice of guilty plea to which rule 37.8 applies, and the adjournment is for not more than 4 weeks;

(b) if the reason for the adjournment was to postpone sentence, include that reason in any such notice to the defendant;

(c) unless the court otherwise directs, make available to the parties any written report to which rule 37.10 applies;

(d) where the court has ordered a defendant to provide information under section 25 of the Road Traffic Offenders Act 1988, serve on the defendant notice of that order unless the defendant was present when it was made;

(e) serve on the prosecutor—

    (i)   any notice of guilty plea to which rule 37.8 applies, and

    (ii) any declaration served under rule 37.11(3)(e) that the defendant did not know about the case;

(f) record in the magistrates' court register the court's reasons for not proceeding in the defendant's absence where rule 37.11(3)(a) applies; and

(g) give the court such other assistance as it requires.

PART 39   TRIAL ON INDICTMENT

39.1   Time limits for beginning of trials

The periods set out for the purposes of section 77(2)(a) and (b) of the Senior Courts Act 1981 shall be 14 days and 8 weeks respectively and accordingly, the trial of a person committed by a magistrates' court—

(a) shall not begin until the expiration of 14 days beginning with the date of his committal, except with his consent and the consent of the prosecution; and

(b) shall, unless the Crown Court has otherwise ordered, begin not later than the expiration of 8 weeks beginning with the date of his committal.

39.2   Appeal against refusal to excuse from jury service or to defer attendance

(1)   A person summoned under the Juries Act 1974 for jury service may appeal in accordance with the provisions of this rule against any refusal of the appropriate court officer to excuse him under section 9(2), or to defer his attendance under section 9A(1), of that Act.

(2)   Subject to paragraph (3), an appeal under this rule shall be heard by the Crown Court.

(3)   Where the appellant is summoned under the 1974 Act to attend before the High Court in Greater London the appeal shall be heard by a judge of the High Court and where the appellant is summoned under that Act to attend before the High Court outside Greater London or before a county court and the appeal has not been decided by the Crown Court before the day on which the appellant is required by the summons to attend, the appeal shall be heard by the court before which he is summoned to attend.

(4)   An appeal under this rule shall be commenced by the appellant's giving notice of appeal to the appropriate court officer of the Crown Court or the High Court in Greater London, as the case may be, and such notice shall be in writing and shall specify the matters upon which the appellant relies as providing good reason why he should be excused from attending in pursuance of the summons or why his attendance should be deferred.

(5)   The court shall not dismiss an appeal under this rule unless the appellant has been given an opportunity of making representations.

(6) Where an appeal under this rule is decided in the absence of the appellant, the appropriate court officer of the Crown Court or the High Court in Greater London, as the case may be, shall notify him of the decision without delay.

39.3 Application to change a plea of guilty

(1) The defendant must apply as soon as practicable after becoming aware of the grounds for making an application to change a plea of guilty, and may only do so before the final disposal of the case, by sentence or otherwise.

(2) Unless the court otherwise directs, the application must be in writing and it must—

    (a) set out the reasons why it would be unjust for the guilty plea to remain unchanged;

    (b) indicate what, if any, evidence the defendant wishes to call;

    (c) identify any proposed witness; and

    (d) indicate whether legal professional privilege is waived, specifying any material name and date.

(3) The defendant must serve the written application on—

    (a) the court officer; and

    (b) the prosecutor.

PART 40 TAINTED ACQUITTALS

40.1 Time of certification

Where a person is convicted of an offence as referred to in section 54(1)(b) of the Criminal Procedure and Investigations Act 1996 and it appears to the court before which the conviction has taken place that the provisions of section 54(2) are satisfied, the court shall make the certification referred to in section 54(2) at any time following conviction but no later than—

    (a) immediately after the court sentences or otherwise deals with that person in respect of the offence; or

    (b) where the court, being a magistrates' court, commits that person to the Crown Court, or remits him to another magistrates' court, to be dealt with in respect of the offence, immediately after he is so committed or remitted, as the case may be; or

    (c) where that person is a child or young person and the court, being the Crown Court, remits him to a youth court to be dealt with in respect of the offence, immediately after he is so remitted.

40.2 Form of certification in the Crown Court

A certification referred to in section 54(2) of the Criminal Procedure and Investigations Act 1996 by the Crown Court shall be drawn up in the form set out in the Practice Direction.

40.3 Service of a copy of the certification

Where a magistrates' court or the Crown Court makes a certification as referred to in section 54(2) of the Criminal Procedure and Investigations Act 1996, the court officer shall, as soon as practicable after the drawing up of the form, serve a copy on the acquitted person referred to in the certification, on the prosecutor in the proceedings which led to the acquittal, and, where the acquittal has taken place before a court other than, or at a different place to, the court where the certification has been made, on—

    (a) the clerk of the magistrates' court before which the acquittal has taken place; or

    (b) the Crown Court officer at the place where the acquittal has taken place.

40.4 Entry in register or records in relation to the conviction which occasioned certification

A clerk of a magistrates' court or an officer of a Crown Court which has made a certification under section 54(2) of the Criminal Procedure and Investigations Act 1996 shall enter in the register or records, in relation to the conviction which occasioned the certification, a note of the fact that certification has been made, the date of certification, the name of the acquitted person referred to in the certification, a description of the offence of which the acquitted person has been acquitted, the date of the acquittal, and the name of the court before which the acquittal has taken place.

40.5   Entry in the register or records in relation to the acquittal

The court officer of the court before which an acquittal has taken place shall, as soon as practicable after receipt of a copy of a form recording a certification under section 54(2) of the Criminal Procedure and Investigations Act 1996 relating to the acquittal, enter in the register or records a note that the certification has been made, the date of the certification, the name of the court which has made the certification, the name of the person whose conviction occasioned the making of the certification, and a description of the offence of which that person has been convicted. Where the certification has been made by the same court as the court before which the acquittal has occurred, sitting at the same place, the entry shall be made as soon as practicable after the making of the certification. In the case of an acquittal before a magistrates' court, the entry in the register shall be signed by the clerk of the court.

40.6   Display of copy certification form

(1) Where a court makes a certification as referred to in section 54(2) of the Criminal Procedure and Investigations Act 1996, the court officer shall, as soon as practicable after the drawing up of the form, display a copy of that form at a prominent place within court premises to which place the public has access.

(2) Where an acquittal has taken place before a court other than, or at a different place to, the court which has made the certification under section 54(2) of the 1996 Act in relation to the acquittal, the court officer at the court where the acquittal has taken place shall, as soon as practicable after receipt of a copy of the form recording the certification, display a copy of it at a prominent place within court premises to which place the public has access.

(3) The copy of the form referred to in paragraph (1), or the copy referred to in paragraph (2), shall continue to be displayed as referred to, respectively, in those paragraphs at least until the expiry of 28 days from, in the case of paragraph (1), the day on which the certification was made, or, in the case of paragraph (2), the day on which the copy form was received at the court.

40.7   Entry in the register or records in relation to decision of High Court

(1) The court officer at the court where an acquittal has taken place shall, on receipt from the Administrative Court Office of notice of an order made under section 54(3) of the Criminal Procedure and Investigations Act 1996 quashing the acquittal, or of a decision not to make such an order, enter in the register or records, in relation to the acquittal, a note of the fact that the acquittal has been quashed by the said order, or that a decision has been made not to make such an order, as the case may be.

(2) The court officer of the court which has made a certification under section 54(2) of the 1996 Act shall, on receipt from the Administrative Court Office of notice of an order made under section 54(3) of that Act quashing the acquittal referred to in the certification, or of a decision not to make such an order, enter in the register or records, in relation to the conviction which occasioned the certification, a note that the acquittal has been quashed by the said order, or that a decision has been made not to make such an order, as the case may be.

(3) The entries in the register of a magistrates' court referred to, respectively, in paragraphs (1) and (2) above shall be signed by the magistrates' court officer.]

40.8   Display of copy of notice received from High Court

(1) Where the court officer of a court which has made a certification under section 54(2) of the Criminal Procedure and Investigations Act 1996 or before which an acquittal has occurred to which such a certification refers, receives from the Administrative Court Office notice of an order quashing the acquittal concerned, or notice of a decision not to make such an order, he shall, as soon as practicable after receiving the notice, display a copy of it at a prominent place within court premises to which place the public has access.

(2) The copy notice referred to in paragraph (1) shall continue to be displayed as referred to in that paragraph at least until the expiry of 28 days from the day on which the notice was received at the court.

PART 41 RETRIAL FOLLOWING ACQUITTAL FOR SERIOUS OFFENCE

41.1 Interpretation
In this Part, 'section 76 application' means an application made by a prosecutor under section 76(1) or (2) of the Criminal Justice Act 2003.

41.2 Notice of a section 76 application
(1) A prosecutor who wants to make a section 76 application must serve notice of that application in the form set out in the Practice Direction on the Registrar and the acquitted person.

(2) That notice shall, where practicable, be accompanied by—

    (a) relevant witness statements which are relied upon as forming new and compelling evidence of guilt of the acquitted person as well as any relevant witness statements from the original trial;

    (b) any unused statements which might reasonably be considered capable of undermining the section 76 application or of assisting an acquitted person's application to oppose that application under rule 41.3;

    (c) a copy of the indictment and paper exhibits from the original trial;

    (d) copies of the transcript of the summing up and any other relevant transcripts from the original trial; and

    (e) any other documents relied upon to support the section 76 application.

(3) The prosecutor must, as soon as practicable after service of that notice on the acquitted person, file with the Registrar a witness statement or certificate of service which exhibits a copy of that notice.

41.3 Response of the acquitted person
(1) An acquitted person who wants to oppose a section 76 application must serve a response in the form set out in the Practice Direction on the Registrar and the prosecutor which—

    (a) indicates if he is also seeking an order under section 80(6) of the Criminal Justice Act 2003 for—

      (i) the production of any document, exhibit or other thing, or

      (ii) a witness to attend for examination and to be examined before the Court of Appeal; and

    (b) exhibits any relevant documents.

(2) The acquitted person must serve that response not more than 28 days after receiving notice under rule 41.2.

(3) The Court of Appeal may extend the period for service under paragraph (2), either before or after that period expires.

41.4 Examination of witnesses or evidence by the Court of Appeal
(1) Prior to the hearing of a section 76 application, a party may apply to the Court of Appeal for an order under section 80(6) of the Criminal Justice Act 2003 for—

    (a) the production of any document, exhibit or other thing; or

    (b) a witness to attend for examination and to be examined before the Court of Appeal.

(2) An application under paragraph (1) must be in the form set out in the Practice Direction and must be sent to the Registrar and a copy sent to each party to the section 76 application.

(3) An application must set out the reasons why the order was not sought from the Court when—

    (a) the notice was served on the Registrar under rule 41.2, if the application is made by the prosecutor; or

    (b) the response was served on the Registrar under rule 41.3, if the application is made by the acquitted person.

(4) An application must be made at least 14 days before the day of the hearing of the section 76 application.

(5) If the Court of Appeal makes an order under section 80(6) of the 2003 Act on its own motion or on application from the prosecutor, it must serve notice and reasons for that order on all parties to the section 76 application.

41.5   Bail or custody hearings in the Crown Court

(1) Rules 19.18, 19.22 and 19.23 shall apply where a person is to appear or be brought before the Crown Court pursuant to sections 88 or 89 of the Criminal Justice Act 2003 (with the modification as set out in paragraph (2)), as if they were applications under rule 19.18(1).

(2) Substitute the following for Rule 19.18:

"Where a person is to appear or be brought before the Crown Court pursuant to sections 88 or 89 of the Criminal Justice Act 2003, the prosecutor must serve notice of the need for such a hearing on the court officer."

(3) Where a person is to appear or be brought before the Crown Court pursuant to sections 88 or 89 of the 2003 Act the Crown Court may order that the person shall be released from custody on entering into a recognizance, with or without sureties, or giving other security before—

(a) the Crown Court officer; or

(b) any other person authorised by virtue of section 119(1) of the Magistrates' Courts Act 1980 to take a recognizance where a magistrates' court having power to take the recognizance has, instead of taking it, fixed the amount in which the principal and his sureties, if any, are to be bound.

(4) The court officer shall forward to the Registrar a copy of any record made in pursuance of section 5(1) of the Bail Act 1976.

41.6   Further provisions regarding bail and custody in the Crown Court

(1) The prosecutor may only apply to extend or further extend the relevant period before it expires and that application must be served on the Crown Court officer and the acquitted person.

(2) A prosecutor's application for a summons or a warrant under section 89(3)(a) or (b) of the Criminal Justice Act 2003 must be served on the court officer and the acquitted person.

41.7   Bail or custody orders in the Court of Appeal

Rules 68.8 and 68.9 shall apply to bail or custody orders made in the Court of Appeal under section 90 of the Criminal Justice Act 2003 as if they were orders made pursuant to an application under rule 68.7.

41.8   Application for restrictions on publication

(1) An application by the Director of Public Prosecutions, under section 82 of the Criminal Justice Act 2003, for restrictions on publication must be in the form set out in the Practice Direction and be served on the Registrar and the acquitted person.

(2) If notice of a section 76 application has not been given and the Director of Public Prosecution has indicated that there are reasons why the acquitted person should not be notified of the application for restrictions on publication, the Court of Appeal may order that service on the acquitted person is not to be effected until notice of a section 76 application is served on that person.

(3) If the Court of Appeal makes an order for restrictions on publication of its own motion or on application of the Director of Public Prosecutions, the Registrar must serve notice and reasons for that order on all parties, unless paragraph (2) applies.

41.9   Variation or revocation of restrictions on publication

(1) A party who wants to vary or revoke an order for restrictions on publication, under section 82(7) of the Criminal Justice Act 2003, may apply to the Court of Appeal in writing at any time after that order was made.

(2) A copy of the application to vary or revoke shall be sent to all parties to the section 76 application unless paragraph (3) applies.

(3) If the application to vary or revoke is made by the Director of Public Prosecutions and—

    (a) the notice of a section 76 application has not been given under rule 41.2; and

    (b) the Director of Public Prosecutions has indicted that there are reasons why the acquitted person should not be notified of an application for restrictions on publication,

the Court of Appeal may order that service on the acquitted person is not to be effected until notice of a section 76 application is served on that person.

(4) If the Court of Appeal varies or revokes an order for restrictions on publication of its own motion or on application, it must serve notice and reasons for that order on all parties, unless paragraph (3) applies.

41.10   Powers exercisable by a single judge of the Court of Appeal

(1) The following powers under the Criminal Justice Act 2003 and under this Part may be exercised by a single judge in the same manner as they may be exercised by the Court of Appeal and subject to the same provisions, namely to—

    (a) order the production of any document, exhibit or thing under section 80(6)(a) of the 2003 Act;

    (b) order any witness who would be a compellable witness in proceedings pursuant to an order or declaration made on the application to attend for examination and be examined before the Court of Appeal under section 80(6)(b) of the 2003 Act;

    (c) extend the time for service under rule 41.3(2); and

    (d) delay the requirement of service on the acquitted person of an application for restrictions on publication under rules 41.8(2) and 41.9(3).

(2) A single judge may, for the purposes of exercising any of the powers specified in paragraph (1), sit in such place as he appoints and may sit otherwise than in open court.

(3) Where a single judge exercises one of the powers set out in paragraph (1), the Registrar must serve notice of the single judge's decision on all parties to the section 76 application.

41.11   Powers exercisable by the Registrar

(1) The Registrar may require the Crown Court at the place of original trial to provide the Court of Appeal with any assistance or information which it may require for the purposes of exercising its jurisdiction under Part 10 of the Criminal Justice Act 2003 or this Part.

(2) The following powers may be exercised by the Registrar in the same manner as the Court of Appeal and subject to the same provisions—

    (a) order the production of any document, exhibit or thing under section 80(6)(a) of the 2003 Act;

    (b) order any witness who would be a compellable witness in proceedings pursuant to an order or declaration made on the application to attend for examination and be examined before the Court of Appeal under section 80(6)(b) of the 2003 Act; and

    (c) extend the time for service under rule 41.3(2).

(3) Where the Registrar exercises one of the powers set out in paragraph (2) the Registrar must serve notice of that decision on all parties to the section 76 application.

(4) Where the Registrar has refused an application to exercise any of the powers referred to in paragraph (2), the party making the application may have it determined by a single judge by serving a renewal in the form set out in the Practice Direction within 14 days of the day on which notice of the Registrar's decision is served on the party making the application, unless that period is extended by the Court of Appeal.

41.12   Determination by full court

(1) Where a single judge has refused an application to exercise any of the powers referred to in rule 41.10, the applicant may have that application determined by the Court of Appeal by serving a notice of renewal in the form set out in the Practice Direction.

(2) A notice under paragraph (1) must be served on the Registrar within 14 days of the day on which notice of the single judge's decision is served on the party making the application, unless that period is extended by the Court of Appeal.

(3) If a notice under paragraph (1) is not served on the Registrar within the period specified in paragraph (2) or such extended period as the Court of Appeal has allowed, the application shall be treating as having been refused by the Court of Appeal.

41.13 Notice of the determination of the application

(1) The Court of Appeal may give its determination of the section 76 application at the conclusion of the hearing.

(2) If determination is reserved, the Registrar shall as soon as practicable, serve notice of the determination on the parties to the section 76 application.

(3) If the Court of Appeal orders under section 77 of the Criminal Justice Act 2003 that a retrial take place, the Registrar must as soon as practicable, serve notice on the Crown Court officer at the appropriate place of retrial.

41.14 Notice of application to set aside order for retrial

(1) If an acquitted person has not been arraigned before the end of 2 months after the date of an order under section 77 of the Criminal Justice Act 2003 he may apply in the form set out in the Practice Direction to the Court of Appeal to set aside the order.

(2) An application under paragraph (1) must be served on the Registrar and the prosecutor.

41.15 Leave to arraign

(1) If the acquitted person has not been arraigned before the end of 2 months after the date of an order under section 77 of the Criminal Justice Act 2003, the prosecutor may apply in the form set out in the Practice Direction to the Court of Appeal for leave to arraign.

(2) An application under paragraph (1) must be served on the Registrar and the acquitted person.

41.16 Abandonment of the application

(1) A section 76 application may be abandoned by the prosecutor before the hearing of that application by serving a notice in the form set out in the Practice Direction on the Registrar and the acquitted person.

(2) The Registrar must, as soon as practicable, after receiving a notice under paragraph (1) send a copy of it endorsed with the date of receipt to the prosecutor and acquitted person.

Attorney-General's Guidelines on Disclosure of Unused Material in Criminal Proceedings

(Issued April 2005)

Introduction

1. Every accused person has a right to a fair trial, a right long embodied in our law and guaranteed under Article 6 of the European Convention on Human Rights (ECHR). A fair trial is the proper object and expectation of all participants in the trial process. Fair disclosure to an accused is an inseparable part of a fair trial.

2. What must be clear is that a fair trial consists of an examination not just of all the evidence the parties wish to rely on but also all other relevant subject matter. A fair trial should not require consideration of irrelevant material and should not involve spurious applications or arguments which serve to divert the trial process from examining the real issues before the court.

3. The scheme set out in the Criminal Procedure and Investigations Act 1996 (as amended by the Criminal Justice Act 2003) (the Act) is designed to ensure that there is fair disclosure of material which may be relevant to an investigation and which does not form part of the prosecution case. Disclosure under the Act should assist the accused in the timely preparation and presentation of their case and assist the court to focus on all the relevant issues in the trial. Disclosure which does not meet these objectives risks preventing a fair trial taking place.

4. This means that the disclosure regime set out in the Act must be scrupulously followed. These Guidelines build upon the existing law to help to ensure that the legislation is operated more effectively, consistently and fairly.

5. Disclosure must not be an open ended trawl of unused material. A critical element to fair and proper disclosure is that the defence play their role to ensure that the prosecution are directed to material which might reasonably be considered capable of undermining the prosecution case or assisting the case for the accused. This process is key to ensuring prosecutors make informed determinations about disclosure of unused material.

6. Fairness does recognise that there are other interests that need to be protected, including those of victims and witnesses who might otherwise be exposed to harm. The scheme of the Act protects those interests. It should also ensure that material is not disclosed which overburdens the participants in the trial process, diverts attention from the relevant issues, leads to unjustifiable delay, and is wasteful of resources.

7. Whilst it is acknowledged that these Guidelines have been drafted with a focus on Crown Court proceedings the spirit of the Guidelines must be followed where they apply to proceedings in the magistrates' court.

General principles

8. Disclosure refers to providing the defence with copies of, or access to, any material which might reasonably be considered capable of undermining the case for the prosecution against the accused, or of assisting the case for the accused, and which has not previously been disclosed.

9. Prosecutors will only be expected to anticipate what material might weaken their case or strengthen the defence in the light of information available at the time of the disclosure decision, and this may include information revealed during questioning.

10. Generally, material which can reasonably be considered capable of undermining the prosecution case against the accused or assisting the defence case will include anything that tends to show a fact inconsistent with the elements of the case that must be proved by the prosecution. Material can fulfil the disclosure test:

    (a) by the use to be made of it in cross-examination; or

    (b) by its capacity to support submissions that could lead to:

        (i)   the exclusion of evidence; or

        (ii)   a stay of proceedings; or

        (iii) a court or tribunal finding that any public authority had acted incompatibly with the accused 's rights under the ECHR, or

    (c) by its capacity to suggest an explanation or partial explanation of the accused's actions.

11. In deciding whether material may fall to be disclosed under paragraph 10, especially (b)(ii), prosecutors must consider whether disclosure is required in order for a proper application to be made. The purpose of this paragraph is not to allow enquiries to support speculative arguments or for the manufacture of defences.

12. Examples of material that might reasonably be considered capable of undermining the prosecution case or of assisting the case for the accused are:

    (i)   Any material casting doubt upon the accuracy of any prosecution evidence.

    (ii)   Any material which may point to another person, whether charged or not (including a co-accused) having involvement in the commission of the offence.

    (iii) Any material which may cast doubt upon the reliability of a confession.

    (iv) Any material that might go to the credibility of a prosecution witness.

    (v) Any material that might support a defence that is either raised by the defence or apparent from the prosecution papers.

    (vi) Any material which may have a bearing on the admissibility of any prosecution evidence.

13. It should also be borne in mind that while items of material viewed in isolation may not be reasonably considered to be capable of undermining the prosecution case or assisting the accused, several items together can have that effect.

14. Material relating to the accused's mental or physical health, intellectual capacity, or to any ill treatment which the accused may have suffered when in the investigator's custody is likely to fall within the test for disclosure set out in paragraph 8 above.

Defence statements

15. A defence statement must comply with the requirements of section 6A of the Act. A comprehensive defence statement assists the participants in the trial to ensure that it is fair. The trial process is not well served if the defence make general and unspecified allegations and then seek far-reaching disclosure in the hope that material may turn up to make them good. The more detail a defence statement contains the more likely it is that the prosecutor will make an informed decision about whether any remaining undisclosed material might reasonably be considered capable of undermining the prosecution case or of assisting the case for the accused, or whether to advise the investigator to undertake further enquiries. It also helps in the management of the trial by narrowing down and focussing on the issues in dispute. It may result in the prosecution discontinuing the case. Defence practitioners should be aware of these considerations when advising their clients.

16. Whenever a defence solicitor provides a defence statement on behalf of the accused it will be deemed to be given with the authority of the solicitor's client.

Continuing duty of prosecutor to disclose

17. Section 7A of the Act imposes a continuing duty upon the prosecutor to keep under review at all times the question of whether there is any unused material which might reasonably be considered capable of undermining the prosecution case against the accused or assisting the case for the accused and which has not previously been disclosed. This duty arises after the prosecutor has complied with the duty of initial disclosure or purported to comply with it and before the accused is acquitted or convicted or the prosecutor decides not to proceed with the case. If such material is identified, then the prosecutor must disclose it to the accused as soon as is reasonably practicable.

18. As part of their continuing duty of disclosure, prosecutors should be open, alert and promptly responsive to requests for disclosure of material supported by a comprehensive defence statement. Conversely, if no defence statement has been served or if the prosecutor considers that the defence statement is lacking specificity or otherwise does not meet the requirements of section 6A of the Act, a letter should be sent to the defence indicating this. If the position is not resolved satisfactorily, the prosecutor should consider raising the issue at a hearing for directions to enable the court to give a warning or appropriate directions.

19. When defence practitioners are dissatisfied with disclosure decisions by the prosecution and consider that they are entitled to further disclosure, applications to the court should be made pursuant to section 8 of the Act and in accordance with the procedures set out in the Criminal Procedure Rules. Applications for further disclosure should not be made as ad hoc applications but dealt with under the proper procedures.

Applications for non-disclosure in the public interest

20. Before making an application to the court to withhold material which would otherwise fall to be disclosed, on the basis that to disclose would give rise to a real risk of serious prejudice to an important public interest, prosecutors should aim to disclose as much of the material as they properly can (for example, by giving the defence redacted or edited copies or summaries). Neutral material or material damaging to the defendant need not be disclosed and must not be brought to the attention of the court. It is only in truly borderline cases that the prosecution should seek a judicial ruling on the disclosability of material in its possession.

21. Prior to or at the hearing, the court must be provided with full and accurate information. Prior to the hearing the prosecutor and the prosecution advocate must examine all material, which is the subject matter of the application and make any necessary enquiries of the investigator. The prosecutor (or representative) and/or investigator should attend such applications.

22. The principles set out at paragraph 36 of *R v H & C* should be rigorously applied firstly by the prosecutor and then by the court considering the material. It is essential that these principles are scrupulously attended to to ensure that the procedure for examination of material in the absence of the accused is compliant with Article 6 of ECHR.

Responsibilities

Investigators and disclosure officers

23. Investigators and disclosure officers must be fair and objective and must work together with prosecutors to ensure that disclosure obligations are met. A failure to take action leading to inadequate disclosure may result in a wrongful conviction. It may alternatively lead to a successful abuse of process argument, an acquittal against the weight of the evidence or the appellate courts may find that a conviction is unsafe and quash it.

24. Officers appointed as disclosure officers must have the requisite experience, skills, competence and resources to undertake their vital role. In discharging their obligations under the Act, code, common law and any operational instructions, investigators should always err on the side of recording and retaining material where they have any doubt as to whether it may be relevant.

25. An individual must not be appointed as disclosure officer, or continue in that role, if that is likely to result in a conflict of interest, for instance, if the disclosure officer is the victim of the alleged crime which is the subject of investigation. The advice of a more senior investigator must always be sought if there is doubt as to whether a conflict of interest precludes an individual acting as the disclosure officer. If thereafter a doubt remains, the advice of a prosecutor should be sought.

26. There may be a number of disclosure officers, especially in large and complex cases. However, there must be a lead disclosure officer who is the focus for enquiries and whose responsibility it is to ensure that the investigator's disclosure obligations are complied with. Disclosure officers, or their deputies, must inspect, view or listen to all relevant material that has been retained by the investigator, and the disclosure officer must provide a personal declaration to the effect that this task has been undertaken.

27. Generally this will mean that such material must be examined in detail by the disclosure officer or the deputy, but exceptionally the extent and manner of inspecting, viewing or listening will depend on the nature of material and its form. For example, it might be reasonable to examine digital material by using software search tools, or to establish the contents of large volumes of material by dip sampling. If such material is not examined in detail, it must nonetheless be described on the disclosure schedules accurately and as clearly as possible. The extent and manner of its examination must also be described together with justification for such action.

28. Investigators must retain material that may be relevant to the investigation. However, it may become apparent to the investigator that some material obtained in the course of an investigation

because it was considered potentially relevant, is in fact incapable of impact. It need not then be retained or dealt with in accordance with these Guidelines, although the investigator should err on the side of caution in coming to this conclusion and seek the advice of the prosecutor as appropriate.

29. In meeting the obligations in paragraph 6.9 and 8.1 of the Code, it is crucial that descriptions by disclosure officers in non-sensitive schedules are detailed, clear and accurate. The descriptions may require a summary of the contents of the retained material to assist the prosecutor to make an informed decision on disclosure. Sensitive schedules must contain sufficient information to enable the prosecutor to make an informed decision as to whether or not the material itself should be viewed, to the extent possible without compromising the confidentiality of the information.

30. Disclosure officers must specifically draw material to the attention of the prosecutor for consideration where they have any doubt as to whether it might reasonably be considered capable of undermining the prosecution case or of assisting the case for the accused.

31. Disclosure officers must seek the advice and assistance of prosecutors when in doubt as to their responsibility as early as possible. They must deal expeditiously with requests by the prosecutor for further information on material, which may lead to disclosure.

Prosecutors

32. Prosecutors must do all that they can to facilitate proper disclosure, as part of their general and personal professional responsibility to act fairly and impartially, in the interests of justice and in accordance with the law. Prosecutors must also be alert to the need to provide advice to, and where necessary probe actions taken by, disclosure officers to ensure that disclosure obligations are met.

33. Prosecutors must review schedules prepared by disclosure officers thoroughly and must be alert to the possibility that relevant material may exist which has not been revealed to them or material included which should not have been. If no schedules have been provided, or there are apparent omissions from the schedules, or documents or other items are inadequately described or are unclear, the prosecutor must at once take action to obtain properly completed schedules. Likewise schedules should be returned for amendment if irrelevant items are included. If prosecutors remain dissatisfied with the quality or content of the schedules they must raise the matter with a senior investigator, and if necessary, persist, with a view to resolving the matter satisfactorily.

34. Where prosecutors have reason to believe that the disclosure officer has not discharged the obligation in paragraph 26 to inspect, view or listen to relevant material, they must at once raise the matter with the disclosure officer and, if it is believed that the officer has not inspected, viewed or listened to the material, request that it be done.

35. When prosecutors or disclosure officers believe that material might reasonably be considered capable of undermining the prosecution case or assisting the case for the accused, prosecutors must always inspect, view or listen to the material and satisfy themselves that the prosecution can properly be continued having regard to the disclosability of the material reviewed. Their judgement as to what other material to inspect, view or listen to will depend on the circumstances of each case.

36. Prosecutors should copy the defence statement to the disclosure officer and investigator as soon as reasonably practicable and prosecutors should advise the investigator if, in their view, reasonable and relevant lines of further enquiry should be pursued.

37. Prosecutors cannot comment upon, or invite inferences to be drawn from, failures in defence disclosure otherwise than in accordance with section 11 of the Act. Prosecutors may cross-examine the accused on differences between the defence case put at trial and that set out in his or her defence statement. In doing so, it may be appropriate to apply to the judge under section 6E of the Act for copies of the statement to be given to a jury, edited if necessary to remove inadmissible material. Prosecutors should examine the defence statement to see whether it points to other lines of enquiry. If the defence statement does point to other reasonable lines of inquiry further investigation is required and evidence obtained as a result of these enquiries may be used as part of the prosecution case or to rebut the defence.

38. Once initial disclosure is completed and a defence statement has been served requests for disclosure should ordinarily only be answered if the request is in accordance with and relevant to the defence statement. If it is not, then a further or amended defence statement should be sought and obtained before considering the request for further disclosure.

39. Prosecutors must ensure that they record in writing all actions and decisions they make in discharging their disclosure responsibilities, and this information is to be made available to the prosecution advocate if requested or if relevant to an issue.

40. If the material does not fulfil the disclosure test there is no requirement to disclose it. For this purpose, the parties' respective cases should not be restrictively analysed but must be carefully analysed to ascertain the specific facts the prosecution seek to establish and the specific grounds on which the charges are resisted. Neutral material or material damaging to the defendant need not be disclosed and must not be brought to the attention of the court. Only in truly borderline cases should the prosecution seek a judicial ruling on the disclosability of material in its hands.

41. If prosecutors are satisfied that a fair trial cannot take place where material which satisfies the disclosure test cannot be disclosed, and that this cannot or will not be remedied including by, for example, making formal admissions, amending the charges or presenting the case in a different way so as to ensure fairness or in other ways, they must not continue with the case.

Prosecution advocates

42. Prosecution advocates should ensure that all material that ought to be disclosed under the Act is disclosed to the defence. However, prosecution advocates cannot be expected to disclose material if they are not aware of its existence. As far as is possible, prosecution advocates must place themselves in a fully informed position to enable them to make decisions on disclosure.

43. Upon receipt of instructions, prosecution advocates should consider as a priority all the information provided regarding disclosure of material. Prosecution advocates should consider, in every case, whether they can be satisfied that they are in possession of all relevant documentation and that they have been instructed fully regarding disclosure matters. Decisions already made regarding disclosure should be reviewed. If as a result, the advocate considers that further information or action is required, written advice should be promptly provided setting out the aspects that need clarification or action. Prosecution advocates must advise on disclosure in accordance with the Act. If necessary and where appropriate a conference should be held to determine what is required.

44. The prosecution advocate must keep decisions regarding disclosure under review until the conclusion of the trial. The prosecution advocate must in every case specifically consider whether he or she can satisfactorily discharge the duty of continuing review on the basis of the material supplied already, or whether it is necessary to inspect further material or to reconsider material already inspected. Prosecution advocates must not abrogate their responsibility under the Act by disclosing material which could not be considered capable of undermining the prosecution case or of assisting the case for the accused.

45. Prior to the commencement of a trial, the prosecuting advocate should always make decisions on disclosure in consultation with those instructing him or her and the disclosure officer. After a trial has started, it is recognised that in practice consultation on disclosure issues may not be practicable; it continues to be desirable, however, whenever this can be achieved without affecting unduly the conduct of the trial.

46. There is no basis in law or practice for disclosure on a 'counsel to counsel' basis.

Involvement of other agencies

Material held by Government departments or other Crown bodies

47. Where it appears to an investigator, disclosure officer or prosecutor that a Government department or other Crown body has material that may be relevant to an issue in the case, reasonable steps should be taken to identify and consider such material. Although what is reasonable will vary

from case to case, the prosecution should inform the department or other body of the nature of its case and of relevant issues in the case in respect of which the department or body might possess material, and ask whether it has any such material.

48. It should be remembered that investigators, disclosure officers and prosecutors cannot be regarded to be in constructive possession of material held by Government departments or Crown bodies simply by virtue of their status as Government departments or Crown bodies.

49. Departments in England and Wales should have identified personnel as established Enquiry Points to deal with issues concerning the disclosure of information in criminal proceedings.

50. Where, after reasonable steps have been taken to secure access to such material, access is denied the investigator, disclosure officer or prosecutor should consider what if any further steps might be taken to obtain the material or inform the defence.

Material held by other agencies

51. There may be cases where the investigator, disclosure officer or prosecutor believes that a third party (for example, a local authority, a social services department, a hospital, a doctor, a school, a provider of forensic services) has material or information which might be relevant to the prosecution case. In such cases, if the material or information might reasonably be considered capable of undermining the prosecution case or of assisting the case for the accused prosecutors should take what steps they regard as appropriate in the particular case to obtain it.

52. If the investigator, disclosure officer or prosecutor seeks access to the material or information but the third party declines or refuses to allow access to it, the matter should not be left. If despite any reasons offered by the third party it is still believed that it is reasonable to seek production of the material or information, and the requirements of section 2 of the Criminal Procedure (Attendance of Witnesses) Act 1965 or as appropriate section 97 of the Magistrates Courts Act 1980[1] are satisfied, then the prosecutor or investigator should apply for a witness summons causing a representative of the third party to produce the material to the Court.

53. Relevant information which comes to the knowledge of investigators or prosecutors as a result of liaison with third parties should be recorded by the investigator or prosecutor in a durable or retrievable form (for example potentially relevant information revealed in discussions at a child protection conference attended by police officers).

54. Where information comes into the possession of the prosecution in the circumstances set out in paragraphs 51–53 above, consultation with the other agency should take place before disclosure is made: there may be public interest reasons which justify withholding disclosure and which would require the issue of disclosure of the information to be placed before the court.

Other disclosure

Disclosure prior to initial disclosure

55. Investigators must always be alive to the potential need to reveal and prosecutors to the potential need to disclose material, in the interests of justice and fairness in the particular circumstances of any case, after the commencement of proceedings but before their duty arises under the Act. For instance, disclosure ought to be made of significant information that might affect a bail decision or that might enable the defence to contest the committal proceedings.

56. Where the need for such disclosure is not apparent to the prosecutor, any disclosure will depend on what the accused chooses to reveal about the defence. Clearly, such disclosure will not exceed that which is obtainable after the statutory duties of disclosure arise

Summary trial

57. The prosecutor should, in addition to complying with the obligations under the Act, provide to the defence all evidence upon which the Crown proposes to rely in a summary trial. Such provision

---

[1] The equivalent legislation in Northern Ireland is section 51A of the Judicature (Northern Ireland) Act 1978 and Article 118 of the Magistrates' Courts (Northern Ireland) Order 1981.

should allow the accused and their legal advisers sufficient time properly to consider the evidence before it is called.

Material relevant to sentence

58. In all cases the prosecutor must consider disclosing in the interests of justice any material, which is relevant to sentence (e.g. information which might mitigate the seriousness of the offence or assist the accused to lay blame in part upon a co-accused or another person).

Post-conviction

59. The interests of justice will also mean that where material comes to light after the conclusion of the proceedings, which might cast doubt upon the safety of the conviction, there is a duty to consider disclosure. Any such material should be brought immediately to the attention of line management.

60. Disclosure of any material that is made outside the ambit of Act will attract confidentiality by virtue of *Taylor v SFO* [1998].

Applicability of these guidelines

61. Although the relevant obligations in relation to unused material and disclosure imposed on the prosecutor and the accused are determined by the date on which the investigation began, these Guidelines should be adopted with immediate effect in relation to all cases submitted to the prosecuting authorities in receipt of these Guidelines save where they specifically refer to the statutory or Code provisions of the Criminal Justice Act 2003 that do not yet apply to the particular case.

Part III

Human Rights—Act and Convention

Human Rights Act 1998

(1998, c. 42)

Introduction

1 The Convention Rights

(1) In this Act 'the Convention rights' means the rights and fundamental freedoms set out in—

(a) Articles 2 to 12 and 14 of the Convention,

(b) Articles 1 to 3 of the First Protocol, and

(c) Articles 1 and 2 of the Sixth Protocol,

as read with Articles 16 to 18 of the Convention.

(2) Those Articles are to have effect for the purposes of this Act subject to any designated derogation or reservation (as to which see sections 14 and 15).

(3) The Articles are set out in Schedule 1.

(4) The Secretary of State may by order make such amendments to this Act as he considers appropriate to reflect the effect, in relation to the United Kingdom, of a protocol.

(5) In subsection (4) 'protocol' means a protocol to the Convention—

(a) which the United Kingdom has ratified; or

(b) which the United Kingdom has signed with a view to ratification.

(6) No amendment may be made by an order under subsection (4) so as to come into force before the protocol concerned is in force in relation to the United Kingdom.

2 Interpretation of Convention rights

(1) A court or tribunal determining a question which has arisen in connection with a Convention right must take into account any—

(a) judgment, decision, declaration or advisory opinion of the European Court of Human Rights,

(b) opinion of the Commission given in a report adopted under Article 31 of the Convention,

(c) decision of the Commission in connection with Article 26 or 27(2) of the Convention, or

(d) decision of the Committee of Ministers taken under Article 46 of the Convention,

whenever made or given, so far as, in the opinion of the court or tribunal, it is relevant to the proceedings in which that question has arisen.

(2) Evidence of any judgment, decision, declaration or opinion of which account may have to be taken under this section is to be given in proceedings before any court or tribunal in such manner as may be provided by rules.

(3) In this section 'rules' means rules of court or, in the case of proceedings before a tribunal, rules made for the purposes of this section—

(a) by the Lord Chancellor or the Secretary of State, in relation to any proceedings outside Scotland;

(b) by the Secretary of State, in relation to proceedings in Scotland; or

(c) by a Northern Ireland department, in relation to proceedings before a tribunal in Northern Ireland—

    (i)   which deals with transferred matters; and

    (ii) for which no rules made under paragraph (a) are in force.

Legislation

3 Interpretation of legislation

(1) So far as it is possible to do so, primary legislation and subordinate legislation must be read and given effect in a way which is compatible with the Convention rights.

(2) This section—

(a) applies to primary legislation and subordinate legislation whenever enacted;

(b) does not affect the validity, continuing operation or enforcement of any incompatible primary legislation; and

(c) does not affect the validity, continuing operation or enforcement of any incompatible subordinate legislation if (disregarding any possibility of revocation) primary legislation prevents removal of the incompatibility.

4 Declaration of incompatibility

(1) Subsection (2) applies in any proceedings in which a court determines whether a provision of primary legislation is compatible with a Convention right.

(2) If the court is satisfied that the provision is incompatible with a Convention right, it may make a declaration of that incompatibility.

(3) Subsection (4) applies in any proceedings in which a court determines whether a provision of subordinate legislation, made in the exercise of a power conferred by primary legislation, is compatible with a Convention right.

(4) If the court is satisfied—

(a) that the provision is incompatible with a Convention right, and

(b) that (disregarding any possibility of revocation) the primary legislation concerned prevents removal of the incompatibility,

it may make a declaration of that incompatibility.

(5) In this section 'court' means—

(a) the House of Lords;

(b) the Judicial Committee of the Privy Council;

(c) the Court Martial Appeal Court;

(d) in Scotland, the High Court of Justiciary sitting otherwise than as a trial court or the Court of Session;

(e) in England and Wales or Northern Ireland, the High Court or the Court of Appeal.

(f) the Court of Protection, in any matter being dealt with by the President of the Family Division, the Vice-Chancellor or a puisne judge of the High Court.

(6) A declaration under this section ('a declaration of incompatibility')—

(a) does not affect the validity, continuing operation or enforcement of the provision in respect of which it is given; and

(b) is not binding on the parties to the proceedings in which it is made.

5 Right of Crown to intervene

(1) Where a court is considering whether to make a declaration of incompatibility, the Crown is entitled to notice in accordance with rules of court.

(2) In any case to which subsection (1) applies—

(a) a Minister of the Crown (or a person nominated by him),

(b) a member of the Scottish Executive,

(c) a Northern Ireland Minister,

(d) a Northern Ireland department,

is entitled, on giving notice in accordance with rules of court, to be joined as a party to the proceedings.

(3) Notice under subsection (2) may be given at any time during the proceedings.

(4) A person who has been made a party to criminal proceedings (other than in Scotland) as the result of a notice under subsection (2) may, with leave, appeal to the House of Lords against any declaration of incompatibility made in the proceedings.

(5) In subsection (4)—

'criminal proceedings' includes all proceedings before the Court Martial Appeal Court; and

'leave' means leave granted by the court making the declaration of incompatibility or by the House of Lords.

Public authorities

6   Acts of public authorities

(1) It is unlawful for a public authority to act in a way which is incompatible with a Convention right.

(2) Subsection (1) does not apply to an act if—

(a) as the result of one or more provisions of primary legislation, the authority could not have acted differently; or

(b) in the case of one or more provisions of, or made under, primary legislation which cannot be read or given effect in a way which is compatible with the Convention rights, the authority was acting so as to give effect to or enforce those provisions.

(3) In this section 'public authority' includes—

(a) a court or tribunal, and

(b) any person certain of whose functions are functions of a public nature,

but does not include either House of Parliament or a person exercising functions in connection with proceedings in Parliament.

(4) In subsection (3) 'Parliament' does not include the House of Lords in its judicial capacity.

(5) In relation to a particular act, a person is not a public authority by virtue only of subsection (3)(b) if the nature of the act is private.

(6) 'An act' includes a failure to act but does not include a failure to—

(a) introduce in, or lay before, Parliament a proposal for legislation; or

(b) make any primary legislation or remedial order.

7   Proceedings

(1) A person who claims that a public authority has acted (or proposes to act) in a way which is made unlawful by section 6(1) may—

(a) bring proceedings against the authority under this Act in the appropriate court or tribunal, or

(b) rely on the Convention right or rights concerned in any legal proceedings, but only if he is (or would be) a victim of the unlawful act.

(2) In subsection (1)(a) 'appropriate court or tribunal' means such court or tribunal as may be determined in accordance with rules; and proceedings against an authority include a counterclaim or similar proceeding.

(3) If the proceedings are brought on an application for judicial review, the applicant is to be taken to have a sufficient interest in relation to the unlawful act only if he is, or would be, a victim of that act.

(4) [*Applies to Scotland only*]

(5) Proceedings under subsection (1)(a) must be brought before the end of—

(a) the period of one year beginning with the date on which the act complained of took place; or

(b) such longer period as the court or tribunal considers equitable having regard to all the circumstances,

but that is subject to any rule imposing a stricter time limit in relation to the procedure in question.

(6) In subsection (1)(b) 'legal proceedings' includes—

(a) proceedings brought by or at the instigation of a public authority; and

(b) an appeal against the decision of a court or tribunal.

(7) For the purposes of this section, a person is a victim of an unlawful act only if he would be a victim for the purposes of Article 34 of the Convention if proceedings were brought in the European Court of Human Rights in respect of that act.

(8) Nothing in this Act creates a criminal offence.

(9) In this section 'rules' means—

(a) in relation to proceedings before a court or tribunal outside Scotland, rules made by the Lord Chancellor or the Secretary of State for the purposes of this section or rules of court,

(b) [applies to Scotland only]

(c) [applies to Northern Ireland only]

and includes provision made by order under section 1 of the Courts and Legal Services Act 1990.

(10) In making rules, regard must be had to section 9.

(11) The Minister who has power to make rules in relation to a particular tribunal may, to the extent he considers it necessary to ensure that the tribunal can provide an appropriate remedy in relation to an act (or proposed act) of a public authority which is (or would be) unlawful as a result of section 6(1), by order add to—

(a) the relief or remedies which the tribunal may grant; or

(b) the grounds on which it may grant any of them.

(12) An order made under subsection (11) may contain such incidental, supplemental, consequential or transitional provision as the Minister making it considers appropriate.

(13) 'The Minister' includes the Northern Ireland department concerned.

8 Judicial remedies

(1) In relation to any act (or proposed act) of a public authority which the court finds is (or would be) unlawful, it may grant such relief or remedy, or make such order, within its powers as it considers just and appropriate.

(2) But damages may be awarded only by a court which has power to award damages, or to order the payment of compensation, in civil proceedings.

(3) No award of damages is to be made unless, taking account of all the circumstances of the case, including—

(a) any other relief or remedy granted, or order made, in relation to the act in question (by that or any other court), and

(b) the consequences of any decision (of that or any other court) in respect of that act,

the court is satisfied that the award is necessary to afford just satisfaction to the person in whose favour it is made.

(4) In determining—

(a) whether to award damages, or

(b) the amount of an award,

the court must take into account the principles applied by the European Court of Human Rights in relation to the award of compensation under Article 41 of the Convention.

(5) A public authority against which damages are awarded is to be treated—

(a) [applies to Scotland only]

(b) for the purposes of the Civil Liability (Contribution) Act 1978 as liable in respect of damage suffered by the person to whom the award is made.

(6) In this section—

'court' includes a tribunal;

'damages' means damages for an unlawful act of a public authority; and

'unlawful' means unlawful under section 6(1).

9   Judicial acts

(1) Proceedings under section 7(1)(a) in respect of a judicial act may be brought only—

    (a) by exercising a right of appeal;

    (b) on an application . . . for judicial review; or

    (c) in such other forum as may be prescribed by rules.

(2) That does not affect any rule of law which prevents a court from being the subject of judicial review.

(3) In proceedings under this Act in respect of a judicial act done in good faith, damages may not be awarded otherwise than to compensate a person to the extent required by Article 5(5) of the Convention.

(4) An award of damages permitted by subsection (3) is to be made against the Crown; but no award may be made unless the appropriate person, if not a party to the proceedings, is joined.

(5) In this section—

'appropriate person' means the Minister responsible for the court concerned, or a person or government department nominated by him;

'court' includes a tribunal;

'judge' includes a member of a tribunal, a justice of the peace and a clerk or other officer entitled to exercise the jurisdiction of a court;

'judicial act' means a judicial act of a court and includes an act done on the instructions, or on behalf, of a judge; and

'rules' has the same meaning as in section 7(9).

Remedial action

10   Power to take remedial action

(1) This section applies if—

    (a) a provision of legislation has been declared under section 4 to be incompatible with a Convention right and, if an appeal lies—

        (i)   all persons who may appeal have stated in writing that they do not intend to do so;

        (ii) the time for bringing an appeal has expired and no appeal has been brought within that time; or

        (iii) an appeal brought within that time has been determined or abandoned;

    or

    (b) it appears to a Minister of the Crown or Her Majesty in Council that, having regard to a finding of the European Court of Human Rights made after the coming into force of this section in proceedings against the United Kingdom, a provision of legislation is incompatible with an obligation of the United Kingdom arising from the Convention.

(2) If a Minister of the Crown considers that there are compelling reasons for proceeding under this section, he may by order make such amendments to the legislation as he considers necessary to remove the incompatibility.

(3) If, in the case of subordinate legislation, a Minister of the Crown considers—

    (a) that it is necessary to amend the primary legislation under which the subordinate legislation in question was made, in order to enable the incompatibility to be removed, and

    (b) that there are compelling reasons for proceeding under this section,

he may by order make such amendments to the primary legislation as he considers necessary.

(4) This section also applies where the provision in question is in subordinate legislation and has been quashed, or declared invalid, by reason of incompatibility with a Convention right and the Minister proposes to proceed under paragraph 2(b) of Schedule 2.

(5) If the legislation is an Order in Council, the power conferred by subsection (2) or (3) is exercisable by Her Majesty in Council.

(6) In this section 'legislation' does not include a Measure of the Church Assembly or of the General Synod of the Church of England.

(7) Schedule 2 makes further provision about remedial orders.

21 Interpretation etc.

(1) In this Act—

'amend' includes repeal and apply (with or without modifications);

'the appropriate Minister' means the Minister of the Crown having charge of the appropriate authorised government department (within the meaning of the Crown Proceedings Act 1947);

'the Commission' means the European Commission of Human Rights;

'the Convention' means the Convention for the Protection of Human Rights and Fundamental Freedoms, agreed by the Council of Europe at Rome on 4th November 1950 as it has effect for the time being in relation to the United Kingdom;

'declaration of incompatibility' means a declaration under section 4;

'Minister of the Crown' has the same meaning as in the Ministers of the Crown Act 1975;

'primary legislation' means any—

    (a) public general Act;

    (b) local and personal Act;

    (c) private Act;

    (d) Measure of the Church Assembly;

    (e) Measure of the General Synod of the Church of England;

    (f) Order in Council—

        (i)   made in exercise of Her Majesty's Royal Prerogative;

        (ii) [*applies to Northern Ireland only*]

        (iii) amending an Act of a kind mentioned in paragraph (a), (b) or (c);

and includes an order or other instrument made under primary legislation . . . to the extent to which it operates to bring one or more provisions of that legislation into force or amends any primary legislation;

'the First Protocol' means the protocol to the Convention agreed at Paris on 20th March 1952;

'the Sixth Protocol' means the protocol to the Convention agreed at Strasbourg on 28th April 1983;

'the Eleventh Protocol' means the protocol to the Convention (restructuring the control machinery established by the Convention) agreed at Strasbourg on 11th May 1994;

'remedial order' means an order under section 10;

'subordinate legislation' means any—

    (a) Order in Council other than one—

        (i)   made in exercise of Her Majesty's Royal Prerogative;

        (ii) [*applies to Northern Ireland only*]

        (iii) amending an Act of a kind mentioned in the definition of primary legislation;

    (b) . . .

    (c) . . .

    (d) . . .

    (e) . . .

    (f) order, rules, regulations, scheme, warrant, byelaw or other instrument made under primary legislation (except to the extent to which it operates to bring one or more provisions of that legislation into force or amends any primary legislation);

    (g) . . .

    (h) . . .

'tribunal' means any tribunal in which legal proceedings may be brought.

(2) The references in paragraphs (b) and (c) of section 2(1) to Articles are to Articles of the Convention as they had effect immediately before the coming into force of the Eleventh Protocol.

(3) The reference in paragraph (d) of section 2(1) to Article 46 includes a reference to Articles 32 and 54 of the Convention as they had effect immediately before the coming into force of the Eleventh Protocol.

(4) The references in section 2(1) to a report or decision of the Commission or a decision of the Committee of Ministers include references to a report or decision made as provided by paragraphs 3, 4 and 6 of Article 5 of the Eleventh Protocol (transitional provisions).

(5) Any liability under the Army Act 1955, the Air Force Act 1955 or the Naval Discipline Act 1957 to suffer death for an offence is replaced by a liability to imprisonment for life or any less punishment authorised by those Acts; and those Acts shall accordingly have effect with the necessary modifications.

22   Short title, commencement, application and extent

(1) This Act may be cited as the Human Rights Act 1998.

(2) Section 18, 20 and 21(5) and this section come into force on the passing of this Act.

(3) The other provisions of this Act come into force on such day as the Secretary of State may by order appoint; and different days may be appointed for different purposes.

(4) Paragraph (b) of subsection (1) of section 7 applies to proceedings brought by or at the instigation of a public authority whenever the act in question took place; but otherwise that subsection does not apply to an act taking place before the coming into force of that section.

(5) This Act binds the Crown.

(6) . . .

(7) Section 21(5), so far as it relates to any provision contained in the Army Act 1955, the Air Force Act 1955 or the Naval Discipline Act 1957, extends to any place to which that provision extends.

Convention for the Protection of Human Rights and Fundamental Freedoms*

(Rome, 4.11.1950)[1]

The governments signatory hereto, being members of the Council of Europe,

Considering the Universal Declaration of Human Rights proclaimed by the General Assembly of the United Nations on 10th December 1948;

Considering that this declaration aims at securing the universal and effective recognition and observance of the rights therein declared;

Considering that the aim of the Council of Europe is the achievement of greater unity between its members and that one of the methods by which that aim is to be pursued is the maintenance and further realisation of human rights and fundamental freedoms;

Reaffirming their profound belief in those fundamental freedoms which are the foundation of justice and peace in the world and are best maintained on the one hand by an effective political democracy and on the other by a common understanding and observance of the human rights upon which they depend;

Being resolved, as the governments of European countries which are like-minded and have a common heritage of political traditions, ideals, freedom and the rule of law, to take the first steps for the collective enforcement of certain of the rights stated in the Universal Declaration,

Have agreed as follows:

Article 1

The High Contracting Parties shall secure to everyone within their jurisdiction the rights and freedoms defined in Section 1 of this Convention.

---

* Reproduced with permission from the Council of Europe.

[1] European Treaty Series, No. 5. Text amended according to the provisions of Protocol No. 3 (ETS No. 45), which entered into force on 21 September 1970, of Protocol No. 5 (ETS No. 55), which entered into force on 20 December 1971, and of Protocol No. 8 (ETS No. 118), which entered into force on 1 January 1990, and comprising also the text of Protocol No. 2 (ETS No. 44) which, in accordance with Article 5, paragraph 3, therefore, has been an integral part of the Convention since its entry into force on 21 September 1970.

Section I

Article 2

1. Everyone's right to life shall be protected by law. No one shall be deprived of his life intentionally save in the execution of a sentence of a court following his conviction of a crime for which this penalty is provided by law.

2. Deprivation of life shall not be regarded as inflicted in contravention of this article when it results from the use of force which is no more than absolutely necessary:

    (a) in defence of any person from unlawful violence;

    (b) in order to effect a lawful arrest or to prevent the escape of a person lawfully detained;

    (c) in action lawfully taken for the purpose of quelling a riot or insurrection.

Article 3

No one shall be subjected to torture or to inhuman or degrading treatment or punishment.

Article 4

1. No one shall be held in slavery or servitude.

2. No one shall be required to perform forced or compulsory labour.

3. For the purpose of this article the term 'forced or compulsory labour' shall not include:

    (a) any work required to be done in the ordinary course of detention imposed according to the provisions of Article 5 of this Convention or during conditional release from such detention;

    (b) any service of a military character or, in case of conscientious objectors in countries where they are recognised, service exacted instead of compulsory military service;

    (c) any service exacted in case of an emergency or calamity threatening the life or well-being of the community;

    (d) any work or service which forms part of normal civic obligations.

Article 5

1. Everyone has the right to liberty and security of person. No one shall be deprived of his liberty save in the following cases and in accordance with a procedure prescribed by law:

    (a) the lawful detention of a person after conviction by a competent court;

    (b) the lawful arrest or detention of a person for non-compliance with the lawful order of a court or in order to secure the fulfilment of any obligation prescribed by law;

    (c) the lawful arrest or detention of a person effected for the purpose of bringing him before the competent legal authority on reasonable suspicion of having committed an offence or when it is reasonably considered necessary to prevent his committing an offence or fleeing after having done so;

    (d) the detention of a minor by lawful order for the purpose of educational supervision or his lawful detention for the purpose of bringing him before the competent legal authority;

    (e) the lawful detention of persons for the prevention of the spreading of infectious diseases, of persons of unsound mind, alcoholics or drug addicts or vagrants;

    (f) the lawful arrest or detention of a person to prevent his effecting an unauthorised entry into the country or of a person against whom action is being taken with a view to deportation or extradition.

2. Everyone who is arrested shall be informed promptly, in a language which he understands, of the reasons for his arrest and of any charge against him.

3. Everyone arrested or detained in accordance with the provisions of paragraph 1(c) of this article shall be brought promptly before a judge or other officer authorised by law to exercise judicial power and shall be entitled to trial within a reasonable time or to release pending trial. Release may be conditioned by guarantees to appear for trial.

4. Everyone who is deprived of his liberty by arrest or detention shall be entitled to take proceedings by which the lawfulness of his detention shall be decided speedily by a court and his release ordered if the detention is not lawful.

5. Everyone who has been the victim of arrest or detention in contravention of the provisions of this article shall have an enforceable right to compensation.

Article 6

1. In the determination of his civil rights and obligations or of any criminal charge against him, everyone is entitled to a fair and public hearing within a reasonable time by an independent and impartial tribunal established by law. Judgment shall be pronounced publicly but the press and public may be excluded from all or part of the trial in the interests of morals, public order or national security in a democratic society, where the interests of juveniles or the protection of the private life of the parties so require, or to the extent strictly necessary in the opinion of the court in special circumstances where publicity would prejudice the interests of justice.

2. Everyone charged with a criminal offence shall be presumed innocent until proved guilty according to law.

3. Everyone charged with a criminal offence has the following minimum rights;
  (a) to be informed promptly, in a language which he understands and in detail, of the nature and cause of the accusation against him;
  (b) to have adequate time and facilities for the preparation of his defence;
  (c) to defend himself in person or through legal assistance of his own choosing or, if he has not sufficient means to pay for legal assistance, to be given it free when the interests of justice so require;
  (d) to examine or have examined witnesses against him and to obtain the attendance and examination of witnesses on his behalf under the same conditions as witnesses against him;
  (e) to have the free assistance of an interpreter if he cannot understand or speak the language used in court.

Article 7

1. No one shall be held guilty of any criminal offence on account of any act or omission which did not constitute a criminal offence under national or international law at the time when it was committed. Nor shall a heavier penalty be imposed than the one that was applicable at the time the criminal offence was committed.

2. This article shall not prejudice the trial and punishment of any person for any act or omission which, at the time when it was committed, was criminal according to the general principles of law recognised by civilised nations.

Article 8

1. Everyone has the right to respect for his private and family life, his home and his correspondence.

2. There shall be no interference by a public authority with the exercise of this right except such as is in accordance with the law and is necessary in a democratic society in the interests of national security, public safety or the economic well-being of the country, for the prevention of disorder or crime, for the protection of health or morals, or for the protection of the rights and freedoms of others.

Article 9

1. Everyone has the right to freedom of thought, conscience and religion; this right includes freedom to change his religion or belief and freedom, either alone or in community with others and in public or private, to manifest his religion or belief, in worship, teaching, practice and observance.

2. Freedom to manifest one's religion or beliefs shall be subject only to such limitations as are prescribed by law and are necessary in a democratic society in the interests of public safety, for the protection of public order, health or morals, or for the protection of the rights and freedoms of others.

Article 10

1. Everyone has the right to freedom of expression. This right shall include freedom to hold opinions and to receive and impart information and ideas without interference by public authority and

regardless of frontiers. This article shall not prevent States from requiring the licensing of broadcasting, television or cinema enterprises.

2. The exercise of these freedoms, since it carries with it duties and responsibilities, may be subject to such formalities, conditions, restrictions or penalties as are prescribed by law and are necessary in a democratic society, in the interests of national security, territorial integrity or public safety, for the prevention of disorder or crime, for the protection of health or morals, for the protection of the reputation of rights of others, for preventing the disclosure of information received in confidence, or for maintaining the authority and impartiality of the judiciary.

Article 11

1. Everyone has the right to freedom of peaceful assembly and to freedom of association with others, including the right to form and to join trade unions for the protection of his interests.

2. No restrictions shall be placed on the exercise of these rights other than such as are prescribed by law and are necessary in a democratic society in the interests of national security or public safety, for the prevention of disorder or crime, for the protection of health or morals or for the protection of the rights and freedoms of others. This article shall not prevent the imposition of lawful restrictions on the exercise of these rights by members of the armed forces, of the police or of the administration of the state.

Article 12

Men and women of marriageable age have the right to marry and to found a family, according to the national laws governing the exercise of this right.

Article 13

Everyone whose rights and freedoms as set forth in this Convention are violated shall have an effective remedy before a national authority notwithstanding that the violation has been committed by persons acting in an official capacity.

Article 14

The employment of the rights and freedoms set forth in this Convention shall be secured without discrimination on any ground such as sex, race, colour, language, religion, political or other opinion, national or social origin, association with a national minority, property, birth or other status.

Article 15

1. In time of war or other public emergency threatening the life of the nation any High Contracting Party may take measures derogating from its obligations under this Convention to the extent strictly required by the exigencies of the situation, provided that such measures are not inconsistent with its other obligations under international law.

2. No derogation from Article 2, except in respect of deaths resulting from lawful acts of war, or from Articles 3, 4 (paragraph 1) and 7 shall be made under this provision.

3. Any High Contracting Party availing itself of this right of derogation shall keep the Secretary General of the Council of Europe fully informed of the measures which it has taken and the reasons therefor. It shall also inform the Secretary General of the Council of Europe when such measures have ceased to operate and the provisions of the Convention are again being fully executed.

Article 16

Nothing in Articles 10, 11 and 14 shall be regarded as preventing the High Contracting Parties from imposing restrictions on the political activity of aliens.

Article 17

Nothing in this Convention may be interpreted as implying for any State, group or person any right to engage in any activity or perform any act aimed at the destruction of any of the rights and freedoms set forth herein or at their limitation to a greater extent than is provided for in the Convention.

Article 18

The restrictions permitted under this Convention to the said rights and freedoms shall not be applied for any purpose other than those for which they have been prescribed.

Part IV

Civil Proceedings—Statutes and Rules

Civil Evidence Act 1968

(1968, c. 64)

11 Convictions as evidence in civil proceedings

(1) In any civil proceedings the fact that a person has been convicted of an offence by or before any court in the United Kingdom or by a court-martial there or elsewhere shall (subject to subsection (3) below) be admissible in evidence for the purpose of proving, where to do so is relevant to any issue in those proceedings, that he committed that offence, whether he was so convicted upon a plea of guilty or otherwise and whether or not he is a party to the civil proceedings; but no conviction other than a subsisting one shall be admissible in evidence by virtue of this section.

(2) In any civil proceedings in which by virtue of this section a person is proved to have been convicted of an offence by or before any court in the United Kingdom or by a court-martial there or elsewhere—

    (a) he shall be taken to have committed that offence unless the contrary is proved; and

    (b) without prejudice to the reception of any other admissible evidence for the purpose of identifying the facts on which the conviction was based, the contents of any document which is admissible as evidence of the conviction, and the contents of the information, complaint, indictment or charge-sheet on which the person in question was convicted, shall be admissible in evidence for that purpose.

(3) Nothing in this section shall prejudice the operation of section 13 of this Act or any other enactment whereby a conviction or a finding of fact in any criminal proceedings is for the purposes of any other proceedings made conclusive evidence of any fact.

(4) Where in any civil proceedings the contents of any document are admissible in evidence by virtue of subsection (2) above, a copy of that document, or of the material part thereof, purporting to be certified or otherwise authenticated by or on behalf of the court or authority having custody of that document shall be admissible in evidence and shall be taken to be a true copy of that document or part unless the contrary is shown.

(5) Nothing in any of the following enactments, that is to say—

    (a) section 14 of the Powers of Criminal Courts (Sentencing) Act 2000 (under which a conviction leading to discharge is to be disregarded except as therein mentioned);

    (aa) section 187 of the Armed Forces Act 2006 (which makes similar provision in respect of service convictions);

    (b) section 191 of the Criminal Procedure (Scotland) Act 1975 (which makes similar provision in respect of convictions on indictment in Scotland); and

    (c) section 8 of the Probation Act (Northern Ireland) 1950 (which corresponds to the said section 12) or any corresponding enactment of the Parliament of Northern Ireland for the time being in force, shall affect the operation of this section; and for the purposes of this section any order made by a court of summary jurisdiction in Scotland under section 383 or section 384 of the said Act of 1975 shall be treated as a conviction.

(7) In this section—

"service offence" has the same meaning as in the Armed Forces Act 2006;

"conviction" includes anything that under section 376(1) and (2) of that Act is to be treated as a conviction, and "convicted" is to be read accordingly.

12 Findings of adultery and paternity as evidence in civil proceedings

(1) In any civil proceedings—

    (a) the fact that a person has been found guilty of adultery in any matrimonial proceedings; and

    (b) the fact that a person has been found to be the father of a child in relevant proceedings before any court in England and Wales or Northern Ireland or has been adjudged to be the father of a child in affiliation proceedings before any court in the United Kingdom;

shall (subject to subsection (3) below) be admissible in evidence for the purpose of proving, where to do so is relevant to any issue in those civil proceedings, that he committed the adultery to which the finding relates or, as the case may be, is (or was) the father of that child, whether or not he offered any defence to the allegation of adultery or paternity and whether or not he is a party to the civil proceedings; but no finding or adjudication other than a subsisting one shall be admissible in evidence by virtue of this section.

(2) In any civil proceedings in which by virtue of this section a person is proved to have been found guilty of adultery as mentioned in subsection (1)(a) above or to have been found or adjudged to be the father of a child as mentioned in subsection (1)(b) above—

    (a) he shall be taken to have committed the adultery to which the finding relates or, as the case may be, to be (or have been) the father of that child, unless the contrary is proved; and

    (b) without prejudice to the reception of any other admissible evidence for the purpose of identifying the facts on which the finding or adjudication was based, the contents of any document which was before the court, or which contains any pronouncement of the court, in the other proceedings] in question shall be admissible in evidence for that purpose.

(3) Nothing in this section shall prejudice the operation of any enactment whereby a finding of fact in any matrimonial or affiliation proceedings is for the purposes of any other proceedings made conclusive evidence of any fact.

(4) Subsection (4) of section 11 of this Act shall apply for the purposes of this section as if the reference to subsection (2) were a reference to subsection (2) of this section.

(5) In this section—

"matrimonial proceedings " means any matrimonial cause in the High Court or a county court in England and Wales or in the High Court in Northern Ireland, any consistorial action in Scotland, or any appeal arising out of any such cause or action;

"relevant proceedings " means—

    (a) proceedings on a complaint under section 42 of the National Assistance Act 1948 or section 26 of the Social Security Act 1986;

    (b) proceedings under the Children Act 1989;

    (c) proceedings which would have been relevant proceedings for the purposes of this section in the form in which it was in force before the passing of the Children Act 1989.

13 Conclusiveness of convictions for purposes of defamation actions

(1) In an action for libel or slander in which the question whether the plaintiff did or did not commit a criminal offence is relevant to an issue arising in the action, proof that, at the time when that issue falls to be determined, he stands convicted of that offence shall be conclusive evidence that he committed that offence; and his conviction thereof shall be admissible in evidence accordingly.

(2) In any such action as aforesaid in which by virtue of this section the plaintiff is proved to have been convicted of an offence, the contents of any document which is admissible as evidence of the conviction, and the contents of the information, complaint, indictment or charge-sheet on which he was convicted, shall, without prejudice to the reception of any other admissible evidence for the purpose of identifying the facts on which the conviction was based, be admissible in evidence for the purpose of identifying those facts.

(2A) In the case of an action for libel or slander in which there is more than one plaintiff—

   (a) the references in subsections (1) and (2) above to the plaintiff shall be construed as references to any of the plaintiffs, and

   (b) proof that any of the plaintiffs stands convicted of an offence shall be conclusive evidence that he committed that offence so far as that fact is relevant to any issue arising in relation to his cause of action or that of any other plaintiff.]

(3) For the purposes of this section a person shall be taken to stand convicted of an offence if but only if there subsists against him a conviction of that offence by or before a court in the United Kingdom or by a court-martial there or elsewhere.

(4) Subsections (4) to (7) of section 11 of this Act shall apply for the purposes of this section as they apply for the purposes of that section, but as if in the said subsection (4) the reference to subsection (2) were a reference to subsection (2) of this section.

(5) The foregoing provisions of this section shall apply for the purposes of any action begun after the passing of this Act, whenever the cause of action arose, but shall not apply for the purposes of any action begun before the passing of this Act or any appeal or other proceedings arising out of any such action.

Civil Evidence Act 1972

(1972, c. 30)

3. Admissibility of expert opinion and certain expressions of non-expert opinion

(1) Subject to any rules of court made in pursuance of . . . this Act, where a person is called as a witness in any civil proceedings, his opinion on any relevant matter on which he is qualified to give expert evidence shall be admissible in evidence.

(2) It is hereby declared that where a person is called as a witness in any civil proceedings, a statement of opinion by him on any relevant matter on which he is not qualified to give expert evidence, if made as a way of conveying relevant facts personally perceived by him, is admissible as evidence of what he perceived.

(3) In this section "relevant matter" includes an issue in the proceedings in question.

Children Act 1989

(1989, c. 41)

96 Evidence given by, or with respect to, children

(1) Subsection (2) applies where a child who is called as a witness in any civil proceedings does not, in the opinion of the court, understand the nature of an oath.

(2) The child's evidence may be heard by the court if, in its opinion—

   (a) he understands that it is his duty to speak the truth; and

   (b) he has sufficient understanding to justify his evidence being heard.

(3) The Lord Chancellor may by order make provision for the admissibility of evidence which would otherwise be inadmissible under any rule of law relating to hearsay.

(4) An order under subsection (3) may only be made with respect to—

    (a) civil proceedings in general or such civil proceedings, or class of civil proceedings, as may be prescribed; and

    (b) evidence in connection with the upbringing, maintenance or welfare of a child.

(5) An order under subsection (3)—

    (a) may, in particular, provide for the admissibility of statements which are made orally or in a prescribed form or which are recorded by any prescribed method of recording;

    (b) may make different provision for different purposes and in relation to different descriptions of court; and

    (c) may make such amendments and repeals in any enactment relating to evidence (other than in this Act) as the Lord Chancellor considers necessary or expedient in consequence of the provision made by the order.

(6) Subsection (5)(b) is without prejudice to section 104(4).

(7) In this section—

'civil proceedings' means civil proceedings, before any tribunal, in relation to which the strict rules of evidence apply, whether as a matter of law or agreement between the parties, and reference to 'the court' shall be construed accordingly; and

'prescribed' means prescribed by an order under subsection (3).

98   Self-incrimination

(1) In any proceedings in which a court is hearing an application for an order under Part IV or V, no person shall be excused from—

    (a) giving evidence on any matter; or

    (b) answering any question put to him in the course of his giving evidence,

on the ground that doing so might incriminate him or his spouse of an offence.

(2) A statement or admission made in such proceedings shall not be admissible in evidence against the person making it or his spouse in proceedings for an offence other than perjury.

Civil Evidence Act 1995

(1995, c. 38)

Admissibility of hearsay evidence

1   Admissibility of hearsay evidence

(1) In civil proceedings evidence shall not be excluded on the ground that it is hearsay.

(2) In this Act—

    (a) 'hearsay' means a statement made otherwise than by a person while giving oral evidence in the proceedings which is tendered as evidence of the matters stated; and

    (b) references to hearsay include hearsay of whatever degree.

(3) Nothing in this Act affects the admissibility of evidence admissible apart from this section.

(4) The provisions of sections 2 to 6 (safeguards and supplementary provisions relating to hearsay evidence) do not apply in relation to hearsay evidence admissible apart from this section, notwithstanding that it may also be admissible by virtue of this section.

Safeguards in relation to hearsay evidence

2   Notice of proposal to adduce hearsay evidence

(1) A party proposing to adduce hearsay evidence in civil proceedings shall, subject to the following provisions of this section, give to the other party or parties to the proceedings—

    (a) such notice (if any) of that fact, and

    (b) on request, such particulars of or relating to the evidence,

as is reasonable and practicable in the circumstances for the purpose of enabling him or them to deal with any matters arising from its being hearsay.

(2) Provision may be made by rules of court—

(a) specifying classes of proceedings or evidence in relation to which subsection (1) does not apply, and

(b) as to the manner in which (including the time within which) the duties imposed by that subsection are to be complied with in the cases where it does apply.

(3) Subsection (1) may also be excluded by agreement of the parties; and compliance with the duty to give notice may in any case be waived by the person to whom notice is required to be given.

(4) A failure to comply with subsection (1), or with rules under subsection (2)(b), does not affect the admissibility of the evidence but may be taken into account by the court—

(a) in considering the exercise of its powers with respect to the course of proceedings and costs, and

(b) as a matter adversely affecting the weight to be given to the evidence in accordance with section 4.

3   Power to call witness for cross-examination on hearsay statement

Rules of court may provide that where a party to civil proceedings adduces hearsay evidence of a statement made by a person and does not call that person as a witness, any other party to the proceedings may, with the leave of the court, call that person as a witness and cross-examine him on the statement as if he had been called by the first-mentioned party and as if the hearsay statement were his evidence in chief.

4   Considerations relevant to weighing of hearsay evidence

(1) In estimating the weight (if any) to be given to hearsay evidence in civil proceedings the court shall have regard to any circumstances from which any inference can reasonably be drawn as to the reliability or otherwise of the evidence.

(2) Regard may be had, in particular, to the following—

(a) whether it would have been reasonable and practicable for the party by whom the evidence was adduced to have produced the maker of the original statement as a witness;

(b) whether the original statement was made contemporaneously with the occurrence or existence of the matters stated;

(c) whether the evidence involves multiple hearsay;

(d) whether any person involved had any motive to conceal or misrepresent matters;

(e) whether the original statement was an edited account, or was made in collaboration with another or for a particular purpose;

(f) whether the circumstances in which the evidence is adduced as hearsay are such as to suggest an attempt to prevent proper evaluation of its weight.

Supplementary provisions as to hearsay evidence

5   Competence and credibility

(1) Hearsay evidence shall not be admitted in civil proceedings if or to the extent that it is shown to consist of, or to be proved by means of, a statement made by a person who at the time he made the statement was not competent as a witness.

For this purpose 'not competent as a witness' means suffering from such mental or physical infirmity, or lack of understanding, as would render a person incompetent as a witness in civil proceedings; but a child shall be treated as competent as a witness if he satisfies the requirements of section 96(2)(a) and (b) of the Children Act 1989 (conditions for reception of unsworn evidence of child).

(2) Where in civil proceedings hearsay evidence is adduced and the maker of the original statement, or of any statement relied upon to prove another statement, is not called as a witness—

(a) evidence which if he had been so called would be admissible for the purpose of attacking or supporting his credibility as a witness is admissible for that purpose in the proceedings; and

(b) evidence tending to prove that, whether before or after he made the statement, he made any other statement inconsistent with it is admissible for the purpose of showing that he had contradicted himself.

Provided that evidence may not be given of any matter of which, if he had been called as a witness and had denied that matter in cross-examination, evidence could not have been adduced by the cross-examining party.

6   Previous statements of witnesses

(1) Subject as follows, the provisions of this Act as to hearsay evidence in civil proceedings apply equally (but with any necessary modifications) in relation to a previous statement made by a person called as a witness in the proceedings.

(2) A party who has called or intends to call a person as a witness in civil proceedings may not in those proceedings adduce evidence of a previous statement made by that person, except—

(a) with the leave of the court, or

(b) for the purpose of rebutting a suggestion that his evidence has been fabricated.

This shall not be construed as preventing a witness statement (that is, a written statement of oral evidence which a party to the proceedings intends to lead) from being adopted by a witness in giving evidence or treated as his evidence.

(3) Where in the case of civil proceedings section 3, 4 or 5 of the Criminal Procedure Act 1865 applies, which make provision as to—

(a) how far a witness may be discredited by the party producing him,

(b) the proof of contradictory statements made by a witness, and

(c) cross-examination as to previous statements in writing,

this Act does not authorise the adducing of evidence of a previous inconsistent or contradictory statement otherwise than in accordance with those sections.

This is without prejudice to any provision made by rules of court under section 3 above (power to call witness for cross-examination on hearsay statement).

(4) Nothing in this Act affects any of the rules of law as to the circumstances in which, where a person called as a witness in civil proceedings is cross-examined on a document used by him to refresh his memory, that document may be made evidence in the proceedings.

(5) Nothing in this section shall be construed as preventing a statement of any description referred to above from being admissible by virtue of section 1 as evidence of the matters stated.

7   Evidence formerly admissible at common law

(1) The common law rule effectively preserved by section 9(1) and (2)(a) of the Civil Evidence Act 1968 (admissibility of admissions adverse to a party) is superseded by the provisions of this Act.

(2) The common law rules effectively preserved by section 9(1) and (2)(b) to (d) of the Civil Evidence Act 1968, that is, any rule of law whereby in civil proceedings—

(a) published works dealing with matters of a public nature (for example, histories, scientific works, dictionaries and maps) are admissible as evidence of facts of a public nature stated in them,

(b) public documents (for example, public registers, and returns made under public authority with respect to matters of public interest) are admissible as evidence of facts stated in them, or

(c) records (for example, the records of certain courts, treaties, Crown grants, pardons and commissions) are admissible as evidence of facts stated in them, shall continue to have effect.

(3) The common law rules effectively preserved by section 9(3) and (4) of the Civil Evidence Act 1968, that is, any rule of law whereby in civil proceedings—

(a) evidence of a person's reputation is admissible for the purpose of proving his good or bad character, or

(b) evidence of reputation or family tradition is admissible—

(i)   for the purpose of proving or disproving pedigree or the existence of a marriage, or

  (ii) for the purpose of proving or disproving the existence of any public or general right or of identifying any person or thing,

shall continue to have effect in so far as they authorise the court to treat such evidence as proving or disproving that matter.

 Where any such rule applies, reputation or family tradition shall be treated for the purposes of this Act as a fact and not as a statement or multiplicity of statements about the matter in question.

 (4) The words in which a rule of law mentioned in this section is described are intended only to identify the rule and shall not be construed as altering it in any way.

Other matters

8 Proof of statements contained in documents

 (1) Where a statement contained in a document is admissible as evidence in civil proceedings, it may be proved—

  (a) by the production of that document, or

  (b) whether or not that document is still in existence, by the production of a copy of that document or of the material part of it,

authenticated in such manner as the court may approve.

 (2) It is immaterial for this purpose how many removes there are between a copy and the original.

9 Proof of records of business or public authority

 (1) A document which is shown to form part of the records of a business or public authority may be received in evidence in civil proceedings without further proof.

 (2) A document shall be taken to form part of the records of a business or public authority if there is produced to the court a certificate to that effect signed by an officer of the business or authority to which the records belong.

 For this purpose—

  (a) a document purporting to be a certificate signed by an officer of a business or public authority shall be deemed to have been duly given by such an officer and signed by him; and

  (b) a certificate shall be treated as signed by a person if it purports to bear a facsimile of his signature.

 (3) The absence of an entry in the records of a business or public authority may be proved in civil proceedings by affidavit of an officer of the business or authority to which the records belong.

 (4) In this section—

'records' means records in whatever form;

'business' includes any activity regularly carried on over a period of time, whether for profit or not, by any body (whether corporate or not) or by an individual;

'officer' includes any person occupying a responsible position in relation to the relevant activities of the business or public authority or in relation to its records; and

'public authority' includes any public or statutory undertaking, any government department and any person holding office under Her Majesty.

 (5) The court may, having regard to the circumstances of the case, direct that all or any of the above provisions of this section do not apply in relation to a particular document or record, or description of documents or records.

10 Admissibility and proof of Ogden Tables

 (1) The actuarial tables (together with explanatory notes) for use in personal injury and fatal accident cases issued from time to time by the Government Actuary's Department are admissible in evidence for the purpose of assessing, in an action for personal injury, the sum to be awarded as general damages for future pecuniary loss.

 (2) They may be proved by the production of a copy published by Her Majesty's Stationery Office.

(3) For the purposes of this section—

    (a) 'personal injury' includes any disease and any impairment of a person's physical or mental condition; and

    (b) 'action for personal injury' includes an action brought by virtue of the Law Reform (Miscellaneous Provisions) Act 1934 or the Fatal Accidents Act 1976.

General

11 Meaning of 'civil proceedings'

In this Act 'civil proceedings' means civil proceedings, before any tribunal, in relation to which the strict rules of evidence apply, whether as a matter of law or by agreement of the parties.

References to 'the court' and 'rules of court' shall be construed accordingly.

12 Provisions as to rules of court

(1) Any power to make rules of court regulating the practice or procedure of the court in relation to civil proceedings includes power to make such provision as may be necessary or expedient for carrying into effect the provisions of this Act.

(2) Any rules of court made for the purposes of this Act as it applies in relation to proceedings in the High Court apply, except in so far as their operation is excluded by agreement, to arbitration proceedings to which this Act applies, subject to such modifications as may be appropriate.

Any question arising as to what modifications are appropriate shall be determined, in default of agreement, by the arbitrator or umpire, as the case may be.

13 Interpretation

In this Act—

'civil proceedings' has the meaning given by section 11 and 'court' and 'rules of court' shall be construed in accordance with that section;

'document' means anything in which information of any description is recorded, and 'copy', in relation to a document, means anything onto which information recorded in the document has been copied, by whatever means and whether directly or indirectly;

'hearsay' shall be construed in accordance with section 1(2);

'oral evidence' includes evidence which, by reason of a defect of speech or hearing, a person called as a witness gives in writing or by signs;

'the original statement', in relation to hearsay evidence, means the underlying statement (if any) by—

    (a) in the case of evidence of fact, a person having personal knowledge of the fact, or

    (b) in the case of evidence of opinion, the person whose opinion it is; and

'statement' means any representation of fact or opinion, however made.

14 Savings

(1) Nothing in this Act affects the exclusion of evidence on grounds other than that it is hearsay.

This applies whether the evidence falls to be excluded in pursuance of any enactment or rule of law, for failure to comply with rules of court or an order of the court, or otherwise.

(2) Nothing in this Act affects the proof of documents by means other than those specified in section 8 or 9.

(3) Nothing in this Act affects the operation of the following enactments—

    (a) section 2 of the Documentary Evidence Act 1868 (mode of proving certain official documents);

    (b) section 2 of the Documentary Evidence Act 1882 (documents printed under the superintendence of Stationery Office);

    (c) section 1 of the Evidence (Colonial Statutes) Act 1907 (proof of statutes of certain legislatures);

    (d) section 1 of the Evidence (Foreign, Dominion and Colonial Documents) Act 1933 (proof and effect of registers and official certificates of certain countries);

(e) section 5 of the Oaths and Evidence (Overseas Authorities and Countries) Act 1963 (provision in respect of public registers of other countries).

16   Short title commencement and extent

(1) This Act may be cited as the Civil Evidence Act 1995.

(4) This Act extends to England and Wales.

Civil Partnership Act 2004

(2004, c. 33)

84   Evidence

(1) Any enactment or rule of law relating to the giving of evidence by a spouse applies in relation to a civil partner as it applies in relation to the spouse.

(2) Subsection (1) is subject to any specific amendment made by or under this Act which relates to the giving of evidence by a civil partner.

(3) For the avoidance of doubt, in any such amendment, references to a person's civil partner do not include a former civil partner.

(4) References in subsections (1) and (2) to giving evidence are to giving evidence in any way (whether by supplying information, making discovery, producing documents or otherwise).

(5) Any rule of law—

(a) which is preserved by section 7(3) of the Civil Evidence Act 1995 or section 118(1) of the Criminal Justice Act 2003, and

(b) under which in any proceedings evidence of reputation or family tradition is admissible for the purpose of proving or disproving the existence of a marriage,

is to be treated as applying in an equivalent way for the purpose of proving or disproving the existence of a civil partnership.

Civil Procedure Rules 1998

(SI 1998, No. 3132 (L. 17))

32.1   Power of court to control evidence

(1) The court may control the evidence by giving directions as to—

(a) the issues on which it requires evidence;

(b) the nature of the evidence which it requires to decide those issues; and

(c) the way in which the evidence is to be placed before the court.

(2) The court may use its power under this rule to exclude evidence that would otherwise be admissible.

(3) The court may limit cross-examination.

32.2   Evidence of witnesses—general rule

(1) The general rule is that any fact which needs to be proved by the evidence of witnesses is to be proved—

(a) at trial, by their oral evidence given in public; and

(b) at any other hearing, by their evidence in writing.

(2) This is subject—

(a) to any provision to the contrary contained in these Rules or elsewhere; or

(b) to any order of the court.

32.3   Evidence by video link or other means

The court may allow a witness to give evidence through a video link or by other means.

32.4 Requirement to serve witness statements for use at trial

(1) A witness statement is a written statement signed by a person which contains the evidence which that person would be allowed to give orally.

(2) The court will order a party to serve on the other parties any witness statement of the oral evidence which the party serving the statement intends to rely on in relation to any issues of fact to be decided at the trial.

(3) The court may give directions as to—

(a) the order in which witness statements are to be served; and

(b) whether or not the witness statements are to be filed.

32.5 Use at trial of witness statements which have been served

(1) If—

(a) a party has served a witness statement; and

(b) he wishes to rely at trial on the evidence of the witness who made the statement,

he must call the witness to give oral evidence unless the court orders otherwise or he puts the statement in as hearsay evidence.

(Part 33 contains provisions about hearsay evidence)

(2) Where a witness is called to give oral evidence under paragraph (1), his witness statement shall stand as his evidence in chief unless the court orders otherwise.

(3) A witness giving oral evidence at trial may with the permission of the court—

(a) amplify his witness statement; and

(b) give evidence in relation to new matters which have arisen since the witness statement was served on the other parties.

(4) The court will give permission under paragraph (3) only if it considers that there is good reason not to confine the evidence of the witness to the contents of his witness statement.

(5) If a party who has served a witness statement does not—

(a) call the witness to give evidence at trial; or

(b) put the witness statement in as hearsay evidence, any other party may put the witness statement in as hearsay evidence.

32.6 Evidence in proceedings other than at trial

(1) Subject to paragraph (2), the general rule is that evidence at hearings other than the trial is to be by witness statement unless the court, a practice direction or any other enactment requires otherwise.

(2) At hearings other than the trial, a party may, rely on the matters set out in—

(a) his statement of case; or

(b) his application notice, if the statement of case or application notice is verified by a statement of truth.

32.7 Order for cross-examination

(1) Where, at a hearing other than the trial, evidence is given in writing, any party may apply to the court for permission to cross-examine the person giving the evidence.

(2) If the court gives permission under paragraph (1) but the person in question does not attend as required by the order, his evidence may not be used unless the court gives permission.

32.8 Form of witness statement

A witness statement must comply with the requirements set out in Practice Direction 32.

(Part 22 requires a witness statement to be verified by a statement of truth)

32.9 Witness summaries

(1) A party who—

(a) is required to serve a witness statement for use at trial; but

(b) is unable to obtain one, may apply, without notice, for permission to serve a witness summary instead.

(2) A witness summary is a summary of—

    (a) the evidence, if known, which would otherwise be included in a witness statement; or

    (b) if the evidence is not known, the matters about which the party serving the witness summary proposes to question the witness.

(3) Unless the court orders otherwise, a witness summary must include the name and address of the intended witness.

(4) Unless the court orders otherwise, a witness summary must be served within the period in which a witness statement would have had to be served.

(5) Where a party serves a witness summary, so far as practicable rules 32.4 (requirement to serve witness statements for use at trial), 32.5(3) (amplifying witness statements), and 32.8 (form of witness statement) shall apply to the summary.

32.10   Consequence of failure to serve witness statement or summary

If a witness statement or a witness summary for use at trial is not served in respect of an intended witness within the time specified by the court, then the witness may not be called to give oral evidence unless the court gives permission.

32.11   Cross-examination on a witness statement

Where a witness is called to give evidence at trial, he may be cross-examined on his witness statement whether or not the statement or any part of it was referred to during the witness's evidence in chief.

32.12   Use of witness statements for other purposes

(1) Except as provided by this rule, a witness statement may be used only for the purpose of the proceedings in which it is served.

(2) Paragraph (1) does not apply if and to the extent that—

    (a) the witness gives consent in writing to some other use of it;

    (b) the court gives permission for some other use; or

    (c) the witness statement has been put in evidence at a hearing held in public.

32.13   Availability of witness statements for inspection

(1) A witness statement which stands as evidence in chief is open to inspection during the course of the trial unless the court otherwise directs.

(2) Any person may ask for a direction that a witness statement is not open to inspection.

(3) The court will not make a direction under paragraph (2) unless it is satisfied that a witness statement should not be open to inspection because of—

    (a) the interests of justice;

    (b) the public interest;

    (c) the nature of any expert medical evidence in the statement;

    (d) the nature of any confidential information (including information relating to personal financial matters) in the statement; or

    (e) the need to protect the interests of any child or protected party.

(4) The court may exclude from inspection words or passages in the statement.

32.14   False statements

(1) Proceedings for contempt of court may be brought against a person if he makes, or causes to be made, a false statement in a document verified by a statement of truth without an honest belief in its truth.

(Part 22 makes provision for a statement of truth)

(2) Proceedings under this rule may be brought only—

    (a) by the Attorney General; or

    (b) with the permission of the court.

32.15   Affidavit evidence

(1) Evidence must be given by affidavit instead of or in addition to a witness statement if this is required by the court, a provision contained in any other rule, a practice direction or any other enactment.

(2) Nothing in these Rules prevents a witness giving evidence by affidavit at a hearing other than the trial if he chooses to do so in a case where paragraph (1) does not apply, but the party putting forward the affidavit may not recover the additional cost of making it from any other party unless the court orders otherwise.

32.16   Form of affidavit

An affidavit must comply with the requirements set out in Practice Direction 32.

32.17   Affidavit made outside the jurisdiction

A person may make an affidavit outside the jurisdiction in accordance with—

(a) this Part; or

(b) the law of the place where he makes the affidavit.

32.18   Notice to admit facts

(1) A party may serve notice on another party requiring him to admit the facts, or the part of the case of the serving party, specified in the notice.

(2) A notice to admit facts must be served no later than 21 days before the trial.

(3) Where the other party makes any admission in response to the notice, the admission may be used against him only—

(a) in the proceedings in which the notice to admit is served; and

(b) by the party who served the notice.

(4) The court may allow a party to amend or withdraw any admission made by him on such terms as it thinks just.

32.19   Notice to admit or produce documents

(1) A party shall be deemed to admit the authenticity of a document disclosed to him under Part 31 (disclosure and inspection of documents) unless he serves notice that he wishes the document to be proved at trial.

(2) A notice to prove a document must be served—

(a) by the latest date for serving witness statements; or

(b) within 7 days of disclosure of the document,

whichever is later.

32.20   Notarial acts and instruments

A notarial act or instrument may be received in evidence without further proof as duly authenticated in accordance with the requirements of law unless the contrary is proved.

PD 32 PRACTICE DIRECTION

WRITTEN EVIDENCE

EVIDENCE IN GENERAL

1.1

Rule 32.2 sets out how evidence is to be given and facts are to be proved.

1.2

Evidence at a hearing other than the trial should normally be given by witness statement (see paragraph 17 onwards). However a witness may give evidence by affidavit if he wishes to do so (and see paragraph 1.4 below).

1.3

Statements of case (see paragraph 26 onwards) and application notices may also be used as evidence provided that their contents have been verified by a statement of truth.

(For information regarding evidence by deposition see Part 34 and Practice Direction 34A.)

1.4

Affidavits must be used as evidence in the following instances:

(1) where sworn evidence is required by an enactment, rule, order or practice direction,

(2) in any application for a search order, a freezing injunction, or an order requiring an occupier to permit another to enter his land, and

(3) in any application for an order against anyone for alleged contempt of court.

1.5

If a party believes that sworn evidence is required by a court in another jurisdiction for any purpose connected with the proceedings, he may apply to the court for a direction that evidence shall be given only by affidavit on any pre-trial applications.

1.6

The court may give a direction under rule 32.15 that evidence shall be given by affidavit instead of or in addition to a witness statement or statement of case:

(1) on its own initiative, or

(2) after any party has applied to the court for such a direction.

1.7

An affidavit, where referred to in the Civil Procedure Rules or a practice direction, also means an affirmation unless the context requires otherwise.

AFFIDAVITS

Deponent

2

A deponent is a person who gives evidence by affidavit or affirmation.

Heading

3.1

The affidavit should be headed with the title of the proceedings (see paragraph 4 of Practice Direction 7A and paragraph 7 of Practice Direction 20); where the proceedings are between several parties with the same status it is sufficient to identify the parties as follows:

	Number:
A.B. (and others)	Claimants/Applicants
C.D. (and others)	Defendants/Respondents
	(as appropriate)

3.2

At the top right hand corner of the first page (and on the backsheet) there should be clearly written:

(1) the party on whose behalf it is made,

(2) the initials and surname of the deponent,

(3) the number of the affidavit in relation to that deponent,

(4) the identifying initials and number of each exhibit referred to, and

(5) the date sworn.

Body of Affidavit

4.1

The affidavit must, if practicable, be in the deponent's own words, the affidavit should be expressed in the first person and the deponent should:

(1) commence 'I (*full name*) of (*address*) state on oath......',

(2) if giving evidence in his professional, business or other occupational capacity, give the address at which he works in (1) above, the position he holds and the name of his firm or employer,

(3) give his occupation or, if he has none, his description, and

(4) state if he is a party to the proceedings or employed by a party to the proceedings, if it be the case.

4.2

An affidavit must indicate:

(1) which of the statements in it are made from the deponent's own knowledge and which are matters of information or belief, and

(2) the source for any matters of information or belief.

4.3

Where a deponent:

(1) refers to an exhibit or exhibits, he should state 'there is now shown to me marked '...' the (*description of exhibit*)', and

(2) makes more than one affidavit (to which there are exhibits) in the same proceedings, the numbering of the exhibits should run consecutively throughout and not start again with each affidavit.

Jurat

5.1

The jurat of an affidavit is a statement set out at the end of the document which authenticates the affidavit.

5.2

It must:

(1) be signed by all deponents,

(2) be completed and signed by the person before whom the affidavit was sworn whose name and qualification must be printed beneath his signature,

(3) contain the full address of the person before whom the affidavit was sworn, and

(4) follow immediately on from the text and not be put on a separate page.

Format of Affidavits

6.1

An affidavit should:

(1) be produced on durable quality A4 paper with a 3.5cm margin,

(2) be fully legible and should normally be typed on one side of the paper only,

(3) where possible, be bound securely in a manner which would not hamper filing, or otherwise each page should be endorsed with the case number and should bear the initials of the deponent and of the person before whom it was sworn,

(4) have the pages numbered consecutively as a separate document (or as one of several documents contained in a file),

(5) be divided into numbered paragraphs,

(6) have all numbers, including dates, expressed in figures, and

(7) give the reference to any document or documents mentioned either in the margin or in bold text in the body of the affidavit.

6.2

It is usually convenient for an affidavit to follow the chronological sequence of events or matters dealt with; each paragraph of an affidavit should as far as possible be confined to a distinct portion of the subject.

Inability of Deponent to read or sign Affidavit

7.1

Where an affidavit is sworn by a person who is unable to read or sign it, the person before whom the affidavit is sworn must certify in the jurat that:

(1) he read the affidavit to the deponent,

(2) the deponent appeared to understand it, and

(3) the deponent signed or made his mark, in his presence.

7.2

If that certificate is not included in the jurat, the affidavit may not be used in evidence unless the court is satisfied that it was read to the deponent and that he appeared to understand it. Two versions of the form of jurat with the certificate are set out at Annex 1 to this practice direction.

Alterations to Affidavits

8.1

Any alteration to an affidavit must be initialled by both the deponent and the person before whom the affidavit was sworn.

8.2

An affidavit which contains an alteration that has not been initialled may be filed or used in evidence only with the permission of the court.

Who may administer oaths and take Affidavits

9.1

Only the following may administer oaths and take affidavits:

(1) A commissioner for oaths;

(2) omitted

(3) other persons specified by statute;

(4) certain officials of the Senior Courts;

(5) a circuit judge or district judge;

(6) any justice of the peace; and

(7) certain officials of any county court appointed by the judge of that court for the purpose.

9.2

An affidavit must be sworn before a person independent of the parties or their representatives.

Filing of Affidavits

10.1

If the court directs that an affidavit is to be filed, it must be filed in the court or Division, or Office or Registry of the court or Division where the action in which it was or is to be used, is proceeding or will proceed.

10.2

Where an affidavit is in a foreign language:

(1) the party wishing to rely on it—

(a) must have it translated, and

(b) must file the foreign language affidavit with the court, and

(2) the translator must make and file with the court an affidavit verifying the translation and exhibiting both the translation and a copy of the foreign language affidavit.

EXHIBITS

Manner of Exhibiting Documents

11.1

A document used in conjunction with an affidavit should be:

(1) produced to and verified by the deponent, and remain separate from the affidavit, and

(2) identified by a declaration of the person before whom the affidavit was sworn.

11.2

The declaration should be headed with the name of the proceedings in the same way as the affidavit.

11.3

The first page of each exhibit should be marked:

(1) as in paragraph 3.2 above, and

(2) with the exhibit mark referred to in the affidavit.

Letters

12.1

Copies of individual letters should be collected together and exhibited in a bundle or bundles. They should be arranged in chronological order with the earliest at the top, and firmly secured.

12.2

When a bundle of correspondence is exhibited, the exhibit should have a front page attached stating that the bundle consists of original letters and copies. They should be arranged and secured as above and numbered consecutively.

Other documents

13.1

Photocopies instead of original documents may be exhibited provided the originals are made available for inspection by the other parties before the hearing and by the judge at the hearing.

13.2

Court documents must not be exhibited (official copies of such documents prove themselves).

13.3

Where an exhibit contains more than one document, a front page should be attached setting out a list of the documents contained in the exhibit; the list should contain the dates of the documents.

Exhibits other than documents

14.1

Items other than documents should be clearly marked with an exhibit number or letter in such a manner that the mark cannot become detached from the exhibit.

14.2

Small items may be placed in a container and the container appropriately marked.

General provisions

15.1

Where an exhibit contains more than one document:

(1) the bundle should not be stapled but should be securely fastened in a way that does not hinder the reading of the documents, and

(2) the pages should be numbered consecutively at bottom centre.

15.2

Every page of an exhibit should be clearly legible; typed copies of illegible documents should be included, paginated with 'a' numbers.

15.3

Where affidavits and exhibits have become numerous, they should be put into separate bundles and the pages numbered consecutively throughout.

15.4

Where on account of their bulk the service of exhibits or copies of exhibits on the other parties would be difficult or impracticable, the directions of the court should be sought as to arrangements for bringing the exhibits to the attention of the other parties and as to their custody pending trial.

Affirmations

16

All provisions in this or any other practice direction relating to affidavits apply to affirmations with the following exceptions:

    (1) the deponent should commence 'I (*name*) of (*address*) do solemnly and sincerely affirm ......', and

    (2) in the jurat the word 'sworn' is replaced by the word 'affirmed'.

WITNESS STATEMENTS

Heading

17.1

The witness statement should be headed with the title of the proceedings (see paragraph 4 of Practice Direction 7A and paragraph 7 of Practice Direction 20); where the proceedings are between several parties with the same status it is sufficient to identify the parties as follows:

	Number:
A.B. (and others)	Claimants/Applicants
C.D. (and others)	Defendants/Respondents
	(as appropriate)

17.2

At the top right hand corner of the first page there should be clearly written:

    (1) the party on whose behalf it is made,

    (2) the initials and surname of the witness,

    (3) the number of the statement in relation to that witness,

    (4) the identifying initials and number of each exhibit referred to, and

    (5) the date the statement was made.

Body of Witness Statement

18.1

The witness statement must, if practicable, be in the intended witness's own words, the statement should be expressed in the first person and should also state:

    (1) the full name of the witness,

    (2) his place of residence or, if he is making the statement in his professional, business or other occupational capacity, the address at which he works, the position he holds and the name of his firm or employer,

    (3) his occupation, or if he has none, his description, and

    (4) the fact that he is a party to the proceedings or is the employee of such a party if it be the case.

18.2

A witness statement must indicate:

(1) which of the statements in it are made from the witness's own knowledge and which are matters of information or belief, and

(2) the source for any matters of information or belief.

18.3

An exhibit used in conjunction with a witness statement should be verified and identified by the witness and remain separate from the witness statement.

18.4

Where a witness refers to an exhibit or exhibits, he should state 'I refer to the (*description of exhibit*) marked '…''.

18.5

The provisions of paragraphs 11.3 to 15.4 (exhibits) apply similarly to witness statements as they do to affidavits.

18.6

Where a witness makes more than one witness statement to which there are exhibits, in the same proceedings, the numbering of the exhibits should run consecutively throughout and not start again with each witness statement.

Format of Witness Statement

19.1

A witness statement should:

(1) be produced on durable quality A4 paper with a 3.5cm margin,

(2) be fully legible and should normally be typed on one side of the paper only,

(3) where possible, be bound securely in a manner which would not hamper filing, or otherwise each page should be endorsed with the case number and should bear the initials of the witness,

(4) have the pages numbered consecutively as a separate statement (or as one of several statements contained in a file),

(5) be divided into numbered paragraphs,

(6) have all numbers, including dates, expressed in figures, and

(7) give the reference to any document or documents mentioned either in the margin or in bold text in the body of the statement.

19.2

It is usually convenient for a witness statement to follow the chronological sequence of the events or matters dealt with, each paragraph of a witness statement should as far as possible be confined to a distinct portion of the subject.

Statement of Truth

20.1

A witness statement is the equivalent of the oral evidence which that witness would, if called, give in evidence; it must include a statement by the intended witness that he believes the facts in it are true.

20.2

To verify a witness statement the statement of truth is as follows:

'I believe that the facts stated in this witness statement are true'.

20.3

Attention is drawn to rule 32.14 which sets out the consequences of verifying a witness statement containing a false statement without an honest belief in its truth.

(Paragraph 3A of Practice Direction 22 sets out the procedure to be followed where the person who should sign a document which is verified by a statement of truth is unable to read or sign the document.)

21
Omitted

Alterations to witness statements

22.1
Any alteration to a witness statement must be initialled by the person making the statement or by the authorised person where appropriate (see paragraph 21).

22.2
A witness statement which contains an alteration that has not been initialled may be used in evidence only with the permission of the court.

Filing of witness statements

23.1
If the court directs that a witness statement is to be filed, it must be filed in the court or Division, or Office or Registry of the court or Division where the action in which it was or is to be used, is proceeding or will proceed.

23.2
Where the court has directed that a witness statement in a foreign language is to be filed:
    (1) the party wishing to rely on it must—
        (a) have it translated, and
        (b) file the foreign language witness statement with the court, and
    (2) the translator must make and file with the court an affidavit verifying the translation and exhibiting both the translation and a copy of the foreign language witness statement.

Certificate of court officer

24.1
Where the court has ordered that a witness statement is not to be open to inspection by the public or that words or passages in the statement are not to be open to inspection the court officer will so certify on the statement and make any deletions directed by the court under rule 32.13(4).

Defects in affidavits, witness statements and exhibits

25.1
Where:
    (1) an affidavit,
    (2) a witness statement, or
    (3) an exhibit to either an affidavit or a witness statement,
does not comply with Part 32 or this practice direction in relation to its form, the court may refuse to admit it as evidence and may refuse to allow the costs arising from its preparation.

25.2
Permission to file a defective affidavit or witness statement or to use a defective exhibit may be obtained from a judge in the court where the case is proceeding.

STATEMENTS OF CASE

26.1
A statement of case may be used as evidence in an interim application provided it is verified by a statement of truth.

26.2

To verify a statement of case the statement of truth should be set out as follows:

'[I believe] [the *(party on whose behalf the statement of case is being signed)* believes] that the facts stated in the statement of case are true'.

26.3

Attention is drawn to rule 32.14 which sets out the consequences of verifying a witness statement containing a false statement without an honest belief in its truth.

(For information regarding statements of truth see Part 22 and Practice Direction 22.)

(Practice Directions 7A and 17 provide further information concerning statements of case.)

AGREED BUNDLES FOR HEARINGS

27.1

The court may give directions requiring the parties to use their best endeavours to agree a bundle or bundles of documents for use at any hearing.

27.2

All documents contained in bundles which have been agreed for use at a hearing shall be admissible at that hearing as evidence of their contents, unless—

    (1) the court orders otherwise; or

    (2) a party gives written notice of objection to the admissibility of particular documents.

Penalty

28.1

(1) Where a party alleges that a statement of truth or a disclosure statement is false the party must refer that allegation to the court dealing with the claim in which the statement of truth or disclosure statement has been made.

(2) The court may—

    (a) excercise any of its powers under the rules;

    (b) initiate steps to consider if there is a contempt of court and, where there is, to punish it;

(Practice Direction RSC Order 52 and CCR 29 makes provision where committal to prison is a possibility if contempt is proved)

    (c) direct the party making the allegation to refer the matter to the Attorney General with a request that the Attorney General consider whether to bring proceedings for contempt of court.

28.2

    (1) A request to the Attorney General must be made in writing and sent to the Attorney General's Office at 20 Victoria Street, London, SW1H 0NF. The request must be accompanied by a copy of the order directing that the matter be referred to the Attorney General and must—

        (a) identify the statement said to be false;

        (b) explain—

            (i) why it is false; and

            (ii) why the maker knew the statement to be false at the time it was made; and

        (c) explain why contempt proceedings would be appropriate in the light of the overriding objective in Part 1.

    (2) The Attorney General prefers a request that comes from the court to one made direct by a party to the claim in which the alleged contempt occurred without prior consideration by the court. A request to the Attorney General is not a way of appealing against, or reviewing the decision of the judge.

28.3

Where a party makes an application to the court for permission to commence proceedings for contempt of court, it must be supported by written evidence of the facts and matters specified in paragraph 28.2(1) and the result of the request to the Attorney General made by the applicant.

28.4

The rules do not change the law of contempt or introduce new categories of contempt. A person applying to commence such proceedings should consider whether the incident complained of does amount to contempt of court and whether such proceedings would further the overriding objective in Part 1 of the Civil Procedure Rules.

VIDEO CONFERENCING

29.1

Guidance on the use of video conferencing in the civil courts is set out at Annex 3 to this practice direction.

A list of the sites which are available for video conferencing can be found on Her Majesty's Courts Service website at www.hmcourts-service.gov.uk.

ANNEX 1

Certificate to be used where a deponent to an affidavit is unable to read or sign it

Sworn at .... this ...... day of .... Before me, I having first read over the contents of this affidavit to the deponent [*if there are exhibits, add* 'and explained the nature and effect of the exhibits referred to in it'] who appeared to understand it and approved its content as accurate, and made his mark on the affidavit in my presence.

Or; (after, *Before me*) the witness to the mark of the deponent having been first sworn that he had read over etc. (*as above*) and that he saw him make his mark on the affidavit. (*Witness must sign*).

Certificate to be used where a deponent to an affirmation is unable to read or sign it

Affirmed at .... this ...... day of .... Before me, I having first read over the contents of this affirmation to the deponent [*if there are exhibits, add* 'and explained the nature and effect of the exhibits referred to in it'] who appeared to understand it and approved its content as accurate, and made his mark on the affirmation in my presence.

Or, (after, *Before me*) the witness to the mark of the deponent having been first sworn that he had read over etc. (*as above*) and that he saw him make his mark on the affirmation. (*Witness must sign*).

ANNEX 2
Omitted

ANNEX 3

VIDEO CONFERENCING GUIDANCE
This guidance is for the use of video conferencing (VCF) in civil proceedings. It is in part based, with permission, upon the protocol of the Federal Court of Australia. It is intended to provide a guide to all persons involved in the use of VCF, although it does not attempt to cover all the practical questions which might arise.

Video conferencing generally

1.

The guidance covers the use of VCF equipment both (a) in a courtroom, whether via equipment which is permanently placed there or via a mobile unit, and (b) in a separate studio or conference room. In either case, the location at which the judge sits is referred to as the 'local site'. The other site or sites to and from which transmission is made are referred to as 'the remote site' and in any particular case any such site may be another courtroom. The guidance applies to cases where VCF is used for the taking of evidence and also to its use for other parts of any legal proceedings (for example, interim applications, case management conferences, pre-trial reviews).

2.

VCF may be a convenient way of dealing with any part of proceedings: it can involve considerable savings in time and cost. Its use for the taking of evidence from overseas witnesses will, in particular, be likely to achieve a material saving of costs, and such savings may also be achieved by its use for taking domestic evidence. It is, however, inevitably not as ideal as having the witness physically present in court. Its convenience should not therefore be allowed to dictate its use. A judgment must be made in every case in which the use of VCF is being considered not only as to whether it will achieve an overall cost saving but as to whether its use will be likely to be beneficial to the efficient, fair and economic disposal of the litigation. In particular, it needs to be recognised that the degree of control a court can exercise over a witness at the remote site is or may be more limited than it can exercise over a witness physically before it.

3.

When used for the taking of evidence, the objective should be to make the VCF session as close as possible to the usual practice in a trial court where evidence is taken in open court. To gain the maximum benefit, several differences have to be taken into account. Some matters, which are taken for granted when evidence is taken in the conventional way, take on a different dimension when it is taken by VCF: for example, the administration of the oath, ensuring that the witness understands who is at the local site and what their various roles are, the raising of any objections to the evidence and the use of documents.

4.

It should not be presumed that all foreign governments are willing to allow their nationals or others within their jurisdiction to be examined before a court in England or Wales by means of VCF. If there is any doubt about this, enquiries should be directed to the Foreign and Commonwealth Office (International Legal Matters Unit, Consular Division) with a view to ensuring that the country from which the evidence is to be taken raises no objection to it at diplomatic level. The party who is directed to be responsible for arranging the VCF (see paragraph 8 below) will be required to make all necessary inquiries about this well in advance of the VCF and must be able to inform the court what those inquiries were and of their outcome.

5.

Time zone differences need to be considered when a witness abroad is to be examined in England or Wales by VCF. The convenience of the witness, the parties, their representatives and the court must all be taken into account. The cost of the use of a commercial studio is usually greater outside normal business hours.

6.

Those involved with VCF need to be aware that, even with the most advanced systems currently available, there are the briefest of delays between the receipt of the picture and that of the accompanying sound. If due allowance is not made for this, there will be a tendency to 'speak over' the witness, whose voice will continue to be heard for a millisecond or so after he or she appears on the screen to have finished speaking.

7.

With current technology, picture quality is good, but not as good as a television picture. The quality of the picture is enhanced if those appearing on VCF monitors keep their movements to a minimum.

Preliminary arrangements

8.

The court's permission is required for any part of any proceedings to be dealt with by means of VCF. Before seeking a direction, the applicant should notify the listing officer, diary manager or other appropriate court officer of the intention to seek it, and should enquire as to the availability of court VCF equipment for the day or days of the proposed VCF. The application for a direction should be made to the Master, District Judge or Judge, as may be appropriate. If all parties consent to a direction, permission can be sought by letter, fax or e-mail, although the court may still require an oral hearing. All parties are entitled to be heard on whether or not such a direction should be given and as to its terms. If a witness at a remote site is to give evidence by an interpreter, consideration should be given at this stage as to whether the interpreter should be at the local site or the remote site. If a VCF direction is given, arrangements for the transmission will then need to be made. The court will ordinarily direct that the party seeking permission to use VCF is to be responsible for this. That party is hereafter referred to as 'the VCF arranging party'.

9.

Subject to any order to the contrary, all costs of the transmission, including the costs of hiring equipment and technical personnel to operate it, will initially be the responsibility of, and must be met by, the VCF arranging party. All reasonable efforts should be made to keep the transmission to a minimum and so keep the costs down. All such costs will be considered to be part of the costs of the proceedings and the court will determine at such subsequent time as is convenient or appropriate who, as between the parties, should be responsible for them and (if appropriate) in what proportions.

10.

The local site will, if practicable, be a courtroom but it may instead be an appropriate studio or conference room. The VCF arranging party must contact the listing officer, diary manager or other appropriate officer of the court which made the VCF direction and make arrangements for the VCF transmission. Details of the remote site, and of the equipment to be used both at the local site (if not being supplied by the court) and the remote site (including the number of ISDN lines and connection speed), together with all necessary contact names and telephone numbers, will have to be provided to the listing officer, diary manager or other court officer. The court will need to be satisfied that any equipment provided by the parties for use at the local site and also that at the remote site is of sufficient quality for a satisfactory transmission. The VCF arranging party must ensure that an appropriate person will be present at the local site to supervise the operation of the VCF throughout the transmission in order to deal with any technical problems. That party must also arrange for a technical assistant to be similarly present at the remote site for like purposes.

11.

It is recommended that the judge, practitioners and witness should arrive at their respective VCF sites about 20 minutes prior to the scheduled commencement of the transmission.

12.

If the local site is not a courtroom, but a conference room or studio, the judge will need to determine who is to sit where. The VCF arranging party must take care to ensure that the number of microphones is adequate for the speakers and that the panning of the camera for the practitioners' table encompasses all legal representatives so that the viewer can see everyone seated there.

13.

The proceedings, wherever they may take place, form part of a trial to which the public is entitled to have access (unless the court has determined that they should be heard in private). If the local site is to be a studio or conference room, the VCF arranging party must ensure that it provides sufficient accommodation to enable a reasonable number of members of the public to attend.

14.

In cases where the local site is a studio or conference room, the VCF arranging party should make arrangements, if practicable, for the royal coat of arms to be placed above the judge's seat.

15.

In cases in which the VCF is to be used for the taking of evidence, the VCF arranging party must arrange for recording equipment to be provided by the court which made the VCF direction so that the evidence can be recorded. An associate will normally be present to operate the recording equipment when the local site is a courtroom. The VCF arranging party should take steps to ensure that an associate is present to do likewise when it is a studio or conference room. The equipment should be set up and tested before the VCF transmission. It will often be a valuable safeguard for the VCF arranging party also to arrange for the provision of recording equipment at the remote site. This will provide a useful back-up if there is any reduction in sound quality during the transmission. A direction from the court for the making of such a back-up recording must, however, be obtained first. This is because the proceedings are court proceedings and, save as directed by the court, no other recording of them must be made. The court will direct what is to happen to the back-up recording.

16.

Some countries may require that any oath or affirmation to be taken by a witness accord with local custom rather than the usual form of oath or affirmation used in England and Wales. The VCF arranging party must make all appropriate prior inquiries and put in place all arrangements necessary to enable the oath or affirmation to be taken in accordance with any local custom. That party must be in a position to inform the court what those inquiries were, what their outcome was and what arrangements have been made. If the oath or affirmation can be administered in the manner normal in England and Wales, the VCF arranging party must arrange in advance to have the appropriate holy book at the remote site. The associate will normally administer the oath.

17.

Consideration will need to be given in advance to the documents to which the witness is likely to be referred. The parties should endeavour to agree on this. It will usually be most convenient for a bundle of the copy documents to be prepared in advance, which the VCF arranging party should then send to the remote site.

18.

Additional documents are sometimes quite properly introduced during the course of a witness's evidence. To cater for this, the VCF arranging party should ensure that equipment is available to enable documents to be transmitted between sites during the course of the VCF transmission. Consideration should be given to whether to use a document camera. If it is decided to use one, arrangements for its use will need to be established in advance. The panel operator will need to know the number and size of documents or objects if their images are to be sent by document camera. In many cases, a simpler and sufficient alternative will be to ensure that there are fax transmission and reception facilities at the participating sites.

The hearing

19.

The procedure for conducting the transmission will be determined by the judge. He will determine who is to control the cameras. In cases where the VCF is being used for an application in the course of the proceedings, the judge will ordinarily not enter the local site until both sites are on line. Similarly, at the conclusion of the hearing, he will ordinarily leave the local site while both sites are still on line. The following paragraphs apply primarily to cases where the VCF is being used for the taking of the evidence of a witness at a remote site. In all cases, the judge will need to decide whether court dress is appropriate when using VCF facilities. It might be appropriate when transmitting from courtroom to courtroom. It might not be when a commercial facility is being used.

20.

At the beginning of the transmission, the judge will probably wish to introduce himself and the advocates to the witness. He will probably want to know who is at the remote site and will invite the witness to introduce himself and anyone else who is with him. He may wish to give directions as to the seating arrangements at the remote site so that those present are visible at the local site during the taking of the evidence. He will probably wish to explain to the witness the method of taking the oath or of affirming, the manner in which the evidence will be taken, and who will be conducting the examination and cross-examination. He will probably also wish to inform the witness of the matters referred to in paragraphs 6 and 7 above (co-ordination of picture with sound, and picture quality).

21.

The examination of the witness at the remote site should follow as closely as possible the practice adopted when a witness is in the courtroom. During examination, cross-examination and re-examination, the witness must be able to see the legal representative asking the question and also any other person (whether another legal representative or the judge) making any statements in regard to the witness's evidence. It will in practice be most convenient if everyone remains seated throughout the transmission.

PART 33 MISCELLANEOUS RULES ABOUT EVIDENCE

33.1 Introductory

In this Part—

    (a) 'hearsay' means a statement made, otherwise than by a person while giving oral evidence in proceedings, which is tendered as evidence of the matters stated; and

    (b) references to hearsay include hearsay of whatever degree.

33.2 Notice of intention to rely on hearsay evidence

    (1) Where a party intends to rely on hearsay evidence at trial and either—

        (a) that evidence is to be given by a witness giving oral evidence; or

        (b) that evidence is contained in a witness statement of a person who is not being called to give oral evidence;

that party complies with section 2(1)(a) of the Civil Evidence Act 1995 serving a witness statement on the other parties in accordance with the court's order.

    (2) Where paragraph (1)(b) applies, the party intending to rely on the hearsay evidence must, when he serves the witness statement—

        (a) inform the other parties that the witness is not being called to give oral evidence; and

        (b) give the reason why the witness will not be called.

    (3) In all other cases where a party intends to rely on hearsay evidence at trial, that party complies with section 2(1)(a) of the Civil Evidence Act 1995 by serving a notice on the other parties which—

        (a) identifies the hearsay evidence;

        (b) states that the party serving the notice proposes to rely on the hearsay evidence at trial; and

        (c) gives the reason why the witness will not be called.

    (4) The party proposing to rely on the hearsay evidence must—

        (a) serve the notice no later than the latest date for serving witness statements; and

        (b) if the hearsay evidence is to be in a document, supply a copy to any party who requests him to do so.

33.3 Circumstances in which notice of intention to rely on hearsay evidence is not required

Section 2(1) of the Civil Evidence Act 1995 (duty to give notice of intention to rely on hearsay evidence) does not apply—

    (a) to evidence at hearings other than trials;

    (aa) to an affadavit or witness statement which is to be used at trial but which does not contain hearsay evidence;

    (b) to a statement which a party to a probate action wishes to put in evidence and which is alleged to have been made by the person whose estate is the subject of the proceedings; or

    (c) where the requirement is excluded by a practice direction.

33.4   Power to call witness for cross-examination on hearsay evidence

(1) Where a party—

    (a) proposes to rely on hearsay evidence; and

    (b) does not propose to call the person who made the original statement to give oral evidence,

the court may, on the application of any other party, permit that party to call the maker of the statement to be cross-examined on the contents of the statement.

(2) An application for permission to cross-examine under this rule must be made not more than 14 days after the day on which a notice of intention to rely on the hearsay evidence was served on the applicant.

33.5   Credibility

(1) Where a party—

    (a) proposes to rely on hearsay evidence; but

    (b) does not propose to call the person who made the original statement to give oral evidence; and

    (c) another party wishes to call evidence to attack the credibility of the person who made the statement,

the party who so wishes must give notice of his intention to the party who proposes to give the hearsay statement in evidence.

(2) A party must give notice under paragraph (1) not more than 14 days after the day on which a hearsay notice relating to the hearsay evidence was served on him.

33.6   Use of plans, photographs and models as evidence

(1) This rule applies to evidence (such as a plan, photograph or model) which is not—

    (a) contained in a witness statement, affidavit or expert's report;

    (b) to be given orally at trial; or

    (c) evidence of which prior notice must be given under rule 33.2.

(2) This rule includes documents which may be received in evidence without further proof under section 9 of the Civil Evidence Act 1995.

(3) Unless the court orders otherwise the evidence shall not be receivable at a trial unless the party intending to put it in evidence has given notice to the other parties in accordance with this rule.

(4) Where the party intends to use the evidence as evidence of any fact then, except where paragraph (6) applies, he must give notice not later than the latest date for serving witness statements.

(5) He must give notice at least 21 days before the hearing at which he proposes to put in the evidence, if—

    (a) there are not to be witness statements; or

    (b) he intends to put in the evidence solely in order to disprove an allegation made in a witness statement.

(6) Where the evidence forms part of expert evidence, he must give notice when the expert's report is served on the other party.

(7) Where the evidence is being produced to the court for any reason other than as part of factual or expert evidence, he must give notice at least 21 days before the hearing at which he proposes to put in the evidence.

(8) Where a party has given notice that he intends to put in the evidence, he must give every other party an opportunity to inspect it and to agree to its admission without further proof.

33.7   Evidence of finding on question of foreign law

(1) This rule sets out the procedure which must be followed by a party who intends to put in evidence a finding on a question of foreign law by virtue of section 4(2) of the Civil Evidence Act 1972.

(2) He must give any other party notice of his intention.

(3) He must give the notice—
    (a) if there are to be witness statements, not later than the latest date for serving them; or
    (b) otherwise, not less than 21 days before the hearing at which he proposes to put the finding in evidence.

(4) The notice must—
    (a) specify the question on which the finding was made; and
    (b) enclose a copy of a document where it is reported or recorded.

33.8 Evidence of consent of trustee to act

A document purporting to contain the written consent of a person to act as trustee and to bear his signature verified by some other person is evidence of such consent.

33.9 Human Rights

(1) This rule applies where a claim is—
    (a) for a remedy under section 7 of the Human Rights Act 1998 in respect of a judicial act which is alleged to have infringed the claimant's Article 5 Convention rights; and
    (b) based on a finding by a court or tribunal that the claimant's Convention rights have been infringed.

(2) The court hearing the claim—
    (a) may proceed on the basis of the finding of that other court or tribunal that there has been an infringement but it is not required to do so, and
    (b) may reach its own conclusion in the light of that finding and of the evidence heard by that other court or tribunal.

PART 34 WITNESSES, DEPOSITIONS AND EVIDENCE FOR FOREIGN COURTS

I WITNESSES AND DEPOSITIONS

34.1 Scope of this Section

(1) This Section of this Part provides—
    (a) for the circumstances in which a person may be required to attend court to give evidence or to produce a document; and
    (b) for a party to obtain evidence before a hearing to be used at the hearing.

(2) In this Section, reference to a hearing includes a reference to the trial.

34.2 Witness summonses

(1) A witness summons is a document issued by the court requiring a witness to—
    (a) attend court to give evidence; or
    (b) produce documents to the court.

(2) A witness summons must be in the relevant practice form.

(3) There must be a separate witness summons for each witness.

(4) A witness summons may require a witness to produce documents to the court either—
    (a) on the date fixed for a hearing; or
    (b) on such date as the court may direct.

(5) The only documents that a summons under this rule can require a person to produce before a hearing are documents which that person could be required to produce at the hearing.

34.3 Issue of a witness summons

(1) A witness summons is issued on the date entered on the summons by the court.

(2) A party must obtain permission from the court where he wishes to—
    (a) have a summons issued less than 7 days before the date of the trial;
    (b) have a summons issued for a witness to attend court to give evidence or to produce documents on any date except the date fixed for the trial; or

(c) have a summons issued for a witness to attend court to give evidence or to produce documents at any hearing except the trial.

(3) A witness summons must be issued by—

(a) the court where the case is proceeding; or

(b) the court where the hearing in question will be held.

(4) The court may set aside or vary a witness summons issued under this rule.

34.4   Witness summons in aid of inferior court or of tribunal

(1) The court may issue a witness summons in aid of an inferior court or of a tribunal.

(2) The court which issued the witness summons under this rule may set it aside.

(3) In this rule, 'inferior court or tribunal' means any court or tribunal that does not have power to issue a witness summons in relation to proceedings before it.

34.5   Time for serving a witness summons

(1) The general rule is that a witness summons is binding if it is served at least 7 days before the date on which the witness is required to attend before the court or tribunal.

(2) The court may direct that a witness summons shall be binding although it will be served less than 7 days before the date on which the witness is required to attend before the court or tribunal.

(3) A witness summons which is—

(a) served in accordance with this rule; and

(b) requires the witness to attend court to give evidence,

is binding until the conclusion of the hearing at which the attendance of the witness is required.

34.6   Who is to serve a witness summons

(1) A witness summons is to be served by the court unless the party on whose behalf it is issued indicates in writing, when he asks the court to issue the summons, that he wishes to serve it himself.

(2) Where the court is to serve the witness summons, the party on whose behalf it is issued must deposit, in the court office, the money to be paid or offered to the witness under rule 34.7.

34.7   Right of witness to travelling expenses and compensation for loss of time

At the time of service of a witness summons the witness must be offered or paid—

(a) a sum reasonably sufficient to cover his expenses in travelling to and from the court; and

(b) such sum by way of compensation for loss of time as may be specified in Practice Direction 34A.

34.8   Evidence by deposition

(1) A party may apply for an order for a person to be examined before the hearing takes place.

(2) A person from whom evidence is to be obtained following an order under this rule is referred to as a 'deponent' and the evidence is referred to as a 'deposition'.

(3) An order under this rule shall be for a deponent to be examined on oath before—

(a) a judge;

(b) an examiner of the court; or

(c) such other person as the court appoints.

(Rule 34.15 makes provision for the appointment of examiners of the court)

(4) The order may require the production of any document which the court considers is necessary for the purposes of the examination.

(5) The order must state the date, time and place of the examination.

(6) At the time of service of the order the deponent must be offered or paid—

(a) a sum reasonably sufficient to cover his expenses in travelling to and from the place of examination; and

(b) such sum by way of compensation for loss of time as may be specified in Practice Direction 34A.

(7) Where the court makes an order for a deposition to be taken, it may also order the party who obtained the order to serve a witness statement or witness summary in relation to the evidence to be given by the person to be examined.

(Part 32 contains the general rules about witness statements and witness summaries)

34.9   Conduct of examination

(1) Subject to any directions contained in the order for examination, the examination must be conducted in the same way as if the witness were giving evidence at a trial.

(2) If all the parties are present, the examiner may conduct the examination of a person not named in the order for examination if all the parties and the person to be examined consent.

(3) The examiner may conduct the examination in private if he considers it appropriate to do so.

(4) The examiner must ensure that the evidence given by the witness is recorded in full.

(5) The examiner must send a copy of the deposition—

    (a) to the person who obtained the order for the examination of the witness; and

    (b) to the court where the case is proceeding.

(6) The party who obtained the order must send each of the other parties a copy of the deposition which he receives from the examiner.

34.10   Enforcing attendance of witness

(1) If a person served with an order to attend before an examiner—

    (a) fails to attend; or

    (b) refuses to be sworn for the purpose of the examination or to answer any lawful question or produce any document at the examination,

a certificate of his failure or refusal, signed by the examiner, must be filed by the party requiring the deposition.

(2) On the certificate being filed, the party requiring the deposition may apply to the court for an order requiring that person to attend or to be sworn or to answer any question or produce any document, as the case may be.

(3) An application for an order under this rule may be made without notice.

(4) The court may order the person against whom an order is made under this rule to pay any costs resulting from his failure or refusal.

34.11   Use of deposition at a hearing

(1) A deposition ordered under rule 34.8 may be given in evidence at a hearing unless the court orders otherwise.

(2) A party intending to put in evidence a deposition at a hearing must serve notice of his intention to do so on every other party.

(3) He must serve the notice at least 21 days before the day fixed for the hearing.

(4) The court may require a deponent to attend the hearing and give evidence orally.

(5) Where a deposition is given in evidence at trial, it shall be treated as if it were a witness statement for the purposes of rule 32.13 (availability of witness statements for inspection).

34.12   Restrictions on subsequent use of deposition taken for the purpose of any hearing except the trial

(1) Where the court orders a party to be examined about his or any other assets for the purpose of any hearing except the trial, the deposition may be used only for the purpose of the proceedings in which the order was made.

(2) However, it may be used for some other purpose—

    (a) by the party who was examined;

    (b) if the party who was examined agrees; or

    (c) if the court gives permission.

34.13   Where a person to be examined is out of the jurisdiction—letter of request

(1) This rule applies where a party wishes to take a deposition from a person who is—

(a) out of the jurisdiction; and

(b) not in a Regulation State within the meaning of Section III of this Part.

(1A) The High Court may order the issue of a letter of request to the judicial authorities of the country in which the proposed deponent is.

(2) A letter of request is a request to a judicial authority to take the evidence of that person, or arrange for it to be taken.

(3) The High Court may make an order under this rule in relation to county court proceedings.

(4) If the government of a country allows a person appointed by the High Court to examine a person in that country, the High Court may make an order appointing a special examiner for that purpose.

(5) A person may be examined under this rule on oath or affirmation or in accordance with any procedure permitted in the country in which the examination is to take place.

(6) If the High Court makes an order for the issue of a letter of request, the party who sought the order must file—

(a) the following documents and, except where paragraph (7) applies, a translation of them—

(i) a draft letter of request;

(ii) a statement of the issues relevant to the proceedings;

(iii) a list of questions or the subject matter of questions to be put to the person to be examined; and

(b) an undertaking to be responsible for the Secretary of State's expenses.

(7) There is no need to file a translation if—

(a) English is one of the official languages of the country where the examination is to take place; or

(b) a practice direction has specified that country as a country where no translation is necessary.

34.13A   Letter of request—Proceeds of Crime Act 2002

(1) This rule applies where a party to existing or contemplated proceedings in—

(a) the High Court; or

(b) a magistrates' court,

under Part 5 of the Proceeds of Crime Act 2002 (civil recovery of the proceeds etc. of unlawful conduct) wishes to take a deposition from a person who is out of the jurisdiction.

(2) The High Court may, on the application of such a party, order the issue of a letter of request to the judicial authorities of the country in which the proposed deponent is.

(3) Paragraphs (4) to (7) of rule 34.13 shall apply irrespective of where the proposed deponent is, and rule 34.23 shall not apply in cases where the proposed deponent is in a Regulation State within the meaning of Section III of this Part.

34.14   Fees and expenses of examiner of the court

(1) An examiner of the court may charge a fee for the examination.

(2) He need not send the deposition to the court unless the fee is paid.

(3) The examiner's fees and expenses must be paid by the party who obtained the order for examination.

(4) If the fees and expenses due to an examiner are not paid within a reasonable time, he may report that fact to the court.

(5) The court may order the party who obtained the order for examination to deposit in the court office a specified sum in respect of the examiner's fees and, where it does so, the examiner will not be asked to act until the sum has been deposited.

(6) An order under this rule does not affect any decision as to the party who is ultimately to bear the costs of the examination.

34.15 Examiners of the court

(1) The Lord Chancellor shall appoint persons to be examiners of the court.

(2) The persons appointed shall be barristers or solicitor-advocates who have been practising for a period of not less than three years.

(3) The Lord Chancellor may revoke an appointment at any time.

II EVIDENCE FOR FOREIGN COURTS

34.16 Scope and interpretation

(1) This Section applies to an application for an order under the 1975 Act for evidence to be obtained, other than an application made as a result of a request by a court in another Regulation State.

(2) In this Section—

> (a) 'the 1975 Act' means the Evidence (Proceedings in Other Jurisdictions) Act 1975; and
>
> (b) 'Regulation State' has the same meaning as in Section III of this Part.

34.17 Application for order

An application for an order under the 1975 Act for evidence to be obtained—

> (a) must be—
>
> > (i)   made to the High Court;
> >
> > (ii) supported by written evidence; and
> >
> > (iii) accompanied by the request as a result of which the application is made, and where appropriate, a translation of the request into English; and
>
> (b) may be made without notice.

34.18 Examination

(1) The court may order an examination to be taken before—

> (a) any fit and proper person nominated by the person applying for the order;
>
> (b) an examiner of the court; or
>
> (c) any other person whom the court considers suitable.

(2) Unless the court orders otherwise—

> (a) the examination will be taken as provided by rule 34.9; and
>
> (b) rule 34.10 applies.

(3) The court may make an order under rule 34.14 for payment of the fees and expenses of the examination.

34.19 Dealing with deposition

(1) The examiner must send the deposition of the witness to the Senior Master unless the court orders otherwise.

(2) The Senior Master will—

> (a) give a certificate sealed with the seal of the Senior Courts for use out of the jurisdiction identifying the following documents—
>
> > (i)   the request;
> >
> > (ii) the order of the court for examination; and
> >
> > (iii) the deposition of the witness; and
>
> (b) send the certificate and the documents referred to in paragraph (a) to—
>
> > (i)   the Secretary of State; or
> >
> > (ii) where the request was sent to the Senior Master by another person in accordance with a Civil Procedure Convention, to that other person,
> >
> > for transmission to the court or tribunal requesting the examination.

34.20 Claim to privilege

(1) This rule applies where—

> (a) a witness claims to be exempt from giving evidence on the ground specified in section 3(1)(b) of the 1975 Act; and
>
> (b) That claim is not supported or conceded as referred to in section 3(2) of that Act.

(2) The examiner may require the witness to give the evidence which he claims to be exempt from giving.

(3) Where the examiner does not require the witness to give that evidence, the court may order the witness to do so.

(4) An application for an order under paragraph (3) may be made by the person who obtained the order under section 2 of the 1975 Act.

(5) Where such evidence is taken—

    (a) it must be contained in a document separate from the remainder of the deposition;

    (b) the examiner will send to the Senior Master—

        (i)   the deposition; and

        (ii) a signed statement setting out the claim to be exempt and the ground on which it was made;

(6) On receipt of the statement referred to in paragraph (5)(b)(ii), the Senior Master will—

    (a) retain the document containing the part of the witness's evidence to which the claim to be exempt relates; and

    (b) send the statement and a request to determine that claim to the foreign court or tribunal together with the documents referred to in rule 34.17.

(7) The Senior Master will—

    (a) if the claim to be exempt is rejected by the foreign court or tribunal, send the document referred to in paragraph (5)(a) to that court or tribunal;

    (b) if the claim is upheld, send the document to the witness; and

    (c) in either case, notify the witness and person who obtained the order under section 2 of the foreign court or tribunal's decision.

34.21   Order under 1975 Act as applied by Patents Act 1977

Where an order is made for the examination of witnesses under section 1 of the 1975 Act as applied by section 92 of the Patents Act 1977 the court may permit an officer of the European Patent Office to—

    (a) attend the examination and examine the witnesses; or

    (b) request the court or the examiner before whom the examination takes place to put specified questions to them.

III   TAKING OF EVIDENCE—MEMBER STATES OF THE EUROPEAN UNION

34.22   Interpretation

In this Section—

    (a) 'designated court' has the meaning given in Practice Direction 34A;

    (b) 'Regulation State' has the same meaning as 'Member State' in the Taking of Evidence Regulation, that is all Member States except Denmark;

    (c) 'the Taking of Evidence Regulation' means Council Regulation (EC) No. 1206/2001 of 28 May 2001 on co-operation between the courts of the Member States in the taking of evidence in civil and commercial matters.

34.23   Where a person to be examined is in another Regulation State

(1) Subject to rule 34.13A, this rule applies where a party wishes to take a deposition from a person who is in another Regulation State–

    (a) outside the jurisdiction; and

    (b) in a Regulation State.

(2) The court may order the issue of a request to a designated court ('the requested court') in the Regulation State in which the proposed deponent is.

(3) If the court makes an order for the issue of a request, the party who sought the order must file—

    (a) a draft Form A as set out in the annex to the Taking of Evidence Regulation (request for the taking of evidence);

     (b) except where paragraph (4) applies, a translation of the form;

     (c) an undertaking to be responsible for costs sought by the requested court in relation to—

        (i)   fees paid to experts and interpreters; and

        (ii) where requested by that party, the use of special procedures or communications technology; and

     (d) an undertaking to be responsible for the court's expenses.

  (4) There is no need to file a translation if—

     (a) English is one of the official languages of the Regulation State where the examination is to take place; or

     (b) the Regulation State has indicated, in accordance with the Taking of Evidence Regulation, that English is a language which it will accept.

  (5) Where article 17 of the Taking of Evidence Regulation (direct taking of evidence by the requested court) allows evidence to be taken directly in another Regulation State, the court may make an order for the submission of a request in accordance with that article.

  (6) If the court makes an order for the submission of a request under paragraph (5), the party who sought the order must file—

     (a) a draft Form I as set out in the annex to the Taking of Evidence Regulation (request for direct taking of evidence);

     (b) except where paragraph (4) applies, a translation of the form; and

     (c) an undertaking to be responsible for the court's expenses.

34.24 Evidence for courts of other Regulation States

  (1) This rule applies where a court in another Regulation State ('the requesting court') issues a request for evidence to be taken from a person who is in the jurisdiction.

  (2) An application for an order for evidence to be taken—

     (a) must be made to a designated court;

     (b) must be accompanied by—

        (i)   the form of request for the taking of evidence as a result of which the application is made; and

        (ii) where appropriate, a translation of the form of request; and

     (c) may be made without notice.

  (3) Rule 34.18(1) and (2) apply.

  (4) The examiner must send—

     (a) the deposition to the court for transmission to the requesting court; and

     (b) a copy of the deposition to the person who obtained the order for evidence to be taken.

PRACTICE DIRECTION

DEPOSITIONS AND COURT ATTENDANCE BY WITNESSES

This Practice Direction supplements CPR Part 34

WITNESS SUMMONSES

Issue of witness summons

1.1

A witness summons may require a witness to:

    (1) attend court to give evidence,

    (2) produce documents to the court, or

    (3) both,

on either a date fixed for the hearing or such date as the court may direct.

1.2
Two copies of the witness summons should be filed with the court for sealing, one of which will be retained on the court file.

1.3
A mistake in the name or address of a person named in a witness summons may be corrected if the summons has not been served.

1.4
The corrected summons must be re-sealed by the court and marked 'Amended and Re-Sealed'.

Witness summons issued in aid of an inferior court or tribunal

2.1
A witness summons may be issued in the High Court or a county court in aid of a court or tribunal which does not have the power to issue a witness summons in relation to the proceedings before it.

2.2
A witness summons referred to in paragraph 2.1 may be set aside by the court which issued it.

2.3
An application to set aside a witness summons referred to in paragraph 2.1 will be heard:

(1) in the High Court by a Master at the Royal Courts of Justice or by a district judge in a District Registry, and

(2) in a county court by a district judge.

2.4
Unless the court otherwise directs, the applicant must give at least 2 days' notice to the party who issued the witness summons of the application, which will normally be dealt with at a hearing.

Travelling expenses and compensation for loss of time

3.1
When a witness is served with a witness summons he must be offered a sum to cover his travelling expenses to and from the court and compensation for his loss of time.

3.2
If the witness summons is to be served by the court, the party issuing the summons must deposit with the court:

(1) a sum sufficient to pay for the witness's expenses in travelling to the court and in returning to his home or place of work, and

(2) a sum in respect of the period during which earnings or benefit are lost, or such lesser sum as it may be proved that the witness will lose as a result of his attendance at court in answer to the witness summons.

3.3
The sum referred to in 3.2(2) is to be based on the sums payable to witnesses attending the Crown Court.

3.4
Where the party issuing the witness summons wishes to serve it himself, he must:

(1) notify the court in writing that he wishes to do so, and

(2) at the time of service offer the witness the sums mentioned in paragraph 3.2 above.

DEPOSITIONS

To be taken in England and Wales for use as evidence in proceedings in courts in England and Wales

4.1

A party may apply for an order for a person to be examined on oath before:

(1) a judge,

(2) an examiner of the court, or

(3) such other person as the court may appoint.

4.2

The party who obtains an order for the examination of a deponent before an examiner of the court must:

(1) apply to the Foreign Process Section of the Masters' Secretary's Department at the Royal Courts of Justice for the allocation of an examiner,

(2) when allocated, provide the examiner with copies of all documents in the proceedings necessary to inform the examiner of the issues, and

(3) pay the deponent a sum to cover his travelling expenses to and from the examination and compensation for his loss of time.

4.3

In ensuring that the deponent's evidence is recorded in full, the court or the examiner may permit it to be recorded on audiotape or videotape, but the deposition must always be recorded in writing by him or by a competent shorthand writer or stenographer.

4.4

If the deposition is not recorded word for word, it must contain, as nearly as may be, the statement of the deponent; the examiner may record word for word any particular questions and answers which appear to him to have special importance.

4.5

If a deponent objects to answering any question or where any objection is taken to any question, the examiner must:

(1) record in the deposition or a document attached to it—

(a) the question,

(b) the nature of and grounds for the objection, and

(c) any answer given, and

(2) give his opinion as to the validity of the objection and must record it in the deposition or a document attached to it.

The court will decide as to the validity of the objection and any question of costs arising from it.

4.6

Documents and exhibits must:

(1) have an identifying number or letter marked on them by the examiner, and

(2) be preserved by the party or his legal representative who obtained the order for the examination, or as the court or the examiner may direct.

4.7

The examiner may put any question to the deponent as to:

(1) the meaning of any of his answers, or

(2) any matter arising in the course of the examination.

4.8

Where a deponent:

    (1) fails to attend the examination, or

    (2) refuses to:

        (a) be sworn, or

        (b) answer any lawful question, or

        (c) produce any document,

the examiner will sign a certificate of such failure or refusal and may include in his certificate any comment as to the conduct of the deponent or of any person attending the examination.

4.9

The party who obtained the order for the examination must file the certificate with the court and may apply for an order that the deponent attend for examination or as may be. The application may be made without notice.

4.10

The court will make such order on the application as it thinks fit including an order for the deponent to pay any costs resulting from his failure or refusal.

4.11

A deponent who wilfully refuses to obey an order made against him under Part 34 may be proceeded against for contempt of court.

4.12

A deposition must:

    (1) be signed by the examiner,

    (2) have any amendments to it initialled by the examiner and the deponent,

    (3) be endorsed by the examiner with—

        (a) a statement of the time occupied by the examination, and

        (b) a record of any refusal by the deponent to sign the deposition and of his reasons for not doing so, and

    (4) be sent by the examiner to the court where the proceedings are taking place for filing on the court file.

4.13

Rule 34.14 deals with the fees and expenses of an examiner.

Depositions to be taken abroad for use as evidence in proceedings before courts in England and Wales (where the Taking of Evidence Regulation does not apply)

5.1

Where a party wishes to take a deposition from a person outside the jurisdiction, the High Court may order the issue of a letter of request to the judicial authorities of the country in which the proposed deponent is.

5.2

An application for an order referred to in paragraph 5.1 should be made by application notice in accordance with Part 23.

5.3

The documents which a party applying for an order for the issue of a letter of request must file with his application notice are set out in rule 34.13(6). They are as follows:

    (1) a draft letter of request in the form set out in Annex A to this practice direction,

    (2) a statement of the issues relevant to the proceedings,

    (3) a list of questions or the subject matter of questions to be put to the proposed deponent,

(4) a translation of the documents in (1), (2) and (3) above, unless the proposed deponent is in a country of which English is an official language, and

(5) an undertaking to be responsible for the expenses of the Secretary of State

In addition to the documents listed above the party applying for the order must file a draft order.

5.4

The above documents should be filed with the Masters' Secretary in Room E214, Royal Courts of Justice, Strand, London WC2A 2LL.

5.5

The application will be dealt with by the Senior Master of the Queen's Bench Division of the High Court who will, if appropriate, sign the letter of request.

5.6

Attention is drawn to the provisions of rule 23.10 (application to vary or discharge an order made without notice).

5.7

If parties are in doubt as to whether a translation under paragraph 5.3(4) above is required, they should seek guidance from the Foreign Process Section of the Masters' Secretary's Department.

5.8

A special examiner appointed under rule 34.13(4) may be the British Consul or the Consul-General or his deputy in the country where the evidence is to be taken if:

(1) there is in respect of that country a Civil Procedure Convention providing for the taking of evidence in that country for the assistance of proceedings in the High Court or other court in this country, or

(2) with the consent of the Secretary of State.

5.9

The provisions of paragraphs 4.1 to 4.12 above apply to the depositions referred to in this paragraph.

Depositions to be taken in England and Wales for use as evidence in proceedings before courts abroad pursuant to letters of request (where the Taking of Evidence Regulation does not apply)

6.1

Section II of Part 34 relating to obtaining evidence for foreign courts applies to letters of request and should be read in conjunction with this part of the practice direction.

6.2

The Evidence (Proceedings in Other Jurisdictions) Act 1975 applies to these depositions.

6.3

The written evidence supporting an application under rule 34.17 (which should be made by application notice—see Part 23) must include or exhibit—

(1) a statement of the issues relevant to the proceedings;

(2) a list of questions or the subject matter of questions to be put to the proposed deponent;

(3) a draft order; and

(4) a translation of the documents in (1) and (2) into English, if necessary.

6.4

(1) The Senior Master will send to the Treasury Solicitor any request—

(a) forwarded by the Secretary of State with a recommendation that effect should be given to the request without requiring an application to be made; or

    (b) received by him in pursuance of a Civil Procedure Convention providing for the taking of evidence of any person in England and Wales to assist a court or tribunal in a foreign country where no person is named in the document as the applicant.

(2) In relation to such a request, the Treasury Solicitor may, with the consent of the Treasury—

    (a) apply for an order under the 1975 Act; and

    (b) take such other steps as are necessary to give effect to the request.

6.5

The order for the deponent to attend and be examined together with the evidence upon which the order was made must be served on the deponent.

6.6

Attention is drawn to the provisions of rule 23.10 (application to vary or discharge an order made without notice).

6.7

Arrangements for the examination to take place at a specified time and place before an examiner of the court or such other person as the court may appoint shall be made by the applicant for the order and approved by the Senior Master.

6.8

The provisions of paragraph 4.2 to 4.12 apply to the depositions referred to in this paragraph, except that the examiner must send the deposition to the Senior Master.

    (For further information about evidence see Part 32 and Practice Direction 32.)

TAKING OF EVIDENCE BETWEEN EU MEMBER STATES

Taking of Evidence Regulation

7.1

Where evidence is to be taken—

    (a) from a person in another Member State of the European Union for use as evidence in proceedings before courts in England and Wales; or

    (b) from a person in England and Wales for use as evidence in proceedings before a court in another Member State,

Council Regulation (EC) No 1206/2001 of 28 May 2001 on co-operation between the courts of the Member States in the taking of evidence in civil or commercial matters ('the Taking of Evidence Regulation') applies.

7.2

The Taking of Evidence Regulation is annexed to this practice direction as Annex B.

7.3

The Taking of Evidence Regulation does not apply to Denmark. In relation to Denmark, therefore, rule 34.13 and Section II of Part 34 will continue to apply.

    (Article 21(1) of the Taking of Evidence Regulation provides that the Regulation prevails over other provisions contained in bilateral or multilateral agreements or arrangements concluded by the Member States and in particular the Hague Convention of 1 March 1954 on Civil Procedure and the Hague Convention of 18 March 1970 on the Taking of Evidence Abroad in Civil or Commercial Matters)

    Originally published in the official languages of the European Community in the *Official Journal of the European Communities* by the Office for Official Publications of the European Communities.

Meaning of 'designated court'

8.1

In accordance with the Taking of Evidence Regulation, each Regulation State has prepared a list of courts competent to take evidence in accordance with the Regulation indicating the territorial and, where appropriate, special jurisdiction of those courts.

8.2

Where Part 34, Section III refers to a 'designated court' in relation to another Regulation State, the reference is to the court, referred to in the list of competent courts of that State, which is appropriate to the application in hand.

8.3

Where the reference is to the 'designated court' in England and Wales, the reference is to the appropriate competent court in the jurisdiction. The designated courts for England and Wales are listed in Annex C to this practice direction.

Central Body

9.1

The Taking of Evidence Regulation stipulates that each Regulation State must nominate a Central Body responsible for—

    (a) supplying information to courts;

    (b) seeking solutions to any difficulties which may arise in respect of a request; and

    (c) forwarding, in exceptional cases, at the request of a requesting court, a request to the competent court.

9.2

The United Kingdom has nominated the Senior Master, Queen's Bench Division, to be the Central Body for England and Wales.

9.3

The Senior Master, as Central Body, has been designated responsible for taking decisions on requests pursuant to Article 17 of the Regulation. Article 17 allows a court to submit a request to the Central Body or a designated competent authority in another Regulation State to take evidence directly in that State.

Evidence to be taken in another Regulation State for use in England and Wales

10.1

Where a person wishes to take a deposition from a person in another Regulation State, the court where the proceedings are taking place may order the issue of a request to the designated court in the Regulation State (Rule 34.23(2)). The form of request is prescribed as Form A in the Taking of Evidence Regulation.

10.2

An application to the court for an order under rule 34.23(2) should be made by application notice in accordance with Part 23.

10.3

Rule 34.23(3) provides that the party applying for the order must file a draft form of request in the prescribed form. Where completion of the form requires attachments or documents to accompany the form, these must also be filed.

10.4

If the court grants an order under rule 34.23 (2), it will send the form of request directly to the designated court.

10.5

Where the taking of evidence requires the use of an expert, the designated court may require a deposit in advance towards the costs of that expert. The party who obtained the order is responsible for the payment of any such deposit which should be deposited with the court for onward transmission. Under the provisions of the Taking of Evidence Regulation, the designated court is not required to execute the request until such payment is received.

10.6

Article 17 permits the court where proceedings are taking place to take evidence directly from a deponent in another Regulation State if the conditions of the article are satisfied. Direct taking of evidence can only take place if evidence is given voluntarily without the need for coercive measures. Rule 34.23(5) provides for the court to make an order for the submission of a request to take evidence directly. The form of request is Form I annexed to the Taking of Evidence Regulation and rule 34.23(6) makes provision for a draft of this form to be filed by the party seeking the order. An application for an order under rule 34.23(5) should be by application notice in accordance with Part 23.

10.7

Attention is drawn to the provisions of rule 23.10 (application to vary or discharge an order made without notice).

Evidence to be taken in England and Wales for use in another Regulation State

11.1

Where a designated court in England and Wales receives a request to take evidence from a court in a Regulation State, the court will send the request to the Treasury Solicitor.

11.2

On receipt of the request, the Treasury Solicitor may, with the consent of the Treasury, apply for an order under rule 34.24.

11.3

An application to the court for an order must be accompanied by the Form of request to take evidence and any accompanying documents, translated if required under paragraph 11.4.

11.4

The United Kingdom has indicated that, in addition to English, it will accept French as a language in which documents may be submitted. Where the form or request and any accompanying documents are received in French they will be translated into English by the Treasury Solicitor.

11.5

The order for the deponent to attend and be examined together with the evidence on which the order was made must be served on the deponent.

11.6

Arrangements for the examination to take place at a specified time and place shall be made by the Treasury Solicitor and approved by the court.

11.7

The court shall send details of the arrangements for the examination to such of

  (a) the parties and, if any, their representatives; or
  (b) the representatives of the foreign court,

who have indicated, in accordance with the Taking of Evidence Regulation, that they wish to be present at the examination.

11.8

The provisions of paragraph 4.3 to 4.12 apply to the depositions referred to in this paragraph.

Annex A Draft Letter of Request (where the Taking of Evidence Regulation does not apply)

To the Competent Judicial Authority of   in the   of

I [*name*] Senior Master of the Queen's Bench Division of the Senior Courts of England and Wales respectfully request the assistance of your court with regard to the following matters.

1

A claim is now pending in the Division of the High Court of Justice in England and Wales entitled as follows [*set out full title and claim number*] in which [*name*] of [*address*] is the claimant and [*name*] of [*address*] is the defendant.

2

The names and addresses of the representatives or agents of [*set out names and addresses of representatives of the parties*].

3

The claim by the claimant is for:-
- (a) [*set out the nature of the claim*]
- (b) [*the relief sought, and*]
- (c) [*a summary of the facts.*]

4

It is necessary for the purposes of justice and for the due determination of the matters in dispute between the parties that you cause the following witnesses, who are resident within your jurisdiction, to be examined. The names and addresses of the witnesses are as follows:

5

The witnesses should be examined on oath or if that is not possible within your laws or is impossible of performance by reason of the internal practice and procedure of your court or by reason of practical difficulties, they should be examined in accordance with whatever procedure your laws provide for in these matters.

6

Either/

The witnesses should be examined in accordance with the list of questions annexed hereto.

Or/

The witnesses should be examined regarding [*set out full details of evidence sought*]

N.B. Where the witness is required to produce documents, these should be clearly identified.

7

I would ask that you cause me, or the agents of the parties (if appointed), to be informed of the date and place where the examination is to take place.

8

Finally, I request that you will cause the evidence of the said witnesses to be reduced into writing and all documents produced on such examinations to be duly marked for identification and that you will further be pleased to authenticate such examinations by the seal of your court or in such other way as is in accordance with your procedure and return the written evidence and documents produced to me addressed as follows:

Senior Master of the Queen's Bench Division
Royal Courts of Justice
Strand
London WC2A 2LL
England

PART 35 EXPERTS AND ASSESSORS

35.1 Duty to restrict expert evidence
Expert evidence shall be restricted to that which is reasonably required to resolve the proceedings.

35.2 Interpretation and definitions
(1) A reference to an 'expert' in this Part is a reference to a person who has been instructed to give or prepare expert evidence for the purpose of proceedings.

(2) 'Single joint expert' means an expert instructed to prepare a report for the court on behalf of two or more of the parties (including the claimant) to the proceedings.

35.3 Experts—overriding duty to the court
(1) It is the duty of experts to help the court on matters within their expertise.

(2) This duty overrides any obligation to the person from whom experts have received instructions or by whom they are paid.

35.4 Court's power to restrict expert evidence
(1) No party may call an expert or put in evidence an expert's report without the court's permission.

(2) When parties apply for permission they must identify—
(a) the field in which expert evidence is required; and
(b) where practicable, the name of the proposed expert.

(3) If permission is granted it shall be in relation only to the expert named or the field identified under paragraph (2).

(3A) tWhere a claim has been allocated to the small claims track or the fast track, if permission is given for expert evidence, it will normally be given for evidence from only one expert on a particular issue.

(Paragraph 7 of Practice Direction 35 sets out some of the circumstances the court will consider when deciding whether expert evidence should be given by a single joint expert.)

(4) The court may limit the amount of a party's expert's fees and expenses that may be recovered from any other party.

35.5 General requirement for expert evidence to be given in a written report
(1) Expert evidence is to be given in a written report unless the court directs otherwise.

(2) If a claim is on the small claims track or the fast track, the court will not direct an expert to attend a hearing unless it is necessary to do so in the interests of justice.

35.6 Written questions to experts
(1) A party may put written questions about an expert's report (which must be proportionate) to—
(a) an expert instructed by another party; or
(b) a single joint expert appointed under rule 35.7.

(2) Written questions under paragraph (1)—
(a) may be put once only;
(b) must be put within 28 days of service of the expert's report; and
(c) must be for the purpose only of clarification of the report,
unless in any case—
(i)   the court gives permission; or
(ii) the other party agrees.

(3) An expert's answers to questions put in accordance with paragraph (1) shall be treated as part of the expert's report.

(4) Where—
(a) a party has put a written question to an expert instructed by another party ; and
(b) the expert does not answer that question,
the court may make one or both of the following orders in relation to the party who instructed the expert—

   (i)   that the party may not rely on the evidence of that expert; or
   (ii) that the party may not recover the fees and expenses of that expert from any other
         party.

35.7   Court's power to direct that evidence is to be given by a single joint expert

   (1) Where two or more parties wish to submit expert evidence on a particular issue, the court
may direct that the evidence on that issue is to be given by a single joint expert.

   (2) Where the parties who wish to submit the evidence ('the relevant parties') cannot agree who
should be the single joint expert, the court may—
   (a) select the expert from a list prepared or identified by the relevant parties; or
   (b) direct that the expert be selected in such other manner as the court may direct.

35.8   Instructions to a single joint expert

   (1) Where the court gives a direction under rule 35.7 for a single joint expert to be used, any
relevant party may give instructions to the expert.

   (2) When a party gives instructions to the expert that party must, at the same time, send a copy
to the other relevant parties.

   (3) The court may give directions about—
   (a) the payment of the expert's fees and expenses; and
   (b) any inspection, examination or experiments which the expert wishes to carry out.

   (4) The court may, before an expert is instructed—
   (a) limit the amount that can be paid by way of fees and expenses to the expert; and
   (b) direct that some or all of the relevant parties pay that amount into court.

   (5) Unless the court otherwise directs, the relevant parties are jointly and severally liable for the
payment of the expert's fees and expenses.

35.9   Power of court to direct a party to provide information

Where a party has access to information which is not reasonably available to another party, the court
may direct the party who has access to the information to—
   (a) prepare and file a document recording the information; and
   (b) serve a copy of that document on the other party.

35.10   Contents of report

   (1) An expert's report must comply with the requirements set out in Practice Direction 35.

   (2) At the end of an expert's report there must be a statement that the expert understands and has
complied with their duty to the court.

   (3) The expert's report must state the substance of all material instructions, whether written or
oral, on the basis of which the report was written.

   (4) The instructions referred to in paragraph (3) shall not be privileged against disclosure but
the court will not, in relation to those instructions—
   (a) order disclosure of any specific document; or
   (b) permit any questioning in court, other than by the party who instructed the expert,
unless it is satisfied that there are reasonable grounds to consider the statement of instructions given
under paragraph (3) to be inaccurate or incomplete.

35.11   Use by one party of expert's report disclosed by another

Where a party has disclosed an expert's report, any party may use that expert's report as evidence at
the trial.

35.12   Discussions between experts

   (1) The court may, at any stage, direct a discussion between experts for the purpose of requiring
the experts to—
   (a) identify and discuss the expert issues in the proceedings; and
   (b) where possible, reach an agreed opinion on those issues.

(2) The court may specify the issues which the experts must discuss.

(3) The court may direct that following a discussion between the experts they must prepare a statement for the court setting out those issues on which—

    (a) they agree; and

    (b) they disagree, with a summary of their reasons for disagreeing.

(4) The content of the discussion between the experts shall not be referred to at the trial unless the parties agree.

(5) Where experts reach agreement on an issue during their discussions, the agreement shall not bind the parties unless the parties expressly agree to be bound by the agreement.

35.13 Consequence of failure to disclose expert's report

A party who fails to disclose an expert's report may not use the report at the trial or call the expert to give evidence orally unless the court gives permission.

35.14 Expert's right to ask court for directions

(1) Experts may file written requests for directions for the purpose of assisting them in carrying out their functions.

(2) Experts must, unless the court orders otherwise, provide copies of the proposed requests for directions under paragraph (1)—

    (a) to the party instructing them, at least 7 days before they file the requests; and

    (b) to all other parties, at least 4 days before they file them.

(3) The court, when it gives directions, may also direct that a party be served with a copy of the directions.

35.15 Assessors

(1) This rule applies where the court appoints one or more persons under section 70 of the Senior Courts Act 1981 or section 63 of the County Courts Act 1984 as an assessor.

(2) An assessor will assist the court in dealing with a matter in which the assessor has skill and experience.

(3) An assessor will take such part in the proceedings as the court may direct and in particular the court may direct an assessor to—

    (a) prepare a report for the court on any matter at issue in the proceedings; and

    (b) attend the whole or any part of the trial to advise the court on any such matter.

(4) If an assessor prepares a report for the court before the trial has begun—

    (a) the court will send a copy to each of the parties; and

    (b) the parties may use it at trial.

(5) The remuneration to be paid to an assessor is to be determined by the court and will form part of the costs of the proceedings.

(6) The court may order any party to deposit in the court office a specified sum in respect of an assessor's fees and, where it does so, the assessor will not be asked to act until the sum has been deposited.

(7) Paragraphs (5) and (6) do not apply where the remuneration of the assessor is to be paid out of money provided by Parliament.

PRACTICE DIRECTION

EXPERTS AND ASSESSORS

This Practice Direction supplements CPR Part 35

Introduction

1

Part 35 is intended to limit the use of oral expert evidence to that which is reasonably required. In addition, where possible, matters requiring expert evidence should be dealt with by only one expert.

Experts and those instructing them are expected to have regard to the guidance contained in the Protocol for the Instruction of Experts to give Evidence in Civil Claims annexed to this practice direction. (Further guidance on experts is contained in Annex C to the Practice Direction (Pre-Action Conduct)).

Expert Evidence—General Requirements

2.1

Expert evidence should be the independent product of the expert uninfluenced by the pressures of litigation.

2.2

Experts should assist the court by providing objective, unbiased opinions on matters within their expertise, and should not assume the role of an advocate.

2.3

Experts should consider all material facts, including those which might detract from their opinions.

2.4

Experts should make it clear—
- (a) when a question or issue falls outside their expertise; and
- (b) when they are not able to reach a definite opinion, for example because they have insufficient information.

2.5

If, after producing a report, an expert's view changes on any material matter, such change of view should be communicated to all the parties without delay, and when appropriate to the court.

Form and Content of an Expert's Report

3.1

An expert's report should be addressed to the court and not to the party from whom the expert has received instructions.

3.2

An expert's report must:
- (1) give details of the expert's qualifications;
- (2) give details of any literature or other material which has been relied on in making the report;
- (3) contain a statement setting out the substance of all facts and instructions which are material to the opinions expressed in the report or upon which those opinions are based;
- (4) make clear which of the facts stated in the report are within the expert's own knowledge;
- (5) say who carried out any examination, measurement, test or experiment which the expert has used for the report, give the qualifications of that person, and say whether or not the test or experiment has been carried out under the expert's supervision;
- (6) where there is a range of opinion on the matters dealt with in the report—
    - (a) summarise the range of opinions; and
    - (b) give reasons for the expert's own opinion;
- (7) contain a summary of the conclusions reached;
- (8) if the expert is not able to give an opinion without qualification, state the qualification; and
- (9) contain a statement that the expert—
    - (a) understands their duty to the court, and has complied with that duty; and
    - (b) is aware of the requirements of Part 35, this practice direction and the Protocol for Instruction of Experts to give Evidence in Civil Claims.

3.3

An expert's report must be verified by a statement of truth in the following form—

I confirm that I have made clear which facts and matters referred to in this report are within my own knowledge and which are not. Those that are within my own knowledge I confirm to be true.

The opinions I have expressed represent my true and complete professional opinions on the matters to which they refer.

(Part 22 deals with statements of truth. Rule 32.14 sets out the consequences of verifying a document containing a false statement without an honest belief in its truth.)

Information

4

Under rule 35.9 the court may direct a party with access to information, which is not reasonably available to another party to serve on that other party a document, which records the information. The document served must include sufficient details of all the facts, tests, experiments and assumptions which underlie any part of the information to enable the party on whom it is served to make, or to obtain, a proper interpretation of the information and an assessment of its significance.

Instructions

5

Cross-examination of experts on the contents of their instructions will not be allowed unless the court permits it (or unless the party who gave the instructions consents). Before it gives permission the court must be satisfied that there are reasonable grounds to consider that the statement in the report of the substance of the instructions is inaccurate or incomplete. If the court is so satisfied, it will allow the cross-examination where it appears to be in the interests of justice.

Questions to Experts

6.1

Where a party sends a written question or questions under rule 35.6 direct to an expert, a copy of the questions must, at the same time, be sent to the other party or parties.

6.2

The party or parties instructing the expert must pay any fees charged by that expert for answering questions put under rule 35.6. This does not affect any decision of the court as to the party who is ultimately to bear the expert's fees.

Single joint expert

7

When considering whether to give permission for the parties to rely on expert evidence and whether that evidence should be from a single joint expert the court will take into account all the circumstances in particular, whether:

(a) it is proportionate to have separate experts for each party on a particular issue with reference to—
  (i) the amount in dispute;
  (ii) the importance to the parties; and
  (iii) the complexity of the issue;
(b) the instruction of a single joint expert is likely to assist the parties and the court to resolve the issue more speedily and in a more cost-effective way than separately instructed experts;
(c) expert evidence is to be given on the issue of liability, causation or quantum;
(d) the expert evidence falls within a substantially established area of knowledge which is unlikely to be in dispute or there is likely to be a range of expert opinion;
(e) a party has already instructed an expert on the issue in question and whether or not that was done in compliance with any practice direction or relevant pre-action protocol;
(f) questions put in accordance with rule 35.6 are likely to remove the need for the other party to instruct an expert if one party has already instructed an expert;
(g) questions put to a single joint expert may not conclusively deal with all issues that may require testing prior to trial;

(h) a conference may be required with the legal representatives, experts and other witnesses which may make instruction of a single joint expert impractical; and

(i) a claim to privilege makes the instruction of any expert as a single joint expert inappropriate.

Orders

8

Where an order requires an act to be done by an expert, or otherwise affects an expert, the party instructing that expert must serve a copy of the order on the expert. The claimant must serve the order on a single joint expert.

Discussions between experts

9.1

Unless directed by the court discussions between experts are not mandatory. Parties must consider, with their experts, at an early stage, whether there is likely to be any useful purpose in holding an experts' discussion and if so when.

9.2

The purpose of discussions between experts is not for experts to settle cases but to agree and narrow issues and in particular to identify:

(i) the extent of the agreement between them;

(ii) the points of and short reasons for any disagreement;

(iii) action, if any, which may be taken to resolve any outstanding points of disagreement; and

(iv) any further material issues not raised and the extent to which these issues are agreed.

9.3

Where the experts are to meet, the parties must discuss and if possible agree whether an agenda is necessary, and if so attempt to agree one that helps the experts to focus on the issues which need to be discussed. The agenda must not be in the form of leading questions or hostile in tone.

9.4

Unless ordered by the court, or agreed by all parties, and the experts, neither the parties nor their legal representatives may attend experts discussions.

9.5

If the legal representatives do attend—

(i) they should not normally intervene in the discussion, except to answer questions put to them by the experts or to advise on the law; and

(ii) the experts may if they so wish hold part of their discussions in the absence of the legal representatives.

9.6

A statement must be prepared by the experts dealing with paragraphs 9.2(i) - (iv) above. Individual copies of the statements must be signed by the experts at the conclusion of the discussion, or as soon thereafter as practicable, and in any event within 7 days. Copies of the statements must be provided to the parties no later than 14 days after signing.

9.7

Experts must give their own opinions to assist the court and do not require the authority of the parties to sign a joint statement.

9.8

If an expert significantly alters an opinion, the joint statement must include a note or addendum by that expert explaining the change of opinion.

Assessors

10.1
An assessor may be appointed to assist the court under rule 35.15. Not less than 21 days before making any such appointment, the court will notify each party in writing of the name of the proposed assessor, of the matter in respect of which the assistance of the assessor will be sought and of the qualifications of the assessor to give that assistance.

10.2
Where any person has been proposed for appointment as an assessor, any party may object to that person either personally or in respect of that person's qualification.

10.3
Any such objection must be made in writing and filed with the court within 7 days of receipt of the notification referred to in paragraph 10.1 and will be taken into account by the court in deciding whether or not to make the appointment.

10.4
Copies of any report prepared by the assessor will be sent to each of the parties but the assessor will not give oral evidence or be open to cross-examination or questioning.

Index

A

Appendix 7 Disclosure: CPIA 1996: Code of Practice under Pt II *336–42*
Attorney-General's Guidelines on Disclosure of Unused Material in Criminal Proceedings (April 2005) *376–83*

C

Children Act 1989
  ss. 96, 98 *396–7*
Civil Evidence Act 1968
  ss. 11–13 *394–6*
Civil Evidence Act 1972
  s. 3 *396*
Civil Evidence Act 1995
  ss. 1–14, 16 *397–402*
Civil Partnership Act 2004
  s. 84 *402*
Civil Procedure Rules 1998
  Rule 32 *402–5*
  Rule 33 *418–20*
  Rule 34 *420–6*
  Rule 35 *435–7*
  Practice Direction (Attendance of Witnesses) *426–34*
  Practice Direction (Experts and Assessors) *437–41*
  Practice Direction (Written Evidence) *405–8*
Codes of Practice (PACE)
  Arrest (Code G) *328–36*
  Detention, Treatment and Questioning (Code C) *226–77*
  Identification of Persons by Police Officers (Code D) *277–313*
  Search and Seizure (Code B) *212–25*
  Stop and Search (Code A) *100–17*
  Tape Recording (Code E) *313–21*
  Visual Recordings with Sound of Interviews with Suspects (Code F) *321–8*
Contempt of Court Act 1981
  s. 10 *19*
Convention for the Protection of Human Rights and Fundamental Freedoms (Rome 1950)
  Arts 1–18 *390–3*
Coroners and Justice Act 2009
  ss. 54, 55, 86–93 *187–91*
Crime (International Co-operation) Act 2003
  ss. 7–17, 19, 29–31 *147–52*
Criminal Appeal Act 1968
  ss. 1, 23 *5–6*
Criminal Cases Review (Insanity) Act 1999
  ss. 1, 2 *146*

Criminal Evidence Act 1898
  ss. 1–3 *2*
Criminal Evidence (Amendment) Act 1997
  ss. 1, 2, 5, Sch. 1 *114–17*
Criminal Evidence (Witness Anonymity) Act 2008
  ss. 10–12 *186*
Criminal Justice Act 1967
  ss. 9–10 *4–5*
Criminal Justice Act 1982
  s. 72 *19*
Criminal Justice Act 1988
  ss. 30–32, 34 *101–2*
Criminal Justice Act 2003
  ss. 51–67, 75–80, 98–129, 132–134, 137–140, Schs 4, 5 *154–84*
Criminal Justice and Public Order Act 1994
  ss. 32–38 *110–14*
Criminal Procedure Act 1865
  ss. 3–6 *1–2*
Criminal Procedure and Investigations Act 996: Code of Practice under Pt II *336–42*
Criminal Procedure Rules 2011
  Part 27 *343*
  Part 28 *344–6*
  Part 29 *346–54*
  Part 31 *354–6*
  Part 33 *357–9*
  Part 34 *359–60*
  Part 35 *360–2*
  Part 36 *362–3*
  Part 37 *363–70*
  Part 39 *370–1*
  Part 40 *371–2*
  Part 41 *373–6*

D

Domestic Violence, Crime and Victims Act 2004
  ss. 5, 6 *184–6*

H

Homicide Act 1957
  s. 2 *3*
Human Rights Act 1998
  ss. 1–10, 21–22 *384–90*

M

Magistrates' Courts Act 1980
  ss. 98, 101, 103, 104, 107 *17–18*
Misuse of Drugs Act 1971
  ss. 5, 28 *8–9*

P

Perjury Act 1911
  ss. 13–14 *2*
Police and Criminal Evidence
    Act 1984
  ss. 1–24A, 26–32, 34–51, 53–58,
    60–67, 71–82, 107, 111, 117, 118,
    Sch. 2A *19–101*
  Code A *192–212*
  Code B *212–25*
  Code C *226–77*
  Code D *179–210*
  Code E *277–313*
  Code F *313–21*
  Code G *328–36*
Practice Directions
  Attendance of
      Witnesses *426–34*
  Experts and Assessors *437–41*
  Written Evidence *405–18*
Prevention of Crime Act 1953
  s. 1 *3*
Protection of Children Act 1978
  ss. 1, 1A, 1B,2 *16–17*
Public Order Act 1986
  s. 5 *101*

R

Rehabilitation of Offenders Act 1974
  ss. 4–7 *9–16*
Road Traffic Act 1988
  s. 172 *107–8*
Road Traffic Offenders Act 1988
  ss. 11–13, 16, 18, 20 *103–7*

S

Sexual Offences Act 2003
  ss. 75–79 *153–4*
Sexual Offences (Amendment)
    Act 1992
  ss. 1–2 *109–10*

T

Terrorism Act 2000
  ss. 118, 120 *146–7*
Theft Act 1968
  ss. 22, 25, 27, 30–31 *6–8*

Y

Youth Justice and Criminal Evidence Act 1999
  ss. 16–39, 41–57, 59, 62, 63, Sch. 1A *117–46*

The Lord Rodger Essay Prize

Sponsored by Oxford University Press

The Statute Law Society ('the Society') invites applications for the Lord Rodger Essay Prize.

The Society is a charitable body, which aims to educate the legal profession and the public about the legislative process, with a view to encouraging improvements in statute law. It was founded in 1968 and has members throughout Britain, Europe and the Commonwealth.

Lord Rodger of Earlsferry SCJ was Chair of the Society from 2002 until his death in 2011. He was involved in the legislative process at various stages of his career and retained a strong interest in the making and interpretation of statute law.

In memory of Lord Rodger, the Society has established an annual essay prize worth £1,000.

➤ Essays submitted must concern one or more of the following topics:
  ➢ the legislative process,
  ➢ the use of legislation as an instrument of public policy,
  ➢ the drafting of legislation,
  ➢ the interpretation of legislation.

➤ Essays may relate to the United Kingdom and/or any other jurisdiction or jurisdictions.

➤ Essays must be written in English and must be between 5,000 and 8,000 words long, including footnotes. They must be preceded by an abstract of no more than 200 words.

➤ Essays may be submitted by anyone who is reading for an undergraduate degree at any University and in any subject; or has held their first (or only) undergraduate degree for not more than five years.

Full information about the prize including entry instructions and deadline details can be found on **www.statutelawsociety.org** and at **www.oxfordtextbooks.co.uk/statutes**

Please refer to the website for submission instructions, and to download an entry form. The closing date for the essay prize is mid-September each year.

The winning essay will be chosen by a jury consisting of three members of the Council of the Society. The prize will be presented by the Chairman of the Law Society, at the Society's Annual Lord Renton Lecture in November.

The prize sum is £1,000. The winning essay will be considered for publication in the *Statute Law Review*, which is published by Oxford University Press, in association with the Society.